MENCKEN

by Carl Bode

Southern Illinois University Press   *Carbondale and Edwardsville*

Feffer & Simons, Inc.   *London and Amsterdam*

For Margaret

Library of Congress Cataloging in Publication Data

Bode, Carl, 1911–
    Mencken.
    (Arcturus books, AB107)
      1. Mencken, Henry Louis, 1880–1956.
[PS3525.E43Z5398 1973]   818'.5'209 [B]
ISBN 0–8093–0627–1   72–11997

ARCT
URUS
BOOKS ®

Copyright © 1969 by Carl Bode
All rights reserved
First published September 1969
Second printing December 1969
Arcturus Books Edition April 1973
This edition printed by offset lithography
   in the United States of America
Designed by Andor Braun

Contents

	List of Illustrations	ix
1	Prehistory	3
2	Baltimore Boy	9
3	Daily and Sundays	27
4	The Apt Apprentice	46
5	The SMART SET Era	59
6	Writers and Rotarians	78
7	Dreiser and the Fruits of Dissidence	103
8	Good Company	131
9	The Paradise of Traders and Usurers	164
10	Mainstay of the SUN	191
11	The MERCURY: *The Web*	207
12	The MERCURY: *Mencken's Mind and Art*	241
13	Mencken, Darwin, and God	264
14	Mencken in Love	279
15	The Circus of Dr. R.	304
16	Friends and Familiars	321
17	The Last Hurrah	344
18	Nighttime at Hollins Street	367
	Memento of an Active Man	377
	Afterword: *The Far Side of the Moon*	381
	Acknowledgments	385
	Notes	390
	Index	437

List of Illustrations

(between pages 22–23)

    H. L. Mencken as a baby

    The Mencken family at Mt. Washington

    Mencken in the Baltimore *Herald* city room

    Mencken, Harry Henkel, and Robert Carter

    Mencken, McKee and Tom Barclay, and Folger McKinsey
        outside Wegner's Restaurant

    The Saturday Night Club members

    Mencken in the *Sunpapers* office

    Self-caricature by Mencken

    George Jean Nathan and Mencken

    Smart Set

    American Mercury

    Mencken is arrested on Boston Common

(between pages 160–161)

    Aileen Pringle, Norma Shearer, Louis B. Mayer, and
        Mencken

    Joseph Hergesheimer celebrating his wedding anniversary
        in Hollywood

    Mencken and Aileen Pringle

    Mencken at the piano

    The backyard wall at 1524 Hollins Street

    Mencken and neighborhood children

    Mencken and the Reverend Herbert Parrish

    Mencken and his bride, Sara Haardt

    Mencken and Clarence Darrow

    Celebrating the repeal of Prohibition

(between pages 292–293)

    The Menckens' passport photo

    Mencken covering the Republican National Convention

    The Saturday Night Club

    Mencken listening to the music of Bach

    Mencken the trencherman, with Paul Patterson and others

    Mencken at home

    Mencken and Nathan

    Mencken at Henry Wallace's Progressive Party Convention

    Mencken and his nurse, Lois Gentry

    Mencken and his brother, August

Mencken

A few words on the subject of this biography

> *A howling hyena . . . A Cinderella with flat feet . . . The private
> secretary of God Almighty . . . The buzzard of American litera-
> ture . . . A plain ass . . . The American Legion's worst enemy . . .
> The boss basilisk . . . A clever and bitter Jew . . . A sweet-
> scented geranium . . . A scribbler plethoric and thinker vacuous
> . . . A mischievous bladder-banger . . . One of those little skunks
> who spread their poison wherever they go . . . A radical Red . . .
> A hardened Germanophile . . . A British toady . . . The boy-
> pervert from Baltimore . . . An 18-karat, 23-jeweled, 33rd degree,
> bred-in-the-bone and dyed-in-the-wool moron . . . Our greatest
> heavy-weight of light thinkers . . . A literary stink-pot . . . A
> dead soul . . . A Baltimore Babbitt . . . The high prophet of the
> latrine school of writers . . . The bilious buffoon from Baltimore
> . . . A damphool . . . A public nuisance.*

Culled from *Menckeniana: A Schimpflexikon* (1928)

1. Prehistory

THE BIOGRAPHY OF a writer is always a distortion. When we see him he is usually away from his desk, traveling to another city, carping at his critics, making love, or supporting causes. Sometimes we glimpse him gathering the material to base his writing on. But we seldom see him at the most important times, the times when he sits poking at his typewriter or scribbling revisions with his pen. What is there to say? Day after day he sat at his desk and wrote. At times the writing went abominably; at times it went agreeably well. Most of the time it simply moved along. The sentences somehow got written, the pages filled. Ordinarily the process was a rather trying one. In April 1920 Mencken, though in his splendid prime, still writes, "I am at work on Prejudices II, and, as usual, cursing God." In May 1923 he says sourly, "I am thinking of giving up literature and returning to the cigar business." Ten years later he observes, "I hope to tackle a revision of 'The American Language' . . . and so must look forward to a dreadful job." A good twenty years pass and he is still complaining, "I have finished my book, and also a chapter for a cooperative history of American literature, projected by a posse of super-pedagogues. This last almost broke my back."

And yet there is a curious fascination about a writer's life, whether it is trying or not, whether it is eventful or dull. Biographers attempt periodically to furnish us with a history or description of this novelist or that poet. When the writer has been something of a public figure as well, the prospect of looking at his life grows the more inviting. Presses print few histories of eminent engineers or notable accountants but seem ready to issue the histories of even minor writers.

It is Mencken the writer who has the chief claim on our curiosity. His style was one of the striking creations of his era, far more dynamic than his solidly conservative ideas. His genius for seizing the unexpected and amusing word, for making the irreverent comparison, and for creating a tone that was not acid but alkaline helped to make him the most readable of American essayists. Robert Frost was not the only person to consider him the greatest one. His gift for using his style as the vehicle for vigorous dissent gave his views a currency enjoyed by those of no other writer. Walter Lippmann could rightly call him, in 1926, "the most powerful personal influence on this whole generation of educated people." His formal treatises, even his own favorite, *Treatise on the Gods,* date rather badly. But some of the essays preserved in the six volumes of *Prejudices,* most of that bumptious book *In Defense of Women,* and his three volumes of reminiscences will probably endure. So will *The American Language,* in which the writer turned scholar and labored for thirty years to perfect a landmark in the study of our speech.

Yet the fact is that Mencken was much more than a writer. In his own eyes he was above all a newspaperman. He liked to feel that he was a typical one, though he was not except perhaps during his short apprenticeship. After that he was a star reporter and then had a brief but brilliant career as a newspaper editor. In point, by the time he reached twenty-one he was Sunday editor of the Baltimore *Herald;* at twenty-three he was city editor; at twenty-four, managing editor; and at twenty-five, editor in chief. Then he shifted to the Baltimore *Sun* as a combination editor and writer. He would stay at the *Sunpapers* for, practically, the rest of his life as a newspaperman, starting in 1906 and continuing till 1948.

He was not long in learning that he liked to write even more than he liked to edit, and so after a few years he put managing a newspaper behind him. However, by then he was done as a regular newsman too. He concentrated instead on the personalized reporting of special events and on the composition of a colorful column christened "The Free Lance." The editor became a journalist; the once anonymous reporter returned under a by-line. From the outset the Free Lance created a sensation by pricking the hides of Baltimore's most sacred cows. Day after day, month after month, Mencken raised impertinence to an art. Soon he was recognized as something of a local pundit. Baltimore modeled its image of him on a supposed likeness which the Sunday *Sun* ran several times in 1913 and 1914. Later labeled "The Subconscious Mencken," it showed a walrus-moustached, choleric old tyrant. The Free Lance was followed by further columns, equally spirited if less rambunctious, most notably the "Monday Articles" which started in the *Evening Sun* in 1920 and ran for eighteen years. Through his columns and other personal journalism and through his covering of key events of his day, including every national political convention from 1920 to 1948 except one, he early became and long remained a legendary figure in the newspaper world. Even today such a veteran reporter as Peter Edson says, "Henry L. Mencken, who came up through the *Baltimore Sun,* is for my money the best news-paperman of this century."

He also developed into one of the great magazine editors of his era. Though he was finished as a newspaper editor by his early thirties, he readily switched to the periodical field and devoted a good part of his most fruitful years to the conduct of two magazines. As co-editor of the *Smart Set,* in some ways a rather sleazy journal, he gave it an intellectual fiber and a literary respectability that no one else could supply. As editor of the *American Mercury* he made it the most stimulating magazine of the 1920s.

Through his writing and editing Mencken became a public personality, internationally known. He did more than write about news; he generated it. His photograph appeared regularly in the papers; there readers saw no moustached grandfather but a youngish man with the face of a hard-boiled cherub, topped by hair parted strictly in the middle. The role he played in the widely publicized Scopes trial and in what was called the "Hatrack" case set him in the center of the stage. When the news came out in 1930 that he was to be married, it seemed that every paper reported the fact and carried a photo of the prospective bridegroom. During most of his career he was what today would be termed a celebrity. As early as 1903 he found it worth while to subscribe to a clipping service.

His relationship to his times was dramatic. From about 1910 to 1917 he led the guerrilla warfare in this country against cultural conservatism, especially Puritanism, its most stubborn form. From 1920 to 1929 he captained the educated minority of Americans so well that it won nearly every battle. But in between, during World War I, he was derided as a pro-German and literary libertine; as a writer he was silenced. And during the decade of the Great Depression his following shrank to a tight band of Tories, while the Marxist critics belabored him and the other critics ignored him. If these thought about him at all, it was only to inquire blandly if he was dead. World War II again saw him silent as a polemicist. Even if he had been able to publish his social or political criticism it is doubtful that anyone would have listened. On the other hand, although he never recovered his influence he now reached the public in a new way, through reminiscence, through his delightful and largely autobiographical *Days* books, *Happy Days, Newspaper Days,* and *Heathen Days.* They started in the late 1930s as sketches in the *New Yorker* and then were collected in book form; they did not end until 1943 when the third and final volume appeared. In their pages he led the public back chiefly to his early days in Baltimore. It was a highly entertaining exercise in nostalgia but it had little connection with his readers' or his own ideas.

He had formed those ideas early and kept them late. Yet he was sensitive, until the Depression set in, to the temper of his times. He felt the climate of opinion; he responded, one way or another, to its changes. For that reason any biography of Mencken should take into adequate account what that climate was. It is of prime importance.

Just as a life of Mencken must explore the public man, it should of course explore the private one. The private one becomes the more noteworthy because of the difference between the two. At times his family and friends, even his newspaper associates, had to remind themselves that the genial Mencken they knew was the roaring critic of American culture.

The private man is also rewarding to discover purely for himself. In some ways he seems simple, in others unusually complex. The problem of getting at him is complicated by the way he kept a firm hold over the facts of his personal life. Many of them, he believed, were nobody's business but his own. He had three biographers during his lifetime; he furnished each of them with so many facts that their books never showed how much was omitted. Though the facts they got were screened, they were offered with such amiability that no one could be resentful. Mencken provided his first biographer, Isaac Goldberg, with such a plethora of information — in the form of a thick autobiographical typescript — that all Goldberg had to do for most of the chapters in his *The Man Mencken* was to water it down with his own diffuse style. Mencken was almost as amiable to the two others.

When in the early 1940s the Princeton historian Julian Boyd collected much of Mencken's correspondence, with a view to issuing a volume of it, he too enjoyed Mencken's friendly cooperation. But it too was tempered, for Mencken had every intention of censoring both the letters he had received and those he had sent. He wrote to his correspondents proposing that they let the letters he had sent them be copied — except for those which might cause embarrassment on either side or, as he put it with an engaging grin, might be athwart Christian doctrine. He for his part would use the same care with their letters. The consequence is that though Boyd was able to copy thousands of letters they present us with a partial portrait only. On the other hand, it can be supplemented by several thousands of other letters we can find. After all, Mencken wrote about one hundred thousand letters throughout his long career and received as many if not more. Yet he himself cheerfully maintained that his correspondence, vast though it was, left out nine-tenths of his story.

He said that a man's autobiography told more of the story than did his letters, though he added that a man almost invariably lied when he undertook it. In his own case the deception proved so gentle and artful that it became literature. In the *Days* books the factual inaccuracies are slight; he showed himself to be a sound scholar who checked his sources. The substantial inaccuracies are those of omission and distortion. He implies that they are simply exaggerations. In the Preface to his first volume he takes a term from his favorite character, Huckleberry Finn, and admits as Huck did to telling "stretchers" here and there. Elsewhere he remarks cheerfully of *Happy Days,* "I should say that it is about eighty per cent. truth. The rest consists of icing on the cake." Yet he does more than exaggerate; he alters and excludes. Once, talking about what he has said of his contemporaries, he warns us, "In no case have I told even so much as half of what I know . . . and the part I have told has always been the least embarrassing part"; his remark is equally true for himself. It should be added that there is nothing sinister in these omissions. He himself was philosophical about them. It was the way of the world, as true for institutions as individuals. As he told a friend about a history of the *Sun* he was helping to prepare, "The story is full of swell stuff but, unfortunately, most of it can't be printed."

The basic point, then, is that the *Days,* which seem to speak so amply of Mencken's childhood and young manhood, are both more and less than biography. They are more because they are masterpieces of genre writing. They are less because of all they neglect to say. Not least important, they skate lightly over the surface of his teens, a time of sporadic enjoyment but also a time of such troubles and frustrations that he at least once considered suicide. No wonder he refrained from writing much about them. So the *Days* books call for biography to supplement and balance them. And they focus only on the young Mencken anyway.

Luckily, we can begin the early history of H. L. Mencken helped by the many things he has told us as well as those he has not.

2. Baltimore Boy

HENRY LOUIS MENCKEN WAS BORN in Baltimore on September 12, 1880 at a cost of ten dollars. The price per pound was more than reasonable. Fat babies were then in high fashion: Henry had cheeks like plum pudding and bulged before and behind. From the start he got all the attention traditionally lavished on the first-born. Family records are fuller of him than of any of the three children who followed. The records suggest that he talked early, dominated the conversation as soon as he could, and was walking by the time he reached fourteen months. He says on the first page of *Happy Days* that immediately after his third birthday he became aware of "the cosmos we all infest." That was when he was lugged to his father's factory to look out at a fireworks display. His first memory was of its gaudy dazzle.

A few weeks later his father moved the Menckens to a new house and thereafter memories multiplied. The cosmos began to define itself and at its center was the substantial residence at 1524 Hollins Street that August Mencken bought.

This was the place where a contented Henry Mencken would live the rest of his life, except for the five years of a very happy marriage to an Alabama girl named Sara Haardt. A red-brick row house with marble steps and marble trim, it proved to be comfortable, convenient, and spacious enough for the Mencken family. But the best thing about it from a small boy's point of view was a backyard fully a hundred feet long. Mencken later testified that it had "room for almost every imaginable boyish enterprise." At various times, railroads ran from one end of the yard to the other, a telephone system appeared of two tin cans connected by a long piece of cotton thread, forts went up or were pulled down. Whatever the enterprises, the setting for them was pleasant. Mencken's mother annually planted a vegetable and flower garden which Henry and his frisky brother Charles, a year and a half younger, annually turned into a Dust Bowl. Mencken's father had a grape arbor erected, and half a dozen vines soon flourished on it. The showpiece of the yard was the summerhouse, with its wooden floor and pointed roof. It could be converted into any backdrop that a child's fancy could wish.

In his earliest years the backyard kept Henry content. But even before he entered F. Knapp's Institute, a German primary school which his grandfather Mencken apparently recommended, his cosmos expanded gradually. It took in the house and yard of his uncle, who had moved next door and was starting a family only a little later than August. It took in the pungent-smelling alley behind 1524, along which small stables and Negro shanties faced one another. Above all it took in Union Square at Henry's front stoop. There before him stretched a city block of tidy lawns, walks, and trees, with at its center a small building which he learned in after years was Baltimore's idea of a Greek temple. It was a good neighborhood for a boy to be in.

In his recollections Mencken emphasizes the fact that he believes his boyhood was an ordinary one. "My early life," he says, "was placid, secure, uneventful and happy." He and his friends ran in safety on the street. There were no automobiles and few streetcars, and wagons had to roll slowly over the bulging Baltimore cobblestones. The boys spun tops on the walks of Union Square. With their schoolboy stockings at half-mast, they played one-two-three or leapfrog or such other forgotten games as run-a-mile and catty. They teetered on top of backyard fences; they explored alley ash cans for treasure; they hiked into the woods, then still nearby, and when well hidden puffed a dried-leaf cigarette. They had fights with gangs of boys from other neighborhoods; they stole and were stolen from; they fled at the prospect of a policeman.

Because August Mencken was a prosperous manufacturer he soon started taking the family away from the stifling heat of Hollins Street in summer. At first he and his brother rented a double house near Ellicott City not far from Baltimore. It stood on a slope above the gorge of the Patapsco River. Henry rambled in the countryside, caught butterflies or lizards, dammed a nearby runlet, learned the look of poison oak, and played with the sons of the owner of the house. August watched benignly. He was a good provider and his young family throve.

At all seasons August Mencken was preeminent in his household. "I never saw him," his son remarked in a private autobiographical note, "in a place of disadvantage or embarrassment; in the small world that he inhabited he always sat at the head of the table." Yet he seldom acted the strict Victorian father of the stereotypes. His children responded to him much more through affection, evidently, than through fear. "The system of criminal justice prevailing at Hollins Street," Mencken says in another such note, "was a very mild one. We were paddled freely for misdemeanors, but always gently and never after the age of six or seven. Most of the other punishments that I heard of from playmates were unknown. We were never sent to bed, or locked in a dark room, or deprived of food. Rewards for good conduct were numerous and frequent. They ran all the way from an extra ration of gingersnaps or animal crackers to excursions on foot, by street-car, by train or by buggy. My brother Charlie and I had the franchise of scraping and devouring the savory gum remaining in the pan after the hired girl had boiled milk in the morning. When we broke the house laws we were threatened with the loss of this franchise, but the threat was never carried out."

As a boy Mencken acquired a host of pleasant memories about his father and later printed some of them in *Happy Days*. But we can find much more information in two other places. One is the chapter entitled "My Father" in the typescript on his life which Mencken prepared to help his first biographer; Goldberg used part but not all of the chapter. The other is exceptionally important, not only because it throws new light on August Mencken but also because it tells us, as little else does, about Henry's mother. It is a box of assorted notes which he made mainly in the early 1940s. These private notes have been hidden away until recently.

In sketching his father for Goldberg, Mencken understandably remembered best either the cases where he saw a strong likeness between his father and himself or where father and son differed dramatically. With the passing of time the other more subtle differences or likenesses had perhaps faded from Mencken's mind. He starts by establishing his credentials for Goldberg through telling him that he knew August better than most boys know their fathers. Then he picks out his father's chief characteristics. First of all, August was a successful businessman who built up Aug. Mencken & Bro. from very modest beginnings to a solid enterprise. His cigar factory grew to be one of the best in Baltimore. And as we shall see, though Henry himself never became a businessman in the ordinary sense of the word, he evidenced much of his father's enterprise and shrewdness. Before Henry reached forty he was beyond financial need; at his death he was that rare creature, a wealthy author. Both August and Henry manifested a respect for what money could buy; both enjoyed their creature comforts. Both extended many of the principles of business into private life. The most important of these, Henry said more than once, was that it was "inexcusably immoral" to break engagements of any kind. This, his chief ethical maxim, he got directly from his father. Both also esteemed competence, in almost everything but politics. While they tolerated, or even liked, a few of the successful professional politicians, their general view of political managers was jaundiced.

August was a conservative Southern Democrat. As was proper for a factory owner with, his son noted, one hundred thousand dollars of "first credit," he viewed the Democrats of William Jennings Bryan's wing of the party with bleak hostility. He also felt a tribal aversion toward avowed Republicans. So did his son, though he ultimately disliked Democrats even more.

August's attitude toward the workingman was one of suspicion and toward trade unionism one of rancor. Though he paid the men in his factory union-scale he never allowed them to organize. Henry, even in the progressive days when the New Deal stood at the peak of its popularity, paraded his conservative sentiments. Men might be going hungry but he could announce that what this nation needed was freedom from debt.

Yet August was more than a stereotyped businessman. His personal life was full of paradoxes that pleased Henry and in more cases than not appeared later in him as well. August was a permanent agnostic in religious matters, as Henry would be, but he was ready to make token compromises if his family wished. He made no protest when his four children were baptized, to their mother's satisfaction, and he allowed them to attend Sunday school for a time. Henry let himself be married by a minister in church because his bride wanted it, but his view of religion was always amiably cynical. In general August was no joiner, and his son reported of him that he disliked clubs and associations and would not join a business organization; yet he was a Freemason and marched in Shriners' parades. Henry himself never cared for formal societies — and indeed found in the businessmen's luncheon clubs one of his broadest targets — yet he helped to start three clubs for his friends and himself, one of which, the Saturday Night Club, became the center of his leisure life. Even on the Saturday evening after his wife's death he stoically joined in its meeting.

Both August and Henry liked listening to music and making it. August played the fiddle but, says his son, very badly. Henry played the piano with thumping abandon; the purpose of each of the three clubs was to make concert music and Henry was a born second piano. August relished good food and drink, a fact attested by the grocers' bills which his son unearthed and pasted in a family scrapbook. Henry found few pleasures more satisfying than a full, well-chosen meal and he proved to be a great boon to the Baltimore brewers.

August customarily read newspapers rather than books while Henry would read books, magazines, and newspapers, all with an unflagging appetite. The books August did read, however, also appealed to Henry; in particular, August enjoyed the works of Mark Twain, who proved to be a favorite of Henry's. August was something of a sportsman. He enjoyed driving fast horses, for instance, though his son reports that he did it awkwardly; and he enjoyed baseball. He became for a brief time in fact a stockholder and vice-president of the Washington, D.C. Baseball club, much to the boy's pride. But Henry soon grew to dislike all sports and even, later, the people who enjoyed them. Neither August nor Henry were ever good at sports; both were thoroughly clumsy. Henry said the last word about this fact in *Happy Days*, "All my genes in that field come from my father, who was probably the most incompetent man with his hands ever seen on earth."

Both liked elaborate jokes. For example, August's second summer place, at Mt. Washington, stood on a rise and after buying it he announced to his neighbors that he intended to christen it "Pig Hill" and cover the slope with pigsties. He even had plans drawn for a splendid piggery with a steeple and applied for a permit to erect it. Though he did not build it, somehow the name "Pig Hill" was thereafter given to the entire settlement and this, Henry says in one of the prime understatements of *Happy Days*, did not make him popular in the neighborhood. Another of August's elaborate jokes was the invention of an imaginary brother Fred, supposedly a minister. August maintained the hoax till his death; then Henry took it over. Fred had become a bishop by that time. After answering a good many polite queries from strangers, Henry finally tired of the joke and announced that Fred had been murdered in Abyssinia.

Henry himself developed a consuming delight in practical jokes and hoaxes. They took many forms in his long career. He had stationery printed for the American Institute of Arts and Letters (Negro), whose aims ranged from uplifting literature to seeking social relaxation. He showered invitations to join on his eminent associates, especially those from the South. He created the Tobacco-Chewers' Protective and Educational League of America and disseminated its propaganda. He had an advertising card printed for a Chinese Kosher restaurant. He sent out concoctions austerely labeled "Old Dr. Mencken's Hell Salts." He established the Loyal Legion of American Mothers, whose aim was to support, among other things, the Volstead Act, the purification of American girls, and idealism. He created the Highland Lake Golf Club (also Negro) and again pressed his Southern friends to join. Along with his personal correspondence he enclosed clippings that amused him, for instance, an announcement from the Israelite Baptist Church. One of the more ingenious of his hoaxes was the creation of the Maryland madstones. These he sent "from the mines of western Maryland" to his friends. They arrived customarily with an official tag testifying that they had been certified by the Maryland State Board of Madstone Examiners. At the bottom of the tag was the warning that anyone using an uninspected madstone would be subject to prosecution. The most durable, the most publicized of his hoaxes was the invention of a history of the bathtub, a history now firmly imbedded in American folklore.

August had a considerable sense of family. He reflected on his distinguished descent with satisfaction, well aware that the Menckenii had included noted men. He was more concerned, however, with the present than with the past, with living relatives rather than dead ancestors. What young Henry learned about his family history came from his grandfather Mencken, and from his mother. Even as a boy he was impressed. He heard about Otto Mencken, professor of morals and politics at Leipzig and founder of the first learned journal in Germany. He heard about Otto's brilliant son Johann Burkhardt, not only a renowned historian but also a scholar with a keen nose for cant who in 1715 had published a satire, *De Charlataneria Eruditorum*, on the frauds that some scholars perpetrate to become popular. He heard about Lüder Mencken, professor, judge, legal oracle, and like his famous kinsmen one of the ornaments of Leipzig. Doubtless the boy heard about the government officials who had been in the family and the affluent merchants, down to his grandfather himself, Burkhardt Ludwig Mencken, current head of the Menckenii in America.

What pride of ancestry August communicated to his son never became pompous, for August was quite capable of putting the family coat-of-arms on the garish cigar boxes that issued from his factory. His sense of family showed itself plainly in the bonds of affection that held his children, his wife, and him together. It showed itself too in his closeness to his brother and his brother's brood. It was at August's instance that his brother had bought the house next door. Throughout the year their offspring played with one another. One of the pictures that Mencken has left us in his box of personal notes is of the Sunday morning rambles in summer. "My father and his brother, who had nine youngsters between them, usually took along four or five on these excursions. There were half a dozen breweries in West Baltimore in those days, each with a beer garden attached, and we became familiar with all of them. My own favorite was in Garrison (then Butchers') lane. It had some fine old trees in its yard, and I greatly admired the huge horses in the adjacent stables. On our walks we would sometimes cross the bridge in Frederick Avenue over the Pennsylvania Railroad tracks. As we looked over the rail my uncle would clap his hands and exclaim 'Bang! Did you see it?' He would then pretend that a fast express had just flashed by — so fast that one could barely see it. My brother Charlie and I, so long back as I can remember, did not believe in this marvel, but some of the younger children apparently did so, for after one express had whirled by they would keep watch for another. Sometimes my uncle would pretend that two had just passed, one in each direction."

An appreciation of family life was one of the most vital things that August passed on to his son. Throughout his life Henry took family responsibilities seriously. As an eighteen-year-old he assumed the official headship of the house on his father's unexpected death. At twenty-one he turned down the job of assistant editor of *Leslie's Monthly* because it meant moving from home to New York. As a mature man his continuing concern lay with his family. A good son and brother, he also became a classically indulgent uncle to his niece

Virginia, Charlie's daughter, giving her full scope at the toy store when she was a child and paying her way through college when she was a young woman.

Although August Mencken was the unquestioned head of his house its central figure was certainly Henry's mother. Even as a petite young woman Anna Abhau Mencken had considerable presence. Upon August's death in 1899, she became the dominant personality in the house and so remained until her own death in 1925, long after her children had grown. Her photographs in a family album show a comely matron whose mouth grows firm as the years pass. Naturally enough Mencken as a child was closer to her than to his father, and so he said later on. Anna Mencken's feeling for family was as strong as her husband's. The result was a web of family ties that time would hardly fray and even disaster would not break. The members of the family were probably unaware of the sturdiness of the bonds being built up during Henry's childhood, but the evidence is impressive to an observer.

There is a revealing letter that his mother sent to Henry when, a ten-year-old, he was on a trip away from home with his grandfather Abhau. She wrote, "I was glad to hear from you and to know that you are both well, and enjoying yourselves. We have not been so well, Charles was home from school two days with swollen tonsils, your little brother had a touch of the grip and the earache. Gertie had the toothache every night. I had to take her to the dentist today. I have not been so well myself . . . and even Papa had a swollen cheek." Nor was this all. She went on to report that grandmother Mencken had been sick in bed for several days and that grandfather Mencken, evidently ailing, had remained about the same but was waiting for a letter from Henry. So was Henry's father: "Papa asked every time he came home if we had a letter from you." She added that everyone was feeling better now but clinched the matter by saying, "I think we are all a little homesick for you."

The reproach to the little boy for leaving home, even briefly and with one of his grandfathers, was certainly not conscious. Yet it would be hard to imagine a better way to remind Henry of family ties than by telling him that everyone fell ill while he went on a pleasure jaunt. It would be hard to see how he could avoid a twinge of guilt at the news the letter contained. The feeling of guilt would be reinforced by further news reaching him on the way home, the news that his grandfather Mencken had died while Henry was absent. Mencken once told Goldberg that almost thirty years later he still recalled seeing the black crepe on the door at Hollins Street. On the other hand, he also said that at the time his first thought was that he could miss school because of the funeral.

Mencken's childhood memories of his mother were homely ones. He recalled, for instance, her kitchen-wisdom, which she doubtless tried to pass on to him. In particular, she liked proverbs and used them often. He well remembered some of her favorites including "Lazy people take the most pains," "A guilty conscience needs no accuser," and "The more haste, the less speed." He recalled some of her household customs. He recalled her patient attempts to teach him "a few tricks" in spite of his colossal clumsiness. She managed to train him to thread a needle and to make a cocked hat out of folded paper. But she could never lead him successfully through the mysteries of the bowknot. Even as an elderly man Mencken remarked that he still could not tie his shoelaces right and that the art of tieing a bow tie remained hidden from him.

He often showed a beguiling combination of tenderness, whimsical appreciation for her crochets, and respect. Looking back on his early days he sketched a picture of her in one of his private notes. He began by remarking that she was a great worrier, able to conjure up more hazards than anyone else he knew. When guests were expected she worried about whether they would arrive safely. When her husband described a project he had thought of, she would discover "difficulties that astonished him." Mencken interjected that he had inherited some but not all of her talent for foreboding. And yet she could rise to an occasion and lay aside her fears. When Mencken told her after his father's death that he intended shortly to leave the family business and look for a newspaper job, he testified that she did not distress him with dismal prophecies of real or imagined risks. In fact she encouraged him and to all appearances was pleased when he found work on the *Morning Herald*.

After he became a newspaperman she adjusted her household routines to his irregular hours. No matter how late he arrived at home, he remembers, she always had a plate of sandwiches waiting. When he became well known she took pride in his achievements even though some of his early writings may have distressed her. If she did not always enjoy having a son who centered his life on controversy, she never complained about it. She herself read rather narrowly. She scanned the *Ladies' Home Journal* from cover to cover but found little time for books. Often her son would commend a new one to her, yet she rarely decided to read it. Notwithstanding, she was far from uninformed. Mencken admired her comprehension and said at the end of this sketch of her, "I do not recall ever opening with her any subject that she could not understand."

From childhood on, Mencken found that his mother ministered to his material comfort to his entire satisfaction. She was an excellent housekeeper, managing the establishment at Hollins Street thoughtfully and well. She inaugurated the domestic routines that Mencken relied on and grew to relish, altering them only for his convenience. In mid-career he remarks, "I am often asked why I never married. The reason is very simple. I have always had a home in Baltimore with my mother and sister that is more comfortable than any I could set up for myself. Moreover, if I left, my mother and sister would be more or less alone." He says nothing about romantic love, nothing about not having met a woman he wanted to marry. When he did speak, at one time, to a winsome Washington girl named Marion Bloom about the possibility of their marrying, she recalls that he suggested that they might live on the third floor of the house at Hollins Street.

The comment on why he never married was made before he fell in love with Sara Haardt. But he did not marry till he was fifty, five years after his mother died. One of the strengths of his marriage when it came was that Sara surrounded him with the same domestic security that his mother had. Though Sara's style turned out to be different from his mother's, the substance was identical. Anna Abhau Mencken presided over a household which kept its Victorian flavor, long after it was out of fashion, both in its setting and its rituals. Sara presided over one in which Victorianism was revived as a mode and given an elegant, artificial finish. Mencken appreciated both.

The tenacity of the ties formed on Hollins Street is nowhere better shown than in the fact that two of the four children, Gertrude and August, never married; one, Henry, did not marry till late; and only Charles married when he was young. Moreover, Hollins Street remained the permanent headquarters of the family. When she was middle-aged Gertrude set up an apartment in North Baltimore and eventually divided her time between a farm near Westminster, Maryland, called "Choice Parcel," and an apartment in Westminster itself. But she was always near enough to take part in important occasions. August, who became an engineer, was away a good deal but still lived in the house for more than half of his life. And Henry lived there nearly seventy years.

The furnishings of the house reflected their attachment. There were naturally alterations over the decades but they were gradual. If they clearly increased the comfort of the house, as did the fireplace that Henry installed in 1917, they were thought good. If not, they were regretted. For example, Mencken once told another of his biographers, William Manchester, that after his mother's death he repapered all the walls in an attempt to brighten up the home — and immediately felt sorry. The fireplace itself, whose history Mencken has described at length, is the more significant because he observes that it helps to make the house independent of the outside world if need be. Writing a good thirty years after the fireplace went in, in the days of World War II and government restrictions, he asserts that if "the maniacs in Washington" ever ration gas (which normally heated his house) the fireplace would always keep the Menckens warm. "It is," he says at the end of its history, "good insurance."

Mencken spoke movingly more than once both about the strength and the durability of his affection for his parents. There was, for instance, the time after his mother's death that he received a note of condolence from Theodore Dreiser. He thanked him, adding, "I begin to realize how inextricably my life was interwoven with my mother's. A hundred times a day I find myself planning to tell her something, or ask her for this or that. It is a curious thing: the human incapacity to imagine finality. The house seems strange, as if the people in it were deaf and dumb." He never felt as near to his father even though he wrote a good deal about him and his father, moreover, was dead before Mencken reached manhood. Yet a generation later he could say to console a friend, "I am sorry indeed to hear of your father's death. You are lucky to have had him with you for so long. My own father died when I was eighteen. That is now thirty-four years ago, but I remember him as vividly as if we had only parted yesterday."

The impression we have of Mencken's boyhood is almost pastoral. There is enough mischief to keep it from cloying but there is no doubt that this is a Baltimore where the grass stays green, the weather sunny. We see Huck Finn here, or better still, Tom Sawyer, bathed in a glow of light. The supporting characters, whether typical or not, appear basically good. They almost constitute an extension of Mencken's family. Mencken's memories are bland. His experiences, in kind if not in degree, turn out to be as amiably ordinary as he said they would.

In many ways he emerges as the classic American boy. In a few but important ways he does not. It develops that, once he had lost his baby-fat, he was thin and weak. He recalls that he was round-shouldered and for a time wore shoulderbraces. He could run fast but was not particularly vigorous otherwise. When he and Charlie boxed, Charlie usually won in spite of the fact that he was younger. He played games readily only as a child. Yet, though he got less exercise than most boys perhaps, he was seldom sick until he reached his teens.

Whatever his physical shortcomings they were more than balanced by his remarkable intellectual gifts. His report cards were models from the beginning. Old Professor Knapp consistently adorned them with compliments in German, for instance, "Macht tüchtige Fortschritte." When he finished Knapp's school he was its star pupil. When he entered the Baltimore Polytechnic School in 1892, his record, after a mediocre start, ended by being equally impressive. His first year's report showed a weakness in geometry and German. On the other hand he received a perfect mark in physiology ("Proof of an interest that still survives!" he later observed). In his last year, the school year of 1895/96, he emerged from the final examinations covered with garlands. His father had offered him a hundred dollars if he graduated at the very top of his class. Cramming with remarkable efficiency, studying by gaslight, he won the money as well as prizes offered at the Polytechnic. His over-all average proved to be above 96; it was the highest reached at the school up to that time.

His interests at the Polytechnic were significant. He especially enjoyed chemistry and English. He wavered, he said, "in those days between an impulse to be a chemist and a great desire to be a writer." In actual fact he wavered even earlier and in a sense would continue to waver later on. Throughout his life he would always decide in favor of writing but never lose an interest in scientific and mechanical processes, in exactly how things worked. Technical knowledge would always attract him as a reader and sometimes as a writer. He would use technical terms when he talked or wrote and he would use them knowingly.

One of the enthusiasms that he brought to his classes at the Polytechnic had started as early as the summer of 1888 when he wandered into the offices of the Ellicott City *Times*, not far from the house the Menckens were renting that summer, and had been entranced by the hand press. He campaigned for a little printing press of his own and received it the next Christmas, along with a font of type. Looking back, Mencken pronounced that the press determined the whole course of his life. Inky but enterprising he printed cards and a rudimentary newspaper. Primitive though his efforts were, they made him aware of the larger world of print and paper. They even allowed him to eye the hallowed Baltimore *Sun* not as an oracle but as an oversize competitor. He plunged with gusto into both the process of printing and the writing of copy.

From then on, the newspaper became his paramount interest but not his only one. For Christmas 1892 he received another influential gift, this time a camera. Through it he quickly got involved in the pleasures of chemistry, since he was as much attracted by the mysteries of how to develop pictures as by the art of taking them. When he entered his chemistry class at the Polytechnic, he discovered that thanks to his home laboratory he understood the subject better than his instructor. Even before, he had devised a way of giving silver photographic prints a brownish or reddish tone by dipping them into a solution with platinum in it. And, prophetically, he had then written up the process, in the first article to come from his pen. Under the heading of "A New Platinum Toning Bath, for Silver Prints" he described how it worked. The article was more than a mere boyhood production. Even this early Mencken had the initiative to submit it to some photographic magazines. They rejected it, but to us at this distance it is hard to see why. Sensible and straightforward, it was to all appearances the work of a knowledgeable writer.

It was also the work of a confirmed reader. For the point of departure in Mencken's experiment was something he had read, in this case an article in the magazine *Photography*. But his interest in reading went back much further. He proved indeed to be a wonder-child, the amazement of his family and assorted other relatives. By Christmas of 1886 he was receiving books and, he assured Goldberg, "making shift to read them." By the time he was eight he had become "a steady and heavy reader." He started his own small library. In addition, he browsed in his father's collection of books; he began to draw books from the nearest branch of the Enoch Pratt Free Library, Baltimore's public library; and he dipped into the collections of a Lutheran Sunday School. He soon tired of the Sunday School library except for its travel books, but he had a card for the Enoch Pratt Library before he was nine years old and he used it for the next sixty years.

Before he was twelve he had plowed at home and abroad through a mass of miscellaneous reading matter, including the novels of Dickens, Chambers's *Encyclopedia, Ben-Hur,* and Edward Bellamy's *Looking Backward.* His most splendid discovery was certainly *Huckleberry Finn.* He reports in *Happy Days,* "Its impact was genuinely terrific. I had not gone further than the first incomparable chapter before I realized, child though I was, that I had entered a domain of new and gorgeous wonders, and thereafter I pressed on steadily faster as I proceeded. As the blurbs on the slipcovers of murder mysteries say, I simply couldn't put the book down."

By the time Mencken reached his teens he was reading systematically and meaningfully. He discovered Thackeray and feasted on his Victorian abundance, finding him nearly as rich as Dickens. From the Victorians he worked back to the great British writers of the eighteenth century, Addison, Steele, Pope, and Samuel Johnson among them. He went back further still to the Renaissance and Shakespeare, and thereafter to Chaucer, whose racier tales delighted him. By the time he was fifteen he had read the whole canon of English classics and had seasoned them with selections from minor works. Though few authors, major or minor, daunted him he found it impossible to read Milton's *Paradise Lost* as well as most of the works by Edmund Spenser.

When young Mencken moved over to modern English letters he especially liked the writing of Rudyard Kipling. The stirring, masculine measures of the *Barrack-Room Ballads* affected him more than any other poetry. He also found in Kipling's short stories, with their vivid action and faraway settings, much to attract him. Of modern Americans he read a variety. Most of the poets apparently made little impression. But he enjoyed some of the novelists and short-story writers, including William Dean Howells, Frank Stockton, Henry James, Stephen Crane, and Richard Harding Davis.

At the end of a passage in the typescript for Goldberg where he sums up his reading, Mencken says expansively, "Altogether, I doubt

1. Mencken once remarked that as a baby he would have butchered beautifully. February 1881; W. L. Cover, Baltimore.

2. The Mencken family before their summer place at Mt. Washington. Charlie, younger than Henry but already huskier; Anna Abhau Mencken; Gertrude; August, still in long-clothes; August Mencken, Sr., and Henry. Summer 1892.

3. Mencken at his desk in the city room of the Baltimore Herald. His interest in the theater is attested by the copy of the New York Dramatic Mirror *displayed on the desk. November 1901.*

4. *Playing poor boy in spite of his dapper clothes, Mencken looks wistfully through the gates of the Baltimore Country Club. Next to him is a local theater manager, Harry Henkel; next to Henkel is Mencken's tutor in the drama, Robert Carter. About 1902.*

5. Behind the Sunpapers' office Mencken entices a willing trio to the liquid delights of Wegner's Restaurant in German (now Redwood) Street. They are the cartoonist brothers McKee and Tom Barclay, with Folger McKinsey between them. About 1910.

6. The Saturday Night Club, looking like a board of directors about to belch, sits for its picture at the Rennert Hotel. Of all the worthies the one who bulks largest is A. H. McDannald, sitting opposite Mencken. November 1913.

7. *Mencken in the* Sunpapers' *office showing that he smokes a pipe as well as Uncle Willies. 1913.*

To Virginia Dashiell

with regards, apology

and veneration

[signature]

8. *Mencken by Mencken. The inscription and caricatures are on the title page of the copy of his* The Philosophy of Friedrich Nietzsche *which he gave to Miss Virginia Dashiell, a* Sun *staffer who later married John Owens. 1916.*

9. *An expansive Nathan and a quizzical Mencken confront Alfred Knopf as he snaps their picture at his summer place in 1923, while the three of them lay plans to found the* Mercury.

The
SMART SET

Edited by
George Jean Nathan
and
H.L.Mencken.

10.   *Their minds were already on the* Mercury *when Mencken and Nathan put together the* Smart Set *for November 1923. Though not a bad number, it certainly lacks the distinction of some of the earlier issues. Among the better authors: Djuna Barnes, Nancy Hoyt, and Charles MacArthur.*

Vol· I FEBRUARY 1924 No· 2

THE
AMERICAN
MERCURY

A MONTHLY REVIEW
EDITED BY H · L · MENCKEN
& GEORGE JEAN NATHAN

50¢
FOR ONE COPY

$5.00
BY THE YEAR

ALFRED · A · KNOPF
PUBLISHER

11. *There is hardly a dull page in the second number of the* Mercury. *Aside from O'Neill's* All God's Chillun Got Wings, *which was Nathan's choice, it is nearly all Mencken's. The pieces include a mordant caricature of the American labor leader by James Cain; a short story, "Caught," by Sherwood Anderson; "The Grammarian and His Language" by Edward Sapir; and Raymond Pearl's highly satisfying "Alcohol and the Duration of Life."*

12. *Mencken marching off to jail, or at least to police headquarters. On Boston Common he has just sold a copy of the April 1926* Mercury *to the Reverend J. Franklin Chase, Boston's leading smuthound, and Chase has had him arrested. April 1926.*

that any human being in this world has ever read more than I did
between my twelfth and eighteenth years."

As a budding writer he proved to be equally spectacular. By the
time he was twelve he was attempting poetry, essays, and plays. Only
scraps are left of his earliest efforts. But the article on the toning bath
for photographs has been preserved and so have several scrapbooks
of his writing in his middle and late teens. We can see his initial successes in the one labeled "Earliest Attempts at Verse and Prose, 1895–
1901." It presents an unexpected picture, the picture of a Mencken
who enjoyed writing poetry as much as, if not more than, he enjoyed
writing prose.

Every sign showed that he possessed intellectual and literary
gifts, from his top grades at the Polytechnic to his steady, energetic
efforts at creative writing. The nature of his talents must have been
as evident to his family as to himself. What was not evident to them
was the depth of his desire to be a newspaperman. He had already
made plans to become one; he was already convinced that it was the
best way to use his ability as a writer and to put him in touch with life.
His father, impressed by Henry's scholastic record, was at least half-
willing to send him on to college, perhaps to the Johns Hopkins
University or to law school at the University of Maryland. Both were
in Baltimore; both looked accessible. But Henry, with the sort of
stubbornness he often showed later on, said no: he had not the smallest
wish to go to college. In effect, he wanted newspaper work or nothing.
The result was that his father took him briskly at his word and con-
signed him to the family business. As Goldberg put it, young Mencken
stepped from the Polytechnic platform where he had delivered the
commencement address into the cigar factory.

He accepted his father's decision and went obediently enough to
work. It was not bad at first, for what he did chiefly was to sit and roll
cigars. However, his father soon wished to promote him to selling
them. "The very idea of selling revolted me," he later said and added,
"I never got over my loathing." Even his father took this repugnance
into account and so Henry settled into being a clerk instead. But the
tensions within him rose. His feelings toward his father shifted slowly
yet strongly. The unquestioning love he felt in childhood became a
more nearly adult affection but one countered increasingly by resent-
ment and frustration. He saw his father more clearly and realized that
he was not only an often amiable if Olympian presence but also a

fallible human being. His father himself felt the change though he made few concessions. One time he told Henry of his own ambition to be an engineer and of the pains he felt from the thwarting of that ambition. Henry was not comforted.

He channeled his frustrations, or as much of them as he could, into working harder at what he really liked. His time for that was cut drastically to nights and weekends. He begrudged every minute that he could not spend in reading or writing. He scribbled so much and so steadily that his rather shapely handwriting began to be a scrawl. He turned to the typewriter and taught himself to type. And before he was eighteen he made a peculiarly American move: he enrolled in a correspondence school to take a course for would-be writers. The school called itself the "Cosmopolitan University"; for Mencken it was all the campus he needed. Throughout the last half of 1898 he sent in his lessons conscientiously; they were read and criticized with equal conscientiousness by his mail-order instructors. Their observations frequently had a point. Some of them Mencken chose to disregard, for example the admonition that he should not "use long and pompous words in funny passages." But he treasured most of the admonitions and certainly must have relished the praise which soon followed. By November he was being commended for his "use of conversational style and of colloquial expressions that prevail in the purlieus of a large city." In a scrapbook entitled "Typescripts of Early Fiction" he preserved at least three of the pieces, two articles and a short story, after they were returned to him decorated with the instructor's red ink.

His evenings and weekends sped but his days dragged by. By the time he was seventeen he was at least playing with the notion of committing suicide. He wrote only a few words about it and that was years later, dismissing it as "the green sickness of youth." But the fact remains that he did consider killing himself. And the stifled impulse to escape doubtless grew stronger all the while.

Many a young man faced with frustration by day has looked for release by night. At his own social level Mencken apparently found little. If during the time he endured the factory he went to parties, took out many girls, or wheeled any of them in a Strauss waltz he left scant reference to it. There is only one girl he mentions to any of his biographers. According to Goldberg this is Mencken's "first real sweetheart," the pretty blonde daughter of a neighbor. He wrote her poetry about love's arrow — "Egad! It was a pleasant payne!" The attachment lasted for several years. And then Goldberg says, "A chaste and virtuous affair it was, yet at the same time, in less glamorous surroundings, the boy was being initiated into the cruder biological realities of sex." This last is something that Mencken must have told Goldberg rather than written; it is missing from the typescript that Mencken prepared for him. Anyway, sex was not enough; even then work came first for him and it had to be newspaper work. To prepare himself further for his profession, he concentrated in his reading at the Enoch Pratt Library on books about newspapers and the famous men who had written for them. He continued to practice his own writing and looked around restlessly for additional instruction. He filled out a form sent him by another correspondence school, the Associated Newspaper Bureau's School of Journalism. Termed a "Student's Test," it was really a questionnaire. The last question was the significant one: it asked about his plans. His answer proved prophetic enough. "Expect to begin as a reporter & after that trust to hard work & luck for something better."

Even before he reached eighteen he had made the decision to break away, although he probably told no one except his mother. "By the summer of 1898," he recalled to Goldberg, "I had fully made up my mind to escape, amicably if possible but if necessary by open rebellion."

Open rebellion, however, in August Mencken's household was no easy matter. All evidence shows that his son could not bring himself to it. Then, probably while Henry was still nerving himself for a clash, August took sick. He was at home on New Year's Eve of 1898 talking with his wife when he suddenly collapsed. Henry ran for Dr. Z. K. Wiley, the family physician. Dr. Wiley lived nearby and came as soon as he could. He found August suffering from a serious kidney infection. The infection grew worse, August went into a coma, and died in two weeks. The shock to Henry, who by chance had been ill himself, of the swift change in his father from a firm, even formidable, personality to a shrunken figure in his coffin must have been traumatic.

August's death was so unexpected that it may well have left his son with the undercurrents of rebellion still surging and no person to direct them at. Now they could never be directed at the father and it would be unthinkable to direct them at his memory. Moreover, Mencken probably felt guilty, after his father's swift removal, for having nourished any impulse to rebel at all. He started to suffer from an affliction that may have been psychosomatic: "a chronic bronchitis that had begun at the time of my father's death" is what he calls it. There was one way in which these emotions could be released, if the person who had them was a writer. It was of course through the writing itself. This was what happened in the case of Mencken.

Not that it was quite so simple. No feeling of submerged guilt kept Mencken from looking promptly for a newspaper job. In the first paragraph of *Newspaper Days* he says that his father was buried on a Sunday and on Monday evening Mencken applied for a job at the *Morning Herald;* fifteen years before writing *Newspaper Days*, he had told Goldberg that the wait was two weeks. Regardless, he went soon. It was a while before he got a job and a good while longer before he started to write the kind of newspaper prose that was fueled by rebellion. But the emotion he had stored up could keep. How long it lasted is anyone's guess but it seems safe to say that it was long enough to shape his tone and manner in their enduring mode. As we shall see, he found the father figures of Baltimore his handiest targets. He came to the conclusion that most of them were either venal or ridiculous anyway, and so made fair game, from the mayor on up, or down. But he found nothing ridiculous about rebellion, especially when it was the rebellion of the young. And probably because his early expressions of his own rebellion, tempered as they usually were with humor, proved successful and congenial he was able to maintain his iconoclasm permanently.

3. Daily and Sundays

BECAUSE MENCKEN'S BEST FRIEND AT the Polytechnic, young Arthur Hawks, went to work for the *Morning Herald* this was the paper Mencken besieged. Shortly after his father's death he waited on its city editor, a long-nosed, balding man named Max Ways. Though city editors were notorious for their violence of temper and abruptness of language, he showed himself amiable enough when he consented to see Mencken. This was in spite of the fact that Mencken did not cut the kind of figure apt to enchant an employer. In *Newspaper Days* he recalls how he looked. Not yet nineteen, he weighed less than 120 pounds. What he lacked in poundage he tried to make up in gloss. He wore his hair long and meticulously parted in the middle, and he sported a high stiff collar set off by an Ascot cravat.

The first evening he appeared, Ways put him through a kindly catechism. Did he have any newspaper experience? The answer was, sadly, No. What prompted him to want to become a newspaper reporter? The answer was, Something like a celestial call. In evidence: he was bursting with literary ardor and had been writing for years. Anything published? Not really.

Ways thoughtfully surveyed the young man and then gave the inevitable verdict. There was no opening now and the odds against one turning up were beyond belief. However, if he still was determined he might present himself again from time to time. Needless to say, if an assignment did develop he would not be paid for it. After all, training a beginner simply added another burden to an editor's already bowed shoulders.

He had underestimated Mencken. He showed up at the *Herald* office each evening, with no speck of Aug. Mencken & Bro's. tobacco dust on him. A month passed. Finally, impressed by his persistence and by the good words for him that Hawks's older brother, also on the *Herald* staff, was saying, Ways gave him an assignment. He sent him to the far suburbs of Baltimore, to Govanstown, in the winter night not long after a blizzard. The Govanstown druggist, "hugging a red-hot egg-stove behind his colored bottles," offered him a news tip. When Mencken plowed his way back to the office toward eleven, he wrote and rewrote his news item. Ways grunted as he accepted it and then as a dividend let him rewrite a church notice.

On February 23, 1899 his first two items appeared. Today they rest on the first page of the scrapbook "Early News Stories: Baltimore Morning Herald." The news story ran to no less than eight lines, under the heading of "Team Stolen":

> A horse, a buggy and several sets of harness, valued in all at about $250, were stolen last night from the stable of Howard Quinlan, near Kingsville, in the Eleventh district. The county police are at work on the case, but so far no trace of either thieves or booty has been found.

Just below this the *Herald* put the other item:

> At Otterbein Memorial U.B. Church, Roland and Fifth avenues, Hampden, Charles H. Stanley and J. Albert Loose entertained a large audience last night with an exhibition of war scenes by the cineograph.

His assignments in the weeks that followed gradually improved. But their source was still the suburbs as a rule, and getting the news meant that he had to spend hours on the jolting trolley cars. Then after gleaning his news he had to return to the office late in the evening to write it up. Meanwhile, he was putting in a full day's work at the cigar factory because the *Herald* was not yet paying him. The result was that he always felt sleepy, though never so sleepy that he was inclined to stop. He labored at the factory from eight to five thirty, went home to eat dinner and change his clothes, and then reported for duty at the *Herald* at seven. Often he failed to come home to Hollins Street till after midnight. However, it was not long before he proved himself and Ways started him on a regular job, at seven dollars a week, so that he could quit the factory. On July 2, 1899 to be precise, Mencken became a fulltime newspaperman.

The scrapbook depicts his progress. In it, and in the others that follow, we can see the detailed story. The first two items are pure routine — a team is stolen, an audience is entertained — and so are a few more. By the next month the stories are becoming longer. They still are not the kind that other reporters would fight over, for instance the extended account of the tenth-anniversary sermon of the Reverend J. Addison Smith on the "Responsibility of the Mothers of Baltimore." Yet they are now stories, not squibs. In later pages we can almost literally see Mencken grow as a reporter. The news is presented with an evident effort to make it good reading. Though the facts are given, they are not there alone: a personal touch has been added.

Some of the credit must go to Max Ways, for he encouraged colorful writing. Mencken responded eagerly to the atmosphere that was created, even trying to liven his weather reports. One hot day in 1899, for example, when it is ninety-seven degrees in the Baltimore shade, he starts his story expansively with the lead: "Those hasty persons who discarded straw hats and negligee attire when the sun coquettishly turned his countenance away from Baltimore last week much more hastily resurrected their light headgear and gauzy garments yesterday." The next year, 1900, he is being allowed to try human-interest stories, sometimes at considerable length. They often show a comic zest. A Berkshire boar breaks loose from the drove and defies anyone to catch him. Mencken describes the action midway: "Then with a wild, unearthly root the porker started on the run down Pratt street. Officer Mitchell, with a rope formed into a lasso, started in pursuit. Before he had gone 10 steps the boar had stopped, turned around, come back, collided with the officer, executed a flank movement and jumped into the falls." Or there is a new "anti-expectoration" law and Mencken uses a long column to forecast its frustrations for the City Hall loafers.

He must have impressed Ways early. His first regular beat within the city was not North Baltimore, the Siberia of that day to reporters, but South Baltimore, which was its Mississippi. It was a vast ghetto, full of news events ranging from razor parties to riots. And it bordered on the waterfront, whose stevedores and brawling seamen provided still more news. The problem lay in the fact that there was so much that it tasked not only a novice like Mencken but also the reporters for the two competing papers, the lowly *American* and the august *Sun*. As the man from the *American* put it one day, "Why in hell should we walk our legs off trying to find out the name of a Polack stevedore kicked overboard by a mule?" The solution they came to could be called creative reporting. The three simply agreed that his name was Ignaz Karpinski, his age was thirty-six, and he left eleven minor children. The scheme worked so well that it was continued systematically till Mencken moved to another beat. Each city editor discovered that his reporter had shown the same regard for exactness as the other two. Obviously all were accurate fellows and so were commended from time to time for their accuracy. No doubt Max Ways was gratified to see that his novice could keep the record straight just as well as the veteran reporters from the two opposition papers.

Mencken was soon promoted to covering the best of beats, central Baltimore. It included the busiest police court in town, the jail, the police headquarters, and the morgue. Above everything, it included the City Hall. But once again there was a problem. This time it was not so much the surplus of news — by now he could cope with that — but the fact that the reporter from the *American* knew his way around far better than either Mencken or the youngster covering the beat for the *Sun*. Mencken and the *Sun* staffer, Frank Kent, who would become a prime political journalist, tried to entice the *American*'s man into the same cosy arrangement that had worked in South Baltimore. He turned them down. After all he was scoring scoops nearly every day on Kent and Mencken. Warmly agreeing that this had to be stopped, they devised a variant of the South Baltimore scheme. Each afternoon they met at ease in a saloon across from the City Hall and invented a fake story for their papers. The next day their editors read it with satisfaction, while the *American* was properly chagrined to see itself beaten out. When its reporter still refused to cooperate they upped it to two fakes and then even more. Thus sandbagged, he surrendered. Thereafter, Mencken says, "the three of us lived in brotherly concord": the veteran dug up most of the important news and Mencken or Kent embellished it.

In view of Mencken's enterprise and accuracy Ways raised him within a year to the eminence of purely political reporting. His police court days came to an end. He was to concentrate on the skullduggeries of City Hall, with no more razor parties or Polish drownings.

With success came wealth; his salary, after its slow start at seven dollars a week, now soared to eighteen.

The central figure at City Hall was Thomas the Sudden. Mayor Thomas Hayes had acquired this nickname because his daily doings were crammed with surprises and outbursts. Mencken characterized him as the most quarrelsome man on earth. He was a Confederate veteran, ancient in Mencken's eyes, and bristling with authority. His feuds, as many as six at a time, furnished Mencken with highly readable news which often reached the edge of libel. Hayes wrangled constantly with the City Council; it consisted, according to Mencken's *Newspaper Days*, of a scattering of intelligent raisins in a big loaf of dunderheads. In view of such news sources it is surprising that Mencken filed any straight news.

Not that he showed open hostility toward the mayor in his reporting, although he was the most conspicuous of authoritarian father figures in Mencken's new world. He preferred to make him a figure of fun with his enormous waterfall moustache, writing about him with an amiable grin. He reported, for instance, in the lead paragraph of one piece, "For the $16.43 which he received as a salary yesterday Mayor Hayes performed duties of such surpassing ease that the average citizen would be willing to discharge them — with the mayoralty worries excluded—for 50 cents."

Mencken climbed another rung of the *Herald's* ladder by contributing what was probably his first editorial, on March 25, 1901. The occasion, naturally, was Mayor Hayes, and in this case his so-called Kitchen Cabinet. It was made up of a group of henchmen even seedier than the City Council. Mencken describes them with elaborate solemnity. The grand vizier is one J. Doyle, "who finds time and strength to stand by his chief whenever the latter has need to be stood by." Among the other Cabinet members are G. Zimmerman, whose duty is to escort the mayor to the elevator "morn and evening and to hold an umbrella over the burgomasterial head when it raineth," and Fire Commissioner Sirich, "viceroy of Walbrook," a suburb of the city. If not hilarious, the editorial is at least readable.

The Kitchen Cabinet gave Mencken a chance to try some more hoaxing. The mayor was inordinately suspicious as well as quarrelsome, and so he enforced a rule of secrecy in the Cabinet meetings. Undaunted, Mencken concocted a story for the *Herald* which purported to tell all that had happened at the latest meeting. The buffoonery worked; the story was followed by others equally convincing. Then one of the members of the Cabinet offered in private to tell Mencken exactly what happened at each secret session if Mencken would treat him well enough. Mencken agreed. After that the stories were fully accurate. His informant was never discovered in spite of the mayor's angry efforts.

But it would be a distortion to see most of Mencken's newspaper pieces as stunts or fakes. The majority were either straight news or feature stories which bore the imprint of his youthful style but could rarely have been identified as his without the help of his scrapbook. Basically he was still a reporter, even after he began to take on editorial responsibilities. He realized that many things could not be dressed up; some defied even the most creative imagination — including garbage. And it can give us perspective to see that the final item in the scrapbook, printed April 27, 1901, begins flatly: "Garbage Contractor Rice's attorneys yesterday assured Superintendent of Street Cleaning Iglehart and the city law officers that he would sign his contract and execute a bond."

Mencken's remarkable rise resulted chiefly from his innate talent. However, he also had the advantage of a newspaper's city room as a college, a college which he convinced himself was the best in the world—or, as he put it later, "a school infinitely agreeable and romantic." If it was not quite that, it was still a very educational institution. And in Max Ways it offered him an ideal instructor in the basics of newspaper writing. Ways read every line that Mencken and the other reporters turned in. The result was that he never missed a factual error or a banal phrase. But, Mencken says, Ways never missed anything of merit either. Whatever he discovered he announced promptly and emphatically. The whole office knew it, "sometimes with the effect of making a young reporter wither to the size of one of the office cockroaches, and sometimes with the effect of making him walk on air."

Above Ways in the *Herald's* hierarchy stood a managing editor. When Mencken arrived he was a florid nonentity, Colonel A. B. Cunningham, who helped Mencken not at all. However, he was soon succeeded by a vastly better man, Robert Carter. With his eyeglasses and trim beard and moustache he looked a bit dandyish. He proved to be not only a person of cultivation but a sensible superior.

He showed a marked relish for the arts, especially music and the drama. He saw Mencken's promise and took a liking to him. Soon he and Mencken were often spending half the night together while Carter discoursed on theatrical or musical matters.

Throughout 1901 and 1902 he taught Mencken much. But Carter was more successful with Mencken than with the *Herald*. Max Ways left; the top management, above Ways and Carter, changed for the worse; the staff deteriorated; the circulation sank. Although Carter was not to blame he resigned in January 1903, to be followed by a man named Lynn Meekins. The two seemed polar opposites. Carter was a convivial cosmopolite, Meekins a prim, abstemious Methodist. Nevertheless, Mencken soon discovered that Meekins also had a good deal to him. And Meekins, like Carter, was impressed by young Mencken and taught him a considerable amount too. For Meekins in his way was even better qualified than Carter. He could not only give Mencken the benefit of years of newspaper work, most recently as chief editorial writer of the Baltimore *American;* he could also counsel Mencken on literary matters. He had been the first managing editor of the *Saturday Evening Post,* he had already published two novels, and he was a frequent contributor to *Harper's Magazine.*

In a passage in *Newspaper Days* Mencken characterizes Meekins and his usefulness: "As an author himself he took a great deal of interest in my own literary strivings. His advice in that department was always sound, and he was ever ready with it. He knew most of the American literati of the Howells generation, and was full of illuminating anecdotes about them. His own writings were in their manner, but he was very hospitable to the newcomers who finally unhorsed them, and he did a great deal of miscellaneous reading even in his busiest days." He advised Mencken about reading as well as writing and set him to going through "many a tome" that he might otherwise have passed by.

Both Carter and Meekins assigned Mencken new editorial responsibilities, which will be described shortly; the result in clock hours was more leisure for him rather than less. Since he no longer labored both day and night one of the things he found time for was a return to his boyhood interest in music. It was an interest already stimulated by his listening to Carter and, once fully regenerated, it would never disappear. Again the newspaper acted as his college. The current music critic on the *Herald* was an Englishman, W. G. Owst, "who was an abyss of thorough-bass," and set him "to studying a textbook of that science." One of the reporters Mencken worked with every day was Lew Schaefer, who dedicated his own no doubt scant leisure to composing piano pieces for children to play. And Mencken's assistant, Joe Callahan, was a devotee of music and also, according to Mencken, the worst violinist in history. Callahan knew many other musicians and music lovers (the two not always being the same) and introduced his boss to the cream of them. It was through him that Mencken met the men who became the nucleus of the Saturday Night Club.

Mencken's education was furthered in many directions, cultural and otherwise. One of the most helpful teachers about the way of the world was Al Goodman, the *Herald's* political reporter. Mencken found Goodman's views on politics highly congenial. Goodman taught that nearly all reformers in public life were either feeble-minded or frauds and that some were both. On the other hand, he considered practical politicians a much shrewder breed. Their intelligence allowed them to be effective officials. They sometimes included thieves in their number but the public's loss through their thievery was far less than from "the insane wastes" of the reformers. It was from Al Goodman's bearded lips that he first heard the maxim, "In politics a man must learn to rise above principle." Goodman knew as many politicos as Callahan knew musicians, and Mencken benefited. He quickly got to know some he had not known before; he delved into what he called their mystery and art; he acquired a fair share of inside information about them. And he formed what came to be his permanent attitude: public amusement at the machinations of all of them mixed with private pleasure at the company of some of them.

Mencken's energy as a newspaper writer was astounding. On a typical day in the spring of 1900, May 24 to be exact, he wrote eight news stories, all different and coming to a total of over four thousand words. He still had energy to spare even after all he devoted to the *Morning Herald.* In the same year he began to prepare articles for out-of-town newspapers. The first to appear made fun of the melodramatic characteristics of that popular theatrical figure, "The Stage Reporter," in the New York *Morning Telegraph* for February 14, 1900. Shortly afterward he did some writing for an abortive newspaper syndicate organized by a man on the staff of the Baltimore *American.* In addition, he wrote many feature articles for the *Sunday Herald,* some grounded on fact, others on its facsimile. Characteristically, he enjoyed doing an imaginary interview quite as much as a real one.

On the other hand, he was not a machine. He began losing weight; his family doctor thought he saw signs of incipient tuberculosis. Max Ways gave Mencken a month off during the summer doldrums and he rested, more or less, by taking a trip on a banana boat to Jamaica. Improved upon his return, he not only resumed his old responsibilities but added a new one. For he printed the first of what would be an unparalleled parade of columns on October 28, 1900.

Christened "Rhyme and Reason," it appeared for several Sundays on the editorial page of the *Sunday Herald* and was composed mainly of poetry from his own versatile pen. In mid-November the column was rechristened "Knocks and Jollies" and given a stronger shot of humor; it ran through February 1901. Meanwhile, the column "Terse and Terrible Texts" began to appear, also freighted with his verse. After "Knocks and Jollies" came the "Untold Tales," a rowdy series set in ancient Rome and illustrated with caricatures. They ridiculed Baltimore politicians under the thinnest of disguises. Through their paragraphs stalked such scurvy figures as J. Cato Catullus, the Whig boss of the ninth ward, and Irius Satticus, the expert ballot-box stuffer — along with the black-hearted newspaper reporter G. Nero Allegretto. Mencken wrote more than thirty of these tales. He once characterized them as a series of buffooneries in which over half the heroes were hanged in the final paragraph.

Then came "Baltimore and the Rest of the World," the most significant of his columns so far. It started out by trying hard to be humorous, then grew into something more personal and individual. It did not abandon humor but subordinated it to Mencken's widening view of life. It showed affection for Baltimore as well as comic irritation. And it was prophetic in distinguishing Baltimore from the rest of the world, for he always cherished Baltimore, even with its blemishes, over any other place. It included character sketches of local celebrities, human-interest items on local events, and wry comments on City Hall issues. Interspersed were some of his own, often Kiplingesque, poems; items from out-of-town papers; and such cosmic reports as "The catsup vs. ketchup controversy is raging in Rochester, N.Y., and all the massive intellects of the town are centered upon it."

In these coltish columns, with their varying titles and tones, we

see Mencken beginning to find himself. The poetry is poor to middling, the humor pawky, the journalism not quite able to mirror the
man. Yet the origins of the Free Lance and of Mencken's lifelong
mode are to be found here.

Mencken's assignments grew steadily better and in the spring of
1901 he got his first chance at a spectacular news story. It was provided by a disastrous fire in Jacksonville, Florida, to which the
Herald sent not only a carload of supplies but Mencken. As he told
the readers of the *Herald,* "For nearly two miles east and west, and
along a path almost a mile wide the fire tore through Jacksonville.
Today the ruins stand like Pompeii."

He preceded the train, which experienced some embarrassing
delays in arriving. He rose to the challenge, however, and sent home
dispatches which were so ingenious in their forecasts that hasty
readers might well have assumed that the train was there already.
His dispatch for May 11 reported that it would pull in on Saturday
morning and would provide meals for three thousand men, women,
and children now in need. He quoted the city's commissary superintendent as predicting that when the *Herald* car was emptied, most
of the recipients of rations would imagine they were dining at the
best hotel in the land. The point was that the standard ration was
composed of such plain staples as potatoes, lard, and bacon, while the
Herald's train was scheduled to bring such savories as fruit, tea, cakes,
and spices. When the train puffed in, the headline to Mencken's dispatch said GOOD THINGS IN THE CAR GREETED WITH CRIES OF JOY. He
implied years later in *Newspaper Days* that he suffered as many
misadventures as the train, that the *Herald's* motives were mixed at
best, and that he was left feeling that "Service is mainly only blah."

Other out-of-town assignments followed the one to Jacksonville
and soon there was no further advance as a reporter that he could
make. Only editorships were left. By the end of 1901, when Mencken
was barely eligible to vote, Carter named him Sunday editor. He set
out to learn his duties with his usual energy. For all his cockiness he
got along well with his colleagues and, equally essential, with the men
who printed the paper. From Joe Bamburger, the black-bearded
foreman, and his assistant, Josh Lynch, he found out more about the
newspaper trade as a trade than he ever did from anyone in the
editorial department except Max Ways. They soon formed the habit
of going out together each Saturday evening after the Sunday supple-

ment was locked up, to have some beer and a local beef stew so cheap and nutritious that Joe called it the Workingmen's Friend.

Mencken needed whatever help he could command. On taking a long, cool look at the *Sunday Herald* he saw that it cried for change in nearly every respect. It ailed from poor comics, vapid drawings of vapid girls, dismal humorous sketches, dreary travel stories, and a fusty page of fraternal news. Out went "The Summer Girl" or "The Spirit of Thanksgiving" in her "hour-glass corset and trailing skirts." Out went the dreary accounts of what life in Lapland or Cochin-China was like. Out went the page of fraternal news. In came a different series of travel articles with some genuine freshness to them. They actually made Lapland look alive. In came the first of the new syndicated comic strips, where readers could smile at such now forgotten characters as Billy Bounce, the Teasers, and Simon Simple. In came such unconscious humor as "What the Press-Agents Say," where Mencken each week printed the most bombastic pronouncements by the hired hands of the theatrical companies.

Not surprisingly, he could not alter everything. For instance, he had to keep the feeble efforts of a descendant of Artemus Ward because he had nothing to replace them. But in general his reforms were so effective that when Lynn Meekins succeeded Carter as managing editor, he promoted Mencken to city editor.

In this next post Mencken's first problem was personnel. Under Carter both the quality and the morale of the staff had suffered. Though it was not entirely his fault, the city room he left to Mencken was a mess. As Mencken said later, the reporters he inherited were either drunkards or morons. He fired some, nursed others, and blue-penciled the copy of the rest.

Looking around him for a model for the *Herald* to follow he turned to the New York *Sun*. On the basis of his browsing through a good many papers, it appeared by far the most sprightly. Its news reporting was clear, its editorial writing mannered but clever. He had already found it helpful for his own style; he tried to make it so for his associates too. In his fashion he tried to recreate the spirited atmosphere of Max Ways's regime. He found it impossible to duplicate the New York *Sun*'s success because his reporters were not as gifted. Nevertheless, he was soon able to give Baltimore what he felt was "a well-run and amusing paper."

It took only a few months to put him on top of his job as city editor. At first he did too much, for he added extensive rewriting to his normal stint of assigning stories and editing them. He stopped that at Meekins's orders. But he had energy to spare, the more so since the paper began running smoothly. Some of the energy he turned to the problem of Sunday night. Every city editor knew that, for news, Sunday was the low point of the week, and yet there had to be a newspaper on Monday. As Mencken pondered this universal problem, his comic sense came to the rescue. He would cope as an editor the same way he had coped as a reporter. One Sunday the story came in that there was a wild man loose in the woods beyond North Baltimore. Each Monday for a month his latest exploits were reported by the *Herald* to the alarmed but interested public. As Mencken admitted in *Newspaper Days*, "I got special delight out of the wild man, for I had invented him myself."

Another source of Sunday news appeared in the guise of a forum that met, Mencken found, each Sunday afternoon above a livery stable in West Baltimore. He dispatched a reporter there with instructions to make the most of whatever happened. He came back with a sensational story about a debate between a Socialist and a Single Taxer which ended with the Socialist's pulling out a butcher knife and the Single Taxer jumping through a window. That the story had only a nub of truth was unimportant. Then Mencken took the next step and had the same reporter, week after week, report on the startling activities at the forum of a whole cast of imaginary characters whose rantings or roarings made news.

It was not long before Mencken was taking an occasional chance with stories on other days of the week. He encouraged the reporters who handed in stories which were either funny or mildly fantastic. Somehow both he and the *Herald* escaped without harm. They were never caught when it mattered.

He now cut a formidable figure, young though he was. He oversaw the activities of about thirty men, some of them twice his age. It was a great occasion, he says in *Newspaper Days*, when he overheard himself referred to as the "Old Man." We can catch a characteristic glimpse of him through one of his copyboys. His copyboy in 1904 was a slight thirteen-year-old, Thomas Doerer. He was paid three dollars a week to run Mencken's errands and do his bidding. While waiting for orders he sat in a chair in Mencken's cubbyhole of an office, ready to jump when Mencken shouted "Boy! Copy!" What Doerer saw was a furiously energetic fellow, always busy, usually brusque. Wearing a dark-green eyeshade he punched away at his typewriter with four fingers, stopping periodically to chew an "Uncle Willie" cigar or spit accurately into the brass cuspidor. Doerer brought him a little package of Mail Pouch tobacco every day to supplement the Uncle Willies. His rolltop desk was crammed with papers. Regardless of whether he was editing the copy of others or writing his own, he worked fast and in an atmosphere of pressure. In spite of his speed he was a stickler for accuracy; he wanted the facts in the pages of the *Herald* to be precise.

Yet at times he could relax, even in the office. There he showed that he could tolerate human foibles as long as they did not interfere with the effectiveness of the paper. He might bellow at Doerer but he could also grin at him and give him a pat on the back. Outside the office he liked to visit the saloon across the street from the *Herald*, to drink a stein of beer and eat box-cheese. The afterhours parties he enjoyed were mainly male ones. Such social life as he took time for failed, as far as we know, to involve girls with backgrounds like his own. Every now and then, however, he would write a note with his stub pen to one of the girls in Baltimore's red-light district and give it to Doerer to deliver.

He got the paper running with a sprightliness it had never shown before, not even under Ways. Then came the Great Fire of Baltimore, which literally and figuratively incinerated the *Herald*.

It began on a Sunday morning, February 7, 1904, while he was peacefully sleeping off a Saturday night. A telephone call from the *Herald*, reinforced by the appearance of *Herald* reporter Lew Schaefer, roused him and sent him to the office at noon. What he found was the start of a conflagration which would burn out a square mile in the center of the city and would go "howling and sputtering on for ten days." Telling about it in *Newspaper Days,* Mencken recalls that it was not till early Wednesday morning that he even took his clothes off and it was not till a week later — the succeeding Sunday — that he returned to Hollins Street for a bath and a change of clothing. He went into the week a boy, full of "the hot gas of youth." He left it "a settled and indeed almost a middle-aged man, spavined by responsibility and aching in every sinew."

But the adventure in between was superb. Sniffing excitement, the reporters of the *Herald* turned up by early afternoon on the first

Sunday and, with the high advantage of being able to look from their office window at the story they were writing, poured out page after page of copy. However, shortly before nine in the evening, the police told the *Herald* staff to clear out because the building next door was to be blown up. Carrying, in effect, their newspaper with them the staff marched to a hotel a few blocks off. Lynn Meekins telephoned the Washington *Post,* forty miles away, and arranged to use its facilities for the night. Meekins, Mencken, and a platoon from the *Herald* took a train to Washington, saw the Capitol by moonlight, and somehow got together a four-page paper. By six thirty the next morning thirty thousand copies reached Baltimore on a Washington milk train and were sold by eight o'clock. The streamer headline was Mencken's: HEART OF BALTIMORE WRECKED BY GREATEST FIRE IN CITY'S HISTORY.

Meekins and Mencken tried frantically to find a good way to publish the *Herald* in Baltimore. They had no luck. Washington was out because the *Post* needed its plant. In desperation they turned to Philadelphia, a hundred miles distant, and arranged with the *Evening Telegraph* to use its plant during off-hours. They used it for five weeks. What with special trains, makeshift offices, and heroic effort, they produced a creditable paper. As a matter of fact, the paper flourished. It abounded in advertising — every burnt-out Baltimore merchant wanted to tell his customers that all was well and that he proposed to continue in business — and it contained a full share of what Mencken termed "juicy news."

Sadly enough, the prosperity proved to be brief. When the *Herald* returned to Baltimore and started to function in an old carbarn, it found that its advertisers were deserting it for the evening papers. The *Herald*'s top management, up above Meekins, made the suicidal decision to put out both a morning and an evening paper with no additions in staff. For a week Mencken and the others tried; then they collapsed. Too late the management was persuaded to kill the idea of two papers prepared by the staff of one. The old morning paper was dropped; the new evening one kept going through desperate straits and stratagems. During this final period the owners made Meekins editor in chief with Mencken following him as managing editor. Then they promoted the two still further, making Meekins president and Mencken editor in chief. But these dizzying promotions were useless gestures. Only a powerful infusion of money and credit would have saved the paper; neither was forthcoming and on June 17, 1906 the *Herald* died.

Its death posed no problem for Mencken, however. All three of Baltimore's bigger dailies offered him a job but the *Evening News* moved fastest. He already had a good friend named Stuart Olivier working on the paper and its publisher, a strong-minded and liberal newspaperman from the Midwest, Charles Grasty, wanted Mencken as news editor. The offer, promptly made, was promptly accepted. Yet it took Mencken only a few weeks to find that he cared less and less for that kind of managing. Besides, the *Sun*, though both statelier and slower than the *News*, soon came up with a pleasant alternative. Its board of directors, at the instance of President Walter W. Abell, resolved to increase the size of its Sunday paper and to draft an editor from outside. His choice was Mencken; the board agreed. On July 30 he started at forty dollars a week. The pay was higher than he had ever earned before and the job was, as he once remarked, more leisurely and literary.

It took most of the newspaper world a while to discover his arrival at the *Sun*. Most but not all. In August he devoted a piece, written with his now characteristic bounce and wit, to the choleric editor of the Louisville *Courier-Journal*, Colonel Henry Watterson. Watterson replied with relish, exclaiming, "Think of it! The staid, old Baltimore Sun has got itself a Whangdoodle. Nor is it one of the bogus Whangdoodles which we sometimes encounter in the side-show business — merely a double-cross betwixt a Gin-Rickey and a Gyas-cutis — but genuine, guaranteed, imported direct from the Mountains of Hepsidam."

No part of Mencken's life as a newspaperman ever remained uneventful but the closest to it was his first four years on the *Sun*. As editor of the *Sunday Sun* he captained a very modest enterprise. As he himself pointed out, it was a paltry thing of twelve pages and a weekly budget of no more than one hundred dollars for material. It took little of his office time, so he soon added the writing of editorials and the reviewing of plays to his job. The trouble with his play reviewing was that it slowly curdled. The more he went to the theater the more he was irked by its bombast. The theater managers complained to the publisher of the *Sun*. Walter Abell protected Mencken in the name of freedom of the press, but Mencken himself gradually wearied of playgoing and resigned from it in 1909.

Though the editorial writing went on longer the ultimate result was much the same. He found that he did not really like to do editorials and that most of his editorials did not amount to much. He later said so himself and speculated about the reason. It was mainly, he decided, his apathy about public issues and political contests. It was not that he failed to enjoy the antics of political buffoons. He did, extremely; and he wrote about such things till the end of his newspaper career. But an editorial was normally an official piece for or against something or someone, and Mencken could see no great difference between buffoons. "The question whether A or B was elected to office always seemed to me to be hollow." Moreover, he was always better at attack than defense and a fair share of editorials were spent in fending. Finally, editorials were anonymous, impersonal. Mencken realized that his most effective writing was done under his own name and dealt with subjects that editorial writers usually shunned.

April of 1910 brought a new owner to the *Sun* and new duties to Mencken, but unfortunately they included writing more editorials instead of fewer. The *Sunpapers*, racked by dissension at the top, were sold to a syndicate headed by the same Charles Grasty who had hired Mencken at the *Evening News* and whom Mencken had quickly deserted. But he bore no malice toward Mencken. Grasty proceeded to shake up the *Sun*. He took personal control of its business affairs, dropped many of its old-fashioned practices, and started it on a program of expansion. Most notably, he established a whole new newspaper, the *Evening Sun*. For managing editor he brought over his managing editor at the *Evening News*, John Haslup Adams, and made Mencken associate editor.

Each day Mencken was supposed to write two editorials and to help Adams as much as he could. Daily he averaged between two and three thousand words of writing besides doing his editorial chores. One day Adams asked him to compose an editorial on the airship. He spent two weeks at it with little result except to remind him of the fact that editorials bored him. "The Weakness of the Aeroplane" could have been written by a hundred other men; only the thrust of the style shows some sign of the individual Mencken. But he also got the chance to write a daily column on the editorial page; this he promptly undertook with gusto.

The first piece appeared on April 18, 1910; the rest followed in rich profusion. They were initialed H. L. M., not signed, but it was clear to Baltimore from the start that here was a real personality. Here indeed, though Baltimore would never put it this way, was Watterson's Whangdoodle. Day after day he put into type the facts, the ideas, the attitudes, and the prejudices he had accumulated in his first thirty years. It has been said that the seeds for his future essays are to be found in the Free Lance columns which followed this series started in April 1910, but that is only partly true. They were often seedlings by the time of the Free Lance; the seeds were sown here before. The titles in this series show it. Sometimes the pieces are short, merely a few paragraphs, but as a rule they are regular articles in what we now know as the Menckenian mode. "Huckleberry Finn," "Wars upon Alcohol," "Joseph Conrad," "The Decay of Swooning," "The Art of Lynching," "The Quacks are Prosperous," "In Defense of the Gallus," "Poor Old Ibsen," "Thoughts on Eating," "Notes on Morals," "French Marriages," "Curbing the Cops," "The American," "The Expurgators," "Spoken American," and "Nietzscheana": these are some of the titles in this promising set.

The articles for the next year start January 2 and end May 6. They are if anything richer, more personalized than before. They stopped in the beginning of May for a pleasant reason. Young Harry Black, son of the largest stockholder in the *Sunpapers*, had been in England where he had seen some of the writing of a British columnist. He enjoyed it and the thought came to him that the *Sunpapers* ought to have a brisk, readable columnist of their own. He decided that they already had someone on the staff who might do the job, this H. L. M., whoever he was. On coming home Black shared his idea with Grasty, who agreed readily. The result was that Grasty invited Mencken into his office and explained what he wanted or at any rate what he thought he wanted: a readable, irresponsible, controversial column. It could tilt a lance at anything except the church. It became of course the Free Lance.

Like most natural wonders the Free Lance looks smaller now than we thought it was. It is not as witty, pugnacious, or capricious as its reputation. No man could be both funny and insulting all the time. Nevertheless, the average for blunt speaking and lively writing is high. And the effect of the column on Baltimore was extraordinary. Today many of the references are obscure; the throwaway lines lack meaning. But for the stiff-collared Baltimorean of the years between 1911 and 1915 the column was often — if tradition can be believed — the first thing he turned to in the paper.

It gave the effect of a brightly colored mosaic. There were quotable sentences from outraged or enthusiastic readers; there were comments in "American" as heard, for instance, on the streetcars; there were assorted jibes and catcalls from Mencken; there were pungent pen portraits; there were items of curiosa; there were his alkaline observations on the politics and politicians of Baltimore. In between he put frantic exhortations: "Boil your drinking water! Watch out for ptomaines! Rush the can! Take a bath! Swat the fly! Don't rock the boat!" His compliments were nearly always left-handed; his pretences at fairness were transparent. For example: "Let me not be unfair to the barbers. Their gross and lamentable incompetence is not unique." The people he prayed to be saved from were a multitude. For example: "From all persons who lift their eyebrows when one mentions sauerkraut, and from fat women who loll grotesquely in automobiles, . . . from barbers with pale, freckled hands, and from neighbors who do not drug their children at night, and from German waiters wearing detachable shirt fronts, . . . from young pests selling tickets for church fairs, and from bassos with prominent Adam's apples, . . . from argumentative Christian Scientists, . . . from street car conductors who are new to the line and don't know the names of streets, . . . from adult males who wear diamonds, and from all boosters of tin-pot fraternal orders, . . . and from persons who believe that 'alright' is an English word."

There were resounding generalities such as "All talk of winning the people by appealing to their intelligence, of conquering them by impeccable syllogism, is so much moonshine." And aphorisms such as "an anti-vivisectionist is one who gags at the typhoid vaccine — and swallows 'Science and Health.'" And pungent similes such as "as porous as a blue law" or "As lethal as a Baltimore Sunday."

Moreover, the column seemed to stop at nothing, or almost nothing. Mencken soon persuaded Grasty to release him from the promise not to attack the church, after the Methodist ministers of Baltimore had obligingly met and attacked Mencken. Grasty, affirming his belief in free speech, let Mencken reply. And, as Mencken later observed, he kept on replying for the next five years.

The wars the Free Lance waged were seldom sullied by victory. "I lost all my battles," Mencken recalled. Yet in a way this was rhetoric, as he himself admitted. If many of his specific causes failed, his general effect was still potent. Baltimore became the better for the Free Lance, even to Mencken's eyes. He conceded that it accustomed the city to the freest of discussion, turning a hidebound community into one where any idea could be entertained. The Free Lance helped to make freedom of thought and action real, and what the Free Lance started in its columns spread throughout the *Sunpapers.*

The Free Lance pieces exhibited a rollicking rebellion resembling nothing else on the American scene. The writing was now far from amateurish, though boisterous to the extent of being slapstick. When Mencken rained his verbal buffets on the head of a Baltimore politician, still his best-loved target, or on a Baltimorean idiocy it was like a Punch and Judy show. But, allowing for comic exaggeration, Mencken meant what he said. The rebellion was real, the criticism purposeful.

The point is that it was never heavy. In its largest dimension the Free Lance represented his basic attitude towards newspaper work and toward life. He treated both like his gaudy girls in the red-light district — whom he enjoyed thoroughly but disrespectfully.

4. The Apt Apprentice

"Baltimore and the Rest of the World": such was the title of the most promising series of columns which Mencken did before the Free Lance. In one way it was a measure of his progress. For he was a Baltimore boy and then a Baltimore man, none more loyal; but from the time he left the Polytechnic his horizons expanded till they took in a good deal of the Western world. Through a period that lengthened into half a century he taught himself systematically, by omnivorous reading and skeptical reflection on that reading. He also learned from others, principally from his seniors at the *Herald* to begin with and thereafter from a variety of well-chosen friends.

We have seen how the *Herald* afforded him both experience and instruction. He boasted in the Preface to *Newspaper Days* that while the respectable young fellows of his generation were college freshmen oppressed by "simian sophomores" and misled by chalky pedagogues, he was at large in Baltimore with a front seat at every show, being enlightened in a hundred interesting ways unknown to college curriculums. "If I neglected the humanities," he says, "I was meanwhile laying in all the worldly wisdom of a police lieutenant, a bartender, a shyster lawyer, or a midwife." Nor did he actually neglect the humanities. His best instructors at the *Herald*, Robert Carter and Lynn Meekins, were both apostles of the humanities and the humanities were not overlooked by other members of the *Herald* faculty.

Moreover, when he worked at educating himself he began by stressing the humanities and above all, literature. That teaching started early, even before he yearned to be on a newspaper. An occasional assignment for homework at the Polytechnic helped but he always stood ready to help himself. He not only read; he wrote. From the outset he wrote, as he said more than once, as spontaneously as a cow gives milk or a dog chases a cat. He wrote and then learned from his writing. He proved perfectly willing to attempt any literary form, with the result that failures and fragments were mingled with his youthful successes. Many of these apprentice papers have been preserved in the scrapbook "Earliest Attempts at Verse and Prose." There is a partial libretto for a comic opera on Bluebeard, with the setting switched from France to the Orient. There are several essays and draft notes for essays, including one on *King Lear* prepared for a class at the Polytechnic in 1895. There is his first short story "Idyl," which opens with "The gossips of the little village of Beaufort had long ago whispered that . . . ." There are similar papers in his scrapbook "Typescripts of Early Fiction." These run from assignments he did for the correspondence school to workmanlike tales composed in his early twenties. The most conspicuous item is the first fifty-two pages of a stagy novel, begun when he was perhaps twenty and set in the time of Shakespeare. A false start if there ever was one, it is ornamented by such dialogue as " 'By St. Hubert,' bellowed my lord, 'I will wait me no waits.' "

Most remarkable in his early writing is the substantial amount of verse. In his late teens he enjoyed composing anything with a beat to it, from everyday doggerel to intricate flights of lyric fancy. There was one period of several weeks when he triumphantly penned a poem a day, so it is no wonder that the first third of "Earliest Attempts at Verse and Prose" abounds in assorted if smudgy stanzas.

His urge to publish was almost as strong as his urge to write, and from his fifteenth to his twentieth year he managed more than once to get his work in print. His first poem to be printed, the matey "Ode to the Pennant on the Centerfield Pole," appeared in the Baltimore *American* in the summer of 1896. It was not long before he published others. When he made his way onto the staff of the Baltimore *Herald* it became his prime outlet, but he also went beyond Baltimore and reached out toward the national magazines. Among those which published — and paid for — his verses from 1899 on were the *Bookman*, the *New England Magazine*, *Leslie's Weekly*, the *National Magazine*, and *Life*.

When his very first book appeared it was *Ventures into Verse* and included at least two dozen pieces which had reached print before. He gave it to the world through the happy accident of having two friends if not three (the number varied in Mencken's recollections) who wanted to launch a press, asked him what to print, and readily issued the little volume in 1903.

From the pieces pasted into the scrapbook to those published in *Ventures into Verse* there is a perceptible progress, evidently the work of an enterprising if impressionable talent. Together they preserve a good part of a whole drawerful of verse that Mencken said he had accumulated at the *Herald*. Looking back later, he announced that much of the drawerful consisted of "dreadful imitations of Kipling, who was then my God." The rest consisted, as he remembered, of "triolets, rondeaux and other experiments in the old French forms that Austin Dobson and Andrew Lang had brought in." And there must also have been at least a few pieces of doggerel.

When *Ventures into Verse* emerged, the hand of Kipling lay on it for all to see. Mencken's imagination had been captured by the manly rhetoric, the thumping rhymes, and the galloping rhythms of the British poet. The opening poem was dedicated to him and its stanzas were exceedingly close to some of his. The first stanza sets the tone.

> *Prophet of brawn and bravery!*
> *Bard of the fighting man!*
> *You have made us kneel to a God of Steel,*
> *And to fear his church's ban;*
> *You have taught the song that the bullet sings —*
> *The knell and the crowning ode of kings;*
> *The ne'er denied appeal!*

At least a third of *Ventures into Verse* is made up of counterfeits of Kipling. The young poet celebrates the joys of war ("Oho! for the days of olden time, / When a fight was a fight of men!") and likewise its griefs ("The transport Gen'ral Ferguson, she headed home again, / With a thousand heavy coffins in her hold"). He writes of the Spanish Main and of the "Filipino Maiden." His very accents are at times those of the Barrack Room, when he speaks about "Gawd" or the "Orf'cer Boy." Every line breathes with adventure, either high or harrowing. He rides to the ends of the Empire, with never a backward glance at the Baltimore he leaves behind.

Kipling we could expect. But after Mencken's poems in the Kip-

ling mode, the most conspicuous in *Ventures into Verse* are his attempts at following the French forms. It is not easy to picture him
masticating Mail Pouch ("I had acquired the sinful habit of tobacco-
chewing in my father's cigar factory") while he composed a rondeau
or a ballade. But he did. He found a genuine challenge in their
complexity and he liked to give them an impish turn.

The remaining poems in *Ventures into Verse* are nearer Mencken's norm. Most have a homegrown wit. There is the pawky comedy,
for example, of "The Song of the Slapstick." Doubtless inspired by his
visits to one of Baltimore's steamy burlesque houses, it begins:

> *Why is a hen? (Kerflop!) Haw, haw!*
> *Toot, goes the slide trombone;*
> *Why is a hen? (And a swat in the jaw!)*
> *And the ushers laugh alone.*

Not only was *Ventures into Verse* published, it had a scattering
of reviews. Most privately printed volumes drop into the abyss; his
was an exception. Out of the approximately one hundred copies his
friends issued, he sent away about a dozen for review. He got a
surprisingly good response from the newspapers. Several newspaper
critics liked it and praised it, not for the imitations of Kipling or the
French forms but for the humor. The Milwaukee *Sentinel*, for instance,
spoke favorably of Mencken's "merry songs." The Chicago *Record-
Herald* found that his verse had "froth, zizz, sparkle and tang."

But even if editors and critics liked the verses he wrote, he himself grew to consider them pleasant trifles. They were too slight to be a
vehicle for his burgeoning ideas. Then too, the techniques that attracted him increasingly were the techniques of prose. The shift was
gradual, though. After he left the halls of the Polytechnic and went to
work in the cigar factory, he borrowed books of both prose and verse
from the shelves of the Enoch Pratt Library. He also patronized a
newsdealer's counter in West Baltimore, which stocked the latest of
the literary journals. The majority of those he bought, he later realized,
were eccentric trash but they did him no harm. He reminisced about
them in his *Prejudices: First Series,* and especially about one called
the *Criterion,* which favored European and experimental literature:
"How, as a youngster, I used to lie in wait for the *Criterion* every
week! . . . That was in the glorious middle nineties and savory pots
were brewing. Scarcely a week went by without a new magazine of

some unearthly *Tendenz* or other appearing on the stands."

After he worked his way onto the *Herald* he discovered that he was close to literature as well as to reporting. And to one department of it above all, the drama. Thanks to Robert Carter he focused much of his literary interest on the stage and channeled much of his belletristic writing into theatrical criticism. Less than a year after Carter's arrival as managing editor, he let Mencken become the paper's second-string theater critic. It meant that the younger man could attend anything from melodrama down to vaudeville. He was happy to review the lighter productions that appeared in Baltimore and readily left the heavyweight drama to Carter. Imagine being paid to sit in a red plush seat and see a show!

With no trouble at all Carter persuaded Mencken to his own astringent idea of how to review drama for the press. "Exact and scientific criticism" was not the object. The object was to amuse rather than to instruct, and it would be easier if the reviewer remembered that most playwrights were merely showmen and most actors idiots.

Mencken's early reviews in the *Herald* have a certain sportiveness but little else. He would have wanted to be lively even if Carter had not recommended it, but the first productions he reviewed were so modest in their aims and effects that he did not need Carter's brisk condescension to the stage. What Mencken showed, as he began to grow in his role of reporter of Baltimore's entertainment, was some attention to the principles underlying that entertainment.

Even when he was watching vaudeville — and enjoying it ungartered — he did not rest his mind. Here he is on the act that received top billing one week in September 1904: "Rice and Prevost, comedy acrobats, who appear just before the biograph, are the most satisfactory entertainers in the company. One of the two — it may be Rice and it may be Prevost — wears the powder of a stage clown, and it is his business to be clownish. To accomplish this he does nothing but fall — first over a chair, then from a table, then from table to chair, and, lastly, from, under, over and into table and chair and chair and table. It is the acme of low comedy and the last word in pure buffoonery, and nothing more genuinely ludicrous has been seen in Baltimore since Weber and Fields' last visit. Horseplay of this sort is a fine art and as far removed from the strenuous endeavors of slapstick and seltzer-syphon operators as is water-color painting from kalsomining."

As his education continued he found most of the shows pleasant
but not nourishing enough for a permanent diet. However, he realized
that the serious drama, particularly as it was developing overseas, had
a good deal to it. Once again he had help with his perceptions; for
shortly after he started reviewing, the newspaper world put another
teacher in his path. This time it was a wispy journalist named Will
Page, who worked as press agent for a better-than-average Baltimore
stock company. He and Mencken grew to be friends and he was the
first to alert Mencken to the tart, tendentious plays of George Bernard
Shaw. Also he increased Mencken's interest in the plays of Henrik
Ibsen, an interest aroused as early as 1900, when Mencken traveled
home from Jamaica on a Scandinavian ship whose captain and captain's wife overflowed with information about the Norwegian dramatist.

The sensational nature of both Shaw's and Ibsen's plays appealed
to Mencken. The company Page was with presented Ibsen's *Ghosts*,
in spite of some misgivings, at the opening of the season of 1902 / 3.
A dramatic sermon on the effects of syphilis, the play had been sup-
pressed in London and was the target of conservative critics on both
sides of the Atlantic. Mencken, beaming, applauded its production in
Baltimore. "I was naturally hot for it," he recalled later. The critics
from the *Sun* and the *American* considered the play deplorable while
the *Herald* was prompt with its praise.

Mencken saw no reason to repent thereafter simply because he
was in the minority. Two years later he interviewed a member of the
Baltimore cast, Virginia Kline, and recalled the impact of the play. In
the face of predictions of failure it had succeeded everywhere but in
New York. "Managers and critics had said that Ibsen was impossible"
but the Baltimore company had "visited scores of cities and everywhere were found playgoers with enough appreciation of the finer
subtleties of life to turn from the platitudes of the day to the red-
blooded preaching of the grim old Norwegian." So spoke Mencken.
Though his style was not yet vintage, his tone was already firm.

He notes in *Newspaper Days* that his education was furthered
by a series of press agents from other theatrical companies who called
at the *Herald*'s office, including one with the unforgettable name of A.
Toxen Worm. They were often more instructive than they meant to
be; through their overblown enthusiasm for local products they confirmed him in his deepening belief that American plays were for the

most part trash. The significant ones were coming from Europe despite the proud cries of the press agents.

As he grew better educated he set his standards higher. The American theater as embodied in Baltimore looked worse and worse to him, although he was reviewing the best of the serious drama now that Carter was gone. If the plays were dreary the players were drearier, even the bearers of flashing names. As the theatrical seasons crept along, he realized that Carter's ironic views were all too right. When the noted Richard Mansfield entered Baltimore to star in Schiller's tragedy *Don Carlos,* Mencken reviewed his performance in the *Herald* of January 10, 1906. He announced that Mansfield's acting alternated between the tiresome and the execrable. He did nothing really well; even his makeup was a botch: "Mr. Mansfield . . . paints upon his face the features of a Don Carlos such as probably never lived anywhere." When the *Herald* stopped publishing, in July 1906, Mencken moved briefly to the *Evening News* and then to the *Sun,* where he stayed. But his point of view remained the same. In the theatrical season of 1905/6 he wrote twenty-three unfavorable notices in a row, according to his count.

Nevertheless, both he and the drama benefited from his reviewing. The drama benefited because he was able, at least to an extent, to widen the Baltimore audience for the controversial European playwrights, especially Shaw and Ibsen. Mencken benefited because the reviewing quickened his interest in Shaw and that interest provided a pivot for his career. Before encountering Shaw, Mencken had proved that his various literary or quasi-literary efforts possessed some appeal for the public. Soon successful, he was also soon dissatisfied. As we shall see, it took Shaw to make him a writer of the kind he really wanted to be, both in approach and format. And Shaw became the subject of his first real book, *George Bernard Shaw: His Plays.*

The fact was that in a few short years Mencken had developed into a passable poet whose slim volume of verse attracted more attention than most. Any later volumes would doubtless have shown increasing depth. Yet poetry palled for him by his early twenties. And he soon proved himself as a short-story writer. In the space of half a dozen years he turned from an amateur into a professional who could sell his fiction not merely to the pulps and cheap syndicates but also to the better magazines, if not the best ones. Before he was through only the journals like the *Atlantic* or the *Saturday Evening Post* held out against him. Yet by the time he passed his mid-twenties, short-story writing likewise palled. He continued to do it from time to time, even in his thirties, but he did it with increasing reluctance.

What was left for him was the essay and once he began to see its possibilities he never abandoned it. It gave him the best vehicle for his views. Years later, when he published his most popular books they were primarily collections of essays: the *Prejudices* furnish the most famous example. Even his treatises, however, such as the *Treatise on the Gods,* resolve themselves into sets of related essays. It may even be that the suggestion for the essay form came from Shaw. After all, the Shaw whom Mencken learned to know was the drama critic as well as the dramatist. He was the essayist as well as the playwright, the author not only of many reviews but of the lively essays which masqueraded as the prefaces to his plays. At the least, Shaw helped him to develop a feeling for the kind of expository prose which led to his brilliant essays.

Mencken found his true style in the course of writing the book about Shaw. Many different ingredients went into it but the combination was unique. There was the love of words, basic to his style, seen at its earliest in the school exercises at the Polytechnic and at its fanciest in the aborted novel on Shakespeare. There was the readiness at writing which was cultivated by his reams of copy at the *Herald* and the *Sun,* copy nearly always pushed by a deadline. And there was the urge to write clearly, in part because of the need to make the mass of newspaper readers understand him but also because he early acquired an admiration for clarity for its own sake. Here, incidentally, he had the help of Thomas Huxley. His was the best English written in the nineteenth century, Mencken felt, with the paramount virtue he wished for his own: it made its meaning unmistakably plain.

Some of the tricks of his style he learned easily from others. He apparently told one of his biographers, Edgar Kemler, that reading the editorial writer Edward Kingsbury of the New York *Sun* showed him how to demolish his opponents by, for example, treating them with mock seriousness and giving them titles or by absurdly crediting them with the characteristics of the great. He never gave up the bestowal of titles on those he disliked including such personages as "Prof. Dr." Woodrow Wilson and "Dr." Franklin Delano Roosevelt. And he often undercut an opponent by terming him "The Arkansas Voltaire" or "The Philadelphia Zola." According to Kemler he learned other things from other, more noted writers: charm and allusiveness from James Gibbons Huneker, the art of the epigram from Ambrose Bierce, ribald lyricism from Rabelais, and an omniscient air from Macaulay.

Some of the tricks of style he devised for himself, including the use of highly spiced or novel words, and of archaisms when they did not cloud his meaning. He began to stud his sentences with expressions like "to have at" and words like "wenching." And he grew adept at the unexpected combination — "vacant" beer bottles, for instance, instead of merely empty ones.

From within himself and from without he compounded the style that was to make him famous. But it was matter as well as manner, and his study of Shaw helped to find the proper matter.

As Mencken observed in *Newspaper Days*, ". . . through Shaw I found my vocation at last. My first real book, begun in 1904, was a volume on his plays and the notions in them, critical in its approach. It was the first book about him ever published, and it led me to begin a larger volume on Nietzsche in 1907, and to undertake a book on Socialism two years later, in the form of a debate with a Socialist named La Monte, now recusant and forgotten. After that I was a critic of ideas, and I have remained one ever since."

Shaw provided Mencken with both the subject for his book and the model for its form. In 1891 he himself had published *The Quintessence of Ibsenism*, which Mencken read eagerly since it was one of his favorites writing on another. That book opened with a general consideration of the plays, went on to analyze them one by one, and concluded with a chapter on "The Moral of the Plays." In treating them Shaw mingled summary with comment. His basic purposes were to make Ibsen clear and to defend him from ignorant attack. Mencken proposed to the firm of Brentano in New York, Shaw's American publisher, that he do a book about Shaw himself along the lines of the *Quintessence*. Brentano declined, so he turned to John W. Luce & Company of Boston because it had just printed an edition — pirated — of Shaw's essay called "On Going to Church." Harrison Schaff of the Luce firm commissioned the book and Mencken worked on it from the summer of 1904 into the next spring.

Schaff and his colleagues were understandably wary about accepting a manuscript from an unknown. When Mencken first outlined the work in a series of letters to them, they made suggestions at various points. When he submitted a portion of the manuscript, probably the first part, they proposed revisions and in fact had the whole introduction rewritten. Because he was a new author Mencken responded the more readily to criticism, yet he retained his reasonableness all his life. Now in writing his *Shaw* he accepted many of the editorial suggestions at once. In the case of those he did not he explained why, as Schaff recalls in a letter, "fully, interestingly and with the warmth characteristic of his personality." A decent book developed, one that the critics could greet with respect.

The morning the galley proofs reached Mencken at the *Herald* was memorable. He could not resist showing them to Lynn Meekins, who was as pleased as he was. "If you live to be two hundred years old," he assured Mencken, "you will never forget this day. It is one of the great days of your life." He happily ordered Mencken to return to his office, lock the door, and proofread the galleys. He did so and years later could still remember the "unparalleled glow" of that experience.

When the book was published in 1905 it reflected something of the delight and sense of discovery with which he had approached Shaw. The world Shaw moved in was the most attractive he could imagine. Above all, it was sophisticated and foreign in contrast to the homely one which embraced Mencken. Its leaders captained the kind of artistic and intellectual revolt that appealed to him. Ibsen had smashed one theatrical taboo after another; Shaw was following him and outdoing him. The horrendous philosophies of Schopenhauer and Nietzsche were being preached by the characters in some of the new plays, especially Shaw's. Shaw was mounting his plays as attacks on middle-class morality. One of his first, *Mrs. Warren's Profession*, dealt with prostitution and, Mencken knew, was refused public performance in England. To the startled public Shaw seemed comfortable only when espousing the ideas of a minority.

So did Mencken. Young as he was, he knew how he felt and what he liked and did not like. If some of his ideas were still a bit amorphous, Shaw helped to crystalize them. The contempt for cant, the satirical attitude toward sacred cows, and the energy of expression were all qualities Mencken shared with Shaw. What he disliked in Shaw he either ignored or scanted. He doubtless disliked Shaw's socialism and in a few years would attack socialism in *Men versus the Man*, his debate with La Monte. But in *George Bernard Shaw: His*

Plays he confined himself to a minimal discussion of it and to inter-preting it, when he did discuss it, in terms of the actions and charac-ters. Even in *Widowers' Houses*, which deals with a family of slum landlords, Mencken pointed out that the important thing was not the capitalism they exemplified but the way they made the audience feel as they clashed on the stage with one another.

It is a fair deduction that Mencken learned much from Shaw that failed to find its way into the book. For the book itself is a modest one. Mencken says that he is going to spend little time on Shaw's social theorizing and will concentrate instead on the plays and how their characters move us. In actual fact the bulk of the book is a series of neat plot summaries. But he deals with issues on occasion, especi-ally in the Introduction to the book. He does so enough to testify that he already sensed the value of ideas as artillery.

In *George Bernard Shaw* we glimpse a young writer in transition. Many of Shaw's views were interesting to Mencken whether he men-tioned them in the book or not. But he was already selecting from his subjects whatever he found most congenial. He was beginning, if only beginning, to picture his subjects in his own image. Though at this point it was still largely Shaw's Shaw that we would see, in the next book it would not be Nietzsche's Nietzsche we would read about but Mencken's.

In form as well as content he was finding himself. The book on Shaw contains one passage that readers will pick out as promising the brilliant Mencken of the future. It is from "By Way of Introduction" and begins, "Darwin is dead now, and the public that reads the news-papers remembers him only as the person who first publicly noted the fact that men looked a great deal like monkeys. But his soul goes marching on. Thomas Huxley and Herbert Spencer, like a new Ham and a new Shem, spend their lives seeing to that. From him, through Huxley, we have appendicitis, the seedless orange, and our affable indifference to hell. Through Spencer, in like manner, we have Nietzsche, Sudermann, Hauptmann, Ibsen, our annual carnivals of catechetical revision, the stampede for church union, and the afore-said George Bernard Shaw."

For several years Mencken could hardly get enough of the drama. He wrote his book on Shaw; he reviewed plays regularly, if more and more caustically, for his newspaper; he talked about the drama with everyone from the press agents to the patrons. And he began to edge toward playwriting himself.

He started with translation. The plays by Ibsen which were acted in America, whether in cosmopolitan New York or in provincial Baltimore, were the translations into British English. Done by the British playwright William Archer, they sounded much too stiff. Mencken got the idea of undertaking a translation more flexible, more idiomatic, and better suited for playing than Archer's version. He interested a friend, Holger Koppel, who was the Danish consul in Baltimore and had the required knowledge of Norwegian. The two men first attacked *A Doll's House* and then *Little Eyolf*. Koppel would call out a literal translation of each speech; Mencken would compare it with two or three German translations on hand; and then the collaborators would draft their own version. For a cross-check they would compare it regularly with a French translation. Finally Mencken would go over the text, smooth it out, and prune the more literary phrases. A decent, usable text resulted. Mencken added an introduction to each play and annotations where he felt them necessary. John W. Luce & Company issued the two plays in 1909, each neatly bound in red and stamped in gold. The reviews were good, the revenues scant. Mencken hoped to bring out further volumes but the idea foundered, mainly because of the publisher's sluggishness. He and the Danish consul finished *Hedda Gabler* but it never saw print.

The next step for Mencken was to write his own plays. Protesting nobly that such attempts had been the downfall of dramatic criticism and that he himself would never do it, he did. In 1903, he says in *Newspaper Days*, he and one Stuffy Davis of the New York *Globe* had organized the Society of Dramatic Critics Who Have Never Written Plays. The membership started small and became smaller. Stuffy proved faithful to his vows, but after Stuffy's death Mencken wrote at least two farces which were actually performed as well as several other plays which were not.

For Theodore Dreiser's rakish *Bohemian Magazine* he wrote a number of pieces including a short farce, "The Artist," in the issue for December 1909. Its trick was that it was a drama without words, for the speeches were all supposedly the mere thoughts of the characters. The simple plot centers on a well-known pianist who gives an afternoon recital. The other characters, if they can be called that, are a janitor, six music critics, six other men, and 1,645 enthralled women. The pianist, an East German, bemoans the gassy state of American beer and labors his way through his routine program. The critics carp as he does so and the women gush. There are a few clever lines and the idea was novel enough to gain the farce some notice. Mencken's publisher Luce issued it in book form in 1912; Mencken himself reprinted it in both the *Smart Set* and his *A Book of Burlesques* in 1916; and two acting versions were published.

He wrote a few more plays in the second decade of the century but he never came close to taking playwriting as seriously as he took the writing of criticism. And the plays he wrote were seldom the sort he commended in his reviews. He liked to write farce himself, complete with gags and braying comedians. He started only one social-problem play, in the manner of Shaw, and he never finished that. But the drama that meant most to him as a critic predicted the kind of fiction he would applaud in the pages of the *Smart Set* and the *Mercury*. It would say something new to the new day. It would be a realistic or even naturalistic drama dealing with contemporary problems. In short it would be the theater of Ibsen and Shaw, as construed by Mencken.

The notices his book on Shaw received offered him considerable encouragement. The more alert of the New York reviewers appreciated it, and here and there in the rest of the country it also earned some praise. It gave him the start of a national reputation. And it helped in getting him invited to write book reviews for the *Smart Set*, thereby launching his career as a professional critic.

5. The SMART SET Era

WHEN THE *Smart Set* first raised its raffish head above Mencken's
horizon, he regarded it with emotions which were for the most part
favorable. In spite of the hollowness of more than one of the magazine's pretensions it had charm as well as certain aims he could
agree with. He realized that the *Smart Set* survived because it opened
an outlet for writers who found the more respectable and stuffy magazines closed to them. It survived because it promised its readers
naughtiness but often gave them literature. It performed the greater
service because it made its appearance in an age of the ordinary,
when the established journals and the prominent publishing houses
united in printing pap. Among the major monthlies *Scribner's* was the
least unfriendly to experimental literature. It offered its two hundred
thousand readers much standard fare but also printed some respectable if conventional fiction. It bought the serials of such routine
writers as John Fox, Jr., whose *The Little Shepherd of Kingdom Come*
and *The Trail of the Lonesome Pine* charmed the subscribers, yet it
accepted the work of Edith Wharton too. The *Atlantic Monthly* became so staid that it had to use social-protest material to spice its
bland essays and stories. The other periodicals were as bad or worse.
It was still the era of Gene Stratton-Porter, Rex Beach, and Harold
Bell Wright. In that fact lay the *Smart Set's* opportunity.

It had little to lose. Its founder stood suspect to begin with. He
was a New York scandalmonger, Colonel William D'Alton Mann, who
started the monthly in 1900 with profits from his gossip weekly *Town
Topics*. Its slogan that it was "A Magazine of Cleverness" dates from

the opening issue. It floundered along in its first decade under one editor after another, never quite sure how the slogan was to be interpreted, never quite certain of its place. Notwithstanding, it managed to attract interesting writers from the outset. And, over the years, it proved to be eclectic in its choice, printing such varied authors as Jack London, John Erskine, James Branch Cabell, and Dreiser. It could not pay them adequately but, up to the point of libel or obscenity, it could print what they had composed.

Its interest in the experimental attracted Mencken. He cared little for its strained attempt at a supercilious tone though he did not mind that it snubbed the hordes of American plebians in the process. Thanks to his newspaper work and his current study of Nietzsche he was coming to the conclusion that the average man, even when reading, was an absurdity. At any rate, in the spring of 1908 he received a letter from the current editor, a young man named Fred Splint, outlining a scheme for a monthly review-article on new books and offering him the job of literary critic. So far Mencken had done little reviewing and less criticism, aside from the pieces on the drama which he had published in the *Herald* and the *Sun;* however, his book on Shaw had showed his potentialities. Understandably he was curious about who had recommended him.

There were three possibilities. The young playwright Channing Pollock was one, for he was both Mencken's friend and the drama critic for the *Smart Set.* Theodore Dreiser was another. He was then head editor of three women's magazines including the *Delineator,* for which Mencken had already been doing writing and revising; and Splint had been one of Dreiser's assistants before moving to the *Smart Set.* The third was Splint's assistant editor, Norman Boyer, an ex-newspaperman from Baltimore who also knew Mencken.

It took some forty years before Mencken found out. He told his biographer William Manchester that he initially assumed, in 1908, that it was Pollock. In 1916 or 1917 he wrote to Pollock, he told Manchester, and ascertained that he was not the man. He thereupon wrote to Dreiser, who said that he was not either. Years passed and it was not till the early 1940s, Mencken added to Manchester, that he wrote to Splint. But then Splint assured him that Boyer had brought up his name. And that was that.

Or was it? For when Mencken was preparing materials for his biographer Goldberg in 1925, he said that he had assumed that the

man who proposed him was either Pollock or Boyer. And when Goldberg came to publish his book he included a letter from Dreiser in
which Dreiser maintained that he both suggested to Splint that the
Smart Set inaugurate a book department and that Mencken was the
man to run it. Afterwards, when Mencken was reminded that Dreiser
now claimed the credit, he replied tartly that the one thing Dreiser
hated was a fact.

Regardless of who recommended him Mencken was interested, if
a bit doubtful, as he took the train to New York. In the office of the
magazine he met another young man, George Jean Nathan, who was
slight, dark, and glossily handsome. It turned out that he was being interviewed for the job of drama critic, to succeed Pollock who planned
to leave in a year, while Mencken was being offered the job of
literary critic. Nathan in fact would not appear in the *Smart Set*
until a year after Mencken.

The accounts of their first meeting vary as much as the accounts
of who recommended Mencken. As Mencken retold the story to
Manchester, the two met on May 8, 1908, in Boyer's office and listened
with fidgets and yawns while Boyer took half an hour to explain the
history, current condition, and plans of the *Smart Set*. Finally released,
the two went out to the street where Nathan suggested, tentatively,
that they have a drink. Mencken broke the ice with a pithy comment,
"Boyer is a horse's ass." As Nathan remembered their momentous
meeting, Mencken introduced himself by saying, "I'm H. L. Mencken
from Baltimore and I'm the biggest damn fool in Christendom and I
don't want to hear any boastful reply that you claim the honor." After
the tiresome session with Boyer they went to a place near the *Smart
Set* office and had a Florestan cocktail. Over the drink and its successors Mencken asserted that he considered the world a mess, with
its clowns getting better pay than they deserved. He argued that the
moral was that he and Nathan should clown in the *Smart Set*, though
not so much for the pay as for the joy of it.

Their meeting must have been something like that; every instinct asserts the fact. But these were memories reported nearly forty
years after the event by Mencken and nearly fifty by Nathan. Some
fifteen years after the event Mencken recalled his hiring and made no
mention of Nathan or of tedious parleyings. Mencken said he went to
see Splint and "Splint forthwith offered me the situation of book
reviewer to the magazine." There was no palaver; Splint hired him

promptly and Boyer gave him "an armful of books" to review. Then he and Boyer "went to Murray's for lunch (I remember a detail: I there heard the waltz, 'Ach, Früling, wie bist du so schön!' for the first time)." There is Mencken but no Nathan.

Whatever the immediate circumstances the two met and liked one another. They soon became close friends and working associates. In appearance and manner they were complete opposites; their rapport seemed all the greater because of it. By 1917, when their friendship reached the full, they were an encyclopedia of information about each other. That year they condescended to share with the public some of that information, after seasoning it with exaggerations and mild insults. What they chose to say, the points they chose to make, told nearly as much about the author as about the subject. What Mencken saw in Nathan revealed something about Mencken; what Nathan saw in Mencken revealed something about Nathan. Using what had become a mutual pseudonym, Owen Hatteras, they put it all in a purple-covered pamphlet called *Pistols for Two*. The technique was pointillistic, with each fact a dot. We see people, Hatteras explained at the beginning, "not as complete images, but as processions of flashing points."

Mencken stippled in the portrait of Nathan with considerable flair. "He is a man of middle height, straight, slim, dark, with eyes like the middle of August, black hair which he brushes back *à la française*, and a rather sullen mouth. . . . He smokes from the moment his man turns off the matutinal showerbath until his man turns it on again at bedtime. . . . He rarely eats meat. . . . He lives in a bachelor apartment, nearly one-third of which is occupied by an ice-box containing refreshing beverages. On the walls of his apartment are the pictures of numerous toothsome creatures. . . . In religion he is a complete agnostic, and views all clergymen with a sardonic eye. . . . He is a hypochondriac and likes to rehearse his symptoms. . . . He never reads the political news in the papers. . . . The room in which he works is outfitted with shaded lamps and heavy hangings, and somewhat suggests a first-class bordello. . . . He writes with a pencil on sheets of yellow paper. He cannot use a typewriter. . . . He has his shoes shined daily, even when it rains. . . . He has never had to work for a living. . . . He would rather have Lord Dunsany in *The Smart Set* once than William Dean Howells a hundred times. . . . He owns thirty-eight overcoats of all sorts and descriptions. . . . He never visits a house a second time in which he has encountered dogs, cats, children, automatic pianos, grace before or after meals, women authors, actors, *The New Republic,* or prints of the Mona Lisa. . . . He hasn't the slightest intention of ever getting married. . . . He has never been to Washington, nor to California, nor to Boston. . . . He has never made a speech, nor delivered a lecture, nor sat on a committee. . . . He looks seven years younger than he is. . . . Like Mencken, he is subject to periodic attacks of melancholia. . . . He believes that twelve per cent of all reformers and uplifters are asses, and that the rest are thieves. . . . In philosophy he is a skeptical idealist, believing that the truth is an illusion and that man is a botch. . . . He has never written a thing that, upon rereading after its appearance in print, didn't seem to him to be chock full of flaws. . . ."

Nathan replied in the same vein about Mencken. Among the points he retaliated with were: "He is five feet, eight and a half inches in height, and weighs about 185 pounds. . . . The things he dislikes most are Methodists, college professors, newspaper editorials (of which, in his time, he has written more than 10,000), Broadway restaurants, reformers, actors, children, magazine fiction, dining out, the New Freedom, prohibition, sex hygiene, *The Nation,* soft drinks, women under thirty, the noncomformist conscience, Socialism, good business men, the moral theory of the world, and the sort of patriotism that makes a noise. . . . The only art that ever stirs him is music. He views literature objectively, almost anatomically. He is anaesthetic to painting. . . . He drinks all the known alcoholic beverages, but prefers Pilsner to any other. . . . He has good eyes and a gentle mouth, but his nose is upset, his ears stick out too much, and he is shapeless and stoop-shouldered. One could not imagine him in the moving pictures. He has strong and white, but irregular teeth. . . . He takes no interest whatever in any sport. . . . He rejects the whole of Christianity. . . . His moral code is from the Chinese and has but one item: keep your engagements. He pays all bills immediately, never steals what he can buy, and is never late for an appointment. He has missed but one train in his life. . . . He is a prompt correspondent, and answers every letter the day it is received. . . . He detests windy days. As between heat and cold, he prefers heat. . . . He never preserves love letters, and never writes them. . . . He says the best place to eat in the whole world is at the basement lunch counter of the Rennert Hotel, Baltimore. The best things to order there are oyster potpie, boiled turkey

with oyster sauce, Virginia ham and spinach, and boiled tongue. . . .
He owns ten suits of clothes, and wears them seriatim. . . . He wears
horn spectacles for reading, but never otherwise. . . . He is very polite to women, particularly if he dislikes them, which is usually. . . .
He wears B.V.D.'s all the year round, and actually takes a cold bath
every day. . . . Every Saturday night he spends the time between 8
and 10 playing music, and the time between 10 and 12 drinking
Michelob. . . . He works in his shirt-sleeves and sleeps in striped
pajamas. . . . His favorite American poet is Lizette Woodworth
Reese. . . . He reads an average of ten books a week, in addition to
those he goes through for reviewing purposes. The subjects he affects
are theology, biology, economics, and modern history. . . . He has a
wide acquaintance among medical men and knows a good deal about
modern medical problems. . . . A healthy man, he yet complains
hourly of imaginary ailments. . . . He is, at bottom, a sentimentalist. . . .
He is opposed to vice crusades, holding that the average prostitute is
decenter than the average reformer. . . . A life-long opponent of
Puritanism in all its forms, he is on good personal terms with many
Puritan reformers, and always reads the tracts they send to him. . . .
He washes his hands twenty-four times a day. . . . He slicks his hair
down like the actor who plays the heroic lieutenant in the military
dramas. . . . He sleeps on a sleeping porch adjoining his office. . . .
Wherever he goes he carries a Corona typewriter. . . . He writes on
cheap newspaper copy-paper. . . . He is a bitter opponent of Christian Science, and has written all sorts of things, from epigrams to long
articles, against it. . . . He detests cut flowers, carpets, the sea-shore,
hotels, zoological gardens, the subway, the Y.M.C.A., literary women,
witch hazel, talcum powder, limp leather book-bindings, aerated
waters, bottled beer, low collars, public libraries, and phonographs.
. . . He chews cigars . . . ."

No one at the *Smart Set* could possibly have realized how brilliant
and colorful a pair were being recruited, or how they would develop
in response to its diverse challenges. But their coming was clear gain
to the magazine, for with every issue they grew more deeply involved.
They soon learned the little about the *Smart Set*'s past that they
thought they needed to know. They began their work by writing in
the field of their assigned specialty, that is, books or drama; but they
gradually became general factotums for the magazine; and they ended
by serving as its joint editors for a decade. At the same time that they

furthered their own careers they drew to the magazine more attention, some of it respectful, than it had ever enjoyed.

The history of the *Smart Set,* both before and during the Mencken-Nathan era, has its patches of haze. We are not sure exactly when the two men met nor in what circumstances. We shall see, a little later on, that there is even some uncertainty about how they handled the manuscripts submitted to them. But the history of the magazine before Mencken and Nathan is vaguer still. It has more than its share of shadowy figures. Several, once the *Smart Set* lay behind them, went on to careers of some distinction and emerged, blinking, into something like the limelight. Most, however, who labored under Colonel Mann are long forgotten. Editors and staff came and went, their movements determined by a combination of financial and office politics. Things seem clearer once Mann leaves. In 1911 the controversial Colonel sold the magazine to John Adams Thayer, something of a genius among advertising men. He also sold Thayer a bill of goods, for the circulation of the magazine was sliding from its peak of one hundred and forty thousand in 1908 and its reputation was worsening. It needed more help than Thayer realized. However, Thayer fancied himself both as a publisher and as an author. His experience as an author was confined to the writing of a distinctly premature autobiography, *Astir,* which came out the year before he bought the *Smart Set;* but his experience as a publisher looked more impressive.

Mencken and Nathan watched him with keen interest. There was a good chance that he would encourage an insurgent tone. He himself had fought against fraudulent advertising in the magazines he was previously with, and when publisher of *Everybody's* he had welcomed the pieces by the angry muckraker Thomas Lawson. In the astounding success of Lawson's exposés, issued afterward by Thayer in book form as *Frenzied Finance,* he had seen how crusading could be made to pay. Though Mencken and Nathan were no reformers, they relished the chance to be aggressive. On the other hand, Thayer itched for respectability and profits. He wanted the approval of his peers in the publishing world and also, so gossip said, of New York society. With these yearnings Mencken and Nathan had less sympathy.

Fred Splint left as editor, to be succeeded by Norman Boyer. As assistant editor Boyer had brought in with Mencken's endorsement a fiery young critic, Willard Huntington Wright, of the Los Angeles *Times*. This was in October 1912. Attracted by Wright's interest in Nietzsche and by his literary criticism, Mencken had told him as early as January that he thought he could get him in on the ground floor of the *Smart Set*. Mencken felt the more confident because Thayer had soon showed that he liked him and valued his advice; in fact Thayer offered Mencken the editorship. However, Mencken had mixed feelings about Thayer and besides he declined to desert Baltimore.

When after a brief tenure Boyer was demoted from the editorship, Mencken proposed that Wright replace him. Thayer agreed. Mencken still had not made up his mind about Thayer. One day he wrote sadly to Dreiser, "Thayer has a munseyized mind," invoking the name of the notorious cheapener of magazines, Frank Munsey. The next day he wrote saying that he thought Thayer could be lured into making the *Smart Set* a good magazine again. It was hard to tell.

Wright lasted for a year, 1913, during most of which he clashed with Thayer. The main trouble as Mencken saw it was that Thayer was cautious about editorial policy, even timid, while Wright was bold. When Wright ran a sex story such as "Daughters of Joy" Thayer blanched but Mencken, though himself no crusader for sex in magazines, considered the story sound, indeed excellent. Mencken did his best to remedy the situation. On the one hand, as he later told a correspondent, he made no less than five trips to New York to calm Thayer's fears about the censors. On the other, he warned Wright not to go too far. "Be very careful with sexual stuff, at least for the present," he suggested.

While he continued to counsel Wright and calm Thayer, he gradually formed his own view of what a magazine should be. "We must get away from the old ideas," he explained to Wright. "We must be genuinely different." How to be different became the subject of many discussions he had with Wright and, more important, with Nathan. These were the discussions that would lead, after assorted detours and the departure of Wright, to the *American Mercury*. But that would happen a decade later; meanwhile, the three settled on a suggestion from H. G. Wells's novel *The New Machiavelli*. There the hero wants to establish a journal of enlightened Toryism to spotlight weaknesses in the Socialist position. Blue was the Tory color and the journal would be the "Blue Weekly." Or if not a weekly, perhaps the

"Blue Review." Incidentally, in the novel the hero's proposal is attacked by someone as being characterized by the ideas of Nietzsche and Shaw and by "Superman rubbish" — all of which commended itself to the three planners. Mencken favored adopting the title as well as the viewpoint. He wrote to Wright, "The more I think of it, the more I am taken by The Blue Weekly. It would be difficult to get a better title. It is the best, by long odds, that has been suggested so far."

The differences between Thayer and Wright ended in a bitter quarrel aggravated by the fact that circulation insisted on shrinking. They both traveled to Baltimore for advice and support, and Mencken advised them to part at once, as gentlemen. This they did, with Thayer paying Wright a good bonus.

Wright left in January 1914, to be followed as editor by a New York attorney and author named Mark Luther. Luther, who had been on the staff before, tried to reform the magazine to suit Thayer. Mencken wrote to Dreiser on March 18, 1914 that it was "now as righteous as a decrepit and converted madame." But respectability was not enough. Circulation continued to slide. Thayer cut costs wherever he could, with the result that Nathan and Mencken did less writing for his magazine and a number of other contributors, including Louis Untermeyer the poet, pulled out. Thayer now stopped asking for advice from Mencken, feeling that Mencken had foisted Wright on him. In a long, gloomy letter to the novelist Harry Leon Wilson written a month after Wright's going, Mencken analyzed the situation. It was so bad that nothing could be done till Thayer left the magazine. The hopes Mencken had earlier for making a decent publisher out of him were gone. Thayer had avoided doing for the *Smart Set* what he could do well and had focused on doing what he could do badly. He had paid no attention to the advertising department and had concentrated on the contents of the magazine. In the process he had demonstrated, Mencken added, the worst taste in literature that could be imagined.

Thayer now looked around wildly for a way out. He told Mencken that he was ready to take a loss of one hundred thousand dollars in order to cut loose from the *Smart Set* and Mencken tried to find a buyer in Baltimore but failed. As Thayer moved toward financial disaster his main creditor, a magazine magnate named Eugene Crowe, entered the picture. He agreed to take over the *Smart Set*. Crowe put in as publisher a young Midwesterner, Eltinge Warner, who was already in charge of another Crowe periodical, *Field and Stream*. The post of editor became Warner's to fill and he turned to George Jean Nathan because they both had the same tailor.

Weird as it sounds, it was true. He and Nathan happened to be passengers together on a vessel returning from England, when he noticed that Nathan was wearing a duplicate of his own stylish gray overcoat. Out of curiosity he struck up an acquaintance and found that they were customers of the same London firm. He also found that Nathan was writing for the very magazine he now published. They grew friendly and Warner asked him to become editor. Nathan agreed, provided that Mencken would be named co-editor. After some haggling with Crowe, who doubtless thought the arrangement odd, the two men became joint editors.

They took over in the issue for October 1914, though Mencken had written to Dreiser as early as August that they were for all practical purposes in charge of the magazine then and that Thayer had packed his goods and gone. At last they had a magazine they could edit. They had watched while their predecessors, in various interesting and instructive ways, were botching the job. They knew what had to be done; they knew what they wanted to do. Neither Mencken nor Nathan wished to be doctrinaire; they saw that they could not afford it. Circulation remained low and the magazine was clearly out of touch with the new, troubled times. And there was the danger of censorship: Puritanism in American was becoming bolder. Yet they were not daunted.

Wright had left them a legacy which presented its own challenges. Despite his deficiencies as an editor, he had clearly tried to maintain a tradition of literary quality. He had assembled an impressive group of authors. Among the European ones were Arthur Schnitzler, Frank Wedekind, and August Strindberg; among the writers from the British Isles were George Moore, D. H. Lawrence, and William Butler Yeats. Among the Americans were Ezra Pound, Huneker, Dreiser, Harriet Monroe, and Sara Teasdale. The catalogue was formidable.

The new editors acted promptly. To cut costs still further they established a truly Spartan regime. With no staff left to them except one secretary, they moved to cheaper quarters and economized on stamps. Yet they moved without regrets and with all the resilience they would need. They complained waspishly to each other and the world, but this was what they wanted and their basic good humor told everyone so.

They fastened immediately on the main problem. It was to maintain a lively magazine with a literary standard without inviting the wrath of the censors and without paying authors anything but the most modest fees.

Because the problem was complicated, there was no completely good answer but lightness of tone seemed the least bad one. And lightness could mean good literature as well as poor. It was not quite the cleverness that had already seemed off-key; it was something broader and better. In the first issue Nathan and Mencken assured their readers that the policy of the *Smart Set* was to entertain them, to give them a good time. "Nothing to 'improve' your mind, but plenty to tickle you," they announced guilefully, sure that they would make literature more palatable to the subscribers than Wright had been able to. They had the help of their personal sense of humor. They had no objection to being tickled themselves.

World War I had started and the widening war presented them with a dilemma. If they ignored the war they were out of step with the times; if they dealt with it the light touch was done. They decided to bar war stories and verse. " 'Dusk in War-Time' is very tempting," Mencken assured Sara Teasdale, who submitted it, but "we have made a strict rule."

Of the ten years, from 1914 to 1924, that they spent as editors, over half were years of struggle. Both men looked at the world with some amusement; both intended to keep a certain zest in their labors. But Mencken's letters to Dreiser and to Ernest Boyd, an Irishman who had become his friend while serving as British consul in Baltimore, repeatedly reveal a magazine that barely kept itself afloat. There were many months when Mencken remained unpaid, months when it took every effort to make the magazine appear. On October 14, 1916, Mencken wrote to Boyd that for a year past he had spent two-thirds of his time worrying about circulation and advertising, and for six months had "slept, eaten and dreamed paper" because of the paper shortage. His anxieties were understandable: this was a magazine that had claimed one hundred and forty thousand readers in 1908 and in 1915 had fifty thousand.

From time to time things looked better, even to Mencken's eye, but all too often for the wrong reasons. For example, in March 1917 he reported dryly to Boyd, "We have boobed the Smart Set, and a series of pifflish articles called 'The Sins of the 400' is making circulation jump." In January 1918 he remarked to Boyd that he was drawing a salary for the first time since the previous April.

The salary soon stopped, however, and the troubles of the *Smart Set* returned. Just about everything happened that could worry a magazine editor. Besides the soaring price of paper, there was the high cost of skilled help. Printers were buying silk shirts and going on strike to add silk socks. The *Smart Set* had to move again from one part of Manhattan to another, and then the government requisitioned its new quarters. There was even a threat by the government to stop all fiction magazines, though Mencken consoled himself by remembering that the *Smart Set* also printed nonfiction.

After the war was over in the autumn of 1918, some troubles ended; others began. But the new ones were smaller and less irksome. Mencken and Nathan had avoided both the influenza epidemic and the military draft; the magazine had managed to emerge each month. Things were looking up. Mencken's beer-barrel chuckle was heard more often in the office; his consumption of soda-mints to soothe his stomach went down.

Then too, in spite of Mencken's inevitable complaints, he was making money, as was Nathan. The reason lay in what Mencken called the "louse magazines." These were shoddy monthlies which Mencken and Nathan, with Crowe's backing, created out of hack fiction, pulp paper, and splashy typography. They catered to the trade that today buys paperbacks with naked girls on the cover. The first that Mencken and Nathan devised they called the *Parisienne* since Paris was supposed to be a well of naughtiness. It began with the number of July 1915. The second, which started a little over a year later, they christened *Saucy Stories*. Though both became money-makers speedily, Mencken and Nathan soon tired of them. They found it harder to edit two bad magazines than one good one. The result was that they sold their interest to Crowe and Warner, who knew a good thing when they saw it, and were paid handsomely. "We escaped," Mencken wrote Boyd in relief, "with enough patriotic gold to finance us for a couple of years." Early in 1920 they started one more, *Black Mask*, a mystery story magazine. After running it for six months they sold their interest in this monthly as well to Crowe and Warner. Crowe was then near the end of his life and, liking both of the brisk young men who worked for him, gave them so high a price that it relieved them "from want permanently."

The full irony of Mencken's finances is revealed in a red-leather record book he started keeping in 1913. It shows that his rewards from the *Smart Set* were meager but from the louse magazines full to overflowing. For all the writing, editing, and worrying he did for the *Smart Set*, it paid him in its worst year only a few hundred dollars and in its best year, 1918, four thousand. It was the louse magazines that let him live in the style he wanted. When he sold his interest in the *Parisienne*, he got nearly five thousand dollars. For his interest in *Saucy Stories*, in its turn, he got nearly ten thousand. And *Black Mask* gave him a first payment of five thousand and notes from Crowe, which were later paid, for at least $7,250 more.

Perhaps if the *Smart Set* had been better off, Mencken and Nathan would not have worked as hard as they did. Nevertheless, they worked with ill-concealed enjoyment. They even showed signs, rare among the general run of magazine editors, of liking authors. True, some were not very likable but as long as they looked promising Mencken and Nathan went out after them. The classic position of the magazine editor had been to sit at a large oak desk waiting for manuscripts to be submitted. Mencken and Nathan searched instead. When they dredged up a likely writer, no salesman buttering up a big customer was more solicitous, more persuasive. Mencken once put it quite moderately: he said simply that they were polite. They were far more. Mencken in particular would send personal notes, would visit ailing authors at their bedside, would send them joke mail to cheer them up, and would eat and drink with them when they neared his neighborhood in New York or Baltimore. He said later on that he cared for very few authors, and yet when he inaugurated the *Mercury* he again treated them well and did all he could for them. On the *Smart Set* he and Nathan could not pay them decently but they tried to make up for that. They even managed somehow to install in the office an Authors' Free Lunch, with such items as herring, cheap cheese, and olives, spread on a marble cemetery slab.

They announced to one another, as well as to anyone else listening, that they were giving their all, whatever the result. In his *Intimate Notebooks* Nathan preserved some of his exchanges with Mencken during this period. He quotes some of Mencken's dire complaints: "Last week, as you know, I took out three different literary wenches, bought and drank at least $50 worth of alcoholic liquor, made enough love to inflame at least two dozen Marie Corellis, didn't get home till dawn, and what will we get? Not a damned thing worth printing! And my health is gone! It's your turn, my boy!" Nathan, for his part, later sprayed him with scattershot, rejecting his complaints and reminding him of his own sacrifices for the cause. "I appreciate that you had to give Huneker a small witch-hazel bottle full of green Chartreuse to put clothes on his last heroine and that, accordingly, I owe the firm something, but too much is too much. Let me urge you not to forget that it was I — a year ago — whom you burdened with the job of keeping Dreiser sufficiently oiled to write 'Sanctuary' for us . . . . I am tired of work, and think I shall marry a rich widow. . . . You are drinking too much. This means more work again for me." He added that Warner had showed up in an outfit of sassafras color, so bright that Nathan had to pull down the shades before looking at it. Too much was indeed too much.

Yet the attention paid to writers by Mencken and Nathan never flagged. The combination of solicitude and wit they offered them was unique. A nice example of the wit was the series of directions solemnly passed out during 1921 and 1922. Mencken prepared them and they appeared in a four-page leaflet, *Suggestions to Our Visitors*. Neatly numbered, they began by announcing when the "editorial chambers" would be open and ended by stating positively that no checks would be cashed. In between were put two dozen items including: "Dogs accompanying visitors must be left at the garderobe in charge of the Portier," "Visitors are kindly requested to refrain from expectorating out of the windows," "Choose your emergency exit when you come in; don't wait until the firemen arrive," and "The Editors assume that visitors who have had the honor of interviews with them in the editorial chambers will not subsequently embarrass them in public places by pointing them out with walking sticks." Though Mencken and Nathan groaned noisily at the trouble they were put to, the results even early in the decade were not bad. Manuscripts of all shapes, sizes, and qualities came in.

Once the manuscripts, solicited or otherwise, arrived in the office they were judged with dispatch. When in 1921 Mencken issued the leaflet *A Personal Word*, on how the *Smart Set* was run, he said that he scanned all the manuscripts first and then sent those to Nathan that he thought worth printing. The ones Nathan agreed on were promptly put into type. The rest went out the window. When in 1947 Mencken recalled the procedure for Manchester, he said that Nathan looked at the manuscripts first, penciled on them his vote for or against, and than mailed them to him in Baltimore. The ones they both liked were accepted. Regardless of the discrepancy in Mencken's stories, it is certain that each editor had a veto. There were ordinarily no editorial conferences since a single negative was enough to bar a manuscript.

However, it was inevitable that at times a mere yes or no was insufficient. There is, for instance, a letter to Nathan of February 2, 1917 in which he analyzes a novel submitted by a writer named Barrett. Mencken breaks down the manuscript into seven sections, finding only two of them with scenes of genuine suspense, and tells Nathan it would be a relief to dispose of Barrett. "The novel *may* get over, but I am so full of doubt of it that I have no enthusiasm." Sometimes a letter making a recommendation will synopsize the plot of a story as well. There is an undated communication from Mencken to Nathan which evidently accompanied a group of manuscripts. Mencken writes a trenchant paragraph about each one that appeals to him and then assures Nathan, "The others are not for us."

But even correspondence could not solve all the problems of editing the *Smart Set*, so Mencken set aside every third week in the month for a trip to New York to talk with Nathan, see authors, and attend to miscellaneous business. There were months when he had to travel to New York more often. His home and headquarters, as well as his heart, still remained at Hollins Street, but this was a period when the Algonquin hotel, across from where Nathan lived, housed him a good deal.

Both Mencken and Nathan kept busy. The answers to authors were prompt and often helpful. For that fact much but by no means all of the credit must go to Mencken. He took an interest in many of the submissions, and if he saw a piece potentially worth printing he did his best to assist the author. He wrote, for instance, on July 12, 1917 to the Chicago newspaperman Vincent Starrett. He had sent in a short story of considerable worth but it dealt with the unpopular and risky theme of transvestite perversion. Mencken noted that he had discussed the story with Nathan. "Since I last wrote to you Nathan has gone through 'The Truth about Delbridge' very carefully. He agrees with me that it is a very fine piece of work but he raises an objection that I confess begins to make an impression on me — that is, the objection that a story dealing with such an abnormality would probably prove very offensive to a great many readers and perhaps bring down upon us the strong arm of certain moral gentlemen who constantly stand by waiting their opportunity. I am not entirely in accord with this idea but his arguments shake me up to some extent. And so I hesitate to definitely take the story. If you see any way to change the ending so that the man need not dress himself up in woman's clothes, I would be inclined to grab the manuscript at once. It has been suggested in the office that it might be possible to get around the matter by making the man hang himself with a doll in his arm but without his present paraphernalia of silk stockings. I incline to believe that this would solve the problem. Please give it your thought and let me hear from you. . . .

"I trust that the two books of piety that I sent to you the other day are giving you the spiritual consolation that all of us need in these hard times."

When Starrett's story appeared in October, the man hanged himself with a "silken girdle" and died holding a doll.

The total effect of their efforts during the decade they dominated the *Smart Set* was imposing. There were periods when Mencken thought he saw few manuscripts of merit. At the end of June 1918, for example, he wrote gloomily to Boyd, who was then in Spain, "The supply of decent ms. over here is next to nothing. I spend whole days writing to authors, begging them for stuff." Nevertheless, the *Smart Set* printed some of the best magazine writing in America, and the contents of many numbers was a credit to both men.

They printed their finest fiction in the years from 1919 to 1922. Here and there in the years before, they had printed some very good stories as well as, in the August 1916 number, one token of things to come, "I'm a Stranger Here Myself" by Sinclair Lewis. It satirized the vacation trip of a pre-Babbitt from Northernapolis and his wife, who announced that they traveled to be broadened and quickened. But the period from 1919 to 1922 was the high point. Scott Fitzgerald's "Babes in the Woods" which he later incorporated into *This Side of Paradise* appeared in the issue for September 1919. His "The Diamond as Big as the Ritz" appeared in June 1922. Sherwood Anderson had several stories accepted and published; the most notable was the moving "I Want to Know Why" in the November 1919 number.

Willa Cather's "Coming, Eden Bower!" appeared in the issue for August 1920. Ruth Suckow's "A Homecoming" appeared in November 1921 and her "The Best of the Lot" a year later. Stephen Vincent Benet's "Summer Thunder" came out in September 1920 and Julia Peterkin's "The Merry-Go-Round" in the issue for December 1921. Those were the works of writers who went on to fame if not to fortune. But there were also some writers now totally forgotten who here and there contributed an admirable story. Both Nathan and Mencken were much impressed with, for instance, "The End of Ilsa Menteith" by a woman who wrote under the pen name of Lilith Benda.

The poetry was less memorable than the prose. Neither Mencken nor Nathan had the feeling for poetry that they had for prose and the pages of the *Smart Set* prove it. Most of the lyrics and ballads are the work of versifiers. The most reputable poets who acted as regular contributors were Sara Teasdale and Louis Untermeyer. Among the irregular ones Ezra Pound and Elinor Wylie stood out.

Nathan and Mencken proved just as eager as Wright to print the work of foreign authors. In "A Note from the Editors" in the issue for February 1922 they boasted of their achievements. Among the British writers, they had introduced Somerset Maugham, Lord Dunsany, James Joyce, W. L. George, and Aldous Huxley. They had also printed a sprinkling of Continental authors in translation. And they had continued the tradition, started by the initial editor of the magazine, of buying stories (cheap) from a society of French authors and printing them in the original. The contract remained in force till 1920 and allowed the *Smart Set* to maintain a cosmopolitan pose that other general magazines could not strike. True, the pieces were short but no other journal regularly offered its readers such an item as "La Lettre" by Arnaud de Laporte, which appeared in the May 1915 number.

In addition both editors had a personal style that added distinction and verve to the magazine. They themselves contributed pieces so frequently that they set the general tone. They veiled themselves behind a score of aliases. Starting early in 1912 both used the name of Owen Hatteras to inaugurate a department called "Pertinent and Impertinent." They remembered that Hatteras was a stormy cape and felt that the name fit a brusque persona. When World War I ended they made him military, giving him the rank of major along with an order of merit. Mencken masqueraded even more than Nathan, writing verse and prose as, among others, Herbert Winslow Archer, Pierre d'Aubigny, William Fink, Amelia Hatteras, Harriet Morgan, George Weems Peregoy, and James P. Ratcliff, Ph.D.

Mencken and Nathan contributed, in fact, to every issue as well as editing it. They felt that they had to do so because, though they received some good manuscripts, they seldom received enough. They complained often about the extra writing required. And yet the creative energy of both editors was abundant; they wrote in good part because they wanted to. Although their customary attitude was one of half-comic martyrdom, every now and then they dropped the mask. In a letter of February 2, 1915 Mencken reminded his partner, "we want to devote more and more space to our own compositions."

They appeared in the *Smart Set*'s pages singly and together. They started new things and abandoned old. One of their best ideas they christened "Répétition Générale," a joint department which appeared first in the April 1919 number of the magazine. It was a pastiche of paragraphs long and short whose point was to be provocative. It ran to five pages in the April number. The opening lines of each of the first few paragraphs set the tone for the many monthly installments which followed: "A dog is a standing proof that most so-called human rights, at bottom are worth nothing"; "Children are not so foolish as their elders sometimes believe them to be"; and "The absurd theory that women have beautiful forms has been pretty well blown up." Though the paragraphs usually failed to stun with their genius or amaze with their cleverness, they succeeded in being sprightly. Readers reported that they liked them and several other magazines took profitable note.

In spite of the horseplay, in spite of the rousing challenge to put out a lively issue every month, Mencken and Nathan kept on talking about the idea of a new magazine. Mencken was especially eager for a change. He had begun to believe that his career broke into ten-year segments and his *Smart Set* decade as an editor was almost up. He was sure that he wanted a journal of ideas; Nathan was less sure. In fact the *Smart Set* suited him rather well and if it had been put on a solid financial basis he would have left it reluctantly. But Mencken's dedication to the new idea and the long friendship of the two men persuaded Nathan.

Throughout the spring and summer of 1923 Mencken hinted to his correspondents that changes were in the making. A new magazine was to be born, he assured them confidentially. It would hit hard and below the belt; there would be no nonsense about fairness when it came to battling the boobs.

The first public notice of Mencken and Nathan's putting away the old to take on the new was posted in the *Smart Set* under the date of October 1, 1923. In it they announced that they were abandoning the editorship and had disposed of their holdings in the Smart Set Company. They said that they had thought about leaving for several years. They had put in six years as staff members and nine years as co-editors, and it was time for them to move.

They were moving, moreover, because the purpose they had set for themselves back in 1908 was accomplished. "That purpose was to break down some of the difficulties which beset the American imaginative author, and particularly the beginning author, of that time — to provide an arena and drum up an audience for him, and to set him free from the pull of the cheap, popular magazine on the one side and of the conventional 'quality' magazine, with its distressing dread of ideas, on the other — above all, to do battle for him critically, attacking vigorously all the influences which sought to intimidate and regiment him."

Both the struggle and the victory were vital not only for Mencken but for his times, and so the battlefield and the battles of the first twenty years of the twentieth century need to be inspected next.

6. Writers and Rotarians

MENCKEN AND NATHAN ANNOUNCED that they were abandoning the *Smart Set* because, for one thing, its battles had been won. As they looked back to 1908 and the beginnings of their connection with the magazine, they felt they could afford to be sanguine. Even that early they had been eager to assault the entrenched enemy; now they had triumphed. The enemy was — to repeat — "all the influences which sought to intimidate and regiment" the American writer. Those influences had been the enemy of the *Smart Set*, of its two brilliant co-editors, and of the people who wrote for it. Seen in retrospect they had been the enemy in particular, and above all, of Mencken.

They constituted the forces of convention, of middling conformity, of Puritan constriction. They were the dominating elements in American life during the first two decades of the twentieth century. To Mencken they came to be symbolized by the Blue-Nose and the Boob, the moralistic reformer and the canting businessman. The opposition to them during those two decades was disparate and often divided. At its core stood the American iconoclast. He was supported by the ideas and preachments of key British and European intellectuals, by the books of a few British and European novelists, and by the problem plays of British and European dramatists. He was supported by some American scientists and social scientists and by some dissident American intellectuals and writers — in fact by occupation he was often one of them, but a more active, contentious one than the others. He knew better than most who the enemy was.

When the roll was called, the iconoclast could list on his side such widely assorted names as Darwin, Huxley, Nietzsche, Dreiser, H. G. Wells, Upton Sinclair, Lincoln Steffens, William James, Freud, James Gibbons Huneker, Mitchell Kennerley, and Harriet Monroe. On the other side were such forgotten but once formidable names as Robert Underwood Johnson, Anthony Comstock, and John Sumner.

The struggle between the two forces was set in a broad social and political context. But the focus, for Mencken and his fellows, was on intellectual and literary issues, especially on the relation of man to society and the distinction between good and bad literature. The locales were New York, Boston, and Chicago; the settings were the offices of publishers, the editorial rooms of magazines, and of course the desks of writers. The literary genres involved were the novel and the lyric.

As far back as the turn of the century Mencken recognized, rebel that he was, the forces he himself must fight against. He found an early inspiration in the books by Thomas Huxley which he borrowed from the library. As Mencken said admiringly, even years after encountering him, "All his life long he flung himself upon authority — when it was stupid, ignorant and tyrannical. He attacked it with every weapon in his rich arsenal — wit, scorn, and above all, superior knowledge. To it he opposed a single thing: the truth as it could be discovered and established — the plain truth that sets men free." When that rich arsenal was directed at religion, it had a particularly powerful effect on Mencken. He said explicitly, "Huxley gave order and coherence to my own doubts and converted me into a violent agnostic."

He was further influenced by several of the leading British historians and social philosophers of Huxley's time. They included Herbert Spencer, Henry Thomas Buckle, and James Anthony Froude. They gave his rebellion historical perspective as well as philosophical range. Their cast of mind was enterprising; it helped to prepare him for the stimulating shock of the writings of Friedrich Nietzsche, who became the subject of his next book after the *Shaw*.

What Mencken needed most, to make his rebellion effective, was a national audience. Baltimore was big but not big enough, for the *Sun* was at best a regional paper. With the book about Shaw he took a definite step toward that audience; the moment he made the connection with the *Smart Set* he began to reach it. He could not have done so at a better time, psychologically.

For the national temper seemed smug and yet uneasy. The most striking demonstration of the temper appeared, as it often does in America, in the broad field of politics. Though the capitalistic imperialism exemplified since the end of the nineteenth century by William McKinley still prevailed, changes were in the making. During the last presidential campaign of that century the Republican politician Albert Beveridge had given a speech called "The March of the Flag." In it he asked the question, "Shall the American people continue their resistless march toward the commercial supremacy of the world?" His answer was yes, under the guidance of God and McKinley. He left no doubt, "A moment ago I said that the administration of William McKinley had been guided by a providence divine. That was no sacrilegious sentence. The signature of events proves it." Yet by 1912 Senator Beveridge had deserted the party of McKinley and was espousing Theodore Roosevelt the Progressive against William Howard Taft. In the same year a Democrat, Woodrow Wilson, was elected president of the United States on a program of change and reform which he characterized as "The New Freedom."

In this massive transit Mencken found much to interest and amuse him, and a good number of attractive targets. The smug capitalism of many businessmen became the subject for his barbs for three decades. The notions of McKinley developed into the doctrines of the "booboisie"; these doctrines along with their advocates offered an ideal subject for Mencken's ridicule. He found less to make fun of in the progressivism of Theodore Roosevelt, but the emergence of Wilson and "The New Freedom" gave him a subject second only to the booboisie. Wilson, austerely and piously doing good, seemed to him the epitome of the political reformer and such reformers always drew his ribald attention.

The slowly shifting moods of politics were only the most obvious instance of the considerable alteration in the American temper. In Henry May's *The End of American Innocence* the temper and its changes have been analyzed admirably. To him it shows itself in the form of a national credo, with as its basic tenet the importance of moral values. Moral values are fundamental to all aspects of life, including politics, education, and literature. Moral judgments can and should be applied not only to individuals but to institutions. A senate can be as right, or as wrong, as a president. To this moralism in the American temper there had been only one real challenge in the nineteenth century, Darwinian evolution and its spectre of a soulless universe. By the time Mencken arrived on the scene, however, evolution had been domesticated into progress; it had been absorbed into American doctrine. But by the end of World War I the national credo had undergone a major modification: moralism had given ground, if grudgingly, to permissiveness; and American innocence had reached an end.

Mencken knew by his early twenties how he stood on the matter of moral values. In his personal code he held to a realistic, rather Continental morality, infused with consideration for others and overlaid with elaborate courtesy to women and heartiness toward men. In his public code he proclaimed himself firmly amoral. For his authority he seized on Nietzsche, who insisted that moral codes were always relative, seldom efficient, and never God-given; furthermore, they interfered with the superman. Because they did, the superman's task was to dispatch them. Mencken said a loud amen, in print.

From the outset he attacked the Puritan stress on morality in literature and art. Usually he made fun of it; sometimes he fought it with savage seriousness. He wrote about it regularly. For inspiration in the struggle he often looked across the Atlantic. He starts an article, for instance, in the Baltimore *Sun* as early as September 1906 by remarking, "England just now is enjoying a very healthy and invigorating reaction against conventional cant and virtue." In another article entitled "The Kill-Joy as a Moses" he looked north of Baltimore and observed that Puritanism dies hard. In the veins of the orthodox New Englander the blood still runs gray. "He has yet a war to wage upon the merry heart. In his sight that day is lost which does not reveal to him some new scheme for hushing the sacrilegious laughter of the world and shutting out the light of the good red sun." In still another he looked at home and jeered at the board of play-censors to be appointed in Baltimore, suggesting that they be protected, on threat of the bastinado, from criticism by others.

At the turn of the century American moralism still dominated literature as it did life. The main literary critics were either conservatives or tame liberals. The conservatives tried to maintain the New England tradition, as they saw it, of American literature and did their humorless best to make every writer fit the tradition. The violence they effected was considerable. Emerson, Walt Whitman, and Mark Twain were each distorted, though in different ways; Thoreau and

Melville were ignored; Poe and Hawthorne were given less than their due; and Lowell, Longfellow, Whittier, and Holmes were praised beyond their deserts. Attempts at frank realism in fiction were still repelled. Even Williams Dean Howells, an early advocate of realism, found himself conforming and becoming an apostle of the fiction that showed the smiling aspects of life. Mencken's considered opinion of Howells was that Boston had overcivilized him and that he failed to see and convey the basic tragedy of man. He had become "a somewhat kittenish old maid — in brief, a giggler." Stephen Crane and Theodore Dreiser, in *Maggie: A Girl of the Streets* and *Sister Carrie* respectively, both issued naturalistic novels against the American grain and both were defeated during this time. As Mencken once put it, "When the mild and *pianissimo* revolt of the middle 90's . . . had spent itself, the Presbyterians marched in and took possession of the works."

Against the voices of the conservatives Mencken now clamored to be heard. He challenged them at many a point, even if for a considerable time few persons appeared to be listening. In the ten years after he joined the *Smart Set's* staff he compiled a bibliography of dissent. Though his book on Shaw was already issued by the time he had his talk with Norman Boyer, *The Philosophy of Friedrich Nietzsche* was in the process of appearing. He put out two plays of Ibsen in 1909, the ones he translated with his friend the Danish consul in Baltimore, and readily would have published more if the two had been successful. He prepared most of a little book printed in 1910 as *The Gist of Nietzsche*. He issued two plays by the controversial French playwright Eugene Brieux, with an extensive preface. In 1918 he edited three plays of Ibsen for the Modern Library. And in his reviews he steadfastly denied that morality had any relation to art except to inhibit it. He grandly declared in *Prejudices: First Series*, "No virtuous man — that is, virtuous in the Y.M.C.A. sense — has ever painted a picture worth looking at, or written a symphony worth hearing, or a book worth reading."

The most significant item in this bibliography of dissent is without doubt the book he wrote on Nietzsche. The truculent German had died by the time the new century started, but his effect on America was only beginning to be felt. As Henry May sees it, "Progress, utility, reason, democracy — the things on which modern civilization prided itself, were to Nietzsche symptoms of sickness and approaching death: joy and health lay only in the self-fulfilling and self-transcending individual." And Nietzsche hymned the superman, the "blond beast." Such preachings were perfidious to the great majority of Americans; to a tiny minority they were gospel. If to Mencken they were not exactly gospel, it was because he never could accept any writer, any thinker, completely. Young as he was when he came to Nietzsche, he already felt he had a royal right to pick and choose. So he selected the doctrines that suited him, and these he expounded in *The Philosophy of Friedrich Nietzsche*, which Luce published in 1908.

As important as what Mencken chose was the spirit of his choice. Neitzsche himself spoke with a hard, evangelical fervor; in this book Mencken's tone was usually dispassionate and detached, at times amused. He wanted the conservatives to lose their temper but did not intend to lose his own in the process. Neitzsche, moreover, was a mystic while Mencken was anything but that. The result was that Mencken's interpretation in *The Philosophy of Friedrich Nietzsche* became not only arbitrary but superficial. For that matter, he criticized others who failed to accept the philosophy "in its surface sense."

Nietzsche propounded a Will to Power as one of his major doctrines. This was a striving in man, not so much to dominate others as to realize and then transcend himself. His self in turn strove to generate further selves. Mencken transformed the Will to Power into the Darwinian contest for the survival of the fittest. Only the most ruthless self survived. To Mencken the laws of natural selection were what produced both the superman and the aristocracy of which the superman became the perfect embodiment. Mencken considered him "the crowning stone of the pyramid," the fittest survivor, in spite of Nietzsche's own repudiation of the doctrine of the survival of the fittest. Mencken treated another of Nietzsche's main ideas, the idea of Eternal Recurrence, just as cavalierly. Nietzsche believed that life on earth went through cycles and that the culmination of each cycle lay in the emergence of the superman. After the superman went his way the cycle started again. To Mencken this represented simply another facet of Darwinian selection: man after evolving into superman was brought low "by catastrophe or slow decline" and then the whole process began anew.

Mencken dealt in the same brisk manner with other tenets of Nietzsche's philosophy. He agreed with Nietzsche's condemnation of Christianity but with much more good nature and again with a Darwinian turn. Nietzsche damned Christianity for preaching and perpetuating the morality of the slave instead of the morality of the superman. Mencken asserted calmly that Christianity hampered the great principle of natural selection by fostering the preservation of the weak and unfit. And even when he did not alter what he found, he gave evidence of using Nietzsche to think through his own ideas, for instance, on women, those weak but artful and cunning creatures.

Mencken was twenty-six when he undertook his book. He plowed through a complete set of Nietzsche in German along with a copy of the biography of him prepared by his sister, and then spread the actual writing over a year. It proved to be the most valuable intellectual exercise he ever had — even more than the book about Shaw — because of his rich response to Nietzsche's ideas, attitudes, and emphases.

His *Nietzsche* was stocked with the seeds of his later works, with specific sections of the *Nietzsche* forecasting specific books. The section on Christianity would be the seed for the *Treatise on the Gods,* the section on women the seed for *In Defense of Women,* and the section on government the seed for some of *Notes on Democracy.* Other parts of the book, even single sentences, provided other predictions of the famous Mencken. For example: "It is evident that skepticism, while it makes no actual change in man, always makes him feel better"; and "school teachers . . . are probably the most ignorant and stupid class of men in the whole group of mental workers." Throughout Mencken's career only one other thinker, William Graham Sumner, would make a deeper impression on him and that would be in areas not covered by Nietzsche.

When the *Nietzsche* appeared it made more than a modest splash. Because nearly all the reviewers knew less about the philosopher than did Mencken, their reviewing had an air of slight insecurity about it. They seldom disagreed in detail with his interpretations, preferring to praise him in general terms for his forceful style — "ardent" was the word the New York *Times* used — and clear presentation. The reviewer for the *Dial* proved to be shrewder than most, for he observed that "the reader is often left in doubt as to where the author is speaking his own views and where he is merely presenting those of Nietzsche." Nevertheless, Mencken failed to outrage the reviewers even of the conservative journals. They admired his efforts at the same time that they thought them misspent. So for that matter did several of the liberal journals. As the *Nation* said, somewhat stiffly, "We can commend the exegesis, though we repudiate the conclusions."

His handling of Nietzsche showed that he was becoming his own man. He proceeded to demonstrate the fact in politics as well as in philosophy. He decided that his political position lay midway between two extremes. He denied the capitalistic imperialism of William McKinley at the same time that he rejected the socialism of Karl Marx. He said so, in effect, in some published articles which in 1909 attracted the attention of Robert Rives La Monte. La Monte, a wealthy professional Marxist, worked for the Baltimore *News* in addition to being a national organizer for the Socialist Party and associate editor of the *International Socialist Review*. They started to exchange letters in defense of their views and then, at La Monte's suggestion, turned them into a book. Accepted by Henry Holt, this was the book that came out in 1910 under the heavy title of *Men versus the Man: A Correspondence between Robert Rives La Monte, Socialist and H. L. Mencken, Individualist.*

Mencken's ideas in the book were clear-cut and, incidentally, would never waver. "I'd change the essential doctrine very little if I had it to rewrite today," he said in 1925.

La Monte preaches a Socialist revolution, with production for use rather than for profit and with the working man keeping a fair share of what he produces. He bases his argument on general good, the good of the average man. Mencken replies by advocating the capitalistic system despite its defects. It is founded on natural law, particularly as observed in Darwin's doctrine of the survival of the fittest. Socialism is not and so it will fail. Mencken, glancing over his shoulder at Nietzsche, favors the system that will allow the superior man full scope. He favors the Man over his opponent's Men. The debate is not acrimonious; there is even some friendly dialogue in the dozen letters. Mencken is satirical at times but much less so than in later works.

In the world of ideas and attitudes Mencken knew almost instinctively which he should favor and which he should attack, whether they were announced by a Nietzsche or a Beveridge or a La Monte. Sometimes he had to ponder but his response was usually swift and sharp, and there was much to respond to. This was not so in the case of the novelists he read; they offered him relatively little. Though the novel was the premier literary form, few novelists in the first decade of the new century showed much interest in political or social ideas. And when they did, the ideas were apt to be repugnant to Mencken. They were apt to be Socialistic rather than Darwinian or mechanistic. Only Dreiser would really use the novel form as Mencken thought it should be used; and throughout this decade Dreiser remained silent, although the aborted publication of *Sister Carrie* in 1900 was still remembered.

Among the handful of social novelists striving for reputation were three Americans along with one Englishman. None aroused in Mencken the powerful, sustained interest that Dreiser did: yet each caught his notice. Though he had mixed feelings about each he read their novels readily enough and usually reviewed them for the *Smart Set*. The Americans were Frank Norris, Jack London, and Upton Sinclair; the Englishman was H. G. Wells.

Norris occupied Mencken's attention the shortest time, partly because he died the earliest. He was a disciple of Zola and in his best fiction showed the effect of environment on the human struggle. But he was likewise a romanticist who liked to tell a strange story, for instance of a wolf-man, and who wrapped his social ideas in a romantic haze. Another story, *The Octopus*, now considered his best, bored Mencken with what he criticized as its "far-fetched mysticism." So did the rest except for *McTeague*, which Mencken called "a wonderfully painstaking and conscientious study of a third rate man." In fact he announced that it was nearly as good as *Sister Carrie*. This was high praise and the more apt because Norris had been in a sense Dreiser's discoverer and had tried his best to get *Sister Carrie* properly published.

Jack London held Mencken's attention, and the public's too, much longer than Norris. His powerful tales of low and primitive life made him well known. He showed himself to be a believer both in evolution and Marxist socialism. Mencken endorsed the evolution but gagged at the socialism. When London preached socialism in his novels they became as devoid of grace, according to Mencken, as *Das Kapital* or Mary Baker Eddy's *Science and Health*. Yet he was a craftsman, a scintillating writer. When he abandoned the role of Great Thinker he could write with charm and even poignant feeling. In spite of many of London's ideas, which Mencken found foolish, he conceded that there was in him "a vast delicacy of perception, a high feeling, a sensitiveness to beauty."

It is probably wrong to say that the only other novelists of social significance both to Mencken and to the world at large were Wells and Sinclair. Certainly others wrote, and sometimes wrote well; certainly others used the novel as a vehicle for social ideas. But none attracted the readers, over a long span of years, that Wells and Sinclair did.

Wells proved himself the more vital and the better novelist of the two. An Englishman and a curious combination of proletarian, propagandist, and mystic, he caught public attention with his science stories and then kept it while he composed Utopian fantasies and social-problem novels. Both in his fantasies and his realistic contemporary fiction, he paid enough attention to the effectiveness of character and plot so that large audiences read him for pleasure as much as instruction. He proved for ten years or so, in a stream of novels, to be a good if not great novelist. His best was *Tono-Bungay,* issued in 1908, about an antihero whose triumphs and mishaps show the badness of the British class system and of capitalism as well. It was a tract for the times.

For a while Wells believed in an evolutionary socialism but then lost faith in it and replaced it with a Utopianism oriented toward science. Mencken read him eagerly to begin with. At first he thought Wells's fiction so good, and was so stimulated by it, that he ignored its burden of social ideas. However, as the second decade of the century went along, he found less and less to like; and even the fact that Wells was forswearing socialism failed to make much difference.

It was true that when Mencken first encountered him Wells was at his best. Mencken wrote about him in one of his neophyte reviews for the *Smart Set* and continued to comment on him for a quarter of a century. But he pronounced Wells's epitaph by 1919 with "The Late Mr. Wells" in the first series of *Prejudices.* He began the essay by giving him his due. Wells at his height, from 1908 to 1912 according to Mencken, was very effective indeed. "He had a lively and charming imagination, he wrote with the utmost fluency and address, he had humor and eloquence, he had a sharp eye for the odd and intriguing in human character, and, most of all, he was full of feeling and could transmit it to the reader." Once past his peak, he declined steadily. For he too became intoxicated with the notion that he was a Great Thinker and had something to teach. He killed himself as a novelist through the "imbecile assumption" that "human beings may be made over by changing the rules under which they live, that progress is a matter of intent and foresight, that an act of Parliament can cure the blunders and check the practical joking of God."

The only American novelist who much resembled Wells in his use of the novel as a vehicle for propaganda and reform was the ebullient radical, Upton Sinclair. Both muckraker and Socialist, he became a national figure in 1906 when his exposé of the Chicago stockyards, *The Jungle,* persuaded President Theodore Roosevelt to call for better conditions in the meat industry. If Mencken ever reviewed *The Jungle* we have no record of it. However, when he started reviewing in 1908 for the *Smart Set* he had something to say about Sinclair's *The Moneychangers,* which came out that year; in 1911 he reviewed *Love's Pilgrimage,* and in 1913 *Sylvia.* In these books his reaction to Sinclair's doctrine clearly affected his view of Sinclair's art.

Reviewing *The Moneychangers* he criticized the course of Sinclair's career in much the same terms that he applied to Wells, "When he started out he loomed big. There seemed to be something of the vigor of Frank Norris, even of Zola, in him. He appeared to sense the sheer meaninglessness of life — the strange, inexplicable, incredible tragedy of the struggle for existence. But then came the vociferous success of 'The Jungle.' The afflatus of a divine mission began to stir in him, and he sallied forth to produce his incomprehensible jehad." The result was bad art, for thereafter he hopelessly confused the job of the novelist with the job of the crusader.

On the other hand, Mencken felt much more kindly toward Sinclair's *Love's Pilgrimage,* praising it for its frankness about the physical side of human life and intimating that he had belabored Sinclair before mainly for his own good. He saw in the book the same sort of conflict that would later interest him in Dreiser's *The "Genius"* — the conflict between the artist and the man of family. And he extolled *Sylvia* for its "striking and truthful picture of Southerners and some of their customs."

In general Mencken's response to the books by Sinclair, which emerged with great regularity as the years went by, could be forecast. If Sinclair's particular target was also his and he did not mind the way Sinclair aimed at it, the review in the *Smart Set* was appreciative. If not, the review was hostile. But Sinclair's attack had to be artful enough. Sinclair, for his part, often scolded Mencken for his apparent prejudice against truth in literature. The result was that, in print and out, the two men disputed enthusiastically. When time finally put a stop to the correspondence, Sinclair wrote sadly to a friend, "I miss his pungent letters."

The dearth of social novelists is odd. So is the dearth of programmatic ones, though they are ordinarily a smaller group anyway. In as lively a form as the novel there ought to have been more than Sinclair and Wells. However, one reason lay in the formidable effectiveness, mentioned earlier, of the conservative critics, who as a group were characterized by an iron gentility. They had first of all the power of their pens But in addition they controlled the editorial policies of the major magazines and set the tone of the major publishing houses. They could keep a writer from being published or, if he was published, they could either ignore him or condemn him. They could be the more potent because in several cases the publishing houses owned their own magazines — for example, the Scribner and the Harper firms. An author the conservatives liked was doubly fortunate, for both magazine and book publication often awaited his work. An author they disliked was doubly damned. Doubtless no geniuses were aborted, no Melvilles or Thoreaus denied a hearing; yet we can wonder.

The leaders among the conservative critics included William Crary Brownell, Robert Underwood Johnson, and Bliss Perry. All were authors in their own right, with an inclination toward the reflective essay or the highly polished poem. All had important connections with publishing. Brownell, who liked to write on Victorian authors, was the chief literary adviser at Scribner's. Johnson, who was a poet and the author of, among other things, *Songs of Liberty*, had been on the staff of the *Century* in its heyday and now acted as its editor; unfortunately the years had narrowed his editorial vision. Perry, whose books included *Whittier* and *The American Mind*, was a Harvard professor and the editor of the *Atlantic*.

As a group the conservative critics plainly agreed on essentials though they varied on the details. Their view of life was moralistic, optimistic, and traditional. And they had a patriotism, or a nativism, that differed from Senator Beveridge's only in being less trumpet-toned. As Bliss Perry wrote in *The American Mind* in 1912, "From the very beginning, the American people have been characterized by idealism. It was the inner light of Pilgrim and Quaker colonists; it gleams no less in the faces of the children of Russian Jew immigrants to-day."

These eminent men did not attack Mencken; they were probably not aware of him. Their successors did, however, in the second decade of the century; to them he was, to steal a phrase from him, a straw stuck in their eye. For his part, Mencken was certainly aware of such pillars of the establishment as Brownell, Johnson, and Perry. Yet he restrained himself, rarely assailing these venerable critics in print. Though he might talk about the "senior castrati" he seldom identified them. Nor did he usually review their books in his *Smart Set* days. He made an exception for Perry's *The American Spirit in Literature*, which he considered completely wrongheaded. Perry had declared that the American spirit in literature was marked by venturesomeness and tolerance. Mencken considered that nonsense, for he believed that it attacked and punished literary heresy with "overwhelming ferocity." It flogged a Dreiser or a Whitman hard.

Mencken found nothing by Robert Underwood Johnson worthy of review, and the only book by Brownell that he appraised was a late one, *The Genius of Style*. About it, Mencken said crisply that a book on style should be done by a stylist, and Brownell could never be accused of having style.

A good illustration of the conservatives' approach to American life was their founding of two cultural senates. Both were designed to institutionalize the conservative way. The first was the National Institute of Arts and Letters, established in 1898; the second was the American Academy of Arts and Letters, established in 1904 as an inner circle for the Institute. Robert Underwood Johnson was its long-time secretary and he once described the Academy's aim as being opposition to sensationalism, utilitarianism, and colloquial English! With the best of intentions the Institute and the Academy helped to consolidate conservative control. Mencken scorned both these bodies and never would have anything to do with them, even when they came bearing gifts from their marbleized mausoleums.

His instinct was sound, for the forces in American literature and life which said no to conservatism were growing. Denied a voice in literature, they managed to make themselves heard in literary journalism. This was particularly true for the so-called muckrakers. They exposed corruption in politics and business vividly and graphically; they pitched on the sordid side of American life. It was Theodore Roosevelt who termed them muckrakers; in doing so he typified the conservative response. One of them was Thomas Lawson of *Frenzied Finance* fame. The greatest was Lincoln Steffens, whose *The Shame of the Cities* became the most popular of the three volumes he wrote during the first decade of the twentieth century. He proved to be more sensational, more iconoclastic, than the others; yet even he made a moral appeal at the bottom. In the opening of *The Shame of the Cities* he writes that his purpose is "to sound for the civic pride of an apparently shameless citizenship."

Curiously, Steffens differed from his fellow muckrakers in more than degree, for he showed an instinctive sympathy toward the very bosses and businessmen he was exposing. He preferred them to the reformers and felt that, with an enlightened citizenry to back them, they could manage the operations of the government better than the doctrinaire doers of good — a view Mencken heartily endorsed.

Another group of men undermining American conservatism were the scholarly skeptics. Their investigations afforded the muckrakers and other independents a theoretical framework. Like Mencken, they were aware that their own mentors were European: Darwin, Huxley, and Spencer especially. The group was made up of scientists and social scientists who looked into the assumptions of the conservatives and failed to find the proof — or even the probability — to validate them.

These investigators remained a minority but it was a significant one, for it was led by William James. Though James died in 1910, his intellectual influence continued. During his rich, varied life he balanced two tendencies. One was a dedication to the measurable and the practical, to the measurement of man and the testing of things by finding out if they worked; the other was an interest in intuition and a concern for religious feelings. John Dewey became his successor in the sense that he likewise opposed the absolutes of conservatism. Yet, relativist that he was, Dewey believed in a science of things and morals and he believed that this science would mean progress toward a better world.

Mencken was attracted by James's pragmatism. He too believed that the test of things lay in their results. And he approved of applying to religion the orderly procedures of research and reflection as James had done in, for instance, *The Varieties of Religious Experience*. On the other hand, he sympathized neither with James's interest in intuition nor in his piecemeal supernaturalism. He was suspicious of a scientist who showed any preoccupation with religious matters unless he disapproved of their transcendental nature. However, he was well aware of James's standing among his peers. He once remarked that James's ideas, "immediately they were stated, became the ideas of every pedagogue from Harvard to Leland Stanford." When his death left a great vacancy Mencken added that "Prof. Dr. Dewey was elected by the acclamation of all right-thinking and forward-looking men." As in James's case, Mencken approved of Dewey's belief in experimental science, in the validity of experience, and in the functional nature of knowledge; at the same time he snorted at Dewey's belief that education could make man the master of his environment. Nevertheless, he stood on James's and Dewey's side. Though both men on occasion raised his hackles he found them much more appealing than their opposition.

A third significant figure among the investigators was the psychologist John B. Watson. In 1913 he proclaimed the doctrine he called "behaviorism," which urged the study of behavior because it was calculable and clear. Though man's mind and motivation were profitless to study, what man actually did could be mechanically determined. Pushed far enough, behaviorism implied that everything could be reduced to measurable, mechanical terms. Every action could be exactly described. Watson's doctrine drew Mencken though he felt that somehow mensuration had gone a little too far.

In literature the doctrines of James, Dewey, and Watson lent themselves to naturalistic fiction, the fiction Mencken favored, the fiction that pictured a grim world where man operated mechanically. This mechanistic view the conservatives strenuously opposed, whether they detected it in some of the writings by the muckrakers, saw it plainly in the expository prose of the social scientists, or encountered it embodied in naturalistic fiction. Not only was it pernicious; it was basically un-American. In Europe it was represented by the most tendentious of writers and thinkers, by the followers of Zola and Ibsen chiefly, as well as the followers of Darwin and Spencer. In the face of conservative hostility the native naturalism in the fiction of the 1890s proved, as was noted earlier, merely a flash. Death silenced Stephen Crane and for a decade Dreiser failed to publish a novel. But in the second decade of the new century his fiction managed to establish itself and then stand out, though it remained thoroughly naturalistic.

The characters in Dreiser's novels moved through a planless, mechanical universe, usually suffering and sometimes triumphing as they wandered along streets whose every house he stopped to describe. He pictured both his characters and his scenes with what was, in the worst sense of the term, scientific accuracy. Though his fiction attracted some of the same people who read Wells and Upton Sinclair, it was clearly differentiated from theirs by its lack of program. In their novels Wells and Sinclair both showed the way to Utopia. Dreiser never did and Mencken approved heartily.

Though Mencken's ideas were oriented toward Europe, there was one great European innovator he regarded with the same mixed feelings he felt for William James or John Dewey. This was Sigmund Freud, the newest of the European thinkers he encountered. He became conscious of him only gradually, quite a while after he was aware of Huxley, Darwin, and even Nietzsche. Once formulated, his attitude toward Freud had a touch of condescension which it would never lose. It was a product of his time as well as of his own impulse. As the early twentieth century saw Freud's ideas, they fixed on sex to so large an extent that it seemed to be the center of human activity. To Mencken the stress on sex was slightly offensive. In his guise as a Baltimore gentleman he felt that many sexual matters should not be discussed. In his guise as a convivial American male he felt that sex was here to stay and should be enjoyed, especially by frisky bachelors, but not analyzed. Yet he was attracted by Freud's intellectual daring, by his European sophistication, and by the curious reasonableness of some of his ideas.

His fairest treatment of Freud prior to the 1920s was "Rattling the Subconscious," in the *Smart Set* for September 1918. He cannot avoid playfulness as he opens his essay-review but he soon admits that "One snickers . . ." simply because one is expected to. For there is something in Freudianism. It has demolished much of the old psychology, substituting for it a new one that avoids the supernatural and shows that the laws ruling human nature are the same as those regulating other matters in space and time. Freud's notion of the subconscious, misinterpreted by some of his Freudians, is essentially sound. That a good deal in the subconscious is sexual is also true. Our culture is in conspiracy against sex, with moralism in the lead, and hopes to suppress it. Freud shows that it cannot do so. Though our culture may shove it down into the subconscious, it will show itself not by direct expression but by permeating the whole cast of our thought. Where Freud has been wrong, and has been corrected by such men as Adler and Jung, is in overlooking the other important matters pushed into the subconscious also.

The Freudian analysts have concentrated too much on individual case histories. Their great opportunity, Mencken urges, is to probe into such widely held notions as "the idea of Puritanism, . . . the idea of uplifting, the idea that the arts are immoral."

Mencken could find among the scientists and social critics a good many Americans who like him turned to Europe with respect and admiration. Among the literary critics, he could find for all practical purposes only two. One was Percival Pollard. Born in Germany and educated in England, he moved to America in 1885 armed with an exceptional knowledge of European literature. To this he soon added a genuine concern for contemporary American literature. He castigated it when he found it sentimental or Puritanical, but he applauded it when it was forthright and cosmopolitan. Mencken read him early and with relish. He met Pollard several years before his death. At one point Pollard stayed in Baltimore for several months; during that time he planned with Mencken a joint translation of some German poetry. Pollard was particularly interested in the drama, and Mencken and Nathan found in one of his books the play *Moral* by the German dramatist Ludwig Thoma, from which they devised a version of their own. Pollard died in Baltimore, as it happened, in 1911. He was cremated there and Mencken was left with the ashes. It took him half a year to persuade the flighty widow to accept them.

The other critic cut a far more commanding figure. He was the ruddy, flamboyant James Gibbons Huneker. Born in 1857 in Philadelphia, he studied piano in Paris and then became a music critic first in Philadelphia and later in New York. For most of the first two decades of the twentieth century he wrote for the New York *Sun* on literature and the arts. He played the part of a cosmopolite with a success that only George Jean Nathan was to equal. Flourishing his cane in all directions, he seemed to be more than one man. What he loved was European and there was, he demonstrated, a good deal of it. He praised Continental composers, artists, and writers long before it was thought decent to do so. His relish for decadence startled his times though he also had an appetite for healthy homegrown fare. Underneath he was in some ways a conservative who shared more of the American temper than he would admit. But he enjoyed the role he played and the titles of some of his books reflect the fact. In 1905 he published *Iconoclasts: A Book of Dramatists*, for example, and in 1909 *Egoists: A Book of Supermen*. He urged Americans toward European culture with an enthusiasm that persisted for forty years.

Mencken happened on Huneker even before the new century opened and was immediately drawn to his writing. It was not long before references to him appeared in Mencken's letters. He reviewed *Egoists* both for the *Smart Set* and the *Sunpapers*. He continued to appreciate Huneker, devoting an entire essay to him in *A Book of Prefaces*. When Huneker gave Mencken the manuscript to read of what proved to be his best book, *Painted Veils*, Mencken wrote a friend gleefully that it was superb — and absolutely unprintable, a riot of witty obscenity.

When Mencken arrived at the *Smart Set* poetry was inaugurating its own revolt against conservatism. Conservatism still insisted that poetry should scan. It was firm in its belief in regularity and form. It insisted also on the moral purpose of poetry, still loving the lyric that ended with an exhortation.

The principal periodicals and publishers for poetry as for prose were situated in New York and Boston. In both places revolt was inhibited, with the result that the most interesting poetry of this period made its appearance in Chicago. Carl Sandburg, Vachel Lindsay, and Edgar Lee Masters produced the best. Sandburg smashed tradition with his blunt, powerful free verse. His most moving poems captured a place, a mood, or an event in a few lines. He epitomized Chicago in terse phrases; he caught the feeling of fog in a single image. His longer lyrics were like Whitman's in their rolling lines and roughened rhythms. Lindsay loved the sound of poetry as much as anyone. His ballads were meant to be chanted or declaimed; at times they were accompanied with stage directions on how to give each passage right resonance. Masters, after a career in conventional verse, found his true voice in his "Spoon River" epitaphs, where he could sum up the life of an Illinois villager in a dozen revealing lines.

The revolt in poetry came later than that in prose and met with slightly less opposition. Sandburg, Lindsay, and Masters did not distinguish themselves until after the start of the second decade of the century. But they represented the blooming of a vigorous growth already under way in Chicago before 1910.

As Mencken himself saw it, the new movement in poetry began about 1912, the year when Harriet Monroe established *Poetry: A Magazine of Verse*. He said in "The New Poetry Movement" in *Prejudices: First Series* that he had read *Poetry* from the beginning and enjoyed it. Though it printed a good deal of extravagant and even nonsensical verse, in the main it "steered a safe and intelligible course." It used the best of the new poetry and ignored the worst. Unlike many another little magazine it did something that particularly commended itself to Mencken: it showed a hospitality to ideas. The credit for these accomplishments belonged to Miss Monroe, an intelligent, tactful woman.

Among the outstanding monuments of the new poetry were, to Mencken, the *Spoon River Anthology*, Vachel Lindsay's "General William Booth Enters Heaven," and — in a rare bit of prescience — Robert Frost's volume *North of Boston*. The most impressive poet was Carl Sandburg. Often crude and banal, he nevertheless could be "simple, eloquent and extraordinarily moving." He often achieved striking effects by surprisingly austere means, for example, in "Chicago" and "Cool Tombs." Second to Sandburg in Mencken's eyes was a poet now totally forgotten, James Oppenheim, who became one of the editors of the *Seven Arts* magazine. His sonorous verse derived from Whitman on the one hand and the Old Testament on the other. His "gorgeous rhapsodies" were partly the result of his inheritance; for Mencken always thought that "the Jew, intrinsically, is the greatest of poets."

Mencken believed that the new movement exhausted itself early. By 1919, when he was issuing his *Prejudices: First Series*, he considered that Vachel Lindsay had suffered a sad decline and that his interestingly barbaric rhythms had degenerated into "elephantine college yells." Robert Frost had hardened into a standard New England bard, a "Whittier without the whiskers." Masters was doomed to mediocrity; Mencken now felt that the "Spoon River" pieces held public attention because they were heavy with sex. Ezra Pound had an excellent ear and without doubt gave a thrilling poetic show. But of late he had become an angry pamphleteer, dropping "the lute for the bayonet."

And yet Mencken grieved in this essay over the fact that the movement was running its course. There were two counts especially in its favor. The influences that shaped it were largely European; and it had been antidemocratic in its avoidance of commonplaces and in its "spirit of daring experimentation." Outside the movement there were several poets interesting to Mencken. The first among them was Lizette Woodworth Reese, a Baltimore poet though Mencken fails to say so, and there were two others, now deep in dust, John G. Neihardt and John McClure.

An eastern audience for the Chicago poets became a possibility and then a certainty in the second decade of the 1900s. Several publishing houses were established in New York with a leaning toward the experimental in literature. They favored not only experimental poetry but also experimental prose; they were ready to issue radical nonfiction as well as fiction. The English esthete Mitchell Kennerley founded his firm in 1906 and developed a list of rebels to print. He produced volumes by Vachel Lindsay along with the works of such Eastern independents as Edna St. Vincent Millay, late of Vassar; Walter Lippmann, then a Socialist thinker; and Van Wyck Brooks, a literary idol smasher. B. W. Huebsch started a firm that by 1905 printed Socialist nonfiction as well as European fiction. The translations from German, French, and Russian literature were the most notable items in his list but he also printed D. H. Lawrence and James Joyce. The brothers Albert and Charles Boni, booksellers in Greenwich Village, issued the work of radicals of several sorts. In the summer of 1915 there appeared the house of Knopf.

With a small staff and scant capital, Alfred Knopf combined independence of taste with an eye for emerging talent. In his list he stressed Russian fiction, for which he had profound respect, but he did not neglect the prose and poetry of other countries. He made his mark early: the year after the firm began he published W. H. Hudson's exotic *Green Mansions*. Within another year he secured such promising writers as Mencken himself, the ultraindependent Pound, the gauzy novelist Carl Van Vechten, and the romantic storyteller Joseph Hergesheimer. His list was more eclectic than those of his compeers, for he did not care as much about rebellion for its own sake as they did.

Awakening to the threat of the new houses, the conservative ones shook themselves and began to issue a revolutionary tract or two. The revolution was apt to be modulated but the fact remains that when the second decade of the century began, convention in literature was losing ground to revolt. Though it did not lose heavily, a dash of dissent became fashionable even in the ancient citadels of publishing in New York and Boston.

The conservative magazines encountered the same challenge as the conservative publishing houses. The founding of *Poetry* in Chicago by Harriet Monroe did not rock the main magazines, yet it was not without influence. It helped to broaden their horizons by persuading them that tolerance toward innovation in poetry could be made to pay; in fact it could even have prestige. Moreover, two intellectual weeklies appeared; each had an impact. One was the *Masses*, a weekly established in 1911. Under the direction of a series of editors, usually Socialist, it favored liberal politics and foreign literature. The other was the *New Republic*. Founded in 1914 by the social critic Herbert Croly, its announced aim was not to amuse its readers but "to start little insurrections in the realm of their convictions." In the field of esthetics the monthly *Seven Arts* appeared. It too made an impression though its span was short, from the fall of 1916 to the fall of 1917. Its aim was to give a hearing to exactly the kind of liberalism and experimentalism that the conservative periodicals still suspected. Its editors and contributors were in several cases the luminaries of the future. The editors included Van Wyck Brooks besides the poet Oppenheim; the contributors included Mencken, Dreiser, Robert Frost, and Sherwood Anderson. Mencken gave them his hard-hitting "The Dreiser Bugaboo" to print.

One already established magazine inclined toward the liberal side for several years during the second decade of the century. This was the *Forum* which, with Mitchell Kennerley as publisher, paid more attention to life than to literature but stood ready to provide an audience for both. In it the bright young men of the new age expounded the doctrines of anticonservatism. They described and invoked the ideas they had gotten from such exotics as Sigmund Freud. They praised the works of the European innovators such as H. G. Wells, and the *Forum* from time to time printed selections from these works. In *The End of American Innocence* Henry May observes that the *Forum* published articles by most of the leading young intellectuals in America.

The conservative magazines made their hesitant concessions to change. At the *Atlantic* in 1909 Bliss Perry left as editor and was succeeded by Ellery Sedgwick, whose background looked far less austere. Significantly, he was Mencken's friend. *Harper's* and *Scribner's* allowed a tinge of rebellion to touch their pages, though the stately *North American Review* remained unmoved.

Mencken, surveying the field of the American magazine, decided that almost everything of merit in the early years of the twentieth century could be traced to the influence of the respected *Century* magazine of the 1880s and 90s. He praised it for its plunge into the politics of those days, its encouragement of new writers, its high level of art work, and the way it won public attention by the "sheer originality and enterprise of its editing." But by the time he pronounced this eulogy in "The American Magazine" in *Prejudices: First Series*, he had to add that the *Century* was now past its prime and was entering old age. Its place had been taken by the muckraking magazines like *McClure's*. However, they themselves soon suffered from a surfeit of success. The exposures by such trenchant journalists as Lincoln Steffens and David Graham Phillips proved more than effective. They drove the most colorful culprits out of public life, so Mencken said, and then there was no one to expose. Currently, and regrettably, the *Saturday Evening Post* stood supreme, with "its new type of American literature for department store buyers and shoe drummers, and . . . its school of brisk, business-like, high-speed authors." There had certainly been a swing from convention to revolt, though now the pendulum seemed to Mencken to be moving back.

When, in the second decade of the century Boston and New York became less unfriendly to innovation, innovation reciprocated by moving east. Yet, except at Harvard, Boston was still not very hospitable; New York City, on the other hand, opened the door more than a crack. Its Greenwich Village emerged as an ideal home for the Chicago iconoclasts and the Midwestern realists, along with a share of young Eastern poets and intellectuals. There were more Eastern intellectuals than poets however, among them Lippmann and Van Wyck Brooks.

With the opening of World War I, rebellion accelerated though so did the reaction against it. The genteel radicals of the Village were joined by street Socialists and a few genuine anarchists. The Russian immigrant Emma Goldman, for one, attracted wide attention. She considered herself not only a political revolutionary but an advocate of new literature, particularly in the field of the drama. Two of her books were *Anarchism and Other Essays* and *The Social Significance of the Modern Drama.* Mencken reviewed them both. He was especially taken with her choice of dramatists, in particular Ibsen, Strindberg, and Shaw, in the drama book. Furthermore he agreed with her thesis, which was that the vision of the artist was a sharper instrument for change than the deeds of the actual revolutionist. However, he deplored her own deeds, which included taking to "cart-tail oratory and jail-life."

On balance, he approved of her for he saw her as a thoroughgoing opponent of Puritanism. She was sound on this issue and to him it remained the most important one. He himself had continued to oppose Puritanism enthusiastically. To his sniping in the Baltimore papers he added, over the years, a good many pungent paragraphs in the *Smart Set,* particularly in "Répétition Générale." The one piece of any length that he wrote for the *Smart Set* was "The American: His New Puritanism," which he printed in the number for February 1914. It provided the underpinning for what proved to be his definitive statement, the essay "Puritanism as a Literary Force."

This came out as part of *A Book of Prefaces,* issued in September of 1917, and ran to more than eighty pages. In it Mencken poured the accumulated observation, reflection, and irritation of a decade. It emerged as the most formidable attack in the history of American letters against Puritanism.

In it he asserts that "the prevailing American view of the world and its mysteries is still a moral one, and no other human concern gets half the attention that is endlessly lavished upon the problem of conduct, particularly of the other fellow." Its effect on American literature has been devastating. In no other literature will one find beauty sacrificed so completely to propriety. Its effect on intellectual matters has been as bad. In a burst of anger Mencken charges, "The Puritan's utter lack of aesthetic sense, his distrust of all romantic emotion, his unmatchable intolerance of opposition, his unbreakable belief in his own bleak and narrow views, his savage cruelty of attack, his lust for relentless and barbarous persecution . . . have put an almost intolerable burden upon the exchange of ideas in the United States."

Now it has turned to law to enforce its views. Now it has produced "the moral expert, the professional sinhound" — in particular, Anthony Comstock and John Sumner. In Comstock it has developed a man of dire effectiveness, and Mencken describes Comstock's legislative and legal triumphs. The new Puritanism under such leadership has been able to intimidate publishers, editors, and even authors. At the end of the essay, however, Mencken says with qualified optimism, "Maybe a new day is not quite so far off as it seems to be."

He was wise in declining to predict when it would come. Puritanism, after losing strength between, say, 1908 and 1915, was now regaining it and would not be badly beaten till well into the twenties. Mencken and Nathan were right in announcing its defeat, from their point of view, by the end of 1923 when they left the *Smart Set*. But they underestimated its resilience, its readiness to rise again, as the Scopes trial in 1925 and Mencken's "Hatrack" case in 1926 would show. The fact was that Puritanism did not realize it was whipped.

Meanwhile, it was clear to the upcoming writers and polemicists that Mencken was not exaggerating Puritanism's current threat. They could cite chapter and verse. They felt themselves and their ideas threatened above all by Puritanism as censorship. If it did not affect directly what they wrote, it affected it indirectly. Their fears were understandable. Quasi-official censorship arose and flourished in Boston and New York. It appeared, if it did not flourish, in many other parts of the country: the Blue-Nose sniffed everywhere. It was a Counter-Reformation directed by conservatism against new attitudes. Public opinion could often be rallied by the moralists who wanted to drive out what they considered indecent literature. They had the government attorneys on their side as a rule and the judges as well. And in the federal postal regulations they found a handy weapon. The Post Office could bar indecent matter from the mails; and if the indecent matter appeared in a periodical twice in a row, it could either cancel the mailing privileges of the periodical entirely or raise its mailing rate. Almost all magazines would have had to suspend publication if forced to mail their issues at first-class rates to their subscribers. As Mencken told Dreiser grimly in the summer of 1916, "the Puritans have nearly all of the cards."

In New York old Anthony Comstock gave a classic demonstration of how the moralists' power could be applied. He had developed very comfortable relations with the legal prosecutors and the bench in New York, and even got himself appointed a special agent for the Post Office. He quickly commanded the cooperation of the major publishers and retained it till the end of his life. As a founder of the Society for the Suppression of Vice and a pillar of the Watch and Ward Society, he labored above all to keep the printed word pure. In his busy life he brought several thousands of people to court and caused the destruction of tons of books, some of which were simply pornography but others of which represented serious literature. Among his more flamboyant activities was a raid in 1913 on Mitchell Kennerley's firm, with a public trial to follow, because Kennerley had issued a naturalistic novel by a lawyer, Daniel Carson Goodman, entitled *Hagar Revelly*. Hagar herself was shown as more sinned against than sinning but that did not deter Comstock. Mencken found the raid revolting.

One of the main devices that conservatism took to preserve its values during the first two decades of the century was legal, as well as extralegal, force. It used censorship, official and unofficial, and used it effectively. But Comstock and his principal successor, John Sumner, could never have succeeded without the help of conservative public opinion. They were able to rally it the more effectively because they seized on the period's most sensitive issue, sex. Soon after the start of the twentieth century it had replaced theology as the site for the bitterest battles. The censors provided the hard edge for American conservatism; they were the militants whose mission it was to make America spotless.

Sumner carried on where Comstock left off, becoming secretary of the New York Society for the Suppression of Vice in 1913. Looking back on his accomplishments Sumner said, in one of his *Who's Who* entries, that he had been "a leader in movements and legislation directed against demoralizing influences in publs., the screen, the stage, etc." However, printed matter was his prime interest, and in literature it was the naturalistic novel. Naturalistic novelists were rare before the end of World War I, as we know, but Sumner harried any he found. Mencken called him, through set teeth, a foul and disgusting son-of-a-bitch.

Sumner's foremost target was Dreiser. He could not have picked a more vulnerable one, for Dreiser had few admirers and fewer friends. Mencken, however, could be counted among both. No novelist meant more to him during the first two decades of the century than Dreiser; no novelist got more of his help. With the onset of World War I Dreiser's difficulties mounted, for he made no secret that his sympathies, like Mencken's, were with the Germans. Years before the war, though, Dreiser had begun to blacken his reputation in the eyes of censors and conservatives.

7. Dreiser and the Fruits of Dissidence

FROM THE FIRST YEAR of the century, in fact, Dreiser found himself in difficulty with both public and private censorship. His initial novel, *Sister Carrie*, was printed in 1900 only after much soul-searching by its cautious publisher, Doubleday. Though Dreiser interpreted the delay as supression of his book, Doubleday's hesitation was understandable. There is no doubt that this account of a farm girl who becomes the mistress of first one man and then another, and ends as a musical-comedy star, affronted the sensibilities of the conservative mind. The wages of sin were supposed to be death or at any rate disaster, especially for the woman concerned. But here is Carrie Meeber, lonely and uneasy as the novel ends but still a success, while her lover Hurstwood becomes a beggar and kills himself.

This to Mencken was a novel of magnitude — he once assured Dreiser that he held it in actual reverence — being assailed on precisely the wrong grounds by the wrong people. Then too, Mencken had a sentimental reason for defending the book: he had been one of the rare readers to see it when it first came out in 1900.

Even that early he had been aware of Dreiser. Exactly when Dreiser became aware of Mencken we cannot be sure. But they were corresponding by August 1907, when he wrote Mencken about doing an edition of Schopenhauer. The embattled novelist whom Mencken had read in 1900 was now the patently successful editor of Butterick Publications' three large magazines for women. The main magazine was the *Delineator* and in his quest for new authors and profitable ideas for it Dreiser came across Mencken. Mencken was branching out into magazine journalism and as a sideline had formed an un-official partnership for writing medical articles. A Baltimore doctor named Leonard Hirshberg provided the information after which Mencken promptly provided the prose. Hirshberg approached Dreiser; Dreiser was interested and commissioned a series on infant care, to come out under Hirshberg's name. Shortly afterward Mencken came to see him.

As Dreiser remembered it, "There appeared in my office a taut, ruddy, blue-eyed, snub-nosed youth of twenty eight or nine whose brisk gait and ingratiating smile proved to me at once enormously intriguing and amusing. I had, for some reason not connected with his basic mentality you may be sure, the sense of a small town roisterer or a college sophomore of the crudest and yet most disturbing charm and impishness, who, for some reason, had strayed into the field of letters. More than anything else he reminded me of a spoiled and petted and possibly overfinanced brewer's or wholesale grocer's son who was out for a lark. With the sang-froid of a Caesar or a Napoleon he made himself comfortable in a large and impressive chair which was designed primarily to reduce the overconfidence of the average beginner. And from that particular and unintended vantage point he beamed on me with the confidence of a smirking fox about to devour a chicken."

Dreiser found Mencken impressive as well as attractive. Their correspondence reflects the fact almost from the start. He responded to Mencken's youthful assurance, learning in the process to respect the cast of his mind. He made the pleasant discovery that his intel-lectual masters were also Mencken's: Darwin, Huxley, and Spencer. And, egoist that he was, he could not help being affected by Menc-ken's admiration of his work and the cogency of his reasons. Dreiser was no theoretician, no self-critic, but he sensed why Menc-ken was right. As the months went along, Dreiser asked Mencken's opinion about manuscripts, suggested him to Splint for the *Smart Set* (or so he liked to remember), and offered to put his name on the masthead of the *Delineator*'s literary supplement.

In 1909 Dreiser took over the little *Bohemian* magazine and promptly invited Mencken to contribute. He wanted the light touch — "something real snappy" he said in a note of July 11 — and Mencken furnished it. During 1909 he published eight pieces there. The only important one was his play without words, "The Artist"; the others were froth like "The Bald-Headed Man," in the October issue. When the *Bohemian* starved to death Mencken was one of the mourners. In 1910, through Dreiser, the Butterick firm published the book *What You Ought to Know About Your Baby*, made up of Mencken's ghost-written articles for the *Delineator*.

The two met at intervals and corresponded constantly, Mencken writing with his usual drive and wit, Dreiser with an elephantine imitation. Systematically the younger man encouraged the older in his work. As Mencken's circle of acquaintances grew and his public increased through his reviews in the *Smart Set*, he made it his business to beat the drum for *Sister Carrie*. "I seize every opportunity," he said in a note of March 14, 1911, "to ram in the idea that your book must be read." The next month Dreiser sent him the manuscript of *Jennie Gerhardt*. The story turned out to be as uncompromising as *Sister Carrie*. With literal exactness and much detail it describes the career of a girl who is seduced, by a senator no less, bears his illegitimate daughter, lives in sin with another man who then marries another woman, and ends by nursing this other man in his final illness. When it was printed Dreiser sent him the first copy to come from the publisher. Mencken found it even better than *Sister Carrie* because the structure was more coherent. It fulfilled his definition of a good novel, he wrote Dreiser, "An accurate picture of life and a searching criticism of life."

The more he thought about it the more enthusiastic he became. Five months after first seeing the manuscript he accorded it the highest praise in his power, for he assured Dreiser that it was, aside from *Huckleberry Finn*, the finest American novel so far. He foresaw that the conservative reviewers would be shocked. They were, and he readily defended *Jennie Gerhardt* against them. His letters in 1911 and 1912 reveal his consistent support of the book and of Dreiser as a noteworthy novelist. He did more than review the book; he campaigned for it.

He did not find Dreiser's *The Financier*, issued in 1912, as exciting. He told Dreiser some of his criticisms, seasoned with abundant praise, and Dreiser was appreciative. Mencken had thought the manuscript too long; when Dreiser sent him a copy of the book he assured him that seventy-seven pages had been cut from the proofs and inscribed the book "in grateful friendship." Mencken warned him that antagonism to *The Financier* was inevitable, because the conservative mind interpreted everything as a moral spectacle and so would consider the hero's "cleanly paganism" disgusting. But he reiterated that he stood on Dreiser's side.

Dreiser's troubles continued. The volume to follow *The Financier*, called *The Titan*, was accepted by the firm of Harper's, put in type by them early in 1914, but then not issued. However, the English publishing house of John Lane, which would soon print Mencken, took over and issued *The Titan* the same year. Mencken found in it "the best picture of an immoralist in all modern literature" and gloated that Anthony Comstock could not touch it because the immorality was fundamental to the conception of the book and never betrayed itself in prurient phrases.

When in August 1914 Mencken and Nathan gained control of the *Smart Set* they planned at once to print some pieces by Dreiser. They settled on his plays since his novels could not be excerpted well and his short stories did not impress them very much. They told Dreiser what they wanted and he mailed them three of his plays, confident that they would be promptly published by the eager editors. They were not, however, and Dreiser wrote indignantly to Mencken. Mencken soothed him enough so that by the end of the year Dreiser sent him the manuscript of his next novel, *The "Genius."* Again Dreiser asked for suggestions about improving the book. This time he declined to accept them, however, and when he inscribed the customary copy to Mencken he wrote "Without change but with best wishes just the same."

John Lane published *The "Genius"* in 1915. Considerably before this, Dreiser had become notorious for his itch to get in bed with every woman he could lay his hands on, and the "Genius" proved to be Dreiser himself in all his open sexual adventuring. The hero, Eugene Witla, is a painter not a writer, but otherwise he is a walking justification for the life that Dreiser led. Though the book ends with Witla penitent and resolved to concentrate on his painting instead of his passions, to the censors the ending seemed mere appeasement. The controversy over the book mounted; the year after it came out the Western Society for the Prevention of Vice was able to ban it from a good many Midwest bookstores. It was also able for a time to have the book barred from the mails. In New York the censors, now captained by John Sumner, denounced the book for both blasphemy and immorality. The American head of John Lane, one Jefferson Jones, stopped distributing it in July 1916.

Dreiser, complaining vehemently to Mencken, found him both sympathetic and practical. As he remarked in his letter to Dreiser of July 28, he had fought the censors often enough to know how they operated. The judges, "eager to appear as moral gladiators," regularly sided with them. Mencken dismissed the charge of blasphemy because it was no crime in American law. The charge of immorality was another matter. He advised compromise and approved of the fact that Jefferson Jones had offered to negotiate with the censors. In that way a few lines might be lost but the book would be saved.

Weighing the matter Mencken said that he and Dreiser were living in a country controlled by Puritans. To meet them head on would ensure defeat; they had somehow to be circumvented. But he added meaningfully, "My whole life, once I get free from my present engagements, will be devoted to combatting Puritanism."

However, once he had a chance to see the capricious cuts Sumner and his associates demanded, he changed his mind about compromising the case. The censors wanted to scissor out seventy-four scenes of "lewdness" (mainly hugging and kissing), one brief essay on the female breast, and eight oaths (such as "God damn" and "Jesus Christ"). The cuts were so silly that he felt sure they would not stand up in court. He now agreed that Dreiser ought to fight and offered to help actively. He recalled his own brush with the censors over one of the so-called louse magazines he and Nathan had started, the *Parisienne*, though it was seldom even risqué. The moralists had taken it to court but it proved so clearly harmless that the case was thrown out.

As he demonstrated to Dreiser, Mencken was the ideal ally in a pitched battle. He did everything he could. He argued, he explained, he expostulated. He gave much of his ample energy and enlisted the energy of others. One of the most useful things he did was to urge the Authors' League of America, in August, to sponsor a campaign to support Dreiser. The League consented and circulated a protest which hundreds signed, including some quite conservative writers. Dreiser himself, however, when sending out copies of the list of protestors, left out the names of certain of the conservatives and added the names of several Greenwich Village hacks who had flattered him. Mencken expostulated and then wrote Ernest Boyd, "The old ass is ruining his case by his folly." Yet Mencken remained loyal. "I am working hard on the Dreiser Protest," he reported to a woman friend in November, "rounding up recreant authors, and sending out twenty or thirty letters a day."

The situation improved when a liberal New York lawyer, John Stanchfield, took over the defense. He moved so aggressively that he daunted Sumner and Sumner offered to compromise. Stanchfield was joined by the Free Speech League, which, as Mencken told Boyd in another letter, had been "collecting evidence against the moralists for many years and [had] accumulated an enormous mass of proofs of their imbecilities." And Mencken continued to enlist authors.

The net result of all these efforts was that Dreiser won, although the victory was of the ragged, inconclusive kind that Mencken himself would later win when he challenged the law for the *Mercury*. The United States district attorney in New York ruled, after Stanchfield entered the case, that The *"Genius"* did not violate the law; the Post Office proceedings ground to a halt; and the court itself merely meditated. In a letter of April 20, 1918 to Boyd, Mencken reported that the matter was still under judicial consideration. That summer the court decided that it should not decide — a tactic so feeble that Mencken was more than kind in terming it merely an evasion.

The currents of the time helped to keep Dreiser and Mencken together. Though Dreiser found Mencken arbitrary on occasion, even arrogant, and Mencken discovered that Dreiser could be an ass, they had a common bond of exceptional strength: both were assailed by the same enemies and for largely the same reasons. The coming of the European war, and America's increasing concern with it, resulted in making Germany and all things German offensive to many Americans. The attacks on German culture reached their height after April 1917, when the United States entered the war, but they began before that. German philosophy was evil; German music was suspect; and German literature was coarse and crude. Even German food had to be tried by fire and then rechristened; the innocent "sauerkraut" became "liberty cabbage," for example. And Americans with German names often had to prove their patriotism.

Both Mencken and Dreiser were in a delicate position. Their names were German; and Mencken in particular had been, and continued to be, an apostle of German culture and an advocate of the German Kaiser against the British Crown. He told Dreiser that his great hope was to see the Germans victorious over England. "May all Englishmen roast forever in hell," he exclaimed to him in December 1914. Dreiser's prime offense in the eyes of his enemies was that he was an immoral Teuton who wrote immoral books. By a kind of sleight of hand unconventionality became unpatriotic. Censorship found a keen ally in patriotism, the two fusing in the public mind to an extent now hard to imagine. They were aided by the efforts of the new conservatives in the critical establishment, several of whom would join together to form the New Humanist movement. Their leader was the Harvard professor Irving Babbitt but their hatchet man was a pinch-faced professor from the University of Illinois, Stuart Sherman.

Sherman made it his grand design to purify American culture; in the process he did not mind destroying the careers of Dreiser and Mencken. He felt that the ideas they espoused, if not their actions, were both immoral and treasonable. Sherman dealt his first sharp blow late in 1915, when he published an attack on Dreiser in the *Nation*. "The Naturalism of Mr. Dreiser" went considerably beyond literary criticism by insinuating that Dreiser's characters were neither Anglo-Saxon nor moral. To us today this is a mild and footless complaint. To Sherman, and to many of his readers, it was a grave charge; by Anglo-Saxons he meant the English and emphatically not the Germans, and the English were virtuous men while the Germans were sinks of evil.

Writing to Dreiser Mencken blasted the essay. "The Nation article is a masterly exposure of what is going on within the Puritan mind, and particularly of its maniacal fear of the German." Some other writers joined him both in private and in public but soon the voices in defense of Dreiser's writing dwindled. The climate grew cold. In the spring of 1917 Mencken wrote to Ernest Boyd from New York that the literary situation reflected the political situation and that Dreiser was being hammered in most of the literary weeklies as a secret agent of the Kaiser.

Despite the altered climate Mencken continued for a time to speak out. Here and there he remarked pungently on Sherman's point of view. But his notable counter-offensive was published in the magazine *Seven Arts* in August 1917. This was "The Dreiser Bugaboo," in which he used the old technique, perfected by Dryden and Swift, of making his enemy look more of a fool than a knave. He stigmatized Sherman as the epitome of all that was dreary in the college professor.

He characterized Sherman's charges as a critic against Dreiser as irate flubdub. He got to the heart of the matter when he said, "I single out Dr. Sherman, not because his pompous syllogisms have any plausibility in fact or logic, but simply because he may well stand as archetype of the booming, indignant corrupter of criteria, the moralist turned critic." Alongside his denunciation of Sherman he put his own persuasive description of Dreiser's gifts as a novelist.

That fall, with the military draft going full strength and American doughboys being sent to France in numbers, Sherman did his patriotic duty to the hilt. He reviewed Mencken's *A Book of Prefaces* for the *Nation* of November 29 under the ironic title of "Beautifying American Literature." He did so with the more relish because one of its four essays was another full-dress defense of Dreiser but more cogent and detailed than "The Dreiser Bugaboo." It was the best balanced appraisal of Dreiser up to that time and made Sherman's attacks look merely vindictive. As a matter of fact each of the four pieces in the book affronted Sherman. The essay on Joseph Conrad eulogized an alien, noted for his somber fiction. The essay on James Huneker constituted a hearty defense of that sophisticated anti-Puritan critic. And the final essay, which became one of Mencken's most famous, seemed to Sherman a tissue of provocations. It was "Puritanism as a Literary Force," which we have described before.

In the *Nation* review of the book he identified Mencken as a leading pro-German and then, using the technique of guilt by association, added all the rebels and dissenters he could think of who were handicapped by Germanic names. Among those on his list were Huneker, Alfred Knopf, and one of Mencken's oldest friends, Louis Untermeyer. In a key passage Sherman summed up his charges against Mencken. Mencken always praised "a Teutonic-Oriental pessimism and nihilism in philosophy"; he always criticized the democratic system of politics; he favored the "subjection and contempt of women"; he relished the idea of a "Master Race"; and he was out of sympathy with Anglo-Saxon civilization. Sherman proclaimed that in consequence Mencken was nothing but an infatuated propagandist.

In public Mencken now declined to carry the controversy further. He decided to bide his time. Brisk battler though he was, he did not feel that he fitted the role of martyr — something he might well have become as the tension of war rose throughout the country. It was easier to be quiet because Dreiser grew resentful toward Mencken; it was easier because the case of *The "Genius"* rested in the courts and he could do nothing about it. He wrote Boyd on December 15, 1917 that he had happened on Dreiser at a restaurant and that they had shaken hands solemnly. That was all.

It became increasingly plain that Sherman spoke with the accents of the day. Nearly all the magazines not previously on his side now came over. There were those which had withstood the austere ideal-ism of Woodrow Wilson when he applied it to domestic problems; but when he said he would use it to make the world safe for democracy, it was a stubborn editor or writer who did not murmur Amen. The *New Republic* and the advance-guard *Little Review* kept their indepen-dence of mind but they had scant company. Even if Mencken had tried to publish his polemics to a national audience, he no longer had the periodicals to publish them in.

After the summer of 1917 he had the entry to only one magazine, his own — or rather, his and Nathan's. Even there he did his writing under pseudonyms and kept it literary or mock-literary. He wrote with wariness; he and Nathan edited with wariness as well. In view of the heightening tension both wanted to avoid any collisions with the censors, whether moral or military. They saved their ammunition, resolving to have the *Smart Set* sit out the war. Meanwhile, the moralists reaffirmed their control of American culture and Mencken dropped out of national notice — though it was not to be for long — for the first time in nearly ten years.

He lost his local audience in the same way and at the same time he lost his national one. In spite of Baltimore's Germanism the war which Germany waged against its enemies found less and less sym-pathy. Month by month the people in Baltimore who wanted Britain and France to win grew stronger. "Beat the Huns" became their slogan.

The change was as clear in the offices of the *Sunpapers* as in the city outside. Part of Mencken's job on the *Evening Sun* was to work closely with its editor, John Haslup Adams. But Adams had developed into an adherent and then almost a worshipper of Woodrow Wilson. It was with elation that he saw him elected Governor of New Jersey and thereafter President of the United States. Furthermore, Adams was an advocate of the British as well as of Wilson. Most of the other members of the *Sun* felt the way he did though not as strongly. They too saw in Wilson's program something of a crusade.

The more the Germans inflamed American opinion against them, the more Mencken cheered them on in the Free Lance. Early in 1915 they decided to use their submarines to destroy the shipping of the Allies. Wilson announced that he would hold the Germans strictly accountable for any American losses. On May 7, 1915 a German submarine torpedoed the British liner *Lusitania* off the coast of Ireland. More than a thousand persons aboard drowned, including 124 Americans. While a tide of hostility swept across the United States, Mencken in Baltimore defended the submarine commander. He asserted that the Germans would not stop with the *Lusitania* and in his columns he predicted the day when the German armies would capture Paris and destroy London. He frequently announced that the war was in its final stage, punctuating his predictions with shouts of "Deutschland Über Alles!"

The letters against the Free Lance multiplied. Opposition outside of the paper swelled; so did opposition within, led by Adams. Outraged by Mencken's stand, he accused him of something close to treason. It is doubtful that any other staff member of the *Sunpapers* went as far as Adams, but it is certain that the *Sun* now favored Great Britain for reasons both of public policy and personal taste.

By October 1915 Mencken was ready to write his final Free Lance piece. It was printed on the 23d. It still hailed Germany, snorted at England, and ridiculed the reports of German atrocities. Next to the bottom of the column was this aphorism, "The truth that survives is the lie that it is pleasantest to believe."

However, the United States was not yet at war so he was not yet quiet. For more than another year he contributed pieces to the *Evening Sun*, not every day but more than once a week, that evidenced an unchastened Mencken. The first two were on Puritanism; the third was on "The War in Its Last Phase" and the fourth was entitled sarcastically, "Are the Germans Immoral? Of Course!" During 1916 the *Evening Sun* published nearly sixty of his articles. Their range remained wide; their dominant tone remained one of insult. Among the subjects that Mencken made fun of were American preparations for war, American college women, America itself ("The Paradise of the Third-Rate"), Christian Science, vice reports, and reformers. Here and there he shared his preferences as well as his prejudices with the public. He sounded his praises for, among others,

Beethoven, Dreiser, Huneker, and Conrad. It seemed the same old Mencken except that the proportion of war pieces fell off.

Reading him, the rulers of the *Sunpapers* found themselves in a state of mingled exasperation and admiration. Early in the autumn of 1916 they arrived at a solution to the Mencken problem that must have struck them as the ultimate in ingenuity. They would send him, if he would be sent, as a war correspondent to Germany: in this way he would be both exiled briefly and legitimized. He proved to be more than willing; in fact he wrote Ernest Boyd that the relief was unspeakable. Conditions in the *Sun* office had become trying and Mencken went there less and less. The re-election of Wilson in November, though Mencken had foreseen it, was an added blow. He left his misguided country shortly after Christmas.

He sailed on the *Oscar II,* where he endured his narrow cabin and read and slept, unscathed by submarines. His ship first touched at Kirkwall in the Orkney Islands, then steamed to Christiana and then to Copenhagen. Disembarking, he journeyed to Berlin and established himself at the best hotel, the Adlon. With Mencken safely across the sea, the *Sunpapers* decided that they could brazen out the matter of his controversial beliefs. The *Sunday Sun* advertised on January 27, the day before his first dispatch appeared, "MENCKEN is not neutral. He is pro German" and went on to suggest that his well-known sympathies would help him to get the inside story.

In Berlin he found the American correspondents and the American embassy full of rumors and tension because diplomatic relations were in the process of being broken off. He wangled his way to the wintry Eastern Front, in Lithuania, where the Germans faced the Russian forces. Baltimore seemed a million miles away. He suffered all the hazards of the war correspondent, from fleas to shrapnel. He saw life in the trenches, finding it less harrowing than he had expected. He also lunched and dined with generals; they ate better than the burghers of Berlin. He saved more than his share of souvenirs, among them the seating chart for one of his lush meals with the high command. He returned to Berlin to find the rumors thicker and the passports held up of all Americans who wished to leave. Then the Germans relented at least for the embassy staff.

Mencken himself made an appeal to a highly influential warrior, General Erich Ludendorff, now back in Berlin after triumphs over the

Russians on the same Eastern Front Mencken had visited. The appeal worked; all doors flew open and, though merely a journalist, he was able to leave Berlin at the same time as the American ambassador. He traveled by train to Berne, then to Paris, and then to Madrid, where he managed to get a stateroom on the Spanish liner *Corunna* which would take him as far as Cuba. The slow, uneventful voyage was a pleasant change. When he reached Havana on March 5 he found a revolution, which the *Sun* asked him to report on. He stayed several days and then headed home to Baltimore, arriving on the 14th.

Meanwhile he had been writing, in spite of hindrances, with much of his usual vigor. The pages of the *Sunpapers* testified to his productivity. There were more than a dozen dispatches from Germany and eight from Havana. And there were a baker's dozen which, under the general title of "The Diary of a Retreat," described what was happening during Mencken's last days in Europe and explained how he got from Berlin to Cuba.

"The Diary of a Retreat" is a rarity in Mencken's writing for it began as an actual journal. It joins reportage to personal experience. He preserved at least a volume of typed excerpts. "The cold here is intense," one of them says. "It is positively painful to walk down Unter den Linden. Soldiers, schoolboys, old men, women and even girls are digging away at the frozen snow. . . . As for me, I am pretty well banged up. The cold came very near fetching me in Lithuania, and now I have a game foot and my nose is swollen and takes on a vermillion cast. A frostbitten nose would be farcical . . . but disconcerting." Mencken enjoyed his journalizing and, shortly after he reached Baltimore, wrote Ellery Sedgwick at the *Atlantic Monthly* that he planned to fashion a book out of it.

Two things helped to make Mencken an outstanding newspaperman. One was his gift of phrase; the other, easier to overlook no doubt, was his enterprise. He managed to get out of Berlin by pulling strings that no other reporter seemed able to pull. He could sail for home before any of his peers because, when he found that no ships were leaving northern Europe on account of the German submarines, he traveled south to Madrid and took a Spanish liner there. When he disembarked in Cuba he again turned things to his advantage.

By good luck he had a friend in Havana, a Danish sea-captain who — as Mencken told the story later in *Heathen Days* — knew everybody worth knowing in Latin America. The captain met him promptly in the Prado and outlined the issues of the revolution with blunt simplicity: the rascals who were out wanted to be in. Then he made arrangements for Mencken to meet the leader of each side, that is, the President of Cuba and the head of the revolutionary junta. Both talked copiously. When Mencken went to send his dispatches he discovered that a young Cuban censor was holding up everything. In this emergency the captain found an American ship in the harbor for Mencken, along with a mate who would carry the virgin copy to Key West, where it could be telegraphed to the *Sunpapers*. The scheme worked perfectly; that night Mencken got a cable from the *Sunpapers* saying that the dispatch was being run and was illuminating and high-toned stuff. The scheme continued to work till the fourth day. Then the mate failed to appear. At the ship, however, Mencken caught sight of a likely looking American at the gangway and threw himself on his mercy. The obliging American took the day's dispatch with him and filed it as the mate had done before. Somehow the few remaining days each provided a passenger to carry the day's dispatch.

Mencken came home in the middle of March and his dispatches ran till the end of the month. Then he and the *Sunpapers* were definitely done with one another, by mutual consent. But he was still a newspaperman and so he cast around for a new paper to write for. The only one he could find was the New York *Evening Mail*, whose managing editor, John Cullen, was a friend of Baltimore days. Its credentials were dubious. Furthermore, the pay was low and Cullen felt that he had to stipulate that Mencken could not write about the war, although the war was the prime contemporary issue and Mencken lived on issues. Notwithstanding, he signed on. He contributed well over a hundred essays to the *Mail* before he was through and they include some of his best. He had reached his splendid prime; the pieces prove it. Some were suggested by Free Lance columns and on inspection proved to be amplifications of them; others were not. Nearly all were enjoyable and astringent.

Here some of his classics made their initial appearance, among them "The Sahara of the Bozart," on the cultural barrenness of the South; "A Neglected Anniversary," his famous hoax on the history of the bathtub; and "Critics and Their Ways," later reprinted as the now well-known "Criticism of Criticism of Criticism." Germany aside, the staple subjects were much as before: American literature, the American language, music, women, the antics of the American Congress, and the imbecilities of the reformers. Three other topics were mentioned here and there; they were not new to Mencken's mind but he would spend more time on them in the next decade. These were science in general and medical science in particular, both of which he respected, and the mores of the businessman, which he did not.

Good though the pieces were, the public saw no more of them after the first week of July 1918. On July 9 the publisher of the *Evening Mail* was arrested as a German agent; a new management took over which had no use for Mencken. Now both newspapers and magazines were closed to him. The double blow was a dismaying one but he had seen it coming. Whatever its bad effects, it did nothing to reduce his vitality as a writer. It simply channeled that vitality into his books.

For that matter, he had been going on — even before the outbreak of World War I — with his writing of books at the same time that he was writing for newspapers and magazines and fighting the battles of the just. True, some of the earlier books were trifles, beginning with the luckless *Europe after 8:15*. Its history started in the first months of 1913, while Willard Huntington Wright was putting in his feverish year as editor of the *Smart Set*. He suggested to Mencken and Nathan that the three of them do a series of articles for the magazine on the gayest of the great cities of Europe. Mencken had recently returned from a trip to Europe — his first in fact — and was ready with two articles, one on London, the other on Munich, which had been commissioned by John Adams Thayer. They appeared in spring. After Wright and Nathan had enjoyed a junket to Europe to get materials for their articles, those went to the *Smart Set* also. The next logical step was to turn them into a book. *Europe after 8:15* came out in a showy yellow and black cover just before the war began. There could not have been a worse time to issue this festive little travelogue, with its pictures, by Thomas Hart Benton, of quaintness and alien carousing. Mencken considered it a complete failure.

It was printed by the American branch of the British publishing house of John Lane. This fact in itself was not very important but it led to the appearance of Mencken's next books. He had obviously impressed the manager of the branch, Jefferson Jones, and Jones had suggested that he do a book for them, which in the course of time became two.

A Little Book in C Major, published by Lane in 1916, was the first.

The musical quotation heading it, Mencken notes in the typescript, is the opening phrase of the German soldiers' song "I had a comrade." The comrade was Theodor Hemberger, a stalwart of the Saturday Night Club, who taught Mencken a good deal about music and was drawn to him closely when the war fever made things difficult for all pro-Germans. The book is composed of 226 epigrams, taken with rare exceptions from the pages of the *Smart Set*. Some of the epigrams now seem merely glib while others retain their barb and wit. A few have become famous including "Love is the delusion that one woman differs from another" and "Archbishop: a Christian ecclesiastic of a rank superior to that attained by Christ."

The second volume from Lane came out the same year, *A Book of Burlesques*. The burlesques in question were pieces — from the *Smart Set*, Dreiser's *Bohemian* magazine, and the *Evening Sun* — of the past several years but with the usual revisions and improvements. The most effective was the short play "The Artist," which had been reprinted twice before Mencken inserted it in *A Book of Burlesques*. Among the others, "Death: A Philosophical Discussion" showed his sharp ear for American speech. While awaiting the minister the pallbearers sit around and talk in the room next to the corpse; clouds of clichés mingle in the macabre atmosphere. "From the Programme of a Concert" contains some technically sophisticated musical fooling in its fake program notes. Understandably the style of most of the pieces is pure slapstick. Unlike *A Little Book in C Major* this one became a success. When Knopf took over and published a revised edition of *Burlesques* in 1920, Mencken salvaged some parts of the *C Major* book by introducing them into it. Years later *A Book of Burlesques* was still one of his favorites, reminding him of his buoyant departed youth.

A Book of Prefaces, printed by Knopf in 1917, has already been mentioned. Its four long essays all show authority. They are not only witty and confident; they are as penetrating as anything Mencken had done up to this time. Again they proved to be the culmination of earlier writings — he said he revised them "from snout to tail" — but once this was done they were so satisfactory that he would change them only slightly in later editions.

Mencken's next effort, *Damn! A Book of Calumny*, represented a return to the trifling. Like its predecessors, it resulted from a chance acquaintance with a publisher. This time it was a rotund and zestful man named Philip Goodman, who became Mencken's firm friend. He asked Mencken to do a book for him and he too got two books instead. The first was *Damn!*, whose flip title was not Mencken's idea and always irritated him. With the help of scissors and library paste he put it together in a week. It is a gathering of short pieces, casual essays in which he simply shuts down after saying what he has to say. Or so he maintains in his Preface. Music, literature, and American life were the general fields he drew on for things to damn or occasionally to praise.

In the same year as *Damn!*, 1918, Goodman published a far better book by Mencken. It grew through its various editions and printings to be one of his most stimulating. It was *In Defense of Women*. In spite of its being based as usual on his previous pieces in the *Sunpapers* and the magazines, it had both artistic unity and the appearance of forthright thought. When he sent a copy to a friend he remarked that it was a mere "jocosity," yet it was much more than that. With a mixture of amiable irony and comic common sense he dealt with such tantalizing topics as: "Woman's Equipment," "Compulsory Marriage," "The Emancipated Housewife," and "Women as Martyrs." And he wrote a section which began prophetically, "The marriage of a first-rate man, when it takes place at all, commonly takes place relatively late."

He said in the book that he found women vastly shrewder and more realistic than men. They had much to gain from marriage while men had little, but multitudes of marriages were being celebrated every day. Women rarely fell in love; men, with their idiotic smirks and eye-rollings, proved to be easy victims to amour.

In politics as well as marriage, in bed or in parlor caucus, women were realists. They had no belief in democracy, for they well understood that certain people must rule while the rest obey. Even sexually they did not covet equal rights, except those suffragettes too plain to capture a husband under normal rules. Women were the more complaisant about the so-called double standard because they realized that the average husband might ogle a pretty face but timidity and apathy would combine to make him do little but look. For one husband who kept a chorus girl there were ten thousand as true to their wives as convicts in a death house.

In social customs women were much more conservative than the talk of the time suggested. The large majority did not smoke or drink. The woman who drank as systematically as men was apt to be mannish herself.

And yet there had been some change in mores; there had been, as Mencken put it in one of his later sections, a transvaluation of values. Women now had more economic security than ever before and so could stand off their husbands more readily if they wanted to. They could even philander discreetly without being publicly branded. Their conduct before marriage did not need to be as strict as it had been. The notion of virginity was now so preposterous that no intelligent person of either sex cherished it. It survived "as one of the hollow conventions of Christianity."

Peering into the future Mencken predicted that female prostitution might even grow respectable. He stoutly asserted the advantages of prostitution for the prostitute, maintaining that she ordinarily liked her work and would not want to trade places with a shopgirl or waitress. "She is quite content," he announced.

Another prediction concerned the future of marriage. He had a warning for American women. Obviously with the drive for woman suffrage on his mind, he said that he foresaw more equality for the female but fewer immunities, more rights but fewer privileges. Women would lose some of their femininity, to the regret of both sexes.

He could not resist ending the book with one more prophecy: the time would come when the wife, especially of the superior man, would have to reconcile herself to her husband's keeping a mistress. It was already well known that many happy marriages admitted "a party of the third part."

The public reception of *In Defense of Women* proved kind. The war was almost over and most critics showed little malice toward Mencken for his stand against it or against Puritanism. A change was in the air and new critics were submerging Sherman. It could be sensed even before *In Defense of Women* came out, for the general treatment of *A Book of Prefaces* a year earlier — aside from its abuse by the Shermanites — was more than respectful. *A Book of Prefaces* was hailed by the New York *Tribune* as the event of the year in literary criticism, by the Washington *Star* as a joy, by the Chicago *News* as the work of a winner. True, the Springfield *Republican* dismissed it as "pithy and nettling persiflage" but the *Republican* stood in the minority. When *In Defense of Women* came out, there were four times as many favorable reviews as unfavorable. It was applauded for its wit, its style, its impishness, its daring. Few reviews resembled that of the New York *Tribune,* which in a change of heart about Mencken exclaimed sourly at the publication of the book, "And this is a day of conservation of print paper!"

The year after *In Defense of Women,* in a brilliant display of versatility, he published the work for which he will probably be longest remembered, *The American Language.* It was issued in a handsome format by Knopf, who now became his permanent publisher.

It dated back to some articles Mencken wrote for the *Evening Sun* in 1910. The very first announced the theme; it was "The Two Englishes." He followed it with "Spoken American," "More American," "American Pronouns," and "England's English." These were printed at a time when newspapers showed more interest in linguistic matters than they ever have since. Mencken's brisk opinions and provocative queries drew added attention to the topic and helped to swell his mail. His widening circle of correspondents sent in additions and occasional corrections. He gathered more material in the next year or so. Then in August 1913 the *Smart Set* carried his essay "The American: His Language." It too attracted attention.

He prepared the original typescript of *The American Language,* as he later recalled, in 1915 or 1916. It ran to less than fifty pages but opened, as the finished book would, by invoking Thomas Jefferson as the first apostle of the American language. The slender typescript grew by uneven accretion, much of it probably in the summer of 1918. By the time it reached print it totaled 374 bulky pages.

From the day he began it, he lamented the fact that professional linguistic scholars were overlooking the splendid subject of our language, even if professional writers such as Ring Lardner were not. So he himself applied his energies to it, though he minimized his results to the end with excessive modesty.

His main idea sounds far more obvious now than it did fifty years ago. It was of course that an American language existed aside from its mother tongue of English. It was a language which had absorbed expressions from the American Indian; had naturalized a substantial group of nouns brought in by the Dutch, the French, and the Spanish; had invented a large number of expressions, such as "scalawag"; had devised catchy new combinations, such as "backwoodsman"; and had given old English words, such as "corn," new meanings. The changes in it were accelerated by the drive of population into new and stimulating territory, the West and the Southwest. The changes were still going on and would continue into the indefinite future, in testimony to an undiminished American inventiveness and energy.

As he saw it, the American language was steadily adding new terms which either simplified old ones or added pungency to them. Even if they did neither they were still different. The total result was that the gap between American English and British English was widening year by year — and widening most of all in the language of daily concerns. We "mailed" letters instead of "posting" them, for example; we rode in "elevators" rather than "lifts." The differences kept on growing not only in vocabulary but in pronunciation and spelling. So did the differences in grammar and syntax, for America was becoming more and more informal, except in the eyes of high school English teachers. "Shall" and "will" were losing their distinction; "should" and "would" were merging into one; and no American could now say "It is I" without feeling like a schoolmarm.

Mencken derided Americans in a dozen different ways but never about the language that they and their forefathers had created. Though he could make fun of the jargon the Rotarians talked in, whenever he regarded the language seriously he was impressed. "Such is American," he says in the original typescript of 1915-16, "a language pre-eminent among the tongues of the earth for its eager hospitality to new words, and no less for its compactness, its naked directness, and its disdain for all academic obfuscations and restraints." And though he was far from a believer in progress in general, he adds that the American language at any rate is progressing. It may end, he forecasts, with our using a new idiom, as different from orthodox English as Russian is from Bulgarian. Years later, observing the increase in international communication, he would go further. In the fourth edition, of 1936, he would predict that American through its mass and vigor would attract English into its orbit and English would become a dialect of American.

Alfred Knopf worried about whether the book would move; so did Mencken. But the first edition of fifteen hundred copies sold out swiftly. The second edition, revised and enlarged by well over a hundred pages, would follow in 1921. The third, again revised and enlarged, would come in 1923; the fourth, corrected, enlarged, and rewritten, would come in 1936. The book's majestic progress would be crowned with the publication of two Supplements, in 1945 and 1948, which would once again be revisions as well as major expansions.

Their basic structure, however, would be the same from the start. With only minor variations, each form of the work would begin with a discussion of the two streams of English. Then a surprisingly spirited parade would follow under a series of solemn headings: the materials of the study, the beginnings of American English, the period of growth of the American language, that language today, American and English, the pronunciation of American, American spelling, the common speech, proper names in America, American slang, and the future of the language. The scholarship would become more and more specific, more and more monumental. A single instance can serve. Mencken would correspond with the Right Reverend J. B. Dudek of Oklahoma City about something as minor as the Czech or Bohemian elements in the American language, and by the end of April 1937, the correspondence would number 175 items. Thanks to such continued, energetic efforts it would take Supplements I and II together to cover the topics previously covered in a single volume — and nearly all the material would be new. The footnotes would multiply in each edition with the result that over half of the final Supplement would be sheer annotation.

The acclaim of the work would grow with its size. Though Mencken felt that the first edition was treated condescendingly by most American specialists, some, including Professor Louise Pound of the University of Nebraska and Professor G. O. Curme of Northwestern University, were hospitable to it. Several of the leading European authorities were impressed. Succeeding editions would be praised by reviewers on both sides of the Atlantic. The influence of Mencken's studies and theses would be seen in the increasing number of books and articles about the American language. It would be acknowledged directly and detected indirectly.

Popular acceptance would keep pace with, and in fact exceed, professional acceptance. The second edition would sell well and soon be exhausted; the third would require five reprintings; the fourth would be reprinted at least fourteen times, even becoming a Book-of-the-Month Club choice and selling more than ninety thousand copies in that form before the end of 1939. This in spite of the Depression. It would end as a classic, something few foresaw when it appeared in 1919.

The year 1919 was further distinguished by Knopf's publishing the first series of Mencken's *Prejudices*. They had been suggested by a Cleveland bookseller named Richard Laukhuff, who had told Knopf that he thought it would pay to collect Mencken's *Smart Set* reviews every two years. Knopf agreed and relayed the suggestion to him. Mencken decided, however, that it would be better to substitute miscellaneous essays for the reviews; and this he did. As usual, some of the essays had started as reviews anyway. But now, revised and amplified, they acquired the kind of authority that had enhanced *A Book of Prefaces*. And their wit was unfailing.

The most memorable pieces were his sardonic analysis of current literary critics, "Criticism of Criticism of Criticism"; his ready if premature good-byes to H. G. Wells in "The Late Mr. Wells" and George Bernard Shaw in "The Ulster Polonius"; and two impressionistic surveys, "The New Poetry Movement" and "The American Magazine."

Prejudices had a winning appeal for most critics who read it. Only a handful showed that to them World War I was not yet over, most notably the one who wrote the review in the Los Angeles *Times* under the subhead of "New York Critic and Admirer of Prussian Kultur Makes Vicious Attack on American Literature, Authors and Institutions." Like *The American Language,* Mencken's *Prejudices* had a distinguished future awaiting them. Five more volumes would emerge, the last in 1927, and each would be read eagerly.

The literary essays in the first series of *Prejudices* represent the cream of his criticism. But elsewhere there was much more, anᵈ much of that was good. Mencken had developed into a noteworthy literary critic, and the chapter and verse for that development can be discovered in the pages of the *Smart Set*. They reflect the fact that he had largely abandoned the criticism of the drama for the criticism of fiction even before he arrived at the *Smart Set*. They show that he had grown disenchanted with the theater, though he would still try his hand at writing a few plays.

The Shaw whom he had defended and lauded in 1909 became "The Ulster Polonius" in 1919, with a platitude at the root of each of his plays. As with Shaw, so with others. Mencken's indictment grew to be a blanket one: "The theatre, when all is said and done, is not life in miniature, but life enormously magnified, life hideously exaggerated. Its emotions are ten times as powerful as those of reality, its ideas are twenty times as idiotic as those of real men, its lights and colors and sounds are forty times as blinding and deafening as those of nature, its people are grotesque burlesques of every one we know." Good-bye to all that.

The pages of the *Smart Set* also reflect the slow shift in emphasis in his reviewing from fiction to nonfiction, the gradual widening of his scope. The progress of his program is revealed clearly, as is the essence of his approach. He could develop under nearly ideal conditions: the *Smart Set* provided him for fifteen years with as good a forum as he could imagine in this highly imperfect world.

The original arrangement in 1908 was that he should do a review-article every month in which he discussed the most important recent books and that he should deal briefly with perhaps a dozen others in an appendix, characterizing each in a sentence or so. His first piece on this plan appeared in the November number under the title of "The Good, the Bad and the Best Sellers." In it he writes about Upton Sinclair's *The Moneychangers* at some length and then considers five other books more briefly. Among them he properly praises Mary Roberts Rinehart's *The Circular Staircase*, which would become a minor classic among mystery stories, and perversely praises the latest novel by the English sentimentalist Marie Corelli. Sure that other critics will sneer at her, he applauds her for what he alleges is a very capable performance. In the appendix he shows his true nature by saying of *Views and Reviews*, "Early essays by Henry James — some in the English language."

He establishes his pattern at once. He starts with a few provocative general observations and then applies them to the book that attracts him most. He begins with Mencken rather than with the author of the book. As a preliminary to his appraisal of Sinclair's volume he speaks about platitudes. "Platitudes have their uses, I have no doubt," he says, "but in the fair field of imaginative literature they have a disconcerting habit of denouncing and betraying one another." He goes on to accuse Sinclair of suffering from the *bacillus platitudae*. Mencken makes his foray in a lively fashion, remembering that he must tease the reader into paying attention. But in style and technique he is not quite the witty, knockabout writer he will become in the next few years.

He responded to his opportunities in the succeeding months with evident elation. He set down the notions and opinions he had formulated. Many would become famous, or notorious, and here in the pages of the *Smart Set* they received their first burnishing. In his review-article for December 1908 he paraded what proved to be some of his most durable opinions. Among them: *Huckleberry Finn* is the greatest American novel; and Conrad's "Youth" is the best story in the world today. He also demonstrated the range of his interest, for the books he noticed varied a good deal from one another. He soon showed his awareness of European as well as English literature. As early as his third essay he wrote about *Silence* by the Russian Leonidas Andreiyeff ("or whatever his name may be — I have seen it spelled in a dozen different ways"). And he revealed a robust appetite for half-baked writing. A trashy novel or a pawky tract would often give him a good deal of diversion.

By the end of his first year his preoccupations were plain. He enjoyed reading and reviewing prose fiction. Though he found little good fiction to respond to, he seldom grumbled. Bad fiction was grist for his mill too. In evidence, some of the titles for his review-articles of the first year besides "The Good, the Bad and the Best Sellers": "Novels and Other Books — Chiefly Bad," "Novels for Hot Afternoons," and "An Overdose of Novels." He made no secret that he preferred realistic novels. He believed that plots should be built on probability, that characters should act as if they moved in real life, and that their actions could be tragic or even dreary as long as they were plausible. What he respected most in a novel could be summed up in Dreiser's *Sister Carrie*, with its painstaking exactness and fidelity to life, with its amoral heroine and its antihero, and with its avoidance of program. He often used it as a standard in his *Smart Set* pieces.

Yet even this early he was not concerned with literature alone. His essay for March 1909 opens with: "Three books designed to reduce and mitigate the horrors of human existence are stretched upon the operating table and invite our exploratory surgery. The first is a treatise upon marriage in all its branches; the second is a tract upon the science of eating; and the third presumes to teach us how to sleep."

Before he finished with the *Smart Set* in December 1923, he wrote — according to the count by William Nolte in *H. L. Mencken, Literary Critic* — 182 critical pieces. What characterized them from beginning to end was their zest, whether in praising the good or excoriating the bad. They were a personal response. When attacked he replied that he was indulging his personal taste, as critics must and should. "Criticism itself," he remarked in a review in 1916, "is no more than prejudice made plausible." Moreover, they were a response not only to literature as art but also to literature as instruction. A social novel by Sinclair could irritate him because of its preachiness, but a naturalistic novel by Dreiser could impress him by the truth of its observation.

Mencken was even brash enough one day to take a deep breath and define the novel. He said it described "interesting, significant and probable (though fictitious) human transactions." Both the cause and the effect of the transactions should be shown and the influence on the characters should be stressed. Elsewhere he expanded on his interest in the novel of background, which dealt with a man's reaction to his often harsh surroundings. He respected the novel which well described one man's battle with his world. The fact that the battle might be lost made it often a better novel, for it was typical of life to defeat its puny antagonists. "The aim in a genuine novel," he announced in 1914, "is not merely to describe a particular man, but to describe a typical man, and to show him in active conflict with a more or less permanent and recognizable environment — fighting it, taking color from it, succumbing to it."

His interest in the role of the environment sprang very probably from his interest in Darwin and his doctrines. Not the least of his reasons for esteeming the novels of Dreiser was that in them the fittest survived.

His interest in character analysis, in the cause and effect of human transactions, was not as strong as his interest in environment. But he wanted a reasonable explanation of why the characters did the things they did. He respected the behaviorist psychology of John B. Watson, with its idea that any human action is the result of mechanical forces we can someday figure out, although we know he thought it could be carried too far. And in spite of some qualms he was much attracted by the depth psychology of Sigmund Freud. He thought that Freud, while at times given to talking wildly, had something quite important to say about the springs of human action. Through his hypotheses Freud was able to dismiss any supposedly supernatural element in human conduct and make plausible certain kinds of action that had not been capable of a rational explanation before.

Mencken's demands for a sense of the power of environment and a probing of motivation were intellectual demands. So were two others, which he made from the time he first concentrated on ideas.

He demanded that the novel exemplify ideas in a forceful way. And he demanded that the ideas be largely congenial to him.

As he said more than once, he was basically after encountering Shaw a critic of ideas. As time passed it became plain that he was interpreting the term generously. He meant not only a critic of the ideas in any given work but also a critic of the ideas of other critics, especially the stuffy, conventional, and Victorian kind. He summed it up in 1923 at the end of his *Smart Set* stint: "My literary criticism has been almost exclusively devoted to attacking and breaking down the formal ideas, most of them devoid of logical content, which formerly oppressed the art of letters in the United States — ideas of form and method, of aim and purpose, or mere propriety and decorum."

Throughout the *Smart Set* period Mencken remained a critic of ideas. He had a program for literature and, moreover, for literary criticism. And yet underneath the program lay an emotional response. There is no doubt that he wished to be moved by what he read. He did not insist that it make him gasp with awe, double up with merriment, or dab at the corner of his eye. But he wanted to become involved in what was happening to the characters in the novel before him and he wanted to feel for their fates. In a number of novels he was indeed moved. Many others left him cold. One of the prime reasons for his abandoning literary criticism was the discovery that the novels of the 1920s — with a few remarkable exceptions such as Sinclair Lewis's — moved him less than novels of the decade before. It was partly his fault, for his sensibilities shrank as he grew older. But regardless of whose fault it was, the new literature made little appeal.

Before he abandoned the flowery field of literature for the vegetable garden of the social sciences, Mencken made a further point about both critical theory and practice. He developed it most fully for "Criticism of Criticism of Criticism," in *Prejudices: First Series,* which had started two years earlier as a review of J. E. Spingarn's book *Creative Criticism.* Hostile to the conventionality of the criticism practiced around him, Spingarn turned back to Goethe and revived two of his great critical precepts. One is that the critic should ascertain what the writer had tried to do; the other, how the writer had gone about doing it. Then the work should be judged in those terms. Each literary work is unique and for that reason all the less susceptible to being judged by a set of permanent conventions. The approach Spingarn advocates he calls "creative criticism." Mencken, however, finds the phrase flamboyant and proposes that this admirable approach be called "catalytic criticism" instead.

He explains that the business of the critic is to be a catalyst, to provoke a reaction between the work of art and the reader. The good critic will see to it that the reaction is both intellectual and emotional. As Mencken puts it at the end of the essay, "Out of the process comes understanding, appreciation, intelligent enjoyment — and that is precisely what the artist tried to produce."

Having made this telling point about criticism, Mencken proceeded to modify it if not reverse it. In "Footnote on Criticism," published first in 1921 and then revised for *Prejudices: Third Series* of 1922, he decided that the job of the critic is not to be a catalyst but rather to express himself. In evidence he even hints that his own motive in devoting himself to the novels of Dreiser was simply to show off. The work of art being criticized is nothing but the platform on which the critic performs his aerial leaps and so wins the applause of the audience. The critical review becomes "a fresh work of art and only indirectly related to the one that suggested it."

By the early 1920s Mencken had established himself as a major American critic. But even before America entered the war he was making a name for himself, and he knew it. The friendly reception of his cluster of books, the *Prefaces,* the *Prejudices, In Defense of Women,* and *The American Language,* softened the blows he felt World War I was dealing him. He maintained much of his reputation as a writer in spite of Sherman and his supporters — and then increased it. It did not seem to onlookers that America's entry into the war seriously interfered with his normal activities. Yet he suffered his bruises both as a professional writer and as a private person.

As the war went along, Sherman and other loyal cultural leaders were recruited to pamphleteer for the Allied cause, while Mencken and Dreiser went into limbo. Sherman's chief contribution, issued in February 1918 and widely distributed, was the pamphlet *American and Allied Ideals: An Appeal to Those Who are neither Hot nor Cold.* In it he assured his uncommitted readers that the Allies, unless their leading spokesmen were black-hearted liars, truly battled for world peace. The best way to comprehend the Allied ideals was in reverse: to avoid reading modern German works, such as those by Schopenhauer and Nietzsche. Looking over their shoulder at Mencken and

Dreiser, Sherman denounced the leaders of German thought and of contemporary Germany. They worshipped power, they defended the rape of Belgium, they rejoiced in the sinking of the *Lusitania,* and they extolled war "as the prime element of their *Kultur."*

During the month before Sherman printed his pamphlet President Wilson presented his peace program of fourteen points, including a permanent league of nations, to the Congress. During the months afterward Allied victories mounted. Over in France the American Expeditionary Force fought in the battles of the Marne, Chateau Thierry, Belleau Woods, and the Meuse-Argonne. By November 1918 the war was won and America had helped to win it.

Mencken in the meantime watched both sardonically and uneasily. He watched sardonically as the nations belabored one another like Punch and Judy. He observed the politicians in their cavortings; he saw the intellectuals whip themselves into a loyal frenzy. He secured several copies of Sherman's pamphlet and sent them to friends. He goggled at the college presidents. In a postwar piece in the *New Republic,* "Star-Spangled Men," he would urge ironically that medals and decorations go to the most deserving among them: "for the university president who prohibited the teaching of the enemy language in his learned grove, heaved the works of Goethe out of the university library, cashiered every professor unwilling to support Woodrow for the first vacancy in the Trinity, took to the stump for the National Security League, and made two hundred speeches in moving picture theatres — for this giant of loyal endeavor let no 100 per cent American speak of anything less than the grand cross of the order."

When the war affected him personally he grew apprehensive or irritable. Because Baltimore was a city with a German cast to it, it tried the harder to be patriotic. By city ordinance German Street became Redwood Street. Mencken's personal experiences left a mark that was never erased. Government operatives, he believed, actually spied on him; Baltimore patriots tried to bully him into buying Liberty Bonds to help finance the war; his neighbors sneered at him. He was even ridiculed and criticized because he kept on playing and defending German music. For a short time he feared that in spite of his many minor ailments the Army might draft him. He wrote his friend Lieutenant Colonel Fielding Garrison of the Medical Corps about the possibility of serving as a medical historian but was snubbed for his effort by Garrison.

He endured, however. A month before the Armistice which ended the war, he told Ellery Sedgwick that his experience had been grim. He assured Sedgwick that after the war he would be glad to write for the *Atlantic* a frank account of how it felt to be an American of German blood in wartime. He added that his trials had changed him a good deal.

The evidence we have shows that the changes were a matter of intensification rather than alteration. Under pressure Mencken revised few of his ideas if any; what he did as the result of the war was to hold on to them more firmly, to assert them even more extremely. He now realized more than ever how powerless the individual could be in struggling against either institutions or the populace. There is no doubt that the war deepened his contempt for both and made him all the more a rebel.

8. Good Company

MENCKEN ALWAYS CONSIDERED World War I an ordeal for him. Yet even when it threatened him most nearly, he could pour his energy into the *Smart Set* and his books. They gave him great relief. His social life too offered him surcease, not only during the period of World War I when he needed it most but also before and afterward. Regardless of circumstance he found that, with his abounding vitality, he had time for both an impressive amount of work and a gratifying amount of play. This held true for years. He could act the role of the newspaperman or the editor, the magazinist or the critic, all day and part of the night; but the rest of the night remained for beer and sociability. He himself was always good company and he helped to make the company around him good. Above all, perhaps, in the Saturday Night Club.

As we look back on it today there was something Homeric about the Club, or if not Homeric at least Wagnerian. Gigantic figures loomed through its alcoholic mists, trumpeting jubilantly or scraping furiously away. Triton blew his wreathed horn. The piano thundered like a pipe organ. The smoky room where the Club met seemed much too small for the music. The few visitors were huddled near the wall as they watched the barbaric richness of the ritual. The invocations, the order of the musical numbers, the chants, the bawdy songs were all set and sanctified. Halfway through each Saturday night, the epic scene changed from the inner to the outer dark. For, the concert done, the Club adjourned to a favorite beer cellar for the remaining festivities. There everyone drank gallons; in between gulps, shouts were exchanged but no ordinary conversation. Often there was a high debate; sometimes, though rarely, a resounding quarrel. Then in the middle of the night an end to the festivities, a bursting out into the open, and brazen-toned farewells as the Club members dispersed.

The Club has become legendary. It is hard now to realize that its members were all too human, that its origins were inadvertent, that its music was sometimes flat, and that even its revels were sometimes a bit mechanical. Notwithstanding, after all the deductions for actuality have been made, it was from the start a fellowship which enjoyed Mencken's allegiance.

The Club was never born; it simply grew. Back at the opening of the century, when Mencken was in his early twenties, he and Joe Callahan, both of the Baltimore *Herald*, and several other musically inclined acquaintances began to get together to play or sing. In 1902 he began to play trios with two other Baltimoreans. He played the piano; Albert Hildebrandt, a benign, balding man who made and sold violins, played the cello; and Samuel Hamburger, a sharp-faced salesman later turned electrician, played the violin. At times Joe Callahan joined them in a quartet. They performed and then they drank and talked. New members were admitted to the infant club when they showed they liked to manage an instrument and hoist a seidel of beer. Since some of their playing was catch-as-catch-can they had to be good sight readers.

The first professional musician to join was Theodor Hemberger, who not only played a fine first violin but was the director of several German singing societies in Baltimore. Through him the Club edged toward competence. He made musical arrangements of the selections the Club aspired to play and in various ways extended the Club's musical horizons. John Wade was the first doctor to join. He had been a professional flute player who worked his way through medical school by performing in a theater orchestra.

Max Broedel, a gifted medical artist from Germany, joined the Club in about 1910 and became Mencken's fast friend as well as first piano to Mencken's second. Broedel had some musicianship to his playing, but it was gradually eroded by Mencken's torrent of enthusiasm. It was not long before both men would jump up and down as they played the strongest, most rhythmical passages on their quivering piano. A notable event in their friendship came in 1916 when, in response to a request from Mencken, Broedel gave him one of his drawings. According to Mencken it was a beauty, depicting a cancer of the uterus; and he alarmed his mother by threatening to have it framed and hung on the wall at Hollins Street.

Gradually the Club became institutionalized. A group photograph taken in November 1913 shows the members and guests at their customary ease in the private room at the Hotel Rennert now reserved for them every Saturday night after their playing. Besides Mencken the members shown include Hemberger, with his Kaiser Wilhelm moustache, the curly-haired Broedel, Wade, and Hildebrandt. Joe Callahan was away. The guests of the evening include Paul Patterson of the *Sun* and Willard Huntington Wright of the *Smart Set.*

Other members were inducted as time went on and various guests, usually brought by Mencken, were allowed to admire the playing and join in the drinking. The common bond for the members, as Mencken observed years later in writing an obituary of Hildebrandt, was love of music — and no bond was better than that. The "amiable weakness for the squeaks of the fiddle and the burble of the flute" created good cheer.

Mencken's convivial energy and his passion for music made him the mainstay of the Club. The men surrounding him at the meetings deferred to him almost automatically, though without any apparent loss of self-respect. Hemberger, for example, smilingly called him his beloved General-Field Marshal. The only insurgent member was a publisher and editor who had known Mencken since the start of the century, Heinrich Buchholz. Because he played no instrument he acted as the Club's music librarian, or, as he sometimes waspishly put it, the Club janitor. More than once he quarreled with Mencken and other members, yet somehow peace always returned. Several other members stood as high in their field as did Mencken but they too grouped themselves about him.

Mencken's devotion to music was not only emotional. He was entranced by the melodies he heard, but he also comprehended the technical virtuosity that went into their composition and production. He himself did amateur composing once the Club began. A composer, a good composer, seemed to him the most notable of creators: his accomplishment ranked far above that of the novelist or the painter. Mencken never set himself up as a critic of music or musical performance, yet he inevitably grew in understanding. For years he collected orchestral scores and studied them. Most important, music made a deeper appeal to him than did anything else even remotely like it. He once said, "When I think of anything properly describable as a beautiful idea, it is always in the form of music." He termed his lack of good musical instruction the great deprivation of his life; as a result of it both the music he wrote and the music he played were less than first-rate. However, these limitations weighed little in comparison with the fact that in his physiology, at its most fundamental level, sound meant more than sight. "The world presents itself to me," he asserted in *Minority Report*, "not chiefly as a complex of visual sensations, but as a complex of aural sensations." The appeal of music was indeed profound.

The programs the Club played represented a compromise of taste, certainly; some members liked one composer or school while others preferred another. Not infrequently Mencken's taste prevailed. It wavered little throughout the years. His chief love was the German Romantics, though he also admired the great Classicist Bach and went on an annual pilgrimage for some years to the Bach Festival at Bethlehem, Pennsylvania. Basically the music he liked best was the kind in which he could let himself go.

He described his preferences in detail in a letter of May 6, 1925 to his biographer Goldberg. He put Beethoven first among all composers, even over Bach, and the first movement of the *Eroica* seemed to Mencken simply unparalleled. The qualities that attracted him to Beethoven were his remarkable dignity and superb workmanship. Next he put Brahms, whose First, Second, and Fourth symphonies were incomparable; and then Schubert, "whose merest belch was as lovely as the song of the sirens." But because Mencken disliked singing, Schubert's songs appealed to him less than they should have. Mozart was to Mencken another superb composer, with at least six perfect symphonies to his credit.

Mencken went on to observe that Haydn wrote much memorable music, that Schumann wrote some, and Mendelssohn a little. Wagner was a masterly technical composer, probably the best musician who ever lived, but in his operas he often acted the mountebank as he tried for theatrical effects. Nevertheless, *Die Meistersinger* was the noblest work of art produced by man. Among the composers then living, Richard Strauss ranked first, especially for his operas, where he handled the orchestra even better than Wagner. Turning finally to the so-called moderns, Mencken said that he preferred to read rather than hear them. And jazz, he predicted, would never last.

With Mencken's help the Club library ultimately contained nearly all of the most noted symphonies as well as the best of chamber music. It also contained a well-thumbed selection of marches, waltzes, and instrumental pieces from operas and light operas.

Almost from the outset the Club had connections with other organizations, both musical and social. At times it was a matter merely of interlocking membership; at times it was the result of off-shooting. The earliest to appear was the Florestan Club, probably named after a composition by Schumann and organized in 1911 by several Baltimore musicians and music lovers. One of its founders was Mencken's tutor in music at the *Herald*, W. G. Owst; another was Theo Hemberger. It was at the Florestan meetings that Mencken first met Max Broedel. This club survived for some years and had as its offshoot the Sunday Dinner Club, which convened every other Sunday and dined and drank well. In the early 1920s a Sunday Night Club was organized by the wife of Hamilton Owens, a new colleague of Mencken's at the *Sun*. It included women along with the men and for the most part played chamber music. Mencken joined in occasionally. In the middle 1920s he organized the "Maryland Free State Association" after Hamilton Owens coined the phrase "Free State" for Maryland. It was a dinner club, with Mencken's friend the biometrician Raymond Pearl and an engaging eccentric, Willie Woollcott, among the regulars recruited from the Saturday Night Club. Its pretext was often the honoring of visiting dignitaries.

However, the heart of Mencken's social life remained the Saturday Night Club. Though it had its lean seasons, and some proved to be quite lean, it always recovered. With the passing of the years it altered very slowly, shifting its locale and membership only under considerable pressure. For a long while it played its music at Hildebrandt's shop and then adjourned to the Hotel Rennert for refreshment. During the "Thirteen Dreadful Years" of Prohibition, from 1920 to 1933, it met at the homes of some of the members though there was a period when Hildebrandt obligingly tried to turn his cellar into a beer hall. In 1933 when it became evident that Prohibition was done, the Club returned to the Rennert. But something was wrong and the Rennert palled on the members. Mencken wrote a friend in June that its gilt chairs and hard, tiled floor left them gloomy.

They made what was to be their final move to Schellhase's Cafe, "an honest German saloon" with the best beer in Baltimore and the keg a mere eight feet away. For the playing that preceded the beer they were now able to return to Hildebrandt's shop, where years ago they had begun to be a concert.

Early and late the Club graciously allowed pictures to be taken. Many of the faces appear and reappear, aging mildly in the process. The Club met, for example, on August 29, 1916 at the country home of a Baltimore poetaster named Folger McKinsey and a photograph records the event. Mencken, Hildebrandt, Hemberger, and Wade are among the members who pose for us, along with some newer ones. They went to McKinsey's each year, as a brass band with instruments, to celebrate his birthday. The picture for 1925 includes Hemberger, Broedel, Willie Woollcott, and Hamilton Owens beating a brass drum. The membership posed on April 24, 1937 for a photograph at its last permanent meeting place, Schellhase's. Mencken sits near the center; Broedel is still there, with his curly hair now white; Raymond Pearl is there; so is Buchholz, looking contentious. So are one or two others of the founding fathers and a sprinkling of newcomers.

The rituals of the Club throve in fertile ground. The accustomed time of starting became eight o'clock. The program took on an almost fixed form: first a march, then an overture and a symphony; then an intermission, called a Saufpause; then a few lighter pieces, and lastly a Strauss waltz. A reasonably representative program, midway in the Club's history, was the one which Mencken outlined to Pearl some time after that distinguished scientist had joined the Club. It opened with *Don Juan* by Richard Strauss, went on to the *Siegfried Idyl* by Wagner, the First Sextet by Brahms, the Tragic Symphony by Schubert, and the *Emperor Waltz* by Johann Strauss, Jr.

Ritual songs emerged and then slowly rose and fell in popularity, from "The Shite Hawk" to "I Am a 100% American." The accustomed way to get rid of an unruly member became Mencken's announcement that the Club would disband and then the quiet reassembling of the rest of the Club next week. The accustomed call for silence when chattering interfered with the making of music was Mencken's strident "Maul halten!" With its raucous rituals consecrated by time, its full-throated worship of music and fellowship firmly established, it became to Mencken something like a church. And he was the pastor, the unquestioned leader of the flock.

Though the faithful might have found it hard to believe, Mencken's cosmos contained more than the Saturday Night Club. Some of his good friends belonged to the Club but others, because they lived outside of Baltimore or for other reasons, seldom if ever darkened its gaudy door. Whether in or out, however, they represented a rich assortment of individuals.

As he looked back over the years while preparing his autobiographical notes in the early 1940s, he remarked that his chief associates had been — in this order — newspapermen, musicians, and professors from the Johns Hopkins Medical School, most of whom were musicians too. But there were not many, surprisingly, in any of the three categories. His letter files were voluminous; the number of his correspondents ran to several thousands. His acquaintance grew wide; there must have been thousands of persons too who met Mencken and then thought they knew him. Yet even when he became a national figure he was not impelled to extend the circle of his good friends very much. And after he reached his fifties the circle shrank. However, within this circle, whatever its size, the social life was intensive. It involved enough eating, drinking, music making, and talking to cover several nights in every week. Sometimes they were full nights, starting early and ending only when Mencken took the late trolley home. This was particularly true for Saturday and Sunday evenings. But there were many other nights when he finished his work shortly before ten and then adjourned with a few intimates to the Rennert or Schellhase's for beer and talk.

Such were his evenings, especially in Baltimore. It should be added that they were mainly spent with men. Before Sara Haardt arrived on the scene he had no constant female companion. There simply was no girl he liked enough to see often. Moreover, in Baltimore he was a very visible celebrity from the time he reached his thirties; he soon became, as one of his correspondents remarked, a cautious man. His evenings in New York, on the other hand, were apt to be more high-style. There he was less of a celebrity but even if he was one, it did not hamper him. Supported by the cosmopolitan Nathan, he made the dinner and night club circuit. Nathan usually had his latest girl along and Mencken had one too. Sometimes he and Nathan wanted less flashy fare, the good food and drink at Luchow's, a convivial restaurant, for instance. Sometimes, after Prohibition arrived, they went to scruffy beer halls or New Jersey bars, searching for a palatable beer or drinkable whiskey. Then they might have girls along or they might not; it almost depended on chance.

Yet the emphasis in New York too was male and Mencken's closest friends besides Nathan were all men. The large majority were about his own age. And both there and in Baltimore the closest friendships were long-lasting. Though time inevitably caused some changes most of the friendships endured, without interruption, for decades. Mencken once observed, in the *Smart Set* for July 1919, that a prudent man, realizing that life was short, every now and then reexamined his friendships and dropped most of them. But this was one of the engaging cases where he declined to take his own advice.

In the second decade of the century George Jean Nathan became and remained Mencken's best friend. No one else, either in New York or Baltimore, was better company for Mencken; no one else combined business with pleasure so attractively, at least until the early 1920s. But during the decade Mencken also found a close friend in Phil Goodman and he remained close until the Depression. Goodman had come from Philadelphia to New York and he was successively advertising man, publisher, and play producer. In writing advertising copy he was first-rate; as a publisher he failed partly because he ran ahead of his time in wanting to sell books cheaply through the drugstores; and as a play producer he enjoyed a meteoric success.

As Goodman's daughter Ruth says, he was a bravura kind of man. Weighing nearly three hundred pounds, he had the joviality and gusto associated with his size. He loved good food and good jokes, and he regarded the world with a freebooter's cynicism that Mencken appreciated. Like Mencken he was a Germanophile. He enjoyed German writing as well as German cooking or German beer. When World War I began he deplored it as a peace-loving Socialist, but he favored Germany and detested England. He had a remarkable skill with words which Mencken recognized, for he asked Goodman to proofread and correct the first two editions of *The American Language*. The volumes survive in his daughter's library and the corrections are many. Goodman's skill and vitality can also be seen throughout the long series of letters he exchanged with Mencken, in which they created a comic, nostalgic world out of old-time Baltimore and Philadelphia. Abundant in detail, the letters are filled with sharply limned characters from the two men's early days, all portrayed with joviality.

Goodman always retained much of the bourgeois Jewish culture out of which he came. This was another of his attractions for Mencken, who savored Jewish food, appreciated Jewish ritual and customs, and found a Jewish atmosphere congenial. To keep the Jewishness from cloying for either man, there was the touch of tartness provided by Goodman's aversion to the Jew of the caricatures and Mencken's stock response to "the Jews of Wall Street" or "the Jews of Hollywood."

Goodman began his publishing with Nathan's *Bottoms Up* and it was Goodman who in 1918 issued Mencken's *Damn! A Book of Calumny* and *In Defense of Women.* Though he proved to be only an indifferent publisher for Mencken, the fact did not impair their friendship. In the hazardous business of producing he soon flourished. During the 1920s he produced six or seven hits, among them *The Old Soak* and *Poppy*, starring the famous comedian W. C. Fields. When the Depression came, one of its first casualties was the theater and Goodman lost all his money.

Meanwhile, however, he could buy anything he wanted, from roast goose to rubies. He could even take a trip to Europe to get some of the choice yeast from Munich's Löwenbrau Brewery, as he did in 1925, to use in his and Henry's home brew. He lived with a lavishness that Mencken admired, open-mouthed. He wrote Dreiser that Goodman's earnings from the first week of one of his hits were nineteen thousand dollars. Goodman played the big-city man to Mencken's small-town boy with a comic grace that amused Mencken for years.

Mencken's Baltimore friends fell for the most part in the categories mentioned before: newspapermen, musicians, and doctors. Two of his closest friends, Carl Schon and Ernest Boyd, were none of these things, however. Carl Schon was a well-to-do craftsman who enjoyed making art objects, some of which Mencken considered very fine. He did a good business, Mencken remembered later, in selling his "odd rings, breastplates, bangles, and so on." A man of social charm, with courtly manners and a love for good living, he became a mainstay of the Sunday Dinner Club. Mencken, respectful toward competence anywhere, found in Schon's craftsman's skill something he could admire. Like Goodman and Mencken, Schon had strong sympathies for Germany which he showed even during World War I. And he was a confirmed agnostic, seeing even less than Mencken in the accepted beliefs about religion.

Much different from Schon but equally interesting to Mencken was Ernest Boyd. A red-bearded Dubliner, he was posted to Baltimore in 1913 as British vice-consul. After he corrected an error Mencken made in the *Evening Sun* about trade between Baltimore and Liverpool, the two men met and became friends. Their main bonds but by no means their only ones proved to be a taste for literature and a distaste for the English. As an Irishman Boyd had his own feelings about his English masters, especially during the war with Germany. He had lived in Germany, in fact, and knew German well enough to pass for a native and to appreciate the nuances of German literature. He had a strong sense of humor and Boyd's widow remembers that the two men loved to joke with one another. Also, Boyd loved horseplay. Nathan reported that Boyd took an unfailing delight in "monkeyshines of an undergraduate order." Nothing was better calculated to endear him to Mencken.

Boyd had another tie with Mencken, a love of music. Mencken saw to it that he was made an honorary member both of the Saturday Night Club and of the Sunday Dinner Club. The clubs showed an unaffected liking for him and accepted him for more than Mencken's sake. At the meeting of the Saturday Night Club of August 3, 1918, for instance, when Boyd was back across the ocean, all the members present drank his health and signed a friendly note to him. Both clubs continued to remember him and Mencken told him so, warmly, in a long letter of February 3, 1919.

The period before Boyd left was the exciting one when Mencken owned a Studebaker. He often paid Ernest and his wife Madeleine the compliment of driving them around Baltimore on Sundays. With Ernest perched next to Mencken on the front seat and Madeleine jouncing in the rear, they would roar off on their excursions. Never intimidated by the lack of roads on the outskirts, Mencken would be as apt as not to drive across fields to show the Boyds some stream or other.

Mencken soon developed a genuine devotion to Boyd's interests. By 1916 he had been transferred from Baltimore to Barcelona, and then to Copenhagen. He grew eager to reenter the United States as a private citizen and Mencken's letters contain many evidences of his efforts to prepare the way for Boyd's return. "I have written to H. B. Sell, of the Chicago *Daily News*," he reports for instance, "suggesting that he make some arrangement with you (paid) for an occasional letter on literary affairs in Britain." On his behalf Mencken wrote to or talked to various American editors and publishers, including those of the *Sunpapers* and of the house of Knopf. He valued Boyd's pungent opinions on many matters and hoped to help in establishing him in America as an authority on Irish literature even more than British; he had already reviewed Boyd's *Ireland's Literary Renaissance* in the *Evening Sun* of November 10, 1916 and praised it.

Mencken's letters to Boyd during this period are loaded with news. On June 29, 1918, for example, he writes that censorship is in full swing and that *Damn! A Book of Calumny* is being accused because it charges George Washington with fornication; that good new books are rare; that Nathan has just finished preparing *The Popular Theatre;* that Max Broedel has had a slice cut from his cheek; that the son of Theo Hemberger is in danger of being drafted; that Dreiser goes from bad to worse and has sent him "a truly ghastly" manuscript; and that there will be no more Michelob beer after November 1.

The war over, Mencken's attempts to pave the way for him proved successful. Boyd joined the editorial staff of a New York newspaper, the *Evening Post,* and became adviser on foreign literature to the Knopf firm. From this base of operations he was able to branch out into free-lance writing. He published four books before the end of 1925, the last of which was the slim volume of mingled biography and critical appreciation called *H. L. Mencken.*

The book testified to how close Boyd was to Mencken and how much he comprehended of several sides of him. Boyd analyzes him as an American, a philosopher, and a critic, devoting a chapter to each aspect. The one on Mencken the American is based on what Boyd knew of Mencken's life; it attempts to relate him to the Baltimore he lived in. There is considerable biographical detail and as much attention to Mencken the man as there is to Mencken the American. The second chapter, on Mencken the Philosopher, surveys the chief ideas and attitudes in his books, starting with *Ventures into Verse.* Boyd pays particular attention to Mencken's conception of Nietzsche, pointing out how much and how magisterially Mencken selects from the German philosopher. He goes on to summarize Mencken's political ideas as shown in his debate with La Monte and to suggest the echoes from Nietzsche. He describes Mencken's political philosophy as seen in the Free Lance and his later writings. Boyd sums up here by saying that Mencken represents the old order of sentimental individualism, with its suspicion of government, its faith in personal effort, its optimistic good humor. The third chapter, on Mencken the Critic, deals with his criticism of literature and his criticism of life. To Boyd both are iconoclastic, vigorous, and of course often humorous. Both attack fraud in many forms, especially when it is moralistic, but praise independence and innovation.

Mencken's reaction to the book was ambivalent. To friends he wrote that the book had charm and insight but was flawed by the fact that Boyd saw him mainly as a literary critic. He was not, Mencken said; he was a social critic or even, as he once put it, a politician. To Boyd himself he wrote, "you have done a damned fine job."

One of the best of Mencken's Baltimore friends was Paul Patterson. In 1911, a little more than four years after Mencken came on the *Sun* staff, Patterson was hired as managing editor of the *Evening Sun*. He proved to be expert not only on the editorial but also on the business side of running a newspaper. In 1919 he became the senior officer of the *Sunpapers* and remained so for a good three decades. He and Mencken established a working relationship which ripened into a permanent friendship. Its foundation was their respect for one another as newspapermen. They had in common an insatiable appetite for work and an ability to learn fast the hard way; they were both proud of the fact that they had become city editors while indecently young and were innocent of a college degree.

Both subscribed to the same professional principles. When Mencken prepared Patterson's obituary for the *Sun* files, in the precautionary way newspapers have, long before the subject's death, he summed them up. The first was freedom of the press, freedom from interference within as well as interference without. He affirmed that Patterson "believed that the only newspaper whose opinions were worth hearing at all was that one which was completely free, and he believed that no paper could be free unless the men who wrote it were free." The second principle was that the prime job of a newspaper was to gather news. If this was an obvious principle in theory, it was always being threatened in practice. It was a mundane, sensible view; Mencken shared it.

For a long time they shared a political philosophy as well. It was a libertarianism in the nineteenth-century tradition. However, Patterson was later to modify it for himself, if reluctantly, while Mencken stood fixed in the old faith. The two men were also Darwinians, with an open belief in the survival of the fittest. Mencken preached it and Patterson practiced it. Once Patterson gained control of the *Sunpapers* he coolly evaluated the people around him, matching one against the other and then giving the prizes to those who survived. But he treated Mencken as a full equal. Mencken treated him in the same way, for he was quite capable of starting a letter to his boss with "Who in hell edits the *Evening Sun* letter column?"

Patterson was solid, matter-of-fact, with an owlish look to him as he stared through his glasses. He enjoyed Mencken's fire and wit, and pleased both himself and Mencken by acting as his straight man. With his slow smile he would give Mencken a line or a cue, or start an ancedote for him to finish. He watched the elaborate splendor of some of Mencken's hoaxes with dignified amusement. The best one came years after the friendship began, during a tour of the South in October 1926 that the men took together. In each state in succession starting with Maryland, Mencken told the reporters interviewing him that its favorite son was presidential timber. He left behind him a series of boomlets that were punctured only when newsmen compared notes and saw that what Mencken had done in Maryland he had done in Virginia, in North Carolina, in Georgia.

Among his friends three men in particular, in their abundantly assorted ways, brought out three sides of his character. They were Philip Goodman, Paul Patterson, and — later than the rest — Raymond Pearl. Through Phil Goodman, who always wore his hat cocked on the side of his head, we can see Mencken as the man about town. Through Paul Patterson, the cool, brilliant newspaper executive, we can see Mencken the newspaperman. Through Raymond Pearl, the biometrician, we can see Mencken the eager if amateur scientist. But we can do more than that. Each man had overlapping interests and they serve to show us Mencken as a coherent human being. Goodman liked literature as well as the good life. Patterson enjoyed the delights of travel as did Mencken. Raymond Pearl was notable for the pleasure he took in music and clubs.

In addition each man stimulated Mencken's impulse to write and each responded to his extraordinary creativity. Phil Goodman maintained for years a rich and racy dialogue in the letters he exchanged with Mencken. Patterson, through his frequent commissioning of feature articles and through his encouragement of Mencken as a columnist to discuss anything that struck his fancy, freed him from newspaper routine and let him concentrate on the sorts of stories he liked

best including the national political conventions, such sawdust cir-
cuses as the Scopes trial, and the windy international conferences.
Raymond Pearl, through his many talks with Mencken, through the
articles he wrote and the reading he proposed for him, fortified
Mencken's scientfic information and provoked the increase in scientific
references in his writing. In the late 1920s Mencken used a larger
number of scientific terms, such as "colloids," both in his letters and his
publications than he had before — and this was only one indication of
his added interest in scientific matters.

Raymond Pearl quickly became Mencken's personal scientist.
When in 1923 Mencken first met him, he was forty-four years old and
in his robust prime. He stood over six feet tall; he weighed well over
two hundred pounds; and he had an exuberant personality. No other
friend of Mencken could match Pearl's intellectual breadth and scientific devotion to the study of man — or his interest in the state of his
own body.

Pearl's younger daughter Penelope remembers how often her
father called a physician to the house about some minor ill, a boil
on his nose, for example, or a nagging ache in his back. Like Mencken
he welcomed medical help in spite of his personal doubts about the
competence of many a physician. Like Mencken he also lived with a
systemic ailment, to which he adjusted as well as he could. Mencken
had hay fever; Pearl had migraine. Each complained volubly about
his ailment to the other, yet each seemed able to rise above it for the
purposes of either business or pleasure. Mencken's hay fever was an
aggravation every autumn; Pearl's migraine came at any time of the
year, in short attacks which caused him great discomfort; but business
went on anyway. So did pleasure. Mencken might appear at a party
hot-eyed and sniffling, yet he appeared; and he gave the impression
of enjoying himself. Pearl often had his migraine attacks on a Saturday, and so says in his diary, but he managed to rally enough to make
his way to the Saturday Night Club, where he blew his French horn
and drank his beer with obvious satisfaction. In a single paragraph in
his diary he could note in the first sentence that he had awakened
with a migraine and in the last that he had come home at two in the
morning after a festive meeting of the Club.

They compared ailments — and remedies — with the animation
of two housewives after a hysterectomy. Mencken, with the amateur's
delight in knowingness, was even readier with the remedies than

Pearl. He was apt to be crisp and caustic in his medical analysis. Here
he is writing on September 1, 1925 about an operation Pearl has had:
"May the great pox of Mesopotamia seize whoever gave you that
ether. All your troubles were due to it. It invariably causes hemor-
rhages in tonsilectomy. Why didn't the scoundrels use ethylene, or use
a local anaesthetic? Novocaine and adrenalin do the trick superbly,
and a shot of scopalamine makes you forget that you are present."
Nor is Mencken above prescribing for Pearl about intimate matters.
In a letter of February 1, 1931 he shares with Pearl his hard-won experience on how to avoid the painful recurrence of piles. He describes the remedy to Pearl and then reassures him with an optimism
the medical profession could envy, "Take care and everything will be
all right."

Mencken responded not only to Pearl's concern with personal ailments but also to his general interest in the human condition. In
turn, Pearl found in Mencken a bright, receptive, and knowing pupil.
It was a delight for Pearl to teach him; in fact as the friendship ma-
tured, it became not so much a teaching as a sharing. He mailed
Mencken offprints of interesting articles, including all of his own
prolific production. He suggested books and monographs to build up
Mencken's scientific background. He published a little volume in
1927 called *To Begin with,* an annotated list of the best works for
the graduate student in science to read when starting out, dedicated it to Mencken, and of course gave him a copy. Pearl found in
Mencken, furthermore, a student who read as omnivorously as he
did. On Mencken's desk there was always a mound of books of all
sorts to review; Pearl's house was piled high with print.

The bulk of Pearl's crowded library was composed of scientific
works. But one of the reasons that Mencken responded so heartily to
him was that his interests went far beyond science. Pearl's daughter
remembers that her father not only subscribed to some of the general intellectual magazines but also, with a gleam in his eye, to the
Police Gazette and *Variety.* He enjoyed the bulging bosoms and
the barbershop vulgarity of the *Police Gazette* and he kept up his
interest in the gossipy side of show business by taking *Variety.*

He also shared with Mencken a rare enthusiasm for a scientist, a
devotion to literature. He was one of the few scientists, surely, who
subscribed to the *Times Literary Supplement.* He especially enjoyed
reading fiction and essays. And he himself enjoyed writing. He had

been nearly as young as Mencken when he sent his first article to a newspaper and was surprised to find that the paper not only printed it but paid him. He continued to write and taught himself to write well. Words were important to him, as they were to Mencken.

But here Mencken became the teacher and Pearl the willing pupil. Through Mencken he was brought in touch with some of the most exciting literature of the 1920s and with the most interesting literary figures. Through Mencken he met such notable novelists as Sinclair Lewis and Scott Fitzgerald. He met such promising new authors as James Cain, who when Pearl first saw him was an established editorial writer but had not yet begun to publish his "hard-boiled" fiction. And Mencken opened the world of the drama to Pearl. First, through the plays themselves, by Ibsen, Shaw, Strindberg, and others, and then through the actors. Although Mencken's interest in the theater had fallen off by the time he became friends with Pearl, he still knew many of the figures on Broadway. Through Phil Goodman if not always through Nathan, Mencken kept up as much as he wished with what was happening on the New York stage. The results for Pearl were uniformly pleasant, including as they did introductions to the actresses Pauline Lord and May Alison. Miss Alison developed into one of Pearl's favorite friends.

When it came to music the two men were evenly matched. Both were devoted to making music as well as hearing it. Mencken invited Pearl to the Saturday Night Club as soon as he considered it feasible, for Pearl had the attitude toward music that the Club liked most. "He had an instinctive preference for good music, just as he had an instinctive preference for good victuals and good wine, and he let it go at that. He was not concerned about the way the thing was written, but only about its effects, and under the influence of those effects he let himself go, and got all the innocent joy that a cat gets out of catnip." So Mencken once recalled. At the Club concerts Pearl played his French horn with emphasis. He was one of the reasons that the Club revived after showing signs of debility.

Like Mencken, Pearl found in the Club a catharsis. Because both men had a Victorian sense of decorum instilled in them in boyhood, they enjoyed their adult rebellion all the more. At the Club they guffawed at one another's jokes and joined in all the jovial gestures with which the membership defied the weekday Victorian world. They would chant the stanzas of a favorite bawdy song and then with deeper relief than they realized, roar out its refrain, "Cried the eunuchs, Give us balls!" When it was Pearl's turn to act as host during the time when the Club met at members' homes, he encouraged his guests to relieve their kidneys from the back porch. They did so with much braying and door-banging, while his wife hid in her room and commanded her small daughters to shut their ears.

The correspondence between Mencken and Pearl reveals a social life so full that only men with extraordinary vitality could have kept it up. They relished good food and drink as well as good company. Besides the club meetings they regularly attended each Saturday night, there were many minor revels, often arranged on a few days' notice. One day in February 1925, for instance, Mencken wrote Pearl, "What of a small and refined party next Sunday evening? Dan Henry has an immense mess of terrapin, and proposes that we make a whole meal of it — you, he, Owens and I. He suggests meeting at one of the wop places. He will bring the terrapin ready cooked, and needing only warming. We can get oysters and other trimmings on the spot." He ends, "If you can spare some sherry bring it along."

When the two men did not dine together, they were apt to "sit together." "An evening's sitting" was Mencken's phrase. Somehow they got something simply through being in one another's company. This was most true in times of crisis. When Mencken's wife died, Pearl went to sit with him at Hollins Street. When Pearl met his only professional defeat — but a stunning one: he was offered a professorship at Harvard and then the offer was withdrawn — Mencken went to his home to sit with him.

They liked their intellectual games and elaborate jokes. Mencken gave Pearl a Christmas present one year which symbolizes their relationship. The present was an oversized paperweight, a beautiful, polished piece of mahogany, with green felt pasted underneath so that it would not scratch Pearl's desk, and on top a long rusty nail finely mounted. With it came a high-toned document from Mencken explaining that the nail had been proved to be from the True Cross. Pearl always cherished the gift. For his part, he once served diamondback terrapin at his house to Mencken. When it was brought to the table Mencken loudly demanded to see its diamonds; and Pearl chortling produced a handful of ten-cent gems that he had bought in the certainty that Mencken would ask.

As Pearl's daughter has remarked, the value systems of the two men were nearly identical. They shared the same assumptions about life. For example, both men were agnostics and felt that the comforts of religion were not for them. Yet both were arrested by it. Mencken took his *Treatise on the Gods* more seriously than any other of his tracts. Pearl read all of St. Thomas Aquinas at least once, and he read periodically in the lives of the saints, usually in his set of volumes by Sabine Baring-Gould.

Besides sharing the same assumptions about life, the two men had similar styles, similar tastes. Not entirely, of course. Mencken could never understand why Pearl took his family camping in Maine each summer. Pearl could not comprehend Mencken's complete citification. But because the interests and personalities of the two men meshed so much, their friendship, once started, never stopped. When Pearl died, Mencken said to a Washington friend, Huntington Cairns, "He was the last man I could talk to in Baltimore."

Yet some friends survived in Baltimore till the end of Mencken's life. One of the closest was the handsome, burly Hamilton Owens, who became editor of the *Evening Sun* in 1922. Mencken soon invited him to meetings of the Saturday Night Club even though he played no instrument. Raymond Pearl persuaded him to try the oboe and he gradually mastered it. He saw the Club in some of its finest hours. For instance, he was at the house of Willie Woollcott when the epic decision was made to play all of Beethoven's symphonies at one sitting except for the Ninth. The members started early, at about seven in the evening; they played the First, Second, and Third before stopping for breath and beer; the hardiest members stayed to finish the Fourth and got into the Fifth before they collapsed. Mencken, the hardiest of all, at the end was still triumphantly upright, banging on the piano.

Mencken and Hamilton Owens drew together both at work and in their relaxations. When mixed company was in order he would bring his delightful wife Olga. When Mencken had his strictly male Bierabende, his "beer-evenings," Owens was less likely to be present, chiefly because he lived some distance away in the suburbs of Baltimore and did not enjoy driving back and forth. But he was a good companion and a thoroughly professional newspaperman; Mencken always found him stimulating.

Mencken, certainly, had enemies as well as friends both in Baltimore and the rest of the world. He also had in Baltimore a magnificent example of the kind of friend who relieved him of the need for enemies. Howard Atwood Kelly, M.D., of the Johns Hopkins University and Hospital, was Mencken's hair shirt.

There is little doubt that Howard Kelly was a great as well as a good man. A pioneer in the use of radium, a surgeon and gynecologist already renowned by the time he met Mencken in 1912, he continued to accumulate kudos and awards during the next decades. Over the years he enjoyed honorary membership in more than a dozen foreign gynecological societies; he received several decorations from foreign governments; he was the author or co-author of standard works on operative gynecology, on the appendix, and on the kidneys, ureters, and bladder. He published extensively in American medical biography and in the biography of medical botanists. His range of outside interests was so catholic that it included even reptiles and trees: he was Honorary Curator of the Division of Reptiles and Amphibians at the University of Michigan and an Educational Member of the American Tree Association.

Some twenty years older than Mencken, he was also a devout old-style Christian who tried unctuously and persistently to win Mencken to Christ. The more Mencken rebuffed him the more he tried, confident of his rightness. However, Kelly's genius as an irritant lay not only in trying to convert Mencken but also in supporting nearly every cause which Mencken warred against. It proved to be almost axiomatic that anything Kelly favored Mencken detested. Exasperating though Kelly was, Mencken maintained a consistent politeness toward him.

When their paths converged in October 1912, Dr. Kelly struck exactly the wrong chord. On the 17th he sent Mencken an invitation to a dinner to be given some medical students in order to interest them in purity. He continued in the same way. On the 31st he said he was sending him a book about the world's present troubles, including prostitution. In the middle of the next month he wrote Mencken, inviting him to meet, of all persons, Anthony Comstock. He assured Mencken that Comstock was the foremost protagonist of pure literature in America if not in the entire world. The month after that he invited Mencken to meet John Summer and hear him speak; he told Mencken that for the Sumner meeting he had taken a box and wanted Mencken in it. He went on to tell Mencken how much Christ had meant to him and ended by asking Mencken if he had ever prayerfully and carefully looked into the New Testament.

Throughout the next year, and the years to follow, he often urged Mencken to get close to God. He also solicited advice from him on how to regenerate prostitutes. At one point, Kelly lamented the partial failure of a scheme to reform the naughty girls. He and his friends had established a home for some of them but it had its problems. More than one of the girls had simply used the home for a shelter after her night's work; he even hinted that a few had gone further. Liberty had grown into licentiousness and now there were house rules which the girls had to obey; moreover, they had to show that they sincerely wished to be saved. In a letter in which he solemnly described how, for these girls, a home had become a house, he concluded by telling Mencken that he prayed for him almost daily.

Howard Kelly's pomposities annoyed Mencken nearly as much as his piety. He would invite Mencken to dinner, for instance, and assure him that the meal would be simple and that Mencken could come in his ordinary day clothes. Or he would apologize for not having invited Mencken because the Kellys did not at the moment have a servant to wait on the table.

In one of his exasperating habits he seemed to parody Mencken. Mencken of course enjoyed sending unconsciously funny pamphlets and cards to his close friends. Kelly, for his part, sent Mencken deadly serious religious books, evangelistic tracts, and even little cards he had printed, such as one entitled *Divine Possibilities*. One time he sent Mencken a printed sheet advertising a conclave of the Lord's Day Alliance. Another time he mailed him a copy of a sermon by Billy Sunday. Kelly's Christmas card was always religious; one year he sent Mencken a "Madonna and Child," writing that it showed "Earth's most glorious motherhood."

Howard Kelly's language was, moreover, so splendidly appropriate to his attitude that Mencken could only wince. Kelly would write, for instance, that a reporter they both knew had now "gone home into glory." His note for Christmas 1914 says about his pious card, "May the splendid spirit of service it breathes be a common bond between you and me."

He improved not at all with acquaintance. Ten years after he first crossed Mencken's path his effect was still salutary. Mencken wrote to a friend in May 1922 that he went to a medical banquet in Washington and had to come home with Kelly. "Three separate times I was on the point of jumping out of the train-window," he admitted.

As it turned out, the dedicated unbeliever had the last word about the dedicated believer. Calling him "the most implacable Christian I ever knew, at least among educated men," Mencken said in a typescript after Kelly's death, "Kelly talked to me of his barbaric religion very often, and almost always in terms of fear. He trembled at the thought of Hell, which was as much a reality to his distorted mind as his own operating-room. A Scotch-Irishman, he had picked up this fear early in youth, and never got rid of it. If he was conscious on his deathbed he must have been horribly scared. He pretended publicly that his faith gave him consolation and comfort, but I could never discover any evidence of this in my frequent palavers with him."

But then there were the girls, Mencken's girls. They helped him to forget Howard Kelly and his kind. More than once Mencken declared that his ideal was a buxom German waitress, apple-cheeked, amiable, and eager to attend to his wants. He also announced that he enjoyed a woman who was abundantly mature—a bit moldly as he once ungallantly put it. His readers were titillated if not shocked at such a taste. There was no need. His words were mainly rhetoric. He did not marry till he reached fifty, and the girls he favored before that were often pert, trim, and bright. As he put it, accurately, in a letter to Fielding Garrison, "I like the little ones."

Mencken felt that his private life was private. When it came to helping his biographers he offered them so much material on other things that it is hard to realize that the pages they produced say almost nothing about any woman but Sara Haardt. And yet he found other women attractive, in several cases very much so. The girls he knew in his twenties have left no record. He was circumspect in Baltimore anyway, but after 1908 he spent more time in Manhattan, where he felt much freer. We can recall that he and Nathan often took girls with them when they went out into New York's night life. The handsome Nathan was beginning a career that would provide ample food for cafe gossips; Mencken was by no means handsome but his vitality had its own appeal. Here and there in the correspondence of the two men an unspecified girl is linked with Mencken; here and there he refers to some girl in his correspondence with others. For instance, he remarks to Dreiser wistfully on February 5, 1913 that one of his old girls got married the other day. But none stood out, up through 1913. In the next year, however, he encountered a girl who genuinely interested him.

She was Marion Bloom, trim and young, who came from a farm near Westminster, Maryland. Currently living in Washington, she had stopped in Baltimore with her sister Estelle and the two of them had met Mencken in his office at the *Sun*. He and Marion were immediately taken with one another. She invited him to Washington and he replied promptly in a note of February 18, 1914, confirming that he would make her a visit. He came and found the occasion to come again. Officially he was gathering material at the Library of Congress for a book on the human condition, something he dubbed his "Homo Sapiens" book. He continued to see her, writing on July 1, for instance, that he planned to spend an afternoon in the Library of Congress and inviting her out with him afterward. Soon she was helping him. They would spend the afternoon going through material and then would have their dinner. As a connoisseur of good food, Mencken would often take her to the Ebbitt House, famous for its planked steak, or to a well-known restaurant named Raucher's. After dinner Marion would go with him to the Union Station to meet the train for Baltimore, except for those adventurous times when he drove his Studebaker.

Liking Marion as he did, he could not refrain from trying to make her a writer. He decided that she could compose epigrams at least and that these might be used for fillers in the *Smart Set*, especially after Nathan and he came into control of the magazine. He sent her an advance copy of the first number under the new editorship, remarking that several of the pieces were good and that he himself appeared there under the names of Hatteras, D'Aubigny, Watson, and Woodruff. Obediently Marion composed epigrams. Accepting some of them a little later on, he swore that she was eighty times as clever as the melancholy literary females whose pictures were printed in the papers.

When Marion moved to New York she often became part of an evening foursome which included Nathan and his current girl, for a time Ann Pennington the dancer. In a letter to Dreiser near the end of 1916, Mencken says, "Marion will come with me, and N will bring a lady." In an earlier letter he had already reported that she was enormously impressed by Dreiser and had emerged from his presence in a state bordering on maryolatry.

Mencken continued to advise her, urging her to write and persevere; but he had the grace to apologize for playing Polonius. He himself was working even harder than usual, trying with Nathan to get the *Smart Set* on its feet. He complained in his correspondence with Marion about all the manuscripts he had to read and all the letters he had to answer. She listened amiably and was rewarded with the compliment that she was "the most genial and tolerant of beauteous hussies."

She wrote a short story, "The Revolt," and Mencken helped her to improve it though not enough, it turned out, to get it into the *Smart Set*. He counseled her, without much success, to try her hand at confessions of a supposedly personal nature.

Sometimes, though with the best intentions, he dominated too much and Marion became resentful. Sometimes, in spite of her vaunted amiability, they quarreled. Thereafter he might write a note of apology, qualified at least once with a hearty "Let us fight, damn each other, and be happy." For her part Marion complained about his power to wound her and about the blows she had taken. In a long letter of November 1, 1916 she pours out her grievances. Not the least is that he infuriates her by hiding a tenderness beneath his cruelty. And she charges that though she has tried to be what he wants her to be, the result for her has been nothing but pain. In spite of this she loves him deeply.

The *Smart Set* for March 1917 carried "Reflections" by Marion L. Bloom. The brief piece describes a man of stocky figure, evidently Mencken, arguing around a point while a woman listens lovingly and follows him with her eyes as he paces back and forth. It ends with her saying passionately to herself, "What a beautiful, beautiful voice he has, and how I love him! But Heavens, how much will I find to hate about him when I have ceased to love him!"

Affecting their relation consciously or unconsciously was the course of the war. While Mencken was worrying about being drafted for a struggle he regarded as misbegotten, Marion was preparing to volunteer as an army nurse. He told Ernest Boyd on June 29, 1918 that she was in Washington in nurse's training. The week before she finished, they spent an evening together in New York. Mencken wrote Marion the next day, in a tone of nostalgic sentiment rare for him, that New York was full of reminiscences of her and that his wishes were the fancies of a romantic young fellow. He vowed that she had all his love. They met once more before she left. Much moved, Mencken wrote, "I shall not forget, my dear — this last visit, nor any of the others. You will believe how much I have loved you when the bad dream is over and we are all secure and happy again. You have been very good to me." She sailed for France at the end of September and, whatever his feelings about the war, Mencken admitted to Boyd that he would miss her a great deal.

In France she found scenes of horror and agony of the kind that she had never imagined. Deeply devoted to the wounded men she served, she stayed in uniform even after the war's end. On her return, early in 1919, she felt that religion alone could explain and alleviate the suffering she had seen; and she was particularly drawn to Christian Science.

If she had any dreams of marriage with Mencken she could not have chosen a worse stumbling block. His hostility toward Mary Baker Eddy and the denomination she founded was complete. Nothing could make him sputter more. When he tried to talk with Marion about it he lectured her instead. Though he assured her from time to time that he thought they could have a meeting of the minds, the introduction of Christian Science into their relation poisoned it. Not at once but gradually. He was well aware that he was a complete skeptic; the fact that he laughed at Christian Science, he told Marion, did not mean that he believed in anything else. Occasionally he could be humorous, quipping that he was making copious notes for their theological discussions, but usually he proved hostile. For her part Marion read in the scientist-philosophers such as Sir James Jeans and Sir Arthur Eddington but they failed to lessen her faith in Mrs. Eddy.

At times her winsome gentleness returned, with all its old effect. She feels, probably rightly, that Mencken was thinking about her when he composed his mellow portrait of the female at her amiable best in the piece he used as a coda for *In Defense of Women*. The time is late on a wintry afternoon; the place is a fireside; and the gentle, low-voiced woman may well be Marion.

They still talked about marriage. Mencken could not make up his mind. Often he dismissed the idea as impossible. At other times it looked highly inviting, and he alternated between wanting a household in the suburbs for them, complete with servants, and suggesting that he and Marion simply occupy the third floor at Hollins Street. After a while Marion herself accused him of wanting to be both married and single. She said that at the most he would make a reluctant husband and such a husband was not for her. Mencken was much distressed; he wrote her a long letter and then tore it up because it was too abject. In the note to her reporting this he added bleakly that he was almost beyond intelligible thought. That was near the end of March 1923.

The pitch of emotion continued to rise through the spring of 1923 and into the summer. Suddenly Marion broke. She made a marriage of desperation with a suitor named Maritzer. She announced it to her sister Estelle, asking her to phone Mencken. After he got the news he wrote Marion, "What am I to say? That I wish you happiness that no one deserves so much as you do. That I have just got out some old letters of yours, and re-read them, and burned them, and now sit down and smoke my pipe, and wonder what in hell it is all about." To her sister he wrote ruefully that the Christian Science fever had simply scared him to death and a marriage would have been hopeless. But he would not forget her, and he did not burn all of the letters. He saved at least three folders and years later gave them to the New York Public Library along with other correspondence.

As his relationship with Marion Bloom grew tenser during the first half of 1923, he turned with some relief to a vivacious New York girl. Beatrice Wilson, nicknamed "Bee," was slight, pert-featured, but with remarkable drive. The world of journalism was a hard one for a young woman to thrive in but Bee was already accomplishing it when she first met Mencken. Though still in her early twenties she proved able to make her specialty the interviewing of celebrities reputed to be hard to interview. Because she signed her pieces B. F. Wilson few among her readers guessed her sex. She submitted a piece to the *Smart Set;* it was accepted and Mencken sent her a note asking her to come to see him. On the lookout for a hard-bitten writer, he was pleasantly surprised by the trim girl who presented herself. He invited her to lunch and soon pronounced himself "mashed" on her.

The half-sheet notes began to come from Mencken, making engagements for cocktails or dinner, planning hoaxes, or advising her about her writing. She remembers that he would come to her apartment, always with a shaker of Prohibition gin so that he could make martinis for them. Sometimes she would be alone when he arrived; sometimes there would be other guests, more or less well known. Mencken found many of them boring and he threatened in one note to curse and swear if Bee invited any American female playwright or British actor. Most celebrities bored him anyway, including various members of the circle of writers and critics who lunched at the Algonquin, where Mencken always stayed. Bee was on the fringes of the Algonquin group and Mencken in his notes sometimes teased her about its most exotic member, Alexander Woollcott, brother of Willie. But certain celebrities did not bore him at all. Of those the one she remembers best is Somerset Maugham.

The *Smart Set* had printed his short story "Miss Thompson," from which emerged the famous play *Rain.* Bee thought it a superb story. When Maugham came to New York on a visit she was able to make arrangements to interview him for one of her magazines and she wrote Mencken about it. The two men met at her apartment. She recalls that both had engagements for later in the evening — Mencken was going to dinner with her while Maugham was to be given a party by his literary agent — but they became so interested in talking with one another that they never stopped till after midnight. Maugham was so intent that his stutter grew pronounced and Mencken often tried to help him out. Yet the ideas went back and forth swiftly; the conversation was brilliant. The men ate the crackers she served and finished her small store of liquor long before they left. Listening to them made it one of the best evenings in her life.

With Bee as with Marion, Mencken was constitutionally incapable of keeping silent about her work. He advised her regularly in 1924 and 1925, and she was grateful for his advice. She felt that there was no sager editor in the country. He counseled her on her business with magazines and syndicates; he analyzed her writing. Always kindly, he seasoned his criticism with praise. About one short story he wrote that it was well done but not new. About another he wrote that it was too sentimental, but he took the sting out of the comment with a joke. When she decided to do a series of sketches about important women he was prompt to help. In a note of September 30, 1925 he suggested such subjects as Virginia Gildersleeve, dean of Barnard College; M. Carey Thomas, ex-president of Bryn Mawr;

and Mabel Boardman, secretary of the American Red Cross. He urged her to get the series launched.

She and Mencken shared a sense of humor and it showed best in the jokes they perpetrated. Most but not all were his idea. "Dear Bee," he writes about one hoax, whose very nature she has long forgotten, "Your scheme intrigues me. It would be a very good joke. Let us discuss it when we meet." But the jokes were only one part of their lively relationship. Their personalities reinforced one another. Hers was never dominant, of course; but though she was flattered by Mencken's attention she was not awed. She remarked once that he looked to her like a cross between a Machiavellian cherub and a Boccaccio priest. She never became as deeply involved as Marion Bloom and late in 1925 married a promising engineer, C. S. Macdonald.

The most noted of the girls that Mencken went with was Aileen Pringle. Famous as an actress both in the movies and on the stage, she was witty, beautiful, and self-assured. She constituted that rarity in Hollywood, an actress with a mind. They met in June 1926 at a party given by mutual friends, the novelist Joseph Hergesheimer and his wife, at their home in Pennsylvania called the Dower House. She was delegated to pick him up at the railroad station, and when she drove there she found him with his gladstone bags loaded down with Maryland terrapin he was bringing along for dinner. Miss Pringle recalls that later the same day she and Mencken were riding together again in an automobile when she got something in her eye. Since she failed to get it out, he offered to help. He looked at her eye and she looked at his china-blue ones so close to her — and so the friendship started.

In August both were guests again of the Hergesheimers. Hergesheimer had a motion-picture camera and so they made an impromptu movie on the lawn. Mencken reported to a friend that the film was very thrilling and mildly salacious. And Aileen was "very amusing."

Their friendship had an unexpectedly solid foundation. Both were national figures ready to respect one another when they met. Mencken was less hostile to Hollywood than might be imagined. He had already given an interview to Bee Wilson which showed a surprising judiciousness about the movies. Miss Pringle had started to read him in the *Smart Set* and had followed him to the new *American Mer-*

cury. She admired excellence; so did he. Both of them were witty; she was almost impish. He enjoyed her flashing good looks and her high style, while she found his roundhouse plainness attractive after a surfeit of Hollywood leading men.

She treated him with a wide-eyed directness that no woman had dared to employ before. She looked candidly at his clothes and decided that they were stuffy. He had always worn old-fashioned buttoned shoes — Marion Bloom had once given him a buttonhook — but now Miss Pringle teased him into wearing laced shoes, and this in spite of the fact that he never learned to tie his laces well. His collars were too high; now he lowered them. He had been used to wearing a belt; now she gave him suspenders, which were currently more fashionable. He reciprocated by being photographed wearing them at his desk and while playing the piano; and he presented the photographs to her. He told her complacently, "You have absolutely no respect for me."

Through her he met the film idol Rudolph Valentino in July 1926 and from the meeting came one of his most compassionate character sketches. Valentino, though enormously popular, had long been mauled by the newspapers. A writer for the Chicago *Tribune* had asserted in a hot-weather piece entitled "Pink Powder Puff" that there were pink-talcum dispensers in some of the men's lounges in Chicago and that he had seen men actually powder their faces. The cause of this effeminization of the American male he laid to Valentino and his movies. Valentino, stopping off in Chicago on his way east, was confronted by a gaggle of reporters who demanded to know what he had to say about the charge. Outraged, he denied it while the reporters grinned. The next thing he did was to send a letter to the writer of the piece challenging him to a duel. He was laughed at. When he reached New York the press confronted him again; the stories that were printed made him look like a fool. Hurt and uncertain of what to do, he asked Miss Pringle to arrange a meeting with Mencken, who, he thought, might advise him.

The three of them dined at her New York hotel. Mencken and Valentino got along well together and Mencken did his best to explain the facts of newspaper life to the sensitive star. With what result would never be known, however, for Valentino died shortly afterward. Mencken reported to Ernest Boyd on the meeting, noting that it was "a very instructive session." Valentino's death touched Mencken and when he sat down to write about him he did so with insight, seeing him as a civilized man trapped in an uncivilized trade. "There was some obvious fineness in him," Mencken observed, adding that even his clothes were not the kind that movie actors usually wore.

When he himself came to Hollywood in the autumn of 1926, as the climax of the Grand Tour started in the East in October with Paul Patterson, he found Miss Pringle waiting for him and Hergesheimer soon to arrive. Hergesheimer, in the mid-1920s at the peak of his reputation, was not above going to Hollywood from time to time to write scenarios and make some money. Though Mencken had once scolded him for selling out to the producers, his view changed when he himself began to get around in Hollywood. He saw that the place was awash with wealth and he no longer blamed Hergesheimer for craving a little of it.

From the day he entered Los Angeles he pleased the press. He discovered the Hollywood reporters to be even more personal and prying in their queries than the New York ones. But he fielded their questions with aplomb, not forgetting as a newspaperman himself to offer them an abundance of quotable if largely impersonal quotes. And the few personal ones were in the typical Mencken manner: for example, "Valentino must have a successor somewhere, and it might as well be me."

His sojourn in Hollywood was brief but epic. It quickly took on the condition of myth, with Miss Pringle as the moon goddess. It is certain that he did some things; it is probable that he did others.

It is certain that he met the Hollywood moguls, who regarded him like dignified mastiffs greeting a terrier. Studio cameramen caught him in noncommital poses with, for instance, Louis B. Mayer, Walter Wanger, and Irving Thalberg. In one photograph he shakes hands gingerly with Mayer. In another Miss Pringle points a movie camera at the two men while the Hollywood star Norma Shearer directs. In still another, incidentally, Mencken and Miss Pringle stand looking at each other; his expression is wonderfully quizzical and her face is a delightful study.

It is certain that he went to the raucous party at the Ambassador on November 19, which celebrated Hergesheimer's wedding anniversary. There is a photo to prove it, a masterpiece of its kind. Hergesheimer sits in the center with a benevolent, Buddha-like smile, holding the wedding cake Miss Pringle bought for him. Behind him, scrutinizing his scalp, stand Mencken and two other men. Miss Pringle sits at Hergesheimer's left smiling prettily and offering a bottle of liquor to Anita Loos, then a movie scriptwriter, who plays the part of a babe in a cradle.

It is probable that he was escorted to a stag party, given by some of Hollywood's prize stallions, which ended at the town's only house of prostitution. He went up its steps and across its pillared porch — it was Frances's on Hollywood Boulevard — readily enough, and he consented to grace the first floor. But none of the girls could entice him to the second. He clung to the piano, which every house was supposed to have, and manfully played "The Battle Hymn of the Republic." The more the girls tried the louder he played.

It is probable that during another party some stallion shook his mane and told Mencken contemptuously that he had never read any of Mencken's goddam books and that Mencken retorted that he had never seen any of the star's goddam pictures — and that that made them both Elks.

It is probable that at one of the affairs Hollywood gave for him he told the young actress Betty Compson about the Baltimore sporting houses he knew when a randy reporter, and she replied, "I thought your face was familiar."

It is certain that he broke all his records by seeing three movies during his stay. One was the premiere showing of "What Price Glory," to which he escorted Miss Pringle while the pavement crowds speculated loudly on who he was.

It is certain that the gaudiest of the parties he went to was given by the movie director James Cruze to mark the end of a picture he had made. Incidentally, his wife was Betty Compson and she was at the party. It was held on Cruze's estate at the edge of the arroyo leading from Los Angeles to Pasadena. Miss Pringle, having picked up Mencken and Hergesheimer in Hollywood, brought them over in the style proper to a movie star. Her limousine was a stately Locomobile, complete with a testy chauffeur named Thomas and a haughty black Chow which sat next to him.

The party proved to be as close to the Hollywood orgy beloved by the press as anything Mencken attended. It came complete with Bacchantes, satyrs, and complaisant nymphs. Even the servants were drawn in, and by the time Miss Pringle was ready to start for home it was clear that her chauffeur had been fraternizing fully. On the

13. *The best publicized of all Mencken's trips was his visit to Hollywood in autumn 1926. Here Aileen Pringle is playing cameraman while Norma Shearer directs Louis B. Mayer to look lively.*

14. Only in Hollywood . . . Joseph Hergesheimer, celebrating his wedding anniversary, sits with the cake while Walter Wanger, Mencken, and John Hemphill (Mrs. Hergesheimer's cousin) examine his brains. The other man standing is James Quirk, editor of Photoplay. *The seated people are John Emerson (Anita Loos's husband) and Helen Klumph (a film critic) on the left, and stars Aileen Pringle and May Alison on the right. The pretty baby in the improvised bassinet is Anita Loos. Autumn 1926.*

15. *Mencken is doubtless about to tell Aileen Pringle, just before he breaks into a grin, that he will take no more nonsense from her. Autumn 1926; Hollywood.*

16. *Baltimore's summers were always long and hot, so Mencken did much of his work in his B.V.D.'s. Here is a fine picture of the upper half of them, crisscrossed by the famous suspenders, taken while Mencken muses at the piano. About 1928; Edgar T. Schaefer, Baltimore.*

17. *Mencken built this wall in his backyard at 1524 Hollins Street and boasted that it would outlast most men's monuments. About 1928; Edgar T. Schaefer, Baltimore.*

18. *No public relations man told Mencken to be nice to the Negro children who lived along the alley behind his house. He liked them and for years bought them little treats.* 1929.

19.   Before: *Mencken just prior to his wedding; he stands with the Reverend Herbert Parrish. August 27, 1930; Baltimore* News American.

20. After: *Mencken and Sara, now married and about to be sprinkled with rice on the way to their honeymoon. August 27, 1930; Baltimore* News American.

21. At Mencken's and Sara's handsome apartment in Cathedral Street, Clarence Darrow stares at the sign Mencken put up to keep his old identity. 1930.

22. Popeyed with triumph Mencken downs the first glass of beer drawn at the Rennert after the repeal of Prohibition. The mysterious hand on the right holding a glass belongs to Hamilton Owens. December 5, 1933; Frank Miller, Sunpapers, Baltimore.

winding roads along the arroyo he got her, Hergesheimer, Mencken, and the dog completely lost. Hergesheimer asked Thomas in a lord-of-the-manor tone if he really knew where he was going, and Thomas told him to drive himself. Mencken had more of a human touch and so when he volunteered to drive, Thomas conceded, "I like you, Mencken, but I hate that son-of-a-bitch, Hergesheimer." Finally the chauffeur released the wheel, lurched into the back seat, and Miss Pringle drove. Dropping Hergesheimer off at the Ambassador, she wearily headed home.

By then it was so late that she invited Mencken to spend the small remainder of the night. She put him in a guest bedroom and then retired to her own room to sleep for a few hours. The next morning the repentant chauffeur came in and Mencken, always mindful of the proprieties, dressed with the speed of light so that the chauffeur would not get the wrong impression. He managed to clothe himself but not to comb his hair. Miss Pringle recalls him standing fully dressed with spikes of hair sticking in every direction, as if the fear of scandal had stood his hair on end.

Their friendship went on to include some sprightly meetings, mainly in New York, some good parties, and a good many letters (in the hundreds according to Miss Pringle). More than once the national press speculated about their marrying and their names were linked in the gossip columns. Their friendship ended, or at least altered its terms sharply, when Mencken became engaged to Sara Haardt in 1930. He wrote Miss Pringle asking for his letters back and returning hers.

Of course Mencken did not confine himself to just one kind of girl. Though he customarily escaped the buxom waitresses he claimed to admire, he could appreciate the attractions of Juno when he saw them. The veteran newspaperman Arthur Krock remembers two cases in point. He recalls a Miss Schultz whom Mencken once squired around. Blonde and blue-eyed, she had a majestic bosom and capacity for beer. He also recalls at least one burlesque queen who appealed to Mencken, the amply endowed leading lady of the Tiger Lilies company in San Francisco. Sara Haardt herself was not slight and she was a bit taller than Mencken. But she had wit, style, and some literary talent; all three were requisites for any young woman who aroused a genuine interest in him. All three were present in Anita Loos, who was pleasantly trim as well. Though a brunette she expertly played the role of what was then called "the dumb blonde" and became Mencken's good friend in the mid-twenties. She was married but had a Hollywood type of marriage which allowed her considerable freedom.

She was mainly a script writer for the films, employed by D. W. Griffith among others. Her base was Hollywood but she sometimes worked in New York. When she did so she stayed at the Algonquin and there she met Mencken. She too had already read him in the *Smart Set*. She recalls becoming part of a Mencken coterie that included Hergesheimer, Nathan, Boyd, and a convivial writer and editor named Thomas Smith. She fell in readily with the pleasant routine that featured dinners at Luchow's and journeys to Union Hill, New Jersey, for a beer better than Hoboken's. She too became enchanted by Mencken's brilliant talk; she still says that Mencken and Aldous Huxley were the two best talkers she ever heard.

In 1923, she remembers, she and others in the group were joking about a certain young woman, blonde and frivolous, whom Mencken was dallying with. Miss Loos thought it would be fun to write a sketch of the girl and send it to Mencken to amuse him. She wrote the sketch and then returned to Hollywood, where she forgot about it for a time. When she returned to New York, however, she mailed it to him. He was highly entertained and at their next dinner at Luchow's announced solemnly, "Young lady, you have committed the great sin. You are the first American who ever made fun of sex." With Mencken's help she placed it in *Harper's Bazar*, whose editor urged her to continue with the adventures of the blonde, now christened Lorelei Lee. The adventures became a book, *Gentlemen Prefer Blondes*, and the book became a best seller. Mencken told Bee Wilson it was a superb book. "It made me laugh like hell," he admitted.

After the advent of *Gentlemen Prefer Blondes* Miss Loos returned to writing movie scripts and made her career at it. She inclines to believe that Mencken always thought of her simply as "a cute kid that wrote a book." When Mencken made his foray into Hollywood she helped Aileen Pringle and others to welcome him, and she remembers joining in jokes they played on Hergesheimer.

During the 1920s there were other girls for Mencken too, first attracted by his fame and then held by his pebble-grained personality. Among them were at least two more movie queens besides Aileen Pringle; there was also, briefly, the dancer Adele Astaire; there was also a wealthy young Baltimore woman. In Washington there was a young opera singer, Gretchen Hood. He told Nathan, "I have turned up a new girl in Washington, and she looks very promising." As with Marion, he decided he had to go to the Library of Congress for materials for his "Homo Sapiens" book and see Miss Hood in the bargain.

Then there was Sara Haardt, more and more frequently mentioned in his correspondence and conversations. For a while there was an overlap with other young women. In one letter to Hergesheimer, of July 27, 1927, he reports both on seeing Sara, who was better looking than ever, and hearing from Aileen, who was working hard at making idiotic movies.

Then by 1929 there was Sara alone.

But meanwhile there was also work. There were the *Sunpapers* to advise, irritate, and embellish. There were countless columns to write for its yawning pages. There was the *Mercury* to plan for, to create, and then to shape, down to its details. There were books to write or edit. There was a whole decade, the 1920s, to confront and indeed dominate. It was the time when the public man would take the center of the stage while the private Mencken relaxed cheerfully in the wings.

9. The Paradise of Traders and Usurers

IT IS HARD TO MARK the beginning of the period when America became what Mencken termed the "Paradise of Traders and Usurers." It may have been 1917 or 1919 or 1920. Regardless of when it started, it went on to include the "Jazz Age"; and the "Jazz Age" included the "Roaring Twenties." But it is easy to mark the end of the period. It came, with a shuddering shock, in the autumn of 1929 when the stock market crash set off the Great Depression.

At any rate, the heart of the period was the decade of the 1920s. Its complexities were considerable, so much so that we are only beginning to realize them; such cant phrases as the "Jazz Age" or the "Roaring Twenties" serve simply to give the idiom of the time. But for Mencken the contours of the decade stood out, clear and sharp. And it was his decade. By now a man in his forties, he had firmly made up his mind about what he saw and how he felt about it. His unpleasant experience during the war had served not to unsettle but to confirm his convictions. His cast of mind lent color to his writing. His famous hyperbole grew if anything more pronounced. It gave an edge to his phrases and sentences; it captured the reader with its trenchant simplicity. His writing was superbly and openly one-sided. When the *American Mercury* emerged he declared that it too would make it a practice to present only one side of a case. That side would be the editor's. Both in his writing and in his editing, he defined the 1920s for himself vividly. His definition was not wrong; it was simply limited. He told the truth if not the whole truth.

He defined it vividly for others too, especially the disillusioned young. Of them Harold Stearns said in 1921, in his *America and the Young Intellectual*, that they disliked "almost to the point of hatred and certainly to the point of contempt, the type of people dominant in our present civilization." These were strong words and were acclaimed by Stearns's sympathizers. The next year he edited a symposium, *Civilization in the United States*, which won recognition as an important book and a manifesto for the new generation.

The book was also a testimonial to the reach of Mencken's influence on the 1920s. Though he appeared in the table of contents simply as one of thirty American contributors — his topic was "Politics" — he had helped Stearns to find a number of the others. Those ranged from writers he had only read to his closest friend, Nathan. Three foreigners were invited to contribute and to explain how they and their countrymen regarded American culture; one of the three was his Irish friend Ernest Boyd.

Though the contributors naturally varied in their point of view, they tended to agree on several important issues; there were striking differences between such contributors as Lewis Mumford and Ring Lardner and Van Wyck Brooks, yet there were similarities also. Stearns himself said in his Preface that three main contentions emerged. Each had the flavor of Mencken. The first was that America failed to practice what it preached. The second was that whatever the nature of its civilization, it was certainly not English. The third was that America was emotionally and esthetically starved.

The essays in the book, again in the mode of Mencken, did not try to provide solutions. It was enough to show how blatant the problems were. With a bow to Mencken some of the essayists also tried from time to time for the light touch. "Often, in fact, we are quite gay," Stearns said. He was wrong. Only Mencken could make the American predicament comic. There lay his chief distinction from the other contributors. At the best they practiced resignation; at worst they felt rebellion or despair. Their response showed itself most tellingly in Stearns himself, for he went on to become an expatriate. But not Mencken. When he was asked why he stayed in the United States if he considered its culture contemptible, he answered that it was for the same reason that a small boy went to the circus or a grown man to the zoo. Mencken saw no reason for going into exile; Hollins Street felt far too comfortable.

Throughout the decade he earned and kept the respect of the

young intellectuals. He also influenced scores of creative writers, of many kinds, including the one who best caricatured the temper of the twenties. This was Sinclair Lewis. He sketched the decade in his sardonic novels and in the process regularly acknowledged the significance of Mencken. In *Main Street,* issued at the opening of the decade, he anatomized American small-town culture better than anyone else. In *Babbitt,* published in 1922, he portrayed a typical businessman in a typical city; in *Arrowsmith* he turned his ironic attention to science and medicine in America. In *Elmer Gantry* he satirized the hypocrisies of religion; in *Dodsworth,* issued at the end of the decade, he wrote about the successful American who grows to see the hollowness of American life. And in *The Man Who Knew Coolidge,* published in 1928, he explored a vein that appealed to Mencken doubly. For in the title story one Lowell T. Schmaltz, once a classmate of President Coolidge, not only delivers a lengthy monologue which strings together all possible Rotarian notions but puts them into purely American speech.

When Lewis wrote *Babbitt* it was partly, as we shall see, because of a suggestion from Mencken; when Lewis wrote *Arrowsmith* he told Mencken he was more interested in Mencken's opinion of it than anyone else's; when Mencken reviewed *Elmer Gantry,* Lewis called the review the finest thing that happened about the book; and when Mencken wrote a pair of good reviews of *Dodsworth,* Lewis exclaimed with gratitude and admiration.

Lewis was a remarkable if tortured artist. And drunk or sober, manic or depressive, he always respected Mencken. From the start Mencken's own feelings about Lewis were mixed; nevertheless, he was bowled over by *Main Street.* He warned Nathan, after Lewis had collared them at a party, to prepare for a terrible shock, "I've just read the advance sheets of the book that *lump* . . . wrote and, by God, he has done the job." Mencken proclaimed to the world that it combined a "Dreiserian ruthlessness of observation with a Cabellian-Rabelaisian richness of humor." His enthusiasm lessened only slightly as the decade moved along. He could still maintain in 1927 that if "there was ever a novelist among us with an authentic call to the trade, then surely it is this red-haired tornado from the Minnesota wilds." And he could not help exclaiming, "What a gallery of American types he has painted!" His admiration was understandable. Though Lewis peopled his pages with grotesques, the personages and actual events of the noisy decade outdid him. It seemed that nature did more than copy art; it burlesqued it.

During the decade the voice of business, with its hearty baritone was heard in the national chorus loudest of all. The voice of politics, though sometimes hoarse or uneven, accompanied it in loyal attempts at harmony. The voice of moralism was also raised, triumphantly at the start because of the appearance of Prohibition but after that more shrilly because of Prohibition's crashing failure. The voice of literature, especially in Lewis's novels of the twenties, added its calculated dissonances. And the voice of the intellectuals, thin and not very clear to begin with, became increasingly emphatic. One of the main reasons was the bright brassy tone that issued from Mencken.

He felt he had to shout to be heard and that there was good reason for the shouting. He saw that, the war finished, the United States was surveying the results with some complacency and then doing its best to return to business as usual. In public affairs the popularly elected leaders, as well as self-elected ones, talked like McKinley or Taft. They acted almost as if the World War had no lessons to teach, one way or the other. He did not have far to go for specific evidence. He rode from Baltimore to Washington to attend the inauguration of Warren Gamaliel Harding. He was apprehensive though he thought that anyone would be better than Woodrow Wilson. But Mencken soon squirmed on his hard wooden seat, for he had to admit that the inaugural address reeked with nonsense. Raising his glance toward heaven, Harding affirmed his belief in the divine inspiration of the Founding Fathers. It was still there for our nation to draw on, he announced, and its lesson was still "noninvolvement in Old World affairs." Though he also asserted that our nation had come to a new understanding of its place in the world, when he descended to specifics it grew clear that it was largely the same old place. Underneath his lumpy rhetoric lay the old isolationism, the old capitalism. The "damnedest bosh," Mencken snorted.

Near the end of his address Harding introduced a compliment to the American woman, who had just been given the vote, and hoped that we might "count upon her intuitions, her refinements, her intelligence, and her influence to exalt the social order." He concluded with an apostrophe to the one term above all others that made Mencken wince, Service. "Service," the new President intoned, "is the supreme commitment of life . . . . I pledge an administration wherein all the agencies of government are called to serve, and ever promote an understanding of government purely as an expression of the popular will."

By popular will he meant the will of business. To its expression he listened obediently. During his aborted term of office, government functioned modestly and then only to assist the commercial interest. His successor Calvin Coolidge, another "slave to Service" as Mencken saw it, carried the notion of restraint still further. In his first address to Congress Coolidge said, "The age of perfection is still in the somewhat distant future, but it is more in danger of being retarded by mistaken Government activity than it is from lack of legislation." Let business, like joy, be unconfined.

Mencken could only marvel. "The United States, I believe, is the first great empire in the history of the world to ground its whole national philosophy upon business." Throughout the decade he played the matador to it, from the biggest of big business, epitomized by U.S. Steel and its head, Judge Elbert Gary, down to the local real estate man who sang the song of Service. From 1920, when he composed Monday Articles on business monopolies ("God Help Us All!" was one title), to 1929, when he discussed part of a new tariff act ("Putting Down Wicked Thoughts"), he expatiated on the asininities as well as the iniquities of trade. In mid-decade he summed the matter up: "the art of trafficking is king — and Judge Gary is its grand vizier, as Cal is its court chamberlain." But he simply jabbed the harder. Only in the 1930s, after the New Deal programs arrived, did he begin to swing around to the defense of business; then he saw some virtue in the big corporations which had survived and the tycoons who still headed them. But those days were far ahead.

During the course of the war the patriotism that emerged was both powerful and paranoid. It focused on being a 100 per cent American by supporting our soldiers in France, subscribing to Liberty Bonds, and searching for spies with German accents. Mencken declined to count himself a 100 per cent American and in fact, after the war, helped to perfect the satirical song on this very theme in the Saturday Night Club's ritual.

Near the end of the conflict Russia, under the impetus of the Bolshevik revolt, changed from being our ally to our enemy. After the war all the American suspicion of radicalism — of socialism and anarchism — focused on the Russian "Reds" and their American sympathizers. The Red Scare became the most spectacular manifestation of patriotic paranoia.

The Red Scare was manipulated by both businessmen and politicians. One aftermath of the war was massive labor unrest, accompanied by strikes, lockouts, and sporadic violence. Another was the disillusionment of the intellectuals, and not only the young ones, about the conduct and consequence of the war. Whether they leaned to the political Left or Right, they were often uneasy, even rebellious. But the trouble in the air, the public was led to believe, came from the Left.

President Wilson's Attorney General, A. Mitchell Palmer, appointed himself leader in the effort at purging the country of radicalism. His aim, Mencken said, was "to scare the boobery with Bolshevist bugaboos." The peaks in his campaign came in November 1919 and January 1920, when he ordered nationwide raids on the "Reds." He tried through his federal agents to sweep them up and to deport them to Russia. Legal process was badly mauled but Palmer's actions offered the American public a kind of catharsis. There were arrests of many individuals and also raids on several left-wing journals.

The most popular magazine in the United States, the *Saturday Evening Post,* voiced the view of the American middle class about such matters. Mencken derided the *Post* as one of the "agents of a delicate and enlightened patriotism." Its editor, George Horace Lorimer, published two editorials in February 1920 that summed up the patriotic position. In the first, headed "Sanctuary," he made a smooth transition from one minority to another: "First we discover that one group of aliens is trying to impose the Kaiser on us as a master, and then that another is plotting to deliver us over to Lenine." He explained that the average American was an innocent fellow with no idea of how wily aliens could be. He must be awakened and the alien menace must be coped with. He must be made to see that free speech is being perverted by the Reds and their friends and that they must not benefit from it. For they want it only to inflame their hearers, to incite them to "free love, free loot, free murder," and untrammeled revolution.

In the second editorial, "Self-Preservation," Lorimer urged that we deport those in our midst "who deplore our individualistic, capitalistic system" and hope to confiscate our capital. In addition, we should prevent the entrance into our country of other aliens with the same radical ideas.

The Red Scare went on for about a year and a half before the people became bored instead of excited. Some who had supported Palmer had second thoughts. As Mencken put it, Palmer "carried the farce to such lengths that the plain people began to sympathize with his victims." Nevertheless, American business profited from it. Organized labor was definitely daunted and the intellectual community was at least a little intimidated.

Mencken's response, however, was prompt and emphatic. He jeered at Palmer as "one of the most obnoxious mountebanks ever in public life." He charged that he was edging and squirming his way toward the Presidency. He called his use of the Attorney General's office "Government by Blackleg" and headed one of his Monday Articles with the term. In the article he catalogued the rascalities of the office. It had, "as a matter of daily routine, hounded men and women in cynical violation of their constitutional rights, invaded the sanctuary of domicile, manufactured evidence against the innocent, flooded the land with *agents provocateurs*, raised neighbor against neighbor, filled the public press with inflammatory lies, and fostered all the worst poltrooneries of sneaking and malicious wretches."

But if political oppression subsided with the Red Scare, moral oppression certainly did not. If Palmer lost, Sumner gained. By and large the patriots were still Puritans and the Puritans still patriots; many of them merely shifted their emphasis. As Mencken once explained to Dreiser, "The professional patriot, at bottom, is bound to be a Puritan — the leopard cannot change his spots." The American Legion soon after it was founded in 1919 became an apostle of purity in literature. Censorship of alien, that is, revolutionary, thought was a menace to the liberals principally at the start of the decade. For example, in March 1920 the threat of it kept Mencken from sending Ernest Boyd not merely Socialist but Irish-American and other such incendiary papers. However, that sort of thing gradually stopped. On the other hand, moral censorship flourished well into the decade. In April 1920 he reported to Boyd that the moralists had just come down on Hutchins Hapgood's *The History of a Lover;* and he continued to report such incidents from time to time for several years. There is no doubt that in the next few years the censors lost none of their zeal and little of their effectiveness — until they collided with Mencken.

Mencken's part in the maiming of moral censorship was so important that it deserves separate attention. The history of the "Hatrack" case, in which a story in the *Mercury* for April 1926 caused the temporary suppression of the magazine, shows him at his bristling best and will be told shortly. Though the "Hatrack" case proved to be his most celebrated stand he helped elsewhere, and especially in his Monday Articles, in the constant struggle for free speech.

Mencken's other great battle with the moralists came over theology. Many of them, particularly in the South, still believed the Bible to be utterly right and Darwin utterly wrong. They stood ready to enforce their belief through the police and the courts as well as through religious channels. Here too Mencken put himself in the center of the contest and took part in its most celebrated case, which occurred the summer before "Hatrack." This was the trial in Tennessee of a teacher named Scopes for suggesting to his pupils that evolution was a fact, in spite of a law which forbade him to say so. This story too will be told a little later.

Though always animated by his rambunctious humor, Mencken's struggles against censorship and for free thought were serious enough. His livelihood was involved as well as his convictions. But his struggle against the third crusade of the moralists, Prohibition, was a game. The forces favoring Prohibition had moved with shrewd effectiveness. But after the war ended and Prohibition became law, it proved to be a stumbling buffoon, easy to hoodwink and delightful to deride. Mencken found both its prewar and postwar history instructive.

He recalled that, though the forces of conservatism in general and moralism in particular had to retreat from time to time during the first fifteen years of the twentieth century, they gave ground grudgingly and when beaten in one stratagem used another. Nevertheless, they were being defeated when they were saved by a heavily armed ally, World War I.

In an atmosphere of gradually growing militance the conservative groups brought about their greatest legislative victory, and it was in the field of morals. Their announced aim was to make the drinking of liquor illegal but their ultimate plan was to make their many millions of countrymen virtuous by law. In effect: be good or be imprisoned. They formed a powerful if uneasy alliance whose main members were the Protestant denominations, especially in the South; the farmers of the Midwest, from the rolling hills of Indiana to the prairies; and the middle-class businessmen, from the country storekeeper to the Kiwanis office-manager. Their captains were professional reformers, bishops, and politicians. And their General Staff was the Anti-Saloon League.

The military metaphor is not mere verbiage. The League's Washington lobbyist, in making his report to the annual convention of 1915, spoke glowingly about the "army that is winning battles, that is taking trenches and breastworks of the enemy, and which finds itself advancing victoriously toward its goal." To the Blue-Nose it was a holy war.

As Mencken watched the war approach its climax step by step, he felt outraged but also amused. He felt outraged because he regarded drinking as a prime pleasure, and a highly personal one. Any intrusions on it were rascally. His duty seemed plain. It was to oppose Prohibition by every means at his command, and above all by ridicule, for he knew his forte was guerrilla warfare. Raising his stein like a standard, he resolved never to desist till Prohibition was defeated.

He felt amused at the perfect comic propriety of the whole campaign. A snuffling Congress passed the Eighteenth Amendment to the Constitution, forbidding the making and selling of intoxicating liquors, and submitted it to the states on December 18, 1917. How appropriate that Mississippi led the parade of states which approved! He watched with perverse satisfaction as one state after another followed Mississippi's example, till there were thirty-five in all. Only one more was needed and Nebraska, the fief of William Jennings Bryan, proved to be the one. By proclamation Prohibition began on January 16, 1920. The Volstead Act, passed to enforce it, took effect the next day. Even beer was banned: Pilsner, Löwenbrau, Michelob — they were all illegal now.

Throughout the campaign he wrote to Ernest Boyd at greater length than to anyone else. His letters reflect both his outrage and his amusement. His denunciations were loud rather than bitter. For instance, when the die was cast and Nebraska ratified the amendment, he wrote Boyd, "All is lost, including honor." But he added that he himself had enough whiskey, wine, and beer to last for two solid years and by that time he hoped to be "far from these Wesleyan scenes." When the law actually went into effect he told Boyd, "The full force of Prohibition now oppresses us. It is indescribably damnable." But he took the drama out of his denunciation by boasting that he was brewing ale at home with tasty results.

He soon found that with a little foresight he could take care of his needs in private, and he made assuaging them in public a field sport. In the search for a decent beer or a palatable whiskey he would speed to the far reaches of Hoboken or to the outermost suburbs of Baltimore. He would experiment with home-brew like an eager housewife, exchanging recipes with friends and vaunting himself as a Braumeister. His interest in drink-making, like his interest in drink-hunting, never flagged. One summer he assured his portly friend A. H. McDannald that the whole process was not only instructive but very beautiful.

In print, early and late, he jibed at the militant moralists. After the wartime *Sunpapers* were closed to his opinions, he voiced them in the New York *Evening Mail*. The captions on his articles tell the story: "Anti-Saloon League Lobby has Congress Badly Scared"; "Dithyrambs on Alcohol"; "Prohibition and Other Malaises"; and so on. The *Mail* articles saw him through mid-1918. Then occurred the period of public silence which lasted from the forced change of management of the *Mail* until the renewal, on Mencken's terms, of his writing for the *Sunpapers*. In February 1920 he inaugurated what became his famous series of Monday Articles and in the third one — the first of many — under the title of "The Millennium Dawns" he derided the Volstead Act. In the same year, masked as Major Owen Hatteras, he snorted in the *Smart Set* at Prohibition. From then on, through the 1920s, Prohibition provoked some of his most pungent writing. It swelled his personal popularity, and only with the stock market crash in 1929 and the Depression that followed did the follies of Prohibition lose their charm for his readers.

The enemies of unorthodox thought and of alcohol were also the enemies of sexual freedom: the mass of middle-class moralists. Their leaders, so far as Mencken could see, were the same censorious Puritans he had been bedeviling for years. The friends of the drive for sexual freedom also seemed to be much the same as the friends of other freedoms. But not entirely; there were some new friends who made Mencken uncomfortable.

He viewed the well-advertised rise of sexual license with mingled emotions. Publicly he was committed to the belief that what the individual did was his own business unless it damaged the welfare of someone else. Privately he asserted that taste as well as principle was involved. He never hesitated, in the proper company, to defend the right of an unmarried couple to seek the surcease of a hotel room; and he himself had done so. But the red-light houses which had attracted him in his high-spirited youth were now at most the places where he went to play piano for his friends or to verify his suspicion that every house harbored at least one girl named Mabel. Promiscuity seemed to him animal, more fitting for the baboon than for man. Among his associates he found its main exponent in Theodore Dreiser and his comments on Dreiser were caustic.

The objections Mencken had to the new freedom in personal conduct were ones, then, of decorum and taste. He was convinced that there was a proper way to do something and an improper way. He tried to do things the proper way, as he saw it. He might observe the proprieties with a look of amusement but he observed them, particularly in his private life. He acted gallantly toward the ladies, kissing their hand when the occasion allowed and rolling his eyes comically at the same moment. Unlike George Jean Nathan, who seldom slept with a girl without all Broadway knowing it, Mencken regarded it as a breach of manners to kiss and tell. Significantly, he relished the humor of sex but disliked dirty stories. He felt a genuine aversion both to sordidness and scruffiness. Brought up in a decorous household, orderly in his personal habits, he wanted life itself to be seemly.

Dreiser was the leading person to represent what Mencken objected to, Greenwich Village the leading place. For Mencken the two were connected as early as 1914, when Dreiser moved to the Village for freedom and adulation. It was then already a Bohemia for artists and writers, for refugees from business and the universities, from, for instance, U.S. Steel or Harvard. After the twenties began, more bright young men from Cambridge and New York settled there; so did eager authors from Chicago; so did radicals, amateur and professional; so did an ample share of adventurous girls.

While some of the disillusioned young crossed the ocean to expatriate themselves as Harold Stearns did, in Paris or perhaps London or Rome, others denied America by going to live in the Village. They helped to make it the country's most celebrated haven for the outsider.

Among the Villagers were serious writers, artists, and intellectuals. What everybody heard about, however, was not the writing or painting so much as the sexual license and blowsy living. And those were what Mencken noticed first of all. Yet when he published his criticism of the Villagers his most important charge was not that they were loose-livers but that they were untalented poseurs.

In his private letters he attacked them on both scores. Writing for instance to Ernest Boyd while Dreiser was being persecuted for publishing *The "Genius,"* he saw them as "mountebanks advocating birth control, free verse, free love and other such juvenile propaganda." They were using Dreiser and Dreiser was an idiot for letting them. His vanity and his lechery made him a prime target. "Let some preposterous wench come in in a long blue smock, and call him 'Master' and he is immediately undone."

Yet for all its scruffiness, the Village won some sympathy from Mencken. Its enemies were his, even if its ways were not his ways. He made his definitive statement on the matter in "The National Letters" in the second series of *Prejudices*, of 1920.

There he led off by describing the Village revolt as the natural reaction of youth to hidebound professors. There were such professors throughout the country and in consequence little Greenwich Villages, but the one in Manhattan was the most prominent. The Village revolts could be traced back to the dogmatism of Irving Babbitt, the pundit Paul Elmer More, and, of course, Stuart Sherman, who all deserved to be rebelled against.

Mencken admitted that he enjoyed the spectacle of the rebellion though the actual writing coming from the Village rebels seldom had any value. Its main weakness lay in its emphasis on technique. It paid more attention to how to say something than to having something to say. Much of its writing was meaningless gibberish — often the work of frauds. Its prose lacked distinction; its verse rarely went beyond a hollow audaciousness. Its drama on the other hand, best exemplified in the one-acters of Eugene O'Neill, had genuine strength; yet it was probably mere luck that O'Neill and one or two other significant playwrights lived in the Village.

In spite of the fact that the writing seemed sterile or ridiculous, it had the merit to Mencken of being a challenge to the stale taste of the literary pedagogues, of the conservative critics. The Village was a place where the beginnings of the new and good could be seen. It was not a place of imitations of imitations. Even its carnality was not bad; it argued that there was still health in American youth.

Mencken closed his comments on the Village in "The National Letters" by a charge, which attracted much attention, that sex in the rest of the country was imprisoned and fermenting. This charge was pure rhetoric, becoming steadily less believable as the decade moved along. It is doubtful that even Mencken believed that sex was imprisoned or fermenting, when before his eye came delightful evidence to the contrary. It was best embodied in the flapper, whom he could not avoid watching with amusement and attention. As a matter of fact she was a mainstay of the *Smart Set* much earlier than the 1920s, as early actually as 1914 when Nathan and Mencken became its editors. She had appeared on the covers then and continued to do so till Mencken and Nathan left the magazine in 1923. Mencken was not alone in finding her every action of some interest.

This young woman gradually shortened her skirts from the ankles to the knees. She shed much of her underclothing, began to use rouge and lipstick, and bobbed her hair. She also started to smoke cigarets and when Prohibition came drank Prohibition-style gin. And she allowed herself more freedom of action, including sexual, than any of her predecessors. She was no innocent. In his sketch "The Flapper" in the *Smart Set* for February 1915, Mencken announced that she was privy to dark secrets and had been taught to take care of herself. She had been converted to the gospel of sex hygiene.

The flourishing sexual freedom of the young female — the young male had long been free — proved to be one of the major developments of the 1920s. Its principal prophets appeared to be Sigmund Freud and Scott Fitzgerald, both well known to Mencken. As the young understood it, Freud preached that sexual freedom was needed for mental and physical well-being. True, it would not guarantee it, but such freedom was a proper adjunct to the human condition. Sexual freedom might indeed end badly, yet its very disaster could have something appealing and romantic to it.

Fitzgerald clothed this exciting idea in his flashy, sometimes brilliant, novels of modern life: in particular *This Side of Paradise* and *The Great Gatsby*. He himself lived, as Mencken saw when their paths crossed in Baltimore, like a character from one of his books. In *This Side of Paradise* the hero, Amory Blaine, goes to Princeton, then to war, and returns to have a pair of love affairs, but he finds no peace in them. Everything is cynical and stylish. In *The Great Gatsby* the main character is a young war veteran, Jay Gatsby, turned boot-legger. On coming back to this country Gatsby meets again the rich girl he has never forgotten, wins her briefly from her rich, hulking husband, and then is shot by a garageman. This hero dies; the other lives. But love proves brittle for them both, as well as for the pretty women they go to bed with. The point here is that in Fitzgerald's fiction the women act as unconventionally as the men.

While Fitzgerald was finishing *The Great Gatsby*, Mencken announced publicly that the female sex fretted in the throes of a delayed adolescence. He spoke about it particularly in a *Nation* piece in 1924 called "The Sex Uproar." He said that there had been a harem rebellion which had knocked the suppression of women to bits. Now freedom was going to the female head. He knew a man who owned a copy of *The Art of Love* which he had lent to twenty-six eager women at their request and fifty more were waiting to pore over its pages. Yet their sexual enterprise had Mencken's official approval: "It gives me delight to see a taboo violated, and that delight is doubled when the taboo is one that is wholly senseless." He applauded in print though he still had his private reservations.

This was the decade, then, when woman became emancipated. This meant not only greater social but also greater economic freedom. She had begun during the war to win the right to work when there was a genuine shortage of men to fill jobs. When the men returned she retreated politely but only part way. More and more women chose to work, at least for a while, instead of marrying the best man who offered himself. Some women continued to work after marriage, and one of the issues of the time was whether it was proper for a married woman to do so. Many still felt that the only place for her was the kitchen or the couch.

Much of the ferment of the twenties came from the controversies about the status of woman. The controversies were seldom marked by a sense of humor; the controversialists when they appeared in print were usually earnest, even tense. The eminent exception was Mencken.

He issued his jovial and treacherous *In Defense of Women* in 1918 and then revised and expanded it in 1922. It is his classic state-ment on the sex, tinctured throughout with his humorous exaggeration. Between the publication of the two versions of it American women had won a smashing political victory, the right to vote. The Nine-teenth Amendment, adopted in 1920, had guaranteed woman suffrage and Mencken's eyes must have sparkled as he watched the result. The issue represented the intersection of two of his main amuse-ments, politics and women. When the women, voting in their first presidential election, helped to oust Woodrow Wilson, Mencken was gratified. It showed that the female was shrewder than the male. She was not taken in by Wilson's sniffling moralism. "Women, as a class," he asserted, "believe in none of the ludicrous rights, duties and pious obligations that men are forever gabbling about."

Women now provided the spice for American politics, but even if they had not, he would have relished the politics of the twenties.

There had never been a time in his experience when politics was as gross or as comically extravagant in its rascality. When Harding — to return to him — was elected president Mencken thought it would be impossible to succeed him with anyone as absurd. Three years later he found to his glee that he was wrong. In his own way Calvin Coo-lidge was just as amazing as Warren Harding.

Harding came on the stage as the common man's President. He radiated the dignified affection of a well-fed mastiff, he opened the White House wide to the visits of the people, and he installed in the White House a dog named Laddie Boy. He inaugurated the era of the broad grin.

As he made his rambling speeches and presidential addresses, his language especially attracted Mencken. Seldom had English been as genially maltreated. Harding's errors were not the vulgar ones; they were simply six inches from being correct. The most widely circulated was his invention "normalcy," but he coined a rewarding number of others such as "betrothment" for "betrothal." His thinking looked as woolly as his vocabulary. He felt that good will could solve most of the problems of the world and that a little luck would solve the rest. To his Cabinet he appointed, according to Mencken, a piquant mix-ture: "three highly intelligent men of self-interest, six jackasses and one common crook." He also appointed his own brother-in-law head of federal prisons and a lawyer from his home town, with a few months of banking experience, as Comptroller of the Currency. Nor did he stop there. He allowed what later was called the "Ohio Gang," from his home state, to make the federal government their feeding trough.

It took a while for the people to realize the evils of government by crony. Harding, however, found out before they did and may have killed himself because of the fact. But the country hailed his death in August 1923 as a martyrdom and he was eulogized from one coast to the other. Mencken memorialized him mock-solemnly as "the sainted Gamaliel."

It was only as the presidency of Calvin Coolidge began that some idea of the goings on in Washington became current. Mencken marveled as he read and heard the details of the so-called Teapot Dome scandal. Not at the corruption — that was par for politics — but at the crudity. Under Senate investigation it was discovered that vast federal reserves of oil at Teapot Dome in Wyoming and at two other fields in California had been leased to private oilmen at rates fabulously profitable to them. This had been done with the connivance of the Secretary of the Interior, who, as Mencken said, had been paid off like a common bootlegger, and the acquiescence of the Secretary of the Navy. The hearings and subsequent trials involved some of the plushiest of business moguls as well as federal officials. Before everything was over, at least a few oilmen left the country and one went to prison, if only on a contempt charge. Most simply brazened out the affair. However, among the politicians the Secretary of the Interior went to jail and the Secretary of the Navy retired from public life. Even the Secretary of the Treasury, Andrew Mellon, was found to be at least marginally involved.

Teapot Dome ranked as the most sensational of the scandals of the 1920s, but the federal government, and its attendant big business, was shot through with misconduct. The legacy of Harding included rampant fraud at the Veterans' Bureau, graft in the office of the Alien Property Custodian, and criminal conspiracy in the Department of Justice. As one scandal exploded after another, Coolidge remained calm. Mencken remarked that he was "as magnificently unruffled as a grass widow at her third wedding." Still, he was honest in the ordinary sense of the word, Mencken conceded, though "a dreadful little cad." Under Coolidge the level of federal probity rose. America's unbelievably rich resources continued to be raided but within the limits of the law.

Though Mencken was most attracted by the bumbler Harding and the flamboyant criminality of his regime, he was also edified by the utter mediocrity of Coolidge. Sitting down each day at his typewriter, he literally did not know where to begin because the flood of things to write about rose so high. "Short of ideas in the Republic of today?" he snorted. "As well try to imagine a Prohibition officer short of money." In his Monday Articles for the *Evening Sun* he simply seized on the likeliest of political topics and then pounded his typewriter with vim. His very first Monday Article, on presidential contenders, was called "A Carnival of Buncombe" and it set the tone.

Besides his column and his newspaper specials on what he regarded as the side shows of American politics, he contributed political pieces to the *Mercury* and other magazines from time to time. He epitomized his point of view in the title of a piece he published in the *Nation* in June 1928, "Clown Show."

Yet because of the fascination of politics and politicians he liked to speculate, with his systematic, energetic mind, about the nature of the political process and what made politicians behave as they did. In particular the operation of democracy interested him. It was so highly praised and it worked so badly.

In the middle of the decade he issued his treatise on the subject. *Notes on Democracy*, in spite of its modest title, was the culmination of fifteen years of writing and more than that of thought. He started to make notes for it about 1910. When he began the actual composition in 1925, he drew not only on those early jottings but also on his work in the *Smart Set*, and on the Monday Articles. Before he finished it, in June of 1926, he drew on the *Mercury* also. He rewrote the old material and added to it a much larger amount of new.

The book has three main sections: on democratic man; on the democratic state; and on democracy and liberty. The thesis goes as far back as the book on Nietzsche which Mencken published in 1908. It is that democracy is a fraud. Somehow the mob man has foisted it upon his more talented neighbor. Through various schemes, prominent among them the program of Christianity, the masses struggle to pull the elite down to their own level. Through trumped-up ethics they try to halter the actions of their betters. The natural leaders of the mob are the Puritans, for Puritanism lies implicit in democracy.

The ideal of the members of the elite is to live a life of liberty, expressing themselves to the full. The way to do it is to reject the pernicious doctrines of the mob and to combat the leadership of the Puritans. Though it will not be easy, there is hope of success; for democracy is so greedy that it may devour itself. Mob man may fall into the pit that he himself has dug.

Notes on Democracy aroused the ire of many reviewers, but for the elect it was the classic expression of the antidemocratic idea. Often the judicious critic, the one neither repelled nor enthralled by Mencken's message, gave it the qualified praise that sounded sweetest of all. For example, Edmund Wilson, reviewing the book in the *New Republic* for December 15, 1926, conceded that it was "one of the best-written and most intensely felt" of Mencken's works. He added that though Mencken had been saying the same thing for years, he had never before said it "in so pungent and so terse a language" or with such satiric force.

The doctrines were potent ones during the next few years. Then came the Great Depression and the doctrines appeared irresponsible. The overwhelming need was for far more equality even at the expense of a great deal of liberty. The *Notes* acquired an additional ill repute because a few of their notions could be seen in the principles which were carrying Adolf Hitler to power in Germany. Hitler was in the process of proving himself to be the superman, self-selected at the head of a Teutonic elite. He was not what Mencken had in mind but Mencken's enemies whispered that he was.

The world of the twenties ended in catastrophe. By November of 1929 the paradise of traders and usurers which Mencken had derided yet intellectually dominated was gone. The transvaluation of values would reach much further than he had ever thought. But before the stock market crash he kept the conscience of the decade. He spoke for it better than any other intellectual. He captained more of its key causes, led more of its battles. They were often successful in spite of his disclaimers. In fact the extent of his successes grew so apparent that by the last two years of the decade there was, here and there, a faint feeling that he had been left with little to do. Here and there a college group called him out of date; a radical journal, or even a conservative one, found him fusty. In 1928 Paul Elmer More still considered him antichrist, the "leader of malignity," while St. John Ervine was nominating him for the Nobel Prize; but in 1929, before the crash, the *Bookman* was already announcing "The Passing of H. L. Mencken." He would have no successor.

There can be little doubt of Mencken's influence on the 1920s.

Most signs suggest that it was both broad and deep. And yet it can stand some specific documentation. Luckily, a surprising amount of evidence can be uncovered for one of the crucial aspects of his influence, in this case on writers and their reception. Assessing the evidence is complicated by his reputation as a caustic critic and by the fact that he personally liked writers more before the 1920s opened than after. But the truth is that his influence continued even though his interest waned. The evidence can be found in two different sources, the yellowing pages of the *Smart Set* and the book shelves of the Mencken Room in the Enoch Pratt Library.

The degree and extent of Mencken's appreciation can nowhere be better seen than in the issues of the *Smart Set* for his first half-dozen years. They prove that he liked American, British, and Continental writers. They prove that he liked realists, romanticists, and classicists, though it must be conceded that he liked realists best. In most cases of course his admiration was not undiluted. The important thing was that he felt it and publicly expressed it.

Though catalogues can be dreary, a catalogue of the prose writers in particular whom he praised in the *Smart Set* is revealing in its catholicity. He found something to appreciate in the work of such varied authors as Leonid Andreyev, Max Beerbohm, Arnold Bennett, Earl Derr Biggers, Gamaliel Bradford, James Branch Cabell, Hall Caine, Willa Cather, G. K. Chesterton, Irvin S. Cobb, Joseph Conrad, Marie Corelli, Richard Harding Davis, Theodore Dreiser, John Galsworthy, David Grayson (Ray Stannard Baker), Thomas Hardy, William Dean Howells, James Huneker, Henry James, Rudyard Kipling, Stephen Leacock, Ludwig Lewisohn, Jack London, Helen Mackay, Somerset Maugham, George Meredith, George Moore, Kathleen Norris, Frank Norris, O. Henry, E. Phillips Oppenheim, Mary Roberts Rinehart, Damon Runyon, Saki (Hector Munro), Upton Sinclair, Hermann Sudermann, H. G. Wells, Hugh Walpole, Edith Wharton, and William Allen White.

The peak period for Mencken's concern for literature was the decade from 1908 to 1918. Within that decade, however, distinctions can be made. He felt most involved during the years up to the start of World War I in 1914 in Europe. After that, a content analysis of his work shows that literature played a decreasing part. The war and America's relation to the war crowded it aside. Literature looked pale next to the hot, full-blooded reality of wartime. After the war

Mencken again turned more of his attention to literature but it never regained its early importance.

Though the evidence shows that he moved into the 1920s with a diminished interest in it he made no apologies for the fact. He stepped briskly. He did not act exactly as if he had rid himself of an encumbrance and so could march the faster. But there was, both in what he said and how he said it, a sense that he was turning from minor matters to more serious ones. He was beginning to find the *Smart Set* too trivial, he told his friends; and part of the triviality was the stress on what he termed "Beautiful Letters." American problems intrigued him more than American literature. The country was full of villainy that asked to be tripped up, while poetry in particular, at any rate most poetry, was making him yawn.

And yet he kept much of his concern for the men and women who produced the literature. He wanted them to prosper, even if he had grown to care less for them as persons. The lot of writers in a commercial culture was at best an uneasy one. Their chief enemies were his enemies: gross commercialism and prurient censorship, jungle ethics and Puritan repression. As the 1920s went along, he found himself still besieged by authors, especially those in want of something. They waited in the raunchy atmosphere of the *Smart Set* office, with its plumber's-calendar decor; later they waited outside the austere little room that housed the *Mercury's* staff. They wrote Mencken both in New York and Baltimore. They phoned him, to his annoyance, at Hollins Street or sometimes simply went to his home and pushed the doorbell. More often than not, he helped them. He doubtless grumbled when he did it but he did it nevertheless.

The affection and respect he aroused in the community of writers was unparalleled. In part it was a tribute to his great influence as a reviewer, advocate, and champion of their causes; in part it was their feeling that literature itself was very important to him. There was patently a lag in their realization that he was finding it less meaningful.

When authors want to tell someone that they value his judgment or esteem his influence they have the amiable habit of giving him a book of theirs. Usually they inscribe it. One entire wall and part of another — nearly two hundred feet of shelf space — in the Mencken Room at the Enoch Pratt Library is nearly filled with such volumes. In many there is an inscription. Sometimes there is more than that, often a letter tipped in, in which the author expands on what Mencken's interest has meant.

Here is massed testimony to Mencken's central importance, for a good decade, as an entrepreneur of letters. It tells as well perhaps as anything what he meant to American literature. The books are shelved alphabetically by author, with the famous next to the forgotten. The eye ranges along the alphabet. Here is Sherwood Anderson, for instance. In a copy of his novel *Dark Laughter* (1925) he has written "Henry L Menchen   More deeply loved and respected by mere men who say nothing about it than any other American I know." In his *Hello Towns!* (1929) he has written "Henry L Menchen. You came to bat for me . . . and if you didn't clear the bags it was only because there was no one on." The Romantic poet Joseph Auslander has inscribed his *Cyclops' Eye* (1926), "For H. L. Mencken . . . because, this side idolatry, I am in admiration as much as any." The biographer Gamaliel Bradford has written in his *D. L. Moody* (1927) "H. L. Mencken with the constant remembrance of much kindness shown to Gamaliel Bradford." Then there is a book by the controversial Virginia novelist James Branch Cabell, one of many by him, *The Cords of Vanity* (1920) in which he writes "For H. L. Mencken this book, which he was virtually alone in not acrimoniously disliking in its first form." From Willa Cather there is a letter tipped into her novel *The Professor's House* (1925) saying, "I hope it is not too late to tell you how glad I am that you liked my book. I've tried to telephone you several times. . . ."

Today the names of Sherwood Anderson and Willa Cather can be found in any history of American literature. But there is not even a niche reserved for the next attester to Mencken's influence, the fluttery Richmond essayist and editor, Emily Clark. In her *Stuffed Peacocks* (1927) she has written, "For H. L. Mencken, without whose persistent encouragement these latest chips would never have flown from so old a block [she was thirty-four at the time] — with contrite apologies for their title, and admiring friendship for himself." From burly Paul de Kruif — no sharper personal contrast to Emily Clark could be found — there is a letter tipped into his book about noted scientists, *Microbe Hunters* (1926), which is pertinent not only as a testimonial from him but also from Sinclair Lewis. Lewis had employed de Kruif to help him with the medical novel *Arrowsmith*.

In this letter de Kruif wrote, about *Arrowsmith,* "The book is going very well. We have completed the preliminary sketches and outline, and Red is now well into the writing. You have a great influence on us. We write the damned thing *at* you most of the time."

No novelist filled Mencken with the precise mixture of irritation and approval that Dreiser did. Dreiser reciprocated and wrote in his best novel, *An American Tragedy* (1925), "Dear Heinrich: As my oldest living enemy I venture to offer you this little pamphlet [a deluxe edition in two volumes]. Don't mind if it emits a destructive gas. Us humans — you know." It was different with the young Scott Fitzgerald. In a copy of the novel that first won him attention, *This Side of Paradise* (1920), he confessed, "As a matter of fact, Mr. Mencken, I stuck your name in on Page 224 in the last proof — partly, I suppose, as a vague bootlick and partly because I have since adopted a great many of your views." In *Tales of the Jazz Age* (1922) Fitzgerald has written "To the notorious H. L. Mencken under whose apostolic blessing five of these things first saw the light," as the tales had, in the *Smart Set.* In 1925 *The Great Gatsby* came out. "Dear Menk," Fitzgerald wrote, "Your letter was the first outside word that reached me about my book. I was tremendously moved — both by the fact that you liked it and by your kindness in writing me about it . . . as you know I'd rather have you like a book of mine than anyone in America."

Not far from the Fitzgerald volumes on the shelf, all esteemed today, is a forgotten curiosity, Alexander Harvey's *The Toe and Other Tales,* published in 1913 but sent to Mencken ten years later with "To America's greatest man of letters H. L. Mencken from a scribbler." Below Harvey's book is a long row of volumes, the work of a writer once supreme in his field and now nearly as much ignored as Harvey. This is Hergesheimer; he and Mencken were friends for forty years. There are letters tipped into many of the volumes. Their tenor is always that of equals, but the evidence is plain that Hergesheimer leaned on Mencken, sometimes more, sometimes less, throughout his career. A letter tipped in *Quiet Cities* (1928), dated December 21, 1921, is typical of the many others. Hergesheimer asks Mencken to give him advice on how to write up a western trip that the *Saturday Evening Post* was about to send him on. "Can you come to the Dower House to go into this with me? . . . My dear Harry, I am very serious about this — an extremely independent person, I still find in your equal independence something vastly encouraging, illuminating, and stirring."

James Huneker, like Hergesheimer one of the lost figures of American literature, sent Mencken *Painted Veils* (1920) with the inscription, "To my old friend, the Attila of American criticism, and the salt of the earth generally." Among the K's is Bernice Lesbia Kenyon, who sang *Songs of Unrest* (1923). She writes warmly, "To Henry Louis Mencken   Of whom the author will remember always (1) The contrast of two evenings in his company; (2) His kindness to young poets whom he thinks old (even ancient); (3) His risky promises in the presence of witnesses; (4) The best typewritten one-line notes of the century; and (5) his elated playing of the bass of the 'New World Symphony' arranged for piano four hands!"

The opposite of Miss Kenyon's overflowing admiration is found in Ring Lardner's astringent response to Mencken's help. He had encouraged Lardner at a time when other critics dismissed him as an amusing sports writer. When sending him his books Lardner customarily pasted in a Menckenian greeting, perhaps only a clipping or an allusive jest, such as for *The Love Nest and Other Stories* (1926): "Yours in the Informal Brotherhood of Parker Duofold Owners the World Over."

Sinclair Lewis fills up a shelf. His inscriptions and tipped-in letters show how correct Paul de Kruif was in saying that Lewis, like him, was writing for Mencken. There is, for instance, the letter tipped into *Babbitt* (1922), "Dear Mencken: You ask about the new novel. . . . It's curiously associated with yourself. A year ago in a criticism of Main Street you said that what ought to be taken up now is the American city — not NY or Chi but the cities of 200,000 to 500,000 — the Baltimores and Omahas and Buffaloes and Birminghams etc. I was startled to read it, because that was precisely what I WAS then planning, and am now doing. But your piece helped me to decide on this particular one as against one or two others which, at the time, I also wanted to do. I think you'll like it — I hope to Christ you do." Then there is the letter tipped into the German translation of *Main Street, Die Hauptstrasse* (also 1922) "Dear Menck," it reads, "Phil Goodman tells me you are going to review Arrowsmith. . . . I am very glad. Naturally, I'm more interested in your review than in that of anyone else — particularly with this book."

Elmer Gantry (1927) was dedicated to Mencken, "with *profound admiration*." Tipped into the Enoch Pratt copy is a letter from Lewis saying, "Dear Menck: I've seen the advance proofs of your review of Elmer. It is of course the finest thing that has happened to me about the book." The letter tipped into *Dodsworth* (1929) says in part, "I have seen your two reviews. A thousand gratitudes & admirations." So it went. Mencken disliked Lewis's drunken rages and disorganization; Lewis disliked Mencken's habit of dominating the conversations he himself itched to dominate. But if these samples from Lewis's letters show anything, it is that he had more respect and affection for Mencken than for any other critic. And he was far from alone.

Another evidence of that fact can be found in the letter from Vachel Lindsay tipped into his *Collected Poems* (1925). Dated May 27, 1924 it is about the proof corrections to his poem for the *Mercury*, "The Trial of the Dead Cleopatra." He writes, "If you take this second proof at all seriously, I will be very glad if you return it to me when you are through, with marginal notes on clarity, etc. I will take *every suggestion*." Mencken's friend Anita Loos, whose comic novel *Gentlemen Prefer Blondes* (1925) was written with Mencken in mind and became a best seller, inscribed a copy for him and apologized amiably for mentioning him in it. Nearby *Gentlemen Prefer Blondes* is an influential book by a noted Harvard critic John Livingston Lowes, *Convention and Revolt in Poetry*, first published in 1919, with a letter of September 6, 1923 tipped in. It was prompted by a bid from Mencken to contribute to the new *American Mercury*. "I'm proud to be asked," Lowes responded, "and I'll gladly send you something. . . . Might I take this opportunity to tell you that your review of *Convention and Revolt* gave me quite shameless pleasure."

The jazz-age novelist Percy Marks won wide if short-lived attention. Inside the cover of his novel about hectic life on a college campus, *The Plastic Age* (1925), he has written "To H. L. Mencken as an expression of my gratitude for his interest in me, and especially for his great kindness in reading the manuscript of this book." There are also the extensive works of George Jean Nathan, almost always with airy inscriptions, though every now and then a touch of the more personal appears. For example, in the *House of Satan*, published in 1926, after a clash with Mencken over how the *Mercury* should be run, Nathan has written "Menck — with the old regards — George."

Zelda Marsh (1927) by Charles Norris, who specialized in writing novels about social problems and was the younger brother of Frank Norris, has an inscription "To Henry L Mencken from his friend, Charles G. Norris" as well as a tipped-in letter saying "Dear Hank:. . . I only arrived in town yesterday — and you're the first person I'm writing to."

Three of Eugene O'Neill's early plays were printed in the *Smart Set* and there is no doubt that he owed more, there and elsewhere, to Nathan than to Mencken. Yet O'Neill has written in a copy of *The Moon of the Caribees and Six Other Plays of the Sea* (1923), "To H. L. Mencken — From whose first letter — and *the* first letter of genuine critical appreciation I ever received — I am proud to quote the following: 'You have done something new and done it well'. Which, if I knew anything of Gaelic, I'd print motto-wise on the red (pen) hand of this O'Neill's crest."

Critics have said a good deal about Mencken's indifference to experimental poetry. Most of what they charge is true, and yet there is a copy of *Umbra* (1920) sent by Ezra Pound from London with the inscription, "Blessings on Henry. Ezra. Drink of Helicon all other bars are closed."

More typical of Mencken's interest is a book by Henry F. Pringle, *Big Frogs* (1928). Within the cover of this collection of sketches of controversial figures of the time, its author has written simply "To H. L. Mencken, who bought my first piece." Not far away on the shelf there is a copy of *Little Henrietta* (1927), a story in verse by Lizette Woodworth Reese. It is inscribed "To Henry L. Mencken from his friend Lizette Woodworth Reese." In a collection of her short stories *Ideals* (1927), the novelist Evelyn Scott has written, "To H. L. Mencken Though no critic's approval has given me more courage than his, this book is sent with no implied stipulations. If he doesn't like it, I expect him to ignore it or 'roast' it. And I will continue to wish there were more in America with his implacable directness."

Upton Sinclair resembled Theodore Dreiser in the blustery ambivalence of his relationship with Mencken. Mencken found him both sanctimonious and socialistic; no combination ever irritated Mencken more. But he respected his best writing and Upton Sinclair recognized the fact. A born evangelist, he wanted to convert Mencken and so sent him *The Book of Life* (1921), which is filled with friendly counsel on solving the problems of mind and body, inscribed "To H. L.

Mencken with the author's appreciation." He also gave him *They Call Me Carpenter* (1922), "A Tale of the Second Coming" inscribed "To H L Mencken with moral urges."

The critic J. E. Spingarn sent a copy of his *Poems* (1924) with an inscription "To H. L. Mencken from his friend." And there is a tipped-in letter of July 3, 1918 with this tribute from Spingarn, "What you have to say about criticism always interests me." The San Francisco poet George Sterling mailed Mencken a copy of his dramatic poem *Lilith* (1919) and wrote, "My dear Mencken, Meet my best girl, Lilith. I hope you'll like her." James Stevens was an American who wrote about American folklore and the Northwest. In his *Brawnyman* (1926) he has written, "For H. L. Mencken   Inscribed as some mark of a younger writer's admiration and respect." Tipped into his *Homer in the Sagebrush* (1928), a book of western stories, is a letter of July 1, 1924 which says, "Dear Mr. Mencken: — I think I'd seem very ungrateful if I objected to any wish of yours concerning the Paul Bunyan stories. I feel that I am writing them for you."

One of Mencken's more important discoveries was an Iowa woman, Ruth Suckow. She composed both novels and short stories and became a prominent regional writer. Her relationship to Mencken can be summed up in a sentence that sounds routine but is not, from a letter of June 13, 1925 tipped into her novel *Cora* (1929): "Dear Mr. Mencken: Thanks very much for your advice about the stories." Sara Teasdale was a poet Mencken liked and she liked him. She had earlier expressed her appreciation for his interest; now in a book of lyrics *Flame and Shadow* (1920) she inscribed her greetings. Beyond Sara Teasdale's slim volume we can see the grim stories of the hobo writer Jim Tully. In *Circus Parade* (1927) he has written "To H. L. Mencken with high appreciation to one who made the book possible." Beyond Tully stand the works of that engaging ex-jewelry salesman, Louis Untermeyer. Mencken and he relished one another's wit, and the inscriptions show it. *Including Horace* (1919) is a book of verse parodies and translations from Horace. Untermeyer dedicated it "To H. L. Mencken more in sorrow than in anger" and inscribed it "for H. L. Mencken, in spite of — everything!" His book of humorous essays *Heavens* (1922) bears the inscription "for H. L. M. . . .with renewed assurance of — yes — respect."

Out of Greenwich Village and from Carl Van Vechten came several books to add to Mencken's library. Among them was the most notable of Van Vechten's novels, *Nigger Heaven* (1926), which is inscribed "for Henry Mencken with reverence & reverences." From John V. A. Weaver, who tried to write his lyrics in the American language, came *In American — Poems* (1921), with its simple inscription "To H. L. Mencken. Very sincerely" and *To Youth* (1928), with its pungent "To H. L. Mencken from his literary bastard." From another, much different poet, the New York imagist John Hall Wheelock, came a copy of *The Bright Doom* (1927) inscribed "for H. L. Mencken with the sincere good wishes of the author." Finally from the short-story writer Thyra Samter Winslow there is the tribute, written into *People Round the Corner* (1927), "For H. L. Mencken. Again a Father with my love."

With her, for our purposes, the alphabet ends. We have been looking at the decade from, to be exact, 1919 to 1929. There are some other inscriptions during the decade that we have not noted, and there are a good many from other decades. They come not only from American writers but from foreign ones, especially British. There are tributes during the twenties from such varied British authors as the scandalmonger Frank Harris, the famous novelist and satirist Aldous Huxley, the lyricist Thomas Moult, the scientist-journalist George Ryley Scott, and the popular novelist Hugh Walpole. There are also some significant omissions, writers Mencken did not like or who did not like him. Yet the coverage is remarkably wide; the shelves are crowded. As Burton Rascoe saw it, Mencken "early established a sort of personal relationship with every promising writer in the country. . . . I have yet to meet a man under thirty-five with articulate ideas who has not a sheaf of those lively, hearty notes whereby Mencken conveys a maximum of good cheer and boisterous comment within a minimum of space." Without a doubt his influence on writing during the 1920s was more marked than anyone else's.

Though during the 1920s Mencken became a national figure — a molder of American attitudes, a shaper of the national taste and temper, a major force in American letters — he also remained a local figure. The fact of World War I had separated him from much of Baltimore and from the *Sunpapers*; nevertheless, he was always both a Baltimorean and a newspaperman. He himself knew it very well.

10. Mainstay of the SUN

BY THE TIME the 1920s opened, Baltimore was once again not only habitable but congenial. Some feeling against the Germans survived, but the main target both for the federal government and for the local patriots was now the "Reds" instead of the pro-Germans. Within the *Sun* office a large majority of the staff members felt that since the war in Europe was over, it should be over in the office too. Mencken had kept in touch with Harry Black, who had served as a paymaster for the Navy, and had often visited with Paul Patterson. Now that the *Sunpapers* were returned to a peacetime basis it was clear that interesting things were going to happen. It soon developed that the *Sun* wanted Mencken back and that Mencken wanted to be back, but there were feelings to be soothed on both sides and proprieties to be observed. The result was a stately minuet which lasted for some months. To Ernest Boyd he wrote on November 9, 1919 that the *Sun* wished him to do some articles but that he would not agree unless he received high pay and the right to publish on any topic.

Two days later Paul Patterson was chosen president of the *Sunpapers* and Mencken's most powerful friend assumed control. Believing that the *Sunpapers* could benefit enormously from Mencken's tart counsel, he invited him to return not only as a writer but as an adviser. Mencken himself would determine how much time he would put in and he would have complete freedom of expression. He liked the shape of the job though the salary offered him of two hundred and fifty dollars a month was not overwhelming. But that was because the job was to be part time, in theory anyway. Furthermore, he no longer needed money: the sale of *Saucy Stories* was in the process of yielding him almost ten thousand dollars. So he started in February 1920, armed with his Uncle Willies and ready for action.

The dwindling opposition to him inside the office was led by dour John Haslup Adams. The enthusiasts for England and the adherents of Wilson subsided one by one. In early March Mencken reported to Boyd that the Wilson party was now confined to Adams alone and he was wavering.

During the first months of the new year arrangements were developed so that Mencken could do his *Sunpapers* writing and advising without infringing on his other work. Patterson relied on him from the outset. National politics were beginning to boil and Patterson urged him to go to the Republican convention in Chicago and the Democratic convention in San Francisco, along with Adams and several other *Sun* staff members. Mencken said yes and went on with his business as usual. But on May 28, shortly before the Chicago convention, he published a piece, "The Armenian Buncombe," in which he remarked that Woodrow Wilson was incapable of telling the truth. Adams became furious. He and another *Sun* man, John Owens, told Patterson that either Mencken stayed home from the convention or they would. Years later Mencken told his biographer Manchester that the two men had threatened to resign if Mencken went along but that he had brought a jug on the train and by the time the *Sun* group reached Chicago the alcohol had dissolved all hard feelings.

Yet some rancor remained. After the Republican convention in Chicago, Mencken told Boyd that because of office strife he was through with the *Sun* as soon as the Democratic convention in San Francisco ended. In October, months after both conventions, Patterson wrote Mencken that Adams still resented his calling Wilson a liar. Mencken by now had completely forgotten about the "Armenian Buncombe" piece, but he looked back in the files and there it was. He assured Patterson that though the statement was true he saw how Adams could be upset by it. However, the *Sun* was beginning to boom, and Mencken found writing for it and advising its managers so stimulating that he worked out a truce with Adams.

Mencken was now at the height of his energies. His vitality was so great that even his outside life as writer and magazine editor could not absorb a half of it. The *Sunpapers* received an abundance, far more than they paid for. He infused a new zest not only in the newer staff members but even in some of the veterans who needed it most. The effect was like lighting a string of firecrackers under the *Sun* swivel chairs.

He paid particular attention to the *Evening Sun.* It soon became a far brighter paper than before. He took an immediate liking to Hamilton Owens, who was named its managing editor early in 1922. Eight years younger than Mencken and with somewhat less newspaper experience, Owens valued his help, the more so since it was never heavy-handed. Mencken would drop into his office nearly every afternoon, talking wittily or explosively about newspaper matters of all sizes. His advice was all the better because it came in small doses. Much of it concerned the artful management of trifles; some of it concerned matters of major policy; and some of it concerned man's view of the world. From the first month Owens accepted many of Mencken's minor suggestions; it was not long before he adopted some of the major ones. And it did not take years before he saw life as a whole in a Menckenian way. During World War I Owens had worked readily enough for the Creel Committee on American propaganda and after the war for an American bank in England. But now he began to see the war and England more nearly as Mencken did. He showed it in both his editing and writing.

Mencken's influence on the *Evening Sun*'s editorial page in particular was electric. With his Monday Articles as the high spot the page, as Owens noted, gained "a reputation for being, at worst, smart-alecky and, at best, witty and pungent." Much of the credit he gave to Mencken.

Mencken's effectiveness was increased by the fact that he never grew irritated when Owens turned down a suggestion. He made it plain that he realized that the ultimate responsibility belonged to Owens, who would have to suffer if any suggestion boomeranged. And he was never irritated when Owens altered a sentence or corrected a statement in his pieces for the paper.

Besides offering suggestions when they met, Mencken sent Owens a small but steady stream of notes or letters. On September 3, 1924, for instance, when he stayed home because of surgery on his foot, he wrote Owens a five-point letter of proposals which included printing a daily photograph of Calvin Coolidge because he looked like an idiot. On May 5, 1925 he tipped off Owens to some good material on "Civilization in Georgia." On September 12, 1928 he suggested that a forthcoming Monday Article could be the germ of the kind of controversy that livens any editorial page and furnished a list of twenty-one Southerners, mainly ministers, whom it might set off. On December 15 of the same year he wrote that one of his own articles, "Fruits of Folly," was feeble stuff and Owens should kill it. On July 28, 1931 he suggested that the *Evening Sun* send a reporter to look into the so-called Scottsboro Case, in which a group of Negroes had been sentenced to death in Alabama for allegedly raping two white girls. He appeared tireless.

Hamilton Owens was open and lively by nature, and his response, as he mastered his new job, to Mencken's breezy counsel was enthusiastic. It was hard for Paul Patterson, the sober senior executive, to be enthusiastic about anything; and yet he too steadily solicited Mencken's advice, both for the betterment of the *Sunpapers* and for his own enlightenment.

Did Patterson need a music critic — this was as early as 1920 — to take the place of one who was ailing? He asked Mencken what he thought about the occasional critiques being done by a member of the staff named Strehlau. It turned out that Mencken liked his work and a little later Patterson, who had been put off by Strehlau's lush adjectives and frequent clichés, asked Mencken to have a talk with him to improve his style. Did Patterson need advice on how to improve the editorials in the *Sun?* He turned to Mencken, mailing him a batch but not telling who had written them, because he wanted an objective opinion. And so on. Mencken for his part not only spoke each day with Patterson in his office but sent him too a stream of communications ranging from notes of two lines to memorandums pages long.

On more personal matters Patterson also asked for Mencken's views. Here, for example, is Patterson appealing to him, again in 1920, after listening to Herbert Hoover, "I heard Hoover make his speech and I thought he talked sense. Am I getting obsessed also? Can't you take time to write me a serious analysis of his speech? I like the man, but I do want to keep a clear head in my judgment of him."

As a rule, far from being carried away by Hoover or anyone else, Patterson was a person of solid convictions. But he had the wit to see in Mencken an associate whose decided, stimulating views provided an ideal complement to his own judicious conservatism. He always listened even though he did not always agree with Mencken or adopt his advice. He wrote to Harry Black, for instance, on March 29, 1922, that he did not believe Mencken was right about a certain matter — Mencken wanted to run a "son-of-a-bitch" editorial calling for a Third Party and blasting the Democratic and Republican Parties because they had grown so gross. Patterson said characteristically, "My feeling is the *Sun* should prepare to go into this whole proposition in a quiet, unassuming, but very thorough, way." Yet he trusted Mencken enough so that he frequently laid aside his caution and did what Mencken suggested.

In the *Sunpapers* during the 1920s a determined struggle for Patterson's mind took place. As a matter of fact, the whole question of the posture of the *Sun* was involved. Shortly after Patterson's election as president he, Harry Black, and Mencken had threshed out a new policy for the *Sunpapers*. As a basis Black had prepared a twenty-three page editorial memorandum which analyzed the papers and proposed improvements. From 1920, when it was prepared, it became known in the *Sun* offices as the "White Paper." But the contests over policy and posture were continuing ones. Patterson's own attitude was by no means rigid.

That Mencken's vivid personality appealed to him was obvious to everyone in the office. However, there were several members of the *Sun* staff who tried consistently to capitalize on Patterson's instinct for moderation. Their leader was John Owens, a distant relation of Hamilton Owens, who was first a political reporter for the *Sun* and then its editor after the death of John Haslup Adams in 1927. John Owens still had reservations about Mencken and they concerned not only Mencken's ideas but also his general attitude toward journalism. After John Owens had been editor long enough to give the paper his personal imprint, Patterson asked Mencken to do a critique of the paper. It was characteristic of Patterson to set up the reaction of opposites.

What did Mencken think of the *Sun* now? His answer took seven pages and gave an eloquent exposition of his idea of the job a newspaper should do. He found the *Sun* generally improved but still feeble especially in its editorials and features. The editorials he accused of being too temperate. Some were noticeably damaged by their self-restraint. "The *Sun* is not a court of justice," he observed. "It is an open and avowed advocate of the Opposition." The *Sun* should be a paper with manifest convictions and the courage of those convictions. It should denounce, expose. It should arouse the emotions of its readers. One of its chief purposes should be to stir up "useful hatreds."

Mencken went on to argue that most men were moved not by appeals to their reason but to their emotions and prejudices. Such appeals were not necessarily low, since it was just as creditable to hate injustice and dishonesty as it was to love the truth.

He ended his memorandum with a vision of the opportunities now spread before the *Sun*. It was rich; it was well staffed; it was respected; it was politically independent. Its only serious competitors were the New York *World* and the St. Louis *Post-Dispatch*. The country lay before it for the taking.

John Owens's answer, equally long and cogent, went promptly to Patterson. In its way it made as persuasive a case as Mencken's memorandum. Its keynote, inevitably, was judiciousness. It conceded a good many minor points. But it flatly disputed Mencken's major assumptions. Mencken assumed that what the *Sun* needed was gusto. John Owens asserted that it was a drug on the market and that there was a place instead for "a few cool, unaffected voices." Both men wished for vigor in the *Sun*, but Owens said that he wanted a vigor based on a mastery of the facts while Mencken wanted one based on pure partisanship. Owens was convinced, moreover, that his own kind of vigor would prove far more profitable to the *Sun*. For Mencken was always making the mistake of underestimating the intelligence of the public. The clearest proof lay in the fact that for eighteen years he had appealed, with scintillating journalism, to the public's emotions; and the public, Owens alleged, had rejected his persuasions every time.

Owens too rose to the occasion as he proceeded with his brief. He fastened on the doctrine of public responsibility. The very fact of the *Sun's* monopoly in the morning field meant that it was read by all conditions of people and had to be more moderate than if it were one of a number of competitors. It had to be broad rather than narrow, factual rather than polemical. The vigor it needed could best be furnished through information. Such was John Owens's case. He concluded it with a dry "God bless us every one."

The judges in the Great Debate were Paul Patterson and Harry

Black. In a memorandum to Patterson, Harry Black summed up the decision: it was a draw; it was a difference about manner rather than matter. What Mencken wanted was that "our wares should be displayed loudly and with brighter lights" while John Owens wanted "the shop window not to have too gaudy colours in it."

This was management's attempt to domesticate the difference of opinion; the difference remained. However, both before and after the Great Debate the *Sun's* basic position was close to Mencken's and only the earth-shaking advent of World War II would alter it.

The *Sun's* stance for most of Mencken's time was that of the nineteenth-century liberal; it favored a maximum of freedom and a minimum of government. Even after the Depression had begun to strike its hammer blows, the *Sun* altered its position slowly, grudgingly. Patterson, Black, and the other managers were willing to grant that Owens had an important point when it came to moderation of manner. But matter — and that meant editorial interpretation of the news — was something else. More and more, as the changes brought on by the Depression and then by the New Deal assaulted them, they inclined politically toward the past — and that meant toward Mencken. In 1934 he was elected to the board of directors of the *Sunpapers* and the board, under the chairmanship of Harry Black, received him warmly.

In the presidential election of 1936 the *Sunpapers* remained officially neutral, but thereafter their editorials on Roosevelt and all his works became more and more Menckenian. Again Patterson listened to the liberals on the *Sun* but again he asked for a summary statement from Mencken. Mencken, baking the bacteria out of himself at Daytona Beach, answered with another notable memorandum. Dated January 1937, about a decade after the one just discussed, it was darkened by a suspicion not only of all governments, beginning with the American, but also of some members of the *Sun* staff.

He asserted that it should be the fixed policy of the *Sunpapers* to look at every news report warily. The New Deal propaganda coming from Washington had reached a high degree of effectiveness. Even reports from congressional committees had to be suspected. He assured Patterson that all those committees now functioning were on the lookout for ammunition against capitalism. The *Sun's* policy should be against the Roosevelt administration at all times; every public official should be considered guilty until proved innocent. The fact, for instance, that Henry Wallace, Roosevelt's Secretary of Agriculture, had failed at his own business should be kept before the public mind.

The scrutiny of the news must be the more intense because there was treason in the castle at the *Sun*. Some of the very writers for the *Sunpapers* were now revolutionaries. "We should be watchful," Mencken cautioned, "of radical propaganda by our own men."

The proper platform for the *Sun* was old-fashioned liberalism, the only one for a decent newspaper. In his final paragraph Mencken summed up the liberal ideals that the *Sun* should battle for: limited government, economy in public services, complete publicity on every public matter, free speech, and freedom of the press. He warned that if radicalism, whether of the extreme Left or the extreme Right, won out over liberalism the job of a newspaper would be gone and so would man's liberties.

Patterson listened soberly and sympathetically. On domestic affairs the *Sunpapers* management stayed with Mencken till the end of the decade, and after. Its subconscious, if a newspaper management can have one, remained Menckenian in this respect.

One of Mencken's assets for the *Sun* was the fact that he could move more easily than anyone else among both the managers and the reporters. He had proved his preference, as early as 1906, for writing over editing. He was admired by most of the reporters on the *Sunpapers* and by most of the editors, and he gave in return a warm if gruff affection. And yet when the yeasty days of the New Deal arrived and reporters began to think of themselves as labor and of the editors as the bosses, he was dismayed. When the Newspaper Guild started in 1933 its organizers tried, naturally, to enlist him as the exemplar of the fearless newspaperman. Though Mencken was touched he somehow could not bring himself to join. The bosses were also his friends. Nor did he change his mind later. He wrote the playwright Sidney Howard, in April 1936, in response to an appeal to support a newspaper strike in the Midwest, that he heartily favored the original aims of the Guild. However, it had degenerated into a sounding board for agitators and seemed to be carrying on something like a Red Crusade. As a result he felt that he had to say no.

Mencken always took an important part in the daily and weekly editorial conferences, from 1920 on. As the years passed he gravitated inevitably toward management. Early in 1938 he went so far as to become an editor again. It was a brief if unforgettable experience, starting on February 8 and ending May 7. At the beginning of the year Hamilton Owens had left the editorship of the *Evening Sun* to become the editor of the morning paper. Owens wanted to promote his right-hand man, Philip Wagner, to the vacant post but Mencken argued against it because he felt that Wagner was not quite ready. Mencken himself grandly offered to take over the job. He stipulated that it would not be for more than three months, which would be long enough for him to gauge the capacities of the *Evening Sun* staff and see if Wagner was the proper man. Owens was surprised at the offer. However, it was probable that Mencken wanted once more to try his hand at running a paper. He also itched to implement his own political ideas and the convictions contained in his memorandum of January 1937. The *Evening Sun* had grown somewhat radical for his tastes and this he wished to correct.

As Hamilton Owens later put it, Mencken assumed command in his usual vigorous if not violent manner. He took to wearing a Princeton beer jacket when at ten each morning he descended to the composing room to make up the editorial page. He brought in a brass spittoon, not only for his cigar stubs but for his chewing tobacco. Breathing hard he tried to recapture the past.

It was the return of one-man journalism. With noisy industry the interim editor parceled out assignments, wrote his editorials, rewrote the editorials of others, and tinkered whenever he could — while his glasses slid on his nose — with the news stories and features to give them the Mencken touch. And stunts of all sorts appeared.

The most notable was one of the new editor's first. On February 10 nearly all of the editorial page of the paper was a mass of dots, more than a million of them. Mencken explained in an editorial note that each represented a federal officeholder. He told his readers that the page was too big to paste in their hat but they might hang it on the wall between the picture of Franklin Roosevelt and their copy of "The American's Creed."

What Mencken was after, in general, was more gusto; plainly he had not forgotten his criticism of the *Sunpapers* of a decade ago for lacking it. However, the human expense of trying to get it became considerable. This was the more true because the gusto Mencken craved was a gusto for conservatism. The *Sun* staffers, conservative, liberal, or radical, were men of self-respect. They were not used to

being dominated, even by Mencken, and the air grew full of argument — or as one embattled reporter, Robin Harriss, put it, "full
of zowie." The arch-liberal on the staff was Gerald Johnson, whose
political writing was so highly regarded that Mencken could not bring
himself to blue-pencil it. Instead he asked Johnson to read up on one
topic after another in order to do editorials on them. But by the time
Johnson was ready to compose an editorial on one subject Mencken
was telling him to read up on another. He published less during this
period than at any other time when he worked for the *Sun*.

As the end of his appointed term approached, Mencken could
hardly wait. "I have two more weeks of servitude," he wrote to his
personal secretary, Mrs. Rosalind Lohrfinck, "and then go on parole.
The three months seem like years."

When the three months ended he announced that the only man
to edit the *Evening Sun* was Phil Wagner. Then he collapsed into the
waiting arms of the Hopkins hospital staff. Everybody was relieved,
especially Mencken.

Thereafter he spent less time on the general affairs of the *Sunpapers*. After he left the hospital he continued for another year to
join in the daily and weekly editorial conferences, but by late 1939 he
found himself facing a determined majority who disagreed with him
on international politics if not national ones. By the beginning of 1941
he confined his policy advising to the meetings of the board of
directors of the *Sunpapers*.

Whatever his views, this withdrawal was the *Sunpapers'* loss rather
than his. For, more than anyone else, Mencken had made the *Sunpapers*
an American institution. This is not to deny that he had colleagues there
of eminence, especially the political writers Frank Kent and Gerald Johnson. But Mencken personified the *Sun* to much of America and rightly
so, since he played a unique and diversified — and in fact paradoxical — role in its destinies.

In the 1930s he was, among other things, both the *Sun's* most
controversial staff member and its unofficial ambassador. Much of the
controversy, though by no means all of it, occurred when he acted as
the *Sun's* conscience. Two classic cases came in 1931 and 1933 when
he flayed the Eastern Shore of Maryland for its lynch mobs. Each
time a Negro had been taken from jail and killed. Cut off from the
rest of the world by Chesapeake Bay and the Atlantic, the Eastern
Shore preserved the mores of an older, bloodier age. When Mencken

published Monday Articles on such subjects as "The Eastern Shore Kultur" (it included lynching), the Eastern Shore farmers and fishermen boycotted the *Sun*, bullied its delivery men, and invaded Baltimore with signs on their Fords or Chevies saying they were proud to be from the Shore. Though the *Sun* let Mencken write unhindered, it squirmed under the boycott and did its best to soothe the Shoremen.

Notwithstanding, the *Sunpapers* from time to time clearly benefited from his great reputation for integrity and indeed from his personal charm. When the *Sun* needed an AP franchise he acted as the principal go-between in the delicate negotiations. When the *Sun*, and in this case explicitly the *Sun* management, needed to make a livable contract with the emerging Newspaper Guild, he helped to develop one suitable to both sides.

He was at his best as a diplomat in one of the *Sun*'s most embarrassing imbroglios. It involved Hitler, Ignatius Loyola, Roman Catholic Baltimore, and the freedom of the press. It took place in the summer of 1934.

One of the *Sun*'s senior foreign correspondents, S. Miles Bouton, had written an article from Germany which ran in the *Sun* of June 18. Toward the end of it he unfortunately compared Hitler to Loyola, the founder of the Jesuit order. The Archbishop of Baltimore at the time was Michael Joseph Curley, a big-jawed Irishman noted for his firmness on behalf of the faith. The reference was brought to his attention and he promptly called for a Holy War against the *Sunpapers*. He preached from his pulpit at the Cathedral, ordering a boycott of the *Sun* until it apologized for its slight to the sainted founder of the Jesuits. Then he left on a sea voyage to Ireland to visit his aged mother. The parish priests and subordinate members of the hierarchy carried on where the Archbishop had left off. Though some showed a measure of restraint a considerable number outdid the Archbishop in their denunciations. One or two compared the *Sun* unfavorably to antichrist.

The *Catholic Review*, the official organ of the archdiocese, carried several sulphurous articles and editorials about the matter, as well as two letters from the Archbishop on the *Sun*'s iniquities. On July 6, for example, it called the *Sun* both a liar and a coward.

The *Sunpapers* were exquisitely uncomfortable. The boycott hurt and so did the publicity. The temptation to apologize with dispatch was substantial. On the other hand, there was the *Sun*'s widely admired advocacy of free speech, both in its pages and outside. Should it repudiate its respected correspondent Bouton and so draw on itself the jeers of the liberal or radical press? As some of the agitated editors of the *Sun* staff pointed out, Bouton had made a very limited comparison and it was arguable that within its limitations his comparison was correct.

The controversy blazed for nearly a month, with, apparently, no one doing anything constructive to end it. Except Mencken. Infidel though he was, he enjoyed the confidence of some of the most influential members of the Catholic hierarchy. Even if he had been critical at times of the Church of Rome, he had never blasted it in print as he had the principal Protestant denominations. Personally he found the dignity of the Catholic ritual attractive, and he saw little sign of the sweaty evangelism that repelled him in the Bible-thumping Protestant churches of the South. With a good deal in his favor, he approached one or two key members of the hierarchy. Though the exact nature of the negotiations was not disclosed their results soon emerged. The *Sun* made something like an apology; the archdiocese dropped its boycott. Baltimore simmered down. Mencken had put in long hours but he merely noted in letters to friends that he had been busy extricating the *Sun* from a bit of trouble.

Gadfly, counsel, and minister though he was to the *Sun*, he made his amplest contribution by his newspaper writing. There is little doubt that throughout the 1920s and into the 1930s he was accepted as the leading newspaperman in the nation. He never did straight reporting; as always whatever he touched had the imprint of his personal style and general attitude. But he was thorough in his inquiries and willing to perform the labor that often was needed for even a brief feature. His specialty was not the single article, however, so much as the series, and particularly the weekly column.

The great standard series he developed in the decade was made up of the Monday Articles for the *Evening Sun*. They were, ordinarily, short essays suggested by some news event. Sometimes they were literary notes or reflections on the curiosa of American culture. The first, which appeared on February 9, 1920, concerned the politicians who yearned that year for the presidency of the United States. It may be recalled that it was "A Carnival of Buncombe." The second was a "Literary Note" on Lizette Woodworth Reese. From then on, week by week, the articles brightened the editorial page with their man-ifold reflections. The richness can only be suggested. In 1921 the *Evening Sun's* subscribers could read about "The Asses' Carnival" (the House of Representatives), the art of swearing, the rhetoric of War-ren Harding, "A Great Moral Sport" (capital punishment), "The Ku Klux Buffoonery," "Doctor Evangelicus" (on Mencken's least favorite physician, Howard Kelly) and "The Blue-Nose Utopia" (Prohibition). In 1922 there were among other articles "A Boon to Bores" (the telephone), "Art and the Mob," "Streets and Their Names," "Notes for an Honest Autobiography," "For Better, for Worse" (on marriage), and "Confederate Notes" (on Southern literature).

The rest of the 1920s rolled along merrily, until the autumn of the last year of the decade. Before that the Monday Articles were like a riverboat panorama, full of gaudy scenes and outlandish creatures. Through the Articles stumbled, strolled, or cavorted such figures as Josephus Daniels, whom Mencken touted as "one of the hollowest and dumbest of Southern politicians"; Cal Coolidge's ghost writer with his leaden "clomp of phrase"; the lovelorn murderer Judd Gray with his lethal sashweight; and, for gentle relief, Franz Schubert in the Danu-bian countryside. The settings included Sloppy Joe's in Havana; the Union Station in Baltimore ("When it is crowded [travelers] are uncomfortable, and when it is empty they are apt to laugh"); Boston (where the "Brahmins . . . lock themselves in their lovely houses, and let the mob roar by"); Bethlehem in Pennsylvania ("The plain and tragic fact is that the beer in Bethlehem is now bad — nay, hope-less"); and the Maryland Penitentiary. The opinions expressed were so typically provocative that one sample should do, on the proverbially carefree schoolboy: "the notion that schoolboys are content with their lot seems to me to be a sad delusion. They are, in the main, able to bear it, but they like it no more than a soldier enjoys trench life. The need to endure it makes actors of them; they learn how to lie — perhaps the most valuable thing, to a citizen of Christendom, that they learn in school. No boy genuinely loves and admires his teacher; the far-thest he can go, assuming him to have all his wits, is to tolerate her as he tolerates castor oil. She may be the loveliest flower in the whole pedagogical garden, but the most he can ever see in her is a jailer who might conceivably be worse."

Throughout the decade few readers of the Monday Articles found them dull. But then came the weakening of the stock market and, near the end of October 1929, the stock market crash. Utterly unprepared, Wall Street experienced a panic. It spread over the country. The bull market was dead; Harding-Coolidge-Hoover prosperity was giving a few final gasps; and the American economy lost billions of dollars and nearly all its self-confidence. Yet Mencken was slow to react. On October 28 his subject was "More Law Enforcement," on November 4 "Hot Dogs," on November 11 "The Origin and Nature of Law," on November 18 "Leaves from a Notebook" (including a few reflections on the stage comedian), and on November 25 "The Charity Racket." December saw three more articles, equally untimely, including one on the Christian Scientists.

Mencken wrote on German beer in the opening article for 1930. Prohibition and liquor remained his most popular topic throughout the year. It was only bit by bit that the Depression entered his writing. In March 1931 he wrote on the proposed veterans' bonus and then, tardily, on hard times, and during the rest of the year he paid more attention to the Depression. In September he acknowledged "The End of an Era." Yet the polemics against Prohibition still prevailed.

The year 1932 saw the beginning of a recognizable if superficial shift of emphasis. Once the national political conventions adjourned and the campaigns ended, with Franklin Roosevelt an enormous winner over the incumbent Hoover, Mencken gave more and more attention to Roosevelt and his attempts at renovating the nation. The trouble was that all the New Deal programs of economic and social reform seemed to Mencken ruddy nonsense. They ran counter to his basic, long-held beliefs in individual liberty and individual responsibility. They denied the doctrine preached, to Mencken's mind and heart, not only by Darwin, Huxley, and William Graham Sumner, but by Benjamin Franklin and Horatio Alger. Increasingly outraged, Mencken used more of the Monday Articles to ridicule the new notions or uphold the old. Roosevelt was king, the New Dealers were wizards and quacks, the federal government was spending us into anarchy. By 1937 the chief topic for the Monday Articles was the iniquities of the President and the New Deal. In January of the next year he issued his final group of Monday pieces; they predicted doom here and overseas. He no longer saw America as such a circus, nor the world either for that matter. His tone had deepened, his range had narrowed.

This is not to say that he paid no more attention to the boob and the booster on the American scene. He returned to them from time to time, exposing them more convincingly than ever before. He demonstrated the hollowness of the "American's Creed" with proof after proof which the Depression obligingly furnished him. His comedy sometimes became black comedy; his rowdy good humor sometimes deserted him. But his wit never lost its bite. The trouble was that the readers' attention wandered. They no longer read Mencken eagerly every Monday.

Nevertheless, the general record of the Monday Articles was magnificent. Over a span of eighteen years, from 1920 to 1938, Mencken published more good writing, through these columns, than any other newspaperman of his era. The Free Lance made him famous locally but the Monday Articles helped to establish his national renown.

He dropped the Monday Articles the week before he undertook his three months as editor of the *Evening Sun.* As soon as they were over and he had recovered from his feverish editorial exertions, he started his weekly article again but this time switched it to the *Sunday Sun.* The Sunday Articles ran from May 16, 1938 until February 2, 1941. Their high spots were Mencken at his best, but otherwise the series showed a further sag. The writing became more brittle, repetitious. The rasp in Mencken's tone grew more pronounced and it was less often offset by the infectious good spirits which had marked his newspaper compositions for so many years before.

This loss of vitality and gaiety had been remarkably slow but it had occurred. Mencken in fact detected it before his readers did. As early as the spring of 1930 he had tried to revive the Free Lance column at Hamilton Owens's suggestion. He found it hopeless. He wrote Owens regretfully that in the days of the Free Lance he had been young and full of gas; now he was an aging, somewhat solemn man. In the decade that followed he proved that he was right. He became a scold though by no means a common one. And yet at the same time that his later Monday Articles and his Sunday Articles were becoming a bit short-tempered he was writing reminiscences for the *New Yorker* about his childhood and young manhood with charming urbanity.

Besides his weekly essays Mencken found much more to occupy him in newspaper writing. He never missed reporting on a national political convention of either party from 1920 to 1948, except in 1944 when he was in limbo. The *Sunpapers* made an elaborate production of covering these conclaves and Mencken enjoyed them to the full. They were the top acts of the American political circus, weird and wonderful. Through his dispatches every four years the candidates marched like clowns around a sawdust ring. Some looked gaudier than others, of course; one or two even looked attractive to Mencken under the grease paint though they were always the ones who lost. Harding, Coolidge, Al Smith, Hoover: what more could any spectator ask?

There were other special series, like those in which he had described the conditions on the Eastern Front in World War I and the revolution in Havana not long afterward. There was the glittering series on the trial of John Scopes in July 1925 for teaching Darwinism in Tennessee. There was the one on the comic-opera Pan American Conference of January 1928 in Cuba. There was the one on the Naval Conference in London of early 1930. There were the two series in 1937 especially for home consumption, on the University of Maryland and on the Johns Hopkins Hospital.

Mencken wrote for other newspapers besides the *Sun* only when an especially tempting opportunity offered itself. He did a series of weekly essays for the Chicago *Tribune* from November 1924 to January 1928. They started out by concentrating on literature but inclined increasingly to social issues. Notwithstanding, they contain some of Mencken's very good literary criticism. This series appeared in the *Tribune* each Sunday and, by arrangement, in the *Evening Sun* the day before. For the New York *American* he did a weekly piece from July 1934 to May 1935 on the American language.

He never tired of newspaper work. One day in a Monday Article he wondered aloud what kept him going at his trade, as he put it. His answer was firm: "My continuous curiosity, my endless interest in the stupendous farce of human existence."

11. The MERCURY: *The Web*

MUCH OF MENCKEN'S GENIUS lay in the drive and dexterity that allowed him to be a newspaperman at the same time that he was an author and editor. One role is enough for an ordinary person. Mencken played all three to the hilt. He became the best-known newspaperman in the country. He became, certainly during the 1920s, the most influential magazine editor in the country. And, within the sphere of the subjects he chose, he became the best-known writer.

We can see him through the decade as the public man. The nationwide interest he aroused is mirrored in the many rows of newspaper clipping books in the Enoch Pratt Library. It is also reflected in the journalistic attempts to reveal the "real" Mencken, of which Edmund Wilson's analysis in the *New Republic* is an incisive example. It is reflected in the pages of the *Mercury*, which became his personal magazine to an extent even greater than has been thought. It is reflected in his public actions on behalf of the *Mercury* and freedom of expression.

And Mencken the private man can be seen beneath the public one, when we search into the inner history of the *Mercury*, especially for its opening years, and uncover the web of personal relationships. He will prove to be both worse and better than he appears.

To the outsider who came in to see the imposing literary personality and editor H. L. Mencken, he often had an unexpectedly cherubic look. The fact made it all the more inviting to attempt to explain the difference between the public and the private man, or

between the mask and the masker. Interviewers and commentators
set themselves to determining just how the two were connected.

Wilson's shrewd sketch, entitled simply "H. L. Mencken,"
appeared in the June 1, 1921 number of the *New Republic*. He begins
with a description of the Mencken persona. "A man has withdrawn
from the tumult of American life into the seclusion of a house in Baltimore. He is unmarried and has surrounded himself with three thousand books. From this point of vantage he watches the twentieth century with detached and ironic dismay. A not ungenial materialist, he
reflects that all human activities are, after all, mainly physical in
origin: inspiration is a function of metabolism; death is an acidosis;
love is a biological phenomenon; idealism is insanity. But the body
is capable of much enjoyment; why worry about its obvious supremacy?"

"Something like this," Wilson goes on to say, "is the comic
portrait which Mencken has painted of himself; he has even pretended that it is the character in which he prefers to be accepted.
But there is, behind this comic mask, a critic, an evangelist and an
artist; there is a mind of extraordinary vigor and a temperament
of extraordinary interest." Because Mencken's mind and character
have by no means been properly explored or understood, Wilson
ventures, in the limited space the *New Republic* allows, to make some
suggestions. The most notable things about Mencken's mind are its
ruthlessness and rigidity. He is a puritan anti-Puritan. His greatest
service to American letters comes from the fact that he is a man of
superior intelligence who, unlike Henry Adams or Henry James, is
saturated with American common life. He draws strength from it at
the same time that he curls his lip at it. As Wilson sums it up, "In the
case of Mencken we have Puritanism and American manners in a
position to criticize" themselves.

Then, in a different vein, there was an unsigned article in the
Bookman for February 1922 beginning: "Picture a butcher's boy with
apple cheeks, who parts his hair in the middle and laughs out of the
side of his mouth, and you have a fair idea of the facial aspect of
Heinie Mencken. He is forty-one, but there are moments when he
looks fifteen. These moments are frequent when he is with George
Jean Nathan. He never knows when Nathan is kidding him and,
although he has been associating with Nathan for over twelve years,
Nathan remains to him an enigma past resolving."

The writer of the *Bookman* essay, who turned out to be Burton Rascoe, ended by saying, "whatever Mencken's destiny or place may become in American literature he will always remain, you may be sure, a warmly human figure. All women, without exception, like him. And all men do too, who have ever met him — scholars, pedants, boozers, preachers, teamsters, politicians, highbrows, lowbrows, and medium brows. That is a test and an achievement. The secret of this is that he is frank and unaffected, courteous, gentle, amiable, wise, jovial, and a gentleman."

Such were two of the Menckens proposed to the reading public. Sometimes the colors were warmer than at others, though none could surpass the rosy glow of the *Bookman's* picture. And this was the way, doubtless, it amused Mencken to be interpreted, this way — or the exact opposite. When Edmund Wilson's article appeared Mencken, urbanity itself, wrote to congratulate him on its "plausibility and eloquence." With a nice turn he particularly praised the "critical penetration" of the second half of the article, where Wilson tried to reach beneath Mencken's comic mask. We can see that Wilson succeeded, at least in part. And we can perhaps go a step further now than he did, since we can watch Mencken in the intimacy of the *Mercury* office.

In one way or another four persons were most closely connected with Mencken and the *Mercury*. Two were friends of long standing, Nathan and Knopf, and two were persons new to him, Edith Lustgarten and Charles Angoff. Edith Lustgarten became the office typist and general secretary. Charles Angoff, a young, red-haired Harvard graduate, became Mencken's editorial assistant. They proved to be all the staff the *Mercury* ever had or needed.

The detailed materials for the understanding of the various relationships are not all available. The main gap is the absence of Nathan's letters to Mencken, which doubtless rest among Mencken's restricted papers in the New York Public Library. Yet the tenor of each relationship can be determined, including the one with Nathan. And they are worth determining, since no set of relationships in Mencken's whole career can tell us more about him than the one centered on the *Mercury*.

The opening of the 1920s found Mencken and Nathan still the best of friends. They had not changed since painting the affectionate if slightly acidulous portraits of one another in *Pistols for Two* in 1917. They now attracted wider and sometimes more envious notice than any other pair of American intellectuals. They were frequently photographed looking quizzically at one another, Nathan the boulevardier and Mencken the Baltimore burgher. The press celebrated the friendship so loudly that it became known from one end of the United States to the other. It received the left-handed compliment in December 1920 of being hit off in a bouncy jingle by a comic poet of the day, Berton Braley. Everybody, it seemed, read it and not a few tried to imitate it. Entitled "Three — Minus One," and first published in the New York *Sun*, it was widely reprinted. Its base was Eugene Field's nursery rhyme about "Wynken, Blynken, and Nod."

> There were three that sailed away one night
>   Far from the madding throng;
> And two of the three were always right
>   And every one else was wrong.
> But they took another along, these two,
>   To bear them company,
> For he was the only One ever knew
>   Why the other two should Be;
> And so they sailed away, these three —
>   Mencken,
>   Nathan
>   And God.
>
> And the two they talked of the aims of Art,
>   Which they alone understood;
> And they quite agreed from the very start
>   That nothing was any good
> Except some novels that Dreiser wrote
>   And some plays from Germany.
> When God objected — they rocked the boat
>   And dropped him into the sea,
> "For you have no critical facultee,"
>   Said Mencken
>   And Nathan
>   to God.
>
> The two came cheerfully sailing home
>   Over the surging tide.
> And trod once more on their native loam
>   Wholly self-satisfied;
> And the little group that calls them great
>   Welcomed them fawningly,
> Though why the rest of us tolerate

> *This precious pair must be*
> *Something nobody else can see*
> *But Mencken,*
> *Nathan*
> *And God!*

Not long before "Three — Minus One" Mencken replied to a set of questions sent him by Rascoe. Among the answers was a "Note on my Relations to Nathan." "No two men could possibly be more unlike, in style and thought," Mencken briskly began. The prime point of contact was their mutual revulsion from American sentimentality. They worked well together because both felt lonely and required some support. And, most vital for their work as co-editors, they seldom found themselves in disagreement about literary matters. Each had a veto on anything submitted to the *Smart Set* and accepted by the other, but they seldom exercised it. What pleased one, pleased both. Outside the magazine they also shared many literary preferences. Both liked "Cabell, Dreiser, Cather, Dunsany, Conrad, Anatole France, etc." Besides having similar literary tastes they had a number of similar attitudes, Mencken said. They agreed in their view of women, their attitude toward money, their reaction to religion, and their "(almost pathological) aversion to worldly failure."

Mencken's appraisal though cursory was authoritative. It was so brief, however, that it simply summed up a good many things. It ignored others, which were either so obvious or so personal that he failed to put them down. In its way the most interesting and suggestive analysis of the relationship of the two men was made by Isaac Goldberg, who wrote a short study of Nathan before his book on Mencken. In both works he asserted that above all it was their innate, cynical levity which united them. Beyond that Goldberg saw a series of major similarities which, on closer inspection, broke down into individual differences.

He characterized the general outlook the two men shared as aristocratic, esthetic, and antinomian. Both men were aristocrats. For Nathan this fact meant an interest only in his few intimates; for Mencken it meant a hearty contempt for the mob and yet, as Edmund Wilson had observed, a preoccupation with common life. A notable example could be found in his aversion to the people and his enchantment with political conventions.

Both men to Goldberg were esthetes. Here the differences under the label were equally marked. For Goldberg realized that beauty to Nathan was almost as important as he alleged it was. He could indeed compose a chapter on esthetics the day the most critical battle of the World War was being fought. Mencken could not. He would want to remold the world, though he would never admit it, so that the beauty he admired could flourish.

When Goldberg termed the men antinomian he meant essentially that they were irreligious rebels who found the world meaningless. Here he also noted a difference. Nathan was much more consistent in his response to the world; his was a unified personality. But Mencken was pulled in two opposing directions; his reaction was again ambivalent. While Nathan rebelled by removing himself from the chaotic universe, Mencken readily wrote about, and often took part in, its incoherent proceedings.

As the exemplar of the "disparity-in-agreement" Goldberg picked out *The American Credo*, which the men issued jointly in 1920. As he points out, the Preface by Mencken consists of a study, running to nearly a hundred pages, of the American character. The credo itself, compiled largely by Nathan, is the work of a dilettante and intended to divert. Among its 488 articles of belief are such museum items as: "That all girls educated in convents turn out in later life to be hell-raisers"; "That fish is a brain food"; and "That it snowed every Christmas down to fifteen years ago." The *Credo* discloses two disparate men, "The one by sheer intellectual curiosity intrigued into the very morass which he is mapping; the other, content with dredging up the mire of superstition and credulousness and letting it stand as silently eloquent evidence."

Goldberg's pronouncement was accurate in the main. But there were differences, as well as similarities, which he did not note. These differences were pleasant and they resulted from the fact that the men's characters contained an effervescent mixture of the complementary. Each man found in the other something he lacked in himself — and esteemed. For example, Mencken, who felt that he looked jug-eared and barrel-shaped, viewed the handsome, dapper Nathan with affectionate respect. Nathan, in turn, rather aloof himself, viewed his friend's bustling sociability with fond wonder.

They liked the lively way their personalities worked on one another and consequently they remained good companions. Each stimulated the other to an impish geniality which showed itself not only in rapid-fire repartee but also in their frequent jokes and hoaxes. At times they could not resist hoaxing one another, but usually they looked around among their friends and acquaintances for subjects. In Dreiser, incidentally, they secured one of their most gullible. He found his mailbox filled, at one point during the *Smart Set* days, with a wild variety of gag presents. They included, Nathan recalls, "small American flags accompanied by scrawls issuing Black Hand threats, letters ostensibly written by the President urging him to come at once to the White House for a confidential talk, menus of Armenian restaurants affectionately inscribed to him by Robert W. Chambers, Elinor Glyn and Harold Bell Wright, frankfurters tied with red, white and blue ribbons, beer-bottle labels, photographs of the Czar bearing the inscription, 'To Theodore, gentleman and scholar — well, anyway, scholar,' and other such nonsense."

One of the most amiable things in their relationship was the rapport about nonessentials. They agreed, for example, about such diverse matters as the time when a woman is loveliest and where to consign all greedy physicians. In a charming passage at the end of *In Defense of Women* Mencken describes Elysium: "It is the close of a busy and vexatious day — say half past five or six o'clock of a winter afternoon. I have had a cocktail or two, and am stretched out on a divan in front of a fire, smoking. At the edge of the divan, close enough for me to reach her with my hand, sits a woman not too young, but still good-looking and well-dressed — above all, a woman with a soft, low-pitched, agreeable voice. As I snooze she talks. . . . I ask you seriously: could anything be more unutterably beautiful?" And Nathan remarks in his *Notebooks,* "A man reserves his greatest and deepest love not for the woman in whose company he finds himself electrified and enkindled but for the one in whose company he may feel tenderly drowsy." Again, in paragraph after paragraph of his letters Mencken refers to his ailments and, often, to the quacks who bungle their attempt to cure them. In his *Notebooks* and elsewhere Nathan recites some of the trying instances from his own experience. For one: "Since the age of fifteen, I have been a periodic sufferer from neuralgic pains in the left eyeball. Seeking relief, I have consulted, by actual count, seventy-one different doctors . . . and I have the honor to report that, for all their wisdom and bills, the damned pain is still there."

It was far from surprising that when the idea for the *Mercury*

began to take shape for Mencken in 1921 and 1922 he saw it as
involving a full partnership with Nathan. After all Nathan had in effect
made him co-editor of the *Smart Set* and he deserved every consideration. Nathan, though equally loyal to Mencken, was more clear-
sighted. He focused on the fact of their fundamental differences,
while Mencken blurred them. Nathan felt an uneasiness mounting
almost to mistrust for the messianic impulse he perceived in his
partner. And the new magazine would invite the impulse to an extent
that the old one never could. Both men were to blame for the break
that was waiting for them, Mencken because he disguised from himself the fact that he and Nathan wanted to produce two different
magazines and Nathan because he knew it but was willing to go
along. Knopf, as the prospective publisher, sensed that trouble lay
ahead. He had seen enough of both men to recognize that their
notions of an ideal magazine stood wide apart.

Gradually during 1923 the plans 'reached their final form. They
were the fruit of almost endless discussions which had started the
autumn before. Sometimes only two of the three men were involved,
sometimes all three. Sometimes Alfred's wife and business partner,
Blanche, joined in. The basic questions were hammered out at
dinner or over drinks or at the Knopf offices. Who should be editor?
Knopf wanted Mencken alone but Mencken, mindful of how Nathan
had pulled him to the top of the *Smart Set* staff, felt that he had to
refuse. Knopf understood and so it was decided that Mencken and
Nathan would act as joint editors. What should be the tone of the
magazine? Mencken fondly recalled the "Blue Review" which a
decade ago he, Nathan, and Willard Huntington Wright had projected
as a journal of enlightened Toryism. Its tone should be Tory, Mencken and Knopf decided; and Nathan went along. What should be the
title of the magazine? Mencken still liked the "Blue Review" but
Knopf, no doubt stroking his British moustache, announced that he
considered it too arty. A dozen titles were mentioned; each was
rejected. Then Nathan suggested "The American Mercury." Knopf
agreed but Mencken jibed at its association with the London *Mercury*,
which he felt was a stuffy journal. However, his two associates convinced him and he even became mildly enthusiastic.

Two fundamental questions remained. One was what to do if the
co-editors flatly disagreed with one another. Knopf knew that he
himself would have to have the deciding vote; Mencken and Nathan

concurred. The other question was financial. How should the shares in the magazine be distributed? It was clearly a Knopf enterprise, so the Knopf firm took a two-thirds interest in the magazine while Mencken and Nathan received one-sixth each.

A hundred other arrangements had to be made; all kinds of minor crises had to be met. But somehow they were. As 1923 went along, Mencken grew more and more excited. The Knopfs were obviously eager too. Nathan alone had misgivings. But if they were marked ones they evidently made no impression on Mencken, judging by his jaunty letters to his friends.

In September Knopf issued a handsome folio announcement, and Nathan's name appeared on it above Mencken's, patently at Mencken's suggestion. But it did not take long for the first clash to develop between the co-editors. It centered on whether the infant *Mercury* should publish a recent play by Eugene O'Neill. Several of his prior plays had been printed in the *Smart Set*. Nathan believed it would help to set the right tone for the *Mercury* and also honor the most interesting contemporary American playwright if *All God's Chillun Got Wings* could be printed in the inaugural issue of January 1924. As it happened, it was submitted too late for that. When it came up for consideration for the second issue, Mencken opposed it. Nathan, embarrassed, stood firm and so Knopf had to adjudicate. He sided with Nathan; the play appeared in the second number. With its patient Negro hero and neurotic white heroine, it proved to be a prophetic work, reflecting credit on the periodical that published it. But it was still literature where Mencken wanted politics.

If he had been slower than Nathan in foreseeing the difficulties of joint editorship, he quickly saw them once the magazine was under way. Furthermore, the differences in policy were heightened by Nathan's reluctance to do his half of the editorial chores. He had always carried his share and more of the job of running the *Smart Set*, but he simply could not command much enthusiasm for the way Mencken was shaping the *Mercury*.

The pivotal year for the partnership proved to be 1924. Looking back later, Mencken said that they got along well enough together the first few months but that it gradually appeared that he would have nine-tenths of the work on the *Mercury* to do. His irritation emerged and then intensified. "I'm going nuts," he told Knopf. True, there had been one or two earlier indications of things to come. For instance,

Emily Clark, the editor of the *Richmond Reviewer*, wrote about Mencken in a gossipy letter to Hergesheimer in September 1923, "I believe
in his heart he thinks Mr. Nathan rather shoddy. He told someone
here that he was 'a miserable little Jew chicken chaser.'" Now in 1924
at Schellhase's in Baltimore or Luchow's in New York, his companions heard him say hard things about Nathan in his gravelly voice.
As for Nathan himself, Mencken saw less of him instead of more, in
spite of the fact that they should have been working together at the
Mercury office. He got nowhere when he tried to talk with Nathan
about the magazine, even over drinks. The months went along. Finally
he sent him several long letters explaining his position and asking for
Nathan's response.

He sent the first on October 15. It came promptly to the point,
"Dear George: — After a year's hard experience and due prayer I
come to the conclusion that the scheme of The American Mercury,
as it stands, is full of defects, and that to me, at least, it must eventually
grow impossible. We can go into my reasons at length, if necessary,
next week. I am proposing to Alfred that a meeting be called for
Wednesday. For the present I state only my conclusions."

They were that the *Mercury* was slipping into superficiality, the
same thing that had ruined the *Smart Set* for him, and that the slipping resulted from the "narrow (and progressively narrowing) circle"
of their common interests. The alternatives he proposed were stark.
Either he would retire from all editorial duties and merely become a
contributor or he would take over the editing entirely and put in
someone to manage the office under him. He added that he inclined
to give up the editing, as well as his stock in the *Mercury*, and to
write a single article each month for the magazine.

Though Nathan's reply is not available its main points can be
reconstructed. His answer was apparently moderate and friendly
but not meek. He appealed to their stimulating experience with the
Smart Set, arguing that its considerable measure of success showed
that the *Mercury* could follow its lively pattern. In fact the initial
success of the *Mercury* under their joint editorship proved it. When
the *Smart Set* went downhill it was because it became too serious.
And he probably appealed to Mencken to take the long view and see
if the future would not dispose of some of the present problems.

Mencken came back with a four-page letter on October 19. It
contained his definitive statement of their damaged relationship. He

began by complaining that he saw nothing ahead of him at the magazine except drudgery. He discounted the initial success of the Mencken-Nathan *Mercury*. It appealed chiefly to newsstand buyers who gabbled about what they read but were not really interested in ideas. It should appeal instead to readers who were serious even if they mocked conventional seriousness. It should appeal to the civilized minority who put their mind to politics.

Responding further to Nathan's letter, Mencken flatly contradicted him: the *Smart Set* did not go downhill because it grew serious but because it had not grown serious enough. He reminded Nathan that he had often proposed that they put solider articles in it but could never get his agreement on their nature. For Mencken personally the consequence was that during the final three or four years of the *Smart Set* he simply slopped along.

He assured Nathan that the *Mercury*, given a body of sensible doctrine, could rise to the position of the *Atlantic* or even higher. But editing it was no job for two men, especially for him and Nathan now. In one blunt sentence after another he listed their differences. They had widely diverging concerns. They saw the world in opposite colors. They agreed only on minor matters. They no longer even played together.

He reiterated that he had far too much routine work to do at the magazine. He should track down ideas, manuscripts, and authors. Instead he was overseeing the make-up man. He could do his job as editor with a "competent slave" but not if he had to be the slave himself.

He ended the letter by saying coolly that he knew Nathan had his own troubles and some were worse than Mencken's. But he proposed a meeting to settle the matter.

Doubtless the meeting was held but there is no record of its adding anything new. Mencken kept to his position, and that was that.

What remained was to negotiate the terms of the separation. Mencken himself referred to it as a divorce and there were similarities. He was the partner who wanted the relationship dissolved. Nathan was the partner who wanted it preserved or, if that proved impossible, at least simulated. He was the one who did not want the neighbors to know. Throughout the negotiations and afterward, Nathan declined to consider that his friendship with Mencken had gone bad. Nothing was wrong, Nathan calmly assured the world, and he kept a slight smile on his face. Privately the two men haggled about terms, but Mencken, who counted on Knopf's support in a crisis, knew that he would win out. The brusque opening of his letter of May 3 shows how matters were going. "Dear George: — The trouble with your revision of the memorandum I drew up is that it both goes too far and not far enough." Publicly an elegiac note, a dignified reference to their past association, began to be sounded here and there by close observers. The note is struck in each of the two books on Mencken which made their appearance in 1925. According to Ernest Boyd in his *H. L. Mencken*, "The association has been long, fruitful, and, in its way, unique in American literature." Goldberg remarked, in *The Man Mencken*, "The Mencken and Nathan association goes down as one of the most interesting in the literary history of England and America. It created an atmosphere all its own; it impressed itself upon a phase of our letters."

According to Knopf an agreement was reached by which Nathan's actual connection with the magazine stopped with the February 1925 number though his name stayed on the cover through July. By now Mencken was much irritated with his old associate. He had Nathan's name removed from the directory in the lobby of the building that housed the Knopf enterprises; he ordered his desk moved from the *Mercury* office to another office tenanted mostly by stenographers; and he saw to it that Nathan was told he could expect only a minimum of secretarial and phone service. It was a war of attrition but Nathan did his best to minimize it. He accepted the changes with jaunty grace at the same time that he bargained for the financial arrangements most favorable to him. He still had his one-sixth share of the *Mercury* stock; it took four more years before he surrendered it and then only at the handsome price of twenty-five thousand dollars. The money could not have come at a better time. He received the first installment in November 1929, a month after the Depression began, and the last in May 1931; while Knopf's and Mencken's stock became wastepaper.

Notwithstanding the rift from 1925 on, both men kept up at least a limited contact, partly for the sake of appearances and partly because Nathan maintained more than a nominal connection with the magazine. He continued to write a monthly piece of dramatic criticism, as he had from the first number, in the department allotted

to him and entitled "The Theatre." Sometimes his criticism seemed
flimsy, but often it was among the liveliest, if most mannered, being
written in America. In addition, he contributed epigrams and light
humor to another department, "Clinical Notes," till the number for
March 1930.

Appearances were further preserved through the fact that both
men continued, as their friends learned, to mail copies of their new
books to one another. Not surprisingly, the inscriptions that Nathan
wrote were more personal than those from Mencken. Their correspondence went on too, though now much diminished. A death or a
marriage could bring back the atmosphere of old times. When Mencken's mother died the letter of condolence from Nathan was as warm
as ever, and from Mencken's reply one would have thought that no
break had occurred. And when Mencken married, there was an
exchange of affable if jocular notes. The most amusing was one that
Mencken sent during the honeymoon, exclaiming to Nathan about
how good it felt to be able to look a hotel detective in the eye.

There are several postscripts to the story of their break about the
Mercury. The first is in an irritable letter that Dreiser sent to Nathan
about the policy of the *American Spectator*. This was a journal that
Nathan organized in 1932 as an answer to the *Mercury*, a journal that
he hoped would do well the things the *Mercury* was not doing and
do better the things that it was. Nathan was the mainspring of the
enterprise but he persuaded four other literary figures to join him on
the editorial board at the start, Dreiser, Cabell, Eugene O'Neill, and
Ernest Boyd. Staring straight at the *Mercury*, the *Spectator* piously
vowed that it would shun "all evangelical crusades on behalf of
belated intellectual, economic, and political side-shows." It failed
after several years but it failed sooner for Dreiser. In his letter, dated
October 7, 1933, he told Nathan bluntly, "Mencken stated the case to
me in regard to you in 1926. It was that from the beginning there had
been a fundamental difference between your points of view; that all
you could contemplate was the frothy intellectual and social interests
of the stage, the Four Hundred, the Bohemian and mentally dilettante worlds, whereas he personally was for serious contemplation of
science, medicine, education, literature and what not. The issue, as
you know yourself, proved fatal."

The second and third postscripts come from Mencken. In a letter
to Knopf on November 13, 1934 he said contemptuously of Nathan,

"We should have thrown him out on his backside and let him yell. It is foolish to be decent in dealing with a rat." Yet in a letter to the hobo novelist Jim Tully on February 12, 1935, he commented for public consumption, "The so-called row with Nathan is completely imaginary. So far as I can recall. I have never had any words with him, and certainly the last time I encountered him he was immensely cordial. We seldom meet simply because the friends of each do not interest the other. Nathan plays with a gang of rich nonentities who seem to me to be extremely tiresome, and I suppose my own friends look pretty much the same to him. The American Mercury business in 1924 apparently left him with some unhappiness, but it simply couldn't be helped."

The last postscript comes from Nathan. Writing in his *Intimate Notebooks* shortly after he had been bought out of the *Mercury* and had said his final farewell to it, he remembered that he and Mencken had differed only twice since the afternoon in May 1908 of their first meeting. What had preserved their friendship over so many years — the *Intimate Notebooks* came out in 1932 — was the conviction that nothing in this world matters very much. "As a result, we weathered storms together that would have wrecked many another friendship; we met with humor many a situation that would have severed men constitutionally more indignant."

Knopf's relationship with Mencken, both during and after the *Mercury* period, provided an illuminating contrast to Nathan's. It was not marked by the prompt burst of good-fellowship that characterized the first meeting of Mencken and Nathan, but once the relationship was established it gained strength steadily if slowly. Many, and quite different, strands came to hold it together: the men's great respect for the professional competence they discovered in one another, their ability to work together smoothly, their mutual interest in music, their moral courage, the extent and variety of their reading, and their readiness to help one another without thought of personal profit. At times its strength would be tested, particularly in the early 1930s, but it would survive without damage.

By 1920 the association was taking its permanent shape. It was now seven years since their first encounter, when the elegant young Knopf traveled to Baltimore to see the man who was a coming literary critic as well as author of the brash Free Lance column. They found one another interesting and met from time to time, ordinarily when

Mencken was in New York to do his share of the chores on the *Smart Set*. Knopf started his publishing firm in 1915 and by 1916 both Mencken and Nathan were enrolled as Knopf authors. The next year the fledgling firm published *Mr. George Jean Nathan Presents* as well as Mencken's *A Book of Prefaces*. But then for a year or so there was something of a rift. Mencken wrote Burton Rascoe that Knopf was dismayed by the attacks of some academic critics on the *Prefaces* as unpatriotic and that he would get no further books of Mencken's to publish. At about the same time Mencken, magnetized by the optimism of his new-found friend Phil Goodman, agreed to let him issue first one of his books and then another. *Damn! A Book of Calumny* and *In Defense of Women* both appeared in 1918 under Goodman's imprint. However, he showed himself to be a slapdash publisher and Mencken, who had continued to see Knopf socially, returned with relief to the house which always published him thereafter.

One of Knopf's attractions was that he wanted from the beginning to put out not only good but good-looking books. He had a more artistic feeling for form and format than any other American publisher. Mencken too liked a handsome book. As early as 1909 he remarked in a review of a book in the *Smart Set*, "The binding is a joy, and the title page and text are masterpieces of the printer's art." And this was considerably before he encountered Knopf.

Their business relationship became a model one. With their mutual respect for technical competence they allowed each other to be undisputed in his specialty. Mencken stuck to his writing, Knopf to his publishing; the results were first-rate. The fact was well demonstrated by the case of *In Defense of Women*, which had sold poorly under Goodman and was to sell capitally under Knopf. When Mencken early in 1921 sent in the typescript of the revised version Knopf suggested publishing it the following spring but added amiably that he would try for the coming autumn if Mencken wished. Mencken's reply was propriety itself, "You are the publisher; not I. I leave all such matters to your judgment." Knopf, for his part, encouraged Mencken to write the best books possible and then issued them in tasteful formats and promoted them well. Also, he paid promptly, a fact that Mencken appreciated for he had suffered at the hands of more than one dilatory publisher. But at the Knopf office there was more than prompt payment to impress Mencken; there was the orderly, efficient handling of all financial arrangements. And Knopf never tried to short-change anyone. In a controversy with Burton Rascoe in the mid-1930s, Mencken called Knopf "perhaps the squarest man in money matters ever heard of." He never altered his view.

The mutual respect was great; the affection followed later. In the Knopf letter files the first letter in which Mencken addresses Knopf as "Dear Alfred" does not come till May 14, 1923, and the first letter in which Knopf calls Mencken "Henry" does not come till July 2. From then on, though, the relationship was close.

It was early in the same year that Knopf and his wife, Blanche, entertained the idea on their own account for a new magazine which would boast Mencken as its editor. Knopf has remarked that they were firmly convinced that a magazine would be no better than its editor and so they felt that Mencken had to be their man. They brought Nathan into the negotiations largely at Mencken's insistence.

After the *Mercury* was in operation and Mencken's wrangle with Nathan began, Knopf's problem persisted of how to be fair to both parties even if he sympathized with Mencken. He reminded Mencken that Nathan could not be wished away, that he owned an equity in the magazine, and that the equity had to be dealt with in proper form. It was on this basis that after much bickering between the co-editors Nathan was finally paid for his share of the *Mercury* stock.

Until the end of the decade the association of Mencken and Knopf was one of almost unruffled friendship. The editor and his publisher developed a technique which worked admirably in solving such problems as appeared. Both men knew the tricky habit that the written word had of hardening positions. So in instances of disagreement they named the issues and then agreed to talk — not write — about them. They made a practice of talking over the finest food and drink. Both prided themselves on being connoisseurs of the table, with the result that differences of opinion dissolved tastefully in glasses of Bernkasteler Doktor or were digested with Maryland terrapin.

They had other interests in common besides good food, among them music. For Mencken music meant two things. The first was the robust relaxation of the Saturday Night Club, with him as second piano hammering briskly at the keys. The second was the emotional response, mentioned before, to melody and form, a deeper and readier response than he ever experienced from literature. Music meant a good deal to Knopf as well. He remembers often attending the sessions of the Saturday Night Club as Mencken's guest and then helping to consume the Maryland seafood and — in Prohibition days — the illegal liquor that were served after the playing. He and his wife took a box, for a decade, at Carnegie Hall for concerts of the visiting Boston Symphony and often when Mencken was in New York he joined them.

The musical tastes of the two men overlapped. We know that Mencken particularly appreciated the works of the great Romantic composers, while Knopf enjoyed many of the great Classical composers as well. But they agreed on the greatness of Bach, whom Mencken was willing to assign a special place in Olympus. It became a custom for them to go together to the famed Bach Festivals held annually in Bethlehem, Pennsylvania.

Mencken discovered the appeal of the Bach Festivals in 1922; and the next year, and for a number of years thereafter, he enjoyed them in company with Knopf. They relished their periodic visits in the unlovely Pennsylvania town to hear the local Bach Choir sing works of Bach better than they were sung anywhere else. Though Mencken was not given to superlatives he wrote in a report to the *Evening Sun* on one of the visits, "The members of the Bach Choir know the B minor Mass so well that their mere singing of the notes is completely perfect." He piled compliment on compliment, leaving no doubt that here was a noble choir, nobly directed.

The Festival had few frills; Mencken and Knopf like that. In Bethlehem their needs were modest. Because the music in a mysterious way made him thirsty, Mencken always found a little illegal refreshment for Knopf and himself to enjoy. Believing that Bach's "grand and heavenly music" was "not for teetotallers," he managed customarily to find beer within ten minutes of his arrival in town. Knopf remembered him failing only once. On that visit he suffered the tortures of thirst for a whole day and a half after arriving. He lamented the fact to Knopf while riding in one of Bethlehem's rare taxis. The driver overheard and asked the magic question, "Do you gentlemen want beer?" He then drove them to an innocent-looking building. There Mencken asked the doorkeeper, "Could you do anything for two poor musicians?" The doorkeeper looked at their credentials — both were carrying scores of the B minor Mass — and let them in. At the end of a corridor they found a huge bar with cold beer, thick sandwiches at a dime each, and a covey of local politicians sitting against the wall with their straw hats tilted comfortably on the back of their heads.

Besides some personal enthusiasms they had other characteristics in common, not the least of which was the courage of their convictions. When Boston's Watch and Ward Society attacked the *Mercury* because of its story "Hatrack," about a village prostitute, Mencken cheerfully rushed to do battle and he had Knopf's full support. He had it in other, similar if less publicized struggles. It extended to both word and deed. We sometimes forget that it took courage for Mencken to write as bluntly as he did and courage for Knopf to print what Mencken wrote. Again and again Mencken attacked individuals and institutions with a freedom no writer enjoys today. He could blast a celebrated bishop, an eminent businessman, a popular idol; he could scarify the Baptists, the Jews, the Christian Scientists. And Knopf continued to publish him. To all appearances this kind of courage came as instinctively to the two men as breathing. But it was not so. They recognized the formidable nature of many of the foes they challenged, and their correspondence proves that they kept in mind the perils of libel and censorship. Their acts of defiance were conscious ones.

The same "Hatrack" case that illustrated the courage of the two men also highlighted another trait they shared. That was a strict, almost Victorian sense of propriety, which barred them from making any money out of the case. With the national attention the *Mercury* received through the trial, the April number containing "Hatrack" could have been reprinted and sold by the thousands. Yet Knopf and Mencken were at one in refusing to print a single extra copy.

A bond of another kind lay in the fact that both men read widely, with eclectic taste. Their rapport as editor and publisher was based partly on this circumstance. Certainly they did not always agree about what was good and what was bad, or what should be published and what should not — *All God's Chillun Got Wings* was a case in point. But when they did not agree they could usually communicate the reason to one another. A highly beneficial result for Knopf of this rapport was that Mencken could and did make constant suggestions to the firm about promising authors and manuscript possibilities on both sides of the Atlantic. After all, he knew and cultivated not only the belletrists but writers of every conceivable sort. Almost from the start he read most manuscripts that came to the *Mercury* office, except for the crudest, which his young editorial assistant Charles Angoff culled out. And, finally, he read all sorts of printed material. He read fast and voraciously, to the benefit of the scope of the *Mercury* and the catholicity of the Knopf list. The variety of his suggestions was remarkable.

Among the poets he proposed to Knopf were John V. A. Weaver and William Carlos Williams. Weaver, an advertising man, attracted Mencken because he was using the American language for poetry. His efforts at putting common city speech into verse were typified in such a poem as "Drug Store", which begins "Pardon me, lady, but I wanta ast you, / For God's sake, stop that tappin!" Knopf issued Weaver's volume *In American* in 1921. William Carlos Williams had passed through an imagist and an expressionist period by the time Mencken commended his lyrics to Knopf and was working his way to a bleaker style suitable for celebrating his gray Jersey city of Paterson. But Knopf, understandably enough, turned at this point to Louis Untermeyer for advice rather than Mencken and rejected Williams's collected poems. Among the writers of fiction two of Mencken's finds were prairie realists, George Milburn and Ruth Suckow. Of her he wrote, "A young woman named Ruth Suckow at Earlville, Iowa has sent in to us a number of very remarkable short stories. She tells me that she is at work on a novel. I suggest that it would be a good idea to send her a friendly note saying that I have told you about her and that you will be glad to read her manuscript when it is finished. I am convinced that she will do excellent work." He also tried to get Knopf to publish Milburn's ironic stories, now undeservedly forgotten.

His happiest suggestion in the field of European letters was made in 1921 when he wrote briskly to Knopf, "if you can get 'Buddenbrooks' at a reasonable price, grab it. It is probably the solidest novel done in Germany for years." Knopf became and remained Thomas Mann's American publisher. But Mencken's advice was not restricted to contemporary classics. Knopf recalls asking him to read the translation of a novel by a Norwegian author, not simply for its literary merits but also to see if it would pass the censors. Mencken reported, "This is now absolutely safe. It is also one of the worst novels I have ever read, or heard of. Such banality is really quite magnificent."

As Knopf himself notes, the net that Mencken cast was amazingly wide. For example, he discovered and then recommended a history of European literature published in, of all places, Shanghai. It seemed to him a book of unusual worth and he thought that an American edition might have a chance. Other histories he commended to Knopf were likewise varied. So were the memoirs. For instance, he urged Knopf to look into the possibility of publishing the recollections of E. W. Howe, the Kansas editor and author; of James Weldon Johnson, the Negro poet and official of the NAACP; of one Henry Tetlow, a perfume manufacturer from Philadelphia; and of the veteran editor of the *Retail Coalman,* who according to Mencken was at work on a book dealing with his reminiscences of forty years in coal and railways.

In the field of nonfiction Mencken's suggestions ranged through — and beyond — both the social sciences and the exact sciences, but he was especially interested in religion and medicine. He had ideas to offer as well as manuscripts to recommend. Knopf reports hearing from Mencken about, for example, a work by Robert Eisler called *The Messiah Jesus and John the Baptist;* and he mentions two ideas that Mencken had in that general connection: one for a good history of Christianity from a scientific point of view ("the general tone of the book ought to be that of Huxley") and the other for "a really decent looking" King James Bible, since all "those issued by the regular publishers have a funereal air, and most of them are bound idiotically."

Mencken's most profitable suggestions came in the field of medicine. There his stellar achievement lay in persuading a Missouri doctor he came across, named Logan Clendening, to write a popular book about the human body and to write it to meet the needs that Mencken foresaw. *The Human Body* became one of the bonanzas on the Knopf list. It sold nearly forty thousand copies in its first edition, over thirty thousand in its second edition, and ultimately nearly half a million in cheap reprints.

Knopf was more than grateful for this unremitting interest of Mencken's in getting good works into print, for it worked to the obvious advantage of his firm. He reciprocated as much as he could. When book manuscripts came to him and he thought they might be used in part in the *Mercury,* he promptly told Mencken. Unfortunately, there were few usable ones; only rarely could a book be success-fully excerpted for the magazine. Regardless, Mencken remained an unofficial but highly esteemed scout for the house of Knopf not only during the *Mercury* period but later on. In 1932 the Knopfs elected him to their board of directors, where he remained an influential mem-ber for many years.

On this pleasant, mutually profitable relationship the affluent 1920s apparently put few strains and those seemed slight. However, the Depression provided a harder test. Though the *Mercury* — and that still meant essentially Mencken — felt the effects of the stock market crash it was slow to admit the fact. So for a year or two were its readers. But once the numbness of the blow wore off they altered their ideas, as did the magazines the *Mercury* competed with. The *Mercury* in the long run suffered more than its competitors because it refused to change enough to suit the changing times. Though Knopf watched wistfully for a major shift he failed to find it. A stubborn Mencken carried into the 1930s the same views that had brilliantly informed the magazine in the 1920s and had matched the views which that decade held.

Yet he proved willing to make other concessions, some of them agreeably surprising to Knopf. In particular he now stood ready to help in merchandising the *Mercury*. As the subscription lists shrank, advertisers became a vital resource. They looked more necessary to Knopf all the time, so he began talking to Mencken about their care and treatment. The burden, for instance, of his letter to Mencken of October 27, 1932 is, Let's be kind to the ad men. Mencken was. Sti-fling his repugnance toward Madison Avenue, he joined Knopf at lunches for advertising managers in which the soft sell was applied for the magazine. He now could write to Knopf almost routinely, "I'll get to the office on Monday afternoon, the 12th. I have put down Tuesday for lunch with the advertising men."

Mencken also tried from time to time to brighten the format of the magazine, in the hope of tempting more readers to buy it. But its general posture remained the same, even in 1932, when the cir-culation sank from sixty thousand at the start of the year to forty-two thousand at its end. Knopf felt hampered in what he could do. Though he now wrote Mencken a number of letters on the lamen-table state of the *Mercury*, he still believed that the essence of a magazine was its editor and that the editor had to be let largely alone. And in spite of everything Mencken was still slow to see the magnitude of the crisis.

Whistling in the dark near the end of the same catastrophic year, 1932, when he was befriending the advertising men, he wrote Knopf, "I suggest that we might print a very effective announcement in January or thereabout, saying that, almost alone among American magazines, the A. M. has closed 1932 without showing a loss." This was technically correct but disingenuous. A loss was prevented only because the magazine had signed a five thousand dollar advertising contract with the American Tobacco Company, which was to cover more than a single year. Yet Mencken went on, "The moral for advertisers is plain: we reach a large class of Americans able to pay 50 cents for a magazine, even after three years of the Depression, and they stick to us faithfully." The *Mercury* published its boast but it had no apparent effect. The year 1933 proved even harder than 1932. By the autumn of 1933 both Mencken and Knopf saw that the only possible solution was a new editor. Mencken himself was ready to resign. He had run out of ideas and enthusiasm; he felt almost eager for relief. Besides, he had worked at the editorship for a decade and that was enough. He announced again that most of his career had been split into ten-year segments; here could be another instance. Knopf agreed and a successor for Mencken was picked, Henry Hazlitt. He was not only a decent literary critic but as much a conservative in economic matters as Mencken.

The friendship of Mencken and Knopf emerged weathered but unharmed by the strains of the *Mercury*. The only formidable episode, a disagreement about Hitler, came in the final months of Mencken's tenure. It was discussed with good temper in spite of the feelings involved. The matter arose when Knopf, late in October 1933, sat reading the proofs for the forthcoming December issue. He saw in the book review department, "The Library," a lead review by Mencken headed "Hitlerismus." It dealt with Hitler's rise to power, with his book *Mein Kampf,* and in passing with several other books about Hitler's Third Reich. The tone of Mencken's review was remarkably even. He criticized Hitler for his gross inhumanity but took the view that in the long run Hitler and his regime would be domesticated. The Third Reich would learn through experience and might even become contemptible rather than horrible.

In analyzing Hitler's book Mencken described the pros and cons of Hitler's case as he saw it. "What he says . . . is often sensible enough," he remarked. He went on briefly to analyze the situation of Jewry in the world. Jewry suffered, he thought, from seeming alien and over aggressive. "The disadvantage of the Jew is that, to simple men, he often seems a kind of foreigner." Then he commented that "Many of the current Jewish leaders in this country are very loud and brassy fellows."

Knopf wrote to Mencken at once. "I've just read your piece on Hitler. Believe me, my own personal feelings are not at stake but I think you gravely underestimate the really terrific concern that many of our supporters have about Hitler. . . . I think it will leave in the minds of a great many readers the idea that you are, yourself, at best lukewarm in your feelings." He added that he considered Mencken's comments on *Mein Kampf* unworthy of him.

As always Mencken replied promptly. He said he was sorry Knopf did not like the Hitler piece. If any customer took it for a defense of Hitler, Mencken could only say that he would have to give up trying to write plain English. It was actually an attempt to "disentangle the facts from the blah of both sides." The discussion ended inconclusively. The piece appeared in the final number for the year. Though it attracted much hostile attention at the time, no recriminations came from Knopf. In spite of the fact that he was put into an extremely uncomfortable position, the only public statement he made was oblique and general.

That statement came in the April 1934 number, where he took a page to talk about the *Mercury*. In Mencken's parting announcement of five months before, in the same December issue that contained "Hitlerismus," he had assured the readers of the *Mercury* that its basic aims and principles would change little. Now with Mencken gone, Knopf showed that he realized what the limitations of the magazine had been. Under the heading "From the Publisher to the Readers of The American Mercury," he made his points. First of all, he stated that he had abandoned the *Mercury's* preoccupation with the American scene. Its coverage would now be world-wide. Secondly, the magazine would now be seriously concerned about the tremendous social, political, and economic problems raised by the world crisis. Thirdly, it would be less interested in the harmless follies of the "Rotarians, Babbitts, and lower inhabitants of the Bible Belt" and much

more interested in exposing the follies and knaveries of those in
high places. However, Knopf sensed that if he went too far in the
other direction he might lose many of Mencken's devoted followers.
So he added that the new *Mercury* would still be more like the old
one than any other magazine.

The two men inevitably met less after Mencken resigned as
editor, but they still met. The correspondence continued, often containing suggestions from Mencken as before about authors with manuscripts that Knopf might use. Though they spent more time in talking
about the annual Bach Festivals in Bethlehem than in going, they
did not stop those pilgrimages either.

Nor did the feeling of intimacy abate. Time mellowed Mencken's
teasing of Knopf; Mencken's sense of humor was no longer as rambunctious as it once has been. His letters to Knopf, and others, no longer
jested as much about Knopf's oriental haberdashery or his levantine
air or his thrift as a publisher; but the warmth remained. Knopf reciprocated. Never renowned for his own sense of humor he found in
Mencken's, even after time blunted it a bit, a source of delight. He
continued to consider Mencken his closest friend and readily admitted
that Mencken had influenced him more than anyone else.

Three desks dominated the *Mercury*'s austere little office during
most of Mencken's time. After the first few issues there was none for
Nathan, who was set outside among the Knopf stenographers. But
there was always a desk for Mencken, which he occupied periodically;
a desk for his editorial assistant; and a desk for the office secretary.
When the *Mercury* advertised for someone to sit at that last desk,
over three hundred replies came in. Half a dozen applicants were
interviewed and quickly found wanting before a slight, bright
young woman named Edith Lustgarten appeared. She had grown
up on New York's West Side determined to make her way and she
was already busy at work for the *Nation* when she applied for the
job at the new *Mercury*. She got it without much trouble.

The record of what she did or of what the office practices were
would be immaterial except for the fact that it throws light on Mencken. The *Mercury* became so much the expression of his character
that the very way he gave dictation or let her dispose of manuscripts
had some significance. Then too, it is an article of the American
Creed that how a man treats his secretary tells us something about
the man.

Edith Lustgarten started in March of 1924 and fell easily into the office routines crystalizing around Mencken. He planned on coming to New York only for a few days once a month but inevitably he came more often as the magazine developed. As it turned out, he averaged two trips a month to the office, usually arriving on Monday and leaving late Wednesday. His very presence was tonic and yet his absences were a boon not only for his new assistant Charles Angoff but also for Edith Lustgarten. These allowed her more than the average responsibilities and she responded eagerly. True, most of her time was taken up in standard office work. She opened the increasingly heavy mail; she took dictation; she did some filing. But because the office was permeated with Mencken's personality, every part of her job was more interesting than it would have been in an average office. She especially enjoyed taking dictation from him. Plunging into his morning's mail, he dictated his answers smoothly and skillfully. And he was a delight to listen to: the shortest note was apt to have its touch of Mencken wit, and between paragraphs of the longer letters Mencken was apt to interject a throwaway line intended for his secretary alone. After the dictating, she swiftly transcribed her notes and set the letters out for Mencken to sign. "Mail has to be answered day by day," he told her with the air of enunciating a great truth.

Her filing was done in a Spartan manner, the most striking thing about it being how little there was. In a magazine that did business for a decade with many of the most notable American writers and intellectuals, the correspondence kept in the office never occupied more than one file cabinet or at the most two. In Baltimore Mencken indulged himself by saving nearly everything of any importance that came through the mails. The result was a host of full manila folders in Hollins Street. In New York he firmly repressed his impulse. He ordered Edith Lustgarten to discard all correspondence with contributors, or would-be contributors, except such significant authors as Sinclair Lewis or Eugene O'Neill. After a while Mencken fell into the habit of holding a house cleaning in the *Mercury* office about twice a year. He and Edith Lustgarten would ransack the existing folders. The cream of the correspondence and the most valuable manuscripts would be sent to Hollins Street, there to be stored for ultimate deposit in the New York Public Library. The rest would be stuffed into wastebaskets. There would be few carbon copies of Mencken's own letters to eliminate because he had told her not to make them except in important cases. In Baltimore he worked best surrounded by books, manuscripts, and letters. In New York he rejoiced at the bareness of the *Mercury*'s modest room. "There never was a business of clutter in the office," Edith Lustgarten has noted.

As she progressed in her job Mencken stood ready to give her added duties. Soon she was answering some of the ordinary correspondence. Her routine phrases often resembled Mencken's. "Dear Mr. Griffing," she would write for example, "Our best thanks for your letter. We are delighted to hear that *The American Mercury* is going so well in Buffalo." She soon helped with the copy-editing and proofreading. She has never forgotten the first issue of the *Mercury* that she was permitted to proofread by herself. She thought it perfect when it left her desk, yet when it came out it had half a dozen typographical errors. She was crushed. Instead of scolding, Mencken reminded her that no one was perfect and that some of the slips might have been the printer's. The excuses were timeworn but well-intended, and they made her feel better. She was also allowed to read an occasional manuscript to see if it was worth consideration. Eventually she even got into the *Mercury*. After she had been in the office for several years she gathered enough courage to ask Mencken if she could attempt to write a few capsule reviews. "Not the big ones," she assured him, "but the little ones." He good-naturedly agreed and thereafter she became an occasional contributor. For her the high point came when Mencken put her name on the letterhead. Beneath "H. L. Mencken, Editor" and "Charles Angoff, Managing Editor" was printed "Edith Lustgarten, Editorial Secretary."

Throughout her years at the *Mercury* she was treated, she feels, with unusual understanding. Mencken proved himself a thoughtful employer. He seldom criticized her for errors and he complimented her for exceptionally good work. For instance, one Saturday in 1931 he wrote, "My best thanks for the excellent way you have handled the MSS, and the office while Angoff was away. Everything worked beautifully." Toward her he showed a Victorian courtesy. She was always "Miss Lustgarten" never "Edith." At times he teased her but only in an old-fashioned gentlemanly manner. Even when the Depression came and the situation in the *Mercury* office grew tense, he never took it out on her.

Toward the end of their association there were two events that

cast a particularly clear light on Mencken. The first one mixed farce
with melodrama; the second was serious throughout.

In April 1935, more than a year after Mencken left the *Mercury*,
its now slightly enlarged office staff led by Edith Lustgarten went out
on strike. The handful of employees had petitioned the new management to recognize the office workers' union and to give them a contract. The new management promptly charged her and another secretary with inefficiency, firing them both. They went out on the street
to picket in protest; with them marched a variegated group of fellow
workers and sympathizers. On an unseasonably cold spring day Mencken came by, and according to the AP story for May 1 the following
dialogue took place, opened by Edith Lustgarten after an exchange
of greetings:

> "Mr. Mencken, in all the years I worked for you, did you
> ever find me inefficient?"
> "Did I fire you?" he retorted. "But I thought you were a
> little bolshevik."
> "Now you know damn well I never was," she replied.
> He said that he didn't like to hear girls swearing. He
> asked if he had ever sworn at Miss Lustgarten. She said
> no, but that he used a lot of "funny words."
> "And I think you girls are a lot of damn fools," Mencken
> added, taking out a handkerchief and pretending to cry
> because of the girl's swearing.
> "I don't like to see you like this — out here in the cold
> wind," he said mildly as he drifted away.
> "Oh, that's all right," she cried reassuringly, "I've got a
> heavy coat and extra underwear."

It was the encounter of two different eras; the muted ending
was perfectly in key. The strike itself fizzled out. Though Mencken
wrote a letter publicly stating that she was far from inefficient, she
stayed fired and soon went to work for another magazine.

The second event involved Edith Lustgarten's husband. She had
married Fred Kean, a science teacher in the New York public schools.
He was ailing at the time of the marriage and by the summer of
1935 had to be hospitalized. Mencken was sympathetic. He wrote
her a letter on July 23. Half is devoted to encouraging her to believe
that her husband will recover, the other half to the strike. "I am still
convinced that the strike was a great mistake. The only persons
who profited by it were the quack radicals who egged it on." Fred

Kean failed to improve and by November was gravely ill. His wife did not know where to turn. In desperation she phoned Mencken in Baltimore. He took charge, made arrangements for Kean's hospitalization in Baltimore, secured the best possible diagnostician in his own Dr. Benjamin Baker, and then stayed by her in the hospital while her husband was operated on for a parathyroid tumor. And he saw to it that when Kean left the hospital the costs of the surgery were no problem. Here once more Mencken was at his best and most generous. Similarly, when in 1940 Kean suffered his final illness and his wife turned again to Mencken, he gave all the assistance he could.

The last time she saw Mencken was in May 1944. She had enlisted in the Women's Army Corps and was about to be sent to North Africa. They lunched together and talked tactfully of old times. He urged her — as he so often did those whom he liked — to put something on paper that could be published. He proposed that she write about herself and her Orthodox upbringing, her various jobs, and now her experiences in the women's army. He reminded her in a letter afterward, "You vowed on a stack of beer mats to send me 5,000 words within three weeks but so far they haven't reached me." Despite the vow they never did.

Mencken's relationship with Edith Lustgarten was friendly throughout its career. His relationship with Knopf could not have been more cordial. And his relationship with Nathan, once the storms of the *Mercury* were over, returned to something like its earlier warmth. But the history of his relationship with Charles Angoff is one of tension, largely unrecognized on both sides to begin with but then mounting till neither could ignore it, and ending on Angoff's side with something close to hatred. This relationship is worth looking at closely, and weighing carefully, because its tension brings out a side of Mencken's character seldom seen otherwise. Its annals start in January of 1925.

Exasperated by Nathan's refusal to do routine editorial work on the *Mercury* and burdened by the hours he himself had to put in, Mencken looked around late in 1924 for what he called a slave. With one, he predicted to Knopf, he could get the business of the magazine done and dispense with Nathan. He found him in Charles Angoff, Harvard '23. In the year since graduation Angoff had been searching for a newspaper job, preferably outside of Boston, a city he considered somewhat uncultivated. So far, however, he had gotten only to the suburbs, where he was acting as man of all work for a pawky suburban weekly called the Revere *Budget*. He had been applying without success to newspaper editors throughout the nation and now he turned to magazine editors also. Among those he addressed was Mencken. An earnest admirer of the *Smart Set* and its successor, Angoff thought he had almost no chance of finding a place on the *Mercury* but some chance of finding one on the *Sun*, so he mailed his letter to Mencken in Baltimore. To Angoff's astonished delight, Mencken was interested in considering him for the *Mercury*. Back in New York, he interviewed him, took him to dinner on Sixth Avenue, and within a week hired him.

Angoff reported to the office shortly after the first of the new year. Waving his cigar Mencken made him welcome. He introduced him to Knopf, who, Angoff thought, looked young and shy; to Nathan, who looked like a movie star; and to Edith Lustgarten. The ceremonies over, Mencken rapidly outlined Angoff's duties. In scope and responsibility, they went considerably beyond what Angoff had anticipated. He was to look through all the manuscripts as they came in, reject the obviously unsuitable ones, and then pass the rest to Mencken. In certain cases he might tell authors how their manuscripts could be revised to make them acceptable. He was to help with the proofreading and make-up of the magazine, and lend a hand with anything else around the office that needed to be done. And he was to be allowed to write an occasional brief review for the *Mercury's* "Check List" of new books. He was not to be a secretary — that was Edith Lustgarten's responsibility — but he was to be a general utility man.

The arrangement promised well. It provided Angoff with an unparalleled opportunity to learn to edit and write. It provided Mencken with a freedom from hackwork and an escape from the brawling rush of New York. He was able to concentrate on what he thought an editor should. That was to look for good authors, to solicit good manuscripts from them, and to shepherd the manuscripts onto the pages of the *Mercury*. In February 1925 he wrote to Phil Goodman that Angoff was proving to be quite competent, "He has already relieved me of much routine drudgery, and I hope to put even more on him." Mencken could now confine his visits to New York to once a month if he really wished. That would have been enough for him to oversee the make-up of the coming issue of the magazine and to put his imprimatur on the whole thing. But inevitably authors, ideas, and assorted business combined to draw him to New York more often.

Notwithstanding, he depended on Angoff increasingly though with some misgivings. Angoff himself soon recognized that his editorial views and his tastes differed from Mencken's, but he felt it proper to defer to Mencken as a matter of course once he had made his protest. Mencken usually listened, if condescendingly. For five brilliant years, from 1925 to 1929, the *Mercury* was so successful that everyone connected with it could feel good. The office ran smoothly and Mencken pitched in from time to time, partly because he no longer had to, to help Angoff and Edith Lustgarten. As Angoff noted, "There was nothing too menial for Mencken to do." He copy-read, he checked facts of doubtful accuracy at the library, he caught errors in editorial style, and he kept a careful eye on the appearance of the magazine. In spite of his jibes at its "whorehouse typography" he appreciated the handsome format of the *Mercury*. In the broadest sense of the word the magazine had style, and he wanted to maintain it.

After the stock market crash of 1929 the situation soured. Angoff was much more directly involved at the *Mercury* than was Knopf, so he felt the effects first. He says in his memoir *H. L. Mencken* that he found himself arguing with Mencken, less mildly than before, about what should go into the magazine. He believed that it should take notice of the enormous changes the crash had caused. He opposed, for instance, running some chapters from Harvey Fergusson's book on the Rio Grande; to him they were not merely dull, they were out of keeping with the tempestuous new era. Mencken — a new, irritable Mencken — let Angoff dispute with him briefly about the chapters. Then he put his foot down, saying, "I've had enough. We'll use the Fergusson. After all, the responsibility is mine." Angoff saw that Mencken was thoroughly annoyed and from that time he dated the first rift between them. According to Angoff, Mencken grew perceptibly cooler to him; in fact the atmosphere of the whole office chilled as the Depression affected the magazine.

Though he was convinced that the *Mercury* needed not only a change of course but a change of heart, Angoff says he tried to maintain a viable arrangement with Mencken. By 1931 Angoff's title had become managing editor; he now did more work and had a little more editorial responsibility. He felt an increased equity in the magazine. He thought the *Mercury* worth saving and its noted editor worth converting. He yearned to make the magazine a vehicle for reform in a moderately Socialist mode. But to Mencken socialism, however diluted, was a fraud; he had not swerved from his course of 1910 when he had debated it with Robert La Monte in *Men versus the Man.*

It was all too plain that he hoped to print in the *Mercury* what he had always printed before. One egregious example made Angoff charge that Mencken was running an antiquarian journal. It was his acceptance of an article "The Tragedy of the Sioux" by Chief Sitting Bull. Mencken wanted it to be the lead item of November 1931. Angoff asserts that he protested so earnestly that Mencken gave in. But only partly and even then he added a typical Mencken touch. He dropped the article to the third place in the table of contents and made the author's name Chief Standing Bear.

But the Mencken touch, once so envied, now seemed frivolous. Mencken himself was the last to see it, unfortunately. Nevertheless, the strain grew with each issue of the magazine; each month the Depression got worse instead of better. The ultimate result for Mencken was never in doubt, and it was hastened by the simple fact that he was growing older. Now in his fifties, he admitted to Angoff, "I'm tired of fighting."

In the last months of 1933, before he actually left, his relationship with Angoff hardened though they still spoke to one another. Then Mencken resigned; the conservative Henry Hazlitt succeeded him as editor; and not long afterward Knopf, unimpressed by Hazlitt's performance, let Angoff succeed Hazlitt. Angoff's satisfaction, it can be guessed, at sitting in Mencken's seat was acute, the more so since he had believed for some time that Knopf preferred his ideas about the *Mercury* to Mencken's. For a few months Angoff had a chance to publish something like the kind of periodical he longed for. It failed to please Knopf. Knopf sold the magazine as soon as he could and Angoff was out. He smarted at the blow and looked around him angrily for the cause of it. His frustration, his bitterness, gradually focused on Mencken. From time to time Mencken told his brother August and his friends that he believed Angoff was writing a book about him and that it would be derogatory in the extreme.

However, the book was slow to appear. It was not till shortly after Mencken died that *H. L. Mencken: A Portrait from Memory* had its first printing.

The book displayed a strangled hostility. But an understandable one. It was the apparent product of a love-hate of the kind that would have brought a gleam to the eyes of Freud. There were in the book the remains of the vast respect that young Angoff had felt for Mencken in the first years of the *Mercury*. There were remnants of the fascination that Mencken's wit, energy, and rowdiness had possessed for him. It was plain from many pages of the book that Mencken would always loom large in his memory. On the other hand, the repugnance showed through almost from cover to cover. The book starts, practically, with Angoff's description of Mencken urinating; it ends in much the same way.

The dominant portrait of Mencken emerging from the book is that of a half-educated bullyboy. Under the strains of the Depression he appears to Angoff an almost monstrous figure. Angoff is capable of writing about him during this period, "We found it difficult to talk about the news of the day with him, for fear he would begin to expose his ignorance, stupidity, callousness, and even cruelty."

The harshness of Angoff's judgment came not only from the abrasions of daily contact but from something deeper in the conflicting psychologies of the two men. The conflict was surely Oedipal in part. They played the roles of father and son, from the day they met. Mencken was forty-four, Angoff twenty-three at the time. Mencken had acquired, almost without trying, an enormous renown; it was not long afterward that Walter Lippmann called him "the most powerful personal influence on this whole generation of educated people." Angoff, on the other hand, had little to recommend him in those days except for a Harvard degree and a handful of clippings. Mencken's actions were infused with zest and rollicking authority. Angoff's were marked by hesitation and a degree of personal clumsiness. His bearing seemed slightly awkward; his speech still bore the traces of Minsk, where he had spent his first few years; the learning he gradually demonstrated was an odd mixture of Harvard and the Talmud.

In the memoir Angoff often described Mencken as ridiculing him, teasing him, or lecturing him. Almost every time Mencken did so, Angoff indicates that he was in the right while Mencken was in the wrong. The father overcame the son not by logic or wisdom but by bombast or raillery. A typical way for Mencken to close off a subject was with a remark like, "Angoff, you should be examined by a regiment of psychoanalysts." During the 1920s Angoff generally gave

way, though with some muttering and blushing. But with the arrival
of the Depression he asserted himself more, he says, standing up to
Mencken mainly because he felt his cause to be just.

There is little doubt that Mencken hectored him from time to
time during the decade they were together and that Angoff felt
aggrieved or irritated. He seldom enjoyed the flamboyance of Mencken's comedy but felt that he had to be polite. He remarks, for
instance, after reporting a bit of teasing by Mencken, "I was in no
mood for his humor at that moment, but I managed to conceal my
irritation." And, whether he realized it or not, his nature and his situation made him the inevitable butt for Mencken. Here is a passage,
soberly reported by Angoff: "One afternoon, he shouted across the
office to me: 'You think highly of John Keats. But do you know that's
only a nom de plume?' This surprised me. 'I thought that was his
real name.' 'God, Angoff, Harvard is some dump, really. Didn't they
teach you that John Keats's real name was Jacob Katz? Of course,
you will keep this valuable information confidential.'" But this whole
side of the Mencken-Angoff relationship can best be summed up in
two lines from the memoir: Mencken, "Boston is the anus of America."
Angoff, "Boston may be the anus of America but that anus produced
the only literature, so far, that this country has."

Mencken could not resist — to put it in the slang of the twenties —
pulling Angoff's leg or trying to shock him. Often Mencken made
statements of the kind that were his trademark, the kind in which he
defends an indefensible position with such spirit that he begins
to convince himself that it is defensible anyway. As Angoff listened
in horror, Mencken expanded on such theses as that Lincoln was a
fraud, that slavery in the South was a salubrious institution which
made the slaves happy, that Tolstoy was a humbug, that New York
would be better off with its subways shut, that Kant was a charla-
tan, that every criminal should be sterilized, and that William Faulkner was a mucker. This was the sort of thing that Mencken liked to
say in front of Angoff. He may even have used some crude four-
letter words in his hearing. Yet Mencken's more sophisticated companions seldom if ever heard him swear. With his splendid vocabulary, as Edith Lustgarten noted, he had no need for what Angoff
termed "this rawness of speech." It is probable that Mencken acted
in Angoff's presence as he acted before no one else.

Here, then, is one reason that Angoff's picture of Mencken

varies so fantastically from that of others. No one has expressed the paradox of the memoir better than a novelist acquainted with both men. He comments, "One of the riddles of the literature on Mencken is the book written by Angoff. . . . He had Mencken using language he never used, with me, or others who knew him, including the four-letter words, and doing obscene things, such as using Poe's grave for a urinal, that are utterly incredible in connection with him." On the other hand, the novelist believes that some things in the book are entirely convincing and suggest to him that Angoff was taking notes for his memoir from the day he went to work for Mencken at the *Mercury*.

The Mencken displayed before us is a deteriorating one. As the memoir goes along, the balance of power shifts perceptibly; Mencken grows weaker, Angoff stronger. To Angoff, Mencken is clearly losing his grip. In the years between 1930 and 1934 he not only becomes tired of managing the *Mercury*, he also becomes less able to do so. More and more is left to Angoff, and the year after Mencken resigns he will become editor. To all appearances the son, in Freudian terms, is triumphing over the father for a time at least.

With the son's victory comes a measure of sympathy for his defeated parent. Shortly before Mencken is to leave the *Mercury* Angoff feels "sorrier and sorrier" for him. But it is not till years later that Angoff glimpses something of the inner nature of the relationship. Then in his autobiographical novel *Summer Storm*, in which he calls himself David Polonsky and refers to Mencken as Brandt, he writes that Brandt "wanted David to like him, to be amused by him, to find fatherly guidance in him, to find something in him that an older and more experienced man can give to a younger man who admires him and finds a certain goodness in his company."

The magnitude of Mencken's achievement, however, in the *Mercury* was something Angoff could never bring himself to appreciate. He showed little awareness of the mind and art that went into the making of the magazine. The effect of that mind and art, as one engrossing number after another came out, was evident to much of America. But not the extent of Mencken's role; that would appear to anyone only on close inspection.

12. The MERCURY: *Mencken's Mind and Art*

THE *Mercury* involved a web of personal relationships, the most important being those of Mencken with Nathan, Knopf, and Angoff. However, there were many more; for Mencken made it one of his major aims to cultivate authors who might contribute to the *Mercury* — and whose contributions would harmonize with the doctrine and tone he desired.

To a startling degree the mind of Mencken became the mind of the *Mercury*. Its notable success gave added weight to the minds which influenced his, since he in turn influenced his writers and consequently the many thousands of readers of the magazine. And it was — to repeat — the most influential magazine of its era. To carry a copy of the green-covered *Mercury* under one's arm was a badge of distinction on college campuses, for teachers and students alike. To find the *Mercury*'s ideas impressive was characteristic of many of the intellectuals who played their own part in molding public opinion. And to adopt some of the *Mercury*'s innovations or attitudes seemed simply good sense to many a competing magazine editor.

Mencken had come a long way. Ernest Boyd once summed up Mencken's progress as he saw it. Writing in his *H. L. Mencken,* he remarked that from 1899 to 1916 Mencken's activities were local and that he reached the public outside of Baltimore largely through the literary criticism he published in the *Smart Set*. His rise to popular fame did not begin till he issued *A Book of Prefaces* in 1917. Then came America's participation in the war and thereafter his

impressive audience of the twenties. Boyd was if anything too conservative about the degree of Mencken's rise. By 1921 he had gone
so high that the journalist John Gunther could only exclaim in humorous admiration; by 1922 he had attained such an eminence that
Burton Rascoe thought there was no other way for him to go but
down.

Gunther declared, "Mr. Mencken has arrived. There can be no
doubt of that." He went on exuberantly, "His name, already the war
cry of the younger generation, is beginning to penetrate all quarters,
even the most holy and reverend. One finds him everywhere. He
no longer devotes all of his time to the *Smart Set,* edited by him
and his spiritual twin, George Jean Nathan, but is beginning to
branch out into other periodicals: the *Yale Review,* the *Century,*
the *New Republic.* I fully expected the stars to fall out of the sky
when I found him announced as a contributing editor of the *Nation.*
When I found an advertisement in the New York *Times,* asking
for first editions of his works, it dawned upon me that soon he
would be a great national institution, like the Follies, or Toasted
Corn Flakes."

Underneath his jocularity Gunther was right. At this point in the
early 1920s Mencken was well on his way to being a national institution. With the establishment of the *Mercury* in 1924 he would
unquestionably become one.

Meanwhile, he already had the entry to the liveliest minds in
America. The journals he wrote for were the ones they saw first. On
the genteel magazines, except for the *Atlantic,* and on the mass
magazines, even the portly *Saturday Evening Post,* he looked with
amiable scorn. He could already reach the elite, and he could reach
whatever part of the general public he wanted through his journalism. He was once again writing abundantly for the *Sunpapers*
and his material was so popular that one of his problems was fending
off the requests to reprint which came from other newspapers. He
thoroughly enjoyed the writing he was doing but the notion of a
new magazine exhilarated him even more. He soon turned his best
attention to the fashioning of the *Mercury.*

He saw it as a golden chance to exploit his personal interests.
If they had been narrow the magazine would have suffered but with
the passing of time they had broadened, contrary to what happens
in most men. Though he had lost much of his concern for what he

liked to call "Beautiful Letters," he had deepened and extended his concern for social science and indeed for science itself. His focus became something he termed "public psychology, *i.e.* the nature of the ideas that the larger masses of men hold, and the processes whereby they reach them." And his general range grew grand indeed: it was the scientific study of man.

That became his preoccupation. Throughout the 1920s, throughout his whole middle life in fact, he stood ready to read anything about this curious creature. Partly because of his oddity, man possessed an almost morbid fascination for Mencken. "No other animal," he had already noted in the *Smart Set* for August 1919, "is so defectively adapted to its environment." The books that passed over his desk for review, especially the ones he saved for his library instead of selling to a book shop, and the monographs and articles he read at the suggestion of friends testified to his wide-eyed curiosity about him. So did the scope and emphasis he determined on for the *Mercury*.

Most notable magazines reflect the taste of one person, bear the imprint of a single mind. As Allen Tate has remarked, "The great magazines have been edited by autocrats." During Mencken's career this held true for periodicals as different from one another as the *New Yorker*, the *Reader's Digest*, and *Time*, as well as for the *Mercury*. Nathan's brief appearance on the cover was a gesture to the past; the *Mercury's* purpose was Mencken's. The advertising announcements, the broadsides, the news releases, and Mencken's own letters all said essentially the same thing. "The aim of The American Mercury will be to offer a comprehensive picture, critically presented, of the entire American scene. It will not confine itself to the fine arts; in addition, there will be constant consideration of American politics, American governmental problems, American industrial and social relations, and American science."

The promise to pay attention to science was particularly noteworthy even though, as Mencken interpreted it, it was not all of science but the science that centered on man.

It may be guessed that most editors of general magazines have felt either indifferent to science or awkward in its presence. Few have welcomed it as cordially as Mencken. When he sent out his spate of letters soliciting contributions to the new journal, he saw to it that some stimulating writers on scientific subjects were among the persons asked. He hoped, he announced, to win as contributors men who stood at the top of their profession and could relate their subject to daily life. Among the notable scientists he named in a letter to Raymond Pearl in August 1923 was the behaviorist John B. Watson. And he assured Pearl that any chapter from Pearl's recent book, *The Biology of Death*, would have made an admirable contribution to the *Mercury*. Searching for additional contributors, he asked Pearl if he knew of others engaged in writing similar to that. Pearl proved willing to look, as did one or two other scientists with a broad acquaintanceship as well as high standing in their fields. But their success proved limited, for even in the case of scientists Mencken required that their attitude toward life be compatible with his. A scientist with an enduring belief in the wisdom of the masses or the nobility of reformers or the beauty of the Baptist Church found a cool welcome in the *Mercury* office. The standards were strict.

Part of the problem lay in the fact that Mencken was looking for more Raymond Pearls. For no scientist met the demands, conscious or unconscious, that Mencken made for the *Mercury* better than Pearl. He was exactly what Mencken wished. His professional credentials, both in quality and quantity, were impeccable. His *Who's Who* entry occupied half a column. It listed four scientific books he had written besides *The Biology of Death* and three more he had collaborated on. It listed honors, national and international, appointments, and professional offices. It listed the many editorships he had held — and editorial experience was in Mencken's eyes a distinct asset. Pearl was currently the editor of one professional journal, which he himself had founded, and had been or was now an associate editor of no less than nine others.

Pearl's early researches, including work on fishes and poultry, had been so varied as to seem miscellaneous. However, by the time he established himself on the Johns Hopkins faculty, he had the same concern as Mencken: man himself, mankind. Or as Mencken put it for Pearl years later: "man as a living creature like any other, man the unstable aggregation of more unstable colloids, man in the process of borning, living and dying, man in health and disease, man developing and man decaying." It was not man as poet or prophet but man as Mencken saw him.

Pearl's knowledge of man the animal was genuinely comprehensive. And his work was already distinguished not only for its substance but for the scientific procedures he was devising. He was the first to apply the techniques of mass measurement. He was a pioneer in computerizing before the day of the computer. Whatever the aspect of man he wished to investigate, he labored to acquire as large a mass of data as possible. Then he did his best, with his punch cards and his files, to measure it as precisely as a person could. Was he going to study the factors involved in longevity? He made it his business to find all living Americans over ninety and then to make the data he derived from them exact and easily accessible. Was he going to study the effects of birth control? Even in this sensitive subject he labored to be both comprehensive and precise. In the course of his investigations of man he devised improvements in biometrics that remain influential today.

Both what Pearl studied and the way he studied it made a profound impression on Mencken. But there was even more to attract him to Pearl. It was that he had a basic attitude toward his work that was not only gratifying because it paralleled Mencken's but useful because it gave Mencken's a scientific sanction.

For Pearl devoted himself both to discovering and describing the new and to demolishing the fallacious and old. "I was especially stimulated," Mencken recalled, "by his relentless and effective war upon bogus facts and false assumptions within his own field. He cleared off, in his time, an immense mass of rubbish, and he opened many an area of investigation that had been long resigned to darkness." In addition Pearl, once again with the sanction of science, shared Mencken's refusal to think that human nature and the human condition could be effectively improved. He declined to mix uplift with his science. As Mencken noted, "There was, of course, no touch of messianic passion in him, and he disliked messiahs as he disliked all other varieties of romantics. Even when, as in the case of the birth-control movement, he found himself in collaboration with persons of a generally constabulary cast of mind, he was always careful to distinguish clearly between the facts in hand and their moral and transcendental implications. On the question of the facts he had plenty to say, and he said it with great clarity, but he had serious doubts about the possibility of perfecting the human race, and he let them be known just as clearly."

Fortified by Pearl's impressive example and encouraged by the fact that Pearl promised to write for the *Mercury* himself, Mencken saw to it that from the start the magazine mirrored his own, already pronounced interest in science.

The opening number, for January 1924, struck the proper note. It revealed a department headed "The Arts and Sciences," which became a fixture in the magazine, and in it was the first article on science. It proved of course to be in the Mencken vein. It was "The Pother about Glands" by L. M. Hussey and it contended that man's virility could not be refreshed by any transplanting of glands. No new gonads for old; no apes unmanned for octogenarians. The second number gave more space to science. This time the department contained an article by Pearl which epitomized scientific study as Mencken wanted it. He gladly tilted a glass to the article. Called "Alcohol and the Duration of Life," it neatly demolished the old besides describing the new. Its thesis was that such evidence as we have shows, contrary to common belief, that moderate drinkers live longer than abstainers as well as longer than heavy drinkers. Besides Pearl's brief but inspiriting contribution, there were two longer articles concerned with man. One was "Osteopathy." The work of Morris Fishbein, it was a free-swinging attack by a doctor on what he regarded as lucrative, malevolent quackery. The other was "Heredity and Uplift" by the zoologist H. M. Parshley. His thesis was that the forces of social reform are mischievous but, in the long run, ineffective in their attempt to interfere with the Darwinian survival of the fittest. He forecast doom for the do-gooders. The third number of the *Mercury* had less science, but the tone had been successfully set and the magazine would keep its interest in science till Mencken left.

He maintained this interest in spite of the difficulty of attracting other scientists of the stature of Pearl as contributors. Yet he was a realist: if he could not attract first-rate men who could write he would attract second-rate men. Actually he was able to get both. He found a number of mature, experienced scientists, if not noted ones, who knew how to write; he found several knowledgeable nonscientists who proved they could popularize science (these were newspapermen including two from the *Sunpapers*); and he encountered and encouraged one restless young scientist who became the most successful popularizer of his time.

Professor Parshley of Smith College's zoology department typified the members of the first group. A perfectly respectable scientist, though not especially eminent, he contributed half a dozen articles before the end of the 1920s. Mencken made him the subject of an editorial note in the July 1929 number. It showed his general outlook to be Menckenian. "I do not believe in Prohibition, censorship, religion, or coeducation," he was quoted as saying. Furthermore, the note reported that he played the double bass, the viola, and the saxophone. As a matter of fact he became a friend of Mencken's, traveling to Baltimore at intervals to sit in with the Saturday Night Club.

The restless young scientist was Paul de Kruif. His academic background — he had a doctorate in bacteriology — was strong enough to earn him posts at the University of Michigan's medical school and at the Rockefeller Institute in New York. He enjoyed science and research but he also itched to write. So he sent a letter to Mencken in 1919 asking if a young man engaged in science should dare to attempt popular writing on the side. Mencken gave him an enthusiastic yes and started him on his career. Gradually de Kruif defined his subject and perfected his style. His field of popular science was new and, to Mencken, exceptionally important. On occasion he met de Kruif in New York, drank beer with him, and as their friendship formed expatiated to him on the fruitfulness of his chosen field. De Kruif began to appear in the magazines, published a trial book, collaborated with Sinclair Lewis on *Arrowsmith,* and then in *Microbe Hunters* produced his own best seller. Mencken was delighted. In a Hoboken beer hall he urged de Kruif to do a whole series of scientific best sellers: a book on physiologists, a book on surgeons, a book on therapists, and so on. But de Kruif had his own ideas for future books and Mencken respected those too.

When the *Mercury* appeared it was just the magazine for de Kruif. He published several articles in it during the 1920s. Mencken continued throughout the next two decades to enjoy de Kruif the writer and de Kruif the man. A hulking fellow, hard-talking, hard-drinking, he too shared something of Mencken's attitude toward life. In spite of his chronicling of great scientific discoveries he felt that the condition of mankind could at best merely be ameliorated. And he felt man to be far from perfectible; de Kruif's own shortcomings convinced him of that.

Mencken took a general interest in man which was wide enough to include studies as different in kind as Pearl's and de Kruif's. He took a specific interest in the human body, beginning with his own.

Watching it work with exasperated wonder he looked often, if somewhat distrustfully, for someone to explain it. Mencken never found him but came closest in the case of Dr. Logan Clendening. This was the man he had helped make the most popular medical authority of his time. Mencken enjoyed his blithe debunking of standard medical notions and threw open the *Mercury* to it. Here again he liked not only the contribution but the contributor's attitude — best exemplified in Clendening by the fact that he listed himself in *Who's Who* as "Free Thinker."

Whatever its condition the human anatomy interested Mencken, but its morbid state proved peculiarly appealing. He had an inexhaustible interest in illness. His own body acted as a laboratory in which the many human ills, major and minor, displayed their power to torment or annoy. He once wrote Nathan listing his current ails: a burn on the tongue (healing), a pimple inside the jaw, a sour stomach, a pain in the prostate, a burning in the gospel pipe, a cut finger, a small pimple inside the nose (going away), a razor cut (smarting), and tired eyes. He learned to be at home in hospitals and went to them, as patient or visitor, with unusual willingness. Moreover, as his experience broadened, he had no hesitation in diagnosing or prescribing for his friends.

The signs of his concern are clear in the *Mercury*. Articles on medicine appear in considerable numbers. There are not only the essays and exposés by Morris Fishbein and Logan Clendening, both regular contributors, but other pieces from a miscellany of medical authors. By the end of October 1926 a round dozen of doctors had published there. And more would publish later. Doctors were not the most frequent contributors — journalists led the list — but they were more numerous than in any other general magazine. Mencken's regard for the medical profession and what it did was manifest; though he liked to call doctors quacks he felt an interest in them almost as lively as his interest in politicians.

To Mencken man and his body came first. But man the social animal, man in society, was also absorbing. Here as his guide he had no Raymond Pearl to listen to or read with. He had, however, the works of William Graham Sumner.

In the field of social science Sumner proved to have more meaning for him than did any other thinker. His ideas are well worth investigating because of how much they anticipated and then confirmed Mencken's. It is true that Darwin provided Mencken with the key principle of the survival of the fittest. It is true that Huxley taught him the techniques of free thought. And Nietzsche's vivid, emotional pronouncements were an enormous stimulus to the young Mencken. They helped to formulate some of his major ideas, led to several of his books, and gave him hints on how to strike an attitude. With an admiring bow to these men, Mencken once said that he learned most by looking across the ocean. But though his mentors were customarily European he was not deaf to what a great countryman had to say. Sumner spoke to Mencken as one American to another: literally and figuratively they talked the same language. More to the point, Sumner spoke with what seemed the voice of paramount good sense.

Sumner's books, Mencken said when middle-aged, "made a powerful impression on me when I was young, and their influence has survived." His impact on Mencken was increased through the works of his chief disciple, Albert G. Keller. Keller succeeded Sumner in his chair at Yale, completed four volumes of Sumner's *Science of Society,* and edited Sumner's essays as well as doing his own substantial work. To Keller Mencken wrote early in 1932, "I have read you for many years, and have the new edition of your 'Societal Evolution' on my desk at this minute." Mencken never met Sumner, who died in 1910, but he kept his memory green. If Nietzsche was the voice of Mencken's youth, Sumner became the voice of his maturity.

Mencken by thirty had realized that he was something of a social Darwinist; and Sumner, as Richard Hofstadter has noted in *Social Darwinism in American Thought,* was the leading social Darwinist in America. His synthesis, to Hofstadter, combined three major forces in our capitalist culture. They were the Protestant ethic, the principles of classical economics, and the doctrine of Darwinian natural selection. Each of these forces impressed Mencken; he watched each operate with some satisfaction. In detail he did not always agree with the way he thought they were working; in general, however, he approved. He found Sumner appealing not only in his ideas as a social Darwinist but in his tone. For in presenting his synthesis, in explaining his views, Sumner shunned an anemic objectivity. He urged the correctness of his findings. In his writing he often showed some of the drive that we associate with Mencken, though he never achieved the rollicking vigor that was Mencken's great asset. During the last two decades of the century he stirred up more attention than any other social scientist.

In public affairs he consistently applied the doctrine that that government is best which governs least. He argued for the individual citizen and against the regime which so officiously represented him. He considered most governmental activities, from the tariff to social reform, an interference with the normal workings of the world. The title of an article he published in 1894 shows the attitude he took. It is called "The Absurd Effort to Make the World Over."

In the article Sumner takes a long, cold look at what he terms the "headlong reformers." If we let them have their way the result would be nightmarish. But Sumner reassures us. Ours is a tough world, hard to change by any feverish human efforts. It has been shaped by "spontaneous forces." The "great stream of time and earthly things will sweep on just the same" in spite of the reformers. He ends his essay with a comment that Mencken found memorable: "That is why it is the greatest folly of which a man can be capable, to sit down with a slate and pencil to plan out a new social world."

Yet some social progress can be made, Sumner concedes. Not through the visionary Utopias of the headlong reformers but through the determined efforts of the individual. Progress, like charity, literally must begin at home. "Let every man be sober, industrious, prudent, and wise, and bring up his children to be so likewise, and poverty will be abolished in a few generations." Progress is individual and moral. The virtues that Sumner selects are significant for their bourgeois quality. They are the ones that were inculcated in Mencken, who admitted cheerfully to being "a larva of the comfortable and complacent bourgeoisie." They are the virtues he exemplified in his own existence and derided only when they were cheapened by the booster luncheon-clubs.

They are, further, the virtues of "The Forgotten Man." He became the subject of one of Mencken's favorites among Sumner's essays. "I only wish," he wrote to Keller, "that such things as 'The Forgotten Man' could be printed as circulars in editions of millions."

They are the virtues of the reader the *Mercury* wanted. In the first issue the editors announced, "The reader they have in their eye, whose prejudices they share and whose woes they hope to soothe, is what . . . Sumner called the Forgotten Man — that is, the normal, educated, well-disposed, unfrenzied, enlightened citizen of the middle minority."

In his famous essay on him Sumner asserted that there was only so much of anything to go around. "If you give a loaf to a pauper you cannot give the same loaf to a laborer." If we pass a law to relieve the idle, it must be at the expense of the industrious. In all the efforts at legislating for social reform the man who always loses, the man who must pay for the efforts, is the honest, productive workman. Sumner observes that when A and B join to make a law to help X, their law always proposes to decide what C shall do for X; and C is the Forgotten Man.

It was out of this construction, surely, that Mencken derived what he called in *Newspaper Days* Mencken's Law: "Whenever *A* annoys or injures *B* on the pretense of saving or improving *X, A* is a scoundrel."

To Sumner the American faith in democracy is a sad piece of self-deception. Democracy in its pure form has never existed anywhere, nor would we want it to. Only in a country like America, with its initial advantage of much land and few people, could it even be neared. Sumner announces, "Let it be understood that we cannot go outside of this alternative: liberty, inequality, survival of the fittest; not-liberty, equality, survival of the unfittest." And he put all his bristling energies on the side of liberty and inequality, on the side, he said, of civilization. He stood ready to be governed by an aristocracy of energy and brains, not by the mob.

Just as Sumner's social Darwinism appealed to Mencken, so did his courage. Sumner proved himself fearless in preaching his doctrines even when they became highly unpopular. As an advocate of free competition he fought the protective tariff in the face of its massive support from the business community. There is just as much bite to his book *Protectionism, the Ism that Teaches that Waste Makes Wealth* as there is to his essay "The Absurd Effort to Make the World Over." And he fought American imperialism, manifested most blatantly in the Spanish-American War. He stood up against this popular, trumped-up war and endured all the hostility that his isolation could bring. Mencken doubtless remembered Sumner's stand when World War I took place and any breath of dissent was seen as sedition.

In Keller, Mencken found a noted follower of Sumner who tempered his doctrines to the twentieth century. Keller put more stress on institutions than on individuals but otherwise, as Hofstadter has said in *Social Darwinism*, "he was as skeptical as his teacher of proposals for a quick or drastic reconstruction of society, and as heartily devoted to a rigidly deterministic view" of social change.

Keller did not appear in the pages of the *Mercury* till 1932 but then his essay was, appropriately, on Sumner. "The Discoverer of the Forgotten Man" ran as the lead article in the November issue and was doubtless occasioned by Franklin Delano Roosevelt's revival and — to both Keller and Mencken — perversion of Sumner's once famous phrase. The Forgotten Man to Roosevelt looked much different than he had to Sumner. To Roosevelt he was the Little Man, the man out of work, the man who needed help. To Sumner, Keller, and Mencken he was the man who held a job, never complained, always paid his way, and so failed to draw the notice of the politicians.

Sumner's attractions for Mencken were, to repeat, permanent and profound. Long after his views had played their part in the editing of the *Mercury*, long after Mencken had left the magazine, those views remained present in Mencken's prose. They were precisely the ideas he preached in his Monday Articles, in the Sunday Articles which succeeded them, in his political dispatches, and in portions of his books. Down to his final book, *Minority Report*, his work is sprinkled with passages that smack of Sumner. He observes in *Minority Report*, for example, "There is a constant accession of governmental authority and power. It works inevitably toward the disadvantage of the only sort of man who is really worth hell room, to wit, the man who practices some useful trade in a competent manner, makes a decent living at it, pays his own way, and asks only to be let alone."

To embody in the *Mercury* the ideas that he drew from Sumner, and Darwin and Huxley, the ideas that he shared with Pearl, and the ideas that were peculiarly his, he had to be both potent and persuasive. He was; he played on his authors like instruments.

Whether his writers were specialists or nonspecialists he worked closely with them, beginning with the first issue. When starting the *Mercury* he reminds us of the conductor of a symphony orchestra as he gets ready for his initial concert. Everything must be right; no detail seems too trifling to be overlooked. We can see striking evidence in a large-paper copy of the first number of the *Mercury*, still preserved, which has letters from the contributors tipped in.

The letters show that he stayed with his authors from, in many cases, ideas to galley proof. He sent back a number of articles for revision, adding suggestions on how the revisions should be made. When necessary he included instructions, exhortations, and even prayers! The authors accepted his dictums with a readiness that testified to how high his reputation stood. For example, James Oneal writes a letter of November 7, 1923, about his article "The Communist Hoax," starting: "Here is the article revised according to your suggestions." John McClure says of his fable "The Weaver's Tale" that Mencken can blue-pencil it at will. George Philip Krapp writes about his "The Test of English" that the cuts Mencken proposes are a great improvement. Woodbridge Riley, author of "The New Thought," carries cooperation still further: "Here is the revised article on New Thought condensed to exactly 18 pages as you requested." Everybody played in harmony and the first issue was superbly orchestrated.

Though he did not quite make the magazine's motto *E Pluribus Unum,* he came close. He told Goldberg in 1925 that he had been forced to spend a great deal of time during the *Mercury's* first year in rewriting accepted manuscripts. But he added that after that time the sort of writing he wanted began to come in.

Potential contributors could soon see what he wanted by leafing through the pages of the issues as they appeared, and the editor could relax some of the strictness of his discipline. In that discipline, not incidentally, lay not only much of the strength the *Mercury* showed from the start but also the seeds of its later deterioration.

Throughout his decade on the *Mercury* he kept in close touch with his contributors. Though he remained an autocrat, three things saved him from seeming an ogre to them. One was his relaxed, humorous air; a quip went with every request. Another was his evident interest in his contributors. The third was the good sense of his suggestions. Usually they were so sound that they carried their own persuasiveness with them. He had the wisdom to see where an opening, for example, could be aided or an argument speeded up, where cuts should be made or material inserted. Or how a vapid title could become an inviting one: for example, he transformed "The Decline of the Negro Churches" into "Black America Begins to

Doubt." The tone of a contribution was a more delicate and personal matter; and he usually let that alone. The content was no problem since he seldom accepted any article he disagreed with.

His correspondence with Dane Yorke, a Maine free-lance writer, shows how beneficial his counsel could be. Yorke became one of the *Mercury*'s most valued authors. Versatile enough to write on anything from Shakespeare to woollen mills, he selected his own subjects, prepared his articles, and then submitted them to the *Mercury*. Mencken readily bought most of them. Any changes he proposed were designed to let Yorke speak more clearly to the public and more forcefully. He knew, better than Yorke, the ways of the *Mercury*'s readers. For instance, when Yorke entitled an article on the vagaries of radio "Regusted Radio," taking the term "regusted" from the slang of a popular program called "Amos and Andy," Mencken pointed out that many readers seldom listened to the radio and would not know what the word meant. About the cuts Mencken suggested from time to time, Yorke himself said that they made his pieces clearer without harming either the sense or the tone. And they also made them more incisive.

Of course this kind of management did not always work. Occasionally Mencken overreached himself. Some of the *Mercury*'s contributors balked, especially the distinguished ones, when he tried to tamper with their style, for example, by inserting the "Prof. Drs." and "Hons." which he liked to use himself. He tried it with Arthur Krock, already a respected political journalist but not yet the pundit he would later become. Krock recalls that he simply revised away Mencken's revisions. Krock's text appeared in print, consequently, as Krock had written it. Here and there Mencken got other kickbacks though journalists in general, particularly his friends from the *Sunpapers*, were apt to be complaisant.

When his contributors were scientists, Mencken had only a few suggestions to make about the details of what they said. When they were popularizers of science he considered that he could make a few more. And when they were social scientists he considered that he could make a good many. The chief reason was that he had been studying in the social sciences systematically for many years — with emphasis on "the public psychology" — and now in the middle and late 1920s he was doing so more than ever. For at the same time that he was editing the *Mercury* he was undertaking research for two treatises to appear in the next decade. From the start he took them seriously; later he was to feel that they were perhaps his permanent contribution to the understanding of our civilization. *Treatise on the Gods* appeared in 1930, *Treatise on Right and Wrong* in 1934. Both were broad gauged. Both dealt with important ideas held by the mass of men and tried to describe how they arrived at them. The extensive critical bibliographies in both books testify to his years of study. They show a Mencken who, in spite of his scoffing at scholars, did his best to be scholarly. His quotations were precise, his details accurate. Looking back long afterward at *Treatise on the Gods,* he said proudly that no one had ever challenged a fact in it.

One other work, which never became a printed book but which Mencken read for off and on during the whole of the twenties, was his projected "Homo Sapiens." Even in manuscript it attested to his learning.

Through all this sustained reading, much of it critical, Mencken became a remarkably well-informed editor. We know he did not allow his studies to overturn his previous ideas, but his ideas now had more definition and documentation than ever before.

The first bound volume of the *Mercury,* for January–April 1924, established the scope and nature of the new journal even more than the first number. Along with the sciences, the social sciences are well represented for a general magazine. There is an article by the celebrated anthropologist Robert Lowie, whom Mencken had promptly lured into contributing, entitled "The Origin and Spread of Culture." It asserts that resourcefulness is not the monopoly of a single culture. Inventions can be found in any part of the globe, and it is perfectly possible that the same thing could be invented by more than one tribe or nation. There are articles in the field of political science, such as "The Tragic Hiram," which is a mock-elegiac essay on Senator Hiram Johnson of California, written by Mencken's colleague on the *Sun,* John Owens. There are articles on linguistics, such as Krapp's "The Test of English." There are articles on history designed to clear away old ideas. The titles suggest the tone: "The John Brown Myth" by Leland Jenks, "The Lincoln Legend" by Isaac R. Pennypacker, "The Drool Method of History" by Harry Elmer Barnes.

These breezy essays are mainly the work of professionals; when they are not they tend to be the work of semiprofessionals at least. Pennypacker, for example, was a retired newspaper editor, but he was also the author of three books about the Civil War. When in succeeding volumes of the *Mercury* the proportion of professionals went down and the proportion of journalists rose, the general level of competence did not sink sharply. In the tenth volume, January–April 1927, for example, there was a journalist rather than a professional sociologist writing in Zelda F. Popkin's "The Changing East Side"; but Pliny Goddard, who contributed "Man in America," was a respected anthropologist; James Oneal, who contributed "The Socialists in the War," was on his way to becoming a major historian of American radicalism; and Lewis Mumford, who contributed "The Machine and Its Products," was already nationally known for his studies in American civilization.

Throughout the 1920s the *Mercury* was a remarkably readable magazine, a galaxy of good articles. But not in the 1930s. Then the magazine became markedly more eccentric, attracting fewer first-rate, and even second-rate, minds. Nineteen twenty-nine, the year of the stock market crash, proved to be the pivotal year. After that it was not only that the articles grew crotchety, it was that — seen against the bleak background of the Depression — they became trivial. The very charge of triviality that Mencken had made against the *Smart Set* could now be turned against the *Mercury*. The extended attempt, in the three numbers for the fall of 1931, to find "The Worst American State" remains a prime example. In the attempt, the social scientists' graphs and statistics were employed to document the *Mercury*'s boisterous charges. The decision that the worst state was Mississippi, joke or no joke, must have looked pointless to many of the remaining readers. They had their own troubles, little relieved by looking down on Mississippi.

The cluster of departments Mencken offered his readers was considered during the twenties to be one of the best things in the *Mercury*. "Americana," seized from the pages of the *Smart Set*, was a collection of splendidly asinine quotations from contemporary life. They were divided by states and each quotation was introduced with a sardonic comment from the editors. "Clinical Notes" too came from the *Smart Set*. It was the well-known "Répétition Générale" shorn of its fancy title and given a little more thrust. As before, it featured epigrams but included an assortment of paragraphs, short and long, designed to amuse. "The Theatre" was Nathan's province, we know, and the main thing left for him after the split with Mencken. In the pieces he wrote for it he helped to consolidate his standing as the country's ablest dramatic critic.

Some other departments, such as "The Library," on current books, stayed in the *Mercury* from the start to the finish of Mencken's tenure. A few more came and went. A few, such as "The Soap-Box," which printed communications from readers, appeared late. Though in general the departments added spice to the *Mercury*, they shared in the decline that accompanied the Depression. "Americana," once the most widely hailed of the departments, now deteriorated in both quantity and quality. The quaint or freakish news items that had once been so diverting no longer sounded very funny.

Similarly, the editorials often acquired an antiquarian flavor. They smelled of the attic. Somehow they did not seem to be prime Mencken any more. A sample, say from the September numbers, can show what was happening; for he wrote either as he had before or not at all. In the September 1930 number, the first of Mencken's editorials was "The Calamity at Appomatox." In his usual half-rallying fashion he defended a favorite thesis, that we would be better off if the South had won the Civil War. In the September 1931 number his first editorial lamented the passing of an aristocratic politician — "One Who will be Missed" was the title — in the person of the late Nicholas Longworth. The remaining editorials were "The Boon of Culture" and an elegy on the passing of the steam locomotive. The September 1932 number contained no editorials whatsoever; current problems were in effect ignored. Nor were there editorials in the September 1933 number, the last September number in which Mencken had a hand.

The omissions were explained clearly enough in the November 1933 leader entitled "What is Going on in the World." In it the departing editor confessed that things were happening too fast for him. Roosevelt's New Deal was altering the laws of man and nature so swiftly that an editor could not keep up. Take for example, said Mencken morosely, the fact that he had spent five nights preparing an editorial on the law of supply and demand, only to find that it had "been repealed by Executive Order." Speaking with Dane Yorke,

Mencken voiced similar complaints about how fast things were changing; there was a new note of querulousness in his correspondence too. And he gulped down more soda-mints than ever before.

His editorial stance in the *Mercury* had presumed a static system, one which needed to be stirred up. But it seemed to the country that it was no longer the system which needed stirring up but Mencken. Notwithstanding, he had led the *Mercury* to heights no one had foreseen. It had become the center of all eyes, and many of them had looked with keen approval.

Though it is easy to exaggerate influence, it is apparent that the influence of the *Mercury* in its first few years on American magazines was greater than that of any other periodical during the decade. It was more than a breath of fresh air; it was a gust that once or twice grew to a gale. By example Mencken showed that a magazine could be controversial without being vindictive, lively without being frenetic, and witty without being silly.

Not that the *Mercury* did not owe its own debts. Mencken openly used the *Smart Set* as a point of departure, and he several times said that he looked to Ellery Sedgwick's *Atlantic Monthly* as a model. He also looked back to the enterprising *Century* in its heyday; he had praised it highly in his *Prejudices: First Series* as well as elsewhere. From a variety of his comments we can see that in both those periodicals he discovered a lively engagement with current events without the shallowness that seemed to him the chief flaw of the *Smart Set*. Besides the *Mercury's* debts to these magazines, there was a larger debt it owed. It was to the new spirit of the times. There was an atmosphere of brash rebellion, of ironic amazement at the condition of American culture when the twenties opened. The spirit was reflected in Mencken's stare of incredulity and delight, the china-blue stare his friends remarked on.

The testimonies of the day on the impact of the *Mercury* ranged from the most general to the most particular. "Have you heard of the revolution on Quality Street where the serious magazines live," asked Leon Whipple in a long article he published in *Survey* magazine once the *Mercury* was well established. He contrasted the sinking circulations of the current *Century*, *Scribner's*, and *Harper's* with the astonishing rise of the *Mercury's* circulation from zero to over sixty thousand by the end of 1925. He maintained that these figures were "index numbers for something in our intellectual life" and that other editors had to take the fact into account or fail. They "heard the thunder of the changing tides. They had to go up or go under." Such pronouncements continued to be made for the next several years.

In the wake of the *Mercury* more than one well-known periodical, as a matter of fact, brightened its form and up-dated its content. The *Bookman,* which came under the editorship of Burton Rascoe, who admired Mencken, discarded its old rather fancy cover in 1927 in favor of a two-toned brown one that resembled the *Mercury's.* It spiced its subject matter as well. *Harper's* not only appeared with a fresh cover (red) and fresh format but also attracted several of the *Mercury's* own contributors, among them Ernest Boyd, Clarence Darrow, and Frank Kent. *Scribner's* began to shy away from literature and embrace current events, so that by the beginning of the thirties it was, according to its editors, a general magazine devoted to contemporary life. Even the austere *North American Review* was said to have been affected. And when a magazine resisted the influence epitomized in the *Mercury,* hard times were ahead for it. In his study Whipple diagnosed the decline of the *Century* and the *Forum,* in particular, as being due to a resistance to that influence.

He had a point. The most successful magazines adapted to the new; the others paid for their refusal. Specific influence is hard to prove but we can find some highly suggestive parallels. There is the case of the *New Yorker,* founded a year after the *Mercury.* Its view of life and its attitude toward its readers were much like those of the *Mercury.* Two of its most profitable devices probably owed something to the *Mercury.* One was the "Profile," the other was the "Talk of the Town." As Angoff remembered it, the idea for the "Profile" was "born in the office of the Mercury." A look at the pages of both magazines will show that their pictures of individuals had much in common. Both Mencken and Harold Ross, editor of the new *New Yorker,* wanted character sketches that seized the essence of a personality. They especially liked to see the significant detail, the descriptive touch that told something about the subject — the way he wore his tie perhaps or how he ate his breakfast. Both were intent on finding "revealing trivia." On the other hand, there were differences too between the character sketches that Mencken accepted in those days and the ones that Ross took. Ross was less crusty than he later became and most of the "Profiles" he printed were kindly ones, while Mencken could enjoy printing a portrait etched in acid.

The "Talk of the Town," which opened each weekly number of the *New Yorker,* bore several resemblances to the *Mercury's* "Clinical Notes." They had in common a sophistication; a concern, once again, with the significant detail; and an urbane style. There were also differences, in particular a tinge of sentiment in the "Talk of the Town" that was foreign to the atmosphere of "Clinical Notes."

And yet there were observations like this one which could have appeared easily in either periodical; it is from the "Talk of the Town" of February 28, 1925:

> I used to think that
>
>> They needed an angel in heaven
>> So God took Caruso away
>
> was the Height of Something in belles lettres, but in that mist of the dawn ahead in which one senses perfection an even higher monument to beauty has taken form out of the haze. It is the following from a new popular song entitled "My Kid":
>
>> He comes downstairs in his little white nightie
>> And says his prayers to God Almighty.
>
> I am told that it is making thousands of better men and women in vaudeville and night club circles.

Another device that the *Mercury* used, notably in its "Americana" department, and the *New Yorker* adopted was the clipping of quaint quotations from the press and reprinting them with a wry comment. The difference lay in the fact that the *Mercury*, underneath, was a serious magazine while the *New Yorker* was humorous. Mencken, on the one hand, assembled news items each month that illustrated the grotesqueries of American culture. For example:

> From a harangue delivered to the Chamber of Commerce of Tucson by the Hon. H. B. Titcomb:
>
>> The person who objects to the ringing of cracked bells from a church tower I do not believe is a good citizen of any community.

The aim in "Americana" was to present items that were not only amusing but ridiculous. Ross, on the other hand, simply hoped to entertain by selecting items like this, for the March 15, 1925 number:

The ladies of the Plum Street Church have discarded clothes of all kinds. Call at 44 North Plum Street and inspect them.

A further tribute to the *Mercury's* success was the emergence of several magazines similar to it in one way or another. In his book on Mencken and the *Mercury*, Marvin Singleton has collected several specimens, all rescued from the dustbin of defunct magazines. There was, for instance, *McNaught's Monthly*, which acquired a cover much like the *Mercury's* though its contents were gentler in tone. Its January 1925 number contained such articles as the satirical "If in Doubt, Pass a New Law," but the prevailing view was more kindly, for instance in "Are Americans Robots? The Case for the Negative." There was *Plain Talk*, whose editors announced, "We shall never be flannel-mouthed or insipid. We shall truckle to no advertisers, kiss no political toe, walk no fences, boast no friends, fear no enemies." Its issue for October 1927 includes such articles as "Why not a Catholic President," "Journalism as Big Business," and "Do We Need Grafters." According to Angoff, Mencken asserted that the magazine was an outright imitation of the *Mercury;* and in Angoff's judgment he was right.

Nothing delighted Mencken more than the imitation in reverse that he inspired in the *Saturday Evening Post.* The weekly bible of the boobs and boosters, it represented his favorite target among the magazines. Much annoyed by Mencken's barbs, its arch-conservative editor, George Horace Lorimer, turned Mencken's device of "Americana" around. Each week he collected news items that showed the positive side of American culture and dressed our civilization to advantage. Did the Kiwanians of Memphis, Tennessee spend twenty thousand dollars to heal a sick child? The *Post* clipped the item and, aping Mencken, headed it: "Astonishing account of one little deal by businessmen in which there was no hope of a cash dividend, as set forth in the columns of the Philadelphia Inquirer." But virtue seldom seems as interesting as vice, and Lorimer's "Americana" failed to flourish. However, every time it appeared it offered Mencken a fund of innocent amusement.

The *Mercury* also enjoyed the compliment of being parodied among the college magazines. Though Mencken more than once denied that he cared anything about the *Mercury*'s influence on students, it was certainly the most talked about of all magazines on college campuses. Its mark could be seen on many a student journal, and at least three of them published parody numbers. The Cornell *Widow* for January 1927, the Northwestern *Purple Parrot* for March 1928, and the CCNY *Mercury* for December 1929 were among those that burlesqued it from green cover to green cover.

Mencken himself summed up the role of the *Mercury* in the magazine world in an editorial marking the end of the *Mercury*'s fifth year. He observed that "Several flattering but naive imitations of it have appeared, and it has obviously influenced the format and contents of more than one of its elders."

He was complacent and understandably so; he could not tell what was waiting for him. In the same editorial he also reported cheerily about his magazine, "Its friends, no doubt, will be glad to hear that it comes to this interesting age in the best of health, and with every hope of afflicting the right-thinking for a long while to come. It has paid off every cent of the capital invested in it, it has no debts, and it is showing a profit — not large, but still safe, steady and sufficient. Its circulation has now gone beyond that of any save a few magazines of its class, and its readers show a charming disposition to stick to it, so that the turnover is small. That portion of its circulation which is represented by annual subscribers continues to grow, both absolutely and in relation to the total monthly sale. Its advertisers, having discovered by experience that it reaches a class of readers who want things of merit and are able to buy them, patronize it faithfully, and many of them increase their bookings of space. In brief, the position of the magazine is sound and satisfactory."

Such smugness did not go unnoticed. The New York *Times* teased him, commenting piously that success had spoiled even the *Mercury*. It had become prosperous by ridiculing the American veneration for prosperity; now it was bragging like any Rotarian about its own affluence. The *Times* apostrophized the often-attacked businessman: "O *homo boobiens*, O Americano, thou hast triumphed!"

From 1929 onward, the influence of the *Mercury* diminished and by the time that Mencken left its influence was almost gone. It waned mainly because of the massive economic changes that emerged in the Depression. But even if they had not occurred, the *Mercury* in its first years set a standard so high that no one could have sustained it. Even the brightest vaudeville turns could not impress, month after month, without new spangles or stunning innovations. Gradually the *Mercury* and its editor began to be taken somewhat for granted. The bouquets became fewer; the amused amazement at the tricks on the high wire subsided.

With the onset of the Depression the general envy of the *Mercury* among other magazines turned to condescension. Its few earlier critics had sounded shrill; now they roared out their invective at the magazine and Mencken. The Marxist Michael Gold used his *New Masses* to address an open letter to Mencken demanding that he retire. "You are a Tory who hates the Soviet Union. Worse than that, you are a white Nordic chauvinist who fears and hates the yellow races." So Gold wrote in his issue for September 1931. He was joined, though with less vituperation, not merely by other Marxist critics but by a large number of moderates who now felt that Mencken was an economic primitive and that his whole cast of mind was wrong for this new day. Gold was even joined by the rare remaining New Humanists who deplored not Mencken's conservatism but his lack of it. Stuart Sherman was dead before the Depression started, but both Irving Babbitt and Paul Elmer More survived into the 1930s to scold Mencken.

Nevertheless, the social contribution Mencken had made was beyond question. It was dramatized in two of the key disputes of the 1920s, the Scopes trial and the "Hatrack" case. The one involved the *Mercury* only marginally but the other centered on it. Both instances showed the country Mencken at his peak.

13. Mencken, Darwin, and God

LONG BEFORE THE ADVENT of the *Mercury*, Mencken had sworn opposition to Puritanism in all its forms. When he created the *Mercury* he continued his war. He found Puritanism, though battered by the times, quite ready to join battle. Easily provoked, it took the initiative in what became the most notorious attempt at censorship during the 1920s, the "Hatrack" case; it took the initiative too in the Scopes trial. But it met in Mencken its most resourceful single opponent. In the Scopes trial, which occurred first, he acted mainly as a reporter but also as a participant behind the scenes. In the "Hatrack" case he played the focal role. And after these two celebrated occasions he wrote and published a book, *Treatise on the Gods*, which he intended as his intellectual instrument for the maiming of Puritanism. In each instance he fought a different kind of battle against a different aspect of Puritanism, but it was all part of his total war.

The Scopes trial, held the year after the *Mercury* started, offered him the most inviting opportunity he would ever have to dramatize his views on science and theology. It all began in March 1925 when the state of Tennessee passed a law against the teaching of evolution. In the Tennessee town of Dayton a young high school instructor in biology, John Thomas Scopes, allowed himself to be indicted in order to test the law.

In the words of his indictment he "did unlawfully and wilfully teach . . . certain theory and theories that deny the story of the divine creation of man as taught in the Bible, and did teach instead thereof that man is descended from a lower order of animals." The moment Mencken read in the newspapers about the forthcoming trial he beamed. He realized that he had here not only an event that could reveal the American boob at his most fatuous but one that could illuminate the clash of two striking American attitudes, the opposition of two American views of life. One, the attitude of the vast majority, was to him fundamentalist, parochial, mean. The other, the attitude of the small minority which counted him as a member, was enlightened, open, liberal. Also he saw that he ought to do more than report the trial; he ought to interpret it on two levels. The first, and surface one, would be that of the customary human circus. The second would be that of the onslaught by the massed forces of darkness against the handful of upholders of the light. Furthermore, he certainly ought to help the upholders of the light.

The trial was not to be held till the summer of 1925 but Mencken began his efforts in spring. By chance he was visiting the novelist James Branch Cabell in Richmond when the most controversial trial lawyer in America, Clarence Darrow, was likewise in Richmond, making a speech. Mencken and Darrow, already acquaintances, met at Cabell's home and discovered in each other a consuming interest in the coming trial. Mencken urged Darrow to volunteer as one of the attorneys for Scopes's defense. He needed only a little urging. The central issue was the freedom of man to use his mind, as Darrow and Mencken both saw it; and it was presented in its most inviting form by the attack of the Bible Belt fundamentalists on the theory of evolution. Darrow had already clashed with the Bible's stern defender, William Jennings Bryan, in the pages of the Chicago *Tribune;* and the report that Bryan had joined the prosecution delighted him. "Nobody gives a damn about that yap schoolteacher," Mencken told him. "The thing to do is to make a fool out of Bryan." The persuasions in Richmond were potent enough so that Darrow promptly telegraphed Dayton from there and offered to assist the defense — the first time in his long career that he had volunteered his services. The two men may have met again in Baltimore, for Mencken long afterward told his friend Huntington Cairns that the strategy of the Scopes trial was planned at his house.

As the date of the trial drew closer Mencken was flushed with excitement. In a letter of May 27 he reported to Sara Haardt, "I have got myself involved in the Tennessee evolutionist trial, as a Consulting Man of Vision to Darrow and Dudley Field Malone," another noted liberal lawyer. He wrote and talked with even more spirit than usual. He polished off eight assorted pieces for the *Mercury;* he commented often about Tennessee in his notes to his friends; and in the Bierabende just before his departure he discoursed at exceptional length about the issues and personalities involved.

His concern was completely understandable. "In a sense," as Manchester has observed in his biography, "the issues at stake were those on which the *Mercury* had been founded, on which his whole life had come to be based." The event would very probably be epic. He had to be part of it. Supported by the shades of Darwin and Huxley, abetted by Raymond Pearl, and accompanied by several colleagues from the *Sunpapers,* he entrained for Tennessee.

He found Dayton a surprisingly attractive small town, its houses set in cool green lawns, its trees stately, its single drugstore almost metropolitan. He found the townspeople decently attired and reasonable in their address to outsiders. The reasonableness was based, however, on the rocklike certainty that they were right in trusting Genesis and that the evolutionists were so wrong that they could be indulged a little. To Mencken and his friends, Daytonians made it politely clear that Scopes could not hope to win and that persons perverse enough to help him, chief among them Darrow, would be demolished by the Bible-wielding Bryan. The only question was how he would do it. Their confidence was convincing. "Will he do it gently," Mencken himself wondered in his opening dispatch of July 9, "or will he . . . make a swift butchery of it?"

Mencken walked the streets in the July swelter talking with the local citizens, hailing his fellow newspapermen, and storing up observations for his lengthy reports to the *Evening Sun* and other papers. Because he had admitted with mock-resignation that there could not be the slightest doubt about the result of the trial, he concentrated on the workings of the legal process in Dayton, on its implications for freedom of thought, and on the human-interest aspect of the trial. He found a splendid gallery of grotesques to report. They were not citizens of Dayton; they were outsiders attracted by the heat of the issues. There was above all Bryan himself, mangy, sweaty, baleful. And there were such others as Colonel Patrick Callahan of Louisville, the self-proclaimed head of two hundred and fifty million Catholic fundamentalists throughout the world; and Pastor T. T. Martin of Blue Mountain, Mississippi, with his mop of snow-white hair, who operated from a room stocked "with pamphlets bearing such titles as 'Evolution a Menace,' 'Hell and the High Schools,' and 'God, or Gorilla.'" Every night the pastor sallied out, preaching fiercely against evolution.

While Mencken fanned himself at the torrid trial or cooled off a little at the drugstore, he watched the human comedy he was describing for his papers. "The thing," he wrote Raymond Pearl, "is genuinely fabulous. I have stored up enough material to last me twenty years." The high point for him was a Holy Roller revival meeting he went to in a mountain glade near Dayton. He reported it in a masterly dispatch that mingled glaring description with bits of compassionate comment. He was watching the revival unobtrusively with some other newspapermen when a young girl in the congregation jumped up and then threw herself on the ground. "'This sister,' said the leader, 'has asked for prayers.' We moved a bit closer. We could now see faces plainly and hear every word.

"What followed quickly reached such heights of barbaric grotesquerie that it was hard to believe it real. At a signal all the faithful crowded up to the bench and began to pray — not in unison but each for himself. At another they all fell on their knees, their arms over the penitent. The leader kneeled, facing us, his head alternately thrown back dramatically or buried in his hands. Words spouted from his lips like bullets from a machine gun — appeals to pull the penitent back out of hell, defiance of the powers and principalities of the air, a vast impassioned jargon of apocalyptic texts. Suddenly he rose to his feet, threw back his head and began to speak in tongues — blub-blub-blub, gurgle-gurgle-gurgle. His voice rose to a higher register. The climax was a shrill, inarticulate squawk, like that of a man throttled. He fell back headlong across the pyramid of supplicants.

"A comic scene? Somehow no. The poor half-wits were too horribly in earnest. It was like peeping through a knot-hole at the writhings of a people in pain."

As the trial went along, its personalities postured in front of him and got most of his attention. But he never lost sight of the issues they embodied. Those were as simple to him as truth versus falsehood. He helped to plan the strategy for the defense, working especially through Darrow. Knowing that Scopes would be judged guilty he concentrated, in his suggestions and his dispatches, on how to discredit the judges. To him they were not only the man on the bench but the whole party of parochialism. He concentrated on trying the fundamentalists of Dayton and Tennessee and of the entire country. He indicted them in each dispatch and forecast trouble for them in the future. Even before the jury was picked he asserted, "The real trial, in truth, will not begin until Scopes is convicted and ordered to the hulks. Then the prisoner will be the legislature of Tennessee."

He shared a desk at the trial with an unusually active and well informed colleague, fiery little Watson Davis of *Science Service*, which gathered news about science for the press. In conjunction with the defense Davis had enlisted a dozen of the leading scientists in America. After their arrival Mencken talked with some of them and with Davis about the issues. He agreed with Davis that freedom of education and freedom of scientific inquiry stood in grave danger. The hope lay in educating the reading public about what the trial really meant.

In their own ways Mencken and Davis did it as well as they could. They wanted the expert testimony brought out, knowing that it would demolish the fundamentalist case. For several days the dozen scientists wilted in the wings while the presiding judge made up his mind whether he would let them talk. Early in the morning of July 17 he announced his decision: no. The courtroom forensics would have to continue to be the center of news interest. The scientific testimony on the issue, which Mencken had wanted so much to hear and report, would not be given. The letdown for him was considerable.

All of a sudden the courtroom palled. He remembered that he had work to do in Baltimore and New York, the *Mercury* to edit, a book and articles to write. He took the next train home, thereby missing the last weird scene that afternoon when Bryan allowed himself to be cross-examined by Darrow on the literal accuracy of the Bible. Darrow made him look more ridiculous than he had ever looked before in his long, motley career. Yes, he believed that Joshua made the sun stand still. Yes, he believed that God made Eve from one of Adam's ribs. Yes. Yes. This was a scene that Mencken much regretted missing.

But he made up for it. Five days after the trial was over and the guilty Scopes had been fined one hundred dollars, Bryan died.

The Monday following, Mencken wrote about him in the *Evening Sun*. What he wrote was the first form of his now noted "Bryan the Flycatcher" obituary. Into it Mencken poured all the frustration he had felt at seeing a trial dominated by sympathies for Bryan; at seeing more closely than he ever had before, the massed forces of primitive prejudice; at seeing Bryan, their captain, in all his sweat-stained amplitude. This was the foe and Mencken had never before felt it so personally. He said the final word on Bryan in the expanded version which appeared in *Prejudices: Fifth Series* in 1926.

Bryan fought his last fight, Mencken wrote there, "thirsting savagely for blood. All sense departed from him. He bit right and left, like a dog with rabies. He descended to demagogy so dreadful that his very associates at the trial table blushed. His one yearning was to keep his yokels heated up — to lead his forlorn mob of imbeciles against the foe. . . . He came into life a hero, a Galahad, in bright and shining armor. He was passing out a poor mountebank."

Once his accumulated wrath at Bryan was discharged, Mencken could assess the situation more calmly. In a Monday Article entitled "Round Two," written a month after the opening of the trial, he decided that the threat to free thought had lessened after the death of Bryan. An antievolution bill up before the Georgia legislature had been rejected. In the Dayton trial Darrow had been able to avoid concentrating on "the puerile question of Scopes' guilt or innocence" and instead had "brought the underlying issues before the country." He had done what Mencken had hoped he would and had attempted to do himself. Mencken even predicted that hereafter things would be better — a quite untypical prophecy. "The Constitutional questions involved in the law will now," he said, "be heard by competent judges and decided without resort to prayer and moving pictures." He wrote one more Monday Article on the trial and then returned briskly to other targets.

The next collision was inevitable but none the less stunning when it occurred. In the Scopes trial the nation had seen, most vividly through Mencken's eyes, the clash between the libertarian forces that he symbolized and the collected might of Southern fundamentalism. There the enemy, from his point of view, was the bemused peasant and his bigoted clergy. It was the illiterate farmer and the proprietor of the general store, the back-country revivalist and the village minister. That enemy, ignorant, unwashed, had the brute strength of the mob. But, the Scopes trial ended and Bryan dead, the other and wilier wing of the forces of night still lay waiting for Mencken and his kind. He still had to overmatch the urban fundamentalist, that is, the Eastern Puritan, and his shrewder leadership. The city deacons, and the knowledgeable ministers who preached before them, were even more formidable than the yokels, not only because they were smarter but also because the East dominated the country and the churches did their earnest best to dominate the East.

The Northeast, New England, was the sphere of their greatest power and Boston was the scene of its greatest concentration. In Boston a combination hard to beat held control. The leadership came from the old New England stock. Its chosen instrument, the New England Watch and Ward Society, was to develop into Mencken's most active opponent; on its letterhead in the mid-twenties were the names of such Puritan dignitaries as Charles W. Eliot, the former president of Harvard University; the Reverend Endicott Peabody, the venerated headmaster of the Groton School; Julian Lowell Coolidge, the Harvard mathematician; Godfrey Lowell Cabot, the millionaire manufacturer and philanthropist; and Thomas Dudley Cabot, his enterprising son. Their most potent popular support came from the Boston Irish, who were born censors. The priesthood to which the Irish looked for guidance was Irish also, and far more Puritan than the French or Italian priesthood of Continental tradition. Though the Irish Catholics and the old-line Protestants bickered over many an issue, on the protection of public morals they stood as one. Irish names on the letterhead of the Watch and Ward Society were rare, but the Irish support for its activities remained solid. There was, as Mencken put it, "a moral alliance between the primeval Puritans of Boston and the interloping Irish Catholics." The result was an extremely effective engine for attacking the saboteurs of civic purity.

The immediate cause of the collision was a piece in the *Mercury* for April 1926. Written by a New York journalist, Herbert Asbury, it was something between an essay and a short story. It concerned an angular small-town prostitute nicknamed "Hatrack." She yearned to reform and to be accepted by the congregation of her village church. When she was rebuffed, as happened regularly, she took what fellowship she could from offering herself to the available men-

folk among the villagers. When they were Protestants she brought
them to the Catholic cemetery; when they were Catholics she
brought them to the Masonic one. The punch line of the piece was
her reply to somebody who tendered her a dollar, "You know damned
well I haven't got any change." The piece was seen by the acid
secretary of Watch and Ward, the Reverend J. Franklin Chase, a
man renowned for his prompt response to the sinful in both literature
and life. He sent a warning notice to the chairman of the Massa-
chusetts Magazine committee, one John J. Tracey, telling him that
the sale of copies of the April issue would in his view violate the
law. And all at once Mencken discovered that the April number
was not being sold in Boston.

The extent of the attack and the nature of its background form
the first part of a massively documented history of the "Hatrack"
affair that Mencken prepared a decade later and left to the Enoch
Pratt Library. It begins, "The assault upon the *American Mercury*
for printing Herbert Asbury's 'Hatrack' was certainly not unantici-
pated in the office of the magazine." From its first issue, as Mencken
went on to say, the *Mercury* had been enthusiastically anti-Puritan.
With an outstandingly anti-Puritan editor, such anti-Puritan contributors as Clarence Darrow, James Branch Cabell, and Margaret
Sanger, and with many an anti-Puritan item in its pages, the *Mercury*
stood at the top of the list of targets for the Puritans of the 1920s.
The magazine was from the outset marked for attack and, if possible, destruction, not the least of its sins being that it jeered at
Puritanism at the same time that it condemned it. Among the most
effective, in Mencken's eyes, of the articles published before "Hatrack" were Duncan Aikman's "Arsenals of Hatred," in October 1924,
and Asbury's own "Up from Methodism," in February 1925.

These broad-scale forays in the *Mercury* were followed by one
aimed especially at Chase. Always fascinated by the nature of his
opponents, Mencken realized the power Chase possessed and used.
Early in 1925 he looked around for someone to prepare an article
on him and his methods. He succeeded, though not without trouble;
"Keeping the Puritans Pure" by A. L. S. Wood appeared in September. It was no literary gem but its bad writing did not disguise
the fact that Chase was pictured as a canting fanatic. He was
furious at the *Mercury*. His anger was compounded when two further
articles appeared with unflattering references to him. The letter he

sent to Tracey on March 27, 1926 threatened legal action against anyone who sold a copy of the April issue. Later he specified "Hatrack" as the source of his complaint; it was "immoral," "unfit to be read," vicious, and degrading.

Mencken realized at once that Chase's action had to be fought or worse would come. He discussed the matter with Knopf and his peppery father, Samuel Knopf, the business manager of the magazine. They decided to call in Arthur Garfield Hays, whose boldness and resourcefulness as one of the assisting attorneys for Scopes had impressed Mencken. Mencken and Knopf went to Hays's office in New York on March 30. He accepted the case, promising to have a strategy ready by the next day. He did. It was for Mencken to take a copy of the banned issue to Boston and there sell it, preferably and defiantly to Chase himself. The advantages were double. The action could then be defended, if need be, in open court and the legality of Chase's move tested; and a sale by Mencken would be an enviable source of attention, particularly useful for arousing those Bostonians already uneasy about Chase's power.

A week after the suppression of the April issue Mencken took the train to Boston, where he and Hays were joined by a local partner of the Hays firm named Herbert Ehrmann. Ehrmann arranged for Chase to meet Mencken on the "Brimstone Corner" of the Boston Common. After a good deal of hedging Chase finally presented himself, received a copy of the magazine, and tendered Mencken a silver half-dollar. With a stroke of inspiration, Mencken bit it to be sure it was not lead. Then Chase saw him arrested by the chief of the Boston Vice Squad and literally marched off to police headquarters.

The trial began the next morning in the Municipal Court. It was heard, through pure luck from Mencken's point of view, by one of the few liberal Boston magistrates, Judge James Parmenter. An old man in a wrinkled gown, he impressed Mencken little to begin with. However, his rulings proved to be regular and fair, with no prejudice attached, and at the end of the day he promised to read "Hatrack" himself and to hand down his decision the following morning. Mencken passed an uneasy night, knowing that he could be found guilty and perhaps even be imprisoned. It was a time for his soda-mints if not sleeping pills. Returning to court he listened to

Judge Parmenter's brief analysis of the merits of the case and then to his decision: "I find that no offense has been committed and therefore dismiss the complaint."

Mencken's invasion of Boston now turned triumphal. He hinted to the swarming reporters that he might sue Chase and the Society for heavy damages on the grounds of libel. He lunched with a crowd of Harvard students and a few professors, among them Felix Frankfurter, at the Harvard Union, delighting them with hearty remarks on the joys of battling for freedom. At the end he presented the Union with a large silk Maryland flag. Late that afternoon, full of Cambridge malt, he took the train to New York. He spent the next day in something like exaltation at the *Mercury* office. Amid the flurry of congratulations he got only part way through the mass of letters, telegrams, and newspaper clippings that Edith Lustgarten dumped on his desk. In the evening he relaxed over dinner with a Saturday Night Club crony. Afterward he bought the latest New York *Graphic* and in it saw a three-line item saying that the April issue of the *Mercury* had been barred from the mails! This ended his euphoria.

While he had been working at the *Mercury* office, Chase had gone to New York too and persuaded the postmaster there to bar the ill-starred issue. It was already distributed, so the order had no direct effect. On the other hand, Mencken knew as well as Chase that if the next issue was also barred from the mails, the magazine could legally lose its second-class mailing privilege — and no magazine could pay its way if its issues had to be mailed first-class like letters.

Both angered and dismayed, he prepared himself to fight off this second attack. He felt the *Mercury* could win in the courts in the long run but that a victory could become as expensive as a defeat. Especially wary of having the magazine barred twice in succession, he removed the lead article of the upcoming May issue — it was Bernard De Voto's "Sex and the Co-ed" — and put in its place a piece as bland as milk, Doris Stevens's "On Learning to Play the 'Cello." Hays promptly won an injunction against Chase and the Watch and Ward, prohibiting them from interfering with the sale and distribution of further copies of the *Mercury*. However, the attempt to get the Postmaster-General to reverse his subordinate's ruling in New York, barring the April issue, did not succeed. On April 28 Hays filed suit for an injunction against the ruling. The injunction was granted but the Post Office appealed.

In the meantime, when Mencken came home to Baltimore after the trial and sat down to read the accumulated clippings, he had a shock. He was accustomed to public abuse, but he now saw with amazement that the newspapers were nearly united in their condemnation of his efforts to defend a freedom that was their bread and butter. There were, he realized, many instances where newspaper publishers disliked him and their editors followed suit. There were also many instances of small-town editors who themselves saw Mencken as a threat to their conservative order. But other instances dumbfounded him. The Boston *Herald,* which he regarded as "a notable journalistic prostitute," attacked him as a matter of course; he was irritated but not surprised. But the New York *Herald Tribune,* one of the most respected of newspapers, ran an editorial on the morning Mencken was acquitted that was venomous.

Its opening paragraph read: "The incurable vulgarity of Mr. H. L. Mencken is mixed with a considerable amount of business acumen. In his latest escapade he has been alert to capitalize to the utmost the egregious bad taste of an article to which the Boston authorities took exception. The case is flagrant enough to urge a stock-taking of current standards of decency in print." The rest of the editorial developed these themes and also, in passing, revived the charge that Mencken was an alien with "nothing to offer in place of the familiar loyalties save a crude faith in the blood and iron of Teutonism."

The standard sneer, found in scores of papers, turned out to be that Mencken had peddled smut and then defended it for the sake of selling more *Mercurys.* The headline over the editorial in the Syracuse *Journal* could have stood for them all: A SPLENDID ADVERTISEMENT.

The support that developed for Mencken among the magazine editors of the country was also less than overwhelming. They were not much more enthusiastic than the newspaper editors. When comments appeared in their editorial pages, they were usually the proper ones in favor of free speech and a free press, but more than one periodical took a dry tone in discussing Mencken's victory. Though hundreds of laudatory letters and telegrams reached Mencken's desk in the weeks following the decision, only a few came from the editors of general magazines. Those who did write Mencken to praise him included O. W. Villard of the *Nation*, Henry Seidel Canby of the *Saturday Review*, and Ellery Sedgwick of the *Atlantic*. Sedgwick was a bit lofty about the whole matter, however.

The aftermath of the case was inconclusive. The Watch and Ward forces were beaten and temporarily cowed. Chase died suddenly and unexpectedly. Instead of disheartening the Watch and Ward people this gave them a scapegoat; they implied that the excesses in the case had been Chase's fault. As the months passed they warily resumed their watching and warding, but the *Mercury's* injunction against them continued to hold and they gave Mencken no more trouble. The *Mercury's* injunction against the postal authorities, however, was finally reversed on their appeal. Though Mencken considered taking the case to the Supreme Court his lawyers advised against it and somehow he never did. The Post Office consequently went unscathed. Defending itself cost the *Mercury* nearly twenty thousand dollars, plus the loss of more thousands of dollars in revenue when skittish advertisers backed off.

Nevertheless, the net gain for both the *Mercury* and Mencken was great. The *Mercury* became the salient American magazine and Mencken the international symbol of freedom of speech.

His third battle in his war against Puritanism was a battle of the books. The fundamentalists, who knew only one book, the Bible, were never forced on Mencken's attention as vividly as at the Scopes trial, but often before and afterward he wondered, in conversation and in print, what made them act the way they did. He was always interested in the nature of his opposition and he often studied it systematically. In this case he expanded his horizon to take in religion as a whole. He soon discovered that a scholarly comparison of religions had the refreshing result of putting all religions on a par. The par, furthermore, was a modest one. Mithra and Yahweh were brothers; the mullah and the minister had the same commodity to sell; the rednecks at Dayton and the black men in Africa yearned for similar reassurance.

Except in *The American Language*, Mencken would never become a true scholar. He was too easily distracted by the quaint or curious in his studies and he could not avoid tailoring his evidence to fit his attitudes. Notwithstanding, we know that in *Treatise on the Gods* he undertook his reading carefully, doing the bulk of it in the late 1920s and issuing the book in 1930. On facts and citations from his reading he was exact. He appended a ten-page bibliographical note to the finished *Treatise* which summed up this reading. At the end of the bibliography he put, with a touch typical of him, "Soli Deo gloria!"

He synthesized his materials with highly professional skill, so that they all came out in the Mencken manner. He divided the book into five sections: "The Nature and Origin of Religion"; "Its Evolution"; "Its Varieties"; "Its Christian Form"; and "Its State Today." His intention, he said, was to describe man's religious patterns and to suggest what needs occasioned them. His attitude he defined as one of amiable skepticism. His method, though he did not say this, was simplistic.

He opens the first section with the announcement that the job of religion is to give man access to his gods so that he can persuade them to treat him well. He then traces its origins from man's prehistoric days. He also speculates on how the priesthood began. This section and those that follow are lent vitality through Mencken's style — theology dims but does not extinguish its brightness — and through his constant introduction of current references. Here is a passage on presidential piety which shows both: "It seems to be generally felt that the President of the United States ought to be a member of some church or other . . . and that he should attend its public ceremonials more or less regularly. Dr. Coolidge began going as soon as he got to the White House, though before that his devotions had been feeble and scanty. Dr. Hoover, after years of backsliding, became a passionate Quaker the moment he was nominated."

The succeeding section, on the evolution of religion, is a tidy masterpiece of its kind. Its explanation of how religion evolved into the forms of today seems, to use a favorite term of Mencken's, quite plausible. For instance, he is artful in hypothesizing on why the Sun God supplanted the Earth Mother. He suggests that man worshipped womanhood for its fertility until he discovered that it took him to make woman fertile. Correspondingly, he worshipped the Earth Mother until he discovered that it took the male sun to make the earth produce its crops. The net effect today is that most of us pray to our Father not our Mother.

The section entitled "Its Varieties" is an expansion of Mencken's premise that all religions are at bottom alike. He maintains, for example, that what the Pope hopes to do by saying mass at St. Peter's is precisely what the Yakut *shaman* intends by going into a sweat bath. When Mencken turns his attention to the varieties of heaven and hell, he is especially deft at anatomizing hell. His thesis in the next section, on Christianity, is that today it shows few elements that can be traced to Christ. And its dependence on the Bible has not helped much. Mencken analyzes the Bible and its oddities, summarizing many of the findings of modern textual criticism of the Bible. Then he goes on to outline the history of the Christian church from the beginning to recent times.

He moves to the final section, on the state of religion and above all of Christianity as it is today, with evident relish. This is the most sparkling, most mordant of the sections. The problem is that except at the very end it holds no surprises. Its virtues are its synthesis and its comprehensiveness. Never before has Mencken been able to bring as much of his artillery to bear. He sees religion degraded today, like most other things, by the "democratic pestilence." He mingles Nietzsche with Darwin as he describes the deterioration. Whatever merit religion has had in the past is lost beyond recovery and in its place science now stands supreme. It too will be degraded by democracy but not yet. Meanwhile, civilized man has become his own god, and who can deny that this is an improvement?

In a sense science has grown to be man's religion. But it is not to be confused with the desperate efforts to reconcile the two. Science and religion can mix only at the expense of the integrity of science. Religion has no genuine use: many of the accomplishments pointed out as its product are really the results of simple, common decency on the part of the human race.

By now Christianity has gone down with the rest of the religions. However, it has left us one lovely, unexpected legacy. That is the poetry of the Bible. "The Bible," Mencken says stoutly, "is unquestionably the most beautiful book in the world." The Jews were unconscious poets, with the result that their records have given Christianity its lush esthetic appeal. Christianity has poetry not only in its core but at its circumference. Not only the Bible but even its saints' legends are apt to be beautiful.

In his last two pages he turns back, picking up his thesis of democratic degradation, and makes a concession about religion and the average man: for that man "there must be faith, as there must be morals." Mencken has watched a hanging and cannot forget it, for the doomed man recited the Twenty-third Psalm as he went to the scaffold. And Mencken remarks, "As an American I naturally spend most of my time laughing, but that time I did not laugh."

In retrospect he pronounced *Treatise on the Gods* by far the best book he had ever published. He thought it smooth in manner, good-tempered, and adroitly styled. Furthermore, he considered it a model of condensation. In 1930 when the book came out it seemed that he was not far from right. It was well received, exhausting two printings before publication. Many critics applauded, until the Depression pushed Mencken and the Gods far from their mind.

At the same time that Mencken was fighting for Scopes and "Hatrack" he was falling quietly, almost urbanely, in love. And in the same year that he published what he regarded as his best book, he also took a wife.

14. Mencken in Love

Sara Powell Haardt Mencken, 1898–1935 the big blue scrapbook reads, compiled by Mencken and now kept in the Enoch Pratt Library. On the first page there is the engraved announcement of her graduation in 1916 from Margaret Booth, her preparatory school in Montgomery, Alabama. Soon after comes her diploma from Goucher College and a rotogravure picture, clipped from the Baltimore *American*, of a rather stern young Sara surrounded by her editorial staff of the Goucher yearbook. Then the fancy card of membership in her sorority, Delta Delta Delta, and below it her grades for her senior year, ten A's and four B's. Then a grayish clipping from the Montgomery *Advertiser* reporting her activities in the suffrage crusade in Alabama; this was during the two years after Goucher when she returned to Margaret Booth to teach. But then a little slip of paper itemizing the medical expenses for her first siege of sickness, which came not long after she went back to Goucher again, this time as an instructor in the English department. "Sanitarium — 24 weeks. $960.00."

Thereafter the pieces of paper move, by fits and starts, backward and forward in time. Their combined effect, however, is to show that the young woman who ultimately married Mencken was a gifted and remarkable person in her own right, and not only the protégée and then wife of a famous public personality. In the course of showing what Sara was like they show us a good deal about Mencken too. They reveal a different side to the man who startled and enchanted the American public when he was finally seen from the perspective of courtship and marriage.

Besides the record in the scrapbook there are the letters that passed between Sara and Mencken. We cannot be sure exactly how many Sara sent because those which Mencken saved seem to fall mainly into a few years. But it is clear that for her part Sara kept every note, telegram, and letter that she got from him. Nearly a thousand communications from Mencken lie in the files of her correspondence now deposited at the Goucher Library. Also, we have the recollections of Sara's two best friends, Sara Mayfield and Anne Rector Duffy. Both observed Mencken with delight as he courted Sara Haardt in his oblique, rather elegant, Victorian way. Sara Mayfield was there the first time that Sara Haardt and Mencken were ever thrown together; this was on a Friday night in April 1923. She was as close to the couple as anyone till she left Baltimore in 1928. Anne Duffy, who met Sara Haardt in 1927, became her good friend by the next year and was privileged to see much of the last two years of the courtship. After Sara and Mencken were married in 1930, Anne remained her close friend and confidante.

Sara Mayfield grew up with Sara Haardt, along with Zelda Sayre (who was to marry Scott Fitzgerald) and Tallulah Bankhead, in the sleepy town of Montgomery. She saw her develop into a winsome, perceptive girl with a lovely skin and luminous eyes. She remembers that Sara was extremely gentle in her manner and as suave as silk. "Sara never crosses anybody," Sara Mayfield recalls hearing her father say. But this did not mean that Sara lacked either will or wit. She early showed signs of having a wry sense of humor; it grew more marked with time and maturity.

After a semester or so up north at Goucher, she mastered the engaging trick of being Southern at the same time that she was satirizing the fact. James Cain, who knew her for years, has remarked that when she used a typically Southern expression she often seemed to put faint quotation marks around it. At Maryland parties Sara's neat, incisive comments enjoyed the more attention because they were delivered with the soft tones of Montgomery.

But Sara was not only beguiling, she was bright. The records show that she always did well in English and that she soon learned to love words. She scribbled verse in high school and composed both verse and prose in college. She came to prefer the short-story form and by the time she graduated from Goucher she was eager for professional publication. At first she got no returns for her trouble except the customary rejection slips. This was understandable because she chose to submit her stories and poems to some of the best-known journals of the twenties. Not least among them was the *Smart Set*. And when one night in 1923 she had a chance to spend a couple of hours next to its co-editor, who also ranked as Baltimore's most colorful personality, it must have seemed a very pleasant bit of luck.

It happened because Sara Mayfield, by then a student at Goucher at the same time that Sara Haardt was an instructor, won a contest for the best short story of the year by a freshman. It was a contest that Sara Haardt had won in her own student days. As it turned out, this year's winner received a dividend: the opportunity to have supper in company with Mencken. The professor in charge of the writing classes was Harry Baker, formerly on the *Smart Set* staff, and he asked Mencken to visit Goucher and talk to his girls about writing for magazines. Mencken agreed, with the proviso that there be no publicity. He made the talk, remarked in passing that writing was no trade for a lady, and enjoyed the experience enough so that thereafter he repeated each spring what he called his lecture to the girls on how to catch a husband.

This first time Sara sat with Baker's class too, eager to learn all she could. When his discourse was done Mencken took Sara Mayfield on his arm and they left for Schellhase's with Baker and his young colleague Sara Haardt behind them. After the four settled down over cracked crabs and beer, Mencken asked Sara Haardt if she had not sent him a story for the *Smart Set*. She said yes, tactfully adding, "You read it very promptly." "Well, send me another," he suggested. "Keep trying, keep plugging." At the end of the evening he turned to Sara Mayfield and said gallantly, "We must do this again soon."

A few weeks later he phoned Sara Mayfield and invited her to lunch with him at Marconi's restaurant. With elaborate casualness he added, "Your friend Miss Haardt, I seem to have forgotten her address. Do you suppose we could bring her along to cheer up Joe?" Joe was Joseph Hergesheimer, who was visiting in Baltimore. The four of them lunched together, but Sara Mayfield soon found that she was cheering up Joe while Mencken and the other Sara were conducting exploratory talks.

The attraction was mutual from the start in spite of some substantial obstacles. For him they were his age, his prominence, and no doubt his professional antifeminism. He was almost eighteen years older than she, and he was so notable a national figure that he could suspect a young woman of being attracted by his reputation instead of his person. Perhaps he was always a little unsure of himself, underneath, in facing the opposite sex. He knew that he failed to cut much of a figure, that he looked like a burgher or a Babbitt rather than a cavalier, and that his clothes were inordinately conservative (Anne Duffy was to say that they seemed to be made of tin). When it came to the reams he had written about women, he knew that some of it could be turned cleverly against him.

For Sara's part, she could have been put off by his fame but she soon saw that he himself did not take it seriously. She could have been put off by his age and by his old-fashioned politeness to her, but this was the sort of treatment that her Southern upbringing had led her to expect from a mature man. Later, as she grew to like him very much, she still could be teasing about him. She could still write to Sara Mayfield and refer to him as the Palm of Learning or the Commander of the Faithful or the Duke of Palmolive. Yet even the few jeers were kindly; for she was drawn not only by his vitality and wit, the kind of wit she learned to enjoy thoroughly, but also by his wisdom. She was after all a beginning writer while he was an experienced, solicitous editor.

What he saw in Sara, more and more, was a combination of most of the elements which had appealed to him in other women. She was clever, literary, and physically attractive. He had made a pose of liking either beer garden waitresses, the more bovine the better, or mellow ladies of uncertain age. Actually, we know that the young women who preceded Sara in his friendship were apt to be alert as well as pretty. In Sara he found a young woman who both greatly liked and respected him. Her wit kept the respect from cloying but there is no doubt that it was great. So was the liking. She soon showed one other characteristic, in spite of herself, that made as powerful an appeal as any. Her health was already delicate and before the first year of their acquaintance was passed she became quite ill. To Mencken — not only the most compassionate and devoted of hospital visitors but also the dedicated student of human ills, beginning with his own — Sara sick proved intensely appealing.

Nevertheless, on the surface the two played their proper parts in a romantic comedy, and would continue to for several years. When the Palm of Learning had his name linked in the newspapers with that of the Hollywood star Aileen Pringle, Sara did not hide the fact that she had read about it; and there was a crispness in the air. When Robin Harriss, a personable reporter of Sara's vintage, took her around the dance floor or went to supper with her, Mencken had his own way of showing that he had heard. Perhaps it was a slight stiffening of manner when he saw Harriss next; perhaps it was a compliment he made to Harriss, more elaborate than need be, about his being a dashing young blade.

Underneath the comedy the respect and affection became mutual. It showed in ways both public and private. In Sara it showed, for example, in the fact, just mentioned, that though she was not given to saving letters, she saved every communication that came to her from Mencken. In Mencken it showed, for example, in his constant invitations to lunch and in his frequent tender to her of advice and literary criticism. And it was significant that he pursued this courtship in Baltimore. New York would have been something else again. There he could squire around a variety of bright young companions even to the glittering dinner clubs, and no one would pay much attention. Though he was a celebrity, New York was sated with celebrities. But in Baltimore he could not walk a block on Charles or Mulberry Street without being hailed. Many people knew him and many more talked about him with relish. So when he began taking a young lady to lunch in Baltimore regularly, it was an announcement of some significance. It was by no means a publishing of the banns — it was widely agreed that Henry Mencken would never marry — but it was at least a pleasant public statement.

Sara took sick shortly before Christmas 1923. Sara Mayfield returned to Baltimore after Christmas vacation to find her in her room feverish and at times nearly delirious. Because at the moment influenza was almost epidemic in Baltimore, she had scant medical attention and no hospital space available to her. And she had no visitors but Sara Mayfield. Mencken was much concerned from the start; he had already been worried by the way she looked at their last luncheon together. The worse she got, the more helpless he felt. He could not telephone her; he could not see her. There was no place in her boarding house for visitors and his sense of propriety barred him from her bedroom. The result was that Sara Mayfield became his main source of bulletins. She too did what she could for the sick girl, but it was not till tuberculosis threatened that Sara Haardt was hospitalized. By the beginning of February she lay in Maple Heights Sanitarium about fifteen miles from Baltimore, and Mencken was reassuring her that in six months she would be as good as new.

The very disease she was fighting deepened his regard, for there was a history, it happened, of tuberculosis on the maternal side of his own family. By word and deed he showed his fondness for her. It was during this period that the notes which started "Dear Miss Haardt" changed to "Dear Sara." The contents of the notes became more personal as well, not so much in what they said as in how they said it. And he was assiduous in his attentions. Though he had always visited sick friends this normally had meant a short trip to a local hospital. Getting to Maple Heights involved not only a train ride but also at the end a hill to climb. As Sara's stay went on, Mencken sometimes joked to her about the decrepit Ford he hired to meet him at the train and drive him up the hill for his visit. When it failed to appear he would arrive at Sara's side puffing from the walk in spite of his gallant attempt to hide the fact. All the while his notes kept on coming, whether he was at home or away. In March he sent her a jeweled pendant, a "modest bauble" he called it, for her twenty-sixth birthday. The warmest notes came after he had been to see her and had returned to Hollins Street. He was apt to write then of how he had enjoyed the visit, of how quickly time had passed, of how much he must have talked. The picture comes back of relaxed afternoons, the two people sipping the sherry he had brought; the brilliant, merry man and the gracious, convalescing young woman. She is all the more attractive because she is convalescing and consequently defenseless. It is after such an afternoon that he sits down, one day in February, and writes to her, "I suspect I'm mashed on you."

Discharged from Maple Heights in September 1924, Sara went home to Montgomery for over a year to finish recuperating and begin a new life. She was determined not to go back to Goucher or any other college; instead she wanted to establish herself as a free-lance writer. She had Mencken's encouragement. From the beginning of 1925 the letters reflect the start of an unusually promising professional career. They show his shrewdness and her quickness in grasping the point of his practical suggestions. He assures her that artistic form is not important; close observation and a moving narrative are what count. Gradually her stories, and an occasional article as well, began to be bought. More than one scout from a New York publishing house read the stories and liked them. Did she have a novel that she was working on, they asked politely. If they had not happened to read her work, Mencken was ready to call it to their attention. George Oppenheimer of the Viking Press, for instance, wrote in March 1925, "My dear Miss Haardt: Mr. H. L. Mencken has been kind enough to tell me about your novel *Career*." The magazine editors warmed to her: "We are glad to accept ['All in the Family'] for The Century Magazine. Our check will go to you in a few days." She published in the new *Mercury* itself. The sophisticated magazine *Vanity Fair* beckoned. "Dear Miss Haardt, I have been talking to Mr. H. L. Mencken about inaugurating a book department in Vanity Fair. I asked Mr. Mencken to undertake this but as his obligations to the American Mercury make this impossible, he has suggested that I get in touch with you."

Then Hollywood called, the Vanity Fair of all Vanity Fairs. The original invitation is gone but the scrapbook includes Sara's draft of her answer, "I should be very glad to accept your offer to come to Hollywood." That the invitation went out was a tribute both to her work and Mencken's influence. Walter Wanger's Famous Players-Lasky studio was engaged in hiring young writers for a five- or six-week stint and then keeping them on if they produced usable scripts. Sara qualified for a bid in her own right. Her short stories were steadily improving and as early as 1925 one of them had made the "Roll of Honor of American Short Stories" in the *Best Short Stories* of that year. But it is also possible that Mencken put her name before Wanger, whom he knew. At any rate, Mencken wrote her a letter saying that she should be prepared to hear from one of the Hollywood moguls.

There were several delays before she actually left for the West Coast. But when she did, she had a five-weeks contract at $250 a week and the promise of $3,750 more if she delivered a usable film play. This looked phenomenally attractive. Yet as soon as she boarded the train Mencken commenced to worry. From that day late in September 1927 until the first of the new year, when she returned, his letters ran to double their customary number. He warned her regularly against the lecherous leading men, the tricky agents, the venal studio officials. She must always be on watch.

He wrote with some reason. For though Sara managed in the middle of studio intrigue to survive for more than twice her original five weeks, it was at a considerable cost. She was exasperated at the double-dealing and evasiveness of her studio bosses. They would promise her something but then postpone it. Clear decisions seemed to be beyond them. They liked her work enough to leaf through a few of her sample scripts but not enough to take her rough draft of a feature film about Confederate refugees in Brazil. She gave the script the working title "The Promised Land." When Famous Players could not make up its mind to option "The Promised Land" she took it to the director James Cruze. But could she sell the script to Cruze, she wondered, after she had prepared it mostly on Famous Players' time? Mencken had a helpful answer for this and many another vexing question. These were the periods when he wrote her two or even three times a day, both to counsel her and cheer her up. She needed cheering, for she found not only the chicanery but also the monotony of Hollywood hard to endure. Like many another writer she felt that she was getting money but little else, that she was not being used to her fullest. There she sat, she wrote Robin Harriss in November, in the Golden Vacuum.

The prospect of Christmas in Hollywood with its pastel pine trees was too much. Sara started back east and did so the more easily because she could now carry one gaudy trophy with her. It was Cruze's payment of fifteen hundred dollars for the option on "The Promised Land." There was also the prospect of thousands more if it became a film; yet even if it did not — and it never did — there remained the windfall of fifteen hundred dollars. She went to Montgomery for Christmas and then to Baltimore in time for New Year's.

Mencken was waiting, perhaps a bit apprehensively. It was not impossible that one reason for her going to Hollywood had been to find out what effect a separation would have on both of them. The answer was now clear: they had grown closer than before. The moment they met they began to talk over the Hollywood experience in a great rush of conversation. Mencken maintained that on balance the experience had been good for her as a writer. She remembered the meaningless days of working and waiting and was not so sure. Still, she also remembered a few real friends in Hollywood, chief among them the rough-diamond Jim Tully, and she would not forget some of the lessons she had learned, especially about the dangers of the loss of integrity.

At the same time she clearly could not live in Baltimore on the proceeds of her short stories. Nor on the royalties from any novel, for in spite of the kind queries no publisher had proved willing to purchase *Career.* She was already composing her second novel, to be called *The Making of a Lady,* and it would see print, but not till 1931. Meanwhile she found part-time employment with both Mencken and Joe Hergesheimer. Hergesheimer needed research done for one of his glossy volumes, *Swords & Roses.* It was a group of elegiac essays about the Southern leaders in the Civil War and he commissioned Sara to do background studies on some of the Confederate figures who would appear in the volume.

For Henry she began doing capsule reviews to be run by the *Mercury* in its "Check List" of new books; this paid her a little and selling the review copies to a Baltimore book shop paid her a little more. She also did some research for him. He was still planning his book on "Homo Sapiens," for which he needed information on a variety of matters including evolution in man and animals. She collected data faithfully and organized it, but he ultimately dropped the subject when he found that Raymond Pearl was planning a like book. Most of the data was dull to both of them and probably would have been to readers. This was not at all true for *Menckeniana: A Schimpflexikon.* With a delight equal to Mencken's, Sara went through the piles of clippings about him in search of the most vicious and vituperative. These evidences of his effectiveness came from all over the United States, systematically collected by his clipping service. They were tangible proof that he could heat tempers everywhere. Sara copied the best — or worst — examples and he persuaded Knopf to publish them in a small book in 1928. "Some salient specimens of the anti-Mencken invective," the note to the book explained.

Joe Hergesheimer testified to Sara's charm during this time. In a passage from his unpublished autobiography he writes, "She was endlessly companionable, a beauty dearer to monological man than any precarious digression. Henry and I lingered evening after evening in her apartment on Read Street steeped in her attentive tact. Drinking traditional Maryland rye we watched Sara's slow consumption of gin, Coca Cola and lime juice incredulously. While Henry applied the salt of a verbal pretzel-bender to the Bible Belt her latent composure was swiftly animated by the amusement that never quite reached her grave eyes. At middle-age Henry and I ignored the shortness of time; we were happy; obviously — in Sara's hands at our best — complacent."

By now Sara was beginning to fill the deepest void in Mencken's life, the one left in large part by the death of his mother. She had died in mid-December 1925 following an operation. Shortly after the funeral, he had written Sara a longer, more moving letter, apparently, than he wrote to anybody else. In it he explained how much his mother had meant to him, how much he had depended on her, and how much of a gap her death would leave in his life. He was already reaching out in Sara's direction. He continued to, with increasing earnestness in the months that followed, and the letters from 1927 on show this graphically. She in turn became more dependent on him. She put it fliply to friends, "Henry buys my gin"; but she too was reaching out not only for affection and counsel, though both were important, but also for comfort in her sieges of ill health. The truth is that in spite of periods of gratifying improvement her health was becoming worse instead of better. She was in the hospital and out. She was operated on twice. The first time she had a cyst cut away; the second time the surgery threatened to be still more serious. For in the summer of 1929 it became evident that one of her kidneys would have to be removed to keep her alive.

The doctors told Henry about the coming crisis before they told anyone else. He wired Sara Mayfield promptly and she came to Baltimore to be with her too. The prognosis looked grim. The doctors intimated to them that the patient had at best three years to live. Even with the damaged kidney out, they could not promise a longer time than that. Numbly Mencken and Sara Mayfield stood in the hospital corridor after hearing the verdict. It was noon on a stifling July day; they looked at one another. There were tears in

Sara Mayfield's eyes and Mencken blew his nose violently. "If she gets well," he vowed, "I'm going to do everything in my power to make them the three happiest years of her life." He added, "You know we had been making plans to be married." She answered, "I gathered so, I hoped so."

Sara Haardt's stay in Union Memorial Hospital lasted five months, from May to September 1929. The letters from Mencken during the next few months are as close to romantic as anything he would ever send. He writes in October to tell her how lovely she is and how she has won his family to her all over again. In December he goes to London to cover the Naval Conference for the *Evening Sun* and he confesses more openly than ever how much he misses her. He misses her, in fact, even before he embarks and he writes that he is tempted to tear up his ticket and come back to Baltimore. In London he becomes still more homesick for her. It is now that we have the first "Dearest Sara" letter. Their separation grows the more poignant because she takes sick again and is forced back into the hospital. Then she is released once more and goes to Montgomery to rest.

The indications are that they decided by the beginning of 1930 to be married that spring. A few persons were told early in the year, some members of the immediate families and such very close friends as Anne Duffy and Sara Mayfield. The two Saras met in Montgomery at the start of spring to buy antiques and Victoriana for the apartment the couple was looking for. The search for furnishings speeded up when Sara Haardt came north again.

As the preparations went on, quietly but busily, Mencken watched with benevolent interest. Sara was still supposed to rest, so much of the planning and decorating of the apartment fell to Anne. She was already something of a professional in the field. She took Sara's taste and skillfully elaborated on it. She found the apartment itself, on the third floor of a brownstone building at 704 Cathedral Street, a desirable as well as a convenient address. Decorating and furnishing it occupied nearly three months. Sara had never realized what work would be involved but she did what she could, willingly and systematically, for Henry's sake. She listed the rolls of wallpaper required, the number of new window shades, the furnishings for the handsome drawing room, the rugs, the mirrors. She contracted for repairs and renovations; with Anne's help she got them done; and then — since the apartment was leased in her name — she signed the checks that paid the bills.

In spite of this flurry of activity the secret of the engagement was well kept. Not only because of Sara's and his wish for personal privacy but also because they realized the newspaper sensation that the Great Bachelor's fall would create. The reporters would be hot after every detail, no matter how minor. On the other hand when the engagement was to be made public, it should be done with zest. There was nothing that Mencken enjoyed more than being the center of a sensation that he himself had started, and this fact is even illustrated by the story of the announcement to his colleagues. Gerald Johnson, Mencken's friend and editorial associate on the *Sunpapers*, was an eyewitness to the occasion.

He still remembers that Paul Patterson, as publisher, had called an editorial meeting at his house to discuss some problem the *Sunpapers* were having. Among those present were John Owens, editor of the morning *Sun;* Hamilton Owens, editor of the *Evening Sun;* J. E. Murphy, managing editor of the same paper, and of course Mencken himself. There was also a last-minute visitor, a friend of John Owens named Louis Jaffé, who edited a Norfolk newspaper. The group held their discussion, made their main decision, and the party was about ready to break up when Patterson said, "John, here is a thing we are going to run tomorrow morning." (This was a Saturday and the item would appear in the Sunday *Sun*.) Patterson handed him the typewritten sheet and suggested, "Read it aloud." So John Owens settled in his chair, fished out his glasses, and began, "August 2, Montgomery, Alabama; special to the *Sun*. Mrs. John Anton Haardt, of this city, today announced the engagement of her daughter, Miss Sara Powell Haardt, to H. L. Mencken, of Baltimore. The wedding will take place September 3."

He stopped and there was a desert of silence. Finally Murphy, sitting on the other side of the room from him, said, "I don't get it." Paul Patterson said, "Don't get what?" Murphy said, "I don't get the catch in it. I don't think it's funny." Patterson said, "Funny! Who said it was funny? It's true. We're running it tomorrow, the lead item on the Society Page." There was another silence. Then the guest, Mr. Jaffé, stood up and said, "I understand, Mr. Patterson, this is a firm announcement of Mr. Mencken's engagement?" Patterson said, "It is." Jaffé turned to Mencken, "Well, in that case, Mr. Mencken, I'll offer you my congratulations."

Mencken broke into a Cheshire grin; nearly everybody stood up; and the conversation became an uproar. But John Owens sat silent with the item in his hand. Presently Mencken said, "Oh well, that's that. Now as to the problem we were talking about. I have another idea in connection with it." So the group returned to the previous discussion for the next five minutes and then the conversation again played out. The silence was broken by John Owens, still sitting under the lamp, who exploded, "Well, I'll be goddam!" That broke up the meeting and it was jovially adjourned.

The newspapers of the nation were delighted. Their readers, in that grim first year of the Depression, needed every titillation they could find and the story of the fall of the Great Bachelor was ideal. The editors turned back to Mencken's *In Defense of Women* and reread with relish the section headed "Late Marriages," which began pontifically, "The marriage of a first-rate man, when it takes place at all, commonly takes place relatively late." Besides this basic text they found a multitude of passages where he had jibed at marriage and the female. The most widely read among the editors, however, remarked that Mencken's capitulation was not unforeseen. Writing for the *Philadelphia Ledger* syndicate on March 17, 1926 he had admitted, "The fact that I remain unmarried at 46 is a mere accident of fate, not due to any enterprise on my part. . . . If any woman of the proper resolution had ever made up her mind to marry me, I'd have succumbed like the rest of the poor dogs. . . . I am a firm believer in monogamy. . . . It is comfortable, laudable and sanitary."

The morning after the meeting at Paul Patterson's, Mencken opened his Sunday paper with some apprehension. He felt very vulnerable. However, his colleagues had treated him well. They were constrained to give the announcement full play yet they did not embarrass him. It ran under a three-decker headline and was followed by biographies of him and Sara. There was also a whimsical editorial, "Footnote to a News Item," in which the *Sun* grandly reassured his loyal legions. This was not a new Mencken, it averred; this was the old one now revealed in his amplest dimensions. He had always loved domesticity; this was simply the first time it really showed in public. The editorial ended, "It is our well-informed, deliberate and reasoned opinion that Mr. Mencken will make a good husband, and a *grand* provider."

Mencken discovered that he liked being engaged. He understood the rules of the newspaper game as well as anyone and was perfectly willing to make a good story better. During the short engagement he gave the United Press an ebullient interview that became "must" copy from Sarasota to Seattle. The format was sedate: the United Press sent him a set of questions and he answered them in writing. But the answers were far from sedate. For instance: Q. — "Have you any of the traditional fluster of a bridegroom-to-be?" A. — "I discern no tremors. Getting married, like getting hanged, is probably a great deal less dreadful than it has been made out." From the time the engagement was announced to the time the honeymooners arrived back in Baltimore — less than three months — enough newspaper clippings were sent Mencken by his clipping service to fill three linear feet of scrapbook on his shelf.

The wedding was stealthily moved up a week, to August 27 instead of September 3. The reason, according to one newspaper later, was to "escape zealous attentions of friends," but everyone recognized that the friends included the nation's panting press. In deference to Sara the ceremony took place in an Episcopal church; in deference to Mencken the church was St. Stephen the Martyr. The service was conducted by an appropriately controversial cleric whom Mencken knew, the Reverend Herbert Parrish. His credentials included a series of critical articles on American religion which Mencken had printed in the *Mercury* and an outspoken book developed from them, *A New God for America*. The bride was accompanied by her mother and one sister and was given away by her brother John. Mencken's two brothers and sister were there too, as were a handful of intimate friends. Pictures were taken after the ceremony, some rice was sportively tossed, and then the bride and groom departed.

Because the idea of a Canadian honeymoon had sounded cool and inviting, they took the train north. But Quebec in particular turned out to be an inferno, so they traveled to Halifax, and then to St. John's. In spite of the heat it was a rewarding journey. They could not quite escape the press; and the press photographer in Montreal took a picture which, Mencken wrote Paul Patterson, made Sara look like "a coon intellectuelle" and him like "a Pittsburgh

23. *Visible proof that a passport photo can be good. The Menckens are about to take a Mediterranean cruise. December 29, 1933; Christhilf Studios, Baltimore.*

24. *Mencken doing what he did better than anyone else:
reporting on a national political convention. This is the one
the Republicans held in Cleveland in June 1936.*

25. *The Saturday Night Club, now mellowed, sitting in its second great
resort, Schellhase's Restaurant. The members present that night have signed
their names. They are, from left to right: H. E. Buchholz, Raymond Pearl,
W. Edwin Moffett, Max Brödel (or Broedel), Adolph Torovsky, Frank Purdum,
Israel Dorman, Mencken, Franklin Hazlehurst, and Louis Cheslock. April 24,
1937.*

26. *A rapt Mencken listens to Bach as played in Bethlehem, while Alfred Knopf holds the camera. May 28, 1938.*

27. *Mencken the trencherman. He concentrates on his meat as Paul Patterson, plate still full, addresses him. Next to Patterson sits James Bone of the Manchester* Guardian, *looking dour; beyond him John Owens wields knife and fork while Hamilton Owens holds a cigaret. November 1940;* Sunpapers, *Baltimore.*

28. *Mencken read best lying down. Comfortably, or even semi-comfortably,*
flat he could go through many a book in an hour or so. Here he is at home
shortly after we entered World War II. March 1942; Helen Taylor, New York
Herald Tribune.

29. *Mencken and Nathan, together again, watch an incident in the human comedy, while Nathan comments. The scene is the famous Stork Club in New York. August 25, 1947.*

30. *Mencken rising, perhaps to ask if Henry Wallace considers him a capitalist stooge. The occasion is Wallace's Progressive Party convention in Philadelphia in July 1948. Leonard McCombe for Life.*

31. Mencken, home from the hos
pital after yet another bout o
illness, brings with him his nurse
Lois Gentry, who will attend hin
at Hollins Street for several years
March 20, 1951.

32. In the backyard at Hollins
Street, where they played as boys,
Mencken and his devoted brother
August stand beside the wood pile
on Mencken's seventy-fifth birth-
day. September 12, 1955; Aubrey
Bodine, Baltimore.

vermin exterminator." But the gains were ample. As Mencken wrote in encouragement to the still unwed Nathan, "It is a grand experience to be able to look a hotel detective in the eye." A highlight of the trip was their visit to Twin Farms, in Vermont, the pastoral retreat Sinclair Lewis had bought for himself and his wife Dorothy. The Menckens inspected the Lewises' brand new son Michael and pronounced him a remarkable infant.

Coming back they stopped off in New York, at the Algonquin of course. Sara Mayfield was living in New York then and promptly received a note from Sara Mencken suggesting that she drop in for breakfast. She arrived about ten. The Menckens were dressed in family style: Sara had her hair in wave clips and Henry was in shirt sleeves with his red suspenders fully revealed. The man who had always kept his coat on in the company of any woman but a loose one now flaunted his newfound domesticity. He acted the genial host as usual, insisting on ordering extra coffee and then discoursing to Sara Mayfield about the trip. He held forth on Canadian beer, whose merits he assessed with all the expertise of a Braumeister. He also showed Sara some photographs his wife had taken, including one that he declared made him look, this time, like a Japanese piewoman. A little later he went out on some business and the two Saras turned to talking about further furnishings for the apartment.

The Menckens settled down in Cathedral Street in an atmosphere of elegance and comfort. The decor was Anne Duffy's and Sara's but Mencken was enough of a person, even under the spell of marriage, to put his own stamp here and there on the apartment. Above the sideboard he set a Pabst beer sign in all its saloonlike glory. On one of the bathroom doors, his own, he fixed not one but two signs for greater security, "Men" and "Gents." On the dining-room wallpaper, which had a formal pattern, he carefully pasted comic-strip figures, cut from the daily newspaper, with the balloons enclosing what they said. The figures were so artfully blended with the background that no one would notice them without standing close. If anyone looked hard, however, there were Mutt and Jeff, the Captain and the Kids, Happy Hooligan, and Krazy Kat all making their pointed comments on the formalities around them.

Soon after they were married, the talented photographer Aubrey Bodine took a picture of the Menckens. In the center Henry sits stolidly as if stuffed while Sara stands solemnly beside him. It is pure Victorian. They gave a copy to Anne Duffy and for her he made an addition on it: a sparkling wedding ring drawn on his finger with fountain-pen ink.

The wind howled outside but it was pleasant within the apartment. The Depression deepened and nobody seemed able to do anything about it. The Menckens would have been less than human if they had not turned to one another. Sara was ready to be sheltered; Henry was ready to shelter and take care of her, the more so because her periodic ill health remained a serious threat. He remembered too clearly that the doctors had predicted that she would live only three more years, and he was determined to make them as good as possible. He saw what was happening to the country at large but felt it keenly only when there was a personal encounter. He could watch the hapless Hoover's halfway measures and feel that their inadequacy was merely to be expected. But when he was stopped by a beggar or asked to buy a five cent apple from a jobless veteran, the Depression came home to him. He said one day to John Owens, "You can't have people starving on your doorstep" and perhaps that summed it up.

The life they established on Cathedral Street was primarily Sara's. Its two levels were both Southern. One was formal and public, the other comfortably private. They hired a cook, Hester Denby, and a maid, Bessie Lee. Both would stay with them till Sara died.

For Hester's use Sara gathered the recipes that she thought would please her new husband's palate. Shortly after her marriage she said in an interview that she would put domesticity ahead of her career, and tokens of her intention are scattered over the early pages of the scrapbook. Here is a penciled dinner menu, there a list of "Things to Try" including custard apples; here is a series of soups, there a note on meats, for instance "Ham: see 60 ways to prepare." Next to her husband she thought she could please herself, so she also scribbled down a few of her own favorite dishes, among them mushroom soup.

Besides being a maid Bessie Lee became something of a practical nurse. She eased life for Sara as much as she could. The patterns of a typical day on Cathedral Street are still fixed in Bessie's memory. The first thing in the morning, Hester the cook would arrive. Bessie herself would appear shortly afterward. By then Hester would have prepared Mencken's breakfast and Bessie's first duty would be to serve it to him. He too would be up early, ready to eat at eight. He wanted to be served promptly and he was. His breakfast would be hearty, perhaps cereal and eggs and bacon. Sara's breakfast would be light and she would eat it later, ordinarily at some time from nine to ten. Then while Mencken would read or write — and on certain mornings dictate to his secretary Mrs. Lohrfinck — Bessie would straighten up the apartment and then look after Sara. She would comb Sara's hair and make her bed. If it was a poor day for Sara, she might make the bed several times as Sara, restless or weak, lay down and got up, lay down and got up again. Mencken's letters tell the melancholy story all too often. He wrote, for example, to his old friend McDannald in March 1931, "You have not heard from me because poor Sara has been laid up with pleurisy, following influenza. She was ill here at home for a couple of weeks, and then had to go to hospital." But soon she improved and life on Cathedral Street became genial again, brightened by what Mencken called "her easy laughter."

Then the comfortable routine would continue. Lunch would be served promptly at one; dinner would come at six except when the Menckens had guests. Sara made a point of never letting Henry lunch alone in the apartment; she made no engagements that would interfere. Right after lunch he would nap briefly. The afternoons would be quiet and companionable. At times the only sound would be the brisk clack of his typewriter. Every now and then there would be something in his reading or writing that he wanted to share. Weeks after his mother had died, he had still caught himself planning a hundred times a day to tell her something. Now he had a wife who appreciated his view of the American cultural circus and subscribed to his sentiments about American letters much more than his mother could have, because she knew much more about it. Often he would shout "Sara" and walk solidly down the hall from his room to her lounge at the far end of the apartment. He would share his tidbit with her, they would laugh together, and then he would wheel around to return to his domain.

These pleasant patterns of household life tell us not only of the circumstances of Mencken's daily existence but also of his attempt to establish a manageable order in his home to counteract the chaos and disorder of the world outside Cathedral Street. His center of gravity shifted from the crowded street to the cloistered apartment. In its atmosphere he found that he could relax better than he ever had before. His writing eased up a bit, though his grumbles about it did not diminish; and his reading took longer but covered a little less. He had always liked to read stretched out, but now he spent more time than ever lying on his leather couch and, between pages, taking an occasional swig from a beer bottle. The apartment ran smoothly; Hester and Bessie saw to that. The inborn inefficiency of the female which he had complained about in *In Defense of Women* did not affect his own household. In this attractive retreat his love for Sara even became demonstrative. He was seen to hold hands with her, a sight which would have shocked his old companions profoundly.

For both of them the novelty of marriage was quite a while in wearing off. Sara observed her new husband with loving interest. She even made some notes headed "Henry." "Oct. 12. Talked about cigar-making. Curved his hand to show how cigar was made." "Nov. 5 *Sunday*. After dinner Henry played Beethoven on the victrola. He deplored my lack of knowledge of music and added that he would teach me some day." He indulged her with much amiability, watching her activities too as she wrote, drank Cokes, entertained company, continued to collect Victorian china and glass and what he called "preposterous Victorian books," and played the role of house-wife and, after that, careerist. He soothed her when she was sick and took her on tours to make her well. As a rule only the prospect of a pleasure trip could persuade them to leave Cathedral Street. In January 1932 they cruised in style through the West Indies; in February and March 1934 they toured the Mediterranean. Closer to home, they made excursions to the houses of a small group of old friends and new: to the Dower House in Westchester, Pennsylvania to see Dorothy and Joe Hergesheimer, to Roaring Gap, North Carolina to visit Elizabeth and Fred Hanes, to Wilmington to see Marcella and Alfred duPont. They went only occasionally to New York; more often Henry took the train alone and returned to Baltimore as soon as he could.

Mencken's young niece Virginia was a periodic weekend visitor to Cathedral Street. She liked to get away from her boarding school and spend time with her indulgent uncle and his attractive wife. In after years Virginia summed up her artless, still vivid impressions

of their marriage: "I never realized until I visited them how well
he had accustomed himself to wedded life. They did everything
possible to make each other happy. For someone who had been a
bachelor for fifty years Uncle Henry certainly had some very good
ideas on how to get along with your spouse. He was extremely polite
(and it wasn't put on) and that was one of his doctrines for a
happy married life. He claimed that it was more important to be
polite after you were married than before. For all the years I had
known him I never heard him refer to anyone as 'Darling' or 'Dear'
till he married Sara. It was a bit of a shock the first time I heard
him use this form of address but I realized that it was entirely sincere and it sounded so natural that I knew he meant it. Sara
seemed to be very docile but I have an idea that she ruled with
the 'iron hand in the velvet glove.' But Uncle Harry was so entranced with her that anything she suggested was fine with him. I
often heard Sara say, 'Henry, I think we should do thus and so' and
they did it, even if it was the farthest thing from his mind."

Their generous affection, even after the novelty of marriage
was gone, easily survived any strains. In particular it survived the
three standard complications of domestic comedy. Mencken, as an
old theatergoer, may have noted that nature once again copied art.
For the things that tested his own marriage were standard comic
fare: the wife's distaste for her husband's cronies, the wife's brother
who is short of money, and the wife's bustling, officious best friend.

Anne Duffy was the friend. Years before, she had had her first
confrontation with Mencken; the result was a draw. Spunky and
outspoken, she alternately irritated and impressed him. He said more
than once to Hamilton Owens, "I hate that woman." Yet when he
had to write her a note it was headed "Dear Anne" rather than
"Dear Mrs. Duffy" or even, once or twice, "My dear Anne" and,
more important, the notes were warm.

Now that Sara was married Anne spent more time with her
rather than less. She lived only two blocks away and felt, considering all she had done to find and furnish the apartment, that it was
the next thing to being her own home. Watching the newlyweds
she rejoiced at their amiable arrangements but could not conquer
the feeling that Henry dominated Sara and that Sara should stand
up for her womanly rights. Anne was a ready conversationalist who
had little hesitation in pointing out to Mencken how he could be-

come an even better husband. Mencken had no desire to see some woman telling him in his own home how he should treat his wife. The disagreements often became spirited and loud enough for Bessie or Hester to hear. Sara took little part; the arguments lay between her husband and her best friend. "Now, Anne, I don't want you interfering with our business," he would say in heavier tones than usual. Her reply, defensive but firm, would be classic: "I'm not interfering, Henry. I'm just trying to help Sara." Henry would hold on hard to his habitual courtesy toward a lady but there would be a stiffness in the apartment for a while. And yet when she was about to end her visit he would call out, "Anne, you going? Come back again."

Mencken's cronies offered the second test. They were members of the Saturday Night Club. Some of them were eminent men, it will be recalled, others simply convivial companions who shared his love for making music and drinking beer. Because it was still Prohibition at the time of his marriage the Club was meeting at the home first of one member and then of another, in order to drink unmolested. When it came to Mencken's turn a slight embarrassment arose. The Cathedral Street apartment was obviously too elegant to let the Club feel at ease, and Sara was enough of a Southern lady to find most of the members a little oafish. In addition, they were all in their various ways devoted to music, and she never really liked music. Still at the start she could not see herself turning away the Club. Anne, however, felt no hesitation. She called the meetings, with feline simplicity, "Henry's beer parties" and advised Sara emphatically against them. "You shouldn't let him have those parties here," she more than once maintained; "he should go to a hotel." Henry, reading two doors away, would close his book and march down the hall to do battle. As before, the argument would be resonant but repetitious. Anne would wrap the mantle of nobility about her, asserting, "I'm doing this for Sara's good." Then for a clincher she would remind him of Sara's ill health: "It upsets her when *these people*" — the term was used with lovely scorn — "come here like this." And Henry would reiterate his own theme: "You can come here any time you want, but I don't want you interfering with my business."

Though sympathizing with Anne's view Sara felt that she had to give the Club a chance. She managed well enough the first time or two. The members came in with shouts and friendly cheers. They were greeted by Sara, who then withdrew. But it was an uneasy relationship and the episode of the chairs soon upset it. The chairs in question were a set of antiques which she had bought and refinished for her dining room. Not long after the set arrived the members of the Club planted themselves on the antiques to make their music. Its hearty strains resounded from wall to wall. Under its hypnotic influence some of the musicians began to rock to and fro or lie on their spines. Here and there, with a creak, a wrench, a chair back parted from its chair. They had cost fifteen dollars a piece to refinish and Sara was fond of them. What she said to her husband after surveying the set is unknown but the Saturday Night celebrations were thereafter held elsewhere as a rule. As Mencken had observed in *In Defense of Women,* "the advantage of women lies in their freedom from sentimentality."

At the same time that Sara was discouraging the Saturday Night Club's beery informality, she was encouraging a different group of Mencken's friends. Her taste for elegance went beyond the furnishings of the apartment, and she began to plan small formal dinners — and occasional luncheons — for the prominent newspaper executives and the well-known writers who formed a prestigious part of Mencken's acquaintance. Sometimes a movie star or other celebrity would appear. One night Lillian Gish was a guest and Bessie was so excited that she begged to stay till the end, although there was always a man hired to do most of the serving. Among the more frequent guests were the Paul Pattersons, Hamilton and Olga Owens, and Anne Duffy and her cartoonist husband, Edmund. After the meal had run its smooth course the group would move to the living room. There Mencken would sit, dinner-jacketed, in one corner and discourse to his guests with a sparkle only slightly dimmed by the new decorum. This was the kind of social life that Sara liked and he was willing to join in it. But he would not forego the Saturday Night celebrations.

If he missed any of his old freedom he said little about it. It was not in his code to complain to others about his wife, and his attitude toward her was always loving. It even transcended the problem of the brother-in-law who needed money. In the first years of the Depression Mencken's own income lessened but it was always ample for Sara's and his needs. Though it sank sharply in 1932, it still averaged over seventeen thousand a year throughout their marriage. But Sara's brother John was a Montgomery businessman who lost out badly in the stock market crash along with an army of others. There were times, consequently, when he wanted to borrow money from Mencken. Sara told her husband to do as he pleased — in fact she was embarrassed by the situation — but he readily wrote any checks that were required. He had the money, he felt, and did not begrudge sharing some of it with her relatives.

Sometimes when Bessie stood combing Sara's hair, Sara would talk about the members of her family. She missed them even though their Montgomery scale of values was by no means always hers. She wanted them to thrive and be happy. Sometimes she would think back to the past and reminisce about her childhood to Bessie. At other times she would speak about her state of health. Quite often she would assure Bessie that she hoped to live to a ripe old age.

And yet for Sara ill health was never far away. In March 1935 Mencken wrote to Jim Tully, "Sara has gone to the Johns Hopkins for some x-rays. She had a painful bout of lumbago, following her months in bed, but she does not seem to be seriously ill." Nor was she then. Something was wrong nevertheless. One afternoon in mid-May she drove out with Anne Duffy into the countryside around Baltimore. Wanting an excuse for a destination they tried to find the Maple Heights Sanitarium. They failed. But they bought some ice-cream "Good Humors" to console them and reached the Duffy apartment around five. Sara seemed tired, lay down to take a nap, and arose as tired as before. "You look like hell," Anne announced bluntly. Sara answered that she often felt bad but that it was the lack of makeup that made her look like hell. So she rested a bit more, put on powder and rouge, and then had supper with the Duffys. She was still tired, so about nine Duffy walked her home. That was a Saturday. She went to bed and stayed there, suffering from what Henry in a letter to a friend described as a mild flu.

By the end of the week the flu had become something undiagnosed but far worse, for raging headache followed raging headache. Mencken promptly put her in the Johns Hopkins Hospital, where it was found that she had tubercular meningitis. Anne tried to see her but the hospital would not allow it. Then Henry phoned and told her, simply, that Sara was going to die. He hung up. A minute later he called again, demanding, "Did you understand me?" Anne said yes but he called once more. He could not comprehend what was actually happening and he projected his incomprehension on Anne.

During Sara's final few days all visitors but Henry were barred from her room. When he was not by her bed he was sitting in the apartment waiting. Anne stayed with him there as much as possible. From time to time the phone would ring in the apartment and a nurse would report on Sara's condition. Mencken and Anne waited out the hours. They played double Canfield; they told old, dismal jokes; they sat. Notes and letters of sympathy began to come in to him. Punctillious even at this tragic time, ready indeed to write so that he did not have to think, he sent out his answers and acknowledgments. To Robin Harriss, for example, he wrote on May 30, "My best thanks for your note. Poor Sara, I fear, is now beyond all help. It seems a dreadful end to her long and gallant struggle." The next day the usual phone calls from the hospital failed to come. Instead the doorbell finally rang and there was Dr. Ben Baker with the news that Sara had died at six that afternoon.

Mencken could not bring himself to stay that night at the apartment. He went back to Hollins Street, where his family tried to comfort him and Raymond Pearl went to sit with him. The next morning he sat in Hamilton Owens's office at the *Sun* and spoke about all that Sara had meant to him. He summed it up poignantly, "When I married Sara, the doctors said she could not live more than three years. Actually she lived five, so that I had two more years of happiness than I had any right to expect."

He was in no condition to deal with the grim ritual of funeral arrangements; his brother August, with some help from Anne, took care of most of it. It was she who decided that the coffin could be open and not shut, but Mencken never looked in it. It was unthinkable not to have some kind of service, so an Episcopal minister who lived near Mencken was asked to conduct it. But it was held in a funeral home, not in church. Besides the immediate families only a few others were present, among them the Knopfs, the Hergesheimers, and the governor of Maryland, Albert Ritchie. After the *1935* service the body was cremated and the ashes buried beside the bodies of Mencken's parents.

In Sara had lain all the qualities that attracted Mencken to women. They were there, in good part, when he first met her at Goucher but they developed, under his sympathetic and interested eye, as she became more and more of a person. She was pretty — almost everyone who knew her says that no photograph did her justice — but she grew prettier. She was at her best, by all accounts, during the years of her marriage. In spite of her illnesses she could even look good on a passport photo; there is an attractive one, taken with her husband, that dates from the time they took their first ocean trip together. James Cain was struck by the rich contrast in her coloring, the contrast between the pale transparent skin and the dark wavy hair. Her voice was low-pitched but vibrant and verged on a delicate growl when she said what she thought about some hapless crony of her husband's. Cain says that he never heard her swear but that profanity, in an astringent way, lurked at times beneath the surface of her voice. She was not funny and she had none of Mencken's compulsion to clown with close friends, but she had plenty of wit of a smoky, ironical kind.

And she had literary talent. Though her work was not for the ages, it made a substantial impression while she was alive. During her brief career her sensitive stories were honored three times by the compilers of the annual volumes of short stories. The one that made the honor roll before she went to Hollywood was followed by another which was printed in the *O. Henry Memorial* volume for 1933 and a third which appeared in the *Best Short Stories* of 1934. Her essays and articles ranged from cute journalism to astute expository prose. Her novel *The Making of a Lady* was no award winner but it pioneered along a path later to be followed by such distinguished Southern writers as Eudora Welty, Carson McCullers, and Flannery O'Connor. When illness forced her to stop writing she was on the brink of an international reputation. It was no wonder that her husband was proud of her ability as well as delighted by her charm.

She was in many ways a Victorian. Her Alabama upbringing had not only taught her a propriety increasingly unfashionable up north; it had given her a sense of values much more in harmony with Mencken's than that of the bright New York girls he usually took out. He found Anita Loos, for instance, thoroughly exhilarating; the wit, vivacity, and glitter that would produce *Gentlemen Prefer Blondes* were like champagne to him. But he married Sara. The

tone of mutual politeness, of basic respect, set during the long courtship survived the enforced intimacies of marriage. It was neither
stiff nor artificial; it was simply old-fashioned. When the Canadian
honeymoon ended and the couple stopped in New York on the way
to Baltimore, Mencken allowed Hally Pomeroy of the New York
World to interview him and his bride. She found them in their suite
at the Algonquin, just as Sara Mayfield was preparing to leave after
her own illuminating visit. The reporter's story, dated September 17,
began "They've been married three weeks and he's still as polite as
he said he would be." Politeness, in fact, turned out to be the theme
of the whole interview. Husband and wife agreed on its importance.
Near the end, after Henry had spoken, with some feeling, about Victorian courtesy Sara summed up the matter. "Henry is Victorian,
though he won't admit it," she noted shrewdly. She added, "So am I."

Finally, there were two other things, of a different order of magnitude, that bound him to her. One was the indomitable way she
faced illness and endured pain. Mencken indulged his hypochondria
with grim relish; he was always cataloging his aches, always complaining. Sara was the opposite. Looking back after her death he
said, "I have never met a more patient person, or a more gallant."
The other was the depth of her own feeling for him. Once they
were married she expressed it without reserve. For his part, when a
business trip separated him from her he often wrote that he missed
her and vowed not to be separated again. When Sara wrote to him,
however, she showed a devotion that few women could equal. Not
infrequently she ended a letter to her husband by saying simply,
"I worship you."

Before her death she had decided that her modest library was
to go to Goucher. On October 30, 1935 Mencken while writing to
Dorothy Hergesheimer said of Joe, "I'll see him tomorrow, and he is
going to Goucher College to sustain me when I hand over Sara's
books. How she would have larfed to see us!"

15. The Circus of Dr. R.

SLOWLY MENCKEN CLOSED the door of Cathedral Street. He would never forget how Sara had put life and warmth into the apartment. Nor would he forget the apartment itself with its ornate, high-ceilinged living room and dining room, its string of smaller rooms beyond — the whole apartment was half a block long — ending with Sara's sitting room. Nor would he forget the Victorian elegance of the furnishings which had charmed and amused him: the black velvet rug, the curio cabinets, the rosewood chairs, and the rest. He hated to leave it; he clung to the memories it contained. Ten days after the funeral he wrote to Dreiser, "My plan is to go on with the house here. It is very comfortable and convenient, and I suppose that I'll have to learn to endure the fact that my wife is no longer in it."

He tried for a while to keep the apartment as it had been left by Sara and he tried to maintain the same routine. In the daytime, with Hester and Bessie still around, he felt that living there could be borne. But the nights, he admitted, were dreadful. Though his bachelor brother August had moved temporarily to Cathedral Street to give him some companionship, he had left again by December to return to Hollins Street. By January of the new year Mencken himself decided to go. He felt the powerful pull of his old home and by the end of March he was back at Hollins Street, in company with August; and there he would remain. The process of moving was complicated and dismal, not only because all the furnishings at Cathedral Street that could not be crowded into Hollins Street had to be disposed of, but also because of what the move symbolized. It put a period to his fullest personal life.

He stepped into the street with a reluctance, brisk though he usually was, that he had never felt before. There had been other times when the world had repelled him, the years of World War I in particular. But now it was much worse. He was older by more than fifteen years; he was set in his ways; and he was emerging from a very agreeable, enclosed existence into a world that had altered far more than he cared to recognize.

The price of his five years of marriage was that it had isolated him, gently enough, from many of his old connections. Part of the isolation was personal; part was political, or social in the broad sense of the word. Sara had her own tastes. Shortly after their engagement was announced his old friend Max Broedel wrote Mencken, mentioning his apprehensions about her attitude toward the Club. Mencken replied grandly, "Let your fears be stilled. The bride is not only in favor of the club, she has actually gone to the trouble to put in a superb beer equipment in the new house." Yet Broedel was right.

In place of the conviviality of the Saturday Night Club sort, Sara offered her husband the more sober social life described previously. Its range was noticeably narrower. The couples who came to Cathedral Street were apt to be prosperous even after the stock market crash, were often prominent, and were almost all political and economic conservatives. The only notable liberals were the *Sunpapers'* Gerald Johnson and his wife. The new friends the Menckens made were understandably as conservative as the old. Among them Marcella and Alfred duPont became perhaps the most congenial. They lived the good life and at their house in Wilmington it was hard not to forget the troubles of the rest of the world.

The years of his marriage also saw Mencken withdraw step by step from the *Mercury*. His train trips to New York decreased; we know that more of the editing was left to Angoff. The emotional equity Mencken had in the magazine began to wither. Once he had edited it with spirit and made it a heady influence on the entire country. Now, with the country radically changed, he did not even want to influence it as much as he had before. The new causes left him cold; the new crises failed to command his concentration. In the early 1930s, before *Time* became an institution and *Newsweek* was started, James Cain had the notion of a weekly magazine of news and opinion for which Mencken would have been the ideal editor. Cain interested Raoul Fleischmann, president of the company that published the *New Yorker,* in the possibility of financing it and tried to interest Mencken in editing it. He got nowhere. Though Mencken declined with all the geniality he used with old friends, he was firm. When Cain pressed him for his reasons he gave a number, but the one Cain thinks most significant was that it would have meant reading the New York *Times* each day. Mencken was not being funny, Cain feels; he was saying that the daily reading of particulars about this deteriorating world was something he no longer cared to attempt.

The facts about the Depression that the *Times* so fully reported seemed to Mencken either unbelievable or weirdly misconstrued. Though he saw more than one effect of the Depression with his own eyes he did not credit them. He did not comprehend it intellectually. He did not feel it emotionally. Every instinct in him as well as every teacher he had ever trusted told him that the Depression either simply was not so or else that it was a minor matter, a purging of excess. As he interpreted the America of the first years after the stock market crash, its malaise had come from extravagance and clumsy leadership, especially that of the incompetent Hoover. Once the leadership was changed and the pains of the purging were past, American would be stronger than ever. Its basic principles and traditional practices remained sound.

The shades of his teachers supported him. Huxley had taught that as long as stupid, ignorant, or tyrannical authority was put down, things would be all right. Nietzsche had taught that the sufferings of the mob meant little; the important thing was for the elite to prevail. Darwin had taught that, regardless of circumstances, the fittest would survive; such was nature's way and there was really no other. And Sumner had taught that any organized attempt to interfere with the processes of nature was stupidity. We should shun the reformers who would have our society try to alter the spontaneous forces of nature. We should depend instead on the individual. As Mencken looked at the poor around him he doubtless recalled Sumner's injunction that if every individual were "sober, industrious, prudent, and wise," poverty would be abolished.

In the presidential election of 1932 Mencken voted against Hoover rather than for Roosevelt. His fundamental position did not change. The chasm widened between his stand and the bulk of American opinion. Nowhere was the cleavage shown more clearly than in one of his Monday Articles for the *Evening Sun.* Writing there under the date of February 13, 1933, he out-Hoovered Hoover. For he announced, "Unless I err gravely, what the people really want is a sweeping and *permanent* reduction in the costs of government." He remained convinced during the depth of the Depression, in some of its most trying hours, that the public yearned for a tax cut.

When Roosevelt — or Dr. R. as he soon dubbed him — was inaugurated Mencken decided to give him the benefit of the doubt. Yet his restraint was short-lived. As early as 1920 he had called Roosevelt an ass and accused him of losing the Democratic presidential nomination for Al Smith, and now he could not suppress a shudder as the new President made his daring moves. In his Monday Article of March 27, 1933, while granting that Roosevelt was receiving deafening acclaim, Mencken predicted that the honeymoon would quickly end. A month later he headed one of the Monday Articles "Vive Le Roi!" as he stared at the imperial Roosevelt. He entitled another "A Day of Reckoning." This kind of warning set the tone for the second half of 1933.

He had a deep-seated objection not only to the policies but also to the propaganda of the New Deal. The efforts by Washington to rally public support for its new measures both amused and dismayed him. On the surface he found the public demonstrations for the National Recovery Act, the NRA, grotesque. The fervid speeches, the slogans, the drives, the attempts to put pressure on any part of the public that would not go along were forbidding as well as funny. They reminded him of the propaganda apparatus of World War I that had silenced his newspaper writing as pro-German and had forced him into isolation. Looking back at the first waves of New Deal propaganda, he declared in his last regular editorial for the *Mercury*, "It was 1917 all over again." He resented the notion that anyone who was supposed to show an NRA sticker and refused was unpatriotic. He felt personally threatened.

Powerful though his feelings were, his language in his published writings remained relatively moderate. He wrote against the New Deal and for old American principles, but he wrote with such persuasiveness and internal logic that he found himself becoming the country's most effective spokesman for the old order. His pieces were often witty and always unmarred by the lunatic conservatism that afflicted much of the writing of the Right. He refused to find a Communist under every Washington desk. He stood firm for freedom of opinion and freedom of the press, even defending the freedom of professors, the "gogues." For instance, he defended George Counts of Columbia's Teachers College against charges of communism and defended a university's right, moreover, to have Marxists on its faculty. A great university, he wrote to one angry conservative on August 23, 1934, "ought to have room in it for men subscribing to every sort of idea that is currently prevalent. Certainly you can't deny that Communism is believed in by a great many people, and that some of them are far from insane."

Mencken's onslaught on Roosevelt and his New Deal was systematic, assured, and amusing. The rhetoric of it, however, was old-fashioned and limited in its effectiveness. Here he is on the bureaucrats brought in to run the NRA, and their fevered activities; this is from the Monday Article in the *Evening Sun* for November 6, 1933: "For weeks on end the complaisant newspapers were full of the gaudy forays and even gaudier encyclicals of these busybodies. The more seasoned of them grabbed columns of space under lynching headlines, and even the neophytes managed to be photographed like kidnappers or movie stars, and so drew great clouds of the catnip of publicity into their nostrils, where it will linger until the Judgment Day, tickling them damnably and ruining them for their trades." And here he is writing off one of their leaders: "The Hon. Grover Aloysius Whalen, the New York flamingo, was their Napoleon." The titles of some of his Monday Articles for 1934 again tell the story: "Sold down the River," "The Piper Passes His Hat," "Utopia Eats Utopia," for example.

By late 1934 he was so doughty an opponent of Dr. R. and all his works that he was invited to give the main speech for the "Loyal Opposition" at the Gridiron Banquet in December. It promised to be one of the liveliest occasions of his career; it turned out to be one of the most traumatic.

The members of the Gridiron Club were, and are, chosen from Washington's most respected newspapermen. There are only fifty members at any one time. Its custom has long been to give dinners, once two but now one a year, that are nationally celebrated for their farcical humor. The members act out original skits before an audience of distinguished guests. The evening's entertainment customarily concludes with two brief addresses, one from an outstanding figure in the "Loyal Opposition," the other from the President of the United States. Both addresses are supposed to be sparked with all the humor the speakers can provide. Both addresses can be the less inhibited because they are off the record, the watchword of the Club being "Ladies always present, reporters never."

The evening of December 8 the dinner began, as usual, promptly at seven thirty when the president of the Club, a newspaperman named James Wright, rose and announced grandly, "Tonight, my friends, we train our field glasses on the compounds of the political pageant; on fantastic floats and floating fantasies. Colorful events of recent months will pass in review." They proceeded to do so, between courses of the dinner. To start with there was a Santa Claus skit. It set the tone: what it lacked in subtlety it made up in slapstick. There was a Rose Bowl skit, a maternity ward skit, and New Deal hotel skit; there was the usual succession of rich foods, with Maryland terrapin as the main dish, doubtless in deference to Mencken.

Shortly after nine the hotel skit was over and Mencken's turn came. President Wright explained that instead of looking on the ground for a Republican critic of the Democrats, the Club had looked up and found a child of the sun, H. L. Mencken of the *Sunpapers*, to do the job. Mencken arose, in his white tie and tails, face flushed, eyes bright, and began in his gravelly Baltimore voice with a bow to FDR, "Mr. President, Mr. Wright, and fellow subjects of the Reich." He had worked over his speech with great care — two versions of it remain in the Gridiron archives and three in the Enoch Pratt Library — but somehow the wit proved to be forced, the luster a little lacking. "Fellow subjects of the Reich" was an example. He spoke dryly of how poor everyone was, "we millionaire reporters" among them. He applauded the circus the populace was seeing: "For if the current flow of so-called ideas is somewhat confusing, it must be admitted that the show going with it is very nifty." He remarked that "Every day in this great country is April Fool day." He told a few jokes.

He ended with an anecdote. Some time ago, he said, he had taken his pastor around Washington. After the tour the pastor spoke

to him: "My boy, you cherish a chimera if you ever hope to turn
out the smart fellows who now own and operate this government.
They have enlisted for all eternity, and they'll still be on deck after
eternity is past and forgotten. They have night and day keys to the
White House, they carry Congress in their vest-pocket, and even
the Supreme Court is far too dignified to menace the seat of their
pantaloons." Mencken finished with a switch: "But perhaps I should
add a detail for the sake of the record. The good man got off his
speech in the middle of Pennsylvania Avenue in the early part of
1932. He was not speaking of the Brain Trust, but of the Anti-
Saloon League." The audience's applause was hearty, their laughter
loud.

More skits followed and more food and then finally, at eleven
fifteen, the remarks by the President. In the Gridiron Club files
there is no record of what he said but Roosevelt's papers at Hyde
Park contain the notes and suggestions on which he based his speech.
There are two alternative openings and a closing section which he
apparently never used, because it is out of key with the rest of
the notes. This closing section is a defense of his administration and
a serious expression of his optimism about the future. The rest of
the notes, some three pages, are the basis for an effective and indeed
devastating joke that he proposed to play on Mencken.

When Roosevelt began to speak, in his ripe eastern accents, he
lustily attacked his hosts themselves, the members of the press. He
urbanely delivered his dire criticisms, one by one. "Most of the evils
that continue to beset American journalism today, in truth, are not
due to the rascality of the owners nor even to the Kiwanian bombast
of business managers, but simply and solely to the stupidity, cow-
ardice and Philistinism of working newspaper men." His hearers,
someone has recalled, sat quiet. "I know of no American who starts
from a higher level of aspiration than the journalist. He is, in his
first phase, genuinely romantic. He plans to be both an artist and
a moralist — a master of lovely words and a merchant of sound ideas.
He ends, commonly, as the most depressing jackass in his community — that is, if his career goes on to what is called success."
There were a few embarrassed snorts and some high color. "A Washington correspondent," added Roosevelt zeroing in, "is one with a
special talent for failing to see what is before his eyes. I have beheld

a whole herd of them sitting through a national convention without once laughing." There were scattered guffaws from the herd.

As he went on, smiling broadly, some members of the press began to recognize the source of these acid observations. One knew them almost from the start, Mencken. He sat there in a state hardly to be imagined. When at the end of the address the audience was informed by FDR that the dire quotations came from the works of his "old friend Henry Mencken," a roar went up. Grinning his triumphant grin Roosevelt was wheeled out and the dinner was done.

The public humiliation left a deep mark on Mencken. The next week he several times assured John Owens at the *Sun*, "We'll even it up"; but he never could. A few months later Phil Goodman's daughter and her husband had supper with Mencken in New York and everything was agreeable till Roosevelt was mentioned. Then Mencken spoke with a heat and bitterness that amazed them.

Only Sara could soothe him, and she died six months after the Gridiron affair. Greatly shaken by her death, still angry over Roosevelt's trick, repelled by the whole course of events in the country, Mencken nevertheless promptly rallied his powerful psychological resources and set out to remake his life. More than one of his friends was to notice that after Sara's death he never quite seemed the same. He stiffened somehow. But they also acknowledged the pulsing vitality of his spirit. The sheer energy that had made him a city editor before he was twenty-five; that had made him the center of nearly any group before he was thirty; that had made him the most dynamic and sparkling conversationalist of his day; that had made him in his peak years the prime influence on American intellectual life: this energy continued to drive him despite his bereavement. He wrote a friend that he was completely dashed and dismayed, yet he turned almost at once to the bleak business of making the best of things.

The Saturday following the funeral he invited the Saturday Night Club to meet at Cathedral Street. It was a joyless occasion, the more so because the Club itself was showing its age and infirmity. The older members found it hard to climb the many steps, burdened as they were with their instruments. But they had their determined concert and followed it by going through the motions of jocularity. Mencken said little. Yet a connection with the past was reaffirmed, as others would be. After he had replied to the hundreds of letters of condolence he and August embarked on the liner *Bremen* for a few weeks of rest and change in London.

On shipboard he submitted to having pictures taken; they show a somber Mencken with sunken eyes. But in mid-Atlantic he wrote Blanche Knopf that he had been lolling about, doing a good bit of reading, and feeling alive again. He had even been enjoying "some mild and delicate boozing." Everything considered it was, he told her firmly, "a very comfortable voyage."

Upon his arrival he gave an interview to a reporter from the London *Daily Express*. It appeared on June 29, 1935 and in it the reporter observed that Mencken was still suffering from the shock of his wife's death. Yet he "would not mention the tragedy that had flung him back on his own resources again, but looked to the future with fine and resilient courage." He assured the reporter that he had an idea for a new book and hoped to begin work on it by Christmas. The idea was one he had considered before and would again, though it would never develop fully. It was to be a manual of advice to young men, free from cant and hypocrisy. It would tell them candidly what Mencken thought, and that would be all to their advantage. "Fellows like us have decided and practical ideas. Suppose a man's wife runs away with someone better looking. We know what he ought to do about it."

He tried to capture the old Mencken air. He continued to try during the holiday and became better at it as he went along. One day he wrote Sara Mayfield that the temperature was eighty three and the English, in their doormat tweeds and ditch-digger under-wear, were dropping like flies; but it was comfortable weather for Baltimoreans and he was beginning in fact to feel pretty well. The high spot was a pleasant day of punting on the Thames with Paul Patterson's son Maclean and some others.

By the time he ended his return voyage he was back to some-thing like his customary form. The press was waiting for him as usual when he docked in New York and the reporters were not disappointed. Having sojourned near, if not with, royalty, he revived an earlier proposal of his by announcing, "What this country needs is an absolute monarchy." He dismissed the political complications, promising that he could write an amendment to the Constitution in ten minutes. He concluded by proposing FDR for the throne. "I think President Roosevelt would make as good a king as he has made a bad President." Newspapers from all over copied the item, grateful again for some engaging paragraphs. He remained a first-rate source of news.

Yet it was now news with a difference. The papers no longer reflected the ardent hostility many publishers and editors had felt so frequently in the 1920s. They now ignored his literary opinions, though those had become fewer anyway in the course of time, but found his political philosophy inviting. While a good many reporters were liberal, probably most of the editors and an overwhelming majority of publishers were conservative. They warmed to Mencken as a sound-money, small-government man and said so with enthusiasm on their editorial pages. And they now stood ready to look benignly on Mencken as an institution. It can be deduced that a fair share of their readers felt the same way. Mencken was still too vital and brash to be a Grand Old Man but he was certainly not the Great Rebel any more. Inevitably, his stature diminished. At the extreme the reaction to him was no longer one of vitriol or venom but of elaborate condescension. For example: an item in the Cleveland *Press* for July 20, a week after the New York interview in which Mencken had come out for an American king. In his column the *Press*'s literary editor, Elrick B. Davis, made a passing reference to "the late H. L. Mencken" and then added in feigned surprise, "What? You say Mencken isn't dead? Extraordinary!"

In the months and then the years after Sara's death, politics became for Mencken a powerful anodyne. Even more than before, he talked about politics, read about politics, and published on politics. Roosevelt grew into a greater rogue as time passed; nothing could stale the infinite variety of his tricks on the American public. So Mencken constantly said and wrote. His preoccupation with the sins of the New Deal helped him to forget Sara. Not that they would not have engrossed him anyway. And most of all, the gaudiest of political spectacles, the national conventions, attracted him. While attending them he complained constantly, but his real regret was that they came only every four years.

He had put it pungently in a letter to Jim Tully after the 1932 conventions. "The two national conventions almost wore me out, but they were such good shows that I held up until the end. The Democratic show, in particular, would have delighted your Christian heart. I howled with mirth for hours on end. Over the radio the thing seems to have been simply a bore, but with the actual delegates in front of one it was a circus. They all looked like comic characters, and some of them smelled like goats, jackasses, pole-cats and other biblical animals." No doubt; but he savored everything about a convention. Now in 1936 he had a dividend coming. Besides the regular Republican and Democratic festivals there would be conventions of two splinter groups, the parties of Father Charles Coughlin, a Catholic priest from Detroit who had gathered a considerable following through his fiery radio sermons against Roosevelt, and of Dr. Francis Townsend, who had made himself the political apostle of the elderly by promising them thirty dollars every Thursday if he came to power.

The sweat, the struggle, the chicanery, the antics, the long hours, the strain of writing: he would not have missed any of them. He had even published a book on the pair of conventions he mentioned to Tully, those of summer 1932, and the Preface to the book gives us a vivid picture of what conventions meant for him. In the Preface to *Making a President* he shows how the whole business looks to the reporter who covers the convention and is constantly propelled by the need to file as much copy, and good copy, on the variegated proceedings as he can. The news of each day, Mencken advises his reader, "does not spring into the world well formed and neatly labeled." Far from it; even when coming from one reporter it may be made up of several different versions, beaten out on his typewriter or written in longhand in between his moves from place to place. Mencken cites as a lurid example Dispatch No. XII in *Making a President*. It embodied the ultimate text of a series of reports, prepared over some very trying hours, on the Democratic convention in Chicago. Part of it he wrote at the *Sun* headquarters in the Blackstone Hotel, part at the Western Union office in the Congress Hotel, and part at a writing desk in the lobby of the Congress.

As those hours alternately dragged and spurted along, Mencken recalls, changing events resulted in changes in the reports even as they were being filed. The few forecasts he made to the reader had to be revised, not only in view of what was happening on the floor of the convention but also in the light of what was happening in

smoky rooms. There were too many places that a reporter needed
to visit. He had to be everywhere, it sometimes seemed, at precisely
the same time. The committees, the state delegations, the candidates' headquarters, the secret as well as the public chambers: from
any one of these might come major moves. And at any time, anywhere, one of the political bosses present might "begin to sweat
important news."

Under such conditions it is no wonder that some of the writing
seems dispirited as well as disorganized. Mencken admits that Dispatch No. XVII, for instance, has a tired air to it too. But it could
hardly be otherwise, in view of the grueling conditions under which
both it and its predecessor, No. XVI, were composed. To get material
for No. XVI he had sat in the convention hall till after one in the
morning, while the delegates were "beating Prohibition to death."
At about two he returned to the Blackstone Hotel and pounded
out his first copy for No. XVI. At about three he ground to a stop.
He took a bath, downed a drink, and tumbled into bed. He was
up again before nine and filed the final batch of copy at ten thirty.
And then he was faced with beginning No. XVII.

The trials involved in preparing XVII proved to be even greater
than those in XVI. Mencken recalls them in the book with dyspeptic
relish. That evening the convention reconvened at eight and stayed
in session throughout the night. Early in the evening the Chicago
heat was awesome. He remarked that his seersucker outfit began
to look like a bathing suit and his necktie "took on the appearance
of having been fried." At three in the morning the temperature
dropped in the convention hall but all this did for Mencken was
make him sleepy. He went out into the parking lot to move around
a bit, found Walter Lippmann there, and sat on the running board
of an automobile to talk with him. When Mencken went back into
the hall he discovered the cowboy humorist Will Rogers sitting in
his seat. The two gossiped for half an hour, while the balloting for
the nomination started and then sluggishly moved along. At seven
in the morning he wandered out to buy himself a breakfast of a
roast-beef sandwich and a beer. He came back to find orders from
the *Sun* office saying that the deadline for the current copy had
been pushed up from ten forty-five to nine. He had left his typewriter at the hotel and so was forced to write with a pencil — a
laborious job for someone who had cut his teeth on his old Corona.

But he managed. The copy was scribbled, filed, edited in Baltimore by the copydesk, and then printed for the *Evening Sun's* eager readers. Dispatch No. XVII done, Mencken finally went to sleep at eleven thirty in the morning.

That, as he explains it, is how the readers got what they read. It was not vintage Mencken but it was satisfying enough. They got a good general idea of the course of the convention. What Mencken provided too, with verve, was what struck the senses. He reported faithfully on what deafened his ear, tickled his nose, and bleared his blue eye. He saw the sessions as a circus, as usual, or even a rodeo. Such chapter titles of *Making a President* as "The Clowns Enter the Ring" and "The Wets Swing into the Saddle" bear this out. And the *Sun* readers got the Mencken turn of phrase, the unexpected, comic word. The lead for Dispatch No. XVI, the one that sapped some of his energy for No. XVII, is still as bright as any reader could ask: "Since one o'clock this morning Prohibition has been a fugitive in the remote quagmires of the Bible Belt. The chase began thirteen hours earlier, when the resolutions committee of the convention retired to the voluptuous splendors of the Rose Room at the Congress Hotel. For four hours nothing came out of the apartment save the moaning of converts in mighty travail. Then the Hon. Michael L. Igoe, a round-faced Chicago politician, burst forth with the news that the wet wets of the committee had beaten the damp wets by a vote of 35 to 17. There ensued a hiatus, while the quarry panted and the bloodhounds bayed."

Though the spirit shown in *Making a President* flagged at times, both the book and the reports that constituted its material can still hold the reader. For Mencken's delight in political conventions is contagious. Vividly he describes Al Smith on the podium: "The great set piece of the debate was the speech of Al Smith. When he suddenly appeared on the platform, his face a brilliant scarlet and his collar wet and flapping about his neck, he got a tremendous reception and the overgrown pipe organ let loose with East Side, West Side in an almost terrifying manner, with every stop wide open and a ton or so of extra weight on the safety valve. Al did a very good job. He had at Lord Hoover with some excellent wisecracks, he made some amusing faces, and he got a huge and friendly laugh by pronouncing the word radio in his private manner, with two d's. He had sense enough to shut down before he wore out

his welcome, and so he got another earsplitting hand as he finished,
with the organ booming again and the band helping."

Mencken's zest made everything interesting, even the stretches
of boredom which both conventions inevitably involved. The important thing about the Democratic convention was that in spite of
Al Smith's Bowery-style opposition it nominated FDR; that and
the fact that it resolved to oppose Prohibition. The important thing,
if there was one, about the Republican convention was that it re-
nominated Hoover, Lord Hoover, as Mencken had created him. But
things did not need to be important to come alive.

With this background of rich, steamy experience, Mencken looked
forward to the 1936 conventions. He wanted everything that he had
had before: the boredom as well as the bravura and blare. He was
not disappointed.

He plunged in gratefully. The carbon copies of his dispatches
from the Republican and Democratic conventions have been pasted
into one of the scrapbooks at the Enoch Pratt Library. They reveal
that the annoyances at the conventions only spurred him to more
vigorous writing. There was in particular one of the Democratic
sessions, the evening one held in Philadelphia's Franklin Field, which
Mencken described in his Preface to the scrapbook. It came after a
day of rain. "The flimsy press-stands under the open sky were all
wet, most of the reporters' typewriters got wet too, and they themselves did not escape. There was no light save from the huge
glares of the news-reel men, and from time to time they turned it
off. While I was at work my soggy typewriter was bucking under
my hands, and not infrequently I was barely able to see its keys.
When Roosevelt entered the field a man and a woman leaped to
chairs in the row in front of me, cutting off my view of the speakers'
stand and almost coming down upon me. I remonstrated angrily,
but finally came to terms with the man. I let him stand up, shutting me off from the stand, on condition that he call off to me what
was going on there. This he did very faithfully until the end of
the meeting." In spite of a blocked view and a wet typewriter
Mencken sent in his usual colorful copy to the *Sunpapers*.

The Republican convention came first, however, and the flow
of reportage began June 7. Mencken, setting the scene, was in fine
form. He began, "The delegates and alternates to the Republican
National Convention are still strung across the country, slowly edging

their way toward Cleveland by train, bus, motorcar and oxcart." He struck the proper note; as it turned out, there was no need for the delegates to hurry. The contest for the presidential nomination was no battle of the giants but it was plain from the start that it was Alf Landon's convention. The quiet governor of Kansas proved able to steam-roller the opposition. It was made up of such presidential impossibilities as Senator William Borah, Senator Arthur Vandenberg, and Colonel Frank Knox. They all craved the nomination but could not collect the feeblest of forces to mount a Stop Landon movement. Their efforts were confined, so Mencken indicated, to putting corks on Landon pitchforks. For at one point early in the proceedings some of the Landon backers, moving in to rehearse a wild, spontaneous demonstration for Alf, made their appearance armed with pitchforks. When they tried to start a parade their pointed forks alarmed the opposition, so they were sent out with orders to get corks to protect the prongs.

Mencken clocked the speeches, reported the drolleries, and explained the customs of political conventions with a sharp eye for their inherent absurdity. As he observed about a typical demonstration to the readers of the *Sun,* "Such hullabaloos, by long usage, have become almost as standardized as baccalaureate addresses or hangings. The partisans of the candidate before the house bring in all sorts of banners, most of them inscribed with idiotic slogans, and parade them up and down the aisles. Friendly delegates join them with the State standards, and a great many strangers get through the police lines and enter into the procession. A squalling young girl always shows up, borne on the shoulders of a couple of delegates far gone in liquor." He characterized the nominating and seconding speeches caustically, sparing no speaker except one attractive female politician. He reported happily on the Republican ex-President. He listened to Lord Hoover speak and noted a significant novelty, a new gesture to accompany his address: Hoover "thrust his left hand into his pantaloons pocket, and began to enforce his points by gently thumping his equator with his right."

The Democratic convention, held in Philadelphia, differed from its Republican predecessor by being dominated not by a colorless Midwestern governor but by the giant figure of the President of the United States. The Republican convention looked like a fist fight by contrast. Roosevelt had his convention so securely under control that there was no hint of any clash and the only problem was to develop some plot interest. "Jim Farley's chief job here," Mencken wrote in beginning his reports, "is to prevent the convention boring both the delegates and the country." As the convention moved along he found that he could give Farley only fair marks for theatrical management. The speeches were all long, the orators either windy or flat. There was, for instance, Jesse Jones, the Texas politician and financier. "The Hon. Mr. Jones is a man of many gifts, but eloquence is not one of them, and he drove people out by the thousand. When he finished at last whole sections of the galleries were empty, and scores of delegates and alternates had fled downtown to see what was left of the Mummers' parade and to get in a few life-savers before the saloons closed."

Mencken admitted that there were two exceptions among the speakers. One was Governor Herbert Lehman of New York, according to Mencken the "real star of the performance" one evening. For Mencken he shone the more brightly so that FDR would shine the less. The other was the least bad of the speakers who seconded FDR's nomination: "The only one of these dub orators who attracted any notice was the Hon. Martin L. Davey, Governor of Ohio. The Hon. Mr. Davey used to be a severe critic of the New Deal, but some time ago, while motoring along a road near the little town of Damascus, Ohio, he suddenly saw a great light, and is now hot for it." Even if Governor Davey's speech seemed to Mencken essentially a series of college yells it drew considerable applause. As to Roosevelt's acceptance speech, "It was received in a friendly way by the huge crowd, but it would certainly be an exaggeration to call it a big success."

And yet Mencken could not laugh at the Democratic convention with the same sympathetic amusement that he had shown in Chicago among the Republicans. The flamboyant figure of Roosevelt made him uncomfortable; the eager New Dealers looked to him like a neurotic cabal. This was not too hard to detect from his dispatches — though they often seemed the same tasty recipe as before — but it also showed in other, less public ways. He could not tolerate personal abrasions with the tough good-humor he once had. Marquis Childs remembers that at one of the Democratic sessions Mencken was approached by another noted reporter, who had been drinking enough so that he felt called upon to hector Mencken. Mencken dismissed him sharply, though they had been acquaintances for years, snapping, "Get away from me, you old drunk."

On the other hand, he got something of a lift from the Coughlin and Townsend conventions. Their sessions threw into prominence personalities so bizarre that even Mencken had not in some cases come across their like before. Their politics proved to be a politics of dissent to such a degree that even he was amazed. These meetings were the sideshow, not the main show, but he bought his ticket readily.

In a letter to Ernest Boyd on October 1 he wrapped it all up. "As you probably have heard," he wrote, "I have been politicking since June 1st. I have covered four big national conventions, have made two campaign tours, and have in addition gone out to Kansas to sit at the feet of the prophet Landon. He is much smarter than he looks, and I shall vote for him with great joy. But my guess is that he'll be beaten by at least two million votes. Such a mountebank as Roosevelt is simply irresistible in a great free Republic." In spite of his closeness to the campaign, incidentally, Mencken was to suffer the fate of most prophets, for Roosevelt's margin turned out to be better than eleven million.

16. Friends and Familiars

AS MENCKEN MOVED into middle age his friendships naturally modulated. The five years, between 1930 and 1935, of his marriage to Sara saw him spend less time in New York and more in Baltimore. Some of the New York friendships weakened, even the one with Phil Goodman. The Baltimore friendships remained strong, however, though the ones connected with the Saturday Night Club changed their nature somewhat after Mencken became a married man. He remained close to his good colleagues on the *Sunpapers* even if he drank less beer with them. The friends he and Sara both enjoyed were inevitably the ones invited to Cathedral Street most often. After Sara's death in 1935, Mencken tried to repair such friendships as had fallen in disuse — particularly with women friends — and even added some new ones. But the Saturday Night Club remained the hub of his social life.

In its heyday the Club had been almost epic. Throughout the 1920s it reached a peak it never achieved again. It gained something like a national renown, or notoriety, thanks mainly to Mencken's eminence. But as the 1930s opened, it began — to use Mencken's phrase — to oxidize. For one thing it lost the lustiness of youth. Though younger members were inducted at intervals, the age level crept upward. The riots were no longer as riotous, the orgies seldom as orgiastic. Most tellingly, the meetings began to break up earlier than before. Then too, starting in fall 1929 there was the gray shadow of the Depression. It touched some members of the Club little but, as time went on, it nearly enveloped others. The Club could ignore the Depression at its meetings only with an effort. Nevertheless, the Club though daunted was not destroyed. It refused to give up.

In fact its underlying characteristic during the 1930s and 1940s was its tenacity. It held on in the face of specific blows as well as general ones. No matter that wrinkles deepened or hair grew gray.

Again and again Mencken foresaw its decline and fall, predicting it freely in letters to his friends. Yet somehow the meetings continued, with Mencken seldom absent. When they conflicted with such holidays as Thanksgiving and New Year's Eve they were held anyhow. Only in the brute heat of Baltimore summers were meetings suspended. Even then there were often hot-weather gatherings such as picnics, outings, and parties, not the least of which was the annual foray of the Club, armed with band instruments, to Folger McKinsey's place on the Magothy River to celebrate his birthday each August 29.

Mencken's correspondence with his friend McDannald, an ex-member of the Club who had left Baltimore to work in New York for the *Encyclopedia Americana,* reflects both its hazardous state in these years and its continued existence, both its ups and its downs. Here is a scattering of examples. On October 17, 1938 Mencken wrote that the Club was flourishing. However, on April 28, 1939 he reported that a former pillar of the Club, Theodor Hemberger, had not come to a meeting for years, nor was he the only absentee. On May 6, 1940 Mencken reported that Israel Dorman, their cellist, was ill. In November he wrote about the sudden death of Raymond Pearl, adding that the Club had already been going downhill for a long while and that his death was probably a fatal blow to it. In October 1941 he recorded Broedel's decease. In November he wrote that the Club had managed to struggle on, partly because Hemberger had returned. But the festivities at Schellhase's were losing their flavor; the show that in the old days ·did not end till one in the morning now subsided an hour and a half earlier. On July 22, 1943 he noted the return to the fold of Ed Moffett and his bull fiddle, which proved to be worth a thousand men. In March of the next year he wrote that Moffett had risen to great heights and that Hamilton Owens had come in as guest artist to play his oboe. The next month he wrote that he had skipped one of the sessions at Schellhase's, for the first time in many years.

Mencken's letter to McDannald of October 19, 1944 offers several items of information, including the fact that Heinie Buchholz was causing so much trouble that the Club had missed two meetings and that the Club was returning to its ancient quarters for playing, the store on St. Paul Street which Al Hildebrandt had once owned. To the members it was a return to the warmth and comfort of the womb; to a more realistic observer, such as James Cain, the quarters were frightful with their cobwebs and clutter of hard chairs, music stands, piano, and makeshift music shelves. In April 1945 Mencken mourned the Club's dilapidated state. In February 1946 he announced biliously that the Club still functioned though some members were senile and others insane. Thereafter references disappear from Mencken's remaining letters to McDannald.

He missed the last two meetings of the next month, an ominous sign, because of ill health. Once back, he managed to stay pretty consistently. We know from other sources that the Club continued, sometimes with barely enough members to play a trio, at other times a dozen strong. Its mortal blow came in 1948 from an entirely understandable cause. Mencken, its leader of leaders, suffered a massive stroke. He partly recovered and hoped to become a regular attendant again, but he never did. There are some pictures of him at a meeting in September 1949. He simply sits in a chair, dull-eyed. On December 2, 1950 the Club voted to dissolve. For a short time a few of the members met anyway for beer and conversation. Yet with Mencken gone nothing seemed the same, and these meetings disappeared too.

However, the Club had made a place for itself in the lives of dozens of people. It had become a Baltimore landmark which visiting great men were invited to praise. Its pull had been powerful, not only for Mencken but also for the others. It offered balm to nearly all. Raymond Pearl's temples might pound with a migraine attack, we know, on Saturday morning, but Saturday night he played his mighty French horn notwithstanding. Mencken might have one of his hundred ails and yet when the appointed evening came he would plant himself at his piano. For over forty years the Club gave him the best of company.

The men Mencken relaxed with at the Club were, with one or two exceptions, very amicable associates. They included several of his closest friends. In addition, he had an astounding number of persons with whom he corresponded or passed an occasional hour.

In his contact with many of them he mixed business with pleasure. They were apt to be writers or newspapermen. From his own point of view as a writer, the most significant were his fellow authors. A handful he considered friends, though always with a reservation of one sort or another; the rest he counted as acquaintances. Joe Hergesheimer was a good friend even if he grew difficult and crotchety in the 1930s. Ernest Boyd was another until he took to drinking too much and arguing too heatedly. James Branch Cabell was still another though he had something of the musty flavor of the antiquarian to him. A list of Mencken's literary acquaintances could cover pages but they were less important to him singly than in bulk.

A few other authors had a meaningful part to play in his life; these, over the years, were both more than acquaintances and less than friends. Or if they were friends they were very prickly ones. Upton Sinclair, Sinclair Lewis, and Theodore Dreiser could be numbered in this small group. In the long run the most noteworthy to Mencken was Dreiser.

Though Mencken declared that during the time America took part in World War I and for several years thereafter he and Dreiser met seldom, it proved impossible for them to ignore one another. Each was a titanic figure; each regarded the other with a blend of respect and exasperation. Dreiser's exasperation had much less reason than Mencken's and Mencken was acutely aware of the fact. Nevertheless, he went on defending and, when he could, helping Dreiser. Inevitably he got small thanks.

Toward the end of 1925 their desultory correspondence and contacts were interrupted by an unpleasant incident which was purely Dreiser's fault. He was engaged in finishing *An American Tragedy* and felt, realist that he was, that he had to see the death row at Sing Sing. Because his antihero was to be executed at the end of the book, he had already visited Sing Sing to observe its atmosphere. But death row was closed to tourists, even distinguished ones like Dreiser, so he got in touch with Mencken. He hoped Mencken would be able to arrange for him to enter in the guise of a newspaper reporter. Mencken looked around among his friends in the newspaper business in New York and decided that James Cain was the most approachable. Cain was then an editorial writer on the New York *World*. He persuaded his city editor to secure permission — it had to be done by court order — to let Dreiser as a

reporter for the *World* not only see death row but interview a
prisoner waiting for execution. Then the interview was to be published in the *World*. What happened could have been predicted
by anybody who knew Dreiser well. He was let into Sing Sing, saw
death row, talked with the doomed prisoner, seized on the impressions he wanted, and promptly forgot that he had to do anything
as his part of the bargain. The *World* expected a five thousand word
article. Dreiser denied that he had agreed to write it and said that
if he did it would cost the *World* five hundred dollars. The city
editor of the *World* blamed not only Dreiser but Mencken and
told him so immediately. Mencken telegraphed Dreiser about the
complaint, adding that he found it personally embarrassing. Dreiser
wired back, "The *World* lies. Your telegram is an insult."

After considerable acrimony the *World* dispatched a reporter
to interview Dreiser about his visit to Sing Sing and printed the
interview. The affair then simmered down and in a letter of December 4 to Dreiser, Mencken remarked that he was glad it had
been settled.

Neither man had forgotten it, however. *An American Tragedy*
was published about the middle of December. When Dreiser sent
Mencken a signed copy it was of the deluxe edition but he inscribed
it, with a typically heavy attempt at jocularity, to his "oldest living
enemy." Though Mencken praised the account of the trial and
execution he had reservations about the first part of the mammoth
book. They displeased Dreiser, the more so because Mencken published them in his review in the *Mercury*. There he dryly advised
his readers to hire their pastor to plod through the first volume for
them but by no means to miss the second. Dreiser was antagonized
and retaliated by sneering publicly at Mencken as a critic, as well
as writing him privately, "Who reads you? Bums and loafers. No-
goods."

Meanwhile, something else had happened to add to Mencken's
sense of injury. It was occasioned by the fact that midway in the
World controversy his mother died. He had entertained Dreiser in
December while she was critically ill and he obviously expected
prompt condolences. But Dreiser failed to write the awaited note
till early in February. During the weeks before that he had been
concurrently traveling with his mistress and quarreling with her, and
he had a good deal on his mind. Notwithstanding, Mencken laid

the lapse to his coldness and bad manners. The over-all result was that he stopped corresponding with Dreiser till the middle 1930s.

In spite of the estrangement he did not abate his admiration for Dreiser's books. In 1930 Sinclair Lewis won the Nobel Prize, the first American writer to receive it. The night the news broke, Mencken went with Phil Goodman and Goodman's daughter Ruth to congratulate Lewis at his New York hotel. Lewis was full of euphoria and liquor. Goodman could not contain his pleasure at the award, but Mencken seemed rather quiet. After they left Lewis's room, they fell silent in the elevator. Then Mencken shook his head, "You know it isn't right. Dreiser should have had it — he's a greater man."

The correspondence was resumed with the inadvertent help of Burton Rascoe. In an introduction he prepared for *The Smart Set Anthology,* to be published late in 1934, he alleged, wrongly, that Mencken had broken with Dreiser because Dreiser refused to contribute to a fund to defend the *Mercury* after it was banned in Boston. There were other errors in the Introduction, which was sent out in pamphlet form as a promotional piece. They cast aspersions on Knopf's integrity as well as Mencken's, charging Knopf with profiting handsomely through the *Mercury's* increased circulation after "Hatrack" was printed.

Mencken and Knopf both received copies of the pamphlet. Mencken wrote Knopf that far from soliciting funds from Dreiser, he had not communicated with him since December 1925. Knopf sent a copy of the inaccuracies to Dreiser, who at once wrote to Rascoe. Dreiser also wrote at once to Mencken, saying that he thought Rascoe had lost his mind and that he was writing Rascoe's publishers about the errors. Thereupon Mencken, touched by Dreiser's prompt response, sent him a letter of thanks that ended the long break. In return Dreiser proposed that they meet again in New York, as genial if armed neutrals, and added that Mencken and his wife were always welcome at his home. In December they met in Manhattan and promptly settled down to arguing as if they had never been interrupted.

Their friendship, however, failed to regain its full strength. Dreiser still had the ability to strike what Mencken regarded as absurd attitudes. His philanderings continued to be notorious and his public actions often appeared as silly as his private ones. Mencken found his love for communism and Russia especially odd. Dreiser had traveled to Russia and discovered Utopia, at least in retrospect. In his letters to Mencken he hymned its virtues and eulogized Stalin. To Mencken it was incredible that a man could be so gulled, except that the man was Dreiser. Mencken bluntly told him, in a letter of April 1, 1943, that communism was a fraud and Stalin nothing but a politician — and worse than most politicians. Considering what Mencken said he thought of politicians this was a devastating insult. Moreover, Dreiser allowed himself to be used by the professional Communists in America just as he had allowed himself to be used years before by the Greenwich Village radicals; and Mencken grimaced as he observed it.

On the other hand some things held them together, so that they could still write and meet, at least at intervals, throughout the late 1930s and early 1940s. An important bond was that they both took a lenient view of Germany and a harsh one of England. Both were revolted by Hitler's treatment of the Jews and yet thought he had some excuse for it. Both men were ardent isolationists before the United States entered World War II. They agreed in their detestation of FDR and his curious, malicious policies. So they wrote chatty if sometimes contentious letters to one another. But the epic encounters were over; the events, reflected by the letters, in the lives of the two elderly men were minor ones. For example, in May 1936 Mencken promised Dreiser a Maryland madstone, designed to cure many of the diseases that plagued mankind. In June of the same year Dreiser asked Mencken to get some seats for him at the Democratic national convention. In October 1938 Mencken found in his crowded archives some copies of early pamphlets relating to Dreiser and offered them to him. Later in the same month he proposed to Dreiser that they meet, along with Edgar Lee Masters, at Luchow's the next time Dreiser came east to New York. And so it went.

On the whole, the correspondence and the reports from observers show that to the end each man maintained his respect for the other's achievements. In the same letter in which Mencken tells Dreiser that communism is a fraud and Stalin nothing but a politician, he amiably disclaims the credit Dreiser has given him for the long battle to publish Dreiser's books in the face of censorship. "You are far too kind," he assures Dreiser with a grateful bow.

On Dreiser's death in California late in December 1945, Mencken sent a statement about him to be read at the funeral service in Forest Lawn Cemetery. It was a balanced judgment rather than the eulogy desired and so failed to be read at the service. But it said precisely what Mencken intended and made as good an epitaph as the circumstances allowed. "While Dreiser lived," it stated, "all the literary snobs and popinjays of the country, including your present abject servant, devoted themselves to reminding him of his defects. He had, to be sure, a number of them. For one thing, he came into the world with an incurable antipathy to the *mot juste;* for another thing, he had an insatiable appetite for the obviously not true. But the fact remains that he was a great artist, and that no other American of his generation left so wide and handsome a mark upon the national letters. American writing, before and after his time, differed almost as much as biology before and after Darwin. He was a man of large originality, of profound feeling, and of unshakable courage. All of us who write are better off because he lived, worked and hoped."

Mencken's men friends were clearly more important to him than the women. Yet he always liked the ladies and, aside from when he was married to Sara, paid them a due share of attention. Throughout the 1920s he kept in touch with the women who interested him most, except when they had the bad grace to be firmly married, and after Sara's death in 1935 he made an effort to meet them again, chief among them Marion Bloom and Aileen Pringle.

With her new husband Marion Bloom had hoped to keep the memory of Mencken as far away as possible. But the marriage proved to be a disaster. By 1926 she was corresponding with him once more and by the next year he was sending her books, including *Notes on Democracy.* Inevitably during this period they discussed the problems of marriage. Mencken wrote on February 4, 1927, quoting himself, "If I ever marry, it will be on a sudden impulse, as a man shoots himself."

She went to Paris for a divorce in 1928. On her return she met Mencken again, and again they were simultaneously drawn together and pushed apart. In July they had a long dinner at one of his favorite restaurants in Baltimore, Marconi's; they argued about some things but agreed about others. In November he wrote — referring to their affection — that they had called for a coroner's inquest before the patient had expired; in fact the patient was walking around, "smoking a cigar and singing like a bird." Marion looked prettier to him than ever. Yet so did Sara Haardt, though he naturally neglected to tell Marion this.

The patient struggled before expiring. Marion and Mencken met off and on during the first part of 1929; and even in fall, after the stock market crash, she remembers walking with him and telling him to buy an apple from a jobless veteran they passed. Nevertheless, before the end of the year they were through and he concentrated all his attention on Sara; and there it stayed. Writing to Edgar Lee Masters near the end of 1934 he remarked that Marion was a strange creature and that he did not know what had become of her.

After Sara's death Mencken began corresponding again with the former Bee Wilson. She still has a letter of March 26, 1936, in which he tells her that he has been moving from Cathedral Street back to Hollins Street and adds that he hopes to see her soon. A month later he writes again and complains about the trials of transferring from one place to another; he says that every time he enters a room in crowded Hollins Street he falls over something. Besides corresponding they met once or twice after her husband died. But the days of the hoaxes were over, for both were soberer than before. Their last contact was by phone.

Aileen Pringle had been a bit hurt when Mencken asked for the return of his letters before he married Sara Haardt. But she got over it and several years after Sara's death she became good friends with Mencken again. As she remembers it, their friendship was resumed in 1939. She was living at the Lombardy Hotel in New York and he would come to see her there. They went out to a variety of places in the city, most often to his old favorite, Luchow's. The onset of World War II and Miss Pringle's British origins made it harder for them to be comfortable with one another, so the friendship lost some of its warmth. In 1944 she married James Cain and Mencken in a note of July 25 congratulated him. Mencken continued to keep in touch with her. In November of the same year, for instance, he could report to Mrs. Hamilton Owens, "Aileen still owns her house at 722 Adelaide Place, Santa Monica, Calif."

Mencken looked up Anita Loos also. From time to time, until

he had his stroke, she saw him in New York. Occasionally she stopped off in Baltimore with friends and then was apt to telephone him.

Such were some of Mencken's reconstituted friendships. He still liked these ladies; nevertheless, his relationships with them now had a summary air. He was losing other old friends through death and it was easy for him to think of himself as alone. Yet such was not the case. His vitality and verve, though diminished, continued to attract fresh friends, new acquaintances. His personal patience and kindliness wore a little thin but never really left him. The range and richness of his new relationships can be seen in his associations with a young society matron, a naval officer, and a nun. Those relationships proved to be by no means summary. And those particular ones reveal a Mencken who is finally softening, though by no means abandoning, one or two of his most cherished prejudices, especially against religion, and reviving one or two of his earliest interests, especially in literature.

The young society matron was Marcella duPont. She and her husband met the Menckens by chance on shipboard. It happened that in January of 1932 Mencken had decided that Sara and he deserved a Caribbean cruise. The weather was bitter in Baltimore, so they embarked on the sumptuous life as lived aboard the North German Lloyd *Columbus*. There they encountered Mr. and Mrs. Alfred duPont. Alfred, an architect, was one of the many members of the Du Pont clan; his wife was a sprightly Denver girl who enjoyed good talk and good writing. She had attractive enthusiasms and a fresh, impulsive way of speaking. The Menckens found Alfred personable enough but they were especially taken with Marcella. For her part, she found them both interesting but was particularly impressed with Mencken. From the start she was sure that he was a great man even if he bore his greatness casually and wittily. After the voyage ended, the Menckens took the initiative in seeing that the acquaintance continued. They invited the duPonts to Baltimore and also visited them in Wilmington. In mid-summer 1934 Marcella wrote Mencken to suggest that the two couples try a tropical cruise. "God knows, I wish we could," he answered. But it was out of the question since Sara and he had just returned from a Mediterranean jaunt on the same ornate ship where they had first encountered the duPonts.

During Sara's last year the two couples had little connection and yet after her death Mencken wrote to Marcella, "How often Sara spoke of you!" When Sara's next birthday came around he could not face staying in Baltimore and went to Wilmington instead to see Marcella. Alfred's role in the friendship inevitably became minor. Mencken sensed that he was a difficult husband and his sympathies lay with Marcella. Though her letters customarily include some description of what Alfred has been doing, Mencken's replies usually confine him to the final paragraph. "My best to the Mister" is all that he is apt to say.

From 1936 till Mencken's stroke in 1948, the correspondence remained constant, the friendship close. To Marcella, Mencken showed a side of himself that during those years he seldom showed to anyone else. Undeniably his best friends were men. The bluff, beery companions of the Saturday Night Club, who scratched when they itched, were near to his heart. But he still enjoyed the company of attractive, understanding women; and after Sara's death he found fewer of them than before his marriage. Now in the late 1930s, shoulders humped, hair thinning, he was no longer the jovial celebrity the girls admired. With Marcella, however, he felt like his old self. She was happy to receive his letters and happier to see him in person.

Their talk was, understandably, more sentient than their writing. Yet even the writing, and especially hers, reveals the establishment of an unusual rapport. The letters of late 1935 and early 1936 begin with "Dear Mr. Mencken" and "My dear Mrs. duPont" but soon the salutations are "Dear Henry" and "Dear Marcella." The complimentary closes move from formality to Mencken's "Yours" and her "Devotedly." Her letter of January 4, 1936 ends "To you more than anybody, a happy 1936," as her interest and concern go out to him. Later they exchange pictures, though he carefully inscribes his both to her and Alfred; but there is always the Mencken touch: his picture shows him in shirt sleeves. When she reports that she is ailing, he becomes distressed and promptly recommends his friend Dr. Edward Richardson, a leading gynecologist. Richardson sees her, decides that she must have a major operation, and after a due interval puts her in Union Memorial Hospital in Baltimore. While she lies there for three weeks, Mencken visits her daily, first hanging his beer-mug sign outside her door; and in the island atmosphere of the hospital there is talk between them as personal as they would ever have. It is a little like his seeing Sara at Maple Heights. Coming home at the end of January 1941, she writes gratefully to him. She closes her long letter with, "I miss your visits more than I can say."

After the operation her affection grows still more evident in the letters. They are sometimes headed "Henry dear" or "Henry dearest"; and they may end, "Please let me know when you would like me to come to see you again." While World War II goes on she is often separated from Alfred, who has joined the Navy. She visits Baltimore every now and then in order to lunch with Mencken at Schellhase's. The war comes to its conclusion. Alfred, who has been increasingly at odds with her, leaves her and Mencken rallies to her support. Their affection continues to be strong. After his stroke, however, he can no longer write and can seldom see visitors. Marcella writes sadly to his secretary on March 22, 1949, "I consider him my very best friend, and it is awfully hard to be so near and not see him." On this note the correspondence draws to its close.

There is no doubt that the two people were compatible. Mencken, gallant and paternal, set the tone; but the relationship was not simple, as we can tell from one letter in which she exclaims, "I wish I had Henry Mencken as a son, at least, to worry me into having no time for sordid thoughts on the war." Notwithstanding, he dominated. Though she retained her own personality, she could not help being directed into some of Mencken's ways. She grew to dislike Christmas and "Christmas Blah" as he did; she adopted some of his turns of phrase, for instance when she wrote about "destroying" a turkey when she meant eating it; she confessed that she had acquired some of his orderliness. He, in turn, was charmed by the eager attention she paid him. At times he played the teacher for her sake. She recalls that when they traveled on the train together it often seemed that he had read up on some subject so that he could illuminate it for her, bringing to it even more than his usual wide knowledge. Swiveling in his parlor-car chair he talked to her about such diverse topics as the geography of America, the private life of Mary Baker Eddy, and the hard lot of the typical farmer's wife. But he was much more to her than a teacher.

He showed a gentleness that she found very moving. As she came to know him, she discovered a man of extraordinary compassion. His private generosities ranged from sending checks to help support an old friend in New York, Madeleine Boyd, to spending a day at the State Department in Washington "to argue for the admission of a family of poor Jews." She learned something of the breadth of his sympathy. It took in a sick Negro; it took in her. When she told him that Alfred had left her, tears filled his eyes. He was, she remarked in an interview, "a man of ideal good will."

She came to believe that the good will was the working side of his religion. In all probability Mencken discussed religion with her as much as with anyone. He signed one of the photos he gave her "the old theologian." As a young man he had described himself as a "violent agnostic," thanks in good part to Thomas Huxley's influence. Now he could perhaps be described as a wistful one. He told Marcella that he had deeply wanted to believe when his mother died and when Sara died, but he had not been able to. He also told Marcella once that when he had shared a room, at convention times, with Frank Kent, Kent had always knelt to say his prayers before going to bed. Then Mencken had watched sardonically but later wished that as a child he had been taught to pray that way.

As time went on they had an increasing number of friends in common. He introduced her to Paul Patterson and several others among the statesmen of the *Sunpapers*, and to some of his New York associates. She introduced him to several of the Du Pont patriarchs and to a sprinkling of artists and musicians. Their closest mutual friends were Joe and Dorothy Hergesheimer, whom the Menckens had brought to Wilmington and the duPonts in 1934. Unfortunately, by the mid-1930s Hergesheimer had passed the zenith of his popularity and productivity. He knew he was a diminishing writer and the knowledge made him no easier to live with. His temper grew short as his stories were rejected. The record of his decline can be seen in the letters between Marcella and Mencken. On May 15, 1936 she reports that a friend saw Hergesheimer and said that he looked bad and seemed at loose ends. Later she writes that Hergesheimer never used to bother her but now she finds that she grows argumentative in his company. Still later she reports on his now frequent, almost paranoid quarrelsomeness at a dinner party. During World War II her letters show that he was often close to finding a good job in Washington but never actually found it. After the war, toward the end of the correspondence, he is barely able to support himself; and his friends meet him only by an effort of will.

Other mutual friends proved much more congenial, especially several of the authors among them: in particular Edgar Lee Masters, Mark Sullivan, and Huntington Cairns. There was good talk about writers and writing. And without doubt writing was a bond between Mencken and Marcella. Most of the young women he liked had a flair for it as well as a liking for literature. Marion Bloom wrote squibs for the *Smart Set;* Bee Wilson was a New York feature writer; Aileen Pringle, though she published little, wrote wittily; Anita Loos concocted one of the best sellers of the 1920s; and Sara of course was both a writer and a teacher of literature. Marcella fitted nicely into this group. She sent Mencken some of her sonnets in the summer of 1938. He exclaimed that they were lovely, adding, "You have a fine ear, which is the gauge of all verse, and in fact of all writing." She more than returned the compliment on reading his current prose. Beginning in 1936 his sprightly reminiscences were appearing piece by piece in the *New Yorker.* They could not have had a more enchanted audience than Marcella and she said so. She read them all as they came out and reread them with undiminished delight when they were incorporated in *Happy Days, Newspaper Days,* and *Heathen Days.*

In prose they had many of the same preferences. They both were much impressed by Hergesheimer's early fiction; they both had reservations about his later work. They liked the same novels, often, and the same books of nonfiction. Only when it came to poetry did they part. As a poet herself, Marcella had a devout admiration for the verses of Emily Dickinson and of a number of other poets old and new including W. H. Auden. Mencken was not always sympathetic. "I fear you greatly overestimate the value of the poetry written by such persons as Auden," he told her once, but he added tolerantly, "maybe that is only my prejudice."

But politics meant more to him than literature and so they discussed politics a good deal. Their views on domestic politics became precisely parallel; on foreign policy they agreed about some things but not others. Marcella was a Western conservative who had married into one of the most conservative clans in the United States. In the depth of the Depression she and her husband could move from a home in the country-club district outside Wilmington to a showplace nearby called Calmar. Her response to the Depression was Mencken's. When he wrote his witty editorials against the New Deal she begged copies for her friends: "Would it be too much trouble, Henry, for you to send me two or three extra copies of this March 4th editorial page of yours?" She was proud to introduce him to some of the senior Du Ponts, in particular, Iréné and Lammot. They all spoke the same language now. Now Mencken could say firmly, as he had not found himself able to before, "Mr. duPont is unquestionably quite right." If he felt constrained in this arch-conservative company he scarcely showed it. He chewed his Uncle Willies while they puffed their Belinda Coronas.

But though he let his hopes influence his political views, he never revealed the absolute disregard of reality that characterized the Du Ponts. In a letter to Marcella of May 5, 1938 he offered his typical blended view. "My belief, as you know, is that Roosevelt is still unbeatable, but he may very easily begin to crack within the next year." What also saved him from bizarre excesses was his sense of humor. He reported gravely to Marcella on the celestial phenomena that accompanied the Republican convention of July 1940; they included the appearance of an angel in the gallery. He continued to see American politics as something of a circus, though not as much as before, and persuaded Marcella to see it that way too.

In foreign affairs it was a little different, if we can judge from the letters. He achieved an attitude toward Hitler that she could not assume. When he visited Germany in the summer of 1938, he wrote her that "The Hitler New Deal seems to be working better than Franklin's." Of course he was being jocular, just as he was in the succeeding sentences: "There is actually a shortage of labor. I made a little tour by car through the backwoods of Saxony, and found the farmers all working from 5 A.M. to 10 P.M. Such hours are good for a farmer. They keep him from thinking about politics and theology." Still, his stand in foreign affairs was extreme. He considered it amusingly extreme, but Marcella could not be as amused as he was. So too when he remarked some months before the attack on Pearl Harbor, "The radio commentators report that the fiend Hitler is on his last legs. Yet there are people who say that prayer has no bite." After Pearl Harbor was bombed, she wrote him soberly that the days before the attack seemed to her now "to have been spent in a distant era."

If he was at his least impressive in commenting on the events in Germany, he was at his shrewdest — despite his bias — in talking about politics in America. For instance: his tolerant and prophetic remark to Marcella on Senator Hugo Black in the face of the uproar caused by his nomination to the Supreme Court, "My guess is that Hugo will make a pretty good judge. Practical politicians often do." All in all Marcella found much in Mencken to assent to and admire, relatively little to dissent from.

Leland Lovette, tall, brown-haired, open in manner, was a lieutenant commander in communications at the Naval Academy when he first met Mencken. He had started reading the *Smart Set* in 1914 while a midshipman at Annapolis. He relished the sophistication and dash that Mencken and Nathan brought to the magazine; but the *Smart Set* was far outside the Navy curriculum and many a time he had to read it stealthily late at night. Once the *Mercury* was established he read that too. He drew various kinds of duty following his graduation from the Academy but, whatever he did, he tried to keep up with Mencken's writing. He began to buy Mencken's books, starting with *In Defense of Women*. By the time he was assigned in the early 1930s to the Naval Postgraduate School at Annapolis, he owned a substantial Mencken library.

One day in the late summer of 1933 he was talking with one of his graduate students about Mencken and mentioned how much he would like to meet him. The student, who turned out to be the son-in-law of Van-Lear Black, then board chairman of the *Sunpapers,* remarked that it could easily be arranged. "I'd give anything to meet the man," was Lovette's hearty assurance. The next week found him invited to a party given by Harry Black, brother of Van-Lear, and there was Mencken. The two men, Lovette remembers, hit it off at once. Lovette was captivated by Mencken, and Mencken, for his part, promptly invited him to Cathedral Street.

What Lovette saw in Mencken at the party was the embodiment of the wit, ease, and vigor of his writing. Here was a man of renown who still liked his beer and pretzels. What Mencken saw in Lovette was a paradox. Here was a man who was service-educated but loved Shakespeare, appreciated a good deal of literature, read Aristotle every now and then, and pondered the enduring questions of life. Mencken told Lovette he was one of the few service people he had met who seemed interested in more than war games and battle plans. "I will always think well of you," Mencken once remarked after the friendship had been established, "because your great desire, like mine, has been to get at the heart of things and not skim the surface."

But in the long run Lovette's most powerful appeal was to a side of Mencken often forgotten. He spoke to the young Mencken, the youthful romanticist, the city boy who felt in the sea and far-away places something that stirred him. This was the Mencken who had begun his writing by copying Kipling's poetry and by concocting adventure stories for the pulps. This was the Mencken who early discovered the enthralling tales of Joseph Conrad. His first sea voyage came before he was twenty, on a tramp steamer to Jamaica. He never forgot how it felt to breathe the salt air, to make a landfall at dawn in the West Indies, to smell the heady smell of the tropics. He told Lovette that his first landfall was one of the most exhilarating moments of his life. He added that nothing had ever given him more pleasure than his cruises to the West Indies. He liked the sea and the tropics both and liked to read about them. And he liked to hear yarning about exotic adventures. The result of all this was that he found Lovette, as he wrote to Raymond Pearl shortly after meeting him, "a very interesting fellow," who was "full of odd information and strange tales."

He was indeed. His experiences were remarkably rich and colorful, so much so in fact that Mencken, who ordinarily monopolized a conversation, often asked him to speak about them. At different times Lovette related how he had captained a gunboat in Chinese waters in the 1920s, had fought with the Chinese river pirates, had met some of the war lords; how — going back earlier, to the period of World War I — he had steamed off the coast of South America searching for the *See Adler,* Count Von Luckner's notorious raider; how he had been on submarine chasers in the Bay of Biscay; and how he had been lucky enough to be in London the night the World War I armistice was signed and the city went wild with joy and relief.

It was not surprising that he often saw himself invited to the Bierabende at Cathedral Street. They started, he discovered, rather promptly and ended promptly too. He recalls that customarily they began at seven thirty and concluded at ten. Two or three other guests were apt to be present also. Sara would come in only to greet them. Mencken and his friends would settle back for beer and conversation. "Lovette, what do you think of MacArthur?" he might begin, as he did one night the year after the general led his troops against the so-called Bonus Army of jobless veterans encamped in Washington during the summer of 1932. The other guests would join in. There might be someone from the *Sun*, Hamilton Owens or Paul Patterson perhaps; occasionally there might be a writer or so. Lovette especially recalls two of the writers because of their habit of ruffling the waters. They were Joe Hergesheimer and Sinclair Lewis. But even they could be good company as well as bad, and some of the evenings were thoroughly rewarding.

As the friendship consolidated itself Lovette felt freer to ask questions about two things that interested him as well as Mencken, literature and theology. Their literary tastes were similar. By the time they met, both had read and reread all of Conrad. Both were drawn by his preoccupation with the sea, by his graphic descriptions of the tropics and the jungle, and by his powerful characterizations. Both, as storytellers themselves, relished the work of a master storyteller. Lovette's favorite was *Lord Jim* but Mencken was most enthusiastic about "Youth." "The greatest short piece ever written," he assured Lovette. He added that there was all of life in it and that he returned to it every year.

Lovette liked dramatic literature and at times questioned Mencken about his own preferences or opinions. What did he think of Shakespeare? Mencken confessed that he could not always respond to Shakespeare's writing but that he was nevertheless a superb playwright. He was at his cleverest in playing to the crowd through his artful use of mob scenes; those in *Julius Caesar*, for example, must have delighted the Elizabethan audiences. His finest play was probably *Hamlet*, as Nathan had often asserted. Yet Shakespeare did not always move him; as Mencken said to Lovette once, "We'll just have to leave him on his pinnacle." Bernard Shaw appealed more to his taste. In fact *Antony and Cleopatra* was a livelier play when done by Shaw than when done by Shakespeare. On the other hand, Shaw was not perfect either. He merited the title of the

"Ulster Polonius" which Mencken had tagged him with years ago. Lovette nodded.

Often the two men discussed American literature. Lovette's tastes were generally Mencken's, and Mencken used to talk to him about Dreiser and Sinclair Lewis, about Carl Sandburg and Edgar Lee Masters, and most of all about Mark Twain and *Huckleberry Finn*. One time he got up on his feet in front of Lovette, banged the table with his beer stein, and asserted, "That Mark Twain was American from the roots. He wrote this great book. It is American life and has youth throughout it." Then he summed up: "Mark had it. One of our greatest, whatever the New England school of thought says."

Lovette found Mencken equally interested in theology. He had published *Treatise on the Gods* in 1930 and had forgotten little that he had taught himself about the subject. He declared to Lovette, "I put in all the philosophy I ever knew in life in that. I put just what I thought." At the end, however, he admitted being left with some questions that refused to be resolved. He did not know whether Jesus was human or divine. He did not know whether there was a cosmic purpose to life. He did not know other important things. He explained to Lovette, as he would to Marcella duPont and later to the nun Sister Miriam, that he was an agnostic, taking the only position that he thought was open to a reasonable man. He and Lovette talked often, at their beer seances, about life and death even if they settled little.

Though literature and theology were the special subjects that the two men discussed, Mencken could no more keep from commenting on current events — at least as seen in the columns of the *Sunpapers* — than he could from drinking beer. He realized that his guest was a military man, so he made an effort to be tactful about sensitive topics. The fact that he failed did not matter much to Lovette. Mencken delivered his opinions with a jovial, crashing finality that robbed them of any personal implication. He denounced the policies, foreign and domestic, of the New Deal. He told Lovette that he detested Hitler but felt sorry for the German people and when the European conflict started was sure we should not intervene. In particular, we should not let England's sly diplomats lure us in. After Pearl Harbor he agreed that the Japanese had to be crushed but he believed, as did Lovette, that it would take several years.

Their friendship had no trouble in surviving the trials of the late 1930s and early 1940s. After the war they dined at intervals with one another. Most often Lovette came to Hollins Street, with its male cheer and meticulous service. The talk was nearly, if not quite, as spirited as before.

Lastly, there was the nun, middle-aged, timid, yet determined. Sister Miriam Gallagher, R.S.M. was thinking of doing a master's thesis, at Catholic University in Washington, on Mencken's old friend the esthete James Huneker and so she wrote Mencken asking if he had any Huneker letters. She also asked if he would see her sometime to discuss Huneker. She said she hoped to do a mainly biographical treatment and in the course of it to stress Huneker's Catholic connections. Mencken could no more consider Huneker a Catholic than he could Alfred Knopf; and he told Sister Miriam so, although not quite in those terms. Unpersuaded, she replied meekly that she understood Huneker to have returned to the Catholic faith in his declining years. Consequently she felt that a religious emphasis would not be out of place.

The time was summer 1937. Mencken was busy as always, dividing his days between his office at home, where he sat writing in his B.V.D.'s, and his office at the *Sunpapers*. The *Sunpapers* proved especially demanding, though it should be noted that he seldom did any news work that he did not wish to do. During the middle part of 1937 he produced two substantial series of articles for the *Sun*, concurrently continuing with his Monday Articles for the *Evening Sun*. In addition, he had just finished seeing a history, *The Sunpapers of Baltimore, 1837–1937*, through the press, to which he himself had contributed one hundred and sixty pages. In spite of all this he was kindness itself to Sister Miriam.

In his letter of July 19 he agreed readily to Sister Miriam's plea for an interview. In fact he invited her to lunch, perhaps to soften the blow of telling her that he had only a few Huneker letters and those were already in print. She responded that her order's regulations forbade her lunching with him though not seeing him. Mencken assured her that if the regulations could be changed he would collect a battery of four or five chaperons, all Catholic, female, and elderly, and throw in his brother August for good measure. He promised that he would give her any information on Huneker he had. He meant it, furthermore, for the request struck a chord. He had always been fond of the old esthete and had respected his critical judgments. In 1929 he had edited a five-hundred-page selection of Huneker's essays for the publishing house of Scribner. He had found Huneker's personal flamboyance — the flourished stick, the cape, and all — attractive rather than repellent. Though he could not see Huneker as a weary sinner collapsing on the bosom of Rome, he was nonetheless pleased that somebody was going to do a study of him.

The result was that Mencken not only met with Sister Miriam but provided all the help he could. His most important suggestion was that she get in touch with Huneker's widow, who would be the main source of biographical information. When Mrs. Huneker ignored Sister Miriam's request, a note from Mencken got her an answer and an interview. Her correspondence with Mrs. Huneker is lost, but it does not take much reading between the lines of the letters exchanged by Mencken and Sister Miriam to see Mrs. Huneker's reaction. Plainly, she was put off by the notion that her late husband could be the subject of a Catholic thesis on his ultimate Catholicity. To her he had always been a sophisticated pagan and the more intriguing because of it. Furthermore, she well knew that his love for the voluptuous and worldly was what had made *Painted Veils* his most widely heralded book. Mencken was skeptical about Sister Miriam's thesis; Mrs. Huneker was surely hostile.

Though he had not seen Mrs. Huneker for some years, he received a note from her immediately after she and Sister Miriam met in New York. He reported this to Sister Miriam in a letter of November 29 and added, out of his liking for her, that he certainly hoped that she and Mrs. Huneker had come to terms. He said he did not know what materials Mrs. Huneker had on her late husband but guessed they must be considerable.

The awkward first meeting with Mrs. Huneker proved, however, to be a bad omen. The correspondence suggests that Sister Miriam never overcame the widow's reluctance. Sister Miriam went on to attempt various approaches to her topic but its innate difficulties slowly submerged her. Though for a time Mencken tried to hearten her, she lost interest in the Huneker thesis and ultimately gave it up.

As it turned out she abandoned not only her thesis topic but her whole graduate program. She suffered a heavy blow when she failed her chief oral examination. She immediately wrote the dismal story to Mencken. On her evidence he agreed that she had been poorly treated by Catholic University. He assured her in a letter of September 29, 1938 that he thought that the examination questions she had been asked were idiotic. Why should anyone care, he demanded rhetorically, whether Puttenham's *Arte of Poesie* had six parts or six hundred? He promised to cut off an ear from one professor who had been particularly troublesome to her. "My opinion of his whole gang," he said, "is very low." They all served to illustrate the imbecility of the learned.

Though she forsook graduate study she by no means forsook Mencken. Her letters kept on coming; he continued to reply with warmth and every appearance of interest. She apologized repeatedly for bothering him and often hoped that something she had said had not offended him. There were times, once he had denied being offended, when he was desperate for material; in one note he talks about the birds and cats in his backyard. But he answered, and the letters were eagerly read by her and shared with some of the other sisters in her order.

Sister Miriam had ambitions to be a poet and even before her disastrous examination she sent Mencken some verses for the *Mercury*. Calling them charming he passed them on to the new editor of the magazine. As time went on he saw more of her poetry and liked it. Though religious verse was far from his favorite he was attracted, it would seem, by the regularity of her metrics and the patent sincerity of the emotions she expressed. Occasionally he found it a little hard to know how to react. For example, about one lyric she sent him he could only remark bravely, "It seems somewhat vague to me, but nevertheless I can grasp its beauty." With this encouragement she brought together a volume of her verse, *Woven of the Sky,* and published it. The book was well enough received to require a second printing. Again with his encouragement, she kept up a general interest in literature and ended by compiling an anthology of American literature which also appeared in print. He even advised her on permissions.

She sent him little Christmas presents including a necktie hanger in 1940, invited him to lecture at the college where she taught, and asked if he would meet her cousin. He accepted the

Christmas presents, contrary to his custom; fended off the attempts to get him to lecture; and gallantly met the cousin and bought her a lunch.

But he went even further in his amiability toward Sister Miriam when he allowed her to try — if only try — to convert him and refashion his religious views. Though she herself had some notion of the magnitude of the task, it did not deter her. Her meek tenacity was combined with such palpable goodness that Mencken could not be anything but patient. Moreover, she represented one of the few denominations he could tolerate. She attacked him hardest when he was most vulnerable, that is, when he was lying on a Johns Hopkins Hospital bed. She sent him an engaging note, some "holy cards" apparently, and a crucifix. He thanked her and added, turning the other cheek, that though he could not offer to pray for her he could at least offer to hope.

In essaying to alter his views she corresponded with him especially about "the truth." To her it was revealed with certainty through her religion; to him nothing was revealed and nothing was certain. He explained his skepticism in a letter of April 26, 1938, written to her while he was temporarily editing the *Evening Sun,* "I see no reason why I should assume that I can determine the truth. It may be, for all I know, completely concealed from mortal man. I have caught some glimpses of it from time to time, but its whole outlines still elude me. It may be that it is of such a nature that the human mind cannot really comprehend it. I am, therefore, disposed to cling to my polite skepticism. I am willing to be convinced, but I refuse to grant that I am under any moral obligation to do so." Clearly neither writer convinced the other. Notwithstanding, they remained if not good friends at least good acquaintances.

Much of the record of these last three friendships — with Mrs. duPont, Admiral Lovette, and Sister Miriam — is a matter of trivia. But it is often revealing trivia. It shows us an aging yet still notable man. True, the Mencken of the late 1930s and thereafter is no longer the center of national attention nor the horrific figure who frightened yet fascinated American conservatism. He is no longer riding, as he once had been, "at a gallop, mud-spattered, high in oath." However, his career is not at an end; some of his finest prose remains to be written.

17. The Last Hurrah

THERE IS NO QUESTION that Sara's death left an aching void in Mencken's existence. He did his best to fill it, however, not only with his friendships but also — and indeed above all — with his work.

His vigorous, salty attacks on the New Deal had already made him far more than a commentator on it. He had become the spokesman of conservatism. Now as the 1930s went along, his typewriter developed into the best weapon the conservative cause could command; and he used it tellingly. The national conventions of 1936 gave him an ideal chance, yet there were always other occasions too. At the end of the decade he would boast that never in his career had he praised a President in print, but his attacks on Franklin Roosevelt were especially enthusiastic.

However, at the same time that he was punishing the politicians with much of the energy of old, he was turning to a very different kind of writing. It also helped to fill the void; it also distracted him from the memory of his life with Sara. It was a retreat to the distant past, to a boyhood in Baltimore so untroubled that it almost seemed too good to be true. This other kind of writing had actually begun a year before Sara's death, partly through the instigation of the *New Yorker*. And the beginning had been made with travel sketches and linguistic essays rather than with autobiographical pieces.

Under the strenuous leadership of Harold Ross the *New Yorker* was finding fresh opportunities in the same Depression that was mauling the *Mercury*. While the *Mercury's* circulation dropped from 62,000 in 1930 to 42,000 in 1932, the *New Yorker's* climbed from about 99,000 in 1930 to 114,000 in 1932. When Mencken announced that he was quitting as editor of the *Mercury*, the *New Yorker* took note. In January 1934 Katharine White of the *New Yorker* staff wrote him that her magazine was inaugurating a department called "Onward and Upward with the Arts." She wondered if Mr. Mencken in his new leisure could care to compose some pieces for it, perhaps on the American language? He answered at once with polite interest and wrote again a week later saying that he could think of several subjects that appealed to him. These were not linguistic alone. He suggested two that obviously derived from the *Treatise on Right and Wrong* which he would publish later in the year. He observed that the schemes of Roosevelt's Brain Trust involved some nice questions in ethics which might be discussed and there was also "something to be said about recent efforts to redefine adultery." But all this would have to keep for a while, since he was about to embark on a Mediterranean cruise with his wife.

Nevertheless, he paid the *New Yorker* a visit before he sailed and ended by agreeing to send some travel notes as well as other pieces to the magazine. By the middle of March he had dispatched his first one, on Cairo, from the steamer *Columbus*. Mrs. White announced that she was delighted with it and with his suggestion of a cover title, "Foreign Parts," for it and its successors. That spring and summer the *New Yorker* printed nine of the pieces, "Athens," "Istanbul," and "Jerusalem" among them, in addition to "Cairo." They were all marked with the Mencken wit but they also showed an unexpected mildness. Sara and the Mediterranean sunshine held off his thoughts of Roosevelt, the New Deal, and the foundering *Mercury*. The exotic scenes he saw stimulated him; the writing went smoothly. The *New Yorker*, seeing the possibility of adding a major author to its regular contributors, was extremely cordial. Mrs. White wrote that she was growing more and more enthusiastic about the series. However, he had a book to finish off first, the last of his treatises, those tomes he took so seriously but which add so little to his permanent fame.

Once Mencken and Sara returned to Baltimore he concentrated on seeing the *Treatise on Right and Wrong* through to publication. As he observed in his Preface, the book grew out of *Treatise on*

the Gods. Among the preliminary remarks he makes, the most characteristic are: that he hates metaphysics and so will avoid finespun
abstractions; that he will avoid defining his terms because everyone
will have a general notion anyway of what he means; and that he
will avoid preaching, which has been the curse of much writing
about ethics.

He contends in the body of the book that moral ideas are much
the same throughout the world. It is widely agreed that some things
are wrong. For us they are defined by the Judaic-Christian tradition.
They are murder, theft, trespass, adultery, and false witness — all
in their basic forms. For the rest of the globe, and in other traditions, they are as a rule also wrong. For example, no tradition sanc-
tions murder.

However, although the wrongs are agreed upon, the authority
for considering them wrong and for prescribing what is right varies
from tribe to tribe, from nation to nation. The main categories of
authority are: the appeal to reason; religious mandate; and instinct.
The category with the least sanction is to Mencken the religious,
and especially the Christian, mandate. He notes in point that it
found itself quite comfortable with the idea of chattel slavery.

In analyzing the course of Christian authority Mencken shows
that he has done his homework and gone through the most important
of the Church Fathers as well as through some of their critics. As
usual he has read thoroughly. He enjoys tracing the historical shifts
and struggles of the Church over the problem of evil and the question of man's free will. At the end he remarks that these matters
have not been settled yet but suggests that at some time in the
future, thanks to the advance of science, they may be.

Mencken describes the spread of Jewish theology over the Western world, laying it to its clarity, simplicity, and good sense. Its
Yahweh possessed an "ingratiating charm and plausibility" for many.
On the other hand, for someone like Mencken this same Yahweh
has some crimes to His account and Mencken cites them, with
chapter and verse from the Old Testament. For him personally there
is a much more plausible and ingratiating deity, Aristotle. He finds
Aristotle's *Nicomachean Ethics* especially admirable and he is much
taken by Aristotle's inductive approach to right and wrong.

Coming down to the present Mencken accuses all varieties of

Christianity of turning their backs on the main modern contribution to ethical theory: the "moral obligation to be intelligent."

Though ethics today seems to be in a state of flux, the changes are less striking than they appear. In particular, while there is plainly more sexual license than there used to be, the increase is not devastating. Current moralists "over-estimate the horse-power of the sexual impulse." Mencken's tone throughout the treatise is sensible, informal. There are many gleams of wit. As we might expect, he is at his best in dealing with wrong rather than right. The critics thought so too.

With the *Treatise on Right and Wrong* out of the way, he returned to his work for the *New Yorker*. The two ideas stemming from the book, on the New Deal and ethics and on the attempts to redefine adultery, proved barren. He had alleged in the course of the *Treatise* that FDR's Brain Trust was trying to depict thrift as antisocial and the man who objected to taxation as a scoundrel, but he himself saw that this was no topic for the *New Yorker*. Nor were the new efforts to define adultery; all they did was to try to narrow the definition so that members of the elite could go to bed with one another without censure.

Instead he took up the suggestion Mrs. White had made about writing some pieces on the American language. The result was that he published half a dozen linguistic notes, from May 1935 to March 1936, all written with a light touch that let *New Yorker* readers enjoy his scholarship at the same time that they learned something from it. The final one is as good an instance as any: "The Dizzy Rise (and Ensuing Bust) of Simplified Spelling." Early in the series Sara died but as soon as he felt able Mencken went ahead. In none of the pieces is there a sign of the tragedy he suffered.

When he finished this second series he went on to his most entertaining and extensive writing for the magazine, which would later be preserved in the *Days* books.

The literary origins of these books, and their partial and prior versions in the *New Yorker*, have attracted scant attention till recently. The assumption has been that because they have an air of ease they represent mere reminiscence. The truth is otherwise: they represent the culmination of Mencken's talents. To create the sketches that ended in the *Days* books he combined his superb aptitudes

as a story teller, as a social historian, and as a comedian. The result
was classic but the preparation was lifelong. The history of the *Days*,
in their composition as well as their subject matter, brings us back
to Mencken's boyhood and youth.

We can recall that he started to write fiction at fifteen with, he
reports, "a brief and dreadful piece entitled 'Idyl,' done in one evening," that he turned for a few years to poetry, and that after 1898
he reverted increasingly to prose. His short stories were still apprentice jobs but they were done with growing effectiveness and at least
a semiprofessional gloss. By the spring of 1900 he had three accepted,
the first being "The Cook's Victory," which came out in the August
1900 issue of *Short Stories*. It concerns the captain of an oyster
boat who objects to the burnt buckwheat cakes his cook serves, and
the way the wily cook wins out. The style is vigorous if overblown.
The narrative has pace although the captain and the cook speak in
the thick dialect fashionable in the fiction of the day.

Even young Mencken's abortive efforts reveal talent. In evidence:
"The Outcast," never published and in fact never even finished but
with a powerful, grisly theme handled with compassion. It is an
account of a man who contracts leprosy and of people's reaction to
him. It is not maudlin; it is emotionally compelling. The style is
straightforward, matter-of-fact. The story opens: "For a long while
the doctors lied to Liscum. This was after they really knew what
was the matter with him. For a much longer while they didn't
know, and there was no need to lie." In succeeding stories the effects
were often original and, for all their crudity, they kept the reader
interested. "The Bend in the Tube," for instance, published in *Red
Book* for December 1904, is a brusque tale of the biter bitten. A
newspaperman tries to kill a colleague by dropping a small bomb
down the speaking tube when the colleague is talking into it. What
the man forgets is that the tube has a bend not far below his own
desk and so he himself is blown up.

By the next year, however, Mencken began to be bored with
these tales and to turn to nonfiction, in the form of literary, dramatic,
and social criticism. By the middle of 1909 he could write to Dreiser,
then a magazine editor asking for contributions, "Let me know
what sort of stuff you want, and I'll make a try at it. Short stories
are a bit beyond me: I have retired from that department." Yet he
did not stop completely. Upon joining Nathan on the masthead of

the *Smart Set,* he found that his job was not only to help edit the magazine but also to assist in filling its gaping pages. The very first number he co-edited contained his short story "The Barbarous Bradley," a triangle affair ending with a fist fight. Thereafter he contributed a number of tales, under the pseudonyms of Owen Hatteras and William Drayham. The most substantial was "The Charmed Circle," billed as "A 20,000 Word Story of Smart Society," in the August 1917 issue. These stories plainly ranked higher than his efforts for the pulp magazines; they had an air of professional sophistication. And yet like their predecessors they were as a rule mechanically plotted, set in stagy locales, and filled with flat characters. To such fiction, once the 1920s began, he would never return.

But at the same time that his interest in contrived stories was ending, his delight in telling embellished tales from his own experience was growing. His friends recalled that his love deepened for the lively anecdote. From the recollections of his childhood and youth, characters and incidents emerged. They became a part of his repertory, the tales his dinner companions chuckled at. Sometimes they got into his correspondence, though that happened more rarely because the letters he liked to write were usually too short for yarn-spinning. Yet the central incident in one of his most widely appreciated sketches, "The Girl from Red Lion, P.A.," appeared in a letter to Edgar Lee Masters of December 1934, where it was synopsized and offered as fact. It appeared thereafter at much greater length in the *New Yorker* in February 1941 and in *Newspaper Days* later in the same year.

The stories that find their final form in the *Days* books are ones of character and milieu. The supporting cast, as it surrounds the youthful Mencken, looks extraordinarily colorful. Its members move through the middle-class Baltimore of the horse and buggy era with style, whether they themselves are middle-class or are the servitors attached to that class. Even when they emerge only briefly, they are apt to be fully realized. This is due in part to the fact that many of them starred in those dinner-table stories that Mencken had been telling for years.

It is also due in part to the effect of the fullest, most flavorsome of all Mencken's correspondences, the correspondence with Phil Goodman. Copies of Mencken's letters to Goodman fill three volumes on the shelves of the Enoch Pratt Library, along with a fourth and smaller volume of extracts from letters of both men. There is more than enough to illustrate their favorite game. It was played on the borderline between fact and fancy. In their letters Mencken and Goodman would go back to their early days, in Baltimore and Philadelphia respectively, and recreate some of the characters they had known and embellish some of the incidents they had figured in.

As the men filled in the outlines of their boyhood world, their zest became all the stronger. They would challenge one another. For instance, after Goodman describes "Harmonie Park," where he has Carl Woehr's Bavarian String Orchestra playing nightly, he briskly confronts Mencken. "Now for some exercises in Mnemonics. What was Woehr's opening selection every Saturday night? And what was his invariable finale? And what was his favorite encore? I burn to give you the answers right here, but I want to see if you really know." Mencken knew, and gave as good as he got. The "Extracts" volume in particular concentrates on the characters that show up often in the correspondence over the years and is clearly one more step toward Mencken's *Days* books and Goodman's autobiographical novel *Franklin Street.*

Midway, the game received a pleasant fillip. Sara Haardt, not yet married to Mencken, liked to haunt the antique shops of Baltimore and started to pick up old portrait photographs to give him. These spurred his fancy and soon he was sending them to Goodman with a character sketch typed beneath. There was, for instance, the anonymous lady he christened "Mrs. Tillie Himmelheber."

According to Mencken she "gave her whole life to good works. Whenever the Damenverein of the Zions Gemeinde gave an oyster supper she got up at 4 A.M. and put in 16 hours making Kartoffelsalat. She had nine separate formulae, all perfect. The best, I think, had chopped bacon in it, with a touch of water cress. She was also adept at Bohnensalat. She never cooked meats, having no gift for it." There was another photograph showing a heavily dressed lady with Jewish features. "No," says Mencken's caption, "you are wrong again. Minnchen Pohlmann was actually a Shicksa, and there are family records to prove it, going back to 1830. She used to say that it was her pince-nez that gave her her levantine aspect. She was, all things considered, the swellest dresser ever seen at the balls of the Darmstaedtter Liedertafel. Moreover, she was literary, and wrote pleasant dithyrambs for birthday parties. She married twice — first, Hugo Steinbach, and, second, Maximilian Encke. Childless, she hoarded and pyramided their estates, and when she died herself she was worth four whole rows of houses." Then there was the photograph of a doe-eyed Negro girl. It was inscribed in Mencken's hand, "Phil du Engel, Ich liebe Dich!" and was signed "Bertha."

The Baltimore of Mencken's boyhood grew in the correspondence with Goodman to look like a landscape by Brueghel, crowded with small but distinct and often comic figures. The correspondence, which had started in 1918, lasted until the early 1930s and then lapsed. It furnished a firm bridge to the *Days* books. Mencken himself, after the friendship had cooled, minimized the importance of the correspondence, conceding that the first sketches for *Happy Days* had come out of it but adding that he had carried over no actual material. Nevertheless, we cannot escape feeling that without Goodman as foil Mencken would not have developed the *Days* sketches as delightfully as he did.

At any rate, out of an abundance of speaking and writing Mencken created the world he pictured with such relish in the *Days* trilogy; and the *New Yorker* crystalized his experiences. For by late 1935, after contributing his pieces on his foreign travels and on the American language, he confessed to Katharine White, "I find myself with a great itch to do a short story, so you may have the dreadful job of reading one before long." She smiled invitingly and early in 1936 Mencken mailed in his first. She was delighted with what she called "the Negro philosopher story" and promptly told him so. She added that it had so much charm that she wondered if he might not have other stories.

It was like pressing a button. Mencken responded the next day, assuring Mrs. White that there were many more where this one came from. Among them he cited the tale of the elderly Negress, Aunt Sophia, who would never return to her native village from the city because there were no parades in the country. He also mentioned that he was thinking of a short piece on his imaginary uncle, who had been created so convincingly by his father that "to this day gaffers meet me on the street and ask how he is doing." Seeing Mencken's reply Ross himself was moved to set down a penciled notation on it, "This is really good news."

So it proved, for everyone concerned, though not as immediately as the *New Yorker* wished. Old Wesley, the Negro philosopher, appeared in type in the issue for April 11, 1936. But then in spite of Mencken's genuine interest a substantial pause followed. The main reason was politics. The national conventions and the presidential campaign exercised their unfailing lures. The tumult of the conventions — this year there were four of them, a bumper crop — and the soot-specked pleasure of riding the campaign train of the Republican candidate, Alf Landon, crowded out thoughts of the past. For Mencken the mind-set of current politics and the mind-set of reminiscence simply did not mix. Aunt Sophie (formerly Sophia) had to wait till the *New Yorker*'s issue of February 20, 1937.

After that Mencken became involved for over a year in a variety of other activities. He acted as general editor as well as contributor to the official history of the *Sunpapers;* he oversaw the publication of his ancestor's *The Charlatanry of the Learned* along with his own extensive introduction to it; he worked away at other books. To his multifarious chores at the *Sunpapers* he added one more in the spring of 1938, we remember, when for three hectic months he performed as the editor of the *Evening Sun.* He recuperated with the help of a stint in the Hopkins Hospital followed by a six-week trip to Europe. In Europe he relaxed and thoughts of old Baltimore began to rise gently to the surface again. Yet it still took time for him to return to the kind of writing the *New Yorker* yearned for.

Meanwhile Ross and his staff were understandably solicitous. Mrs. White hinted politely to Mencken that they had been watching and waiting. She wondered what hope there was of some stories from him soon. Or another editor might murmur that he didn't want to pester him, but ——. Finally their reward arrived. Another manuscript, which was to be the first of more than a score, came from Baltimore in March 1939 and Ross was relieved. He told St. Clair McKelway, the editor who after this was to handle many of Mencken's contributions, that it was heartwarming to know that Mencken would be in the magazine again. McKelway passed the comment on to him, adding that he himself hoped that Mencken would prepare enough of the new sketches to make a book.

This he was now ready to do; in fact he was eager to set more sketches down. Years earlier Sara had wanted him to. She had grown to realize their literary potentialities, for her husband's anecdotes about his boyhood had amused her nearly as much as they had the Saturday Night Club. Shortly before her final illness she had made Blanche Knopf promise to keep him at the task. As much impressed by the idea of the *Days* sketches as Sara, Mrs. Knopf agreed; and she kept her promise. Now in 1939 Mencken felt the time was ripe. The enthusiasm of the Knopfs and the interest of the *New Yorker* speeded the new sketches.

The first the *New Yorker* printed was "The Ruin of an Artist." This was a frisky account of Mencken's boyhood adventures with the piano and the piano teachers who more or less taught him. In subject and style it set the tone for the rest of the series. Thereafter the focus was on Mencken the schoolboy and his family. The "Baltimore blackamoors" played their part but it was a supporting one. Old Wesley and Aunt Sophie were no longer featured. "Memoirs of Deceased Pedagogues," "Recollections of Academic Orgies," "The Schooling of a Theologian": these and the sketches that followed provided a banquet for the readers of the *New Yorker*. There were nine sketches in all, published at intervals from May to November of 1939, and they were composed with consistent felicity. They "read fine" as McKelway put it. The conclusion of "Larval Stage of a Bookworm" is a pleasant example: "Thus launched upon the career of a bookworm, I presently began to reach out right and left for more fodder. When the Enoch Pratt Free Library of Baltimore opened a branch in Hollins street, in March, 1886, I was still a shade too young to be excited, but I had a card before I was nine, and began an almost daily harrying of the virgins at the delivery desk. In 1888 my father subscribed to *Once-a-Week*, the predecessor of *Colliers*, and a little while later there began to come with it a long series of cheap reprints of contemporary classics, running from Tennyson's poems to Justin M'Carthy's 'History of Our Own Times'; and simultaneously there appeared from parts unknown a similar series of cheap reprints of scientific papers, including some of Herbert Spencer. I read them all, sometimes with shivers of puzzlement and sometimes with delight, but always calling for more. I began to inhabit a world that was two-thirds letterpress and only one-third trees, fields, streets and people. . . . I read everything that I could find in English, taking in some of it but boggling most of it.

"This madness ran on till I reached adolescence, and began to distinguish between one necktie and another, and to notice the curiously divergent shapes, dispositions and aromas of girls. Then, gradually, I began to let up.

"But to this day I am still what might be called a reader, and have a high regard for authors."

The pieces he now produced defied categorizing. Though the elements could be traced, the form Mencken gave them made them nearly unique. He called them short stories or simply stories but they were far from the routine tales he had brought out a generation earlier. They were too extended to be called anecdotes. They were too actual to be local-color fiction. They were too exuberant and personal to qualify as social history. Perhaps the best way to put it is that they constituted the human comedy of young Mencken in old Baltimore. The writing was supple and deft, avoiding quaintness, condescension, and sentimentality. And above all it had the apparent artlessness which concealed the skills and resources he drew on.

The contents of these sketches tell us a great deal about Mencken. But the way he prepared them and the way he dealt with the periodical which published them are revealing too. They show a thorough, thoughtful man. So for that matter do the first two series of pieces he wrote, on his travels and on the American language; but the third series furnishes the best example.

He impressed Ross with the meticulousness of his scholarship. Ross had an almost pathological distrust of the accuracy of authors but Mencken never let him down. For his domestic pieces he went back to the prime sources, the crowded archives of a family that seemed to have saved everything. The Mencken household bills, the report cards, the souvenirs, and a vast litter of other items still survived. He dug through all this and verified his roseate recollections. In addition, he encountered a trove of facts he had never known. He had early been told, for example, the minute and hour of his birth. But when he consulted the archives he also found how much his momentous delivery had cost. Dr. Buddenbohn's bill had been kept: it was for ten dollars; and so Mencken informed the world.

Mencken went far in applauding the *New Yorker*'s zeal for factual correctness and he went even farther in his unexpected willingness to see his text edited. Celebrated as a strong-minded editor himself, he responded from the start with great politeness to the *New Yorker*'s editorial suggestions. "Your proofroom is very watchful," he remarked to Mrs. White in one letter, "something that deserves high praise in this careless world. I have followed all its suggestions save one. The letterhead of Reid's simply says Reid's Hotel, not Reid's Palace Hotel. The guide-books are often wrong in such details." A scholar speaking to scholars, he summed up the matter, "In nearly every case I have taken spellings, addresses, etc. from local documents."

The *New Yorker's* copy editing was unbelievably strict and old-maidish, down to the use of more commas than had been fashionable for fifty years. But Mencken acquiesced to it so civilly that Ross and his associates were charmed. They had not expected such sensible professionalism, forgetting perhaps that Mencken's ego was not that of a prima donna but of a working newspaperman. He was ready both to rewrite and be rewritten. Nor did he share the usual illusion of authors that every word is sacred. As he had told Mrs. White about one of the travel sketches, "If any cuts are necessary let me know and I'll make them promptly." He proved to be just as agreeable about cuts made by the staff itself. He urged the *New Yorker* to set its most bilious copy editors on his work and to order them to "chop it freely." The *New Yorker* took an excerpt from one of his good-natured letters and put it on the wall in its main corridor, hoping that it would be seen by "some of the over-sensitive writers we have such a hell of a time with."

Mencken showed his consideration in more than mechanics. For instance, he realized that Ross worried morbidly that a wicked word or lewd insinuation might creep into the columns of his magazine. Mencken understood. He had been a determined crusader for freedom of print, with the Dreiser case and the "Hatrack" case as his liveliest battles for the cause; yet he deferred to Ross's notions of propriety. When Mencken proposed an article about American swearing he promised, in consequence, "I'll be very careful in the piece on naughty words" and added that it would be censor-proof.

The choicest of choice fruit of all this cooperation was the group of *New Yorker* sketches that Mencken proceeded to put into book form in *Happy Days, 1880–1892.* He had expanded them somewhat and now added nine more to plump out the book. Knopf published it in January 1940. The reviewers and the public greeted the volume with pleasure. Here was an old friend taking them far from the Depression and the war in Europe, back to the days of Everyman's childhood. The book managed to find a niche on the nonfiction best-seller lists and stayed there till spring. The genial reception it had was summed up in the *Atlantic Monthly*'s verdict: "A book to be read twice a year by young and old, as long as life lasts."

On receiving his gift copy from Mencken, Dreiser wrote that he was reading and chuckling, reading and chuckling, as he went along. He urged Mencken to press on to later periods, announcing that "This country needs just such an autobiography."

The moment the last sketch for *Happy Days* arrived at the *New Yorker* McKelway too encouraged Mencken to start another round. He announced fervently that he hoped to God Mencken was going ahead and that the *New Yorker* would be able to see every chapter — after all, the venture had been a great success from the *New Yorker*'s point of view. However, the year 1940 saw only a single piece appear, "Downfall of a Revolutionary," and Mencken would not collect it for several years. In addition, it developed that some of McKelway's colleagues failed to share his enthusiasm. Two of them in interoffice memos to Ross declared that readers were tired of "Mencken-Baltimore reminiscence." They ended in fact by returning one sketch.

Mencken himself recognized the need for a change. The first decade or so of his life still contained unmined material — it was "virtually unlimited" in Mencken's phrase — but he took the *New Yorker*'s division of opinion seriously. The problem lay in what to do next. The second decade of his life, the teens, failed to stir him. Actually, they included enough somber memories to put him off. He said later that his teens were so like any other teens that he hesitated to write about them — though the same thing held true for his childhood and had not hampered his writing in the slightest.

But the third decade, filled with his light-hearted experiences as a young reporter, stood waiting. The adventures were adult, even slightly bawdy, and their world though still Baltimore was wider than in *Happy Days*. However, they would bring no blush to a Christian cheek, Mencken predicted, and — he could have added — no flush to the irascible face of Ross. He was right, and the *New Yorker* once again grew pleased and eager.

Nine sketches in a row, later to be collected in *Newspaper Days, 1899–1906*, appeared in the *New Yorker* during 1941. The first to be printed became the most famous. It was "The Girl from Red

Lion, P.A." mentioned before. It concerned a rural lass who one night let her beau go too far. Sure that nothing but a life of sin was left open for her, she tearfully entrained for Baltimore and any brothel where she could start her scarlet career. Mencken described how his fellow reporter, Percy Heath, reassured her with some fancy phrases in Miss Nellie's establishment, a high-toned house where chance had deposited her. "The girl, of course, took in only a small part of this, for Percy's voluptuous style and vocabulary were beyond the grasp of a simple milkmaid. But Miss Nellie, who understood English much better than she spoke it, translated freely, and in a little while the troubled look departed from those blue eyes, and large tears of joy welled from them. Miss Nellie shed a couple herself, and so did all the ladies of the resident faculty, for they had drifted downstairs during the interview, sleepy but curious. The practical Miss Nellie inevitably thought of money, and it turned out that the trip . . . had about exhausted the poor girl's savings, and she had only some odd change left. Percy threw in a dollar and I threw in a dollar, and Miss Nellie not only threw in a third, but ordered one of the ladies to go to the kitchen and prepare a box-lunch for the return to Red Lion." The pieces that followed were all genial, spirited accounts of his salad-days experience in the newspaper world. At their end Ross observed warmly to Mencken that he was probably "the most enlightened man writing today."

To these sketches Mencken added enough more to fill out the second book. Knopf issued it in the autumn of 1941. Again critics remarked on Mencken's good nature, skill, and lucid charm. Again the public showed interest, though it declined to buy the book in very large numbers. But the consensus was that Mencken had done the nearly impossible: he had followed a unique book with an excellent sequel.

Six weeks after *Newspaper Days* reached the bookstores, the attack on Pearl Harbor took place and the full weight of World War II fell on America. Mencken had already stopped writing for the *Sunpapers* — his final contribution until after the war appeared anonymously October 28 — and would not begin again until 1948. He now thought that the United States had to defeat the Japanese and the Germans too. However, the recollection of what he regarded as the aberrations of World War I remained fresh and he felt a deep distaste for the way World War II was being waged. He believed that he could say nothing about it in public. Even if he wanted to, the government's official censorship and the press's unofficial one would prevent him. So he confined himself to letters and personal talk. His tone was dry. Writing to Dreiser in March 1943, he termed the war "the current crusade to save humanity." Writing to Manfred Guttmacher, the Baltimore psychiatrist who had just entered military service, he spoke about "this cruel war" with sarcastic overtones, just as he had earlier when referring to "the fiend Hitler" in a letter to Marcella duPont.

He channeled his still formidable energies entirely into non-political writing. He had already felt, in the spring of 1941, an extraordinary burst of vitality which had enabled him to write his sketches at the rate of three thousand words a day. This was his all-time high but it did not sink much in the months that followed. In 1942 he shepherded a dictionary of quotations on its laborious way through to publication in 1,347 close-packed pages. And he shaped the third and last group of recollections for the *New Yorker,* which became the nucleus of the book *Heathen Days.*

These sketches proved to have little coherence as a group and represented a slight falling off in quality. In terms of their background this was understandable. Mencken remained uncomfortable about his teens, though he did two pieces set in this period, "Adventures of a Y.M.C.A. Lad" and "The Educational Process." Incidentally, these two failed to appear in the *New Yorker* but were included in the book. Because *Newspaper Days* had recently been issued he felt he could not print any more newspaper sketches for some time. That left the period of his later life. However, as he wrote the bookseller Ben Abramson, he hesitated to issue any sketches about it since there were too many persons still alive who might be embarrassed. As a matter of fact, he tactfully roamed back and forth in time. When *Heathen Days* came out the first sketch was dated 1890 and the last 1936.

Notwithstanding their miscellaneous nature, the *New Yorker* accepted and printed a string of them, and several including "A Dip into Statecraft" and "Notes on Paleozoic Publicists" showed Mencken in top form. Mencken in his Preface modestly averred that he was merely offering a set of "random reminiscences," but they were more than that. The touch continued to be adroit. In "The Educational Process," for instance, he commented on one of his schoolmasters at the Polytechnic, "He was a competent teacher, and rammed the mysteries of algebra into his boys with great success. Some of them actually became so proficient that they could solve the problems he set to them without any sort of cheating." And of himself in those days he said, "Nor was I the bright and shining sort of youngster who may be expected to attract adult notice and favor; on the contrary, I was more unprepossessing than otherwise, with a bulging cranium, round shoulders, bow legs, and very little show of the prancing masculine gorgeousness that developed later."

With the publication of *Heathen Days* the close association between Mencken and the *New Yorker* appeared at an end. It published only one piece of his in 1944, one in 1945, and none in the next two years. However, in 1948 the relationship revived. The magazine printed not only a piece called "Love Story" and a sketch about Dreiser but also a series of seven pieces under the general heading of "Postscripts to the American Language." Then, in the middle of more writing, Mencken had his stroke.

Seen in retrospect the relationship was immensely valuable to him. It throve when he needed it and it made the *New Yorker*, after the *Smart Set* and the *Mercury*, his most rewarding magazine.

Without question his reminiscences represent his last, best writing. But they by no means used all his energy. Nor did his newspaper articles. There was still enough left for various pieces of literary journeywork, mainly editing. One piece of editing began and ended as a labor of love. It was *Southern Album*, an anthology of Sara's fiction which he issued in 1936, the year after her death. His Preface proved to be moving without being sentimental; somehow even the biographical data he gave had emotional overtones.

He also produced a work of familial piety during the next year. It was the edition mentioned earlier of a book by one of his ancestors which he had encountered with whoops of joy. In the eighteenth century Johann Burkhardt Mencken (or if you will, Johann Burkhard Mencke) had viewed the scholars of his day with the same wry condescension that would be all too plain two centuries later in his distinguished descendant. *The Charlatanry of the Learned* illustrated the fact that no roguery is new. Mencken had it translated from Latin into English and himself contributed more than forty pages of preface.

The last substantial piece of journeyman work he performed

was *A New Dictionary of Quotations on Historical Principles.* Knopf printed it in 1942, but it represented labor for Mencken that went back many years further. When he gave Paul Patterson a copy he reported that he had first called for a new quotation book in an article in the *Evening Sun* in 1911 and that shortly afterward he himself began to gather note-cards for the purpose. He looked specifically for quotations that interested him but were not in any of the existing volumes. He continued with dogged industry, and help for a time from Charles Angoff when he was on the *Mercury.* As World War II approached, Mencken used some of his enforced leisure to work at the dictionary of quotations. In itself it is a useful reference tool and it also indicates both Mencken's tenacity and his interest in the writings of others.

It may also indicate at least one more thing: his still unfailing, sometimes pixyish humor; for the reader, as he riffles through the entries, can be struck every now and then by the pleasant suspicion that Mencken himself is the author of certain items. The source listed is usually obscure and foreign, Balkan perhaps. The citation may read simply "Ukrainian proverb," for instance; but the voice muffled by the foreign accent may be that of Owen Hatteras or C. Farley Anderson or indeed H. L. Mencken.

He did another editorial chore also, much more minor but still worth mentioning. He contributed an introduction to the Memorial Edition of Dreiser's *An American Tragedy* issued in 1946. He had already given his valedictory on Dreiser's death the year before, in a memorial message which had not been read or printed. Now he had a chance to offer a final estimate of Dreiser. It was a very favorable one but he discovered that even after Dreiser's death he could not stultify himself. He still felt compelled to say that he thought that part of the book's high reputation was due to its sheer bulk. He remained astringent to the end.

Although his published writing dwindled in the mid-1940s, he never stopped work. He concentrated on preparing volumes of reminiscences that covered the period after *Newspaper Days,* the period, as he had said, when he had to consider the feelings of people still alive. He had long thought about writing up his recollections of this era. He wanted to describe his experiences as an author and editor and to continue in full detail the record of his experiences as a newspaperman which he had begun in *Newspaper*

Days. In late 1941 he told Ellery Sedgwick that he intended to do a companion volume to *Newspaper Days* on his "magazine adventures." Here and there in letters to his friends we can catch a glimpse of the work in progress. There is, for instance, the letter of April 17, 1942 to the novelist H. L. Davis in which Mencken mentions ruefully that he has wasted nearly a year on "a long record that can't be published." There is the letter of February 23, 1943 to Dreiser asking him to explain, if he will, some puzzling references that Mencken has found on going through his files of correspondence with him. Then there is the letter of August 17, 1945 to the novelist James Farrell. Mencken opens by telling Farrell that he is "playing with an idea of doing a sort of chronicle of my adventures as editor" and follows by confessing that he already has put a sizable part of it on paper. He says that he wants to make it as interesting as possible and so will use some rather intimate accounts of people he has known. He hastens to add that he will allow nothing to be printed in his lifetime that will mortify anyone — an assurance the more advisable because he has just asked Farrell for some personal information.

For three years after the letter to Farrell he continued writing. Feeling that his literary days were near an end, he worked resolutely. He depended more and more on the clerical assistance of Mrs. Lohrfinck. In years past she had usually typed clean copies from his own typewritten drafts but after the early 1940s he found it increasingly easy to dictate to her instead of typing his compositions first himself. In May 1948, six months prior to his stroke, he told Huntington Cairns that he had already dictated an account of his magazine experiences running to over six hundred thousand words and that he thought it probably would run to a million words before he was through. He never made the million but at least he had a productive half year more.

As a matter of fact he produced an imposing amount in his final years of writing. In all he finished a four-volume set of typescripts entitled "My Life as Author and Editor," a three-volume set entitled "Thirty-five Years of Newspaper Work," a five-volume diary, and a four-volume compilation entitled "Letters and Documents Relating to the Baltimore *Sunpapers.*"

Along with this spate of dictating he managed two more pieces of editing. He culled his out-of-print writing for the most interesting selections, preferably those with "a certain ribaldry" to them, dropped in a few unpublished items, christened the resulting book *A Mencken Chrestomathy,* and mailed it to Knopf. It came out the year after his stroke but all the work had been finished before. And he put together most of the notes which would make up *Minority Report,* his last book, which will be mentioned later.

At the same time that he was dictating his manifold memoirs, and adding a little editing on the side, he was doing his final stint at the *Sun.*

Though the outbreak of World War II chilled the relationship between Mencken and the *Sunpapers* it was not destroyed. It is true that after February 2, 1941 he published nothing in the *Sunpapers* except for the unsigned obituary of Max Broedel. And he told more than one person privately that he kept no hand in the *Sun's* editorial affairs. Yet the *Sun* was more than a paper to him; it was a way of life. He continued to see his good friends on the staff. In spite of the fact that the meetings became fewer and a bit awkward they were not abandoned. Perhaps the best indication that he was willing to keep up a connection was the fact that he stayed on the payroll. If he had really been finished with the *Sun* he would not have accepted a cent.

Throughout the war he continued to serve on the board of directors. He also suggested an occasional news story or feature to his longtime colleagues. In 1943 and 1944 he assisted in an enterprise that had a particular attraction for him. It was a projected stylebook for the *Sunpapers,* designed to solve, with harmony and consistency, the problems of capitalization, punctuation, and general usage encountered in writing for any newspaper. Maclean Patterson, Paul's son, prepared the rough copy and at the end of April 1943 sent it to Mencken with a plea for his advice. For thirty years he had thought off and on about some of these problems and he was impressed by the way Maclean Patterson was attacking them. Mencken told him that it was the best stylebook he had ever seen and that he would be willing to do what he could to make it even better.

No one could have been a more knowing adviser. He drew on his double background as a newspaperman and as a student of the American language. His counsel was shrewd, if salted with crotchets such as "I favor capitalizing the names of the seasons, as we capitalize the names of the days of the week." In the fall of 1944 he prepared a succinct preface. Facing the facts of linguistic life, he said, "A stylebook does not pretend to lay down the rules of correct English. In America those rules are in a state of flux. They are determined, such as they are, not by the fiats of grammarians and schoolma'ams, but by the practice of good writers. The best a newspaper can do is try to maintain a reasonable uniformity. Often it must choose arbitrarily between two forms both of which have support in logic and good usage." He added a cautionary paragraph against such banalities as "to contact" and the imitation of the style of *Time* magazine, noting that a good newspaperman did not ape bad models.

Mencken's concern for the *Sun* continued. It was diminished by exasperation at the paper's wayward editorial policy, its stubborn support of Roosevelt's war, yet it never came close to disappearing. Roosevelt died and Mencken wrote sarcastically to a friend a few days later that the news had almost floored him but that he had now recovered somewhat and no longer woke at night sobbing. The Germans surrendered and then the Japanese. The urge to return to old interests and business as usual became as powerful for most Americans as it had been after World War I ended. Somehow the Russians refused to let this happen; nevertheless many Americans made the effort. Among them were the managers of the *Sunpapers* and Mencken himself. Though some stiffness still existed during the months immediately following the war, it became clear that it need not be permanent. The initiative, however, had to come from the *Sun*. There was a certain difference of opinion on the staff about taking it, but Paul Patterson and Hamilton Owens made it plain that they wanted Mencken back. It had been the same way after World War I.

Because they were astute men they did not hurry him. The postwar seduction of Mencken was accomplished slowly and tactfully, taking nearly two years. The crucial occasion was the approach of the national political conventions, still his best-loved entertainment. As early as November 1947 Maclean Patterson wrote him about resuming his writing for the *Sun*. He replied with almost, but not quite, a firm no. There the matter rested for the remainder of that year. The Pattersons waited, counting on the growing excitement and political ballyhoo of the campaigns to warm Mencken's interest. When he was in New York the following March, the *Herald Tribune* carried an interview in which he said he would probably go to the conventions in spite of his age rather than have "some young punk" cover them. He predicted that as a result of his activity he would come home on a shutter but he consoled himself by adding that it would be a heroic death.

The item was dropped on Maclean Patterson's desk and he moved in at once. He sent a copy of the clipping to Mencken with a note to remind him that the *Sun* was holding both a seat and a hotel bed for him at each convention. Then Maclean wrote jubilantly to his father, who was in the hospital, "It looks as though Mr. Mencken is weakening!" His father urged him on and also promised to talk to Mencken. He did so, assuring Mencken that he would not have to do any writing if he did not wish it. He could promise this the more easily because he knew that it would be physically impossible for Mencken to sit at a national convention without drumming on his typewriter. Moreover, by now it was clear that there would be three conventions instead of two, and the third — to be held by Henry Wallace and his Progressives — would provide the garish color that most fascinated him. On April 14 Mencken confessed to Maclean Patterson, "God knows I itch to see all three conventions." And so he went.

Everyone gained. From the time Mencken turned in his first dispatch it was clear that he still led the field. Though past its prime, his picturesque prose held up well through column after column. Here he is, for instance, explaining to the reader about the Southern politicians who had sworn to unseat President Truman at the Democratic convention: "The species, in fact, is excessively bellicose and even blood-thirsty, and there has not been a Democratic convention in history in which it did not stage a gory bout. Even at the lovey-dovey convention of 1936, with everyone gassed and enchanted by the smell of jobs, some of the Southerners, led by the late Cotton Ed Smith of South Carolina, put on an insurrection against letting colored delegates from the North make speeches."

Much as he enjoyed reporting the conventions that nominated President Truman and Thomas Dewey, he enjoyed the Progressive Party convention more. He watched Henry Wallace and his variegated crusaders with a gourmet's relish. The journalist Alistair Cooke has given the best picture of Mencken at the Progressives' meetings. In the *Atlantic Monthly* for May 1956 he printed his recollections as

"Last Happy Days of H. L. Mencken." They portray a Mencken of
continuing energy and crusty charm, who even won a compliment
from Wallace, a phenomenal feat at that frantic caucus. When he
joined his fellow newspapermen in the celebrations that accompanied
the convention, he showed his old skill in creating comic uproar. His
blue eyes beamed, his grin widened, his gravelly voice held the
crowd.

If the Wallace dispatches failed to reach the level of his best
earlier reporting they nevertheless showed his mark plainly. Like
the dispatches from the other two conventions, they were still good.
"The delegates," he wrote in one piece on the Progressives, "taking
them one with another, have seemed to me to be of generally low
intelligence, but it is easy to overestimate the idiocy of the partici-
pants in such mass paranoias. People of genuine sense seldom come
to them, and when they do come, they are not much heard from.
I believe that the percentage of downright half-wits has been definitely lower than in, say, the Democratic Convention of 1924, and
not much higher than in the Democratic Convention of this year."
The passage has his old bluntness and clarity as well as much of
his old vitality. Yet something is gone, perhaps the telling, individual
phrase that had always marked even the short notes written to his
friends.

Once he and the *Sunpapers* came together again Mencken resumed his regular advising as well as his writing. He revived the
habit of afternoon visits to the office. He dropped in daily on Paul
Patterson among others, with wicked jeers about the *Sunpapers'*
shortcomings and prompt praise for their achievements. And as had
been his custom before the war, he offered not only editorial advice
but news tips as he puffed his cigar. Up to the last month of his
active life he made suggestions. If he did not see the *Sun* staff
member he wanted, he wrote him a note. By then Maclean Patterson was an editor at the *Sun* and received a number of notes
from him. There was, Mencken wrote him, for instance, old Dr.
Slemons dying in Los Angeles, who ought to have an obituary as a
former Hopkins man. There was a saloonkeeper whose fiftieth anniversary at the bar was coming up. There was A. Philip Randolph,
the veteran Negro labor leader; he deserved much more attention
from the press than he was getting.

The Wallace dispatches appeared in July and were followed

in late summer and early fall by sixteen other pieces. The last two of them saw print in November. One asserted that the nation got what it deserved in electing Harry Truman. The other blasted Baltimore for jailing some Negroes and whites who had tried to play tennis together at Druid Hill Park. This piece appeared on November 9. Two weeks later came his crippling stroke.

After his all too partial recovery it was proposed that he start going again to the office; it would give him something to do. He refused. His speech and memory were brutally impaired and it would have been a mockery for him to return. But he had given the *Sunpapers* as much as he could as long as he was able. In Alfred Knopf's judgment his first loyalty was always to the *Sunpapers*.

18. Nighttime at Hollins Street

MENCKEN'S INTEREST in the human body was ardent. It started with his own body of course. He was always taking his temperature, literally or figuratively. He mentioned his current complaints in a thousand letters and when he catalogued those complaints they stretched from Baltimore to New York. His battle with hay fever, waged anew each autumn, epitomized all his efforts, for it was conducted with unrelenting vigor but only rare success. Fortunately his ills long remained minor ones. They were aggravations which could be dealt with in a spirit, paradoxical though it sounds, of irritable good humor. They never mastered him: he would appear at a dinner, for instance, hoarse-voiced or red-eyed but still droll.

Even if he saw himself as afflicted by a multitude of minor ills, he recognized that his basic condition was good. He passed through his first half century with hardly a scar. When in his fifties he began going to his young medical friend, Dr. Benjamin Baker, he appeared the picture of health.

However, near the end of July in 1939 he suffered what he himself realized was at least a slight stroke. We lack the details but we know he found one day that he felt fuzzy, that the left side of his face was stiff, and that he could not move his left arm. Dr. Baker promptly put him in the Johns Hopkins Hospital. Happily his stay was brief, his recovery quick. By the middle of August, when he was vacationing with his friends the Hanes family in North Carolina, his host Dr. Fred Hanes could write Dr. Baker that he was again in good shape with no evidence of physical disability.

Dr. Hanes added that he thought the seizure had been a warning to Mencken and that he would thereafter take advice more readily. Close friend though Dr. Hanes was, his prediction proved only partly right. Mencken would take advice when it suited him.

But the slight stroke did have one characteristic consequence. As early as June 1940 Mencken began to keep a deathwatch. On the one hand, he continued to send the *New Yorker* the mellow stories which captivated Harold Ross. On the other hand, he inaugurated a grim diary of his decay. It survives in the form of a sheaf of typescripts, perhaps fifty pages in all.

Given his knowledge of medicine plus his hypochondria, it is no wonder that he observed with fascination his slow slide downhill. He starts his first extant note by saying that he approaches his sixtieth birthday in impaired physical condition but without any mental impairment that he can see. He remarks that he has already enjoyed a longer life than many a Mencken and that his life has been a good one. He feels little regret. The world has treated him well; he has been very successful, in view of what he considers to be his modest equipment. The trouble is, he says in a later note, that the equipment is wearing out. There was a time when he could work without interruption, except for meals and a brief nap, from ten in the morning to ten at night. That time has plainly passed.

His response, however, is not one of resignation but the reverse. The spring of 1941 sees him writing more productively than ever before. But when his energy lags he begins to force himself. The result can be deduced from a note of June 1, 1942, where he reports a caution from Baker's partner, Dr. Charles Wainwright, that he must either ease off or risk a severe stroke. He seems to take Wainwright seriously, for he tells himself that he will give his remaining energy to the final arrangement of his papers. The decision has a funereal air about it. But then, having made his decision, he unexpectedly feels better and so he again undertakes a fair amount of writing. Thereafter he has his ups and downs, including another slight stroke. He discovers by the end of 1942 that he must spend more and more time resting on his couch. Nevertheless, he turns to preparing the record of his magazine experiences and makes considerable headway. His mental state is still good, so he can no more keep from writing than from breathing. He even labors at the supplement to *The American Language,* an arduous and tedious job.

As late as June 10, 1944, he can announce that his mental state remains satisfactory. His physical state is dismal, though; he has acquired at least three handicaps. These are a heart condition, a very sensitive throat, and the slight and transient but ominous strokes. By the end of February 1945 he is compelled to report that his mental abilities are being affected as well. He observes gloomily that his mind is deteriorating. He becomes nervous and confused whenever he sits down at his typewriter.

The year 1945 proves to be the worst so far, with his mental powers declining along with his physical ones. Although his eyesight has been growing bad this is the first year he suffers from double vision. And he has had nightmares off and on for years, but now there are more of them. He dreams often of trying to catch a train and failing; he dreams of straining or struggling. One day he dejectedly remarks about his general condition, "As life peters out nearly every item of its routine becomes unpleasant." Yet his powerful vitality has by no means vanished. Nor has his invention. Even if his memory for words has weakened he continues to have ideas for subjects to write on.

His last good year is now arriving. It runs from the spring of 1946 to the spring of 1947. His health is better than it has been, he testifies, for the past four or five years. By summer he is in trouble, however. In early August he suffers from what Dr. Baker tells him is another slight stroke. But it is actually less slight than the ones before. The consequence is that for days he cannot even sign his own name, let alone compose or type. Only toward the end of the month does he note that his handwriting seems to be improving, as is his typing.

Through other sources than his diary we know that during the fall and winter of 1947 he worked as well as he could. He got things done, though the references about his "oxidizing" rose in his letters to friends. He endured the Baltimore summer of 1948 with no major setbacks and then began his annual grappling with hay fever. At intervals his brother August and Mrs. Lohrfinck thought they saw new signs of strain. If they remarked on them he was apt to dismiss the matter with a wry joke. But the record in the diary is somber. The final typescript that we have is dated October 9, 1948. In it he complains of both stomach and heart trouble, as well as of a further loss of memory.

Yet his correspondence shows that presidential elections still amused him, and he had a chuckle left as the people spoke in their hoarse tones and voted for Harry Truman instead of Thomas Dewey.

His crippling seizure did not come till a fortnight after the election. Up to that time he tried his best — as he had for nearly a decade — to keep up a good front, to maintain his visits to the *Sun* office, and to repeat the ordinary motions of daily life.

But on the evening of November 23 he called at Mrs. Lohrfinck's apartment to read through the typing she had done for him the day before and then to take her to dinner. About seven thirty he told her he felt bad and had a headache. She got him a drink hoping that it would help him. He took it, but the glass slipped from his hand and he began to talk incoherently. Alarmed, she called Dr. Baker. When he arrived he found Mencken pacing back and forth, ranting. He got him to the hospital, where it was seen that he had been the victim of a severe stroke. Though the hospital rallied all its formidable resources, his condition grew worse. For a few days it seemed that he would die. He did not. But he shortly discovered that whatever the condition of his general health, he had lost most of the faculties which lent meaning to his life. He could no longer read or write. And he could no longer speak except haltingly. Once he realized all this he threatened to kill himself.

August and others did their utmost to reassure him. He responded somewhat and began to improve. By the third week of his hospital stay he was walking around with assistance; after the fifth week he was discharged.

An old, incapacitated man, he was taken back to Hollins Street. There arrangements were made to give him the best possible care, with August in particular devoting most of his time to him. His general condition continued to grow better but the fact merely highlighted the extent of his specific losses. In March 1949 Dr. Baker called in a consultant, whose report has been preserved. On first glance the consultant saw a signal improvement. But when he made some tests he found that Mencken not only could not read but could not comprehend much that he heard. The consultant said that the extent of incomprehension was concealed by the remnants of Mencken's remarkable facility with language, but the sad fact was that he could understand only part of what anyone said. Yet if he was successful in sensing the drift of conversation, then he seemed able to understand some of the details.

The consultant suggested various possible remedies. He told August to get Mencken to try to read some poetry he knew well or read his own books. He told him not to have Mencken stay at any task longer than half an hour, however. He recommended that he be taken to the movies and plays and that he should continue with his gardening in the backyard when the weather allowed. He might even be taken fishing during the summer months. Meanwhile, he should be cheered up as much as he could.

Baker's partner, Dr. Philip Wagley, who was to become Mencken's friend for the final half dozen years of his life, saw him in April 1949. His case notes give a forbidding picture. He found a discouraged Mencken well aware of the extent of his disaster. Even Sara's death had not stunned him like this catastrophe. He could not find the spirit in him to rally. He declined to try a program of training in rereading. He refused the offer of a news magazine blown up to a size where even his dimmed eyesight might see it. He did not want anyone to read to him, he said, nor did he even want to listen to phonograph records — and this in spite of the deep attraction music had possessed before. Now that he had been struck down, he seemed to wish no alleviation of his misery.

The next year he felt better and showed some gains. He could read words on a map, such as "Louisiana," "Mississippi," and "Maryland." Yet when he picked up the New York *Times* he failed to read more than one or two headlines. He often talked about being half-dead or dead. And there was many a day when he bitterly regretted staying alive. He would stand at the window, looking out on Union Square with tears in his eyes, and wish that his miseries were over.

Life went on, nevertheless, and it was somehow made manageable with August's help. Mencken grew to talk more freely. But as he talked, his permanent defect always showed itself. Again and again he could not think of the right word, of the word he needed to describe a thing or finish a sentence. Sometimes he could not summon the word at all. At other times he produced something that sounded like it but had a different meaning. There is a short list of such words in one of the medical documents. He said "scoot" when he meant "coat"; "ray" when he meant "rain"; "yarb" when he meant "yard." He gradually learned to improvise, to pantomime some of the words that would not come. For example, if he could not recall the word for drinking, he would raise an imaginary glass to his lips. Or if he could not recall the word for ham, he would shape the outline of a ham with his hand.

As time went on, August developed a remarkable verbal rapport with his brother. He became expert in supplying the word which Mencken was blocked from using. He learned to look to August, and August provided the proper term. It made the process of conversation less painful to everyone involved.

Inevitably some visitors made Mencken feel more at ease than others. He felt decidedly comfortable with Dr. Wagley, so Wagley visited him socially in the evening every now and then as well as professionally during the day. The day after an evening visit by him in September 1950, Mencken spoke about his condition and its prospects, and his words were transcribed. They offer us a moving account of his own view. "I gave a long tale of my troubles last night. He (the doctor) was in the house to see me and my brother was present. Fortunately, I can talk to him very easily, but I never feel like doing it in the morning. . . . My words do not begin to live until afternoon. . . . My worst trouble is that I simply can't write my account in detail. As soon as I begin the subject I shake up on it and in a little while I can't say what I want to say. It is my opinion that my mind has been destroyed completely."

Yet at times he seemed to improve. In point, the next month he went to the hospital for treatment and then returned, according to Mrs. Lohrfinck, in the best of spirits. However, within a week after her rosy report he was admitted to the hospital, near death. This time he had evidently suffered a heart attack. For a long while he lay critically ill and x-rays showed that his heart had become much enlarged. He was finally sent home in March 1951 after more than five months.

Life at Hollins Street recommenced. It would have gone more dismally than before except for the fact that this time he brought with him the efficient young woman who had been his day-nurse at the hospital. Named Lois Gentry, she stayed with him on private day-duty for nearly three years in all. He also had an orderly who helped him to get up and dress each day. As soon as Miss Gentry arrived she fell into the routine of the household. She would come every morning after he was up and do whatever nursing duties were necessary. For a while they were substantial but then Mencken recovered enough so that he could even return to some morning work with Mrs. Lohrfinck. He and Mrs. Lohrfinck would adjourn to the second-floor study and answer, or at least acknowledge, such letters as came in. In addition they would go over the correspondence he intended to present to the New York Public Library. Thousands of letters to him had accumulated. They would throw out some and keep many others. The letters from him would not be there of course, but the shorthand notes for them still existed in Mrs. Lohrfinck's notebooks and these too in a good many cases she would transcribe for presentation to the Library. About an hour before lunch, or sooner if he had to, he would stop and rest. Mrs. Lohrfinck would gather her papers and leave. Then lunch would be served, the big meal of the day. It was an old-fashioned formal meal. Mencken, still presiding, always wore coat and tie. Miss Gentry sat on his right, August on his left.

After lunch he and she would go into the back garden in all except the worst weather. Even if it rained they went out of the house and sat just inside the little shed. Then another nap for Mencken and then listening to the radio or — a late concession — watching television. Art Linkletter was one of his favorites in both mediums. Mencken watched television chiefly to make fun of it. He had not lost his sense of humor entirely and was amused by the new medium's gaucheries. He also liked the fatuous movies which were beginning to be shown on television. He found the Tarzan films especially preposterous and enjoyable. On radio, the opera was Mencken's favorite, especially the Saturday afternoon broadcast of the Metropolitan. This he could appreciate seriously, for his love of music had returned in part.

In good weather he and Miss Gentry sometimes took a walk. They would make their way around Union Square or perhaps go as far as the drugstore to get a handful of cigars. His doctor still allowed him a cigar after lunch every day and at times another one at night. Mencken seldom bought expensive ones; as a rule he chose the Uncle Willies on which he had chewed for fifty years. Often he would buy some chocolates for the Negro children who lived in his alley.

One of Miss Gentry's duties was to see to it that her patient obeyed the doctor's orders. However, Wagley was young and Mencken sometimes ignored his advice. When that happened, her job was to be kind but firm and see to it that Mencken did not tire himself by gardening, for instance, or neglect to take the pills Wagley prescribed.

On the whole his health improved during the time she was with him. Consequently, for the last year or so of her stay she became less of a nurse and more of a companion. She learned that he still could tell a good story, even if haltingly, and that he liked to reminisce about his childhood. He told her a good deal that she recognized in *Happy Days* when she came to read it. Working in the Mencken household grew so easy that she became bored. Because she knew she was beginning to stagnate she left, though with considerable regret, in the autumn of 1953.

Mencken now seemed well enough to make it unnecessary to replace her. After some months William Manchester, whose life of Mencken had appeared in 1950, was employed as a reader for him. He came to Hollins Street every morning regularly from the summer of 1954 to the summer of 1955. He read to Mencken and listened to him as well. He became a valued companion, with his fresh humor and good spirits. In the evenings other visitors appeared. August discouraged those he thought might upset his brother as well as those he thought frivolous — and this included all females except Blanche Knopf. The most faithful attendants were close friends in Baltimore: Hamilton Owens, Louis Cheslock, and two or three more. Alfred Knopf came from New York when he could. Dr. Arnold Rich and other old or new alumni of the Saturday Night Club waited on him every now and then to pay their respects.

To fill in the hours and days of the crippled man remained a grave problem, notwithstanding. There were various attempts to bring him back into his literary work, or at least a part of it. All failed but one. It was discovered that he could still make a simple editorial judgment on something he had written before, especially if he could take it bit by bit. This remaining talent led to his last book, *Minority Report*.

It started as a collection of miscellaneous notes from his files. He had written a multitude of them (thousands, he says in the Preface prepared prior to his stroke) and shoveled them together. If we can judge from internal evidence he probably wrote most of those to go into *Minority Report* in the years from 1939 to 1941. During 1948, in the months preceding the stroke, he pretty well finished the job. But then the manuscript was lost in the confusion following his critical illness, not to be found for several years. Once found, however, it furnished exactly the sort of mild stimulus Mencken needed. He spent many an hour with Mrs. Lohrfinck while she took the notes one by one and read them slowly to him. He would either approve at once of including them in the book or eliminate them, or else tell how to revise them. If they seemed to call for extensive revision he could not of course manage it and they were dropped. He vetoed some of the notes because they were poorly phrased, others because their content might give undue offense, for example when they were strident on the subject of the Jews. But an ample selection remained.

When his and Mrs. Lohrfinck's job was done she typed the notes again and forwarded them to the Knopf office in New York. There they apparently received a second screening before going to the printer, though there was still enough fire in them to let the Knopf office advertise that the book they became was controversial. It appeared in May 1956, four months after he died. One of its aphorisms read, "Moderation in all things. Not too much life. It often lasts too long."

Meanwhile, public interest in Mencken and his works, never entirely lost, rose bit by bit. The biographies by Manchester and Edgar Kemler (Kemler's like Manchester's came out in 1950) received good reviews and considerable attention. The clipping books at the Enoch Pratt Library show a steady trickle of references to him in newspapers and magazines. In 1955 he had his seventy-fifth birthday and Baltimore, led by the Pratt Library, celebrated the memorable occasion.

Sometime during the early morning of January 29, 1956 he died in his beloved Baltimore row-house. His last waking hours carried some reminiscences of his once full-blooded life. Toward the end of the winter afternoon he stretched out on the couch in his second-floor office, listened to a portion of *Die Meistersinger* on his radio, and then took a nap. On awakening he came down to supper. August had built a cheerful fire as usual and his friend Louis Cheslock was present. Mencken complained to them of not being well but, according to August later, drank two Gibsons and felt the better for it. The conversation was good in spite of his speech handicap. Shortly after nine he excused himself and returned to his bedroom. Again he listened to the radio, this time to a symphony, and then went to sleep. He died at about three or four in the morning, apparently peacefully, of what was found to be a coronary occlusion. Long before, he had specified the only eulogy he wished and he had put it so winningly that it has become famous: "If, after I depart this vale, you ever remember me and have thought to please my ghost, forgive some sinner and wink your eye at some homely girl."

To help August, Hamilton Owens made the arrangements for the funeral. They were in line with Mencken's own wishes. He and Hamilton had more than once discussed the lack of a proper funeral service for the unbeliever. Since there was none, the arrangements were Spartan. After the body was laid out in a little funeral home less than a block from Hollins Street, Owens simply stood up to say a few words. He explained to the handful of friends present that Henry had wanted no ritual of any sort. All he wanted was for them to gather round and see him off on his last journey. Having said that, Owens stopped and the body was carried out. Only the brothers August and Charlie accompanied it to the Loudon Park Cemetery, where it was cremated and the ashes deposited next to Sara's in the Mencken family plot.

19. Memento of an Active Man

THE VALEDICTORY was fond. Newspapers throughout the nation noted Mencken's death. The reporters, columnists, and editors who composed his obituaries recognized that a preeminent figure in their field had passed away. They announced that as a newspaperman he had known no peer and that he had been in a class by himself as a satirist, nonconformist, and debunker. Their accounts were often affectionate as well as respectful, and seasoned with kindly anecdote. Though they recalled that he had been the nation's number-one gadfly they swathed the recollection in sentiment. They had lost the feeling for the old Mencken, for the man who had goaded much of the nation, who had caused tempers to climb and foreheads to flush. Only here and there could the response be found that he himself would have relished. But at least one paper had exactly the right reaction. It was the *Jersey Journal* of Jersey City and it quoted a Washington minister. His verdict on the deceased was: "He loved his drunken pals. He loved to swear in the presence of ladies and archdeacons. To him, everything was a racket—God, education, radio, marriage, children."

That was a farewell Mencken would have prized, a fit farewell for the man best memorialized—in his prime—in this fashion:

THE FOLLOWING resolution was unanimously adopted at a State meeting of the Knights and Women of the Ku Klux Klan at Little Rock, Ark., Sept. 7, 1925:

WHEREAS, One H. L. Mencken is the author of a scurrilous article recently published in the Baltimore Sun, describing the Klan parade in

Washington, D.C., August 3, in which he viciously slurs and insults the good women and the patriotic men who marched in that parade to the number of more than 100,000, declaring that there was not an intelligent or comely face among them, that they looked like a gang of meat cutters and curve greasers on a holiday and many other slanders and insults too vile and indecent to be repeated, therefore be it:

RESOLVED, By the Knights of the Ku Klux Klan of Arkansas, a State which the said Mencken has in times past slandered as "a land of morons," that we condemn in the strongest possible language the vile mouthings of this prince of blackguards among the writers of America, to whom virtue, patriotism and democracy are only a subject upon which to expend the venom of a poisonous pen; that we further condemn the Baltimore Sun for heaping insults upon the good men and women of America, and that we commend the course of the Baltimore Chamber of Commerce in protesting against the calumny too degrading and false to come from the heart of one who is not himself a moral pervert.

RESOLVED FURTHER, That copies of this resolution be sent to the Baltimore Sun, National Courier, Baltimore Chamber of Commerce and H. L. Mencken.

Afterword: *The Far Side of the Moon*

THE STOREHOUSE of Mencken material is the Mencken Room at the Enoch Pratt Library in Baltimore. Here are nearly all of Mencken's typescripts, more than a hundred volumes of his personal clipping books, and family scrapbooks full of photographs and many other kinds of memorabilia. Here too are copies of all his printed works, both in English and in translation. Lining the walls of the room are two thousand books from his personal library. In file drawers in the next room lies the bulk of his correspondence with fellow Marylanders, either in the original or in copy.

The second great source of Mencken material is the Princeton University Library. In 1942 the historian Julian Boyd, then the head librarian and a friend of Mencken's, started to gather letters to and from Mencken because he hoped to edit a selection of them. He won Mencken's approval for the project. Though both Mencken and his friends did some screening, in the end they turned over a great deal of correspondence. The copying went ahead busily for several years despite the fact that Boyd never found the leisure to edit the collection he had planned. The richest harvest was gathered between 1942 and 1944. Thanks to his enterprise the Princeton Library now includes uncounted thousands of copies—no one knows how many—of letters from Mencken and to him. The copies range from facsimile reproductions, photostat or microfilm, to more or less accurate transcriptions; in addition there is a scattering of originals. In spite of Mencken's precautions the result is an often illuminating mass of letters.

Here and there throughout the country other letters were deposited but these collections were small compared to the vast holdings at Princeton. However, Mencken made a major gift to the New York Public Library. To it he presented both important manuscripts and a very large number of letters. The letters were either originals from many of his literary correspondents or copies of his own letters which were transcribed by Mrs. Lohrfinck from her notebooks. This collection he closed to everybody before 1971. With it he deposited a set of the two unpublished works of his mentioned earlier, "My Life as Author and Editor" in four volumes and "Thirty-five Years of Newspaper Work" in three volumes. No one would be allowed to look into either set until 1991. He gave copies of the same seven volumes, subject to the same restrictions, to the Dartmouth College Library and to the Enoch Pratt Library. Lastly, he gave the Enoch Pratt Library nine more volumes, which he restricted till 1981. They are the five-volume diary and the four volumes entitled "Letters and Documents Relating to the Baltimore Sunpapers."

The prohibitions pose a major problem for the student of Mencken. Should all efforts to write his life be abandoned till 1971 or 1981 or even 1991? Perhaps. Nevertheless, several factors persuaded me, for one, to go ahead. The first was the existence of an enormous amount of material already available in manuscript form or otherwise. Projection is always risky, and yet it appeared to me probable that even the large restricted holdings at the New York Public Library would not change the basic lines of Mencken's life nor alter my fundamental interpretations. Somewhere with each succeeding hundred letters the law of diminishing returns must come in. Moreover, copies of many of the letters were obviously to be found at Princeton. How great the proportion was, no one could say. But if I had to guess, I would estimate it at least a third.

The restriction on Mencken's reminiscences about his work as author and editor and about his newspaper experiences poses a like problem. So does his diary. What he says in all those volumes may modify if not upset a considerable number of conclusions. On the other hand, it may not. I decided to take the risk. My guess is that the far side of the moon is much like the side we already see.

Moreover, I wanted to do two things that no biographer had done before. Neither depended on unlimited access to biographical data. One was to analyze Mencken's writing in relation to his life. The other was to describe the relation between his life and times.

More personally: another factor that encouraged me to go ahead and write the biography was the interest and assistance of Mencken's brother August. I turned to him often from the time in the early 1960s when I began my research until his death in May 1967. There were some matters, private ones, that he was unwilling to talk about. But for many matters he could not only furnish recollections but also check my factual accuracy.

I was further influenced by the fact that many of Mencken's friends, as well as several enemies, had memories of him that they were willing to share with me. In about half of the most important cases it turned out that

I could tape the interviews. In the other cases I took notes. Several times the person I was interviewing gave me notes he himself had prepared. There were some persons I saw only once. Most I saw more than that and I spoke many times with a number of the main persons for my purpose.

The persons I interviewed were among the last links with Mencken's past. Their recollections were unique, irreplaceable. If I had waited till 1991 to speak with them, they would no longer have been available nor would I. The years when I was gathering my material saw the passing of some of his closest associates including his secretary Mrs. Lohrfinck, his best friend on the *Sunpapers*, Hamilton Owens, and of course his brother August.

Not infrequently the persons I interviewed told me something with the stipulation that I could not give the source. This fact accounts for some though certainly not all of the undocumented statements in this biography. As William Manchester observed in the Introduction to his life of President Kennedy, if he had not promised to keep his informants anonymous he would have had little information to print.

Acknowledgments

MY GREATEST DEBTS are to an individual and two institutions. The individual is the late August Mencken; the institutions are the Enoch Pratt Library and my own university, the University of Maryland.

It was August Mencken's interest, as much as anything, that made me decide to undertake a biography of his brother. I have already spoken of the assistance he gave me; it would have been hard to work without it. I should add that it was given under the most pleasant possible conditions: at lunch in Marconi's, for instance, or along with beer in the backyard of 1524 Hollins Street.

The Enoch Pratt is a superb public library, with a particular interest in Mencken. The relation between the man and the institution was long and rewarding on both sides. Throughout his career it was his constant resource and he said so. My work in its Mencken Room brought me into contact with many members of the staff but the one I turned to most often was Mr. Richard Hart, head of the humanities division. He never failed me. My obligations are also great to Miss Betty Adler, the Library's Mencken specialist, who read my manuscript for fact and often rescued me through her extensive knowledge, and to Mr. Edwin Castagna, director of the Library.

The Graduate School of my university systematically and generously supported my work on Mencken. I know the pressures that prompt any institution to want a quick return on an investment; the Graduate School's patience, as I went along in my own way, was exemplary. I am also grateful to my department, the Department of English, which gave me reduced teaching schedules from time to time along with clerical and research assistance.

I owe many debts as well to other institutions and individuals. The

Princeton University Library, with more Mencken correspondence available than any other library, was generous in the access it allowed me. I found Mr. Alexander Clark, curator of manuscripts, especially helpful. For help in my work with the extensive Dreiser-Mencken correspondence at the University of Pennsylvania Library I want particularly to thank Mrs. Neda Westlake; at the Cornell University Library I want to thank Dr. George Healey; at the Georgetown University Library, its librarian Mr. Joseph Jeffs; and at the Library of Congress, Dr. John Broderick. To make the best use of these and other libraries, I was aided by two grants from the American Philosophical Society; once again this distinguished organization facilitated my research.

In the course of my work Mr. Alfred A. Knopf shared his recollections of Mencken with me and also let me scan a considerable amount of correspondence between him and Mencken. I am grateful for that and likewise for permission from Alfred A. Knopf, Inc. to quote from these books by Mencken, listed in order of publication: *A Book of Burlesques; A Book of Prefaces; In Defense of Women; The American Language; Prejudices,* First through Sixth Series; *Notes on Democracy; Treatise on the Gods; Making a President; Treatise on Right and Wrong; Happy Days; Newspaper Days; Heathen Days;* and *Minority Report.* The same firm has given me permission to quote from *Pistols for Two,* jointly composed by Mencken and George Jean Nathan under the pseudonym of "Owen Hatteras" and from a compilation entitled *Menckeniana: A Schimpflexikon,* which Sara Haardt prepared.

For permission to quote from many letters by Mencken, as well as from his typescripts and family documents, I am indebted to the executor of the Mencken estate, the Mercantile-Safe Deposit and Trust Company of Baltimore, and particularly to Mr. William G. Frederick of its staff.

The chance to interview persons who knew Mencken was invaluable. I am grateful that I was able to get their recollections of Mencken from: Judge Thurman Arnold, Dr. Benjamin Baker, Miss Marion Bloom, Mrs. Ernest Boyd, Mr. James Bready, Mr. James Cain, Mr. Huntington Cairns, Mr. Louis Cheslock, Mr. Marquis Childs, Mr. Rodney Crowther, Mr. Watson Davis, Mr. George Dixon, Mr. Thomas Doerer, Mrs. Edmund Duffy, Mrs. Marcella duPont, Mr. A. D. Emmart, Mr. James T. Farrell, Miss Lillian Gish, Mrs. Augustus Goetz, Miss Jane Grant, Dr. Manfred Guttmacher, Sir William Haley, Mr. R. P. Harriss, Mr. Gerald Johnson, Mrs. Fred Kean, Mr. Alfred A. Knopf, Jr., Mr. Arthur Krock, Mrs. Charles Lappin, Mrs. John W. Lohrfinck, Miss Anita Loos, Admiral Leland Lovette, Mrs. C. S. Macdonald, Mrs. Lois Macks, Professor Kemp Malone, Mr. William Manchester, Miss Sara Mayfield, Mr. Stuart Olivier, Mr. George Oppenheimer, Mr. and Mrs. Hamilton Owens, Mr. John Owens, Mr. Maclean Patterson, Mrs. Paul

Patterson, Mrs. Robert Poindexter, Dr. Penelope Pearl Pollaczek, Miss Aileen Pringle, Dr. Arnold Rich, Mr. George Schuyler, Mr. Lawrence Spivak, the Right Reverend W. F. Stricker, Mr. C. P. Trussell, Mr. Louis Untermeyer, Dr. Philip Wagley, Mr. Philip Wagner, and Mrs. Marthe Ward.

I also benefited in my research from information given me by: Dr. Nicholas Alter, Professor Robert Baker, Mr. Montgomery Belgion, Professor Joseph Blotner, Professor Guy Forgue, Professor Ronald Gottesman, Professor and Mrs. William Hedges, Mr. Herbert Mitgang, Mr. Drew Pearson, Professor Moses Rischin, Professor Mark Schorer, and Mr. H. Allen Smith.

For the opportunity to see and draw on correspondence with Mencken I am grateful to these persons: Miss Marion Bloom (her own correspondence), Mr. Melville Cane (as executor of Sinclair Lewis's will, for Lewis's correspondence), Mr. Harold J. Dies (as trustee of the Dreiser Trust, for Dreiser's correspondence), Mrs. Marcella duPont (her own correspondence), Mr. James A. Genthner (Charles Abhau's correspondence), Mrs. Augustus Goetz (her father Philip Goodman's correspondence), Mrs. Joseph Hergesheimer (her husband's correspondence), Miss Olga Kelly (her father Dr. Howard Kelly's correspondence), Mr. Nicholas C. Lindsay (his father Vachel Lindsay's correspondence), Mr. Ferner Nuhn (as executor of Ruth Suckow's estate, for her correspondence), Mr. Maclean Patterson (his own and his father Paul Patterson's correspondence), Dr. Penelope Pearl Pollaczek (her father Raymond Pearl's correspondence), Mrs. C. Grove Smith (her father F. Scott Fitzgerald's correspondence), and Mr. James Stevens (his own correspondence).

Many writers inscribed the volumes they presented to Mencken and I appreciate the permission I have received to quote from several inscriptions of exceptional length. They include inscriptions by: Theodore Dreiser (permission from Mr. Harold J. Dies), F. Scott Fitzgerald (permission from Mrs. C. Grove Smith), and Bernice Lesbia Kenyon (Mrs. Walter Gilkyson).

For permission to quote from material that has not seen print I am indebted to: Mr. John Gunther (typescript on Mencken), Mrs. Joseph Hergesheimer (extract from her husband's autobiography), Mrs. David Morrison (extract from a television script), and Mrs. Hamilton Owens and the Oral History Collection, Columbia University (extract from the typescript of an interview with Mr. Owens). For permission to reprint published material I am indebted, first of all, to the *Sunpapers* of Baltimore for a good many phrases, and occasional longer passages, which Mencken wrote in the *Sunpapers*. I am also indebted to: Professor Charles Angoff (for material from his *H. L. Mencken: A Portrait from Memory* and from *Summer Storm*), the *New Yorker* (for an extract from its "Talk of the Town" department), Mr. George M. Rascoe (for an extract from Burton Rascoe's "The Literary

Spotlight, V"), the University of Pennsylvania Press (for brief extracts from the *Letters of Theodore Dreiser*, edited by Robert Elias), and Mr. Edmund Wilson (for an extract from his *New Republic* article "H. L. Mencken").

I owe a debt to each of the four books on Mencken which appeared before his death. Each contributed to my understanding of Mencken. Isaac Goldberg's *The Man Mencken* (1925) is based on facts furnished by Mencken himself; that is both its strength and its limitation. Ernest Boyd's *H. L. Mencken* (1925) is a brief biographical and critical study by a friend who knew Mencken as a writer as well as a man. Edgar Kemler's *The Irreverent Mr. Mencken* (1950) is an urbane biography by a young admirer who got much of his information from talking with Mencken. William Manchester's *Disturber of the Peace* (1950) is a vivid, detailed story of Mencken's life. It too benefited from the fact that its author could consult with his subject. Of these four books only one is documented, however. That is Edgar Kemler's and its documentation is not extensive. Quite properly, that meant that a new biographer like me had to begin afresh in assembling all possible data and in sifting evidence.

A fifth book, Charles Angoff's *H. L. Mencken: A Portrait from Memory* (1956) came out shortly after Mencken's death. To me it lacks perspective because of its author's antipathy to Mencken and all his works; if the book had been documented we would have been better able to assess Professor Angoff's charges. Nevertheless, it deserves careful consideration since it comes from someone who worked for Mencken over nearly a decade and studied him at length.

I drew here and there in my own book from each of the foregoing volumes and have acknowledged my specific debts in my notes. I have not drawn on two other, more recent books but I should say something about both. The first is Professor Guy Forgue's encyclopedic *H. L. Mencken: L'Homme, L'Oeuvre, L'Influence* (1967). Published in Paris, it reached me only after the great bulk of my investigating was over. The second is Sara Mayfield's *The Constant Circle* (1968). Miss Mayfield, who grew up with Sara Haardt, wrote her warmly appreciative volume on the Menckens against a background of close acquaintance. I would have gone to *The Constant Circle* often, except for the fact that Miss Mayfield had generously given me abundant information before the book appeared.

The pictures in my book come for the most part from the Mencken Room, where they are pasted into scrapbooks. Whenever I have found a more specific source, I have cited and acknowledged it in my text. In addition, I want to record my special thanks to: the *Sunpapers* (for the caricature of Mencken by Bertha Kelley and the photograph by Fred Miller of Mencken celebrating the end of Prohibition), the Mercantile-Safe Deposit and Trust Company (for the caricature of Mencken by Mencken himself),

Mr. Alfred A. Knopf (for the snapshots of Mencken with Nathan and of Mencken in Bethlehem), Mr. Edgar T. Schaefer (for the photographs of Mencken at the piano and in his backyard), *Life* (for Mr. Leonard McCombe's photograph of Mencken at the Wallaceite convention), and Mr. Aubrey Bodine (for the photograph of Mencken with his brother August). I also want to say a word of appreciation for the painstaking work by Mr. William Ochs of Baltimore, which resulted in the best possible reproductions.

At the Southern Illinois University Press my editor was a longtime friend, Mrs. Harry T. Moore. I owe more than a simple acknowledgment both to her and to the director of the press, Mr. Vernon Sternberg.

I wish to acknowledge the research assistance at the University of Maryland of Mr. George Bell, Miss Lorraine Janus, and Miss Marguerite Bloxom and the secretarial help, mainly typing, of these members of the English Department's office staff: Mrs. Paul Chadha, Mrs. Joseph DiCarlo, Miss Donna Hull, Miss Mary Kirkpatrick, Miss Linda Koelker, Mrs. Bruce Piringer, Mrs. Stephen Tranum, and Mrs. Loretta Willie. In addition, I had help in typing drafts from Miss Mary Slayton of the Department and from Mrs. Kayton Moses of Baltimore in transcribing tapes.

Lastly, I want to express my appreciation to the students in my Mencken seminar who shared some of their knowledge of Mencken with me, especially Dr. Herbert Simpson, who has become a specialist in the Mencken-Nathan relationship. Dr. Simpson has also helped in the proofreading of my manuscript.

University of Maryland   CARL BODE
College Park, Maryland

Notes

Abbreviations

AN 1925   The autobiographical notes compiled by Mencken, in the form of a two-hundred-page typescript, to help Isaac Goldberg write his *The Man Mencken* (1925). They are deposited in the Mencken Room of the Enoch Pratt Free Library in Baltimore.

AN 1941   The miscellaneous autobiographical notes Mencken composed chiefly from 1941 on, but especially in the early 1940s. They are deposited in the Mencken Room.

Angoff   *H. L. Mencken: A Portrait from Memory* (1956) by Charles Angoff. The source used is the paperback edition.

EPL   Enoch Pratt Free Library, Baltimore.

Goldberg *The Man Mencken* (1925) by Isaac Goldberg.

Kemler   *The Irreverent Mr. Mencken* (1950) by Edgar Kemler. The source used is the corrected paperback edition.

Manchester *Disturber of the Peace: The Life of H. L. Mencken* (1950) by William Manchester. The source used is the slightly revised paperback edition retitled *H. L. Mencken: Disturber of the Peace.*

MB   *H. L. M.: The Mencken Bibliography* (1961) compiled by Betty Adler with the assistance of Jane Wilhelm.

NYPL   New York Public Library.

Pennsylvania University of Pennsylvania Library.

Princeton Princeton University Library.

In the Notes to each section of the book I have tried to cite my main sources and acknowledge my debts. At times I have not been able to do this. Some information reached me with the understanding that the source would not be disclosed. (William Manchester has previously made the point. Some years after writing his life of Mencken he wrote one of the late President Kennedy. In the Introduction he observed, sensibly, that if he had not promised to keep his informants anonymous he would have had little information.)

In the Notes the page number of the text is given first, followed by the first three words of the sentence or passage to be annotated.

The scrapbooks cited are in the Mencken Room of the Enoch Pratt Library. I have used their short titles as given on the title page.

1 *Prehistory*

Page 3 "I am at": Mencken to Louise Pound, April 23 [1920]; *Princeton.*

Page 3 "I am thinking": Mencken to Theodore Dreiser, May 31 [1923]; *Pennsylvania*

Page 3 Ten years later: Mencken to Louise Pound, October 31, 1933; Duke University Library.

Page 3 A good twenty: Mencken to George Jean Nathan, February 8, 1945; Cornell University Library.

Page 4 Robert Frost was: Herbert Faulkner West, *The Impecunious Amateur Looks Back* (1966), p. 162.

Page 4 Walter Lippmann could: Lippmann's review of Mencken's *Notes on Democracy; Saturday Review of Literature,* December 11, 1926.

Page 4 He would stay: Except for a brief stint with the New York *Evening Mail* in World War I. Aside from that stint, he did no newspaper writing during either World War.

Page 5 Later labeled "The": The so-called caricature was the work of McKee Barclay of the *Sunpapers.* It was first entitled "An Inductive Synthesis," the idea being that a study of Mencken's splenetic columns had resulted in this cartoon of him.

Page 5 Even today such: Peter Edson's tribute to Mencken is in *The Press in*

Washington (1966), edited by Ray Eldon Hiebert, p. 25.

Page 5 As early as: The clippings go back to 1903. They have been collected and pasted in clipping books and are deposited in *EPL.* Mencken recalls in a *Smart Set* review (LI, 1917, 397–98) that he paid a clipping bureau five dollars for seventeen clipped reviews of his first book, *Ventures into Verse,* when it appeared in 1903.

Page 7 After all, Mencken: The estimate of the magnitude of Mencken's correspondence was given me by his brother August Mencken in our interview of November 29, 1966.

Page 7 Yet he himself: Mencken, *Minority Report,* p. 281.

Page 7 Elsewhere he remarks: Mencken to Joseph Hergesheimer, December 5, 1939; *Princeton.* He called *Happy Days* a mixture of fact and fiction, in a letter to his uncle Charles Abhau, who would have been in a position to know; Mencken to Charles Abhau, December 5, 1939; collection of Mr. James A. Genthner.

Page 7 Once, talking about: *Minority Report,* p. 59.

Page 7 As he told: Mencken to Marcella duPont, September 26, 1936; her collection.

2 Baltimore Boy

There are two basic sources for this chapter. One is the volume "Autobiographical Notes, 1925" in EPL. It is a typescript of some two hundred pages by Mencken; he prepared it as an aid to Isaac Goldberg, his first biographer. Goldberg, who knew little about him, sent him questions. Mencken answered them so fully and coherently that in effect he wrote a good part of Goldberg's book. He made some errors in his recollections but they are generally small factual ones. *The Man Mencken* was published in 1925. (The chapters in *AN 1925* dealing with Mencken's early life helped to suggest the content for some of the sketches that appeared in the *New Yorker* and were ultimately collected and expanded in *Happy Days.*) The other basic source is a box of miscellaneous autobiographical notes which Mencken set down from 1941 on. In the citations from *AN 1941* that follow, I use the first words of each note as a catchword since the notes are for the most part unpaged and unconsecutive. Supplementary data comes from a variety of sources. It is specifically documented except in a few cases where the source is confidential. In my interpretation of Mencken's relationship to his parents I have gotten help from Shirley Dinwiddie's paper, done in my seminar, "The Hearth and the Sword: A Study of Personality Variables in H. L. Mencken."

Page 9 Mencken later testified: *AN 1925*, p. 47.

Page 10 "My early life": *Happy Days,* p. vii. All quotations and citations from the three *Days* books are from the first collected edition, *The Days of H. L. Mencken* (1947).

Page 11 "The system of": *AN 1941*, note beginning "The system."

Page 12 Before Henry reached: His two account books in *EPL* and the third in the keeping of his executors show a steady increase in income and capital, except for a dip during the Depression. At his death he left an estate estimated at nearly $400,000.

Page 12 The most important: *Minority Report,* p. 50.

Page 12 Men might be: This is a standard theme in Mencken's Monday Articles from about 1932 till the end of the decade.

Page 13 Henry said the: *Happy Days,* p. 17.

Page 14 Henry himself developed: There is a scrapbook in *EPL* in which Henry's brother, August, assembled some of the joke and hoax items, such

as the printed letterheads for imaginary organizations. One of Mencken's most elaborate hoaxes was the invention of the Maryland madstones which he sent to his friends complete with official tag. Mr. A. D. Emmart of the *Sunpapers* still has his madstone and reports that its efficacy has by no means decreased with the passing of the years. Mencken first printed his imaginary history of the bathtub in the New York *Evening Mail* for December 28, 1917. There he solemnly alleged that the bathtub was unknown till the 1840s, was installed in the White House in the 1850s, and that President Millard Fillmore took the first presidential bath. By the time Mencken was middle-aged the story had become part of the American legend; his ponderings on the matter are contained in "Melancholy Reflections," which he wrote for the Chicago *Tribune* of May 23, 1926. It also appeared in several other papers and has since been reprinted at intervals.

Page 14 August had a: Mencken notes his father's pride of family in *AN*

1925, p. 41. In *AN 1925* he modernizes the spelling of his ancestors' names and I have followed his practice.

Page 15 What pride of: The family coat-of-arms on the cigar boxes is preserved in a sample pasted into the scrapbook "August and Anna Mencken and their Children," II, 150.

Page 15 One of the: *AN 1941*, note beginning "The old brewery."

Page 15 At twenty-one he: *AN 1925*, p. 109.

Page 15 A good son: Mencken's indulgence toward his niece is reflected in, for instance, his letter to Miss Marion Bloom of July 18 [1919]; her collection. His correspondence with Virginia (in *EPL*) shows him supporting her in college.

Page 16 Even as a: Mencken's childhood memories of his mother are preserved chiefly in *AN 1941*.

Page 16 Naturally enough Mencken: Mencken, copy of his communication to William Manchester, August 13, 1948; *EPL*.

Page 16 She wrote, "I": In the scrapbook "August and Anna Mencken and their Children," II, 147.

Page 17 Mencken's childhood memories: *AN 1941*, note beginning "My mother's liking."

Page 17 He recalled her: *AN 1941*, note beginning "I was clumsy."

Page 17 Looking back on: Mencken's character sketch of his mother is in *AN 1941*, note beginning "My mother was."

Page 18 In mid-career he: *AN 1925*, p. 191.

Page 18 When he did: Mentioned in my interview of August 18, 1965, with Miss Marion Bloom.

Page 19 For example, Mencken: *Manchester*, pp. 264–65.

Page 19 The fireplace itself: *AN 1941*, note beginning "The fireplace." In the note Mencken describes the alterations made in the house as the decades went along. In sum total they

were considerable, but spread over the years they suggest permanence, not change.

Page 19 He thanked him: Mencken to Dreiser, February 5 [1926]; *Princeton*.

Page 19 Yet a generation: Mencken to the Right Reverend J. B. Dudek, September 9, 1932; *Princeton*.

Page 20 In many ways: Data for this paragraph is from the chapter "My Boyhood and School Days," *AN 1925*.

Page 20 Old Professor Knapp: *AN 1925*, p. 60.

Page 21 Looking back, Mencken: *Happy Days*, p. 202.

Page 21 Under the heading: The text of "A New Platinum Toning Bath" is printed in *Goldberg*, pp. 82–83.

Page 21 They rejected it: *Newspaper Days*, p. 57.

Page 21 By Christmas of: *AN 1925*, p. 70.

Page 22 He reports in: *Happy Days*, p. 167.

Page 22 At the end: *AN 1925*, p. 73.

Page 23 As Goldberg put: *Goldberg*, pp. 89–90.

Page 23 "The very idea": *AN 1941*, note beginning "My life has."

Page 24 The school called: Mencken's relations with the Cosmopolitan University are shown in the documents in the scrapbook "Earliest Attempts at Verse and Prose, 1895–1901."

Page 24 Some of them: *Ibid.*, p. 64.

Page 24 By November he: *Ibid.*, p. 78.

Page 24 He wrote only: *AN 1941*, note beginning "My life has."

Page 24 If during the: He was probably too clumsy to like dancing.

Page 24 According to Goldberg: *Goldberg*, p. 84.

Page 24 He wrote her: *Kemler*, p. 18.

Page 25 And then Goldberg: The boy was indeed initiated into the cruder realities of sex; his medical record at eighteen shows a case of chronic urethritis.

Page 25 He filled out: The test is

pasted in the scrapbook "Childhood and Schooldays, 1880–96," p. 81. He gives his age as nineteen but he was clearly younger.

Page 25 "By the summer": *AN 1925,* p. 81.

Page 25 He started to: *AN 1925,* p. 85.

Page 26 In the first: *Goldberg,* p. 95 for the reference from the biography.

Page 26 But the emotion: Some of it went into the short stories he wrote.

In one year, apparently, 1900, he produced four which had as their point the successful defiance of authority. Two, both unpublished, are dated 1900 and are preserved in the scrapbook "Typescripts of Early Fiction." They are "The Conquest of the Cop" and "The Exploit of Kelly and Razorback." "The Cook's Victory" was published in 1900 and "The Flight of the Victor" in 1901, the former in *Short Stories* and the latter in *Frank Leslie's Popular Magazine.*

3 *Daily and Sundays*

Mencken's own stories, as collected in *Newspaper Days, 1899–1906,* must furnish the background for any history of his early development as a newspaperman. (There is nothing substantial in print on his whole newspaper career.) For its relation to his writing there is Douglas Stenerson, "Mencken's Early Newspaper Experience: The Genesis of a Style," *American Literature,* XXXVII (1965), 153–66.

Page 27 In *Newspaper Days:* P. 3.

Page 27 Not really: He had published some doggerel in the Baltimore *American* but did not feel it tactful to tell Ways.

Page 28 Finally, impressed by: Mencken inscribed a copy of *Ventures into Verse* to him with "To my old friend Wells Hawks who put me in the business." The date is June 14, 1903, and the inscribed copy is listed in *A Census of Ventures into Verse* (1965) compiled by Betty Adler, p. 20.

Page 28 On February 23: From the start Mencken clipped his news stories and saved them for pasting in his scrapbooks. With the principal exception of some early stories for the *Herald* which were lost in Baltimore's Great Fire and some early and miscellaneous pieces for the *Sunday Sun,* his newspaper writing has been preserved in the scrapbooks.

Page 28 Today they rest: Mencken dates this scrapbook 1899–1901.

Page 29 One hot day: August 21, 1899.

Page 29 A Berkshire boar: January 18, 1900.

Page 29 Or there is: February 12, 1900.

Page 30 As the man: *Newspaper Days,* p. 262. Mencken tells the whole story in the chapter called "The Synthesis of the News."

Page 30 Thereafter, Mencken says: *Ibid.,* p. 265.

Page 31 With success came: *Ibid.,* p. 40.

Page 31 Mencken characterized him: *Ibid.,* p. 41.

Page 31 Hayes wrangled constantly: *Ibid.,* p. 45.

Page 31 He reported, for: "Early News Stories: Baltimore Morning Herald," p. 292.

Page 31 Undaunted, Mencken concocted: *Newspaper Days*, pp. 50–51.

Page 32 However, he also: Mencken's tribute to Ways is found in "Max Ways as H. L. Mencken Knew Him," *Sun*, June 6, 1923. He takes a more dyspeptic view of his early instruction at the *Herald* in *Minority Report*, p. 292. And in a letter to H. C. Byrd, June 7, 1937 (*EPL*) he says, "I learned a good deal from studying the writings of an editorial writer on the old New York Sun named [Edward] Kingsbury."

Page 32 With his eye-glasses: Mencken describes his debt to Carter in *Newspaper Days*, pp. 111–12, in particular.

Page 33 In a passage: *Ibid.*, p. 163.

Page 33 He advised Mencken: *Ibid.*

Page 33 It was an: Except for a time after his stroke.

Page 33 The current music: *Ibid.*, p. 141.

Page 34 And Mencken's assistant: *Ibid.*, p. 142.

Page 34 It was from: *Ibid.*, p. 143.

Page 34 On a typical: *AN 1925*, p. 85.

Page 35 Max Ways gave: The trip made an impression on Mencken which was never erased. It not only made him feel somewhat better, it opened new horizons for him.

Page 35 Christened "Rhyme and": On November 18, 1900 "Rhyme and Reason" was renamed "Knocks and Jollies." It ran well into February 1901. "Terse and Terrible Texts" appeared irregularly from December 3, 1900 to May 13, 1901; in all there were nineteen of the "Texts." "Baltimore and the Rest of the World" ran from May 20, 1901 to September 23 and usually appeared on Mondays, Wednesdays, and Fridays. The first of the "Untold Tales" appeared in the final "Knocks and Jollies" column in February. Those that followed, thirty-two in all, came out at intervals in either the *Sunday Herald* or the *Morn-*

ing Herald. They were spread out over a little less than a year, the final one appearing on February 2, 1902.

Page 35 Interspersed were some: For example, the columns for February 9 and 16, 1902, which are here referred to.

Page 36 As he told: "Early Newspaper and Magazine Work, 1899–1905," p. 24.

Page 36 He quoted the: *Ibid.*, p. 21.

Page 36 He implied years: *Newspaper Days*, p. 94.

Page 36 By the end: Mencken describes his editorial responsibilities in *Newspaper Days*, pp. 127–39.

Page 37 Out went the: By pure luck Mencken was able to buy some better travel articles and he substituted those.

Page 37 As Mencken said: *AN 1925*, p. 88.

Page 37 He found it: *Ibid.*

Page 38 As Mencken admitted: P. 137.

Page 38 He dispatched a: *Newspaper Days*, p. 138.

Page 38 His copyboy in: The data in the rest of the paragraph and in the paragraph following comes from my interview with Thomas Doerer, May 3, 1966.

Page 39 What he found: *Newspaper Days*, p. 277.

Page 39 He went into: *Ibid.*, p. 278.

Page 41 Its board of: *The Sunpapers of Baltimore*, p. 268.

Page 41 The pay was: *Newspaper Days*, p. 313.

Page 41 Watterson replied with: On August 25, 1906, Colonel Watterson took more than a full column to tease Mencken in return. The quoted paragraph opens the editorial.

Page 42 "The question whether": *AN 1941*, note beginning "I was never."

Page 42 "The Weakness of": This editorial is pasted into the scrapbook "Editorials and Other Articles, The

Baltimore Evening Sun, vol. I, 1910–1912," p. 75.

Page 43 It became of: The Free Lance started on May 8, 1911 as "The World in Review"; the next day it became "The Free Lance." It ended on October 23, 1915.

Page 44 And, as Mencken: *AN 1925*, p. 94. He recalls the full story in "The Wowsers State Their Case," *Evening Sun*, January 17, 1927.

Page 44 "I lost all": *Ibid.*, p. 95.

Page 45 The Free Lance: *Ibid.*

Page 45 When Mencken rained: Mencken says, in an addendum to a letter, that he never attacked a man who could not hit back and that he often insisted in the *Sun's* letting those whom Mencken attacked answer in the letters columns. Mencken to Burton Rascoe, summer 1920(?); *Pennsylvania.*

4 *The Apt Apprentice*

Page 46 He boasted in: *Newspaper Days*, p. ix.

Page 47 Many of these: "Earliest Attempts at Verse and Prose, 1895–1901."

Page 47 There is his: Mencken says in the note prefixed to "Idyl's" handwritten pages that it was "strongly influenced by the contemporary *Ladies Home Journal* school!" The piece is dated March 28, 1896.

Page 47 His first poem: Mencken saved many of the letters accepting his poetry and pasted them into "Earliest Attempts at Verse and Prose."

Page 47 When his very: Mencken lists the two dozen poems printed before *Ventures into Verse; AN 1925*, pp. 123–24.

Page 48 He gave it: The publishing history of *Ventures into Verse* is complicated by Mencken's varying recollections. Sometimes there are two friends who want to do the publishing, sometimes three; there are three members of the firm according to the imprint in the volume itself. There were either seventy-five or one hundred copies printed or slightly over one hundred; Mencken paid either thirty dollars or sixty dollars toward the cost of printing. The story is told, and the

variants noted, in *A Census of Ventures into Verse* compiled by Betty Adler. Mencken's own most comprehensive account is in *Newspaper Days*, p. 64.

Page 48 Looking back later: *Newspaper Days*, p. 62.

Page 49 The Milwaukee *Sentinel:* July 28, 1903.

Page 49 The Chicago *Record:* August 17, 1903.

Page 49 He reminisced about: *Prejudices: First Series*, p. 129.

Page 50 "Exact and scientific": *Newspaper Days*, p. 112.

Page 50 Mencken's early reviews: His first steps in criticism are documented in the scrapbook "Editorials, Dramatic Reviews and Other Contributions to the Baltimore Morning Herald and the Baltimore Evening Herald, 1904–1906."

Page 50 Here he is: *Ibid.*, p. 26.

Page 51 This time it: *Newspaper Days*, p. 122.

Page 51 Also he increased: *Ibid.*, p. 91.

Page 51 "I was naturally": *Ibid.*, p. 123.

Page 51 "Managers and critics": "Editorials, Dramatic Reviews and Other Contributions to the Baltimore Morning Herald and the Baltimore Evening Herald, 1904–1906," p. 27.

Page 52 When the noted: *Ibid.*, p. 164.

Page 52 In the theatrical: *Newspaper Days,* p. 126. He may have been exaggerating the number, to make a good story.

Page 52 In the space: The record of Mencken's early success as a short-story writer is preserved in the scrapbooks "Typescripts of Early Fiction" and "Early Newspaper and Magazine Work, 1899–1905."

Page 53 Mencken found his: The book on Shaw came out in 1905 and Mencken (twenty years later) put the next year as the point when his true prose style developed; *AN 1925,* p. 125. It might be best to say that the writing of his *Shaw* allowed his style to jell and that the jelling came in 1906.

Page 53 Here, incidentally, he: Mencken notes his admiration for Huxley's style in *AN 1925,* p. 74.

Page 53 He apparently told: *Kemler,* pp. 30–32. Kemler sets Mencken's stylistic maturing a little later than Mencken does himself.

Page 54 As Mencken observed: *Newspaper Days,* p. 74.

Page 54 Mencken proposed to: The facts about his publication of the book on Shaw are contained in *AN 1925,* pp. 125, 137.

Page 55 In the case: Schaff's letter of August (?), 1925 is printed in *Goldberg,* pp. 371–77.

Page 55 "If you live": *Newspaper Days,* p. 307.

Page 56 It is from: *George Bernard Shaw: His Plays,* p. x.

Page 57 He interested a: The circumstances of Mencken's and Koppel's translations are given in the Introduction to *A Doll's House,* which Luce published in 1909.

Page 57 In 1903, he: *Newspaper Days,* p. 121.

Page 58 He wrote a: In a scrapbook called "Attempts at Plays" there are three more dramatic efforts: *John Smith: A Fantastic Comedy; Morals,* based on a German drama by Ludwig Thoma and put into American speech by Mencken in collaboration with George Jean Nathan; and *The Goat,* which exists only in an extended synopsis and Act I. But one farce in which he collaborated with Nathan was both published and often at the point of being produced. Called *Heliogabalus,* it dealt with the infatuation of a randy Roman emperor with a Christian maiden. Knopf printed it in 1920 and it quickly sold out. Mencken describes its tangled history in the acting script "Heliogabalus: A Buffoonery," p. 1; *EPL.*

5 *The* SMART SET *Era*

The most judicious study of the *Smart Set* and Mencken's relation to it is the extensive Introduction by Carl Dolmetsch in his *The Smart Set: A History and Anthology* (1966). Mencken's own recollections, of those now available, are set down in the typescript of an interview he gave William Manchester on June 2, 1947 (copy in *EPL*), along with some corrections in his letter to Manchester of June 16, 1947 (copy in *EPL*).

Page 60 At any rate: *Manchester,* p. 57 (though the Manchester interview puts the time of year later).

Page 60 There were three: In the Manchester interview Mencken said that he wrote to his friend Channing Pollock, then drama critic at the *Smart Set,* and asked him whether the job had been offered at his suggestion. Pollock said no. Then Mencken thought of Dreiser, wrote him, and Dreiser also said that he had not suggested Mencken for the job. Then Mencken wrote Splint, who said that Norman Boyer had suggested him. Two weeks after the Manchester interview Mencken wrote Manchester (June 16, 1947; copy in *EPL*) making the slight correction mentioned above. That is, he said that he simply assumed that Pollock had proposed him and so did not bother to write Pollock till long afterward. He discovered in 1916 or 1917 that Pollock was not responsible for the suggestion, when Pollock apparently wrote confirming the fact in answer to Mencken's query. Then Mencken said he wrote Dreiser and got Dreiser's no. And it was not until the early 1940s that Mencken wrote Splint and was told about Boyer. Consequently, Mencken observed to Manchester, he was in ignorance for some forty years as to who had recommended him.

Page 61 And when Goldberg: Dreiser's communication to Isaac Goldberg, August 24, 1925, printed in *Goldberg*, pp. 380–81. This was also once Mencken's understanding: *AN 1925*, p. 110.

Page 61 As Mencken retold: *Manchester*, pp. 57–58. Dolmetsch (p. 25) puts their first meeting a year later.

Page 61 As Nathan remembered: In his "The Happiest Days of H. L. Mencken," *Esquire*, XLVIII (1958), 146–50.

Page 61 Some fifteen years: Mencken's recollections in "Fifteen Years," *Smart Set*, LXXII (1923), 139.

Page 65 The history of: But Dolmetsch's study has helped a good deal.

Page 66 Attracted by Wright's: Mencken to Willard Huntington Wright, January 16 [1912]; *Princeton*.

Page 66 Mencken felt the: Manchester interview. According to Dolmetsch, Thayer offered the editorship to Nathan after offering it to Mencken.

When both refused he named Boyer managing editor. Dolmetsch says further that Wright himself persuaded Thayer to make him editor, over Boyer, after first persuading Thayer to make him an associate editor.

Page 66 When after a: Manchester interview.

Page 66 One day he: Mencken's pessimistic view of Thayer is given in the letter to Dreiser of November 12 [1912]; *Pennsylvania*. The optimistic one is given in the letter of November 11 [1912]; *Pennsylvania*.

Page 66 When Wright ran: Mencken to Willard Huntington Wright, before June 1913; *Princeton*.

Page 66 On the one: Mencken to Harry Leon Wilson, February 8, [1914]; *Princeton*.

Page 66 "Be very careful": Mencken to Willard Huntington Wright, before August 1913; *Princeton*.

Page 66 "We must get": *Ibid.*

Page 66 But that would: H. G. Wells, *The New Machiavelli* (1911), p. 391.

Page 67 He wrote to: Mencken to Willard Huntington Wright, March 17 [1913(?)]; *Princeton*.

Page 67 The differences between: Mencken to Harry Leon Wilson, February 8 [1914]; *Princeton*.

Page 67 Mencken wrote to: Mencken to Dreiser, March 18, 1914; *Pennsylvania*.

Page 67 In a long: Mencken to Harry Leon Wilson, February 8 [1914]; *Princeton*. The letter outlines the whole story of the magazine's troubles at this time.

Page 67 As Thayer moved: Manchester interview.

Page 68 The post of: Dolmetsch authenticates this story (pp. 44–45), though Mencken told Manchester a slightly different version (Manchester interview).

Page 68 They took over: Mencken to Dreiser, August 13 [1914]; *Pennsylvania*.

Page 68 To cut costs: Manchester interview.

Page 69 "Nothing to 'improve' ": "The November Number of Smart Set," *Smart Set*, XLIV (1914), 37.

Page 69 "Dusk in War-Time": Mencken to Mrs. Ernest Filsinger (Sara Teasdale), February 23 [1915]; *Princeton*.

Page 69 On October 14: Mencken to Ernest Boyd, October 14, 1916; *Princeton*.

Page 69 For example, in: Mencken to Ernest Boyd, March 20, 1917; *Princeton*.

Page 70 In January 1918: Mencken to Ernest Boyd, January 8 [1918]; *Princeton*.

Page 70 "We escaped," Mencken: Mencken to Ernest Boyd, October 14 [1916]; *Princeton*.

Page 70 Crowe was then: *AN 1925*, p. 114.

Page 71 The full irony: The book is deposited in *EPL*. Mencken actually started the book in 1914 but incorporated the figures for 1913 in it.

Page 71 Mencken once put: Manchester interview.

Page 71 He quotes some: *The Intimate Notebooks of George Jean Nathan* (1932), pp. 98–106 *passim*.

Page 73 There is, for: Mencken to Nathan, February 2 [1917]; Cornell University Library.

Page 73 There is an: Mencken to Nathan, according to internal evidence written early in 1915; Cornell University Library.

Page 73 He wrote, for: Mencken to Vincent Starrett, July 12, 1917; *Princeton*.

Page 74 At the end: Mencken to Ernest Boyd, June 29 [1918]; *Princeton*.

Page 75 Neither Mencken nor: For Mencken, Nathan put it pungently when he reported, "he succumbs . . . to any poem about a dog (however bad)"; *Pistols for Two*, p. 31.

Page 75 Starting early in: The two men were engagingly casual about some of their writing. For instance, Owen Hatteras's "Litany for Magazine Editors" was printed under Nathan's name in the *Bookman*, XXXXIII (1916), 280–83, and under Mencken's in his *A Book of Burlesques* the same year.

Page 75 Mencken masqueraded even: Mencken's pseudonyms are listed in *MB*, pp. 348–49.

Page 76 In a letter: Mencken to Nathan, February 2 [1915, apparently]; Cornell University Library.

6 *Writers and Rotarians*

Page 78 To Mencken they: Of course when it came to businessmen his barbs were not directed at Rotary and the Rotarians alone. He could be caustic too about the Kiwanis Clubs, about the Lions, and others; his general target was the businessmen's service societies.

Page 79 The literary genres: The drama was also involved, chiefly in New York, but to a lesser degree; see Chapter 4 for Mencken's attitude.

Page 79 As Mencken said: "Thomas Henry Huxley, 1825–1925," *Evening Sun*, May 4, 1925.

Page 79 He said explicitly: *AN 1925*, p. 74.

Page 79 He was further: *Ibid*.

Page 80 During the last: Indianapolis *Journal*, September 17, 1898.

Page 80 In Henry May's: First published in 1959; the source used here is the paperback edition of 1964.

May's book concentrates on the years between 1912 and 1917.

Page 81   He starts an: *Sun,* September 22, 1906.

Page 81   In another article: *Sun,* November 5, 1909.

Page 81   In still another: *Sun,* March 13, 1910.

Page 82   Even William Dean: Obituary of Howells, *Evening Sun,* May 13, 1920.

Page 82   He had become: Mencken to Harry Leon Wilson, September 4 [1911]; *Princeton.*

Page 82   As Mencken once: "Fifteen Years," *Smart Set,* LXXII (1923), 140.

Page 82   Though his book: Or Fred Splint—we can take our choice.

Page 82   He grandly declared: P. 198.

Page 82   As Henry May: P. 195.

Page 83   Young as he: The relation of Mencken's ideas to Nietzsche's and the extent of Mencken's reliance on him are described in Edward Stone, "Henry Louis Mencken's Debt to Friedrich Wilhelm Nietzsche" (Master's thesis, University of Texas, 1937).

Page 83   For that matter: *The Philosophy of Friedrich Nietzsche,* p. viii.

Page 83   Mencken considered him: *Ibid.,* p. 261.

Page 83   To Mencken this: *Ibid.,* p. 117.

Page 84   He plowed through: Mencken outlines the circumstances of the composition of the book about Nietzsche in *AN 1925,* pp. 125–26.

Page 84   For example: "It": *The Philosophy of Friedrich Nietzsche,* pp. 215, 217.

Page 84   They seldom disagreed: New York *Times,* September 15, 1908.

Page 84   The reviewer for: July 1, 1908.

Page 85   As the *Nation:* April 2, 1908.

Page 85   He said so: Mencken's account of the origins of *Men versus the Man* is in *AN 1925,* pp. 127–28.

Page 85   "I'd change the": *Ibid.,* p. 128.

Page 86   But he was: In his *Vandover and the Brute* the lycanthropy is made figurative but it is still there. Vandover even goes naked on all fours.

Page 86   Another story, *The:* "Various Bad Novels," *Smart Set,* XL (1913), 159.

Page 86   So did the: Mencken was reviewing *McTeague,* originally issued in 1899, because it had just come out in a fifty cent edition. *Ibid.*

Page 86   This was high: Norris was working for the publisher Doubleday and tried his best to smooth the way for *Sister Carrie.*

Page 86   When London preached: Mencken crisply sums up London's merits and demerits in *Prejudices: First Series,* pp. 236–39. The quotation is on p. 239.

Page 87   "He had a": P. 22.

Page 87   He killed himself: *Ibid.,* p. 33.

Page 88   Reviewing *The Moneychangers: Smart Set,* XXVI (1908), 156.

Page 88   On the other: *Smart Set,* XXXIV (1911), 156.

Page 88   And he extolled: *Smart Set,* XL (1913), 160.

Page 89   The result was: Some of the briskest contention is embodied in their correspondence now in the Lilly Library at Indiana University.

Page 89   When time finally: Upton Sinclair to Huntington Cairns, November 4, 1953; Library of Congress.

Page 89   As Bliss Perry: P. 73.

Page 90   Mencken considered that: "The Coroner's Inquest," *Smart Set,* LIX (1919), 141.

Page 90   About it, Mencken: "What is Style?", *Mercury,* IV (1925), 381.

Page 90   Mencken scorned both: After Mencken's stroke in 1948, he was offered the Gold Medal of the Academy. His secretary, Mrs. Rosalind Lohrfinck, was not clear about the implications of the offer and so she accepted on his behalf. When he and his brother August became aware of what had happened August tried to decline the medal. However, it would have proved too embarrassing to say no at this late date, and so the medal was officially awarded. August Mencken's file of letters on the matter is in *EPL.* He also told me the story on June 7, 1963.

Page 92 He once remarked: *Prejudices: First Series,* p. 61.

Page 92 When his death: *Ibid.,* p. 62.

Page 93 He cannot avoid: "Rattling the Subconscious," *Smart Set,* LVI (1918), 138.

Page 94 Their great opportunity: *Ibid.,* p. 140.

Page 94 Mencken read him: He once said that he learned more from Pollard than from anyone else except Robert Carter, especially about the value of a critic's concentrating on a few men; in addendum to an undated letter to Burton Rascoe, probably written late in 1919; *Pennsylvania.*

Page 94 He met Pollard: A sketch of Mencken's relations with Pollard, along with the macabre story of his funeral, is in *Kemler,* pp 47–50. Mencken himself reminisced about Pollard's end in *AN 1941,* note beginning "The matter referred," and also says something about him in *Prejudices: First Series,* pp. 129–31.

Page 95 Mencken happened on: *Prejudices: First Series,* p. 129.

Page 95 When Huneker gave: Mencken to Fielding Garrison, November 17, 1919; *Princeton.*

Page 96 Though it printed: *Prejudices: First Series,* p. 84.

Page 96 Often crude and: *Ibid.,* p. 86.

Page 96 His "gorgeous rhapsodies": *Ibid.,* p. 87.

Page 96 By 1919, when: *Ibid.,* p. 89.

Page 96 Robert Frost had: *Ibid.,* p. 90.

Page 96 But of late: *Ibid.*

Page 97 The influences that: *Ibid.,* p. 95.

Page 97 The first among: Mencken told Fielding Garrison that he thought the best recent poetry was in Sandburg's *Chicago Poems,* Oppenheim's *The Book of Self,* and McClure's *Airs and Ballads.* Mencken to Fielding Garrison, June 2, 1919; *Princeton.*

Page 98 In *The End:* P. 295. As a matter of fact, the *Forum* had already begun to turn liberal when Kennerley became its publisher in 1910.

Page 99 Mencken, surveying the: "The American Magazine," *Prejudices: First Series,* p. 174.

Page 99 Currently, and regrettably: *Ibid.,* pp. 176–77.

Page 100 He was especially: "Critics of More or Less Badness," *Smart Set,* XXXXIV (1914), 152–54.

Page 100 It provided the: However, in between "The American: His New Puritanism" and "Puritanism as a Literary Force" he did an interesting newspaper article. Called "Notes for a Proposed Treatise upon the Origin and Nature of Puritanism," it appeared in the *Evening Sun* of October 25, 1915.

Page 100 In it Mencken: P. 198.

Page 100 In a burst: *Ibid.,* pp. 201–2.

Page 101 At the end: *Ibid.,* p. 283.

Page 101 As Mencken told: Mencken to Dreiser, July 28 [1916]; *Pennsylvania.*

Page 101 In New York: His story is told in full in Heywood Broun and Margaret Leech, *Anthony Comstock: Roundsman of the Lord* (1927).

Page 102 Looking back on: *Who's Who in America, 1928–1929.*

Page 102 Mencken called him: Mencken to Burton Rascoe, May 9 [1919]; *Pennsylvania.*

7 Dreiser and the Fruits of Dissidence

Page 103 This to Mencken: Mencken to Dreiser, March 3 [1911]; *Pennsylvania.*

Page 103 Then too, Mencken: His fellow Baltimorean, the playwright George Bronson Howard, had given him a copy toward the end of 1900; *AN 1925*, p. 74.

Page 103 But they were: Dreiser to Mencken, August 23, 1907; *Pennsylvania.*

Page 104 A Baltimore doctor: Mencken summarizes the process in the inscription to his gift copy of *What You Ought to Know about Your Baby* for Paul Patterson's collection of Menckeniana; collection of Maclean Patterson.

Page 104 As Dreiser remembered: *Goldberg*, p. 379.

Page 104 Their correspondence reflects: The great bulk of the Dreiser-Mencken correspondence is at the University of Pennsylvania Library, but a considerable number of duplicates are in the collections of the Princeton University Library. I have depended chiefly on the holdings at the University of Pennsylvania. Occasionally I have had to draw on Robert Elias's admirable published edition of Dreiser's letters (3 vols., 1959). There are twenty-one envelopes of letters from Dreiser among Mencken's restricted papers in the New York Public Library, according to the typescript volume "Correspondents in H. L. Mencken's Letter File New York Public Library," *EPL.*

Page 104 He wanted the: Dreiser to Mencken, July 11, 1909; Elias, *Letters of Theodore Dreiser*, I, 92.

Page 104 During 1909 he: By now they were close friends and exchanged visits. Mencken's letter of November 15 [1909], for instance, outlines a program for a visit by Dreiser to Baltimore which includes dinner and a burlesque show; *Pennsylvania.*

Page 105 "I seize every": Mencken to Dreiser, March 14 [1911]; *Pennsylvania.*

Page 105 When it was: Dreiser's inscription in Mencken's copy; *EPL.*

Page 105 Mencken found it: Mencken to Dreiser, April 23 [1911]; *Pennsylvania.*

Page 105 It fulfilled his: *Ibid.*

Page 105 Five months after: Mencken to Dreiser, September 20 [1911]; *Pennsylvania.*

Page 105 Mencken had thought: Dreiser to Mencken, October 24, 1912; *EPL.*

Page 105 Mencken warned him: Mencken to Dreiser, December 10 [1912]; *Pennsylvania;* the book is in *EPL.*

Page 106 Mencken found in: Mencken to Dreiser, March 23 [1914]; *Pennsylvania.*

Page 106 When in August: "We are practically in charge of the magazine. Thayer has packed his goods and left." Mencken to Dreiser, August 13 [1914]; *Pennsylvania.*

Page 106 They settled on: Mencken liked Dreiser's short story "The Lost Phoebe" but Nathan did not. And Mencken may have been using Nathan as a shield.

Page 106 They were not: Dreiser to Mencken, October 13, 1914; Elias, *ibid.*, I, 178–79.

Page 106 Mencken soothed him: Mencken to Dreiser, October 14, 1914; Elias, *ibid*, I, 179–80; and Dreiser to Mencken, October 15, 1914; Elias, *ibid.*, I, 180–81; and Dreiser to Mencken, November 30, 1914 (saying he was sending Mencken *The "Genius"*); Elias, *ibid.*, I, 183.

Page 106 This time he: Inscription in *EPL* copy.

Page 106 Considerably before this: Dreiser's sexual life is described in W. A. Swanberg's outstanding biography *Dreiser* (1965), as is the controversy over *The "Genius."*

Page 107 As he remarked: Mencken to Dreiser, July 28 [1916]; *Pennsylvania.*

Page 107 But he added: *Ibid.*

Page 107 The censors wanted: *Kemler*, p. 79.

Page 107 He recalled his: *AN 1925*, p. 114.

Page 107 He did everything: Some of the opening efforts are described in Mencken's letter to Gordon Ray Young, September 2, 1916; *Pennsylvania.* He added that if the moralists beat Dreiser they would go on to undreamed-of excesses.

Page 107 Mencken expostulated and: Mencken to Ernest Boyd, October 9, 1916; *Princeton.*

Page 108 "I am working": Mencken to Marion Bloom, letter undated but envelope postmarked November 15, 1916; collection of Miss Bloom.

Page 108 The situation improved: Mencken to Dreiser, November 13, 1916; *Pennsylvania.*

Page 108 Stanchfield was joined: Mencken to Ernest Boyd, November 13, 1916; *Princeton.*

Page 108 In a letter: Mencken to Ernest Boyd, April 20, 1918; *Princeton.*

Page 108 He told Dreiser: Mencken to Dreiser, November 12 [1914] *Pennsylvania.*

Page 109 "May all Englishmen": Mencken to Dreiser, December 15 [1914]; *Pennsylvania.*

Page 109 Sherman dealt his: In the issue for November 2, 1915.

Page 109 "The Nation article": Mencken to Dreiser, December 8 [1915]; *Pennsylvania.*

Page 109 In the spring: Mencken to

Ernest Boyd, [April (?), 1917]; *Princeton.*

Page 110 He characterized Sherman's: I (1917), 509.

Page 110 He got to: *Ibid.*, p. 511.

Page 110 He did so: The essay is entitled simply "Theodore Dreiser."

Page 111 He wrote Boyd: Mencken to Ernest Boyd, December 15 [1917]; *Princeton.*

Page 112 While a tide: Besides this Free Lance column of May 8, 1915, others that show Mencken's pro-German attitude include those dated June 25, September 11, and October 16; all of 1915.

Page 112 "The truth that": But the opposition had the last word; in the letters to the editor the *Evening Sun* printed "An Answer to Mencken from the Trenches in Flanders," December 18, 1915.

Page 113 He proved to: Mencken to Ernest Boyd, October 14 [1916]; *Princeton.*

Page 113 He sailed on: He tells the story of his voyage in letters to his mother; scrapbook, "Germany, 1917," *passim.* This is not the typescript account of his experiences in Germany mentioned below.

Page 113 Disembarking, he journeyed: Mencken tells the story of his German adventures in the typescript "Berlin, February, 1917 . . . Being the Diary of H. L. Mencken"; *EPL.*

Page 113 He saved more: They are in the scrapbook "Germany, 1917."

Page 114 Meanwhile he had: Aboard ship going home, he wrote fifty thousand words in ten days and sent his reports on events in Germany to the *Sun* when he docked at Havana. Most of what he sent was published; some, he recalled later, was killed. *AN 1925*, p. 48.

Page 114 "The cold here": "Berlin, February, 1917," p. 12.

Page 114 Mencken enjoyed his: "More of it will go in my book, 'The Diary of a Retreat,'" Mencken to Ellery Sedgwick, April (?), 1917; *Princeton.*

Page 114 By good luck: Mencken's own zestful account of his adventures in Havana is in "Gore in the Caribbees" in *Heathen Days.*

Page 115 Then he made: "At work on the revolution all day. I have managed to reach . . . both sides." This was on March 6. "Berlin, February, 1917," p. 189; *EPL.*

Page 115 Mencken came home: The final dispatch appeared on March 29, 1917.

Page 115 Then he and: He still had friends in the office but he also had enemies. One was John Haslup Adams, who told him that all persons of German blood deserved the troubles they were having. Mencken never forgave him. "Minority Report: H. L. M.'s Notes," April 5, 1940; *EPL.*

Page 115 The only one: He himself reported that he was induced to write for the paper by Cullen. The publisher was Dr. Edward Rumely, who was already being investigated by the federal government as a possible German agent and did not wish to inflame the authorities further by inviting Mencken to write pro-German pieces for the *Evening Mail.* Rumely was later sentenced to Sing Sing. Mencken describes the episode in his letter to Ernest Boyd of July 23, 1918; *Princeton.*

Page 116 Good though the: *Ibid.*

Page 116 Its history started: *AN 1925,* p. 131.

Page 116 Mencken had recently: Mencken to Harry Leon Wilson, May 27 [1913]; *Princeton.*

Page 116 The next logical: *AN 1925,* p. 131.

Page 117 The comrade was: "Carbon Copy of Original Typescript of A Little Book in C Major"; *EPL.*

Page 117 Years later A: Mencken to Daniel M. Henry, quoted in Mary Elizabeth Starin, "An Eastern Shore Friend," *Menckeniana,* No. 22 (1967), 8.

Page 117 Again they proved: The texts which provide the basis for this statement can be found in *EPL.*

Page 118 The first was: *AN 1925,* p. 132.

Page 118 When he sent: Mencken to Harry Rickel, November 4 [1919]; *Princeton.*

Page 119 A Book of: *Tribune* for December 16, 1917; *Star* for November 11, 1917 (however, the *Star* had some reservations); *News* for December 12, 1917; *Republican* for October 21, 1917. On the whole the reviews, both in the newspapers and in the magazines, were mixed but with the good predominating.

Page 119 When In Defense: Among the favorable reviews were those in the New York *Globe* for October 28, 1918, the Detroit *Journal* for November 2, 1918, the Washington *Star* for October 20, 1918, and the San Francisco *Bulletin* for January 11, 1919.

Page 119 Few reviews resembled: On the other hand, on the same day, the year before, when the *Tribune* had praised *A Book of Prefaces* it had also printed one of Stuart Sherman's blasts against Mencken.

Page 120 It dated back: *AN 1925,* pp. 132–33 ff.

Page 120 He prepared the: "The American Language . . . Original Typescript, 1915–16," Preface; *EPL.*

Page 120 The slender typescript: *AN 1925,* p. 133.

Page 121 "Such is American": "The American Language . . . Original Typescript, 1915–16," p. 43.

Page 121 Alfred Knopf worried: But by June 30, 1919 Knopf's royalty statement showed that 1,373 copies had been sold; and this meant, when review copies had been deducted, nearly all available. Statement in *EPL.*

Page 122 Mencken would correspond: The correspondence: *Princeton.*

Page 122 Though Mencken felt: Mencken to Bernard Smith, July 25, 1930; *Princeton.*

Page 123 Mencken decided, however: *AN 1925,* p. 134.

Page 123 Only a handful: Los Angeles *Times,* November 30, 1919.

Page 123 The literary essays: The definitive piece of work on Mencken in this field has been done by William H. Nolte in *H. L. Mencken: Literary Critic* (1966).

Page 123 Mencken's indictment grew: *Prejudices: First Series,* p. 217.

Page 125 Before he finished: P. 45.

Page 125 "Criticism itself," he: "A Soul's Adventures," *Smart Set,* XLIX (1916), 153.

Page 126 Mencken was even: "A Road Map of the New Books," *Smart Set,* XXVII (1909), 153.

Page 126 "The aim in": "The Anatomy of the Novel," *Smart Set,* XLIII (1914), 153.

Page 127 He summed it: Mencken, typescript, 1923, for George Müller, the Munich publisher of the German edition of *In Defense of Women; EPL.*

Page 128 The critical review: P. 87.

Page 128 Sherman's chief contribution: Published by the Committee on Public Information.

Page 129 In a postwar: *New Republic,* September 29, 1920.

Page 129 He wrote his: Mencken to Fielding Garrison, August 30, 1918; *Princeton.*

Page 130 A month before: Mencken to Ellery Sedgwick, October 8 [1918]; *Princeton.*

8 *Good Company*

Page 132 In 1902 he: *AN 1925,* p. 154. There is a good sketch of the history of the Club in Louis Cheslock's affectionate *H. L. Mencken on Music* (1961), pp. 207–15.

Page 132 The first professional: Cheslock, *ibid.,* pp. 207–8.

Page 132 Max Broedel, a: Mencken, undated note on Broedel (or Brödel); *Princeton.*

Page 133 A group photograph: "Photographs and Other Portraits of H. L. Mencken, 1881–1936," p. 11. However, Wright's name is not given beneath the photograph.

Page 133 The "amiable weakness": Mencken, "The End of a Happy Life," *Evening Sun,* November 21, 1932.

Page 133 Hemberger, for example: Theodor Hemberger to Mencken, September 1, 1916; *EPL.*

Page 133 Several other members: Especially in the middle and late periods of the Club's existence. An example from the middle period is Raymond Pearl, from the late period Dr. Arnold Rich.

Page 133 He himself did: Several of his compositions are in *EPL.*

Page 134 He once said: *Happy Days,* p. 196.

Page 134 He termed his: He bewailed the lack in *Happy Days, ibid.* Disagreeing with Mencken's own estimate of his musicianship Louis Cheslock says that it was good; "Mencken—The Musician," *Sun,* September 9, 1956. Writing a quarter century after the event, he remembers the first time he heard Mencken play; it was with "proficient dignity" and "fine sensitivity to dynamics and mood."

Page 134 "The world presents": P. 47.

Page 134 Basically the music: Mencken to Fanny Butcher, February 20, 1921; *Princeton.*

Page 134 He described his: *Goldberg,* pp. 178–83.

Page 134 Next he put: The quotation on Schubert is from *ibid.,* p. 179.

Page 135 It also contained: The point about operas and light operas is that Mencken liked their music when instruments played it, but the human voice left him indifferent.

Page 135 The earliest to: Emile Odend'hal, "I Remember . . . Mencken's Florestan Cocktail," *Evening Sun,* October 28, 1956.

Page 135 This Club survived: Mencken, undated note on Max Broedel; *Princeton.*

Page 135 In the early: Hamilton Owens, Oral History interview, July 24, 1958, p. 47; copy in collection of Mrs. Hamilton Owens.

Page 135 In the middle: "Hamilton Owens at Opening of the Mencken Room," typescript; collection of Mrs. Hamilton Owens. Originally a recording, it has been transcribed in *Menckeniana,* No. 23 (1967), 4–9.

Page 135 During the "Thirteen": Mencken to Max Broedel, July 23, 1923; *Princeton.*

Page 135 Mencken wrote a: Mencken to Jim Tully, June 29, 1933; *Princeton.*

Page 135 For the playing: The move is noted in a photo of April 24, 1937, "H. L. Mencken: Photographs and Drawings, Mostly Made in 1937–1938," p. 7.

Page 136 The Club met: "Photographs and Other Portraits of H. L. Mencken, 1881–1936," p. 25.

Page 136 The picture for: *Ibid.,* p. 57.

Page 136 The membership posed: "H. L. Mencken: Photographs and Drawings, Mostly Made in 1937–1938," p. 7.

Page 136 A reasonably representative: Mencken to Raymond Pearl, November (?), 1927; collection of Dr. Penelope Pearl Pollaczek.

Page 136 The accustomed call: "Hamilton Owens at Opening of the Mencken Room," typescript; collection of Mrs. Hamilton Owens.

Page 137 As he looked: *AN 1941,* note beginning "As a newspaper man."

Page 137 And after he: *Ibid.,* note beginning "It would be false."

Page 138 Mencken once observed: LIX, 67.

Page 138 But during the: Mencken tells the story of his relations with Goodman in the introduction to the volumes of typescript copies of their correspondence; *EPL.*

Page 138 As Goodman's daughter: My interview with Ruth Goodman Goetz, October 2, 1963; this interview and those of May 22, 1964 and July 23, 1964 supplement—and to a certain extent correct—Mencken's account prefacing the volumes mentioned above.

Page 139 Though he proved: "Letters to Philip Goodman," I, 1.

Page 139 Meanwhile, however, he: *Ibid.,* p. 3. That he went especially for the yeast is a story I have also heard from August Mencken (my interview, November 29, 1966).

Page 139 He wrote Dreiser: Mencken to Dreiser, September 10 [1923]; *Pennsylvania.*

Page 139 He did a: *AN 1941,* note beginning "One of my."

Page 139 And he was: "Violent agnostic" was Mencken's term.

Page 139 Much different from: The information about Ernest Boyd comes in good part from my interview with his widow, Madeleine Boyd, of June 24, 1963.

Page 140 Nathan reported that: *The Intimate Notebooks of George Jean Nathan* (1932), p. 61. He further characterized Boyd as a remarkably well-informed hedonist who could talk with anybody; *ibid.*, pp. 53–63 *passim.*

Page 140 At the meeting: Mencken to Ernest Boyd, August 5 [1918); *Princeton.*

Page 140 Both clubs continued: Mencken to Ernest Boyd, February 3 [1919]; *Princeton.*

Page 140 "I have written": Mencken to Ernest Boyd, undated letter probably of 1917; *Princeton.*

Page 141 Mencken's letters to: In fact for this period the letters to Boyd are the best single source of information about what Mencken is doing and thinking.

Page 141 On June 29: Mencken to Ernest Boyd, June 29 [1918]; *Princeton.*

Page 141 He published four: The volume on Mencken was slim indeed, running to only eighty-nine pages.

Page 142 He was not: Mencken to Jim Tully, May 27 [1925]; *Princeton.*

Page 142 To Boyd himself: Mencken to Ernest Boyd, August 30 [1925]; *Princeton.*

Page 142 One of the: The factual data on Patterson's career is given in *The Sunpapers of Baltimore.* Information about his relationship with Mencken comes from their correspondence now in the collection of Patterson's son Maclean; from my interviews with Maclean Patterson of January 12 and August 17, 1965; from my interview with his mother and him of February 8, 1965; and from a veteran member of the *Sunpapers* staff.

Page 142 When Mencken prepared: Copy in the collection of Maclean Patterson.

Page 143 Once Patterson gained: Patterson-Mencken correspondence, collection of Maclean Patterson; and my interview with Mrs. Paul Patterson, February 8, 1965.

Page 143 Mencken treated him: Mencken to Paul Patterson, January 10 [1923]; collection of Maclean Patterson.

Page 143 With his slow: My inter-

view with James Cain, June 3, 1963.

Page 144 Raymond Pearl quickly: The personal information on Pearl which follows comes almost entirely from my two interviews with his younger daughter, Dr. Penelope Pearl Pollaczek, of February 23 and February 24, 1965. It is supplemented by my examination of his diaries and his correspondence with Mencken. The diaries, the letters from Mencken, and some carbons of the letters from Pearl are all in her collection.

Page 146 "He had an": Mencken, "Raymond Pearl," *Sun,* November 24, 1940.

Page 167 One day in: Mencken to Raymond Pearl, February 17, 1925; collection of Dr. Penelope Pearl Pollaczek.

Page 148 When Pearl died: My interview with Huntington Cairns, May 7, 1963.

Page 148 For instance, he: Hamilton Owens, Oral History interview, July 24, 1958, pp. 48–49; copy in the collection of Mrs. Hamilton Owens.

Page 149 On the 17th: Howard A. Kelly to Mencken, October 17, 1912; the Kelly correspondence is all in *EPL.*

Page 149 On the 31st: *Ibid.*

Page 149 In the middle: *Ibid.*, November 17, 1912.

Page 149 The month after: *Ibid.*, December 29, 1912.

Page 150 In a letter: *Ibid.*, October 12, 1913.

Page 150 One time he: *Ibid.*, November 10, 1915.

Page 150 Another time he: *Ibid.*, April 9, 1914.

Page 150 Kelly's Christmas card: *Ibid.*, December (?), 1926.

Page 150 Kelly would write: *Ibid.*, April 9, 1914.

Page 150 His note for: *Ibid.*, December 24, 1914.

Page 150–51 Mencken wrote to: Mencken to A. H. McDannald, May 2 [1922]; *EPL.*

Page 151 Calling him "the": *AN 1941*, note beginning "The most implacable."

Page 151 As he put: Mencken to Fielding Garrison, February 23, 1921; *Princeton.*

Page 152 For instance, he: Mencken to Dreiser, February 5 [1913]; *Pennsylvania.*

Page 152 She was Marion: My interview with Miss Bloom, July 27, 1965.

Page 152 She invited him: Mencken to Marion Bloom, February 18 [1914]; collection of Miss Bloom. It should be added that Mencken put the year on few of the letters he sent her but she preserved a good many of the envelopes, so that most of the letters can be dated from them. Most of the postmarks are legible. The letters to her that follow are from her collection. Three folders of letters from her are in the restricted correspondence Mencken sent to *NYPL.*

Page 152 He continued to: *Ibid.*, July 1 [1914].

Page 152 After dinner Marion: He assured Dreiser that it made at least twelve miles an hour on level roads. Mencken to Dreiser, probably November 19, 1915; *Pennsylvania.*

Page 152 He sent her: Mencken to Marion Bloom, November 11 [1914].

Page 152 Accepting some of: *Ibid.*, undated; but the envelope is postmarked November 24 and the year is presumably 1914.

Page 152 In a letter: Mencken to Dreiser, apparently December 27, 1916; *Pennsylvania.*

Page 152 In an earlier: *Ibid.*, November 2 [1915]; *Pennsylvania.*

Page 153 Mencken continued to: Mencken to Marion Bloom, undated but probably early 1915.

Page 153 She listened amiably: *Ibid.*, undated but in envelope dated April 23, 1915.

Page 153 Thereafter he might: *Ibid.*, undated but perhaps October 27, 1916.

Page 153 In a long: Marion Bloom to Mencken, November 1, 1916; copy made by Miss Bloom.

Page 153 It ends with: LI (1917), 31.

Page 153 He told Ernest: Mencken to Ernest Boyd, June 29 [1918]; *Princeton.*

Page 153 Mencken wrote Marion: Mencken to Marion Bloom, letter marked with pen, September 21, 1918.

Page 154 Much moved, Mencken: *Ibid.*, undated but with envelope dated in pencil 1918.

Page 154 She sailed for: Mencken to Ernest Boyd, September 28 [1918]; *Princeton.*

Page 154 On her return: My telephone interview with Miss Bloom, May 25, 1968.

Page 154 He was well: Mencken to Marion Bloom, September 11; year dated in pencil as 1919 or 1920.

Page 154 Occasionally he could: *Ibid.*, April 4; year probably 1920 or 1921.

Page 154 For her part: My interview with Miss Bloom, July 27, 1965.

Page 154 She feels, probably: Mencken first printed it in "Répétition Générale," *Smart Set*, LXV (1921), 40.

Page 154 At other times: My interview with Miss Bloom, July 27, 1965.

Page 155 After a while: Marion's letter of accusation is lost: Mencken's reply, telling her that he has torn up his long letter and is distraught, has been preserved by her; March 24 [1923].

Page 155 She announced it: Undated memorandum of Miss Bloom.

Page 155 After he got: Mencken to Marion Bloom, August (?), 1923; copy made by Miss Bloom. Incidentally, he did smoke a pipe at times.

Page 155 To her sister: Mencken to Estelle Bloom Kubitz, August 10, 1923; copy made by Miss Bloom.

Page 155 She submitted a: My interview with the former Beatrice F. Wilson, now Mrs. C. Stuart Macdonald, July 26, 1964.

Page 155 The half-sheet notes: Mencken's correspondence with Mrs. Macdonald remains in her possession. Her own is apparently lost. It is not in *NYPL.*

Page 156 Mencken found many: Mencken to "Bee" Wilson, March 15 [1925(?)].

Page 156 Bee was on: Actually, she had merely met Woollcott. My letter from Mrs. Macdonald, August 16, 1968.

Page 156 When Maugham came: My interview with Mrs. Macdonald, October 1, 1963.

Page 156 About one short: Mencken to "Bee" Wilson, June 12 [1925(?)].

Page 156 About another he: *Ibid.,* July 20 [1925]. Mencken does not give the year but mentions that he has just returned from the Scopes trial.

Page 157 "Dear Bee," he: *Ibid.,* March 15 [1924 or 1925].

Page 157 She remarked once: My interview with Mrs. Macdonald, July 26, 1964.

Page 157 They met in: Letter to me from Aileen Pringle, April 3, 1968.

Page 157 Miss Pringle recalls: My interview with Miss Pringle, May 24, 1963.

Page 157 And Aileen was: Mencken to Fielding Garrison, August 5, 1926; *Princeton;* Miss Pringle is not identified by name in the letter but recalls the incident.

Page 158 She treated him: The bulk of the information to follow comes from my interview with Miss Pringle.

Page 158 Mencken reported to: July 26 [1926]; *Princeton.*

Page 159 "There was some": "Valentino," *Evening Sun,* August 30, 1926.

Page 159 When he himself: The most extensive account of Mencken's visit to Hollywood is in *Kemler,* pp. 220–

21 and 225–28. It varies considerably both from the account in *Manchester* and Miss Pringle's recollections. It is obvious that here Mencken was of little help to his biographers; he plainly enjoyed the legends that grew up around his foray.

Page 159 Though Mencken had: *Kemler,* p. 220.

Page 159 And the few: *Manchester,* p. 263.

Page 159 Studio cameramen caught: Prints of the pictures mentioned here are to be found in the scrapbook "Photographs and Other Portraits of H. L. Mencken, 1881–1936."

Page 160 It is probable: The stag party story is from *Manchester,* pp. 263–64, with local color from an anonymous informant of mine.

Page 160 It is probable: Mencken apparently gave the Betty Compson story to both Kemler and Manchester.

Page 160 It is certain: Mencken boldly confessed to seeing the three movies in an interview with James Quirk, under the title of "The Low-Down on Hollywood," in *Photoplay* magazine for March 1927.

Page 160 It is certain: The account of the Cruze party and its aftermath is from my interview with Miss Pringle of May 24, 1963, amplified by our telephone interview of November 29, 1968.

Page 161 He wrote Miss: My interview with Miss Pringle, May 24, 1963. Jame Cain also mentions the matter in his letter to Mencken of June 19, 1946; Library of Congress.

Page 161 The veteran newspaperman: My interview with Arthur Krock (in company with Huntington Cairns), June 25, 1963.

Page 161 All three were: The information to follow comes chiefly from my interview with Miss Loos of October 30, 1964.

Page 162 With Mencken's help: *Bazar,* spelled that way in those days.

Page 162 "It made me": Mencken to "Bee" Wilson, November 7 [1925].

Page 162 During the 1920s: For various reasons, principally personal but also connected with limitations of space, I am not able to go into these friendships.

Page 163 In Washington there: She was the daughter of a veteran Washington correspondent for the AP, Edwin Hood.

Page 163 He told Nathan: Mencken to Nathan, March 2 [1926]; Cornell University Library.

Page 163 In one letter: Mencken to Hergesheimer, July 27, 1927; *Princeton*.

9 *The Paradise of Traders and Usurers*

Page 165 Of them Harold: *America and the Young Intellectual*, pp. 11–12.

Page 165 "Often, in fact": *Civilization in the United States*, p. viii.

Page 165 He warned Nathan: Mencken to George Jean Nathan, October 27(?), 1920; quoted in *Manchester*, p. 161.

Page 165 Mencken proclaimed to: "Peasant and Cockney," *Evening Sun*, January 3, 1921.

Page 166 He could still: "Lewis and his Novel," *Evening Sun*, March 21, 1927.

Page 166 And he could: *Ibid.*

Page 167 But Mencken soon: "Gamalielese," *Evening Sun*, March 7, 1921.

Page 168 His successor, Calvin: "Autopsy," *Evening Sun*, November 10, 1924.

Page 168 "The United States": "Golden Age," *Prejudices: Fifth Series* (1926), p. 272.

Page 168 In mid-decade he: "The Golden Age," *Evening Sun*, February 9, 1925.

Page 169 His aim, Mencken: "A Carnival of Buncombe," *Evening Sun*, February 9, 1920.

Page 169 Mencken derided the: "The Voter's Dilemma," *Evening Sun*, November 3, 1924.

Page 169 In the first: *Saturday Evening Post*, February 7, 1920. Here and elsewhere in this chapter I have been guided in the interpretation of social events especially by *Progressivism and Postwar Disillusionment, 1898–1928* (1966), edited by David Shannon.

Page 169 In the second: *Ibid.*

Page 170 As Mencken put: "A Carnival of Buncombe," *Evening Sun*, February 9, 1920.

Page 170 He jeered at: "The Intelligentsia," *Evening Sun*, March 16, 1920.

Page 170 In the article: "Government by Blackleg," *Evening Sun*, September 27, 1920.

Page 170 As Mencken once: Mencken to Dreiser, January 3, [1919]; *Pennsylvania*.

Page 170 For example, in: Mencken to Ernest Boyd, March 12 [1920]; *Princeton*.

Page 170 In April 1920: Mencken to Ernest Boyd, April 3 [1920]; *Princeton*. The book finally appeared anonymously as *The Story of a Lover*, to the accompaniment of mixed reviews.

Page 172 The League's Washington: The Reverend E. C. Dinwiddie in *Proceedings* (1915), p. 55.

Page 172 For instance, when: Mencken to Ernest Boyd, January 18 [1919]; *Princeton*.

Page 173 When the law: Mencken to Ernest Boyd, December 6 [1921(?)]; *Princeton.*

Page 173 One summer he: Mencken to A. H. McDannald, July 1 [1926]; *EPL.* In 1930 Mencken kept a record of his brewing, including both processes and recipes. For example: 5 oz. Bohemian hops, 3 lbs. corn; brewed October 17; bottled October 22. He adds that in this batch one bottle exploded. "Book Orders" notebook, p. 15; *EPL.*

Page 174 Privately he asserted: In conversations with, for instance, Stuart Olivier, James Cain, and Dr. Manfred Guttmacher.

Page 175 Writing for instance: Mencken to Ernest Boyd, October 9, 1916; *Princeton.*

Page 175 "Let some preposterous": Mencken to Ernest Boyd, March 9 [1918]; *Princeton.*

Page 177 Yet their sexual: "The Sex Uproar," *Nation*, July 23, 1924.

Page 178 "Women, as a": *In Defense of Women* (1922), p. 130.

Page 178 There had never: The politics, and indeed the flavor, of this period is caught remarkably well in two works I have drawn on. The first is the final volume of Mark Sullivan's *Our Times* (1935), which goes to 1925. The second is Frederick Lewis Allen's *Only Yesterday: An Informal History of the 1920's* (1931).

Page 178 To his Cabinet: "Moral Reflections," *Evening Sun*, February 25, 1924.

Page 179 This has been: "Teapot Dome," *Evening Sun*, February 4, 1924.

Page 179 Mencken remarked that: "Exit," *Evening Sun*, March 4, 1929.

Page 179 Still, he was: On Coolidge's honesty: "Twilight," *Evening Sun*, October 17, 1927. On his caddishness:

"The Voter's Dilemma," *Evening Sun*, November 3, 1924.

Page 180 "Short of ideas": "Off the Grand Banks," *Evening Sun*, September 7, 1925.

Page 180 He epitomized his: "Clown Show," *Nation*, June 27, 1928.

Page 180 In the middle: Mencken summarizes how *Notes on Democracy* was composed in his inscription to the typescript he gave to Alfred Knopf; *EPL.*

Page 181 *Notes on Democracy:* Mencken remarked that most of the notices were "furiously hostile." Headnote to additional typescript in *EPL.*

Page 181 In 1928 Paul: Paul Elmer More, "The Demon of the Absolute," *New Shelburne Essays*, I (1928), 2–11. St. John Ervine, "America and the Nobel Prize," *Philadelphia Inquirer*, December 16, 1928. Anon., "The Passing of H. L. Mencken," *Bookman*, LXX (1929), 186–88.

Page 182 He found something: The list of writers is based on William Manchester's analysis in his Master's thesis, "A Critical Study of the Works of H. L. Mencken as a Literary Critic of the Smart Set Magazine, 1908–1914" (University of Missouri, 1947); *EPL.*

Page 184 Here is massed: Nearly all the sources are to be found in the text itself. Additional information follows.

Page 184 From Willa Cather: The date of her letter is February 27, doubtless 1925.

Page 184 From burly Paul: The date of his letter is April 2, probably 1926.

Page 185 "Dear Menck," Fitzgerald: His letter on *The Great Gatsby* is tipped into *Flappers and Philosophers* and is dated May 4, 1925.

Page 186 There is, for: The date of his letter tipped into *Babbitt* is January 21, 1922.

Page 186 "Dear Menk," it: The date of his letter is March 16, doubtless 1922.

Page 187 Tipped into the: The date of his letter is March 24, doubtless 1927.

Page 187 The letter tipped: The date of his letter is April 12, doubtless 1929.

Page 188 Zelda Marsh (1927): The date of his letter is merely "Wed the 19th."

Page 190 As Burton Rascoe: Quoted in Ernest Boyd, *H. L. Mencken* (1925), p. 77.

10 *Mainstay of the* SUN

Page 191 To Ernest Boyd: Mencken to Ernest Boyd, November 9 [1919]; *Princeton.*

Page 191 He liked the: Red account book; *EPL.*

Page 192 In early March: Mencken to Ernest Boyd, March 3 [1920]; *Princeton.*

Page 192 Years later Mencken: *Manchester*, pp. 172–73.

Page 192 After the Republican: Mencken to Ernest Boyd, June 17, 1920; *Princeton.*

Page 192 He assured Patterson: I have not found Patterson's letter but its existence is implied in Mencken's answer of October 10 [1920], in the collection of Patterson's son Maclean.

Page 193 He took an: The basis for the description of Mencken's relationship to Hamilton Owens is my series of interviews with him from October 1962 through 1964. These are supplemented by Owens's remarks in "Hamilton Owens at Opening of the Mencken Room"; typescript, collection of Mrs. Hamilton Owens.

Page 193 With his Monday: "Hamilton Owens at Opening of the Mencken Room."

Page 193 On September 3: Mencken to Hamilton Owens, September 3 [1924]; collection of Mrs. Hamilton Owens.

Page 194 On May 5: Mencken to Hamilton Owens, May 5, 1925; collection of Mrs. Hamilton Owens.

Page 194 On September 12: Mencken to Hamilton Owens, September 12 [1928]; collection of Mrs. Hamilton Owens.

Page 194 On December 15: Mencken to Hamilton Owens, December 15 [1928]; collection of Mrs. Hamilton Owens.

Page 194 On July 28: Mencken to Hamilton Owens, July 28, 1931; *Princeton.* The sentence was never carried out.

Page 194 It was hard: Data about the relationship on the *Sunpapers* of Paul Patterson to Mencken is drawn chiefly from the correspondence, now in the collection of Maclean Patterson, supplemented by interviews with Maclean Patterson and with a veteran *Sun* staff member.

Page 194 Did Patterson need: All the correspondence basic to this paragraph took place during 1920.

Page 194 Here, for example: Paul Patterson to Mencken, February 25, 1920; copy in the collection of Maclean Patterson.

Page 195 He wrote to: Paul Patterson to H. C. Black, March 29, 1922; copy in the collection of Maclean Patterson. Actually Mencken was elaborating on an idea of Black's.

Page 195 As a basis: *The Sunpapers of Baltimore* (1937), edited and in part written by Mencken, pp. 369–73.

Page 195 His answer took: Mencken

to Paul Patterson, July 21 [1928(?)]; collection of Maclean Patterson.

Page 196 John Owens's answer: John W. Owens to Paul Patterson, undated memorandum; collection of Maclean Patterson.

Page 197 In a memorandum: H. C. B[lack] to Paul Patterson, undated memorandum; collection of Maclean Patterson.

Page 197 Dated January 1937: Mencken to Paul Patterson, memorandum and accompanying note; collection of Maclean Patterson.

Page 198 When the Newspaper: My interview with August Mencken, September 10, 1963.

Page 198 He wrote the: Mencken to Sidney Howard, April 14, 1936; copy in the collection of Maclean Patterson.

Page 199 At the beginning: Hamilton Owens, Oral History interview, July 23, 1958, pp. 63–64; copy in the collection of Mrs. Hamilton Owens.

Page 199 As Hamilton Owens: *Ibid.*, p. 64.

Page 199 He took to: Philip Wagner,

"Mencken Remembered," *American Scholar*, XXXII (1963), 267.

Page 200 The arch-liberal was: *Manchester*, p. 330.

Page 200 "I have two": Mencken to Mrs. Rosalind Lohrfinck, April 22, 1938; *Princeton*.

Page 200 Two classic cases: My interview with August Mencken, July 22, 1964.

Page 201 When the *Sun:* My interview with Hamilton Owens, November 30, 1962.

Page 201 The Archbishop of: The course of the controversy is reflected in the pages of the *Catholic Review* for June 22, June 29, July 6, July 13, and July 20, 1934.

Page 203 The opinions expressed: "Travail," *Evening Sun*, October 8, 1928.

Page 205 He wrote Owens: Mencken to Hamilton Owens, April 15, 1930; collection of Mrs. Hamilton Owens.

Page 206 He never tired: "Off the Grand Banks," *Evening Sun*, September 7, 1925.

11 *The* MERCURY: *The Web*

Page 208 Then, in a: "The Literary Spotlight, V," *Bookman*, LIV (1922), 551–54.

Page 209 Such were two: The principal appreciations of Mencken for the years 1920–22 are listed in *MB*, pp. 298–304.

Page 209 When Edmund Wilson's: Mencken to Edmund Wilson, May 26, 1921; *Princeton*.

Page 209 The main gap: The typescript list of Mencken's correspondents whose letters are restricted in *NYPL* notes that there are three envelopes of, presumably, Nathan's letters. Over 360 letters from Mencken to Nathan are deposited at the Cornell University

Library, but they do not begin in numbers till 1923. There is one letter there from Nathan to Mencken.

Page 210 It received the: In the New York *Sun*, December 6, 1920.

Page 211 Among the answers: The "Note" is part of an addendum to an undated letter to Burton Rascoe, probably written late in 1919; *Pennsylvania*.

Page 211 In its way: It was entitled *George Jean Nathan: A Critical Study* (1925) and issued as one of the "Little Blue Books" published by Haldeman-Julius.

Page 211 He characterized the: *Goldberg*, pp. 218–23.

Page 212 The *Credo* discloses: *Ibid.*, p. 223.

Page 213 They included, Nathan: *The Intimate Notebooks of George Jean Nathan*, p. 42.

Page 213 In a charming: 1922 edition, pp. 207–8.

Page 213 And Nathan remarks: *The Intimate Notebooks of George Jean Nathan*, p. 306.

Page 213 For one: "Since": *Ibid.*, p. 281.

Page 213 It was far: For my account of the origins of the *Mercury*, particularly as they concerned Mencken and Nathan, I have drawn mainly on *Kemler*, pp. 163–66; M. K. Singleton, *H. L. Mencken and the* American Mercury *Adventure* (1962), pp. 28–37; Alfred Knopf's extensive recollections; a few recollections of August Mencken (my interview of November 12, 1963); and Herbert Simpson's University of Maryland dissertation, "Mencken and Nathan" (1965).

Page 214 And the new: At one point, in fact, a plan was discussed with the Knopfs to take over the *Smart Set;* Mencken's annotations, apparently, on the *Princeton* transcript of his letter to Alfred Knopf of March 5, 1923.

Page 214 A dozen titles: Singleton, *H. L. Mencken and the* American Mercury *Adventure*, p. 33.

Page 214 One was what: From Mencken's point of view, as Knopf recalls it, the chances of a clash were not great. Knopf has told me that in those days the partnership was so solid that Mencken could not conceive of its being broken.

Page 215 The other question: The memorandum of agreement on which the *Mercury* was ultimately based is dated December 11, 1923. Besides giving Knopf the deciding vote, it specifies that "Mencken and Nathan agree to work as editors without salary until such time as all agree, by mutual consent, that salaries, and their

amount, shall be paid"; J. C. Lesser (treasurer of Alfred A. Knopf, Inc.) to me, November 19, 1965.

Page 215 In September Knopf: Copy in *EPL*.

Page 215 But it did: Knopf's recollections as shared with me.

Page 215 Looking back later: *AN 1925*, p. 116.

Page 215 "I'm going nuts": *Kemler*, p. 171.

Page 215–16 For instance, Emily: Quoted in *Ingénue among the Lions*, edited by Gerald Langford (1965), p. 185. The date of the letter is supplied in brackets.

Page 216 He sent the: Mencken to Nathan, October 15(?); Cornell University Library. The year is not given in this letter or the succeeding ones but here it is surely 1924; for Mencken says in *AN 1925*, p. 116, "Toward the end of 1924 — that is toward the end of our first year — I notified Knopf and Nathan that there would have to be a rearrangement."

Page 216 Mencken came back: The letter is in the Cornell University Library.

Page 217 Mencken himself referred: Mencken to Philip Goodman, April 28, 1925; "Letters to Philip Goodman," vol. I; *EPL*.

Page 218 The brusque opening: Mencken to Nathan, May 3, probably 1925; Cornell University Library. But Knopf says the actual negotiations were long and tiresome.

Page 218 According to Ernest: P. 9.

Page 218 Goldberg remarked, in: P. 217.

Page 218 According to Knopf: Knopf's recollections.

Page 218 He had Nathan's: Knopf's recollections.

Page 218 He still had: Knopf's recollections.

Page 219 When Mencken's mother: Nathan wrote in fact as soon as he learned that she was seriously ill;

Mencken replied on December 12 [1925]; Cornell University Library.

Page 219 The most amusing: Mencken to Nathan, undated letter but noted as being written during the first week of September 1930; Cornell University Library.

Page 219 Staring straight at: In a direct hit at Mencken the *Spectator* also remarked in its opening editorial that "Another defect of the average magazine is that its editor often permits himself to remain in harness long after his imaginative oats have given out and the magazine thereafter continues simply as a matter of habit."

Page 219 In his letter: Dreiser to Nathan, October 7, 1933; *Pennsylvania*.

Page 219 In a letter: The letter is in the Knopf files.

Page 220 Yet in a: Mencken to Jim Tully, February 12, 1935; *Princeton*.

Page 220 "As a result": P. 94.

Page 220 Knopf's relationship with: My main source for the relationship between the two men has been the Knopf files. Kept over many years, they are now incomplete. There are evident gaps in the correspondence, and here and there I judge that letters have been removed or lost. I have been able to supplement these files with Knopf's recollections. Herbert Simpson's dissertation, mentioned before, has also been a help; so have the recollections of Alfred A. Knopf, Jr., about the later part of the relationship.

Page 220 By 1920 the: Knopf's recollections.

Page 221 Mencken wrote Burton: Knopf's recollections. But it should be added that neither Knopf nor Mencken's brother August could recall even a temporary rift.

Page 221 As early as: "Books for the Hammock and Deck Chair," *Smart Set*, XXVIII (1909), 158.

Page 221 Mencken stuck to: His only repeated complaint to others was that he had to do too much of the promotional work for his books, work that the Knopf firm should have done.

Page 221 Mencken's reply was: *Letters of H. L. Mencken* (1961), ed. Guy Forgue; p. 227.

Page 222 In a controversy: Mencken to Theodore Dreiser, November 21 [1934]; *Pennsylvania*.

Page 222 In the Knopf: There is, however, a letter for February 4, 1921 which Knopf begins with "Dear Menck." And there may be others which I have not seen.

Page 222 Knopf has remarked: Knopf's recollections.

Page 222 Until the end: On the other hand, things did not look that way to Mencken when he was old and becoming ill. In the typescript notes on his physical state now in *EPL* he wrote (August 18, 1945) about the "difficulties with Nathan and the Knopfs" which followed the launching of the *Mercury*. However, he saved the particulars for the detailed history of his magazine days.

Page 222–23 Music meant a: Knopf's recollections.

Page 223 They relished their: Knopf's recollections. However, they missed the Festivals from 1925 to 1927.

Page 223 Though Mencken was: *Evening Sun*, May 21, 1928.

Page 223 Knopf remembered him: The search for beer in Bethlehem figures vividly in the recollections Knopf shared with me.

Page 224 When Boston's Watch: The "Hatrack" case is described in some detail in Chapter 13 of this book.

Page 224 A highly beneficial: Knopf's recollections are clear on how this arrangement worked in general. It should be added that the chapter and verse fill a whole series of files in the Knopf office.

Page 225 Weaver, an advertising:

Mencken to Knopf, December 13, 1919; Knopf files.

Page 225 William Carlos Williams: Knopf's recollections.

Page 225 Of her he: The letter about Ruth Suckow was actually addressed to Franklin Spier of the Knopf firm; August 9, 1921; Knopf files.

Page 225 He also tried: He succeeded with Miss Suckow but not with Milburn.

Page 225 His happiest suggestion: Knopf's recollections.

Page 225 Mencken reported, "This": Mencken to Knopf, April 2, 1921; Knopf files.

Page 226 It seemed to: Mencken to Knopf, August 3, 1931; Knopf files.

Page 226 For instance, he: Knopf's recollections.

Page 226 Knopf reports hearing: On Eisler, Mencken to Knopf, November 18, 1931; Knopf files. On a good history of Christianity, Mencken to Knopf, (?); Knopf files. On an attractive looking Bible, Mencken to Knopf, (?); Knopf files.

Page 226 There his stellar: Knopf's recollections.

Page 227 In 1932 the: Knopf to Mencken, August 4, 1932; Knopf files.

Page 227 The *Mercury* in: Singleton's *H. L. Mencken and the* American Mercury *Adventure*, pp. 215–38, describes the magazine's melancholy decline.

Page 227 Though Knopf watched: The situation is revealed in the general tenor of the Knopf-Mencken correspondence and, though in exaggerated form, in *Angoff*, pp. 206–25.

Page 227 The burden, for: Knopf files.

Page 227 He now could: Mencken to Knopf, December 2 [1932]; Knopf files.

Page 227 But its general: Ayer's *Directory*, however, shows somewhat different figures. It gives the circulation as slightly over 62,000 for 1930 —

not 1931 — and slightly over 42,000 for 1932.

Page 228 Whistling in the: Mencken to Knopf, November 23 [1932]; Knopf files. The analysis of the *Mercury's* annual profit or loss furnished me through the courtesy of J. C. Lesser of the Knopf firm shows a slight loss for the year, a bit over fifty dollars. Mencken nevertheless wrote Phil Goodman that the magazine was getting through 1932 with a profit of more than five thousand dollars; Mencken to Goodman, November 7, 1932; "Letters to Philip Goodman," vol. III; *EPL.*

Page 228 Yet Mencken went: *Ibid.*

Page 228 Mencken himself was: So he wrote a number of friends, including Boyd, Pearl, Sedgwick, Eugene Saxton, and Harry Leon Wilson. He publicly announced his departure in "Ten Years," *Mercury*, XXX (1933), 385.

Page 228 He saw in: "Hitlerismus" appeared on pp. 506–10 of the December number (vol. XXX).

Page 229 "I've just read": Knopf to Mencken, October 24, 1933; Knopf files.

Page 229 As always Mencken: Mencken to Knopf, October 26, 1933; Knopf files.

Page 229 In Mencken's parting: That is, "Ten Years."

Page 229 Under the heading: *Mercury*, XXXI (1934), xi.

Page 230 He continued to: His most moving tribute to Mencken was "For Henry with Love," *Atlantic Monthly*, CCIII (1959), 50–54.

Page 230 When the *Mercury*: My description of Edith Lustgarten Kean's relationship to Mencken and the *Mercury* is based principally on our interviews of October 1, 1963 and February 19, 1964, her collection of notes and letters from Mencken, and some correspondence between her and me. It was Nathan who told her about the three hundred applicants; our interview of October 1, 1963.

Page 230 She had grown: *Ibid.*

Page 231 Edith Lustgarten started: On March 17, 1924; our interview of February 19, 1964.

Page 231 As it turned: Letter to me from Edith Lustgarten Kean, September 20, 1965.

Page 231 "Mail has to": Our interview of October 1, 1963.

Page 231 Her filing was: The description of the office practice is for the most part from my interview with Mrs. Kean of October 1, 1963.

Page 232 "There never was": *Ibid.*

Page 232 Her routine phrases: Edith Lustgarten to ———— Griffing, June 4, 1924; copy in the collection of Mrs. Kean.

Page 232 She has never: Our interview of October 1, 1963.

Page 232 "Not the big": *Ibid.*

Page 232 For instance, one: Mencken did not give the day and month on this note; collection of Mrs. Kean.

Page 233 "I am still": Mencken to Edith Lustgarten Kean, July 23, 1935; collection of Mrs. Kean.

Page 233–34 Fred Kean failed: Mencken's help in Mr. Kean's illnesses is described in my interview with Mrs. Kean of October 1, 1963.

Page 234 The last time: *Ibid.*

Page 234 He reminded her: Mencken to Edith Lustgarten Kean, September 28, 1944; collection of Mrs. Kean.

Page 234 And his relationship: There was a steady dribble of correspondence throughout the 1930s and 1940s and into the period after Mencken's stroke; as noted earlier, the letters by Mencken are at the Cornell University Library while the letters by Nathan are apparently in the collection Mencken restricted at *NYPL.*

Page 234 But the history: To my regret my efforts to obtain information from Mr. Angoff personally were for the most part unsuccessful. However,

he gave me an interview on November 17, 1964; and we have exchanged a number of letters following the finishing of my book.

Page 234 In the year: *Angoff,* p. 19. Angoff was 23 when he wrote Mencken.

Page 235 To Angoff's astonished: Mencken's account is in his typescript history of the "Hatrack" case, vol. I, 101 and 101–2, footnote.

Page 235 Angoff reported to: On January 25, 1925.

Page 235 He introduced him: *Angoff,* p. 27.

Page 235 In February 1925: Mencken to Philip Goodman, February 4 [1925]; "Letters to Philip Goodman," vol. I; *EPL.*

Page 236 As Angoff noted: *Angoff,* p. 190.

Page 236 He opposed, for: *Ibid.,* p. 208.

Page 236 Then he put: *Ibid.,* p. 209.

Page 237 He yearned to: This was August Mencken's judgment, though he put it more strongly to me; our interview of February 12, 1963. Angoff himself says he wanted to make it a cultural magazine; *Angoff,* pp. 221, 228.

Page 237 One egregious example: *Angoff,* p. 212.

Page 237 Now in his: *Ibid.,* p. 216.

Page 237 From time to: Mencken expressed the same sentiments in his correspondence with the Knopf firm's lawyer; Mencken to Benjamin Stern, September 28, 1939; Knopf files.

Page 238 The book starts: *Angoff,* pp. 22, 232. At the end of the book Angoff describes Mencken's taking him to Poe's tomb and telling him that he had suggested to his Saturday Night Club cronies that "we all piss on his grave."

Page 238 Angoff is capable: *Angoff,* p. 214. And yet in the introduction he announces, "My purpose is simply to describe Mencken . . . as a personal friend"; p. 9.

Page 238 Angoff's were marked: My interview with Edith Lustgarten Kean, February 19, 1964.

Page 238 A typical way: *Angoff*, pp. 104–5.

Page 239 He remarks, for: *Ibid.*, p. 50.

Page 239 Here is a: *Ibid.*, pp. 86–87.

Page 239 But this whole: *Ibid.*, p. 44.

Page 239 With his splendid: I have not found anyone who knew Mencken well who recalled his using the kind of language Angoff ascribes to him.

Page 240 Then in his: *Summer Storm* (1963), p. 33. On the other hand, there is a hardening rather than a softening in his attitude toward Mencken as described to me in his letter of December 20, 1968.

12 *The* MERCURY: *Mencken's Mind and Art*

Page 241 Writing in his: Pp. 66–67.

Page 242 By 1921 he: The Gunther quotation in the next paragraph is contained in an undated typescript he sent Mencken with a covering letter of September 21, 1921; *EPL*. Rascoe's comment occurs in his "Notes for an Epitaph," New York *Evening Post*, March 4, 1922.

Page 243 His focus became: quoted in Ernest Boyd, *H. L. Mencken*, p. 81.

Page 243 "No other animal": LIX, 62.

Page 243 As Allen Tate: "The Function of the Critical Quarterly," *Southern Review*, I (1936), 558.

Page 243 "The aim of": This was the language in, among other places, the announcement as printed in the New York *Times* of August 18, 1923.

Page 243 When he sent: His omnivorous reading of the past fifteen years had kept him in touch with the best scientific writing offered the public.

Page 244 Among the notable: Mencken to Raymond Pearl, August 8 [1923]; collection of Dr. Penelope Pearl Pollaczek.

Page 244 Or as Mencken: Mencken, "Raymond Pearl," *Sun*, November 24, 1940.

Page 244 And his work: My interview with Dr. Penelope Pearl Pollaczek, February 23, 1965.

Page 245 "I was especially": "Raymond Pearl," *Sun*, November 24, 1940.

Page 245 As Mencken noted: *Ibid.*

Page 246 The third number: Mencken's interest in science remained strong. When he was asked in 1938 what he liked to read most he answered, "In general I prefer books dealing with the exact sciences"; Mencken to James H. Gipson, April 15, 1938; *Princeton*.

Page 247 "I do not": *Mercury*, XVII (1929), xlvi.

Page 247 So he sent: De Kruif, *The Sweeping Wind* (1962), p. 7.

Page 247 And he felt: *Ibid.*, *passim*.

Page 248 He once wrote: *Manchester*, p. 72.

Page 249 Sumner's books, Mencken: Mencken to Albert G. Keller, January 5, 1932; *Princeton*.

Page 249 To Keller Mencken: *Ibid.*

Page 249 His synthesis, to: Richard Hofstadter, *Social Darwinism in American Thought* (1944), p. 37.

Page 250 It is called: It appeared in the *Forum*, XVII (1894), 92–102.

Page 250 "Let every man": Sumner, *Essays*, I, 109.

Page 250 They are the: *Happy Days*, p. viii.

Page 250 He became the: Douglas C. Stenerson analyzes Sumner's influence in "The 'Forgotten Man' of H. L. Mencken," *American Quarterly*, XVIII (1966), 686–96.

Page 250 "I only wish": Mencken to Albert G. Keller, January 5, 1932; *Princeton*.

Page 250 In the first: P. 28.

Page 251 "If you give": "The Forgotten Man," reprinted in *Summer Today* (1940), p. 3. Sumner first gave it in 1883 as a lecture.

Page 251 It was out: *Newspaper Days*, p. 32.

Page 251 Sumner announces, "Let": Quoted by Hofstadter at head of Chapter 3, *Social Darwinism in American Thought*.

Page 252 Keller put more: Hofstadter, *Social Darwinism in American Thought*, pp. 133–34.

Page 252 Sumner's attractions for: As Keller said in his article, Sumner was "of the Darwinian type" and Mencken was a thoroughgoing Darwinist.

Page 252 He observes in: P. 17. Incidentally, though Mencken was no joiner, he belonged in the 1940s to the William Graham Sumner Club.

Page 252 We can see: The issue with the letters is in *EPL*.

Page 253 John McClure says: His letter to Mencken is undated.

Page 253 George Philip Krapp: George Philip Krapp to Mencken, September 15, 1923.

Page 253 Woodbridge Riley, author: Woodbridge Riley to Mencken, November 6, 1923.

Page 253 He told Goldberg: *AN 1925*, p. 118. Still earlier, in September 1923, he told Ernest Boyd bluntly that the manuscripts coming in were "mainly crap"; September 28 [1923]; *Princeton*.

Page 253 Or how a: *Manchester*, p. 181.

Page 254 Yorke became one: Menc-ken to Dane Yorke, October 9, 1933; *Princeton*.

Page 254 Versatile enough to: Mencken once suggested a subject to him but it failed to work out.

Page 254 For instance, when: Dane Yorke, typescript on his work for the *Mercury*, designed to accompany the copies of his correspondence with Mencken at *Princeton*.

Page 254 He tried it: My interview with Arthur Krock, June 25, 1963, before our taping session.

Page 255 Looking back long: *AN 1941*, note beginning "Treatise on the Gods."

Page 255 One other work: The idea of the "Homo Sapiens" book long attracted him even though he said he gave it up because Raymond Pearl was doing it.

Page 255 There is an: Mencken had named Robert Lowie to Raymond Pearl as one of the distinguished scientists he wanted to attract to the *Mercury*; Mencken to Pearl, August 8 [1923]; collection of Dr. Penelope Pearl Pollaczek.

Page 257 Speaking with Dane: Dane Yorke, typescript on his work for the *Mercury*; *Princeton*.

Page 258 Mencken openly used: On modeling the *Mercury* on the *Atlantic*: for instance, my interview with August Mencken, September 10, 1963.

Page 258 He also looked: He particularly praised the *Century* in *Prejudices: First Series*, p. 174.

Page 258 "Have you heard": "The Revolution on Quality Street, Part I," *Survey*, LVII (1926), 119–24, 177–79; and "The Revolution on Quality Street, Part II," LVII (1927), 427–32, 469–72.

Page 259 *Scribner's* began to: K. S. Crichton to Dane Yorke, June 27, 1930; *Princeton*. The Depression helped but did not initiate the change.

Page 259 As Angoff remembered:

"The Inside View of Mencken's Mercury," *New Republic*, September 13, 1954. However, Jane Grant recalled otherwise in her *Ross, The New Yorker and Me* (1968), p. 122. According to her, several features, including the "Profiles" and the "Talk of the Town," got their start in an unsuccessful weekly called *The Home Sector* which Harold Ross edited before the *New Yorker*.

Page 261 In his book: *H. L. Mencken and the* American Mercury *Adventure*, pp. 182–87.

Page 261 There was *Plain:* Mencken asserted that this magazine was an outright imitation of the *Mercury*, according to Angoff, who agreed; Charles Angoff, "Mencken: Prejudices and Prophecies," *Saturday Review*, August 10, 1963.

Page 261 Did the Kiwanians: *Saturday Evening Post*, May 21, 1927.

Page 262 He observed that: *Mercury*, XV (1928), 407.

Page 262 In the same: *Ibid.*

Page 262 The *Times* apostrophized: In the issue for November 23, 1928.

Page 263 The Marxist Michael: *New Masses*, VII (1931), 3.

13   *Mencken, Darwin, and God*

Page 264 In the Tennessee: According to Scopes, many years after the event, he was merely a substitute biology teacher who agreed, at the suggestion of townspeople, to test the law. He believes that some of the businessmen in Dayton thought it would put the town on the map and help business. John T. Scopes and James Presley, *Center of the Storm: Memoirs of John T. Scopes* (1967), p. 61.

Page 264 In the words: The text of the indictment of Scopes was printed in the *Evening Sun* for July 13, 1925, from the UP release.

Page 265 By chance he: There are variations in the accounts of the way Darrow became involved in the case, but it certainly appears that Mencken played a part. In after years he told Huntington Cairns that he persuaded Darrow by arguing that the important thing was not the defense of Scopes but the assault on Bryan; copy of Cairns's account, May 21, 1948; collection of Huntington Cairns.

Page 265 "Nobody gives a": *Manchester*, p. 193.

Page 265 In a letter: Mencken to Sara Haardt, May 27, 1925; *Princeton*.

Page 266 He polished off: He said he had to do the eight, in a letter to Goodman, June 27 [1925]; "Letters to Philip Goodman," vol. I; *EPL*.

Page 266 "In a sense": *Manchester*, p. 191.

Page 266 He found Dayton: The immediate background for this section on the Scopes trial is Mencken's dispatches to the *Sunpapers*. From July 9 through July 18 the *Evening Sun* printed a dispatch from him every day except Sunday the 12th. In addition he devoted six Monday Articles to it; the first appeared June 15 and the last September 14. His most extensive — but time-mellowed — account is in *Heathen Days*, pp. 214–38. In addition, thére is John Scopes's own story in *Center of the Storm*.

Page 267 "The thing," he: Mencken to Raymond Pearl, *Kemler*, p. 185.

Page 267 He reported it: No dispatch better showed his involvement; *Evening Sun*, July 13, 1925.

Page 268 Even before the: Mencken's dispatch, *Evening Sun*, July 10, 1925.

Page 268 He shared a: My interview with Watson Davis, June 15, 1965.

Page 268 Darrow made him: L. S. de Camp, *The Great Monkey Trial*, pp. 381–410.

Page 269 The Monday following: "Bryan," *Evening Sun*, July 27, 1925.

Page 269 Bryan fought his: The piece is an untitled editorial in *American Mercury*, VI (1925), 158–60; and in its final form, quoted here, an item in *Prejudices: Fifth Series* (1926), "In Memoriam: W. J. B." The quotation is on pp. 71–72.

Page 269 In a Monday: August 10, 1925.

Page 270 There was, as: With as much thoroughness as he had ever done anything, in 1937, a decade after the event, Mencken put together the records of the "Hatrack" case. They included not only his documented history of the case but painstakingly as-sembled legal appendixes; the eight typescript volumes are in *EPL*. The quotation is from the first volume, p. 2. In my account I depend most on Mencken, and the paragraphs that follow are largely based on his type-script volumes.

Page 274 Its opening paragraph: The *Tribune*'s blast is in the issue for April 7, 1926.

Page 274 The headline over: Printed in the issue of April 7, 1926.

Page 276 Here is a: *Treatise*, p. 28.

Page 277 "The Bible," Mencken: *Ibid.*, p. 345.

Page 278 In his last: *Ibid.*, p. 352.

Page 278 And Mencken remarks: *Ibid.*, p. 353.

Page 278 In retrospect he: *AN 1941*, note beginning "Treatise on the Gods." He said much the same thing in another note beginning "But in my own."

14 *Mencken in Love*

Page 279 Sara Powell Haardt: Menc-ken himself compiled the scrapbook, subtitled "Letters, Documents, and Souvenirs, 1898–1935." My guess is that he did so during the months fol-lowing her death and that he started out with his usual determination to be orderly. The first items were easy to arrange but thereafter there were so many that he simply pasted them in as he came to them. I do not believe that he could bring himself to be more thorough; I think he tried briefly and then gave it up.

Page 280 Besides the record: The let-ters between Mencken and Sara in the Goucher College Library are now closed to scholars and have been since 1963. I was fortunate in being able to examine them before that. Professor and Mrs. William Hedges of the Goucher faculty also examined them before they were closed and, in an interview of June 19, 1963, shared their recollections of them with me.

Page 280 But it is: Another testimony to her regard for him, since she saved very few letters from others, as Menc-ken noted when he compiled the scrapbook; p. 38.

Page 280 Sara Mayfield was: The in-formation from Miss Sara Mayfield is contained for the most part in the tape of my extended interview with her on July 15, 1963. The supplementary data comes from my correspondence with her since that time, as well as from copies of letters to her from Sara Haardt (beginning June 28, 1927) and from Mencken (beginning October 10, 1928). Since this chapter was written Miss Mayfield has published her *The Constant Circle: H. L. Mencken and His Friends* (1968), a warmly human and anecdotal book of reminiscences about Mencken, his wife, and their associates.

Page 280 Anne Duffy, who: The information from Mrs. Edmund Duffy comes from three interviews, May 22, July 26, and November 16, 1964, the most important being the first.

Page 280 "Sara never crosses": My interview with Miss Mayfield, July 15, 1963.

Page 280 James Cain, who: My interview with James Cain, June 3, 1963.

Page 280 The records show: Sara's academic career at Goucher is summarized in the scrapbook, p. 10. Incidentally, she was elected to Phi Beta Kappa.

Page 281 It happened because: My interview with Miss Mayfield, July 15, 1963.

Page 281 The professor in: Mencken remembered that it was through Baker that he met Sara Haardt. Baker had been on the *Smart Set* staff before joining the Goucher faculty, and one day he asked Mencken to speak to his class on the elements of magazine writing. Typescript by Mencken in the Harry T. Baker correspondence file; *EPL.*

Page 281 When his discourse: My interview with Miss Mayfield, July 15, 1963.

Page 282 She could still: For instance in her letter to Sara Mayfield of June 28, 1927; *Princeton.*

Page 283 When Robin Harriss: My interview with R. P. Harris: April 1, 1963. Background information is contained in his memorandum to me dated March 31, 1963, and my examination of some of his correspondence with Sara Haardt and Mencken from July 7, 1927 to May 30, 1935.

Page 283 Sara took sick: My interview with Miss Mayfield, July 15, 1963.

Page 283 Mencken was much: Menc-

ken to Sara Haardt, December 27, 1923; *Princeton.*

Page 284 It was during: These are among the letters at Goucher.

Page 284 Discharged from Maple: Moreover, Sara found that the president of Goucher wanted to get rid of her, in spite of the protestations of such devoted colleagues of hers on the faculty as Professor Ola Winslow and Professor Marjorie Hope Nicolson.

Page 285 Gradually her stories: The record of her rise is in the scrapbook and in her letters to Sara Mayfield which are in Miss Mayfield's collection.

Page 285 George Oppenheimer of: Scrapbook, p. 40.

Page 285 The magazine editors: The letter from the *Century* is in the scrapbook, p. 40.

Page 285 The sophisticated magazine: *Ibid.*, p. 49.

Page 285 The original invitation: *Ibid.*, p. 21.

Page 285 At any rate: My interview with Professor and Mrs. William Hedges, June 19, 1963.

Page 285 But when she: The letter from Herman Mankiewicz spelling out the terms of her contract is on p. 50 of the scrapbook.

Page 286 He warned her: And against the "Jews of Hollywood."

Page 286 There she sat: Sara Haardt to R. P. Harriss, November 22, 1927; collection of Mr. Harriss.

Page 286 It was Cruze's: Her contract with Cruze for "The Promised Land," full of clauses, is on pp. 56–59 of the scrapbook.

Page 286 It was not: Though she had no hesitation in telling Sara Mayfield that she was devoted to Mencken; Sara Haardt to Sara Mayfield, December 4, 1927; collection of Miss Mayfield.

Page 286–87 The moment they: On Sara's tales about her Hollywood experiences see, for instance, Mencken's letter to Joseph Hergesheimer of January 3, 1928; *Princeton.*

Page 287 It was a: Sara Haardt wrote Sara Mayfield that she had finished work for Hergesheimer on all of the Confederates but two, as of her letter of June 28, 1927; collection of Miss Mayfield.

Page 287 She collected data: The data is among her papers at the Goucher College Library.

Page 287–88 In a passage: Hergesheimer's typescript autobiography, p. 8 of the chapter on Mencken; copy in the collection of Huntington Cairns.

Page 288 He wired Sara: He also wrote Sara Mayfield; an index of the closeness of the two Saras is that Mencken said in his letter to her of June 29, 1929 that he was writing about the operation to no one else; collection of Miss Mayfield.

Page 289 The letters from: The only ones to approach them in warmth are some that he wrote to Marion Bloom.

Page 289 Decorating and furnishing: The renovation and furnishing of the Cathedral Street apartment are documented in the scrapbook. For example, orders for some of the repairs are on p. 25; some of the articles she wanted for the apartment are listed on p. 27; the lease she signed is on p. 109.

Page 290 He still remembers: My interview with Gerald Johnson, June 13, 1963. Other accounts are in general agreement with it.

Page 291 The silence was: Mencken to Max Broedel, August 4, 1930; *Princeton.*

Page 291 He felt very: His apprehensions about the *Sun*'s handling of the story of the engagement are noted in his letter to Hamilton Owens of August 4, 1930, as well as his relief about the way it was actually treated; collection of Mrs. Hamilton Owens.

Page 292 The format was: The interview was carried by many of the papers the UP served.

Page 292 The reason, according: Mencken's apprehensions about the press are typified in his letter to Hergesheimer saying, "What I fear is that the local Hearst sheet may get on to it, and give us a ride"; Mencken to Joseph Hergesheimer, July 31, 1930; *Princeton.*

Page 292 In deference to: The details about the wedding are drawn from the *Sunpapers* reports of the following day and the recollections of Mr. and Mrs. Hamilton Owens (my interview with Mr. and Mrs. Owens, February 28, 1963).

Page 292 But Quebec in: Mencken to, among others, A. H. McDannald, September 5 [1930]; *EPL.*

Page 292 They could not: Mencken to Paul Patterson, September 1, 1930; collection of Maclean Patterson.

Page 293 As Mencken wrote: Mencken to George Jean Nathan; undated letter but noted as being written during the first week of September 1930; Cornell University Library.

Page 293 A highlight of: Mark Schorer, *Sinclair Lewis* (1961), p. 538.

Page 293 Sara Mayfield was: My interview with Miss Mayfield, June 15, 1963.

Page 293 Above the sideboard: Mencken's personalized additions to the Cathedral Street decor were described to me by Mrs. Edmund Duffy in our interview of May 22, 1964. They are corroborated in general by the photographs of the apartment pasted into the scrapbook and by the recollections of such a visitor as Theodore Maynard in his *The World I Saw* (1938), pp. 283–85.

Page 294 He said one: Mencken's comment was recalled by John Owens in my interview with him of September 23, 1964.

Page 294 Both would stay: Hester went with Mencken to Hollins Street, in fact, and worked there till her death.

Page 294 Shortly after her: Interview dated September 17 [1930] given to Hally Pomeroy of the New York *World*.

Page 294 Besides being a: The account of the Menckens' daily life on Cathedral Street comes chiefly from my interview with their maid, Mrs. Bessie Lee Poindexter, on October 15, 1963. It is supplemented by the recollections of Mrs. Edmund Duffy in the interviews of May 22 and July 26, 1964.

Page 295 He wrote, for: Mencken to A. H. McDannald, March 2, 1931; *Princeton*.

Page 295 Sara made a: Sara Haardt Mencken to Alfred Knopf, January 25, 1933; Knopf files.

Page 295 Weeks after his: Mencken to Theodore Dreiser, February 5, 1926; *Princeton*.

Page 295 Often he would: My interview with Mrs. Bessie Lee Poindexter, October 15, 1963.

Page 296 He was seen: By Sara Mayfield among others; my interview of June 15, 1963.

Page 296 She even made: Sara's notes on her husband are in the scrapbook, p. 30.

Page 296 As a rule: Mementoes of the Menckens' tours are pasted in another scrapbook, "Clippings Carbons and Souvenirs Including Music, 1893–1938," p. 74 ff.

Page 296 In after years: The excerpt from Mrs. David Morrison's recollections of life on Cathedral Street come from the script of a television program she took part in in Lancaster, Pennsylvania, after Mencken's death; collection of August Mencken.

Page 297 Anne Duffy was: Mencken's attitude toward Anne Duffy was certainly ambivalent. A description of his negative reaction is contained in my interview with Hamilton Owens of May 8, 1963. His positive reaction can be detected in his letters to her now in *EPL*.

Page 298 The disagreements often: The course of Henry's and Anne Duffy's relationship as seen within the Cathedral Street apartment is ascribed in my interview with Mrs. Bessie Lee Poindexter, October 15, 1963.

Page 299 The chairs in: *Ibid.*

Page 299 As Mencken had: *In Defense of Women* (rev. ed. 1922), p. 177.

Page 299 At the same: Sara's attitude toward the Saturday Night Club including some of its most eminent members is described in my interview with Hamilton Owens, May 8, 1963 and also in my interview with James Cain, June 3, 1963.

Page 299 Her taste for: James Cain attended more than one of these parties; my interview with him of June 3, 1963.

Page 299 One night Lillian: My interview with Mrs. Bessie Lee Poindexter, October 15, 1963.

Page 299 It was not: However, James Cain remembers a plaint by Mencken about Sara's medical expenses; my interview of June 10, 1963.

Page 299 Though it sank: The data is in Mencken's red account book; *EPL*.

Page 300 But Sara's brother: My interview with Mrs. Bessie Lee Poindexter, October 15, 1963.

Page 300 In March 1935: Mencken to Jim Tully, March 12, 1935; *Princeton*.

Page 300 One afternoon in: My interview with Mrs. Edmund Duffy, May 22, 1964.

Page 301 To Robin Harriss: Mencken to R. P. Harriss, May 30 [1935]; collection of Mr. Harriss.

Page 301 The next morning: Hamilton Owens, "H. L. Mencken: A Personal Note" in Guy Forgue, *Letters of H. L. Mencken* (1961), pp. xi–xii.

Page 301 Besides the immediate:

Hamilton Owens made a list of the persons, aside from members of the family and *Sun* staffers, who attended the funeral and gave it to Mencken; copy in the collection of Mrs. Hamilton Owens.

Page 302 In spite of: One passport photo is a double one, taken with Henry, and she looks charming; "Clippings Carbons and Souvenirs Including Music, 1893–1938," p. 80.

Page 302 James Cain was: He mentions it in a memorandum to me of February 12, 1964.

Page 302 When illness forced: At

her death she left an incompleted novel entitled *Plantations;* my interview with Miss Sara Mayfield, June 15, 1963.

Page 303 Looking back after: As Mencken answered the hundreds of letters of condolence that came to him, he remarked again and again on Sara's patience under pain and — he used the word often — her gallantry. For example: Mencken to Ernest Boyd, June 4, 1935; *Princeton.*

Page 303 On October 30: Mencken to Mrs. Joseph Hergesheimer; *Princeton.*

15 *The Circus of Dr. R.*

Page 304 Nor would he: I saw the apartment in 1964 through the courtesy of its occupant at the time, Mrs. Eleusinia Neff.

Page 304 Nor would he: The particulars about the furnishings come from the orders and bills in the scrapbook "Letters, Documents, and Souvenirs, 1898–1935" and from the photographs at the end of the scrapbook.

Page 304 Ten days after: Mencken to Dreiser, June 11 [1935]; *Princeton.*

Page 304 But the nights: Mencken to Harry Rickel, January 14, 1936; *Princeton.*

Page 304 Though his bachelor: My interview with August Mencken, June 7, 1963.

Page 304 He felt the: Mencken to Mrs. Joseph Hergesheimer, March 10, 1936; *Princeton.*

Page 305 The price of: Among the comments about Sara's inadvertently helping to isolate Mencken from the world are those made by James Cain in my interview of June 3, 1963 and Ruth Goodman Goetz in my interview of July 23, 1964.

Page 305 Mencken replied grandly:

Mencken to Max Broedel, August 7, 1930; *Princeton.*

Page 305 Among them Marcella: The two couples first met on a cruise early in 1932. My interview with Mrs. duPont, March 20, 1965.

Page 305 In the early: My interview with James Cain, June 3, 1963.

Page 306 In the presidential: "I voted for Roosevelt too, but what could we do? The alternative was to vote for that horrible cream-puff, Hoover." Mencken to A. H. McDannald, February 22, 1936; *EPL.*

Page 307 As early as: In "An American Troubadour," *Evening Sun,* December 27, 1920.

Page 307 A month later: May 1, 1933.

Page 307 He entitled another: June 19, 1933.

Page 307 Looking back at: *Mercury,* XXX (1933), 262.

Page 308 He stood firm: Mencken to Roscoe Peacock, August 16, 1934; *Princeton.*

Page 308 A great university: *Ibid.,* August 23, 1934; *Princeton.*

Page 308 By late 1934: My account of the Gridiron Club dinner is based on a variety of sources. The chief ones are: a black looseleaf notebook in the Gridiron archives in Washington which contains the history of the functions for 1934; the draft suggestions for FDR's speech, now in the Roosevelt archives in Hyde Park; the drafts of Mencken's speech in the Gridiron archives and *EPL* also; and the observations of Arthur Krock (my interview of June 25, 1963) and Marquis Childs (my interview of June 2, 1964).

Page 311 The next week: My interview with John Owens, September 24, 1964.

Page 311 A few months: My interview with Ruth Goodman Goetz, May 22, 1964.

Page 311 The Saturday following: My interview with August Mencken, November 12, 1963.

Page 312 On shipboard he: The pictures are pasted in "Photographs and Other Portraits of H. L. Mencken, 1881–1936."

Page 312 But in mid-Atlantic: The letter to Blanche Knopf is from her files and was dated by her as June 18, 1935.

Page 312 One day he: Mencken to Sara Mayfield, July 12 [1935]; collection of Miss Mayfield.

Page 312 The high spot: My interview with Maclean Patterson, January 12, 1965.

Page 312 Having sojourned near: Reported in, among other papers, the New York *Herald Tribune* for July 13, 1935.

Page 313 He had put: Mencken to Jim Tully, July 13, 1932; *Princeton.*

Page 314 In the Preface: The full title of the book is *Making a President: A Footnote to the Saga of Democracy* (1932).

Page 314 The news of: *Ibid.*, p. iv.

Page 315 And at any: *Ibid.*, p. vi.

Page 315 To get material: *Ibid.*, p. vii.

Page 315 He remarked that: *Ibid.*, p. viii.

Page 315 He had left: This was the time when he finally shelved his Corona for a Remington Noiseless; Mencken to Philip Goodman, June 21, 1932, "Letters to Philip Goodman," vol. III; *EPL.*

Page 316 The lead for: *Making a President,* pp. 133–34.

Page 316 Vividly he describes: *Ibid.*, p. 142.

Page 317 The carbon copies: "Dispatches to the Baltimore *Sun* from the Republican and Democratic National Conventions, June 1926."

Page 317 There was in: The preface is on a Western Union blank.

Page 318 As he observed: *Evening Sun,* early edition(?), June 11, 1936.

Page 318 He listened to: *Ibid.*, June 11, 1936.

Page 319 "Jim Farley's chief": *Ibid.*, June 22, 1936.

Page 319 "The Hon. Mr.": *Ibid.*, June 26, 1936.

Page 319 "The only one": *Ibid.*, June 27, 1936.

Page 319 As to Roosevelt's: *Ibid.*, June 28, 1936.

Page 319 Marquis Childs remembers: My interview with Marquis Childs, June 2, 1964.

Page 320 On the other: His relationship with Dr. Townsend perfectly represents the combination of kindliness and professional cynicism with which he regarded politicians. In spite of what he usually said about them, they sensed that he liked them. When Dr. Townsend issued his autobiography *New Horizons* in 1943, he sent a copy to Mencken inscribed "To H. L. Mencken from his friend Dr. F. E. Townsend" in his uneven, old-man's script; *EPL.*

Page 320 In a letter: Mencken to Ernest Boyd, October 1, 1936; *Princeton.*

16 *Friends and Familiars*

Page 322 On October 17: Mencken to A. H. McDannald, October 17, 1938; *EPL.*

Page 322 On April 28: *EPL.*

Page 322 On May 6: *EPL.*

Page 322 In November he: *Ibid.,* November 20, 1940; *EPL.*

Page 322 In October 1941: *Ibid.,* October 27, 1941; *EPL.*

Page 322 In November he: *Ibid.,* November 11, 1941; *EPL.*

Page 322 On July 22: *EPL.*

Page 322 In March of: *Ibid.,* March 20, 1944; *EPL.*

Page 322 The next month: *Ibid.,* April 3, 1944; *EPL.*

Page 322 Mencken's letter to: *EPL.*

Page 323 To the members: James Cain's memorandum to me, April 21, 1964.

Page 323 In April 1945: Mencken to A. H. McDannald, April 2, 1945; *EPL.*

Page 323 In February 1946: *Ibid.,* February 18, 1946; *EPL.*

Page 323 We know from: My interview with August Mencken, November 12, 1963; my interview with Louis Cheslock, April 18, 1963 (I may be wrong by a few days on this date).

Page 323 Its mortal blow: The stroke occurred on November 23, 1948.

Page 323 On December 2: Louis Cheslock, *H. L. Mencken on Music,* p. 215.

Page 324 He persuaded his: My interview with James Cain, June 3, 1963.

Page 325 Dreiser wired back: Dreiser to Mencken, November 28, 1925; *Pennsylvania.*

Page 325 The affair then: Mencken to Dreiser, December 4 [1925]; *Pennsylvania.*

Page 325 When Dreiser sent: The inscribed copy is now in *EPL.*

Page 325 They displeased Dreiser: "Dreiser in 840 Pages," *Mercury,* VII (1926), 379–81.

Page 325 Dreiser was antagonized: *Kemler,* p. 172.

Page 325 Meanwhile, something else: W. A. Swanberg, *Dreiser* (1965), p. 299, quotes a letter from Mencken to Helen Dreiser, whom Dreiser had left sitting in his car in the street while he chatted with Mencken. She was then his mistress; he had not yet married her. In the letter Mencken says that he resented both Dreiser's leaving her in the cold and his aloof indifference at Mencken's mother's illness. Years later Mencken wrote Alfred Knopf cryptically that Dreiser had come to Baltimore with his girl and disgusted him so much that he resolved to have no more to do with him; Mencken to Knopf, November 20, 1934; Knopf files.

Page 326 The night the: My interview with Ruth Goodman Goetz, October 2, 1963.

Page 326 The correspondence was: The episode is described from Mencken and Knopf's point of view in Knopf's recollections.

Page 326 Mencken wrote Knopf: Mencken to Knopf, November 20, 1934; Knopf files.

Page 326 Dreiser also wrote: Dreiser to Mencken, November 20, 1934; *Pennsylvania.*

Page 326 Thereupon Mencken, touched: Mencken to Dreiser, November 21 [1934]; *Pennsylvania.*

Page 326 In return Dreiser: Dreiser to Mencken, November 24, 1934; *Pennsylvania.*

Page 327 Mencken bluntly told: *Pennsylvania.*

Page 327 An important bond: For example, Mencken to Dreiser, April 1,

1940; "I needn't tell you that your blast against the English gave me great delight"; *Pennsylvania*.

Page 327 They agreed in: Mencken sent Dreiser a pamphlet with a satirical poem in it entitled "Oxiline" and directed against FDR. It is copyrighted 1939. This is in addition to the letters with passages assailing FDR. *Pennsylvania*.

Page 327 For example, in: Mencken to Dreiser, May 26, 1936; *Pennsylvania*.

Page 327 In June of: Indicated by Mencken's answer of June 29, 1936; *Pennsylvania*.

Page 327 In October 1938: Mencken to Dreiser, October 14, 1938; *Princeton*.

Page 327 Later in the: *Ibid.*, October 31, 1938; *Princeton*.

Page 327 "You are far": Mencken to Dreiser, April 1, 1943; *Pennsylvania*.

Page 328 But it said: The *Pennsylvania* copy is marked "Hollywood Memorial Program Message 1945."

Page 328 Throughout the 1920s: From the early 1920s on, one of Mencken's close friends was Blanche Knopf. Their relationship was both personal and professional. Though the Knopf files show the development of the professional side in detail, they lack information — except for a few references — about the personal side. Furthermore, I had little chance to talk with Mrs. Knopf about the relationship. Faced with this paucity of information I can only speculate, though with some confirmation from other sources. At any rate, I believe that by the middle 1920s she considered Mencken her best friend, as he was her husband's. I believe that she turned to him more than once in time of trouble. Sometimes it was physical trouble, most notably in 1936 when she needed the best medical help she could get and Mencken gladly made all the arrangements. When the trouble was emotional she turned to him too. I wonder about the implications of the fact that in her letter file for 1924 there is only one item and that the letter file for 1929 is missing, while the adjoining files are full. But I believe we get a hint here and there from the files of other years. On February 17, 1928, for instance, she writes Mencken urging him to come up for a Sunday visit and saying emphatically that she would be "Goddam glad" to see him. I have been told — by someone in a position to know — that she and her husband, both imperious personalities, were at odds by the end of the decade and that Mencken, out of his firm friendship for both, helped to keep them together. I believe that she continued to depend on him. A letter remains, for example, of May 31, 1933 in which she says that there are a good many things she wants to speak with him about privately. I also believe that she and her husband long competed for Mencken's regard, even in such a thing as seeing a book of his through the press. In point, her letter of February 25, 1941 in which she talks about his forthcoming *New Dictionary of Quotations*. She says she wants to settle the issue of who is to "make the book," she or her husband. If they both have a hand in it, it will be a mess. She adds defensively that Mencken should choose the person he prefers and she would not blame him for preferring Alfred.

Page 328 By 1926 she: Mencken to Marion Bloom, October 25 [1927]; collection of Miss Bloom.

Page 328 Mencken wrote on: *Ibid.*, February 4 [1927]; collection of Miss Bloom.

Page 328 She went to: My telephone interview with Miss Bloom, May 25, 1968.

Page 328 In July they: Mencken to Marion Bloom, July 24 [1928]; collection of Miss Bloom.

Page 328 In November he: *Ibid.*, November 25, 1928; collection of Miss Bloom.

Page 329 Marion and Mencken: My interview with Miss Bloom, August 18, 1965.

Page 329 Writing to Edgar: Mencken to Edgar Lee Masters, December 15, 1934; *Princeton.*

Page 329 A month later: Mencken to Mrs. C. Stuart Macdonald, April 30, 1936; collection of Mrs. Macdonald.

Page 329 Their last contact: My letter from Mrs. C. Stuart Macdonald, August 16, 1968.

Page 329 Aileen Pringle had: James Cain to Mencken, June 19, 1946; Library of Congress.

Page 329 As she remembers: My interview with Aileen Pringle, May 24, 1963.

Page 329 In 1944 she: Mencken to James Cain, July 25, 1944; Library of Congress.

Page 329 In November of: Mencken to Mrs. Hamilton Owens, November 13, 1944; collection of Mrs. Owens.

Page 330 Occasionally she stopped: My interview with Anita Loos, October 30, 1964.

Page 330 His personal patience: He made a genuine effort to be polite and responsive. Here he is, for example, replying to a friend from Texas, Mrs. Josiah Combs: "The fact that you and your husband keep a pet turtle is interesting indeed." Mencken to Mrs. Josiah Combs, May 31, 1938; *Princeton.*

Page 330 There they encountered: My account of the friendship between Marcella duPont and Mencken is based mainly on their correspondence and on interviews with Mrs. duPont. She has saved all his letters except for some from 1945, which were

burned by mistake, and she has kept carbons of her own letters. Our interviews came on December 3 and 12, 1962 and March 20, 1965 and were supplemented by telephone conversations during 1963 and 1964.

Page 330 "God knows, I": Mencken to Marcella duPont, August 19, 1934; collection of Mrs. duPont.

Page 331 During Sara's last: *Ibid.*, June 14, 1935.

Page 331 When Sara's next: My interview with Mrs. duPont, March 20, 1965.

Page 331 When she reports: *Ibid.*

Page 331 While she lies: *Ibid.*

Page 332 She closes her: Marcella duPont to Mencken, February 1, 1941.

Page 332 They are sometimes: "Please let me know" concludes her letter of February 15, 1943.

Page 332 Marcella writes sadly: Marcella duPont to Mrs. Rosalind Lohrfinck, March 22, 1949.

Page 332 Mencken, gallant and: Marcella duPont to Mencken, May 25, 1944.

Page 332 She recalls that: My interview with Mrs. duPont, March 20, 1965.

Page 333 His private generosities: Mencken's help to Ernest Boyd's widow is also mentioned in my interview with Mrs. Boyd of June 24, 1963. "To argue for" is from his note to Mrs. duPont of March 5, 1943.

Page 333 When she told: My interview with Marcella duPont, March 20, 1965.

Page 333 He was, she: *Ibid.*, December 12, 1962.

Page 333 He told Marcella: *Ibid.*, March 20, 1965.

Page 333 He also told: *Ibid.*

Page 333 Later she writes: Marcella duPont to Mencken, April 12, 1938.

Page 333 Still later she: *Ibid.*, November 29, 1940. But she also says he was lamblike before the explosion.

Page 333 After the war: Shortly before the end of the war Mencken comments on Hergesheimer's troubles in a letter to Alfred Knopf, March 17, 1945; Knopf files. Hergesheimer's bad state later on is remarked in my interview with Mrs. duPont of December 12, 1962 and with Huntington Cairns of September 19, 1962.

Page 334 He exclaimed that: Mencken to Marcella duPont, June 25, 1938.

Page 334 They could not: Marcella duPont to Mencken, February 8, 1940, for example. Her applause is scattered through her letters.

Page 334 Mencken was not: Mencken to Marcella duPont, October 31, 1946.

Page 335 When he wrote: Marcella duPont to Mencken, March 30, 1938.

Page 335 Now Mencken could: Mencken to Marcella duPont, May 5, 1938.

Page 335 He reported gravely: *Ibid.*, July 10, 1940.

Page 335 When he visited: *Ibid.*, July 1, 1938.

Page 335 So too when: *Ibid.*, April 22, 1941.

Page 336 For instance, his: *Ibid.*, November 17, 1937. On the other hand (to keep a biographer humble) he wrote Sara Mayfield that he thought Black would probably make a bad judge; Mencken to Miss Mayfield, August 19, 1937; *Princeton*.

Page 336 He had started: My interview with Admiral Leland Lovette, August 13, 1964.

Page 336 One day in: *Ibid.*, June 1, 1964.

Page 336 The student, who: *Ibid.*, August 13, 1964.

Page 337 "I will always": *Ibid.*

Page 337 He told Lovette: *Ibid.*, March 4, 1965.

Page 337 The result of: Mencken to Raymond Pearl, September 20, 1933; collection of Dr. Penelope Pearl Pollaczek.

Page 337 His experiences were: Lovette not only told Mencken about his adventures but also wrote about them to him. For example: his letter from China of September 3, 1934 now tipped into his presentation copy, to Mencken, of his *Naval Customs, Traditions, and Usage* in *EPL*.

Page 338 He recalls that: My interview with Admiral Lovette, August 13, 1964.

Page 338 "The greatest short": *Ibid.*

Page 338 Yet Shakespeare did: *Ibid.*

Page 339 One time he: *Ibid.*

Page 339 He declared to: *Ibid.*

Page 339 Mencken delivered his: Mencken's comments on both national and international affairs are recalled by Admiral Lovette chiefly in the interview of March 4, 1965.

Page 339 Their friendship had: Their correspondence continued into the postwar years. An example is Mencken's pleasant note of May 13, 1946, now in the collection of the Admiral's widow, Mrs. Leland Lovette.

Page 340 Sister Miriam Gallagher: The letters from Mencken to Sister Miriam, sixty-four in all, have been deposited in the Georgetown University Library. The first is dated July 19, 1937 and the last April 24, 1943. The heaviest years are 1937–39. Her letters to him are in the restricted collection at *NYPL*.

Page 340 She also asked: The friendly tone of Mencken's reply of July 19, 1937 suggests that there had been more than one preliminary letter.

Page 341 He reported this: Incidentally, he responds to Sister Miriam's report that her Mother Superior classes him with Hemingway by remarking that Hemingway seems to him "a predominantly foolish fellow." But in his next letter, December 1, 1937, he retracts partly and calls Hemingway "a rather amusing fellow."

Page 342 There were times: Mencken to Sister Miriam, May 13, 1938.

Page 342 Calling them charming: *Ibid.*, April 7, 1938.

Page 342 For example, about: *Ibid.*, March 6, 1939.

Page 343 She sent him: Mencken thanked her in a note of December 30, 1938.

Page 343 Notwithstanding, they remained: Mencken's kindliness continued. It was apparent even in random meetings with others. In point, the experience of Dr. Curtis Davis, cited in his letter to me of March 25, 1968. In the summer of 1941 he was a graduate student at Duke University in search of a subject for a dissertation. He too thought of Huneker. As the son of a Baltimore doctor who had treated Mencken, he had no trouble in arranging to see him about Huneker. Mencken invited Davis to an evening at Schellhase's. When he went there he found Mencken drinking beer with friends in a back booth. He had expected to encounter a "brusque, barbed, witty, and ironic" man; instead he met a generous Mencken who made Davis feel he was the center of attention. He told him about Huneker and gave him all the information he could.

Page 343 He is no: "At this point enters, at a hard gallop, spattered with mud, H. L. Mencken, high in oath"—Stuart Sherman, "Mr. H. L. Mencken and the Jeune Fille," New York *Times*, December 7, 1919.

17 *The Last Hurrah*

The title for this chapter is taken from Edwin O'Connor's novel.

Page 344 At the end: Mencken's remark is dated April 24, 1939 in the typescript "Minority Report: H.L.M.'s Notes"; *EPL*. It is undated in the book, p. 174.

Page 345 While the *Mercury*'s: Figures from Ayer's *Directory* for 1931 and 1933.

Page 345 In January 1934: Mrs. K. S. White (the wife of E. B. White) to Mencken, January 24, 1934; *Princeton*. The citations and quotations from Mencken's correspondence with the *New Yorker* which follow come from a Princeton microfilm of Mencken originals and *New Yorker* carbons.

Page 345 He answered at: Mencken to Mrs. K. S. White, January 26 and February 3, 1934; *Princeton*.

Page 345 Mrs. White announced: Mrs. K. S. White to Mencken, April 7, 1934; *Princeton*.

Page 345 That spring and: They are listed in *MB*, p. 150.

Page 345 Mrs. White wrote: Mrs. K. S. White to Mencken, April 20, 1934; *Princeton*.

Page 346 Its Yahweh possessed: *Treatise on Right and Wrong*, p. 148 for the quotation.

Page 346 Coming down to: P. 219 for the quotation.

Page 347 Current moralists "over-estimate": P. 247.

Page 347 The result was: They are listed in *MB*, p. 152.

Page 347 The literary origins: A descriptive outline of the genesis of the *Days* books is provided by Brother James Atwell's "Eclipse and Emergence," *Menckeniana*, No. 24 (Winter 1967), 1–7.

Page 348 We can recall: Introduction, "Typescripts of Early Fiction."

Page 348 In evidence, "The": *Ibid.*, 59–69.

Page 348 By the middle: Mencken to Dreiser, after July 11, 1909; *Princeton.*

Page 349 The very first: XLIV (1914), 31–46.

Page 349 But at the: Mencken's interest in his childhood and youth was quickened by writing his autobiographical notes for Isaac Goldberg to use in his biography.

Page 349 The central: Mencken to Edgar Lee Masters, December 15, 1934; *Princeton.*

Page 350 "Now for some": Philip Goodman to Mencken, "Extracts," p. 60; *EPL.*

Page 350 There was, for: The photographs of "Mrs. Himmelheber" and others come to me from Ruth Goodman Goetz, who has also furnished the background information about them.

Page 351 The correspondence, which: The correspondence may have continued, at least in the form of a few letters, till Goodman's death. But if so, these letters have been lost. The Depression, New Deal socialism, and the rise to power of Hitler all served to pull the two friends apart.

Page 351 Mencken himself, after: His comment is in Volume I of the correspondence, p. 5.

Page 351 Nevertheless, we cannot: I wonder if another suggestion for the Mencken-Goodman character sketches with photos, like that of Mrs. Tillie Himmelheber, came from a book in Mencken's possession? It was Frank Wing's *The Family Album* (1917), inscribed to Mencken by the author. It is made up of folksy, rather funny character sketches written on each left-hand page and "daguerreotype" drawings on the right-hand side.

Page 351 For by late: Mencken to Mrs. K. S. White, December 21, 1935; *Princeton.*

Page 351 She was delighted: Mrs. K. S. White to Mencken, January 17, 1936; *Princeton.*

Page 351 Mencken responded the: Mencken to Mrs. K. S. White, January 18, 1936; *Princeton.*

Page 351 Seeing Mencken's reply: *Ibid.*

Page 352 Mrs. White hinted: Mrs. K. S. White to Mencken, September 29, 1937; *Princeton.*

Page 352 Or another editor: St. Clair McKelway to Mencken, August 10, 1938; *Princeton.*

Page 352 He told St.: McKelway reported Ross's enthusiastic response in a letter to Mencken of March 13, 1939 and said that the *New Yorker* could use an almost unlimited number of such pieces.

Page 353 Shortly before her: My interview with Mrs. Alfred Knopf, April 1, 1963.

Page 353 They "read fine": St. Clair McKelway to Mencken, April 7, 1939; *Princeton.*

Page 353 Thus launched upon: In this reference and the others after it the edition used, it probably should be noted again, is the first collected one, *The Days of H. L. Mencken* (1947).

Page 354 For his domestic: *Happy Days,* Preface, pp. v–vi.

Page 354 "Your proofroom is": Mencken to Mrs. K. S. White, April 27 [1934]; *Princeton.*

Page 355 As he had: Mencken to Mrs. K. S. White, April 6, 1935; *Princeton.*

Page 355 He urged the: Mencken to St. Clair McKelway, April 8 [1939]; *Princeton.*

Page 355 The *New Yorker:* St. Clair McKelway to Mencken, April 11, 1939; *Princeton.*

Page 355 When Mencken proposed: Mencken to Mrs. K. S. White, March 23, 1935; *Princeton.*

Page 356 The genial reception: CLXV (1940), unnumbered page.

Page 356 On receiving his: Dreiser to Mencken, December 17, 1939; *Pennsylvania.*

Page 356 He announced fervently: St. Clair McKelway to Mencken, September 19, 1939; *Princeton.*

Page 356 Two of them: The memos are undated but probably were written in January 1940.

Page 356 They ended in: The sketch was on Hoggie Unglebower. Mencken made it the opening sketch of *Heathen Days* after first seeing it printed by *Esquire* in September 1940.

Page 356 The first decade: "Virtually unlimited" — Mencken to St. Clair McKelway, September 22, 1939; *Princeton.*

Page 356 He said later: Mencken speaks of the typicality of his teens in a letter to Ben Abramson, October 2, 1941; Yale University Library.

Page 356 But the third: Mencken suggested in a letter of January 20 [1940] to Ross that he might write about his early newspaper experiences; *Princeton.*

Page 356 Nine sketches in: They are listed in *MB*, p. 157.

Page 357 Mencken described how: *Newspaper Days*, p. 237.

Page 357 At their end: Harold Ross to Mencken, November 19, 1941; *Princeton.*

Page 358 Even if he: Mencken speaks about official and unofficial censorship in, for instance, his letter to Harry Elmer Barnes of July 18, 1944; *Princeton.*

Page 358 Writing to Dreiser: Mencken to Dreiser, March 19, 1943; *Pennsylvania.*

Page 358 Writing to Manfred: Mencken to Dr. Manfred Guttmacher, October 7, 1942; Guttmacher collection.

Page 358 He had already: He mentions the burst of energy in *Heathen Days*, Preface, p. vi.

Page 358 However, as he: Mencken to Ben Abramson, October 2, 1941; Yale University Library.

Page 358 Notwithstanding their miscellaneous: They are listed in *MB*, p. 157.

Page 358 In "The Educational": *Heathen Days*, p. 43.

Page 359 And of himself: *Ibid.*, p. 42.

Page 359 It published only: However, we know from Mencken's account book of 1944–48 that the *New Yorker* paid him a yearly retainer of $100 whether it published him or not. When it began to print him again, after World War II, the price it paid for his pieces climbed sharply. Prior the end of the war he was receiving on the average of $275 for each item. After the war he got more than twice as much. "Love Story" (November 1947) brought him $875.

Page 359 The magazine printed: "Postscripts to the American Language" are listed in *MB*, p. 160.

Page 360 When he gave: The copy is now in the collection of Maclean Patterson.

Page 361 In late 1941: Mencken to Ellery Sedgwick, November 1, 1941; *Princeton.*

Page 361 There is, for: Mencken to H. L. Davis, April 17, 1942; *Princeton.*

Page 361 There is the: Mencken to Dreiser, February 23, 1943; *Pennsylvania.*

Page 361 Then there is: Mencken to James Farrell, August 17, 1945; *Pennsylvania.*

Page 361 He depended more: The information about Mencken's changing patterns of work is from my interview with Mrs. Lohrfinck, October 11, 1962.

Page 361 In May 1948: Huntington Cairns, unpublished memoir of May 21, 1948 on Mencken.

Page 362 It is true: The obituary appeared in the *Sun* October 28, 1941.
Page 362 And he told: He said so even as late as the fall of 1947, for instance in his letter to Mrs. Rufus Gibbs, November 26, 1947; collection of Norman James.
Page 362 Perhaps the best: The record is contained in two black account books, one for 1928–43 and the other continuing from 1944 till November 1948. The record shows that his *Sunpapers* salary was $1,000 a month at its peak; that it was cut to $750 a month starting in February 1941; and that it was cut further to approximately $416 a month (or $5,000 a year) starting March 1, 1946. There it stayed till his stroke. His *Sunpapers* director's fees of $20 per session continued too till the stroke.
Page 362 In 1943 and: The story is in the correspondence in the collection of Maclean Patterson.
Page 362 His counsel was: Mencken to Maclean Patterson, February 22, 1944.
Page 363 Roosevelt died and: Mencken to A. H. McDannald, April 25, 1945; *EPL.*
Page 363 There was a: My interview with Hamilton Owens, February 28, 1963.
Page 363 As early as: Maclean Patterson to Mencken, November (?), 1947; collection of Mr. Patterson.
Page 363 When he was: "About People," New York *Herald Tribune,* March 26, 1948.

Page 364 The item was: Maclean Patterson told me about the incident and showed me the pertinent letters when I interviewed his mother and him on February 8, 1965.
Page 364 On April 14: Mencken to Maclean Patterson, April 14, 1948; collection of Mr. Patterson.
Page 364 Here he is: Typescript of the dispatch, June 10, in the collection of Mr. Patterson.
Page 364 In the *Atlantic*: CXCVII (1956), 33–38.
Page 365 "The delegates," he: Typescript of the dispatch in the collection of Mr. Patterson.
Page 365 There was, Mencken: Mencken to Maclean Patterson, April 21, 1948; collection of Mr. Patterson.
Page 365 There was a: *Ibid.,* July 1, 1948.
Page 365 There was A.: *Ibid.,* October 28, 1948.
Page 366 This piece appeared: It was "Equal Rights in Parks," *Sun,* November 9, 1948.
Page 366 In Alfred Knopf's: Knopf's recollections as shared with me. The *Sunpapers,* incidentally, were loyal too. A year and a half after Mencken's stroke they voted him an annual pension of $7,500; E. P. Kavanaugh, secretary of the *Sunpapers,* to Mencken, March 31, 1950; *EPL.*

18 *Nighttime at Hollins Street*

Page 367 When in his: However, here and there, there were indications of what the future would bring. In April 1938 he went to Dr. Baker because of a peculiar sensation about his heart; a month later he saw Dr. Baker about a vague epigastric pain.

Dr. Baker's memos of April 12 and May 16, 1938 in his file on Mencken.
Page 367 However, near the: Dr. Baker, interval note, April 14, 1941.
Page 367 By the middle: Dr. F. M. Hanes to Dr. Benjamin Baker, August 18, 1939; in his file on Mencken.

Page 368 It survives in: The type-script was deposited in *EPL* after August Mencken's death.

Page 368 He starts his: It is dated June 9, 1940.

Page 368 The spring of: He wrote his uncle, Charles Abhau, on September 12, 1941 that in spite of his troubles he had been able to get more words on paper during 1941 so far than in any year since 1924; letter in the collection of James A. Genthner.

Page 369 One day he: Entry of March 20, 1945.

Page 369 Even if his: Entry of December 15, 1945.

Page 369 It runs from: Entry of March 31, 1947.

Page 369 In early August: Entry of August 6, 1947.

Page 370 But on the: Rosalind Lohrfinck, undated typescript; *EPL*.

Page 370 In March 1949; Dr. Theodore Lidz to Dr. Benjamin Baker, March 22, 1949; in Dr. Baker's file on Mencken.

Page 371 His case notes: Preserved in Dr. Baker's file on Mencken.

Page 371 He found a: Dr. Philip Wagley, notes of April 5, 1949.

Page 371 There is a: Unsigned note dated September 6, 1950; in Dr. Baker's file on Mencken.

Page 372 They offer us: Typescript dated September 1, 1950; in Dr. Baker's file on Mencken.

Page 372 In point, the: Rosalind Lohrfinck to Dr. Philip Wagley, Oc-tober 5, 1950; in Dr. Wagley's file on Mencken.

Page 372 He was finally: Document, dates 10-12-50 — 3-20-51, apparently prepared by Dr. Robert M. Paine with Dr. Wagley as visiting physician; in Dr. Wagley's file on Mencken.

Page 372 Named Lois Gentry: The details that follow come mainly from my interview with Lois Gentry Macks, March 11, 1964. They are supplemented by the recollections of August Mencken.

Page 372 He also had: The orderly was Renshaw ("Rancho") Brown.

Page 374 After some months: My interview with William Manchester, October 7, 1964.

Page 374 He had written: They fill a box in *EPL* and a sizable number are not included in the book.

Page 375 He spent many: My interview with Rosalind Lohrfinck, October 2, 1962. Incidentally, she was the person who resurrected the manuscript; August Mencken to Alfred Knopf, November 19, 1955; carbon in *EPL*.

Page 375 One of its: P. 239.

Page 375 Toward the end: My interview with August Mencken, July 2, 1962.

Page 376 Long before, he: *Smart Set*, LXVI (1921), 33.

Page 376 To help August: My interview with Hamilton Owens, May 8, 1963.

Memento of an Active Man

Page 377 His verdict on: Issue of February 6, 1956.

Page 377 The following resolution: Copy in the collection of Mrs. Hamilton Owens.

Afterword

Page 381 In file drawers: There is also a small amount of correspondence with non-Marylanders. There are also some three thousand books in this room that he accumulated for *The American Language.*

Page 381 In 1942 the: The Knopf files contain the story of the project, of Mr. Boyd's struggles to find enough time to carry it out, and of his eventual decision to give it up. However, when Guy Forgue undertook to do a selection from Mencken's letters, he found his main source in the collection assembled in the Princeton Library under Mr. Boyd's direction. The selection appeared as *Letters of H. L. Mencken* (1961).

Page 381 Though both Mencken: He wanted to protect both his friends and himself. For example, he wrote Dreiser that he had gone through Dreiser's letters to him with some care and found them harmless; Mencken to Dreiser, July 16, 1942; *Pennsylvania.*

Page 381 The letters were: We are sure the *NYPL* has the letters from authors. It probably has copies of some of the letters he sent them. August Mencken wrote Knopf, after Mencken's death, that *NYPL* had only the letters from authors, not to them; August Mencken to Knopf, January 30, 1957; carbon in *EPL.* But Mrs.

Lohrfinck transcribed a good deal of Mencken's own correspondence from her notebooks and I believe that some of the transcriptions are in *NYPL* also. In his will Mencken states that *NYPL* is to have the letters from authors and "documents relating to them" — largely, I suppose, letters by Mencken.

Page 382 With it he: The general statement about the manuscripts and their restrictions is summarized in the *Publishers Weekly* for November 4, 1957. The specifications for the gift to Dartmouth are given in the College's announcement; New York *Herald Tribune,* September 15, 1957. The specifications for the gift to the Enoch Pratt Library are given in its announcement; Baltimore *Sun,* July 14, 1957. Incidentally, in Guy Forgue's *H. L. Mencken: L'Homme, L'Oeuvre, L'Influence* (1967) there is a reference (p. 29) to further materials in the Enoch Pratt Library: "Personal Diaries" in sixteen volumes and "The Days of H. L. Mencken" in six volumes.

Page 382 I turned to: My last interview with him came on March 1, 1967. I was out of the country when he died.

Page 383 As William Manchester: To restate a point I made in the introduction to the Notes.

Index

Abell, Walter W., 41

Abhau, Carl Heinrich, 16

Abramson, Ben, 358

"Absurd Effort to Make the World Over, The," 250, 251

Adams, Henry, 208

Adams, John Haslup, 42, 111, 112, 191, 195, 404

"Adventures of a Y.M.C.A. Lad," 358

Aikman, Duncan, 271

"Alcohol and the Duration of Life," 246

Alger, Horatio, 204

Alison, May, 146

All God's Chillun Got Wings, 215, 224

America and the Young Intellectual, 165

"American, The," 43

American Academy of Arts and Letters, 90, 400–401

American and Allied Ideals: An Appeal to Those Who are neither Hot nor Cold, 128

American Credo, The, 212

"American: His Language, The," 120

"American: His New Puritanism, The," 100

American Language, The: genesis of, 120; main idea, 120–21; ramifications, 122; reception, 122; mentioned, 3, 4, 123, 128, 138, 275, 368

"American Magazine, The," 99, 123

American Mercury, The: early plans for, 66–67, 76–77; final plans, 214–15; rift between M and Nathan,

215–20; M's association with Knopf, 222, 224, 227–30; M's work with Edith Lustgarten, 230–32; M's work with Charles Angoff, 234–40; M's shaping the *Mercury,* 242–58; stress on science, 243–48; stress on medicine, 248; influence of William Graham Sumner's social Darwinism on M and the *Mercury,* 248–52; M's managing of contributors, 252–54; decline of *Mercury,* 256–58, 263; influence of *Mercury* on other magazines, 258–62; mentioned, 5, 58, 71, 108, 157, 163, 164, 171, 180, 183, 187, 207, 209, 213, 225, 226, 233, 241, 260, 261, 262, 264, 266, 268, 270, 271, 273, 274, 275, 285, 287, 292, 305, 307, 325, 326, 336, 342, 345, 359, 360

American Mind, The, 89

"American Pronouns," 120

American Spectator, 219

American Spirit in Literature, The, 90

American temper, The

—*circa* 1900–1919: Puritanism, 78–80; moralism in literature, 81–82; avoidance of social-protest fiction, 85–89; domination by conservative critics, 89–90; the growth of anti-conservative forces, 90–95; the revolt in poetry, 95–97; conservative concessions, 98–99; Puritan counter-reformation, 101–2

—*circa* 1919–1929: M and the disillusioned young, 164–66; influence of business on government, 167–68; the Red Scare, 168–70; Puritanism, 170–78; the Prohibition campaign, 171–73; sexual freedom, 173–74, 176–77; M and Greenwich Village, 174–76; M and the status of women, 177–78; M and the politics of the 1920s, 178–81

—*circa* 1929–1941: the Depression and the New Deal, 306–11, 313, 317, 319–20

—World War II and after, 363–66

American Tragedy, An, 185, 324, 325, 360

Anarchism and Other Essays, 99

Anderson, C. Farley, 360

Anderson, Sherwood, 74, 98, 184

Andreyev, Leonid, 125, 182

Angoff, Charles: editorial assistant at *Mercury,* 235–36; rift with M, 236–40; hostile view of M in his *H. L. Mencken: A Portrait from Memory,* 237–40; mentioned, 209, 225, 231, 232, 241, 259, 261, 305, 360

Anti-feminism, 118–20

"Anti-Saloon League Lobby has Congress Badly Scared," 173

Archer, Herbert Winslow, 76

Archer, William, 57

"Armenian Buncombe, The," 192

Arrowsmith, 166, 184, 185, 186, 247

"Arsenals of Hatred," 271

"Art and the Mob," 203

"Artist, The," 57, 104, 117

"Art of Lynching, The," 43

Asbury, Herbert, 270–71

"Asses' Carnival, The," 203

Astaire, Adele, 162

"Athens," 345

Atlantic Monthly, 52, 59, 89, 98, 114, 130, 217, 242, 258, 275, 356, 364

Auden, W. H., 334

Aug. Mencken & Bro., 12, 28

Auslander, Joseph, 184

"Autobiographical Notes, 1925," 11 *passim*

"Autobiographical Notes, 1941—," 11, 15, 17, 392

Babbitt, 166, 186

Babbitt, Irving, 109, 175, 263

"Babes in the Woods," 74

Baker, Benjamin, Dr., 234, 301, 367, 369, 370

Baker, Harry, 281

"Bald-Headed Man, The," 105

Baltimore *American,* 30, 33, 34, 47, 51, 279

"Baltimore and the Rest of the World," 35, 46, 395

Baltimore *Evening News,* 41, 42, 85

Baltimore *Herald:* M's work at, 27–40; as reporter, 28–35; training by Max Ways, 29, 36; training by Robert Carter, 32–33; training by Lynn Meekins, 33; as columnist, 35–36; as editor, 37–41; as drama critic, 50–52; experiences recollected in *Newspaper Days,* 356–57; mentioned, 4, 17, 26, 46, 47, 48, 53, 55, 60, 132, 135

Baltimore *Sunpapers:* M as editor of *Sunday Sun,* 41; as editorial writer for *Evening Sun,* 42; as columnist for *Evening Sun,* 42–45; as author of Free Lance column, *Evening Sun,* 43–45; growing rift over World War I, 111–15; M as war correspondent in Germany, 113–14; rejoins *Sunpapers,* 191–92; M's effect on *Evening Sun,* 193–94; M's work with Paul Patterson, 194–98; M on function of a newspaper, 195–96, 197–98; M as editor of *Evening Sun,* 198–200; M settles *Sunpapers'* dispute with Archbishop Michael Curley, 201–2; M's writing for *Sunpapers,* 202–6; M's Monday Articles for *Evening Sun,* 202–5, 308, 314–20; M's Sunday Articles for *Sun,* 205; diminished relationship during World War II, 362–63; M resumes fulltime work, 364–66; mentioned, 4, 5, 7, 21, 30, 51, 52, 53, 60, 81, 95, 117, 118, 120, 133, 135, 140, 141, 142, 143, 148, 152, 163, 173, 180, 190, 223, 236, 242, 246, 254, 255, 266, 269, 289, 290, 291, 301, 304, 307, 311, 321, 333, 336, 338, 339, 340, 343, 346, 352, 357, 360, 382, 383

Bamburger, Joe, 36
Bankhead, Tallulah, 280
"Barbarous Bradley, The," 349
Barnes, Harry Elmer, 255
Barrack-Room Ballads, 22
Beach, Rex, 59
"Beautifying American Literature," 110
Beerbohm, Max, 182
Bellamy, Edward, 22
Benda, Lilith, 75
"Bend in the Tube, The," 348
Benet, Stephen Vincent, 75
Ben-Hur, 22
Bennett, Arnold, 182
Benton, Thomas Hart, 116
"Best of the Lot, The," 75
Best Short Stories, 285, 302
Beveridge, Albert, Senator, 80, 85, 89
Bierce, Ambrose, 54
Big Frogs, 188
Biggers, Earl Derr, 182
Biology of Death, 244
Black, Harry, 43, 191, 195, 197, 336
Black, Hugo, Justice, 336
Black Mask, 70, 71
Bloom, Estelle, 152, 155
Bloom, Marion: M's friendship with, 152–55, 328–29; mentioned, 18, 156, 157, 158, 163, 334, 408
"Blue-Nose Utopia, The," 203
"Blue Review," 67, 214
"Blue Weekly," 66, 67
Bodine, A. Aubrey, 293
Bohemian Magazine, 57, 104, 105, 117
Boni, Albert, 97
Boni, Charles, 97
Bookman, 47, 181, 208, 209, 259
Book of Burlesques, A, 58, 117
Book of Life, The, 188
Book of Prefaces, A: "Puritanism as a Literary Force," 100–101; "Theodore Dreiser," 110; book in general, 117; mentioned, 95, 119, 123, 128, 221, 241
"Boon of Culture, The," 257
"Boon to Bores, A," 203
Boston *Herald*, 274
Bottoms Up, 139
Bouton, S. Miles, 201
Boyd, Ernest: M's friendship with, 139–42; Boyd writes *H. L. Mencken*,

141–42; mentioned, 69, 70, 74, 107, 108, 109, 111, 113, 153, 154, 158, 162, 165, 170, 172, 173, 175, 191, 192, 218, 219, 241, 242, 259, 320, 324
Boyd, Julian, 7, 381, 436
Boyd, Madeleine, 140, 333
Boyer, Norman, 60, 61, 62, 65, 66, 82
Bradford, Gamaliel, 182, 184
Braley, Berton, 210
Brawnyman, 189
Brieux, Eugene, 82
Bright Doom, The, 190
Broedel, Max, 132, 133, 135, 136, 141, 305, 322, 362
Brooks, Van Wyck, 97, 98, 99, 165
Brownell, William Crary, 89, 90
Bryan, William Jennings: M's contempt for, 268–69; mentioned, 172, 265, 266, 270
"Bryan the Flycatcher," 269
Buchholz, Heinrich, 133, 136, 323
Buckle, Henry Thomas, 79
Buddenbohn, C. L., Dr., 354
Buddenbrooks, 225
Butterick Publications, 103, 105

Cabell, James Branch, 60, 182, 184, 211, 219, 265, 271, 324
Cabot, Godfrey Lowell, 270
Cabot, Thomas Dudley, 270
Cain, James M., 146, 280, 302, 305, 306, 323, 324, 329
Caine, Hall, 182
Cairns, Huntington, 148, 265, 334, 361
"Cairo," 345
"Calamity at Appomatox, The," 257
Callahan, Joe, 34, 132, 133
Callahan, Patrick, Colonel, 266
Canby, Henry Seidel, 275
"Career," 285, 287
"Carnival of Buncombe, A," 180, 202
Carter, Robert I., 32, 33, 36, 37, 46, 50, 52
Cather, Willa, 75, 182, 184, 211
Catholic Review, 201
CCNY *Mercury*, 262
Century, 89, 99, 242, 258, 259, 285
Chambers, Robert W., 213

"Charity Racket, The," 204
Charlatanry of the Learned, 14–15, 352, 359
"Charmed Circle, The," 349
Chase, J. Franklin, Reverend, 271, 272, 273, 275
Cheslock, Louis, 374, 375
Chesterton, G. K., 182
"Chicago," 96
Chicago *Daily News,* 119, 140
Chicago *Record-Herald,* 49
Chicago *Tribune,* 158, 206, 265
Chief Sitting Bull ("Chief Standing Bear"), 237
Childs, Marquis, 319
Christianity: attack in *The Philosophy of Friedrich Nietzsche,* 83–84; attack in *Treatise on the Gods,* 275–78; M softens view, 333; attack in *Treatise on Right and Wrong,* 346–47
Circular Staircase, The, 124
Circus Parade, 189
Civilization in the United States, 165
Clark, Emily, 184, 216
Clendening, Logan, Dr., 226, 248
Cleveland *Press,* 313
"Clinical Notes," 219, 256, 260
"Clowns Enter the Ring, The," 316
"Clown Show," 180
Cobb, Irvin S., 182
Collected Poems, 187
Colliers, 353
"Coming, Eden Bower!" 75
Compson, Betty, 160
Comstock, Anthony, 79, 100, 101, 102, 106, 149
"Confederate Notes," 203
Conrad, Joseph, 43, 110, 113, 125, 182, 211, 337, 338
Convention and Revolt in Poetry, 187
Cooke, Alistair, 364
"Cook's Victory, The," 348
"Cool Tombs," 96
Coolidge, Calvin, 168, 178, 179, 193, 203, 204, 206, 276
Coolidge, Julian Lowell, 270
Cora, 189
Cords of Vanity, The, 184
Corelli, Marie, 72, 124, 182

Cornell, *Widow,* 262
Coughlin, Charles, Reverend, 314, 320
Counts, George, 308
Crane, Stephen, 22, 82, 92
Creative Criticism, 127
Criterion, 49
"Criticism of Criticism of Criticism," 115, 123, 127
"Critics and Their Ways," 115
Croly, Herbert, 98
Crowe, Eugene, 67, 68, 70, 71
Cruze, James, 160, 286
Cullen, John, 115
Cunningham, A. B., Colonel, 32
"Curbing the Cops," 43
Curley, Michael Joseph, Archbishop, 201
Curme, G. O., 122
Cyclop's Eye, 184

Damn! A Book of Calumny, 117–18, 139, 141, 221
Daniels, Josephus, 203
Dark Laughter, 184
Darrow, Clarence, 259, 265, 266, 267, 268, 269, 271
Dartmouth College Library: collection of Mencken materials, 382
Darwin, Charles, 79, 81, 83, 85, 91, 92, 93, 104, 126, 171, 204, 249, 252, 266, 277, 306
Das Kapital, 86
d'Aubigny, Pierre, 76, 152
Davey, Martin L., Governor, 319
Davis, Curtis, 431
Davis, Elrick B., 313
Davis, H. L., 361
Davis, Richard Harding, 22, 182
Davis, Watson, 268
"Day of Reckoning, A," 307
Days books: background and genesis, 347–51; mentioned, 6, 7, 8
"Death: A Philosophical Discussion," 117
"Decay of Swooning, The," 43
De Charlataneria Eruditorum. See *Charlatanry of the Learned*
de Kruif, Paul, 184, 185, 186, 247

de Laporte, Arnaud, 75

Delineator, 60, 103, 104, 105

Denby, Hester, 294, 296, 298, 304

De Voto, Bernard, 273

Dewey, John, 91, 92, 93

Dewey, Thomas, 364, 370

Dial, 84

"Diamond as Big as the Ritz, The," 74

"Diary of a Retreat, The," 114

"Dip into Statecraft, A," 358

"Discoverer of the Forgotten Man, The," 252

"Dithyrambs on Alcohol," 173

"Dizzy Rise (and Ensuing Bust) of Simplified Spelling, The," 347

D. L. Moody, 184

Dobson, Austin, 48

"Doctor Evangelicus," 203

Dodsworth, 166, 187

Doerer, Thomas, 38, 39

Doll's House, A, 57

Dorman, Israel, 322

"Downfall of a Revolutionary," 356

Drayham, William, 349

"Dreiser, Bugaboo, The," 98, 109, 110

Dreiser, Theodore: M's early relationship with, 103–11; M's support of Dreiser's novels, 105–8; M's rift with Dreiser, 324–26; reconciliation, 326; M's estimate of Dreiser's importance, 328; mentioned, 19, 57, 60, 61, 66, 67, 68, 69, 72, 79, 82, 86, 88, 90, 92, 93, 98, 101, 102, 114, 125, 126, 127, 128, 129, 139, 141, 152, 170, 174, 175, 183, 185, 188, 211, 213, 219, 304, 327, 339, 348, 355, 356, 358, 359, 360, 361, 427

"Drug Store," 225

Dudek, J. B., Right Reverend, 122

Duffy, Anne Rector: acquaintance of M and friend of his wife, 297–98; mentioned, 280, 282, 289, 290, 293, 294, 299, 300, 301

Duffy, Edmund, 299

Dunsany, Lord, 62, 75, 211

duPont, Alfred, 296, 305, 330, 331, 332, 333, 334

Du Pont, Iréné, 335

Du Pont, Lammot, 335

duPont, Marcella: M's friendship with, 330–36; mentioned, 296, 305, 339, 343, 358

"Earliest Attempts at Verse and Prose, 1895–1901," 23, 47

"Early News Stories: Baltimore Morning Herald," 28

"Eastern Shore Kultur, The," 201

Eddington, Arthur, Sir, 154

Eddy, Mary Baker, 86, 154, 332

Edson, Peter, 5

"Educational Process, The," 358

Egoists: A Book of Supermen, 95

Ehrmann, Herbert, 272

Eisler, Robert, 226

Eliot, Charles W., 270

Ellicott City *Times,* 21

Elmer Gantry, 166, 187

Encyclopedia, Chambers's, 22

End of American Innocence, The, 80, 98

"End of an Era, The," 204

"End of Ilsa Menteith, The," 75

"England's English," 120

Enoch Pratt Free Library: collection of Mencken materials, 381–82; mentioned, 22, 25, 49, 183, 207, 279, 309, 317, 349, 353, 375

Erskine, John, 60

Ervine, St. John, 181

Europe after 8:15, 116

Everybody's, 65

"Expurgators, The," 43

Farley, James, 319

Farrell, James T., 361

Faulkner, William, 239

Fergusson, Harvey, 236

Field and Stream, 68

Field, Eugene, 210

Financier, The, 105, 106

Fink, William, 76

Finn, Huckleberry, 7, 19, 22

Fishbein, Morris, Dr., 246, 248

Fitzgerald, F. Scott, 74, 146, 176, 185, 280

Flame and Shadow, 189

"Flapper, The," 176

Fleischmann, Raoul, 306

"Footnote on Criticism," 128

"For Better, for Worse," 203

"Foreign Parts," 345

"Forgotten Man, The," 250

Forum, 98, 259

Fox, John, Jr., 59

Frankfurter, Felix, 273

Franklin Street, 350

"Free Lance, The," 4, 5, 36, 43, 44, 45, 46, 112, 141, 205, 220

"French Marriages," 43

Frenzied Finance, 65, 91

Freud, Sigmund, 79, 93, 94, 98, 126, 176, 238

Freudianism: M's mixed view of, 93–94

"From the Programme of a Concert," 117

"From the Publisher to the Readers of The American Mercury," 229

Frost, Robert, 4, 96, 98

Froude, James Anthony, 79

"Fruits of Folly," 194

Gallagher, Miriam, Sister: M's friendship with, 340–43; mentioned, 330, 339

Galsworthy, John, 182

Garrison, Fielding, Dr., 129, 151

Gary, Elbert, Judge, 168

"General William Booth Enters Heaven," 96

"Genius," The, 88, 106, 111, 175

Genius of Style, The, 90

Gentlemen Prefer Blondes, 162, 187, 302

Gentry, Lois: M's nurse, 372–74

George, W. L., 75

George Bernard Shaw: His Plays: genesis and analysis, 54–56; mentioned, 52, 79

Germany, 108–14, 129–30, 228–29, 335–36

Ghosts, 51

"Girl from Red Lion, P.A., The," 349, 356–57

Gish, Lillian, 299

Gist of Nietzsche, The, 82

Glyn, Elinor, 213

Goddard, Pliny, 256

"God Help Us All!" 168

Gold, Michael, 263

Goldberg, Isaac, 6, 11, 17, 21, 22, 23, 24, 25, 26, 60, 61, 134, 211, 212, 218, 253

Goldman, Emma, 99–100

Goodman, Albert, 34

Goodman, Daniel Carson, 102

Goodman, Philip: M's friendship with, 138–40; influence of Mencken-Goodman correspondence on M's *Days* books, 349–51; mentioned, 117, 118, 143, 146, 186, 221, 235, 321, 326

Goodman, Ruth, 138, 311, 326

"Good, the Bad and the Best Sellers, The," 124, 125

"Government by Blackleg," 170

Grasty, Charles, 41, 42, 43, 44

Gray, Judd, 203

Grayson, David, 182

Great Gatsby, The, 176, 185

"Great Moral Sport, A," 203

Green Mansions, 97

Greenwich Village, 174–76

Griffith, D. W., 162

Gunther, John, 242

Guttmacher, Manfred, Dr., 358

Haardt, John, 292, 300

Haardt, Sara. *See* Sara Haardt Mencken

Hagar Revelly, 102

Hamburger, Samuel, 132

Hanes, Elizabeth, 367, 368

Hanes, Frederick, Dr., 296

Hapgood, Hutchins, 170

Happy Days, 1880–1892: genesis and analysis, 353–56; mentioned, 6, 7, 9, 11, 13, 22, 334, 351, 374

Harding, Warren Gamaliel, 167, 178, 179, 203, 204, 206

Hardy, Thomas, 182

Harper's Bazar, 162

Harper's Magazine, 33, 99, 258, 259

Harris, Frank, 190

Harriss, R. P., 200, 283, 286, 301

Harvey, Alexander, 185
"Hatrack" case, The: 270–75; mentioned, 5, 101, 171, 224, 263, 264, 278, 326, 355
Hatteras, Amelia, 76
Hatteras, Owen, 62, 75, 152, 173, 349, 360
Hawks, Arthur, 27
Hawks, Wells, 28
Hayes, Thomas, Mayor, 31
Hays, Arthur Garfield, 272, 273, 274
Hazlitt, Henry, 228, 237
Heathen Days, 1890–1936: genesis and analysis, 358–59; mentioned, 6, 114, 334
Heavens, 189
Hedda Gabler, 57
Hello Towns! 184
Hemberger, Theodor, 117, 132, 133, 135, 136, 141, 322
Hemingway, Ernest, 430
Henry, Daniel, 147
Henry, O., 182
"Heredity and Uplift," 246
Hergesheimer, Joseph, 97, 157, 159, 160, 161, 162, 163, 185, 186, 216, 281, 287, 296, 301, 303, 324, 333, 334, 338
Hildebrandt, Albert, 132, 133, 135, 136, 323
Hirshberg, Leonard, Dr., 104
History of a Lover, The, 170
Hitler, Adolf, 181, 201, 228, 229, 327, 335, 339, 358
"Hitlerismus," 228, 229
H. L. Mencken, 141–42, 218, 241
"H. L. Mencken," 208
H. L. Mencken: and the American Mercury *Adventure,* 261
H. L. Mencken: A Portrait from Memory, 236, 237–40
H. L. Mencken, Literary Critic, 125
Hofstadter, Richard, 249, 252
Hollywood, M's trip to: 159–61
Holt, Henry, 85
"Homecoming, A," 75
Homer in the Sagebrush, 189
"Homo Sapiens," 152, 163, 255, 287
Hood, Gretchen, 163

Hoover, Herbert, 194, 204, 206, 276, 294, 306, 307, 316, 317, 318
"Hot Dogs," 204
House of Satan, 187
Howard, Sidney, 198
Howe, E. W., 226
Howells, William Dean, 22, 33, 62, 82, 182
"Huckleberry Finn" (by M), 43
Huckleberry Finn, 105, 125, 339
Hudson, W. H., 97
Huebsch, B. W., 97
Human Body, The, 226
Huneker, James Gibbons, 54, 68, 72, 79, 94, 95, 110, 113, 182, 186, 340, 341
Hussey, L. M., 246
Huxley, Aldous, 75, 162, 190
Huxley, Thomas, 53, 56, 79, 91, 93, 104, 204, 226, 249, 252, 266, 306, 333

Ibsen, Henrik, 51, 52, 56, 57, 58, 82, 92, 100, 146
Iconoclasts: A Book of Dramatists, 95
Ideals, 188
"Idyl," 47, 348
Igoe, Michael L., 316
"I'm a Stranger Here Myself," 74
In American—Poems, 190, 225
Including Horace, 189
"In Defense of the Gallus," 43
In Defense of Women: genesis and analysis, 118–20; mentioned, 4, 84, 128, 139, 154, 177, 213, 221, 291, 296, 299, 336
Intimate Notebooks of George Jean Nathan, The, 71, 213–20
Ireland's Literary Renaissance, 141
"Istanbul," 345
"I Want to Know Why," 74

Jaffé, Louis, 290, 291
James, Henry, 22, 182, 208
James, William, 79, 91, 92, 93
Jeans, James, Sir, 154
Jefferson, Thomas: American language, 120

Jenks, Leland, 255
Jennie Gerhardt, 105
Jersey Journal, 377
"Jerusalem," 345
Jews, The, 96, 229, 333, 375, 422
John Greenleaf Whittier, 89
John Lane Company, 106, 116
Johnson, Gerald, 200, 290, 305
Johnson, James Weldon, 226
Johnson, Robert Underwood, 79, 89, 90
John W. Luce & Company, 54, 57, 58, 83
Jones, Jefferson, 107, 116
Jones, Jesse, 319
"Joseph Conrad," 43, 110
Joyce, James, 75, 97
Jungle, The, 88

Kean, Fred, 233, 234
"Keeping the Puritans Pure," 271
Keller, Albert G., 249, 250, 251, 252
Kelly, Howard, Dr.: M's acquaintance with, 149–51; mentioned, 203
Kemler, Edgar, 53, 375
Kennerley, Mitchell, 79, 97, 98, 102
Kent, Frank, 30, 200, 259, 333
Kenyon, Bernice Lesbia, 186
"Kill-Joy as a Moses, The," 81
Kingsbury, Edward, 53
Kipling, Rudyard, 22, 48, 182, 337
Kline, Virginia, 51
Knapp, Friedrich, Professor, 20
Knapp's Institute, 10
"Knocks and Jollies," 35, 395
Knopf, Alfred: first meeting with M, 220; business relationship as M's publisher, 221–22; mutual interests, 222–24; M as literary scout for Knopf's firm, 224–26; efforts to salvage *Mercury,* 227–30; mentioned, 97, 110, 117, 121, 123, 209, 214, 215, 218, 234, 235, 236, 237, 241, 272, 287, 301, 326, 340, 353, 362, 366, 374, 415
Knopf, Alfred A., Inc., 97, 120, 122, 141, 215, 225, 226, 227, 355, 357, 360, 375

Knopf, Blanche, 214, 222, 312, 353, 374, 428
Knopf, Samuel, 272
Koppel, Holger, 57
Krapp, George Philip, 253, 255
Krock, Arthur, 161, 254
"Ku Klux Buffoonery, The," 203

Ladies' Home Journal, 18
"La Lettre," 75
La Monte, Robert Rives, 54, 55, 85, 141, 237
Landon, Alfred, Governor, 318, 320, 352
Lardner, Ring, 120, 165, 186
"Larval Stage of a Bookworm, The," 353
"Last Happy Days of H. L. Mencken," 365
"Late Mr. Wells, The," 123
Laukhuff, Richard, 123
Lawrence, D. H., 68, 97
Lawson, Thomas, 65, 91
Leacock, Stephen, 182
"Leaves from a Notebook," 204
Lee, Bessie, 294, 295, 296, 298, 299, 300, 304
Lehman, Herbert, Governor, 319
Leslie's Monthly, 15
Leslie's Weekly, 47
"Letters and Documents Relating to the Baltimore *Sunpapers,*" 361, 382
Lewis, Dorothy Thompson, 293
Lewis, Michael, 293
Lewis, Sinclair: M's praise of, 166, 326; importance of M to, 166, 185, 186–87; mentioned, 74, 127, 146, 167, 184, 231, 247, 293, 324, 338, 339
Lewisohn, Ludwig, 182
Life, 47
Lilith, 189
Lindsay, Vachel, 95, 96, 97, 187
Linkletter, Art, 373
Lippmann, Walter, 4, 97, 99, 238, 315
"Literary Note," 202
Little Book in C Major, A, 116–17
Little Eyolf, 57
Little Henrietta, 188

Little Review, 111

Little Shepherd of Kingdom Come, The, 59

Lohrfinck, Rosalind, Mrs., 200, 295, 361, 369, 370, 372, 373, 375, 382, 383

London, Jack, 60, 86, 182

London *Daily Express,* 312

Longworth, Nicholas, 257

Looking Backward, 22

Loos, Anita: M's friendship with, 161–62, 329–30; mentioned, 160, 187, 302, 334

Lord, Pauline, 146

Lord Jim, 338

Lorimer, George Horace, 169, 261

Los Angeles *Times,* 66, 123

Louisville *Courier-Journal,* 41

"Louse magazines," 70–71, 107

Love Nest and Other Stories, The, 186

Love's Pilgrimage, 88

"Love Story," 359

Lovette, Leland: M's friendship with, 336–40; mentioned, 330, 343

Lowes, John Livingston, 187

Lowie, Robert, 255

Luce. *See* John W. Luce & Company

Ludendorff, Erich, General, 113

Lustgarten, Edith: office secretary at *Mercury,* 230–32; goes on strike after M leaves, 233; M helps when her husband falls ill, 233–34; mentioned, 209, 235, 236, 239, 273

Luther, Mark Lee, 67

Lynch, Josh, 36

Mackay, Helen, 182

Maggie: A Girl of the Streets, 82

Main Street, 166, 186

Making a President: genesis and analysis, 314–17

Making of a Lady, The, 287, 302

Malone, Dudley Field, 265

Manchester, William, 19, 60, 61, 73, 192, 266, 374, 375, 383

Man Mencken, The, 6, 218

Mann, Thomas, 225

Mann, William D'Alton, Colonel, 59, 65

Mansfield, Richard, 52

Man Who Knew Coolidge, The, 166

"March of the Flag, The," 80

Maritzer, Lou, 155

Marks, Percy, 187

Martin, T. T., Pastor, 266

Marx, Karl, 85

Masses, 98

Masters, Edgar Lee, 95, 96, 327, 329, 334, 339, 349

Maugham, W. Somerset, 75, 156, 182

May, Henry, 80, 82, 98

Mayer, Louis B., 159

Mayfield, Sara, 280, 281, 282, 283, 284, 288, 289, 293, 312

McClure, John, 97, 253

McClure's, 99

McCullers, Carson, 302

McDannald, A. H., 173, 295, 322, 323

McKelway, St. Clair, 352, 353, 356

McKinley, William, 80, 85, 167

McKinsey, Folger, 136, 322

McNaught's Monthly, 261

McTeague, 86

Meekins, Lynn, 33, 37, 38, 40, 46, 55

Mein Kampf, 228, 229

Mellon, Andrew, 179

"Memoirs of Deceased Pedagogues," 353

Mencken, Anna Abhau, 16–18

Mencken, August (M's father): M's view of, 11; comparison with his father, 11–13, 15; M's struggle against his father 23–26; mentioned, 9, 10, 14, 16

Mencken, August (M's brother): takes care of M after M's crippling stroke, 370–72, 374; mentioned, 18, 19, 237, 301, 304, 312, 340, 369, 373, 375, 376, 382, 383

Mencken, Burkhardt Ludwig, 15, 16, 17

Mencken, Caroline Gerhardt Belz, 16

Mencken, Charles, 10, 11, 15, 16, 18, 20, 376

Mencken, Gertrude, 16, 18

Mencken, Henry Louis: as newspaper-man, 4–5, 21, 26, 27–45, 111–15, 191–206, 307–20, 356–57, 362–66;

reputation, 4, 6, 241–42, 274–75, 313, 377, 391; childhood, 9–12, 15–16, 19–21, 23, 353–54; with his father, 11–13, 15, 23–26; ancestry, 14–15; hoaxes, 14, 213, 392; with his mother, 16–18; closeness of his family, 18–19; schooling, 20, 353; early writing, 21, 23–25, 46–49, 47–49, 50–52, 54–56, 57–58, 397; self-education, 21–24, 353; reporter, editor, columnist on Baltimore *Herald*, 28–35, 37–41, 356–57, 395; variously as writer, columnist, editor, advisor on Baltimore *Sunpapers*, 41–45, 111–15, 191–206, 307–20, 362–66; as critic of drama, literature, ideas, 50–52, 54–56, 123–28, 127; develops individual style, 53–54; as playwright, 57–58; on *Smart Set*, 59–77; association with Nathan, 61–64, 68–77, 137–38, 209–13, 215–20; hypochondria, 64 *passim*; as magazine editor, 68–77, 70–71, 207–63; writing for *Smart Set*, 75–76; feud with Stuart Sherman, 109–11, 128–29; writing for New York *Evening Mail*, 115–16; men friends, 137–49, 321–28; association with Philip Goodman, 138–40, 349–51; association with Dreiser, 103–11, 324–26, 328; association with Ernest Boyd, 139–42; association with Paul Patterson, 142–43, 194–98; association with Raymond Pearl, 144–48, 244–45; association with Hamilton Owens, 148, 193–94; women friends, 151–63, 328–36; friendship with Marion Bloom, 152–55, 328–29; friendship with Beatrice Wilson, 155–57, 329; friendship with Aileen Pringle, 157–61, 329; trip to Hollywood, 159–61; friendship with Anita Loos, 161–62; 329–30; Red Scare, 168–70; influence on writers of the 1920s, 183–90, 252–54; on *American Mercury*, 214–63; association with Alfred Knopf, 220–30; association with Edith Lustgarten, 230–34; association with Charles Angoff, 235–40; Scopes trial, 264–69; "Hatrack" case, 270–75; association with Sara Haardt, 281–301, 304–6; Gridiron Banquet, 308–11; friendship with Marcella duPont, 330–36; association with Leland Lovette, 336–40; association with Sister Miriam Gallagher, 340–43; writing in *New Yorker*, 344–45, 347, 351–59; as short-story writer, 348–49, 394; declining health, 367–76

—views on literature: composition a chore, 3; reliability of autobiography, 7; social novel, 86–89; puritan critics, 90; "New Poetry" movement, 95–97; romantic literature, 337–39

—views on other matters: puritanism, 5, 78–79, 81, 89–90, 100–102, 170–78, 264, 269–78; Nietzsche's superman, 83; socialism, 85; Freudianism, 93–94; sympathy for Germany, 108–14, 129–30, 228–29, 335–36; anti-feminism, 118–20; science, 144–45, 243–48; Prohibition movement, 171–73; sexual freedom, 173–74, 176–77; Greenwich Village, 174–76; status of women, 177–78; politics, 178–81, 204, 306–20, 334–36, 363–65; Jews 96, 229, 333, 375; religion, 264–69, 333, 339, 343, 346–47

Mencken, Johann Burkhardt (Johann Burkhard Mencke), 14, 15, 352, 359
Mencken, Lüder, 15
Mencken, Otto, 14
Mencken, Sara Haardt: 279–303; her character, 280, 282, 286, 288, 294, 299, 301–3; her writing, 280–81, 285–86, 289, 302; courtship by M, 281–84, 286, 288–89; engagement to M, 289–92; marriage to M, 292–303; view of Saturday Night Club, 298–99; final illness, 300–301; aftermath of marriage for M, 304–6; mentioned, 9, 18, 137, 151, 161, 163, 265, 311, 313, 321, 328, 329, 330, 331, 333, 334, 338, 344, 345, 347, 350, 352, 359, 371, 376
Mencken, Virginia, 16, 296
Mencken Chrestomathy, A, 361–62
Menckeniana: A Schimpflexikon, 2, 287
Men versus the Man: A Correspondence between Robert Rives La Monte,

Socialist and H. L. Mencken, Individualist, 55, 85, 237

Mercury. See *American Mercury*

Meredith, George, 182

"Merry-Go-Round, The," 75

Messiah Jesus and John the Baptist, The, 226

Microbe Hunters, 184, 247

Milburn, George, 225

Millay, Edna St. Vincent, 97

"Millennium Dawns, The," 173

Milwaukee *Sentinel,* 49

Minority Report: genesis and analysis, 362, 374–75; mentioned, 134, 252

"Miss Thompson," 156

Moffett, W. Edwin, 322

"Monday Articles," 5, 168, 170, 171, 173, 180, 193, 194, 201, 202, 203, 204, 205, 206, 252, 296, 307, 308, 340

Moneychangers, The, 88, 124

Monroe, Harriet, 68, 79, 96, 98

Montgomery *Advertiser,* 279

Moon of the Caribbees and Six Other Plays of the Sea, The, 188

Moore, George, 68, 182

Moral, 94

More, Paul Elmer, 175, 181, 263

"More American," 120

"More Law Enforcement," 204

Morgan, Harriet, 76

Moult, Thomas, 190

Mr. George Jean Nathan Presents, 221

"Mrs. Tillie Himmelheber," 350

Mrs. Warren's Profession, 55

Mumford, Lewis, 165, 256

Munsey, Frank, 66

Murphy, J. E., 290

Music: at Saturday Night Club, 131–36; M's love for, 133–34; M's preferences in, 134–35; Bach Festival, 223–24

"My Father," 11

"My Life as Author and Editor," 361, 382

Nathan, George Jean: first meeting with M, 61–62; M's picture of Nathan, 62–63; Nathan's picture of M, 63–64; as co-editor of *Smart Set,* 68–77; M's friendship with, 137–38; renown of M's friendship with, 209–11; comparison of M and Nathan, 211–13; rift over *Mercury,* 215–20; mentioned, 65, 66, 67, 78, 94, 106, 107, 111, 116, 139, 140, 141, 146, 151, 152, 153, 162, 163, 165, 166, 174, 176, 187, 188, 208, 214, 221, 222, 230

Nation, 63, 85, 109, 110, 177, 180, 230, 242, 275

National Institute of Arts and Letters, 90

"National Letters, The," 175, 176

National Magazine, 47

"Naturalism of Mr. Dreiser, The," 109

"Neglected Anniversary, A," 115

Neihardt, John G., 97

New Dictionary of Quotations on Historical Principles, A: genesis and analysis, 359–60; mentioned, 358

New England Magazine, 47

New God for America, A, 292

New Machiavelli, The, 66

New Masses, 263

"New Platinum Toning Bath, for Silver Prints, A," 21

"New Poetry" movement, 95–97

"New Poetry Movement, The," 96–97, 123

New Republic, 63, 98, 111, 129, 181, 207, 208, 242

Newspaper Days, 1899–1906: genesis and analysis, 356–57; mentioned, 6, 26, 27, 31, 33, 36, 38, 39, 46, 51, 54, 57, 251, 334, 349, 358, 360, 361

Newsweek, 305

New York *American,* 206

New Yorker: M's contributions, 344–45, 347, 351–59; mentioned, 205, 243, 259, 260, 306, 334, 349, 368, 420, 433

New York *Evening Mail:* M's writing for, 115–16; mentioned, 173

New York *Evening Post,* 141

New York *Globe,* 57

New York *Graphic,* 273

New York *Herald Tribune,* 274, 363

New York *Morning Telegraph,* 34

New York Public Library: collection of Mencken materials, 381–82; mentioned, 155, 209, 231, 373
New York *Sun*, 37, 53, 94, 210
New York *Times*, 84, 242, 262, 306, 371
New York *Tribune*, 119
New York *World*, 196, 303, 324, 325
Nietzsche, Friedrich, 54, 55, 56, 60, 66, 67, 79, 81, 83, 84, 85, 93, 128, 141, 180, 249, 277, 306
"Nietzscheana," 43
Nigger Heaven, 190
Nolte, William, 125
Norris, Charles, 188
Norris, Frank, 86, 88, 182, 188
Norris, Kathleen, 182
North American Review, 99, 259
North of Boston, 96
Northwestern *Purple Parrot*, 262
Notebooks. See The Intimate Notebooks of George Jean Nathan
"Note from the Editors, A," 75
"Note on My Relations to Nathan," 211
"Notes for an Honest Autobiography," 203
Notes on Democracy: genesis and analysis, 180–81; mentioned, 84, 328
"Notes on Morals," 43
"Notes on Paleozoic Publicists," 358
"Novels and Other Books—Chiefly Bad," 125
"Novels for Hot Afternoons," 125

O'Connor, Flannery, 302
Octopus, The, 86
"Ode to the Pennant on the Centerfield Pole," 47
O. Henry Memorial Prize Stories, 302
Old Soak, The, 139
Olivier, Stuart, 41
Oneal, James, 253, 256
O'Neill, Eugene, 175, 188, 215, 219, 231
"On Going to Church," 54
"On Learning to Play the 'Cello," 273
Oppenheim, E. Phillips, 182
Oppenheim, James, 96, 98
Oppenheimer, George, 285

"Origin and Nature of Law, The," 204
"Osteopathy," 246
"Outcast, The," 348
"Overdose of Novels, An," 125
Owens, Hamilton: M's association with, 148, 193–94; mentioned, 135, 136, 147, 195, 199, 205, 290, 291, 299, 301, 322, 338, 363, 374, 376, 383
Owens, John, 192, 195, 196, 197, 255, 290, 291, 294, 311
Owens, Olga, 148, 299, 329
Owst, W. G., 33, 135

Page, Will, 51
Painted Veils, 95, 186, 341
Palmer, A. Mitchell, 169, 170
"Paradise of the Third-Rate, The," 112
Parisienne, 70, 71, 107
Parmenter, James, Judge, 272, 273
Parrish, Herbert, Reverend, 292
Parshley, H. M., 246
"Passing of H. L. Mencken, The," 181
Patterson, Maclean, 312, 362, 363, 364, 365
Patterson, Paul: M's friendship with, 142–43; working relationship with, 194–98; mentioned, 133, 159, 191, 192, 290, 291, 292, 299, 333, 338, 360, 363, 365, 407
Peabody, Endicott, Reverend, 270
Pearl, Raymond: M's friendship with, 144–48; role in M's stress on science in *Mercury*, 244–45; mentioned, 135, 136, 143, 246, 247, 248, 252, 266, 267, 287, 301, 322, 323, 337, 407
Pennington, Ann, 152
Pennypacker, Issac R., 255, 256
People Round the Corner, 190
Peregoy, George Weems, 76
Perry, Bliss, 89, 90, 98
Personal Word, A, 72
"Pertinent and Impertinent," 75
Peterkin, Julia, 75
Philadelphia *Evening Telegraph*, 40
Philadelphia *Inquirer*, 261
Philadelphia *Ledger*, 291
Phillips, David Graham, 99

Philosophy of Friedrich Nietzsche, The: genesis and analysis 82–85
Photography, 21
"Piper Passes His Hat, The," 308
Pistols for Two, 62–64, 209
Plain Talk, 261
Plastic Age, The, 187
Poems, 189
Poetry: A Magazine of Verse, 96, 98
Police Gazette, 145
"Politics," 165
Politics, and M: 178–81, 204, 306–20, 334–36, 363–65 *passim*
Pollaczek, Penelope Pearl, 144, 145, 147
Pollard, Percival, 94, 401
Pollock, Channing, 60, 61
Pomeroy, Hally, 303
"Poor Old Ibsen," 43
Popkin, Zelda F., 256
Poppy, 139
Popular Theatre, The, 141
"Postscripts to the American Language," 359
"Pother about Glands, The," 246
Pound, Ezra, 68, 75, 96, 97, 188
Pound, Louise, 122
Prefaces. See A Book of Prefaces
Prejudices: genesis of, 123; additional series, 123; mentioned, 3, 4, 49, 53, 82, 87, 96, 99, 127, 128, 139, 175, 258, 269
Princeton University Library: collection of letters from and to M, 7, 381
Pringle, Aileen: M's friendship with, 157–61, 329; mentioned, 162, 163, 283, 328, 329, 334, 409
Pringle, Henry F., 188
Professor's House, The, 184
"Prohibition and Other Malaises," 173
Prohibition movement, and M: 171–73 *passim*
"Promised Land, The," 286
Protectionism, the Ism that Teaches that Waste Makes Wealth, 251
"Puritanism as a Literary Force," 100, 110
Puritanism: characterization of, 78–79; M's attack on, 79; effect on literature,

81–82; decried in M's *The Philosophy of Friedrich Nietzsche*, 83–84; the conservative critics, 89–90; decried in M's "Puritanism as a Literary Force," 100–101; manifested through censorship, 100–102; manifested in onslaught on Dreiser's novels, 105–8; postwar censorship, 170–71; the Prohibition campaign, 171–73; in "Hatrack" case, 270–75
"Putting Down Wicked Thoughts," 168

"Quacks are Prosperous, The," 43
Quiet Cities, 185
Quintessence of Ibsenism, The, 54

Randolph, A. Philip, 365
Rascoe, Burton, 190, 209, 211, 221, 222, 242, 259, 326
Ratcliff, James P., 76
"Rattling the Subconscious," 93
Reader's Digest, 243
"Recollections of Academic Orgies," 353
Red Book, 348
Red Scare, The, 168–70
Reese, Lizette Woodworth, 64, 97, 188, 202
"Reflections," 153
Religion, and M, 264–69, 333, 339, 343, 346–47 *passim*
"Répétition Générale," 76, 100, 256
Retail Coalman, 226
Revere *Budget*, 235
"Revolt, The," 153
"Rhyme and Reason," 35, 395
Rich, Arnold, Dr., 374
Richardson, Edward, Dr., 331
Richmond Reviewer, 216
Riley, Woodbridge, 253
Rinehart, Mary Roberts, 124, 182
Ritchie, Albert, Governor, 301
Rogers, Will, 315
Roosevelt, Franklin Delano: M's opposition to him and his New Deal,

204, 307–11, 313, 317, 319–20; mentioned, 53, 197, 198, 199, 252, 306, 314, 318, 327, 335, 344, 345, 347, 363

Roosevelt, Theodore, 80, 88, 91

Ross, Harold, 259, 261, 344, 351, 352, 354, 355, 356, 368

"Round Two," 269

"Ruin of an Artist, The," 353

Runyon, Damon, 182

"Sahara of the Bozart, The," 115

Saki (Hector Munro), 182

"Sanctuary," 169

Sandburg, Carl, 95, 96, 339

Sanger, Margaret, 271

"Sara Powell Haardt Mencken, 1898–1935," 279, 280, 285, 394

Saturday Evening Post, 33, 52, 99, 169, 185, 242, 261

Saturday Night Club, The: genesis, 131; growth, 132–36; and Sara Haardt Mencken, 298–99; decline and end, 321–23; mentioned, 13, 34, 117, 140, 144, 146, 148, 168, 222, 223, 247, 273, 305, 311, 352, 374

Saturday Review of Literature, 275

Saucy Stories, 70, 71, 191

Sayre, Zelda, 280

Schaefer, Lew, 34, 39

Schaff, Harrison, 54, 55

Science: M's interest in, 144–45, 243–48

Schon, Carl, 139

"Schooling of a Theologian, The," 353

Schopenhauer, Arthur, 55, 103, 128

Schubert, Franz, 134, 136, 203

Schumann, Robert, 134, 135

Science and Health, 86

Science of Society, 249

Science Service, 268

Scopes trial, The: 264–69; mentioned, 5, 101, 144, 171, 206, 263, 270, 272, 275, 278, 420

Scott, Evelyn, 188

Scott, George Ryley, 190

Scribner's, 59, 99, 258, 259

Sedgwick, Ellery, 99, 114, 130, 258, 275, 361

"Self-Preservation," 169

Sell, H. B., 140

Seven Arts, 96, 98, 109

"Sex and the Co-ed," 273

Sexual freedom, 173–74, 176–77

"Sex Uproar, The," 177

Shame of the Cities, The, 91

Shaw, George Bernard, 51, 52, 53, 54, 55, 56, 58, 60, 67, 100, 123, 127, 146, 338

Shearer, Norma, 159

Sherman, Stuart: M's feud with, 109–11, 128–29; mentioned, 119, 175, 263

Short Stories, 348

Silence, 125

Sinclair, Upton, 79, 86, 87, 88–89, 93, 124, 126, 182, 188, 324

Singleton, Marvin, 261

Sister Carrie, 82, 103, 105, 125

Sister Miriam. *See* Gallagher, Miriam, Sister

Smart Set, The: M's appointment as book-reviewer, 60–62; first meeting with Nathan, 61–62; writer for *Smart Set*, 65–67; co-editor with Nathan, 68–77; M's sympathetic treatment of writers, 71–74; reasons for leaving the *Smart Set*, 77, 216–17; trends in M's reviewing, 123–28; mentioned, 5, 58, 59, 64, 78, 79, 82, 86, 87, 88, 90, 93, 95, 100, 101, 104, 105, 106, 111, 116, 117, 120, 131, 133, 138, 152, 153, 155, 156, 157, 162, 173, 176, 180, 182, 183, 185, 188, 211, 213, 214, 215, 221, 235, 241, 242, 243, 256, 258, 281, 334, 336, 349, 359

Smart Set Anthology, The, 326

Smith, Alfred E., 206, 307, 316, 317

Smith, E. D., Senator, 364

Smith, Thomas, 162

Social Darwinism: in M's *The Philosophy of Friedrich Nietzsche,* 83; as preached by William Graham Sumner, 248–52; in M's opposition to the New Deal, 306–8

Social Darwinism in American Thought, 249, 252

Social novel, 86–89

Social Significance of the Modern Drama, The, 99
"Song of the Slapstick, The," 49
"Sold down the River," 308
Songs of Liberty, 89
Songs of Unrest, 186
Southern Album, 359
Spencer, Herbert, 56, 79, 91, 92, 104, 353
Spingarn, J. E., 127, 189
Splint, Fred, 60, 61, 65, 104
"Spoken American," 43, 120
Spoon River Anthology, 95, 96
Springfield *Republican,* 119
"Stage Reporter, The," 34
Stanchfield, John, 108
Starrett, Vincent, 73, 74
"Star-Spangled Men," 129
Stearns, Harold, 165, 174
Steffens, Lincoln, 79, 91, 99
Sterling, George, 189
Stevens, Doris, 273
Stevens, James, 189
St. Louis *Post-Dispatch,* 196
Stockton, Frank, 22
Stratton-Porter, Gene, 59
Strauss, Richard, 134, 136
"Streets and Their Names," 203
Strindberg, August, 68, 100, 146
Stuffed Peacocks, 184
Suckow, Ruth, 75, 189, 225
Sudermann, Hermann, 56, 182
Suggestions to Our Visitors, 72
Sullivan, Mark, 334
Summer Storm, 240
"Summer Thunder," 75
Sumner, John, 79, 100, 102, 106, 107, 108, 149
Sumner, William Graham: influence on M's ideas, 248–52; mentioned, 84, 204, 306
"Sunday Articles," 205
Sunpapers of Baltimore, 1837–1937, The, 340
Survey, 258
Swords & Roses, 287
Sylvia, 88
Syracuse *Journal,* 274

Taft, William Howard, 80, 167
Tales of the Jazz Age, 185
Tate, Allen, 243
Teasdale, Sara, 68, 69, 75, 189
"Terse and Terrible Texts," 35, 395
Tetlow, Henry, 226
Thalberg, Irving, 159
Thayer, John Adams, 65, 66, 67, 68, 116
"Theatre, The," 219
They Call Me Carpenter, 189
"Thirty-five Years of Newspaper Work," 361, 382
This Side of Paradise, 74, 176, 185
Thoma, Ludwig, 94
"Thoughts on Eating," 43
"Three—Minus One," 210
Time, 243, 305, 363
Times Literary Supplement, 145
Titan, The, 106
To Begin with, 145
Toe and Other Tales, The, 185
Tono-Bungay, 87
Townsend, Francis, Dr., 314, 320
Town Topics, 59
To Youth, 190
Tracey, John J., 271, 272
Trail of the Lonesome Pine, The, 59
"Tragedy of the Sioux, The," 237
Treatise on Right and Wrong: genesis and analysis, 345–47; mentioned, 255
Treatise on the Gods: genesis and analysis, 275–78; mentioned, 4, 53, 84, 148, 254, 262, 339, 346
"Trial of the Dead Cleopatra, The," 187
Truman, Harry S, 364, 366, 370
"Truth about Delbridge, The," 73
Tully, Jim, 189, 220, 287, 300, 313, 314
Twain, Mark, 13, 81, 339
"Two Englishes, The," 120
"Typescripts of Early Fiction," 24, 47

"Ulster Polonius, The," (by M), 123, 338
Umbra, 188
Unpublished works by M: "My Life as

Author and Editor," 360–61; "Thirty-five Years of Newspaper Work," 361; five-volume diary, 361; "Letters and Documents Relating to the Baltimore *Sunpapers*," 361. *See also* "Homo Sapiens"
Untermeyer, Louis, 67, 75, 110, 189, 225
"Untold Tales," 35, 395
"Up from Methodism," 271
"Utopia Eats Utopia," 308

Valentino, Rudolph, 158–59
Vanity Fair, 285
Van Vechten, Carl, 97, 189, 190
Varieties of Religious Experience, The, 92
Variety, 145
Ventures into Verse: genesis and analysis, 47–49; mentioned, 141, 396
Views and Reviews, 124
Villard, O. W., 275
"Vive Le Roi!" 307

Wade, John, Dr., 132, 133, 136
Wagley, Philip, Dr., 371, 372, 374
Wagner, Philip, 199, 200
Wagner, Richard, 134, 136
Wainwright, Charles, Dr., 368
Wallace, Henry, 198, 364, 365
Walpole, Hugh, 182, 190
Wanger, Walter, 159, 285
Warner, Eltinge, 67, 68, 70, 72
"Wars upon Alcohol," 43
Washington *Post*, 40
Washington *Star*, 119
Watson, Irving S., 152
Watson, John B., 92, 126, 244
Watterson, Henry, Colonel, 41, 395
Ways, Max, 27, 28, 29, 30, 32, 33, 35, 36, 37, 39
"Weakness of the Aeroplane, The," 42
Weaver, John V. A., 190, 225
Wedekind, Frank, 68
Wells, H. G., 66, 79, 86, 87–88, 89, 93, 98, 123, 182

Welty, Eudora, 302
"Wets Swing into the Saddle, The," 316
Whalen, Grover Aloysius, 308
Wharton, Edith, 59, 182
"What is Going on in the World," 257
What You Ought to Know about Your Baby, 105
Wheelock, John Hall, 190
Whipple, Leon, 258–59
White, Katharine, 345, 347, 351, 352, 355
White, William Allen, 182
Whitman, Walt, 81, 90, 95, 96
Widowers' Houses, 56
Wiley, Z. K., Dr., 25
Williams, William Carlos, 225
Wilson, Beatrice: M's friendship with, 155–57, 162, 329, 334, 409
Wilson, Edmund, 181, 207, 208, 209, 211
Wilson, Harry Leon, 67
Wilson, Woodrow, 53, 80, 111, 112, 113, 129, 167, 178, 192
Winslow, Thyra Samter, 190
Women, role of, 118–20, 173–74, 176–78
Wood, A. L. S., 271
Woodruff, Robert W., 152
Woollcott, Alexander, 156
Woollcott, Willie, 135, 136, 148, 156
Worm, A. Toxen, 51
Woven of the Sky, 342
Wright, Harold Bell, 59, 213
Wright, James, 309
Wright, Willard Huntington, 66, 67, 68, 69, 75, 116, 133, 214
Wylie, Elinor, 75

Yale Review, 242
Yorke, Dane, 254, 257
"Youth," 125, 338

Zelda Marsh, 188
Zola, Emile, 86, 88, 92